EXPLORING CRIMINAL JUSTICE

THE ESSENTIALS

THE CRIMINAL

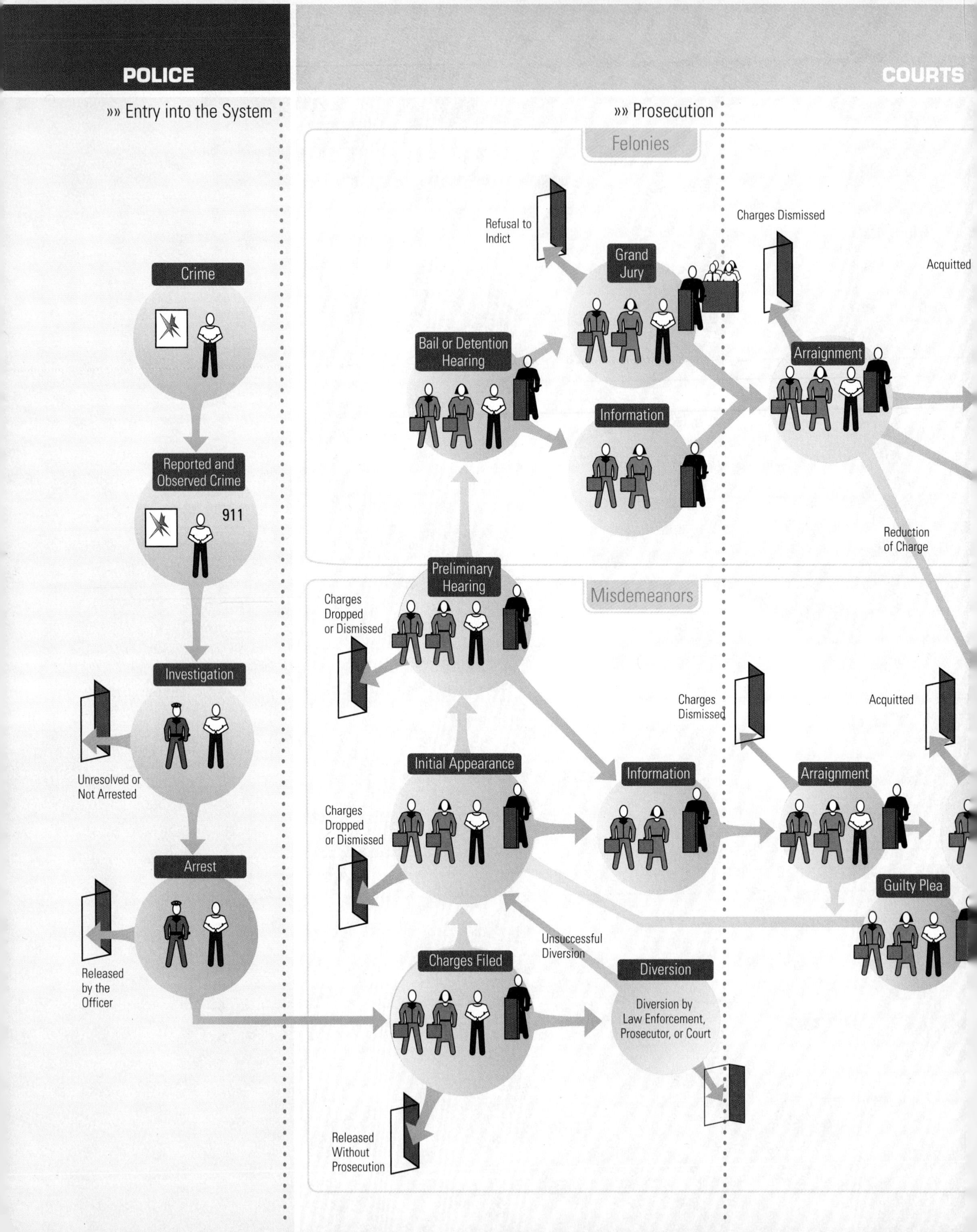

POLICE

COURTS

»» Entry into the System

»» Prosecution

Felonies

Misdemeanors

Crime

Reported and Observed Crime

911

Investigation

Unresolved or Not Arrested

Arrest

Released by the Officer

Charges Filed

Released Without Prosecution

Initial Appearance

Charges Dropped or Dismissed

Preliminary Hearing

Charges Dropped or Dismissed

Bail or Detention Hearing

Grand Jury

Refusal to Indict

Information

Charges Dismissed

Arraignment

Acquitted

Reduction of Charge

Information

Charges Dismissed

Arraignment

Acquitted

Guilty Plea

Unsuccessful Diversion

Diversion

Diversion by Law Enforcement, Prosecutor, or Court

USTICE SYSTEM

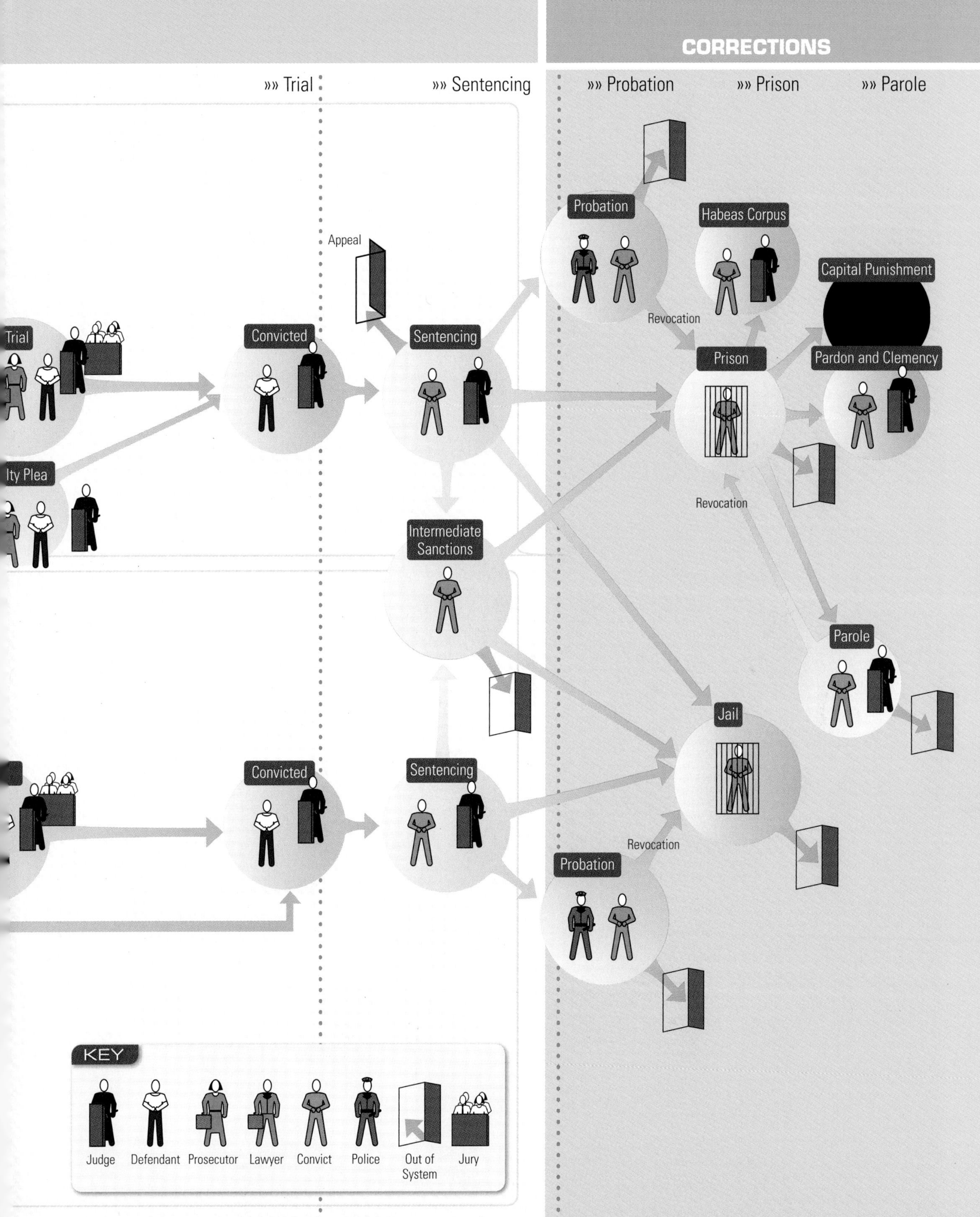

EXPLORING CRIMINAL JUSTICE
THE ESSENTIALS

ROBERT M. REGOLI, PHD
Professor
Department of Sociology
University of Colorado at Boulder

JOHN D. HEWITT, PHD
Professor
School of Criminal Justice
Grand Valley State University

JONES AND BARTLETT PUBLISHERS
Sudbury, Massachusetts
BOSTON TORONTO LONDON SINGAPORE

World Headquarters
Jones and Bartlett Publishers
40 Tall Pine Drive
Sudbury, MA 01776
978-443-5000
info@jbpub.com
www.jbpub.com

Jones and Bartlett Publishers Canada
6339 Ormindale Way
Mississauga, Ontario L5V 1J2
Canada

Jones and Bartlett Publishers International
Barb House, Barb Mews
London W6 7PA
United Kingdom

Jones and Bartlett's books and products are available through most bookstores and online booksellers. To contact Jones and Bartlett Publishers directly, call 800-832-0034, fax 978-443-8000, or visit our website www.jbpub.com.

Substantial discounts on bulk quantities of Jones and Bartlett's publications are available to corporations, professional associations, and other qualified organizations. For details and specific discount information, contact the special sales department at Jones and Bartlett via the above contact information or send an email to specialsales@jbpub.com.

Production Credits
Chief Executive Officer: Clayton Jones
Chief Operating Officer: Don W. Jones, Jr.
President, Higher Education and Professional Publishing: Robert W. Holland, Jr.
V.P., Sales and Marketing: William J. Kane
V.P., Design and Production: Anne Spencer
V.P., Manufacturing and Inventory Control: Therese Connell
Publisher: Cathleen Sether
Acquisitions Editor: Jeremy Spiegel
Editorial Assistant: Kyle Hoover
Production Director: Amy Rose
Senior Production Editor: Renée Sekerak
Production Assistant: Jill Morton
Marketing Manager: Jessica Faucher
Manufacturing and Inventory Control Supervisor: Amy Bacus
Interior Design: Anne Spencer
Cover Design: Kristin E. Parker
Assistant Photo Researcher: Jessica Elias
Composition: Publishers' Design & Production Services, Inc.
Cover and Title Page Images: Officers at WTC disaster, Courtesy of Andrea Booher/FEMA; Judge and officer outside cell, © Corbis/age fotostock; Background © unopix/ShutterStock, Inc.
Chapter Opener Image: © AbleStock
Text Printing and Binding: Courier Kendallville
Cover Printing: Courier Kendallville

Library of Congress Cataloging-in-Publication Data
Regoli, Robert M.
Exploring criminal justice : the essentials / by Robert M. Regoli and John D. Hewitt.
p. cm.
ISBN-13: 978-0-7637-5648-2
ISBN-10: 0-7637-5648-2
1. Criminal justice, Administration of—United States. I. Hewitt, John. II. Title.
HV9950.R446 2009
364.973—dc22

2008053147

6048

Printed in the United States of America

13 12 11 10 09 10 9 8 7 6 5 4 3 2 1

DEDICATION

To John, my dear friend, who has stood with me through thick and thin, never wavered in his support, and has always seen the good during our hard times. No one could ever be as blessed with a coauthor who, not once in our long friendship, has ever dropped the ball.

—Robert M. Regoli

To my mother, Sally Mann Hewitt, who taught me the joys of learning and the value of debating ideas and who still, at 96, models for me a lively and engaging intellectual curiosity.

—John D. Hewitt

BRIEF CONTENTS

CONTENTS

Part IV Corrections

FOREWORD

The public frequently views crime through the lens of the media, the government, politicians, or the representatives of the criminal justice system. Historically, criminal justice policies have been based on sensationalized cases and a "quick fix" mentality rather than a reasoned approach to a societal problem. By contrast, when researchers and academics study crime and the criminal justice system, they examine specific theories, policies, and procedures. They focus on the causes and correlates of crime, the fluctuations in the crime rate, the existing and promising programs, and the overall trends in criminal justice. It is, in fact, a very complex system.

In explaining the criminal justice system and its evolution in their new book, *Exploring Criminal Justice: The Essentials*, authors Bob Regoli and John Hewitt strike a nice balance. They sensitize us to the complexity of the criminal justice system, illustrating with real-world examples how the system deals with crime. Through their approach, students can make sense of the complexities. The result is a text that is highly readable.

Students will find this book interesting and challenging. The authors endeavor to enlighten students in an objective manner through published research that will prompt discussions about the criminal justice system's ability to understand and address crime and to ensure justice in our society. These are laudable goals, and the authors should be commended for their excellent work.

The criminal justice system is poised for expansion. It is anticipated that there will be many employment opportunities for criminal justice students in the next 5 to 10 years. We have already witnessed the prison boom, the increased attention to preventing terrorism, and the technological advances in all areas of the criminal justice system. However, this most recent expansion goes beyond recruiting more professionals and constructing more prisons. We will also be confronting serious economic challenges. Economic constraints will force us to re-evaluate the war on drugs, the cost of prison versus community correctional programs, the application of technology, and the role of the federal government.

As noted, this text affords students the opportunity to become familiar with research and its connection to criminal justice policy. The authors' approach is balanced and inclusive; they enlighten the reader about the major issues and problems and illustrate that objective research is the cornerstone of criminal justice policy. In short, students will have the foundation for future courses and further reading.

Because crime is a part of our social, educational, and entertainment world, we may be inclined to assume that it is a simple problem that can be solved relatively easily. Through education, we learn that there are no easy solutions to the crime problem. We also become familiar with highly successful strategies and programs in existence. Rather than adopting a single stance, Bob Regoli and John Hewitt have relied on their extensive teaching, researching, and writing experience to provide students with an introduction to the study of crime and criminal justice that is both challenging and rewarding.

Alida V. Merlo
Professor
Department of Criminology
Indiana University of Pennsylvania

ACKNOWLEDGMENTS

The people we have worked with at Jones and Bartlett continue to be spectacular! Our editor, Jeremy Spiegel, not only is a most wonderful and gracious person, but also someone whose knowledge of the publishing business from top-to-bottom is unparalleled. His guidance, direction, critical assessment, and encouragement is what made it possible for us to "keep on keeping on." We will forever be grateful for what he has taught us.

Many colleagues, some of whom are personal friends and others whom we have not yet met, unselfishly shared information, insights, and criticisms with us and helped us grow and formulate our ideas about crime and justice. Our appreciation to these people extends well beyond the gratitude we express here, but we do thank you and each of you will always hold a special place in our hearts: Alissa Ackerman, Geoff Alpert, Alex Alverez, Rosalie Arndt, Lee Ayers, Patrick Bacon, Sarah Bacon, Rachel Bandy, Gregg Barak, Tom Barker, Deborah Barrett, Allison Bayless, Kevin Beaver, Janet Behrens, Joanne Belknap, Ingrid Bennett, Richard Bennett, Mark Berg, Dennis Blewitt, Bob Bohm, Kevin Borgeson, Mary Callahan, Lisa Campione, Todd Clear, Meda Chesney-Lind, Shannon Coffey, Mark Colvin, Peter Conis, Allison Cotton, Herb Covey, Sarah Corcoran, John Crank, Bob Culbertson, Frank Cullen, Lois DeFleur, Walter DeKeseredy, Matt DeLisi, Brendan Dooley, Delbert Elliott, Raymond Foster, Lisa Fowler, John Fuller, Rebekah Garrett, Patrick Gerkin, Sarah Getman, Arif Ghayur, Michelle Goetz, Lindsey Grall, Richard Grossenbacher, Ed Grosskopf, Mark Hamm, Amy Harrell, Kraig Hays, Laura Hettinger, Eric Hickey, Andy Hochstetler, Michael Hogan, Lou Holscher, Charles Hou, James Houston, Lisa Hutchinson, Peter Iadicola, James Jabbour, Eric Jensen, Christopher Kierkus, Inge King, Brian Kingshott, Beverly Kingston, Blair Lachman, Paul Lasley, Ed Latessa, Richard Lawrence, Stephanie Lichtenauer, Andrea Light, Jeff London, Katie Lowe, Stacy Mallicoat, Andy Miracle, Tina Miracle, Marilyn McDowell, Jean McGloin, Doug McKenzie, Scott Menard, Gloria Mendoza, Bill Miller, Tiare Moorman, Katie Murphy, Hal Pepinsky, Alex Piquero, Nicky Piquero, Mark Pogrebin, Joycelyn Pollock, Eric Poole, Hillary Potter, Eric Primm, Beverly Quist, Michael Radelet, Ronald Reed, Tom Reed, Adam Regoli, George Rivera, Geoff Rivers, Richard Rogers, Clarence Romig, Vincent Sainato, Fred Sams, Joe Sanborn, Jeff Shrink, Eric Schwartz, Marty Schwartz, Madison Serdinak, Rajshree Shrestha, James F. Short, Jr., Larry Siegel, Chad Simcox, Victor Strieb, Terry Thornberry, Larry Travis, Beverly Quist, Jay Watterworth, Laura VanderDrift, Amanda VanHoose, Michael Vaughn, Regina Verna, Jerry Vito, Jules Wanderer, Tom Winfree, Ralph Weisheit, John Wright, Christine Yalda, and Joanne Ziembo-Vogl.

There is no doubt that some very important people in our lives were unintentionally omitted from the list. Please accept are heartfelt apology for the omission. Other colleagues selected to review the book improved the text in innumerable ways. Each went beyond what was asked and provided us with insights that we considered seriously and in most instances incorporated into *Exploring Criminal Justice: The Essentials.* There is no way to put into words how much your guidance along the way has meant to us.

Writing does not take place in a vacuum, and authors are not unaffected by—nor do they fail to affect—those closest to them. Our children, Adam, Andrea, Eben, and Sara;

our grandchildren, R.J., Zoë, Henry, Hugh, and James; and especially our wives, Debbie and Avis, have sacrificed and shared with us in so many ways as we often obsessed over our writing. They stood alongside us, provided encouragement, support, tolerance, patience, and humor, and are appreciated much more than they ever will know.

PREFACE

Although more than 1.5 million people are currently confined in state and federal prisons in the United States, crime in this country has actually been declining for the past decade—that is, at least until recently, when there has been a small increase in offenses committed. Whether this upward trend will continue and what the future holds are hotly debated topics among criminologists. Nonetheless, some of the most recent data produced by the Federal Bureau of Investigation suggest that both reported crimes and arrests are at their lowest levels since the early 1970s, and national surveys of victims report similar declines in victimization rates. The number of people under sentence of death and the number of actual executions each year have fallen dramatically since they reached their peak in 2000. The U.S. Supreme Court heard arguments for only half the number of cases in 2008 than it did in 1987.

Do these trends mean that policymakers have discovered how to control (or possibly even eliminate) crime? The answer is emphatically *no*. Criminologists are not sure why crime has declined or, conversely, why there was a small increase in the amount of serious violent crime reported to police in both 2006 and 2007. Certainly, expenditures on the criminal justice system have not declined; some states spend more on their prison systems than they do on public education. The criminal courts are clogged with cases, and local communities continue to build more jails and detention centers. Since the terrorist attacks of September 11, 2001, the criminal justice system has faced a plethora of new challenges—for law enforcement, in the detection and response to terrorist activity; for the courts, in the detention and prosecution of alleged terrorists; and for corrections, in the incarceration of those convicted of terrorism.

Many students of criminal justice are curious to know about how crime is changing and how the criminal justice system is responding to those changes. Some students have already decided to major in criminal justice, while others are just beginning to explore what this major has to offer. We wrote *Exploring Criminal Justice: The Essentials* to be a useful guide for all students interested in learning more about the U.S. criminal justice system.

More than 60 years of collective college teaching experience has taught us that students come to courses with a variety of backgrounds and expectations. We believe this truism is especially valid for students taking their first course in criminal justice. Some students have family members who work in the system as police officers, attorneys, counselors, or probation, parole, or correctional officers. Other students have already had firsthand experience in the system, either as full-time employees, volunteers, or perhaps even crime victims, criminal offenders, or members of a jury. Students also come to this course with knowledge of the criminal justice system based on television dramas such as *CSI* and *Law and Order*, documentaries, news programs, films, music, and other media, including comic books and violent video games. The common ground that these students share is an interest in learning more about the criminal justice system and its operation.

A good textbook is more than just a compendium of facts and figures, flow charts, and case studies. Recognizing that fact, *Exploring Criminal Justice: The Essentials* engages students in an exploration of the intricate details of the criminal justice process.

It breathes life into the criminal justice system by examining its many components and investigating how they operate in relationship to one another as well as considering the people who work in the system and what they do.

In responding to the needs of professors and their students, we have provided a text that is complete, current, clearly written, and engaging. The issues, research, policies, programs, and court cases are presented and discussed in a balanced manner intended to foster discussion and debate in addition to learning and greater understanding. We hope that both professors and students will benefit from this text as they explore our presentation of the criminal justice system and its processes.

REVIEWERS

Randolph Grinc
Caldwell College

Barry Harvey
Alvernia College

William Kelley
Auburn University

Helen Lim
California Lutheran University

Stewart Lawrence Weisman
Cazenovia College

Joseph A. Reilly
Drexel University

Linda Fleischer
Essex Community College

Elizabeth Marsal
East Carolina University

Jennifer Girgen
Florida State University

Special thanks to the following people for their contributions to the text.

Thomas Blomberg
Dean and Professor of Criminology and Criminal Justice
Florida State University

Mark D. Cunningham, PhD, ABPP
Clinical and Forensic Psychologist
Lewisville, TX

Cassia Spohn
Professor of Criminal Justice
Arizona State University

Clyde L. Cronkhite
Retired Chief of Police, Santa Ana, CA
Professor of Law Enforcement and Justice Administration
Western Illinois University

Kim Budreau
Sergeant, Medford Police Department
Medford, OR

Lorenzo M. Boyd
Former Deputy Sheriff, Suffolk County, MA
Assistant Professor of Criminal Justice
Fayetteville State University

Diana Reynolds Clayton
Assistant Professor of Criminal Justice
Rogers State University

Jeffrey S. Cohen
Attorney at Law
Office of the Alternate Public Defender
County of Los Angeles

Pablo Cortes
Chief Judge
Wyoming District Court
Wyoming, MI

Art Beeler
Warden
Federal Correctional Complex
Butner, NC

Judith Simon Garrett
Deputy Assistant Director
Division of Information, Policy, and Public Affairs
Federal Bureau of Prisons
Washington, DC

Betsy Matthews
Associate Professor
Department of Correctional and Juvenile Justice Studies
Eastern Kentucky University

James Burfeind, PhD
Professor and Chair of Sociology
University of Montana

Scott J. White, PhD
Former Intelligence Officer
Assistant Professor of Criminal Justice
Westfield State College

Amy Harrell
Department Chair
Business Technologies
Nash Community College

Peter J. Conis
Instructor
Department of Sociology
Iowa State University

Lee Ayers
Associate Professor
Department of Criminology and Criminal Justice
Southern Oregon University

The study of criminal justice must first begin with the social and historical context of both crime and justice. This section examines the nature of criminal justice in society (past and present), extending beyond the components of the criminal justice system (namely, the police, courts, and corrections) to consider its foundations.

Chapter 1 looks at how society defines crime and provides a brief overview of both the criminal justice system and the criminal justice process. The origins of this system are the focus of Chapter 2, which presents the development of criminal law over time and the ways that law defines crime and criminal responsibility. Focusing on crime, its criminals, and its victims, Chapter 3 discusses the nature and extent of crime, identifies who are the most likely offenders and victims, explains why people commit crime, and explores which social policies might be implemented to prevent crime.

How society defines, measures, and explains crime and criminal victimization provides the necessary framework to understand the organization and operation of the U.S. criminal justice system.

PART

I

Crime and Criminal Justice

POLICE

CHAPTER

1

Overview of Criminal Justice

OBJECTIVES

1 Define crime and explain how what is called "criminal" changes over time.

2 Describe the impact (if any) of crime control legislation on crime reduction.

3 Identify the three primary components of the criminal justice system.

4 Explain the principal functions of the police, courts, and corrections.

5 List the steps in the criminal justice process.

6 Understand the role of public perceptions on crime control policy.

PROFILES IN CRIME AND JUSTICE

Thomas Blomberg
Dean and Professor of Criminology and Criminal Justice
Florida State University

My decision to become a criminologist reflected several interrelated considerations. Generally, I found criminology and its search for the causes and control of crime to be inherently interesting and important. More specifically, my introduction to the field of criminology came through the research and writing I was doing for my undergraduate honors thesis at the University of California at Berkeley. My thesis topic was U.S. prisons. In the course of my readings and writings on the past, present, and future of prisons in the United States, it became clear to me that prisons were, at best, a very limited response to crime and, at worst, a policy rife with ineffectiveness and negative consequences.

Upon completion of my thesis and with my growing interest in criminology and its role in public policy, I abandoned my plans to enter law school and embarked upon my graduate studies in criminology. For the past 35 years, I have been a university professor conducting research, writing, teaching, and mentoring undergraduate and graduate students. Five years ago, I became Dean of the College; this administrative role has limited my teaching, but not my mentoring functions. In fact, my role as mentor has expanded with the Deanship to include faculty as well as students. While being Dean is different from being a professor, the rewards are very satisfying, particularly in relation to seeing the development and contributions of the faculty and students you are working with.

I truly love research, writing, and teaching. I found teaching to be particularly exhilarating when I was actively engaged in "scientific discovery" through my research and writing. To be giving a lecture to a graduate seminar of 12 students or a large undergraduate course with 100 or more students and to see "the light bulbs go on," and to see and feel the students' interest and enthusiasm for the material being presented, is truly a gratifying experience. Further, to be presenting research results and policy recommendations to practitioners or policymakers is both very satisfying and challenging. In sum, I believe what makes these research, writing, teaching, and presentation experiences so special is that, in conducting the work of criminology, we are dealing with timely issues that have the potential to make life better for all of society's members.

The challenge faced by individuals who desire to pursue careers in criminology is that it is a very competitive field. To get into the best criminology graduate programs requires excellent academic credentials. Once admitted into graduate school, the competition gets even greater to continue to excel in your coursework and research and to successfully publish while you are in graduate school. For example, when we are recruiting entry-level assistant professors out of graduate school, we look for those candidates who have already established a research agenda and the beginning of a publication record. As many criminologists assert about human behavior, "the best predictor of future behavior is past behavior." After being hired, new assistant professors must hit the ground running by teaching typically two courses per semester, conducting research, submitting manuscripts to peer-refereed journals, and providing service to their department, college, university, and profession. The often-heard claim "Publish or perish" is real.

Criminology research and teaching, like so many professions, has its share of "ups and downs." I regularly advise new PhDs leaving our college to begin their respective academic careers, "Do not take the professional ups any more seriously than the professional downs." Career trajectories travel through an obstacle course that must be navigated through various twists, turns, and ups and downs. Among the best advice I received from my major professor as I was beginning my academic career was to develop a lifestyle in which my work—namely, research and writing—was a part, but not the total, of my life. I was further advised to develop specific amounts of research and writing to be accomplished on a daily basis and, once that amount of research and writing was accomplished, to turn my attention to other nonacademic matters. My advice, then, is to work hard, do your very best, and take your work, but not yourself, too seriously. Challenge yourself to have a balanced professional and personal life.

Introduction

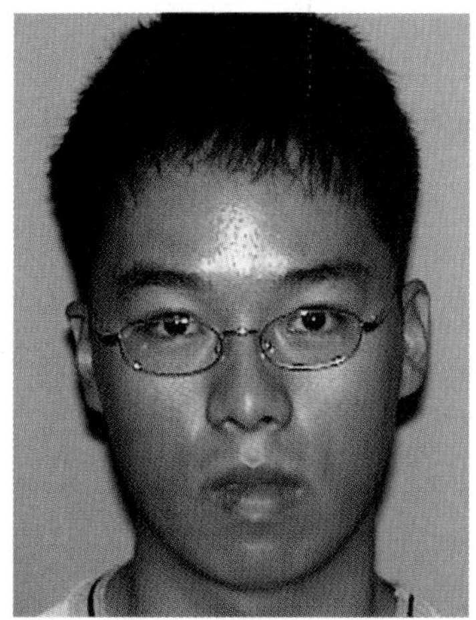
On April 16, 2007, Seung-Hui Cho killed 32 people at Virginia Tech University.

On April 16, 2007, Seung-Hui Cho perpetrated the deadliest mass killing in modern U.S. history when he murdered 32 people and attempted to murder 29 others before killing himself at the campus of Virginia Polytechnic Institute and State University (Virginia Tech) in Blacksburg, Virginia.[1] As awful as Cho's conduct was, it is important to remember that it is not only psychotic killers like Cho who commit serious violent crimes, producing widespread concern. Sometimes criminal justice personnel themselves commit appalling crimes.

Such was the case with Rodney King, who was captured in a 12-minute videotape by George Holliday that turned what would have been a forgotten, albeit violent, encounter between Los Angeles police and King into one of the most widely watched and discussed incidents of its kind. The videotaped beating of King has proven itself to be one of the most horrifying, racially charged incidents of excessive police force ever exposed. Across the nation, millions of Americans were shocked by the fuzzy video images of four officers from the Los Angeles Police Department (three white and one Latino) beating an African American man—Rodney King—with their batons. Believing that King was dangerous and possibly under the influence of drugs, the officers felt the force they used to subdue him was justified. Even so, the officers were indicted on charges of "assault by force likely to produce great bodily injury" and "filing false reports." A jury of 10 whites, one Latino, and one Asian voted to **acquit** the officers, which is a verdict of not guilty in a criminal case.

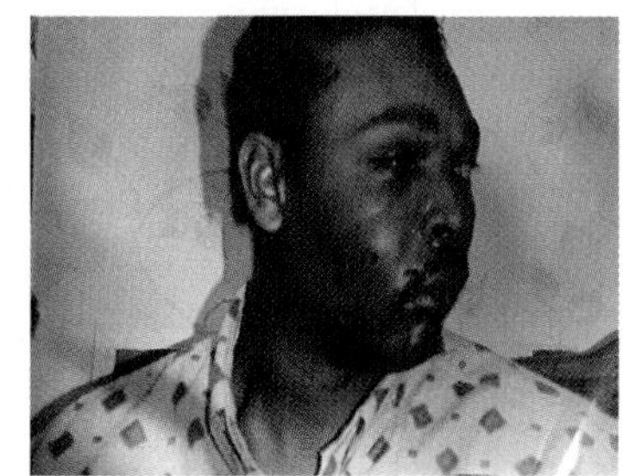
Rodney King was the victim of one of the most notorious incidents of police brutality in U.S. history.

The verdict triggered massive rioting in Los Angeles, which ultimately left hundreds of buildings damaged or destroyed and dozens of people dead.[2] During this turbulent time, King appeared on national television, pleading for peace: "People, I just want to say, you know, can we all get along?"[3] Unfortunately, the truth is that people cannot. Throughout history there have always been people—whether killers like Cho, the four Los Angeles police officers, or ordinary citizens—who fail to "get along."

The Problem of Crime

Crime exists in all societies. The nineteenth-century French sociologist Émile Durkheim observed this and went on to suggest that crime is normal and that it could not be eliminated. For Durkheim, even in a society of saints, deviance will occur.[4] The behavior of some people will depart from the established **norms**—the rules and expectations by which society guides the behavior of its members. Depending on the degree of departure, a person's actions may be defined as "criminal." Because certain behavior is "right," by default other behavior must be "wrong." What distinguishes one society from another are the behaviors they define as "normal, appropriate, or law-abiding" versus "deviant, inappropriate, or criminal." Behavior that is considered criminal varies *between* societies because people living in different countries, for instance, hold different beliefs about what is right and what is wrong and, therefore, establish different standards or expectations for behavior. For example, in the United States possession of marijuana is a crime and convicted violators may be punished. In contrast, in the Netherlands, even though marijuana is not legal, for the past 30 years the Dutch have tolerated its use and adults over age 18 may smoke it in more than 1000 coffee shops throughout the country with no fear of being arrested.[5]

Durkheim also believed that crime is functional and is necessary for a society to progress because it may lead to needed social change.[6] After the massacre at Virginia Tech, for example, the university put in place policies to more closely monitor troubled students, installed interior locks on classroom buildings, and implemented an Internet-based message board to alert the campus to emergencies. Other universities, such as the

FOCUS ON CRIMINAL JUSTICE

Drug Policy in the Netherlands

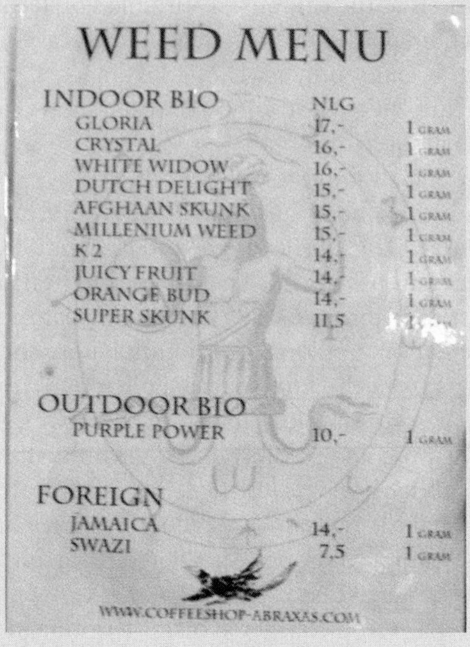

In the United States, the government has declared a war on drugs. It imposes severe penalties for possession of marijuana and hashish (cannabis), which U.S. drug laws classify as Schedule I drugs—placing them in the same category as heroin, cocaine, and LSD. Although the legal penalties for possession of these drugs in each state vary greatly, federal law provides for a prison term of up to life in prison for someone who distributes 1000 pounds or more of marijuana as well as a maximum $200,000 fine. People who are caught with even very small amounts of these drugs may face the forfeiture of their cars, homes, or other possessions.

In the Netherlands, the government views these drugs quite differently. Beginning in the mid-1970s, the Netherlands quietly decriminalized the personal use of marijuana and hashish. Dutch drug policies were changed. Believing that the policies underlying the U.S. war on drugs and their criminalizing impact on individuals were harmful to society, the Dutch designed their approach to limit the negative and stigmatizing effects of drug use on individual users. They did so by drawing a clear distinction between "hard" drugs, such as opiates, and "soft" drugs, such as cannabis, and gave law enforcement priority to controlling the production, importation, and trafficking of hard drugs. Dutch law enforcement also decided to ignore the sale of small amounts of cannabis for personal use. Dutch officials believed that if cannabis was decriminalized, thereby separating the soft and hard drug markets, it would reduce the likelihood that marijuana users would come into contact with heroin users. This way, young people experimenting with marijuana would be less likely to become involved with more dangerous and addictive drugs. The Dutch drug policies were also aimed at normalizing the drug problem. That is, the Dutch admitted that extensive cannabis use had gained a firm foothold in society, as was the case with alcohol and tobacco, and that it was far more realistic to try to reduce the personal and social harms associated with drug use through education and "user-friendly" treatment programs.

In Amsterdam, there are more than 400 coffee shops where people can legally buy and smoke marijuana and hashish. These shops provide a relaxed environment where people can use the drugs, listen to music, engage in relaxed conversations, enjoy refreshments, and play video games, darts, and pool. They also provide a controlled environment, reinforcing tolerance of soft drug use, while condemning the sale or use of harder drugs. No other drug may be sold or used, and the shops may not advertise or sell cannabis to people younger than age 16.

Although there is minimal support for decriminalizing marijuana in the United States, groups such as the National Organization for the Reform of Marijuana Laws (NORML) and the American Civil Liberties Union (ACLU) do support its legalization. In states such as Oregon, the penalty for possession of less than 1 ounce of marijuana has been reduced to a misdemeanor; in Boulder, Colorado, persons arrested for possession of less than 1 ounce of marijuana receive a $100 fine.

In contrast to the views espoused by supporters of the legalization of marijuana, the U.S. Drug Enforcement Agency and the American Academy of Pediatrics see marijuana as a "gateway" drug and insist that its decriminalization would lead to greater use of harder drugs owing to increased experimentation that would erode public morals. Indeed, many Americans believe that decriminalizing cannabis would lead to a dramatic increase in drug use. A recent study suggests that this perception is not accurate. Craig Reinarman and his colleagues tested the premise that punishment for cannabis use deters use and thereby benefits public health. Comparing the cannabis habits of users in Amsterdam and San Francisco, the researchers found no evidence to support claims that criminalization reduces use or that decriminalization increases use.

Sources: "Drug War Facts," available at www.drugwarfacts.org, accessed August 12, 2008; "Response to the American Academy of Pediatrics Report on the Legalization of Marijuana," *Pediatrics* 116:1256–1257 (2005); Manja Abraham and Hendrien Kaal, *Licit and Illicit Drug Use in the Netherlands* (Amsterdam: Mets and Schilt, 2002); Rudolph Gerber, *Legalizing Marijuana* (New York: Praeger, 2004); Craig Reinarman, Peter Cohen, and Hendrien Kaal, "The Limited Relevance of Drug Policy," *American Journal of Public Health* 94:836–842 (2004).

University of New Hampshire, have also taken steps to improve campus safety. At New Hampshire, roof-mounted loud speakers stand ready to shout out instructions during emergencies. Similar loudspeaker systems are now in place at Northwestern University and the University of Vermont, among other colleges. In addition, in the wake of the shootings at Virginia Tech, the U.S. Education Department proposed new rules that would permit school administrators to share confidential data on troubled students. The rules would allow medical personnel in school clinics, for instance, to disclose information to security personnel without a student's consent, if the student is considered to be a threat.[7] There is ample evidence that throughout history, society has been transformed by the behavior of persons who violated social norms, such as Cesar Chavez, Mohandas Gandhi, Jesus, Martin Luther King, Jr., and Socrates. In their own lives, these people were sometimes called "criminal" because they opposed the policies and practices of the ruling class. The ability of social deviants to change the world around them continues today.

The nineteenth-century French sociologist, Emile Durkheim, believed crime is normal in society and cannot be eliminated.

It is also important to know that *within* a society crime varies over time and place. The amount of crime in a community will typically mirror the patterns of nonconforming

Headline Crime

Denver Bans Pit Bulls

For hundreds of years, owning the dog of your choice was permitted in the United States. No more—at least not in Denver, Colorado. In 1989, Denver passed an ordinance banning pit bulls or pit bull mixes. The ordinance prohibits any person from owning, possessing, keeping, exercising control over, maintaining, harboring, or selling a pit bull (or mix) in the city and county of Denver. Originally, any person who violated the law was subject to a $999 fine and/or one year in jail. Today, if someone is caught owning a pit bull (or mix), on the first offense, the city puts a microchip in the dog's ear and the owner must immediately move the dog outside the city and county. If the owner does not comply, on the second offense, the dog is destroyed. It is, however, permissible to transport a pit bull directly through Denver, from a starting point outside of Denver to another destination outside of Denver, provided that the pit bull (or mix) remains in the vehicle.

In 2004, a state law was passed barring cities and counties from enacting breed-specific legislation regulating dogs. Denver stopped enforcing the ordinance but challenged the state law in court, claiming the law violated Denver's home-rule rights. In 2005, the ordinance was reinstated after the state law was successfully challenged in court. Animal rights activists once again filed a lawsuit against the city and county of Denver. Then, in 2008, a federal judge dismissed a suit by three women who claimed the ban was unconstitutional.

In 2005, when Denver reinstated its ban, the neighboring cities of Aurora, Castle Rock, Commerce City, Lakewood, and Lone Tree adopted laws either outlawing pit bulls and other dangerous dogs or revising their vicious-dog ordinances. These cities feared that Denver's cast-off pit bulls might be dumped in their cities.

Since Denver reinstated its ordinance in 2005, 1667 pit bulls (or mixes) have been euthanized and 2318 dogs have had microchips inserted into their ear and moved out of the city or county. According to a Denver Assistant City attorney, the city ban on pit bulls is warranted because a pit bull "will try to rip flesh, like a shark." A federal Centers for Disease Control and Prevention study of deaths caused by dogs between 1979 and 1998 nationwide found that pit bull-type dogs caused 66 deaths out of a total of 238 fatalities involving at least 25 breeds of dogs.

Sources: April Washington, "Mixed Results on Dog Bans," *Rocky Mountain News*, April 21, 2008, p. 6; John Ensslin, "Federal Suit Contests Denver's Pit Bull Ban," *Rocky Mountain News*, April 21, 2008, available at http://www.rockymountainnews.com/drmn/local/article/0,1299,DRMN_15_5474747,00.html, accessed August 11, 2008; "Denver Pit Bull Owners Sue Denver," *The Denver Post*, April 29, 2008, available at http://www.denverpost.com/ci_5628087, accessed August 11, 2008; Jeff Kass, "Denver Pit Bull Ban Draws Dog Lovers' Ire," *The Boston Globe*, July 6, 2005, available at http://www.boston.com/news/nation/articles/2005/07/06/denver_pit_bull_ban_draws_dog lovers_ire/, accessed August 4, 2008.

behavior that are of greatest concern to either *a significant number of people* or *a number of significant people*.[8]

For example, during much of the eighteenth and nineteenth centuries in the United States, alcohol use was widespread. People consumed alcohol on a regular basis, and street fights were common, albeit rarely sanctioned. Even though these practices are less prevalent today, the public now views them as more problematic and appropriate for regulation by the criminal justice system. Similarly, drug use in the late nineteenth century was of very little concern—even housewives used heroin openly—and drugs such as marijuana, heroin, and cocaine were not criminalized until the early twentieth century.[9]

National Efforts to Fight Crime

In the 1970s and 1980s, the social climate changed dramatically. In this period, the use of illicit drugs was perceived as a growing problem. Toward the end of the 1980s, First Lady Nancy Reagan launched the widespread "Just Say No" campaign, reflecting how drugs had become a major public concern. In a 1989 public opinion poll, 64 percent of the respondents identified drugs as the number one problem facing the nation. It was in this climate that punishment for drug law violations became more severe. By the early 1990s, even though drug use had declined, arrest rates for drug offenses remained high, and about 30 percent of all new admissions to federal prison were people convicted of drug-related offenses.[10]

Toward the mid-1990s, there was a decline in public concern over the drug problem; only about 6 percent of respondents in a 1993 Gallup Poll responded by saying that drug abuse was the single most important problem facing the country.[11] In this shifting climate, there was apprehension over the dramatic impact of the enforcement of drug laws on increasing prison populations; politicians and judges called for changes in society's response to drug use, including a de-emphasis on arrests and imprisonment and a greater emphasis on prevention and treatment. Few people were surprised when less than five months after taking office, President Bill Clinton recommended major cuts in the federal drug policy office annual budget (from $17.3 million to $5.8 million) and reduced the drug policy staff from 147 to 25.[12]

Changing definitions and perceptions regarding the crime problem, as well as adjustments in the criminal justice system, are consistent with Durkheim's observations about how the boundaries of conventional behavior vary over time and place. What the boundaries are and how they should be enforced, along with the role of the criminal justice system, will always be topics of debate. But this dilemma does not come without significant cost to society. The cost, for example, of maintaining the criminal justice system complex in the United States is enormous. The country spends more than $200 billion annually and employs more than 2 million people to provide police protection ($94 billion), corrections activities ($65 billion), and judicial and legal activities ($45 billion).[13] Since 1982 there has been a significant increase in the amount of money spent on each of the criminal justice functions (see FIGURE 1–1).[14]

Even though a large amount of money is spent fighting crime, very little is actually known about how to prevent crime and what its causes are. To attack the crime problem, over the past 40 years the U.S. Congress has passed no fewer than five important pieces of significant legislation:

- Omnibus Crime Control Bill and Safe Streets Act of 1968
- Comprehensive Crime Control Act of 1984
- Crime Control Act of 1990
- Violent Crime Control and Law Enforcement Act of 1994
- USA Patriot Acts of 2001 and 2005[15]

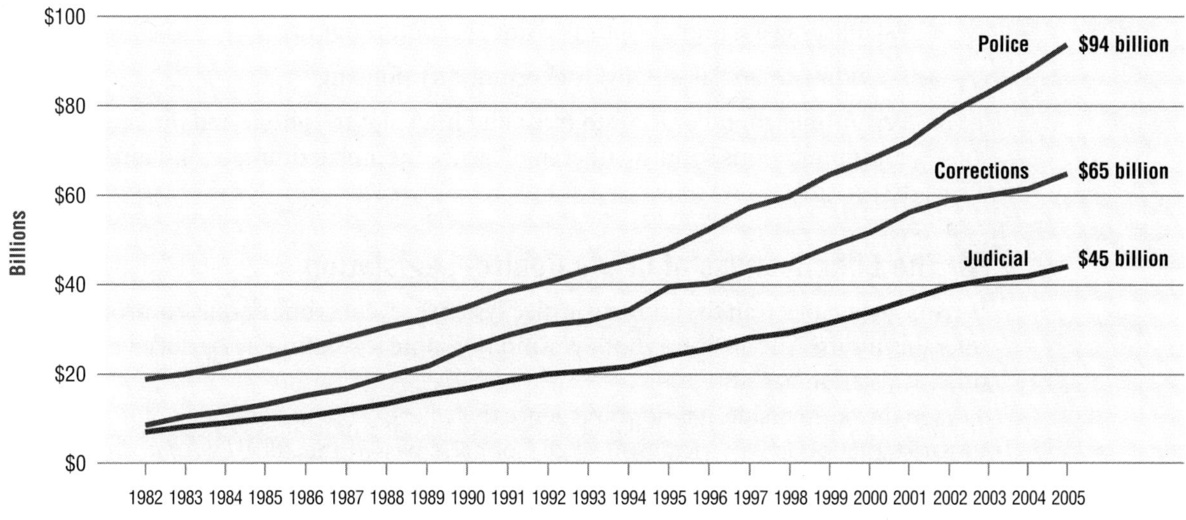

FIGURE 1-1 Direct Expenditure by Level of Government, 1982–2005

Source: Local Governments Spend More on Criminal Justice than State Governments or the Federal Government (Washington, DC: U.S. Department of Justice, 2007), available at http://www.ojp.usdoj.gov/bjs/glance/expgov.htm, accessed October 12, 2008.

The purpose of each act has roughly been the same—to control, regulate, and prevent crime, particularly as crime rates soared from 1960 to 1991 (see FIGURE 1-2). In reaction to the failure of these measures to significantly reduce crime, Congress also has taken other steps:

- Increasing education and training for law enforcement officers
- Seizing the assets of drug traffickers
- Requiring mandatory minimum sentences for chronic criminal offenders
- Developing alternative reform programs for prison inmates

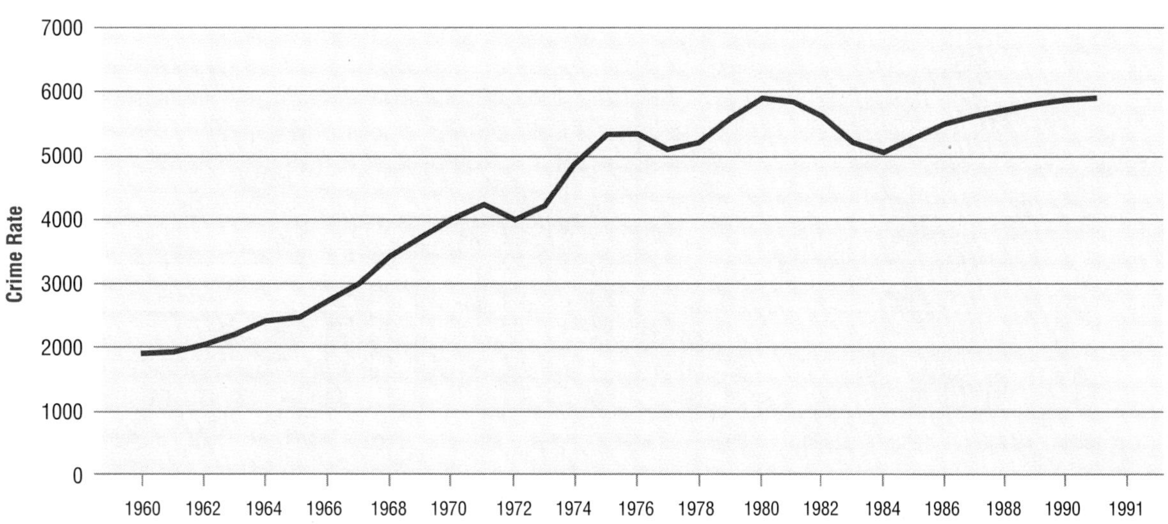

FIGURE 1-2 Crime Rate in the United States (per 100,000 people)

Source: Federal Bureau of Investigation, Crime in the United States, 2007 (Washington, DC: U.S. Department of Justice, 2008).

- Establishing a national victim's compensation program
- Providing financial support for community policing
- Permitting federal officials to track and intercept telephone and other electronic communications so as to gather intelligence to combat domestic and international terrorism[16]

The Effectiveness of Crime Control Legislation

Is crime inevitable? Can the criminal justice system prevent crime or only control it within tolerable limits? The answer is both yes and no; some legislation has reduced crime and other legislation has not.

On the positive side, it is no coincidence there have been no domestic or international terrorist attacks on American soil since Congress passed the 2001 *USA Patriot Act* and approved the *USA Patriot Improvement Act* in 2005.[17] Although critics claim the United States is less safe today than it was prior to the invasion of Iraq, on its face, some evidence suggests the opposite. It is also no accident that the crime rate decreased to levels not seen since the late 1960s following the passage of the *1990 Crime Control Act* and the *1994 Crime Bill.*[18] However, the overall lowering of the crime rate in some cities, such as New York, San Francisco, and Seattle, has been attributed to a number of factors, including changes in the economy, longer prison sentences and amount of time served, better policing and patrolling strategies, and legalization of abortion (see Chapter 3).[19]

Alternatively, some of the crime legislation passed by Congress did little to reduce crime. The *1968 Omnibus Crime Control Bill* and the *Comprehensive Crime Control Act of 1984*, for example, had only a negligible impact on the crime rate.[20] In fact, crime soared during the 1970s and early 1980s. Yet, curiously, throughout most of this period, the public did not perceive crime to be much of a problem. It was not until the early 1990s that public perceptions on the seriousness of crime changed, and they changed very quickly. By August 1994, shortly before Congress voted on the *Violent Crime Control and Law Enforcement Act*, 37 percent of Americans believed that crime was the most important problem facing the nation; today, only about 2 percent believe this to be true (see FIGURE 1–3).[21]

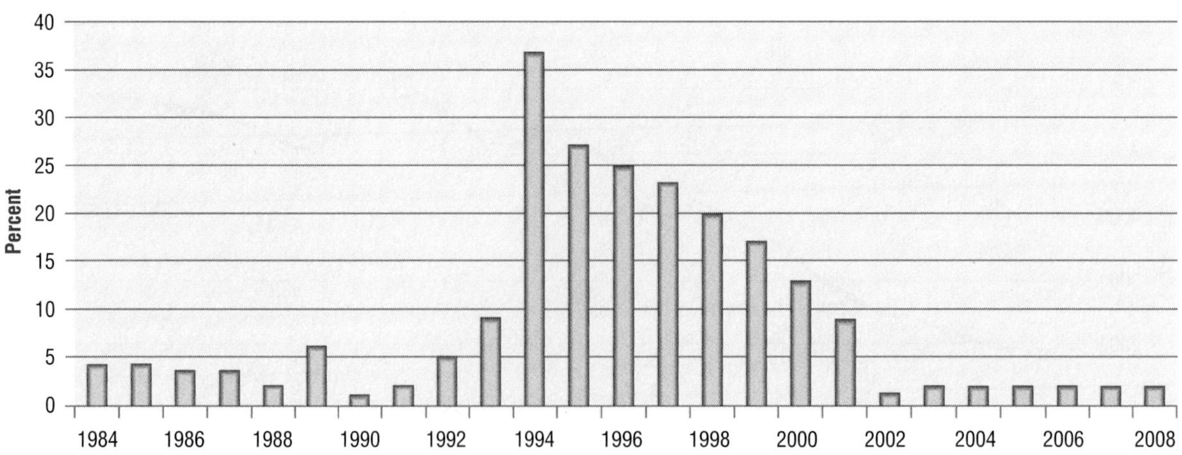

FIGURE 1–3 Percent of Americans Who Believe Crime Is the Nation's Most Important Problem, 1984–2008

Source: Ann Pastore and Kathleen Maguire, *Sourcebook of Criminal Justice Statistics, 2003*, 31st ed. (Washington, DC: U.S. Department of Justice, 2006), available at http://www.albany.edu/sourcebook/pdf/t212006.pdf, Table 2.1, accessed October 12, 2008; CBS News/*New York Times* Poll, March 28–April 2, 2008, available at http://www.pollingreport.com/prioriti.htm, accessed October 12, 2008.

Crime Control in the United States

It is no understatement to say that it is difficult for a heterogeneous society to agree on the nature of the crime problem or on ways to control it. Which behaviors should be considered crimes? Which limitations (if any) should be imposed on law enforcement officers when they are enforcing the law? How severely should criminals convicted of violent offenses be punished? Opinions differ, yet maintaining order in society is one of the primary functions of government. The criminal justice system in a democratic nation will be held accountable to its citizenry with respect to how it goes about maintaining order and ensuring due process.

Crime control in the United States is under the domain of the **criminal justice system**, which establishes many of the rules that govern social interaction, enforces the standards of conduct necessary to protect individuals and the community, and establishes the punishments for violating those rules in an effort to help people live together in peace and unity. More specifically, agencies and procedures in the criminal justice system investigate criminal conduct, make arrests, gather evidence, bring charges against alleged offenders, conduct trials, impose sentences, and carry out punishments to battle the problem of crime.

The Structure of the Criminal Justice System

The United States does not have a single, monolithic criminal justice system that is centralized and controlled by a national government. Instead, the U.S. criminal justice system is a loosely coupled system made up of three major components—law enforcement, courts, and corrections—that operate across federal, state, and local levels (see TABLE 1-1).

- **Federal Level.** The **federal criminal code** defines federal crimes. Dozens of federal government law enforcement agencies enforce laws, such as the Federal Bureau of Investigation (FBI) and the Drug Enforcement Administration (DEA). The federal government also has a system of courts, including District Courts, Courts of Ap-

TABLE 1-1 Criminal Justice System Agencies

	Federal	State	Local
Law enforcement	Federal Bureau of Investigation Drug Enforcement Administration Secret Service U.S. Marshals	State police Highway patrol State Bureau of Narcotics State Fish and Game	Municipal police County police Town constables
Courts	U.S. Supreme Court U.S. Courts of Appeal U.S. District Courts Federal Magistrates	State supreme court State court of appeals	Criminal court City or town court Justice of the Peace court Traffic court Juvenile court
Corrections	Federal Bureau of Prisons Federal probation Federal parole	State department of corrections State parole	County jail City lock-up County probation Community corrections

peals, and the U.S. Supreme Court, as well as a system of corrections, including the Federal Bureau of Prisons and federal probation and parole agencies.

- **State Level.** Each state has a criminal code that defines state crimes and provides statutes setting punishments for offenders. Every state also has its own system of law enforcement, courts, and corrections for both adult and juvenile offenders.
- **Local Level.** Counties and cities have sheriff's departments and municipal (city) police agencies, city lock-ups and county jails, community corrections programs, and city and county criminal courts, Justice of the Peace courts, and town courts.

Each agency has its own distinctive operating system, though the jurisdictions and activities of these organizations may overlap. For example, the Virginia Tech shootings were investigated by federal, state, local, and campus law enforcement agencies.[22] In that instance, the crime occurred on the university campus (campus police) located in Blacksburg, Virginia (city and state police), and was characterized as a terrorist act (federal law enforcement). Because of this overlap, "turf wars" can occur, with the various criminal justice agencies not cooperating smoothly or effectively. Conflicts may arise from differences in opinion about how crime should be controlled and how justice should be achieved. Because one of the most important functions of law enforcement is to investigate crime and apprehend criminals, officers often see defense attorneys as working against them when they obtain acquittals for defendants. Similarly, police may feel that judges contribute to the crime problem when they hand out reduced sentences to chronic offenders. Sometimes federal and local prosecutors may engage in battles when, after investigating criminal activity and preparing cases for prosecution, each party wants to control the investigation and receive recognition for any success.

Tensions also exist between the courts and corrections personnel. Although state prison administrators may believe they are best suited to establish institutional rules and policies, federal judges sometimes intervene on behalf of inmates, declaring single institutions or even entire correctional systems to be in violation of inmates' constitutional rights. Also, in an effort to get tough on crime, local judges may sentence increasing numbers of offenders to prison—only to aggravate the problem of prison overcrowding. Even within a prison, the demands and interests of correctional officers (e.g., security) may conflict with those of treatment staff.

More typically, the different parts of the criminal justice system work together very well. Prosecutors cooperate with police to investigate crimes, such as drug trafficking, and often assist officers when evaluating evidence to ensure that it will later be admissible in court. Judges review and sign search and arrest warrants brought to them by police. At trial, law enforcement officers are frequently witnesses for the prosecution. When offenders are released from prison and on parole, they are supervised by parole officers, who work closely with law enforcement to monitor their activities.

Law Enforcement

In the United States, there are more than 17,000 local, state, federal, and special law enforcement agencies (e.g., campus police) that collectively employ roughly 1 million people, nearly 90 percent of whom work for state and local agencies (see TABLE 1-2).[23] Most Americans are aware of their local police and sheriff's personnel because they see them almost daily, patrolling streets, managing crowds, and making traffic stops.

The most important goals of police are to enforce the law and to maintain order. To achieve these goals, law enforcement officers are actively engaged in crime prevention, investigating reported crimes, participating in community-based programs, such as the Police Athletic League, and arresting criminal suspects. Officers also respond to domestic disturbance calls, settle disputes, calm loud parties, and remove drunks and transients from city streets.

TABLE 1-2 Number of Police Agencies and Number of Full-Time Sworn Officers

Type of Agency	Number of Agencies	Number of Full-Time Sworn Officers
TOTAL	**17,941**	**836,787**
All State and Local	17,876	731,903
Local police	12,776	446,974
Sheriff	3,067	175,018
Primary state	49	58,190
Special jurisdiction*	1,481	49,393
Constable/marshal	513	2,323
Federal	65	104,884

*Special jurisdiction law enforcement agencies include campus, airport, harbor, railroad, and mass transit police.

Sources: Bureau of Justice Statistics, http://www.ojp.usdoj.gov/bjs/lawenf.htm, accessed April 24, 2008; Brian Reaves, *Federal Law Enforcement Agencies* (Washington, DC: U.S. Department of Justice, 2006); Peter Horne, "Policewomen," *The Police Chief* 73:56–61 (2006).

State and local law enforcement officers also provide citizens with valuable services and regulate traffic. Over time, the **service function** performed by these officers has changed dramatically. Early in the twentieth century, for instance, police provided shelter for the homeless. Today, however, the service activities of officers include opening locked car doors, searching for lost children, providing citizens with directions, assisting the elderly, and more. When officers are performing traffic duties, for example, you will often see them directing vehicles at concerts and sporting events, investigating accidents, enforcing speed limits and other traffic laws (such as running a red light and failure to wear a seat belt), and arresting motorists who are driving under the influence of alcohol or drugs.

There are 65 federal law enforcement agencies that employ more than 105,000 persons; these agencies include the U.S. Secret Service, the Capitol Police, U.S. Customs, the U.S. Mint Police, and the Bureau of Indian Affairs.[24] Like state and local police, federal law enforcement agencies also do more than enforce federal laws. For instance, the U.S. Park Police has a Traffic Safety Unit (TSU) that coordinates the force's alcohol and speed enforcement programs and handles all fatal motor vehicle collisions within its jurisdiction. In addition, the TSU instructs Park Police personnel, as well as other local, state, and federal agencies, in the use of radar, laser, accident investigation, forensic scene mapping, and standardized field sobriety testing, as well as other policing operations.[25]

Courts

The United States has a dual system of courts, composed of parallel court systems at the federal and state levels. Every state (plus the District of Columbia and all U.S. territories such as Guam, Puerto Rico, and the Virgin Islands) has its own court system. Each state court interprets and applies state laws, whereas the federal court applies federal laws. These systems operate largely independently. Occasionally, however, cases at the state level that involve constitutional issues are appealed to the federal courts. Nearly all decisions decided by the U.S. Supreme Court originated from cases originally filed at the state level.

Both federal and state court systems are organized into three tiers: lower courts, intermediate appellate courts, and courts of last resort, also known as supreme courts. The lower courts are further divided into courts of limited jurisdiction and general trial courts, or courts of general jurisdiction. Courts of limited jurisdiction handle the majority of criminal cases, dealing with infractions of city ordinances (e.g., abandoned vehicles, loud music, failure to remove snow from sidewalks, and dog leash laws) and

Andrea Yates killed her five children by drowning them in the family bathtub. At her first trial she was convicted of first-degree murder but her conviction was overturned on appeal. At her second trial, Yates was found not guilty by reason of insanity.

misdemeanors (e.g., shoplifting and disorderly conduct). More than 3000 general trial courts operate in the United States, plus 94 U.S. District Courts that hear felony cases.[26]

The lower courts are the first to hear a case. The process begins with an **initial appearance**, which is the first appearance in court of a person who has been arrested, to hear charges read, be advised of his or her rights, and have bail determined. If it is determined that the suspect probably committed the crime, bail is then set depending on the seriousness of the crime and counsel is assigned to suspects who cannot afford an attorney. Guilty pleas are accepted from misdemeanant defendants who decide to forfeit their right to a trial. If the defendant pleads "not guilty," a trial is held to determine the guilt or innocence of the alleged offender or a plea agreement is negotiated with the prosecutor. If an offender is found guilty at trial, he or she is then sentenced by the court.

Intermediate appellate courts hear appeals of cases brought to them from the lower courts. They do not retry cases, but rather review transcripts from cases and hear testimony on issues concerning violations of legal procedure, such as the admission of illegally obtained evidence, which may form a basis for overturning or modifying a lower court's decision. In 2002, for instance, Andrea Yates was sentenced to life in prison for murdering three of her five children.[27] The jury rejected the insanity defense, concluding that Yates knew right from wrong at the time she killed her children. In 2005, the case was appealed to the Texas First Court of Appeals, which reversed the conviction because an expert witness for the state, Dr. Park Dietz, had presented false testimony when he said that Yates might have been influenced by a particular episode of the *Law and Order* television program, though no such episode ever aired. Given that one or more jurors might have been influenced by this false testimony, a new trial was ordered. At this second trial, Yates was found not guilty by reason of insanity and sentenced to a state-run, maximum-security mental hospital.[28]

The U.S. Supreme Court has jurisdiction over all cases involving federal or constitutional issues. It reviews federal district court decisions as well as decisions appealed from state courts focusing on issues of federal law. The U.S. Supreme Court does not have jurisdiction over cases involving state law or violations of a state's constitution. In these instances, each state's own Supreme Court is the final arbiter of justice.

Corrections

Federal, state, and local correctional systems are responsible for the custody, punishment, and rehabilitation of convicted offenders. In 2006, more than 2.2 million individuals were incarcerated in local, state, and federal corrections facilities (i.e., jails, halfway houses, correctional and detention centers, reformatories, and prisons) in the United States. In addition, more than 4 million offenders were on probation and an additional 1 million offenders were on parole.[29]

The Federal Bureau of Prisons operates more than 175 prisons, including detention centers, medical centers, prison camps, and penitentiaries. There are an additional 1300 state-run correctional facilities that house persons convicted of state-level crimes. Nearly 400,000 people work in state correctional systems, and more than 35,000 individuals work for the federal correctional system.[30]

Both federal and state correctional systems classify inmates based on various factors, such as the seriousness of the offense committed, treatment needs, and perceived dangerousness. Once an inmate is classified, he or she is assigned to a suitable facility or program. Offenders who are convicted of felonies are typically confined in prisons, although they may be sentenced to a term in jail; persons convicted of misdemeanors are detained in local jails or minimum-security corrections facilities. Correctional institutions are categorized as super-maximum-, maximum-, medium-, minimum-, or low-security facilities.

The primary functions of correctional institutions are to provide offenders with treatments, punish them for their wrongdoings, and shield society from any harm they might otherwise cause. Sometimes these institutions offer counseling, job training, and education to aid in the rehabilitation of offenders. Community corrections, including probation and parole services, focus on reintegrating offenders into society through supervision and participation in counseling that works to resolve job, family, education, and drug- or alcohol-related problems.

As part of her community service for drunken driving and possession of cocaine, a Los Angeles court ordered Lindsay Lohan to spend two days working in a morgue to show her graphic evidence of dead bodies.

The Criminal Justice Process

The structure of the criminal justice system is different from the criminal justice process.[31] The structure refers to the institutions, agencies, and personnel who enforce and apply the criminal law. The **criminal justice process** is a complex process that includes the stages discussed in this section.

Law Enforcement

Initial Contact

For most people, their initial contact with the criminal justice system begins with the police. Usually, it entails an officer observing a crime in progress, a victim or a witness reporting a crime, or an ongoing investigation providing law enforcement officials with enough evidence to take action.

Criminal Investigation

Once the police determine that a crime has been committed, they will gather evidence and may identify a suspect. Occasionally a suspect is apprehended at the crime scene, but most often he or she is identified later through information obtained from victims and witnesses, physical evidence (e.g., blood or hair samples, fingerprints, tire marks), or informants.

Arrest and Booking

If police believe that a suspect committed a crime, they arrest him or her. Once an arrest is made, authorities will book the individual, which involves recording the name of the

Headline Crime

The False Confession of John Mark Karr

In 2006, John Mark Karr voluntarily confessed to police that he had killed, drugged, and had sex with 10-year-old JonBenet Ramsey. Karr was arrested and charged with criminal offenses related to the murder. Before Karr's first scheduled appearance in a courtroom, however, Boulder (Colorado) District Attorney Mary Lacy dropped the charges against Karr after DNA tests failed to tie him to the crime, despite his own statements of involvement. This case demonstrated that when a prosecutor thinks there is insufficient evidence to proceed with a prosecution, he or she will likely dismiss the charges, which Lacy did.

Source: Tom Kenworthy, "Ramsey Suspect's DNA Not a Match," *USA Today*, August 29, 2006, pp. 1A, 3A

person arrested, the place and time of the arrest, the reason for the arrest, and the name of the arresting authority. At booking, suspects also are fingerprinted, photographed, and placed in holding cells, where they await further interrogation.

Courts

Charging

After making an arrest, police turn over the information they have gathered about the crime to the prosecutor, who decides which charges, if any, will be filed with the court. The prosecutor may decide either to dismiss the case, leading to the suspect's release, or to proceed with the case.

Initial Appearance, Preliminary Hearing, or Arraignment

If the case proceeds, the defendant next makes his or her initial appearance in court, where the charges are read, bail is set, and the defendant is informed of his or her rights. If the defendant is charged with a misdemeanor, he or she may enter a plea. If this plea is "guilty," the judge may impose a sentence immediately.

If the defendant is charged with a felony, he or she may choose to not enter a plea at the initial appearance. Instead, a judge may schedule a preliminary hearing to determine probable cause (i.e., to determine that there is sufficient evidence that a crime was committed and that the accused person likely committed it).

In cases where a defendant has been indicted by a grand jury and probable cause has been established through the grand jury investigation, the defendant's first appearance in court is at an arraignment, where the trial date is set.

Bail and Detention

Following the initial appearance, many defendants post bail (a sum of money that the arrested person pays to guarantee that he or she will appear at future hearings). As an alternative to posting bail, most jurisdictions allow "good risk" defendants to make a personal promise to appear in court, called release on recognizance (ROR).

Defendants who cannot post bail or who do not qualify for ROR will be transferred to the city or county jail, where they are likely to remain until their arraignment date. Some defendants are not eligible for bail because they are viewed by the court as posing a serious threat to the community (including victims or witnesses who may testify against the defendant) or because they are likely to abscond (run away). These defendants are held in preventive detention.

On December 5, 2008, a Las Vegas Judge sentenced O. J. Simpson to at least 15 years in prison for leading an armed hotel room confrontation over sports memorabilia in 2007. Simpson will be eligible for parole in 9 years.

Plea Bargaining

Very few cases actually go to trial. In fact, nearly 95 percent of all cases resulting in felony convictions never reach a jury. Instead, they are settled through plea bargains in which a defendant agrees to plead guilty in exchange for some consideration, such as prosecutors dropping a charge or count or making a recommendation for a reduced sentence.[32]

Trial

Defendants who choose to go to trial are guaranteed the right to a trial by jury, although they may request a bench trial, in which the judge alone determines guilt or innocence. In either situation, the trial concludes with one of three possible verdicts: not guilty (acquittal), guilty (conviction), or undecided (hung jury). When a trial ends in a hung jury, the prosecutor may refile the charges and prosecute the defendant again.

Sentencing and Appeals

Following a guilty plea or a verdict, a sentencing hearing is set. The judge decides the appropriate sentence by considering both characteristics of the offense and characteristics of the offender that might increase or decrease the severity of the sentence (known as aggravating or mitigating factors) as well as other relevant materials. Often, the sentence the judge can impose is limited by law.

If defendants believe they were unfairly convicted or sentenced, they may appeal their verdicts or sentences to an appellate court. This court reviews the lower court's transcripts solely for procedural errors, such as admission of illegally obtained evidence. If an appellate court determines significant errors were made at trial, it may overturn the conviction and order a new trial or vacate the sentence and order a new sentencing hearing.

Quarterback Michael Vick was sentenced to 23 months at a federal minimum-security prison in Leavenworth, Kansas, after pleading guilty to dog fighting charges.

Corrections

Probation

A convicted offender may be placed on probation, a sentencing option typically involving a suspended prison sentence and supervision in the community. The conditions of probation might include paying a fine, participating in psychological counseling, taking part in a drug or alcohol treatment program, obtaining a job, or regularly reporting to a probation officer. If the offender violates any of these conditions, the court may revoke his or her probation and return the probationer to prison.

Incarceration and Rehabilitation

If the court decides that probation is not an appropriate sentence, the offender may be incarcerated in jail (for misdemeanor convictions and some felony convictions) or placed in prison (for longer-term imprisonment).

Release and Parole

Few offenders serve their full prison sentence. Some are released early as a result of earning "good time reductions" in their sentences; others receive parole, a type of conditional release. If released early, the offender is supervised in the community by a parole officer and must follow a set of clearly articulated conditions. If any of the conditions are violated, the offender may be returned to prison.

Perceptions of the Criminal Justice System

A goal of the criminal justice system is to achieve justice. To do so, the system must balance both the rights of the victim and the rights of the accused. When considering the meaning of justice, several questions come to mind with respect to the behavior of the criminal justice system and its agents:

- When should police officers use force? How much and what type of force should they use?
- When should convicted offenders be eligible for probation and returned to the community?
- How should the courts use their resources to balance the needs of victims, their families, and the public against the rights of the accused and convicted?

Developing a positive public view of the criminal justice system is necessary for it to function effectively and efficiently across all three components: law enforcement, courts, and corrections. If citizens believe the criminal justice system is corrupt or that it places the rights of the accused above the rights of victims, then they will be less likely to cooperate with criminal justice officials, thus putting the entire system in jeopardy.

Police

Since the 1960s, public opinion polls have reported that generally the majority of the U.S. public holds a favorable view of the police.[33] To ensure effectiveness, the police depend on the public's support, participation, and assistance in providing information that helps them to solve crimes and make arrests.

Citizens will usually report a crime to the police only if they believe that:

- The offense is serious enough to warrant official intervention.

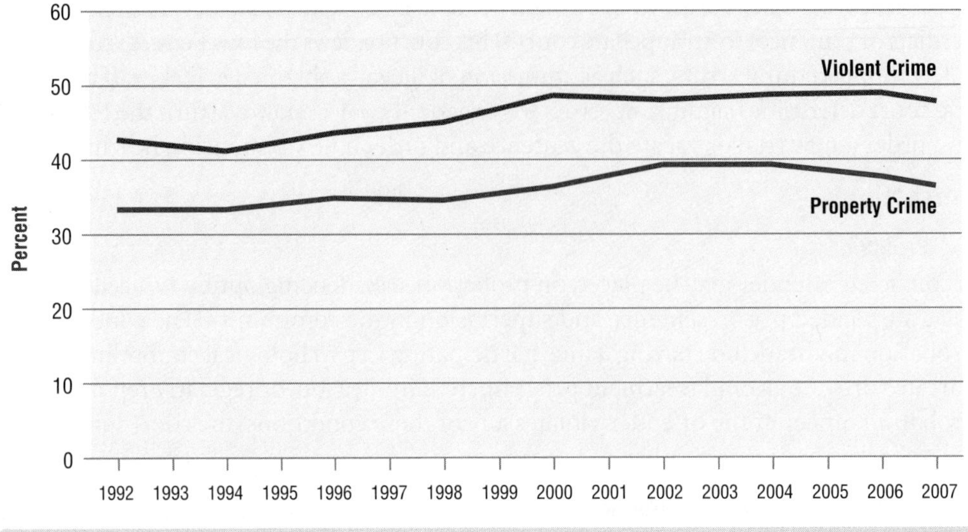

FIGURE 1-4 Percent of Serious Crime Reported to Police, 1992–2007

Source: Shannon Catalano, *Criminal Victimization, 2005* (Washington, DC: U.S. Department of Justice, 2006); Michael Rand and Shannon Catalano, *Criminal Victimization, 2006* (Washington, DC: U.S. Department of Justice, 2007).

- Police will respond to their request.
- Police will provide a useful service at the crime scene.

During 2006, 49 percent of all violent victimizations and 38 percent of all property crimes were reported to the police (see FIGURE 1-4). Rape and sexual assault were less likely to be reported to the police than robbery and aggravated assault. Robbery and aggravated assault were equally likely to be reported to police. Fifty-seven percent of robberies and 59 percent of aggravated assaults were reported to the police in 2006. As in previous years, most motor vehicle thefts were reported to the police. About 81 percent of these victimizations were reported to the police in 2006.[34] A few of the reasons the crime reporting rate is not higher include:

- Fear of retaliation
- The individual's decision to handle the matter informally
- The crime is minor
- Police will not be able to do anything
- Reluctance to bother the police[35]

Courts

In 2006, 80 percent of all Americans reported having confidence in the courts and the criminal justice system.[36] This confidence is critical to the effective operation of the courts not only because some judicial officials depend on public support for reelection, but also because public participation is necessary for forming citizen juries and providing witness testimony.

In addition, jury duty requires people to take time away from their jobs and family, disrupts their normal routines, and offers little compensation. If people see jury duty as more of an inconvenience than a civic responsibility, they are more likely to try to find ways to avoid serving.

With the exception of expert witnesses, witnesses receive no remuneration for their time or testimony. For many people, being questioned on the witness stand causes anxiety and is very unpleasant. Negative experiences in the court may lead to a reduced willingness to cooperate in the future.

Corrections

Prisons and jails must have public support for funding to build, staff, and operate corrections facilities. Although most Americans favor building new prisons, reformatories, halfway houses, and detention centers, few want them near where they live, a phenomenon now commonly called the NIMBY (Not in My Back Yard) syndrome. Yet, some communities have lobbied their legislatures to build new facilities in their towns as a way of providing jobs and to bolster the local economy.[37]

It is becoming common for citizens to openly protest persons who cooperate with police or those who work for police as paid informants.

Criminal Justice in Popular Culture

Popular culture also may affect public perceptions of the criminal justice system. Through the repetition of certain themes and content, popular culture may potentially either distort or confirm viewers' beliefs about the real world. For instance, television programs such as *Bones*, *Boston Legal*, *Cold Case*, *CSI*, *Dexter*, *Homicide*, *Law and Order*, *New Amsterdam*, and *Without a Trace* often provide exaggerated images of crime and justice.

One report found that violence was portrayed on more than 80 percent of television programs. Murder alone accounted for nearly one-fourth of all television crimes; in reality, murder accounts for only 1 percent of all violent crime and only 0.2 percent of all serious crimes reported to the police.[38]

The high rates of arrest and conviction of criminals on television are also fictional. A crime is cleared when a law enforcement agency makes an arrest, charges at least one person with the commission of a crime, and turns the case over to the court for prosecution.[39] Typically, for all serious violent and serious property crimes in a particular year, the **crime clearance rate** is about 20 percent.[40] In some instances law enforcement agencies may clear a crime as a result of "exceptional means." Examples of exceptional clearances include, but are not limited to, the death of the offender (e.g., suicide, justifiably killed by police or private citizens), the victim's refusal to cooperate with the prosecution after having identified the offender, or the denial of extradition because the offender committed a crime in another jurisdiction and is being prosecuted.[41] Today, increasing numbers of witnesses—particularly ones who witnessed serious violent crimes—are refusing to cooperate with law enforcement investigations with such regularity that their silence is driving down the crime clearance rate for homicide and other violent crimes. The Police Executive Research Forum recently reported a 78 percent decrease in the willingness of witnesses to testify, and a 45 percent drop in solved cases. As is shown in TABLE 1-3, witnesses are pressured into silence in a variety of ways.

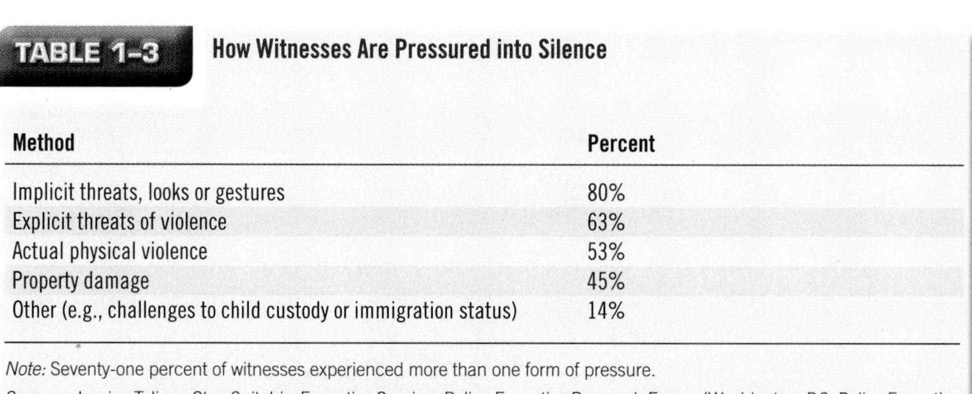

TABLE 1-3 How Witnesses Are Pressured into Silence

Method	Percent
Implicit threats, looks or gestures	80%
Explicit threats of violence	63%
Actual physical violence	53%
Property damage	45%
Other (e.g., challenges to child custody or immigration status)	14%

Note: Seventy-one percent of witnesses experienced more than one form of pressure.

Sources: Jessica Toliver, *Stop Snitchin*, Executive Session, Police Executive Research Forum (Washington, DC: Police Executive Research Forum, 2008); Kevin Johnson, "Witness Troubles Stymie Police," *USA Today*, March 24, 2008, p. 1A.

FOCUS ON CRIMINAL JUSTICE

Criminal Justice and Popular Culture

Film, the Internet, music, television, and video games are powerful forces in shaping the values of contemporary American culture. The first films to focus on crime and criminal justice were released in the early 1930s, when movies filled with gangsters and crooks became popular. These films followed a pattern established in radio programming that presented the listening public with an underlying moral lesson: Villains do not win and heroes never lose. They also stressed the importance of good over evil, truth over lies, and civilization over anarchy. Many films in the 1960s and 1970s, such as *Bonnie and Clyde* and *The Godfather*, also emphasized the theme of good versus evil, despite their glorification of outlaws and mobsters.

A second theme of crime films, which emerged after the turbulent 1960s, reflected a conservative public backlash against crime and what was perceived to be an ineffective criminal justice system. In the 1970s, a number of vigilante movies were released, including *Dirty Harry*, *Sudden Impact*, and the *Death Wish* series. These films blamed crime on liberal permissiveness and hypocrisy, and showed that the crime problem could be solved only by resorting to violence.

More recent crime films have focused on injustices within the criminal justice system, illustrating problems caused by racial and ethnic tensions, gang violence, and illegal drugs. *Boyz 'N the Hood*, *American History X*, and *Traffic*, for example, presented rather bleak images of society's ability to solve pervasive social problems.

On television, police have dominated images of crime and its control for several decades, starting in the 1950s with programs such as *Dragnet* and *Highway Patrol*, and more recently with shows such as *Bones*, *Law and Order*, and *CSI*. Television also presents a mythology about crime: The offender's guilt is clear, and police are portrayed as keepers of the peace and protectors of the public. Of more significance is that television shows the law being applied equally to all citizens—black and white, female and male, poor and wealthy—illustrating the notion that no citizen is above the law.

Criminal courts have also been portrayed on television through both older and more contemporary shows (*Perry Mason*, *The Practice*, *Ally McBeal*, and *Boston Legal*). These programs provide a brief but distorted portrayal of defense attorneys, prosecutors, and judges. Unlike in real life, nearly all the criminal cases presented on television go to trial and few are plea bargained.

Viewers have the opportunity to see the "realities" of the criminal justice system through "infotainment," or programs that blend news with entertainment. Programs such as *Cops* show real or recreated events in which police officers arrest and interact with victims and witnesses. A 24-hour cable channel, truTV (originally called The Courtroom Television Network), also presents live coverage of criminal trials. It was launched in 1991 to inform viewers about the inside workings of the criminal justice system.

Music has also been one of the most pervasive and accessible elements of popular culture. Folk music and the blues have always contained images of outlaws, gunfights, and prison, whereas country music has usually emphasized people languishing in prison, the hangovers and pains from drinking, fighting, lost love, and occasional challenges to unjust intrusions of authority. Some contemporary rock and rap songs also contain images of crime, violence, and the injustice of the criminal justice system. Songs such as the Beatles' "Maxwell's Silver Hammer," Bob Marley's "I Shot the Sheriff," Timbuk3's "Bank Robber," and those reflecting acceptance of drug use, such as Eminem's "My Fault" and J.J. Cale's "Cocaine," present challenges to conventional morality and law.

While critics complain about the glorification of crime and extensive violence in film, music, television, and video games, the target of many individuals is the content of "gangsta rap" music that discusses forcible rape, murder, violent

(continues)

(continued)

robbery, and the sexual exploitation of women. Defenders of gangsta rap argue that these songs and their messages reflect the economic and social frustrations of the urban underclass and provide a window into urban culture. At the same time, artists such as Biggie Smalls, Busta Rhymes, Eminem, 50 Cent, Ludacris, N.W.A., and Tupac have been criticized for degrading women and glorifying drugs and violence. Critics complain that these artists encourage adolescents to take unnecessary risks, consume drugs, and commit violent crime, thereby putting unnecessary strain on law enforcement agencies that are already operating with sparse and meager resources.

Sources: Ray Surette, *Media, Crime, and Criminal Justice*, 3rd ed. (Belmont, CA: Wadsworth, 2006); Nicole Rafter, *Shots in the Mirror: Crime Films and Society* (New York: Oxford University Press, 2006); Elayne Rapping, *Law and Justice as Seen on TV* (New York: New York University Press, 2003); Harry Benshoff and Sean Griffin, *America on Film* (Malden, MA: Blackwell, 2004).

Additionally, television news and documentaries may affect public perceptions of crime and justice by their emphasis on dramatic violent crime and crimes committed by public figures. In fact, it has been found that the more television people watch, the more likely they are to be afraid of becoming a crime victim.[42] Some studies point to the possibility that frequent viewing of violence on television may contribute to crime by increasing the aggressive behavior of viewers. Fortunately, however, there is little evidence to suggest that when citizens sit on juries to make decisions about the guilt or innocence of a suspect that they are influenced by what they may have previously viewed on television or film.[43]

WRAPPING IT UP

Chapter Highlights

- There is crime in all societies. To respond to crime, societies establish laws prohibiting certain behaviors, define the rules that govern the enforcement of law, and create institutions and systems for responding to crime.
- The criminal justice system is an interrelated set of subsystems that operate horizontally and vertically across federal, state, and local levels. The laws and jurisdictions of each subsystem sometimes overlap, which often leads to conflicts among the various agencies.
- The criminal justice process is composed of well-defined legal rules that specify the procedures through which suspects enter and are treated by the criminal justice system.
- The perceptions citizens hold of the criminal justice system may affect whether they will assist the police, court, and correction systems in carrying out their duties.

Words to Know

acquit A verdict of not guilty.

crime clearance rate The percentage of crimes for which law enforcement agencies make an arrest, charge at least one person with the commission of a crime, and turn the case over to the court for prosecution.

criminal justice process The procedures that occur in the criminal justice system, from a citizen's initial contact with police to his or her potential arrest, charging, booking, prosecution, conviction, sentencing, incarceration or placement on probation, and appeals (if any).

criminal justice system A complex set of interrelated subsystems composed of three major components—police, courts, and corrections—that operate at the federal, state, and local levels.

federal criminal code The legal code that identifies and defines federal crimes.

initial appearance A defendant's first appearance in court to be informed of the charge(s), advised of his or her rights, and to have bail determined.

norms The rules and expectations by which a society guides the behavior of its members.

service function Role of police to assist citizens with noncriminal matters, such as opening locked car doors.

Think and Discuss

1. Is the amount of crime in our society normal, or have we simply come to define the level of crime that we have as being normal?

2. Why are perceptions of crime and justice so important to our thinking about crime and to the daily operation of the criminal justice system?

3. The crime rate has generally decreased during the past decade, and only a very small percentage of Americans believe crime is the nation's most serious problem. Why do you believe the crime rate has dropped? Do you feel safer today than you did only a few years ago?

Notes

1. "Massacre at Virginia Tech," available at http://www.cnn.com/SPECIALS/2007/virginiatech.shootings/, accessed July 26, 2008.
2. Solomon Herbert, "King Litigation May Spur Healing or Unrest: Rodney King's Civil Lawsuit against the Los Angeles Police Department," *Black Enterprise*, September, 1992, available at http://www.findarticles.com/p/articles/mi_m1365/is_n2_v23/ai_12539601, accessed May 7, 2008.
3. Rodney King, "Quotation of the Day," *The New York Times*, May 2, 1992, p. 6A.
4. Émile Durkheim, *The Rules of Sociological Method*, translated by Sarah Solovay and John Mueller (New York: Free Press, 1885/1938), p. 68.
5. "Amsterdam Coffee Shop Directory," available at http://www.drugpolicy.org/global/drugpolicyby/westerneurop/thenetherlan/, accessed July 26, 2008; "Drug Policy around the World," available at http://www.drugpolicy.org/global/drugpolicyby/westerneurop/thenetherlan/, accessed July 7, 2008.
6. Émile Durkheim, *The Division of Labor and Society* (New York: Free Press, 1893/1964); Durkheim, note 4.
7. Sue Lindsey and Dionne Walker, "Va. Tech Study: Add Security, Help for Troubled Students," *USA Today*, August 23, 2007, p. 5A; Greg Toppo, "College on the Alert in Low-Tech Ways, Too," *USA Today*, April 15, 2008, p. 4D; "Easing Campus Privacy Rules," *The Week*, April 4, 2008, p. 4.
8. Armand Mauss, *Social Problems as Social Movements* (Philadelphia: Lippincott, 1975).
9. Erich Goode, *Drugs in American Society*, 7th ed. (New York: McGraw-Hill, 2007); George Gallup, Jr., *The Gallup Poll* (Princeton, NJ: Gallup Poll, September 1993); Gary Burden, "U.S. Drug Policy May Be in for a New Look," *Law Enforcement News* 15:5 (1993).
10. George Gallup, Jr., *The Gallup Poll* (Princeton, NJ: Gallup Poll, September 1989).
11. Gallup, note 9; Burden, note 9.
12. *The Violent Crime Control and Law Enforcement Act of 1994* (HR 3355) (Washington, DC: U.S. Government Printing Office, 1994).
13. Kristen Hughes, *Justice Expenditures and Employment in the United States, 2003* (Washington, DC: U.S. Department of Justice, 2006).
14. Hughes, note 13.
15. U.S. Congress, HR 1572; *The Omnibus Crime Control and Safe Streets Act* (P.L. 90-351) (Washington, DC: U.S. Printing Office, 1968); *The Comprehensive Crime Control Bill of 1984* (P.L. 98-473) (Washington, DC: U.S. Government Printing Office, 1984); *The Crime Control Act of 1990* (P.L. 101-647) (Washington, DC: U.S. Government Printing Office, 1990); *The Violent Crime Control and Law Enforcement Act of 1994* (HR 3355), note 12; *USA Patriot Act of 2001* (HR 3162 RDS) (Washington, DC: U.S. Government Printing Office, 2001); *USA Patriot Improvement Act of 2005* (HR 199) (Washington, DC: U.S. Department of Justice, 2006).
16. Federal Bureau of Investigation, *Crime in the United States, 2007* (Washington, DC: U.S. Department of Justice, 2008); *The Omnibus Crime Control and Safe Streets Act*, note 15; *The Comprehensive Crime Control Bill of 1984*, note 15; *The Crime Control Act of 1990*, note 15; *The Violent Crime Control and Law Enforcement Act of 1994*, note 12; *USA Patriot Act of 2001*, note 15; *USA Patriot Improvement Act of 2005*, note 15.

17. *USA Patriot Act of 2001*, note 15; *USA Patriot Improvement Act of 2005*, note 15.

18. *The Crime Control Act of 1990*, note 15; *The Violent Crime Control and Law Enforcement Act of 1994*, note 12.

19. Steven Levitt and Stephen Dubner, *Freakonomics*, rev. ed. (New York: HarperCollins, 2006).

20. *The Omnibus Crime Control and Safe Streets Act*, note 15; *The Comprehensive Crime Control Bill of 1984*, note 15.

21. Ann Pastore and Kathleen Maguire, *Sourcebook of Criminal Justice Statistics, 2003*, 31st edition (Washington, DC: U.S. Department of Justice, 2006), available at www.albany.edu/sourcebook/pdf/t212006.pdf, accessed August 4, 2008; "CBS News/*New York Times* Poll, March 28–April 2, 2008," available at http://www.pollingreport.com/prioriti.htm, accessed August 2, 2008.

22. David Maraniss, "That Was the Desk I Chose to Die Under," *The Washington Post*, April 19, 2007, p. A01; Federal Bureau of Investigation, "School Shooting: Role of the FBI at Virginia Tech," available at http://www.fbi.gov/page2/april07/shootings041607.htm, accessed August 2, 2008.

23. Data on the number of federal, state, local, and campus police agencies is available at http://www.ojp.usdoj.gov/bjs/lawenf.htm, accessed August 1, 2008.

24. Brian Reaves, *Federal Law Enforcement Officers* (Washington, DC: U.S. Department of Justice, 2004), available at http://www.ojp.usdoj.gov/bjs/abstract/fleo04.htm, accessed August 2, 2008.

25. Information on the U.S. Park Police, Traffic Safety Unit, is available at http://www.nps.gov/uspp/traffsaf.htm, accessed August 2, 2008.

26. Information on U.S. courts is available at www.uscourts.gov/, accessed August 1, 2008.

27. Laura Parker, "Yates Rejects State's Plea Offer," *USA Today*, February, 28, 2006, p. 3A.

28. "Woman Not Guilty in Retrial in the Deaths of Her 5 Children," *The New York Times*, July 27, 2006, available at http://www.nytimes.com/2006/07/27/us/27yates.html, accessed August 6, 2008.

29. William Sabol, Heather Couture, and Paige Harrison, *Prisoners in 2006* (Washington, DC: U.S. Department of Justice, 2007).

30. Available at http://www.bop.gov/, accessed August 7, 2008.

31. The discussion is derived from John Ferdico, Henry Fradella, and Christopher Totter, *Criminal Procedure for the Criminal Justice Professional*, 10th ed. (Belmont, CA: Wadsworth, 2008).

32. Available at http://www.pbs.org/wgbh/pages/frontline/shows/plea/etc/synopsis.html, accessed August 12, 2008.

33. Catherine Gallagher, Edward Maguire, Stephen Mastrofski, and Michael Reisig, *The Public Image of the Police* (Alexandria, VA: International Association of Chiefs of Police, 2001).

34. Michael Rand and Susan Catalano, *Criminal Victimization, 2006* (Washington, DC: U.S. Department of Justice, 2007).

35. Rand and Catalano, note 34.

36. "Americans Have Confidence in Courts, Justice System," available at http://www.uscourts.gov/newsroom/confidence.html, accessed July 19, 2008.

37. Sharon Dunn, "Progress on Ault Prison Is Dragging," *Greeley Tribune*, September 10, 2006, available at http://www.greeleytrib.com/article/20060910/NEWS/109100090/-1/rss02, accessed July 27, 2008; Kevin Dayton, "Prison Keeps Impoverished Town Alive," *Honolulu Advertiser*, October 3, 2005, available at http://the.honoluluadvertiser.com/article/2005/Oct/03/ln/FP510030313.html, accessed August 5, 2008; Ryan King, Marc Mauer, and Tracy Huling, *Big Prisons, Small Towns* (Washington, DC: Sentencing Project, 2003), available at www.soros.org/initiatives/justice/articlespublications/publications/bigprisons20030201/bigprisons.pdf, accessed August 4, 2008.

38. Donald Shelton, The *CSI* Effect: Does it Really Exist?," *NIJ Journal* 259:1–6 (2008); Andrew Thomas, "The *CSI* Effect: Fact or Fiction," *Yale Law Review* 115:70–72 (2006); Katherine Ramstand, *The CSI Effect* (New York: Berkley Trade, 2006); Ray Surette, *Media, Crime, and Criminal Justice*, 3rd ed. (Belmont, CA: Wadsworth, 2006); Danlo Yanich, "Kids, Crime, and Local Television," *Crime & Delinquency*

51:103–122 (2005); Kathryn Greene and Marina Krcmar, "Predicting Exposure to and Liking of Media Violence," *Communication Studies* 56:71–93 (2005); Franklin Gilliam, Jr., and Shanto Iyengar, "Prime Suspects: The Influence of Local Television News on the Viewing Public," *American Journal of Political Science* 44:560–573 (2000).

39. Federal Bureau of Investigation, note 16.

40. Federal Bureau of Investigation, note 16.

41. Federal Bureau of Investigation, note 16.

42. Kenneth Dowler, "Media Consumption and Public Attitudes toward Crime and Justice," *Journal of Criminal Justice and Popular Culture* 10:109–126 (2003).

43. Donald Shelton, Young Kim, and Gregg Barak, "A Study of Juror Expectations and Demands Concerning Scientific Evidence: Does the '*CSI* Effect' Exist?" *Vanderbilt Journal of Entertainment and Technology Law* 9:331–368 (2006).

CHAPTER

Criminal Law: The Foundation of Criminal Justice

OBJECTIVES

1 Grasp the relationship between civil and criminal law, and describe how the law distinguishes among different levels of seriousness.

2 Identify the essential elements of a crime, including *actus reus* and *mens rea*.

3 Know the meaning and uses of the various justifications, excuses, and exemptions that may bar legal liability.

4 Understand the Constitutional amendments that deal with due process, the rights of the accused, and the applicability of these principles.

PROFILES IN CRIME AND JUSTICE

Mark D. Cunningham PhD, ABPP

Clinical and Forensic Psychologist
Lewisville, Texas

As a board-certified forensic psychologist, I travel from Dallas to other parts of the country. Most of my work involves evaluations and testimony related to sentencing decisions in death penalty cases. Evaluations for capital sentencing require extreme breadth, typically meaning a retrieval of all available records and extensive interviews of the defendant, the defendant's immediate and extended family, and numerous other third parties. These evaluations are also literature intensive, drawing on research linking adverse developmental factors to criminal violence and on correctional data that inform risk assessments of future prison behavior. When in the office or in my seat on an airplane, I review and analyze these records and research findings as I prepare reports or testimony.

I also author scholarly publications regarding standards and special considerations in capital evaluations, perform research regarding capital offenders, participate in investigations of rates and correlates of prison violence, and teach workshops. I enjoy the intellectual stimulation, as well as the constantly changing routine and travel of this work and scholarship.

I came to these professional roles by a circuitous route that was part professional evolution and part serendipity. My doctoral training was in clinical psychology, and my early practice focused on providing treatment services. This experience would later prove invaluable in developing the clinical skills that I would bring to bear in the forensic arena. Over time, I was called on to provide expert witness evaluations for the courts. My increasing involvement in forensic cases led to a several-year process of intensive reading and workshop attendance in pursuit of board certification in forensic psychology. The sustained board preparation reawakened the scientist in me and also resulted in my first capital case referral. My scholarship and practice in the capital sentencing arena grew from there.

Introduction

Throughout history, the creation and evolution of law have been instrumental in promoting and regulating social behavior. Aristotle, for example, believed that law is the essence of social order: Good social order can be built only on good law; bad law can also produce social order, but such order may not be desirable.[1] Law, however, is not inherently good or bad, nor has it always accomplished its goals. Law is good to the extent that it is used or adhered to lawfully. If those individuals who are responsible for administering law fail to operate according to the accepted rules, law may become oppressive and a tool of manipulation.

Laws are formalized rules that prescribe or limit actions. Criminal law is one category of law, which consists of the two subcategories of substantive criminal law and procedural criminal law. **Substantive criminal law** identifies behaviors considered harmful to society, labels those behaviors as crimes, and specifies their punishments. **Procedural criminal law** specifies how crimes are to be investigated and prosecuted. Together, substantive criminal law and procedural criminal law form the foundation of the U.S. system of criminal justice.

Common Law and the Concept of *Stare Decisis*

Although the early legal codes laid a foundation for formalizing principles and customs into law, it was the emergence of English common law that held the greatest significance for the development of criminal law in the United States. The tradition of **common law** allowed judges to determine which behaviors constituted crimes and what appropriate punishment should be imposed when they were violated, thus establishing a body of law common to the entire nation.

One of the most important concepts operating in common law was the doctrine of precedent, or *stare decisis* (literally, "to stand by the decisions"). This doctrine allows courts to interpret and apply law based on previous court decisions. According to *stare decisis*, judges were required to decide new cases in a manner consistent with principles established in prior cases. To the extent that a new case was substantially similar to a previous one, the judge was required to interpret the law in the same way and follow the precedent. Judges were not supposed to create laws, but they could study past legal decisions, discover the principles embodied in them, and apply those principles to new situations.[2]

All laws in the United States must be in accordance with the Constitution.

Contemporary Sources of Criminal Law

Criminal law in the United States has largely grown out of English common law, which was first brought over to America during the colonial period. However, Americans desired a codified system of law to provide greater uniformity, standardization, and predictability. As a result, the states and the federal government began to formalize law by developing statutes and by drawing upon a number of other sources—case law, administrative rules, and the constitutions of the various states and the federal government.

Statutes

Criminal law is contained in written codes called **statutes**. According to the balance of powers established in the Constitution, the law-making function resides in the legislative branch rather than in the judicial branch of government. Congress and state legislatures are responsible for enacting statutes that define crimes (substantive laws) and specify the applicable penalties for their violation as well as law governing legal procedures (procedural laws).

Case Law

Case law is a continuation of the common-law tradition in which judicial decision making in individual cases involves interpreting existing law, looking at relevant precedent decisions, and making judgments about the legitimacy of the law. Because gaps will inevitably exist between what a legislative body intends when it passes a law and what actually happens when that law is enforced, the practice of case law allows the courts to interpret the law as they apply it.[3]

Administrative Rules

The rules, orders, decisions, and regulations established by state and federal administrative agencies are another source of law. The Federal Trade Commission (FTC), Internal Revenue Service (IRS), Food and Drug Administration (FDA), and Environmental Protection Agency (EPA), for example, have all established a multitude of rules and regulations that have the full force and effect of law. These agencies investigate and impose criminal sanctions for such violations as securities fraud, the willful failure to pay income tax, the intentional sale of contaminated food, and the dumping of toxic wastes.

Constitutions

The U.S. Constitution and each of the 50 state constitutions are the final arbiters of substantive and procedural law. A law enacted by a state legislature may be found to be in violation of either that state's constitution or the U.S. Constitution. Federal laws, regulations, or administrative acts may be judged only against the U.S. Constitution. In addition, the Bill of Rights, which was added to the U.S. Constitution in 1791, includes protections afforded to defendants in criminal prosecutions (such as the right to counsel, prohibitions against illegal search and seizure, and the right to due process), reflecting the framers' fear of a strong centralized government.

Conceptualizing Crime

Crime is an intentional act or omission in violation of criminal law, committed without defense or excuse, and sanctioned (i.e., punishable) by the state. Crime is essentially a legal construct, because the law narrowly defines the specific elements of the forbidden act and the conditions under which they occur. For example, intentionally taking the life of another person may or may not constitute a crime. Although it would be a crime for a person to intentionally kill his or her spouse to collect life insurance, it would not be a criminal act for a police officer to intentionally kill an armed suspect in self-defense.

Crime is also a failure to act (e.g., not paying income tax). At various times in history, a condition of being or status was included in definitions of crime. For example, during the seventeenth century, Massachusetts Bay Colony made it a crime to be a Quaker. Until 1962, in California it was illegal to "be addicted to the use of narcotics" (the statute was eventually declared unconstitutional by the U.S. Supreme Court).[4]

Seriousness of the Crime

Generally speaking, acts that are defined as crimes are considered more serious violations of norms (rules that regulate behavior) than are noncriminal acts. Nevertheless, perceptions of the seriousness of certain crimes may vary between different times, cultures, and societies. According to public opinion polls, most Americans agree that violent crimes are more serious than property crimes, but there are gradations—most people see a parent's assault on a child as more serious than a husband's assault on his wife, and selling heroin is generally considered to be a more serious crime than selling marijuana.[5] In the United States, people who engage in sexual relations before marriage may be breaking the law in some states (e.g., Florida, Michigan, Mississippi, North Dakota, and Virginia), though there is little chance of prosecution. In China, however, persons engaged in the same behavior may be charged with prostitution (for the female) and rape (for the male).[6]

Mala in Se Crimes versus *Mala Prohibita* Crimes

In the early development of criminal law, all crimes were considered wrong for one of two reasons: They were considered inherently wrong or evil (***mala in se***) or they were wrong merely because they were prohibited by a criminal statute (***mala prohibita***). Only nine common-law crimes were classified as *mala in se* offenses:

- Murder
- Manslaughter
- Rape
- Sodomy
- Robbery
- Larceny
- Arson
- Burglary
- Mayhem

These offenses were also the first group of crimes to be referred to as felonies. The *mala prohibita* crimes, by comparison, were considered less serious and consequently were classified as misdemeanors.

The significant historical distinction between these two categories of crimes reflects perceptions of the degree of public harm they present. Because *mala in se* crimes were believed to be inherently evil and to pose a major threat to the social order, it was understandable that they would be sanctioned by the law and more severely punished. *Mala prohibita* crimes, such as public drunkenness, loitering, prostitution, and gambling, did not carry the same broad moral condemnation. TABLE 2-1 presents a brief list of examples of *mala in se* and *mala prohibita* crimes today.

The basic distinction between these two groups of crimes persists in present-day criminal law. The offenses classified as *mala in se* crimes have largely remained the same, but the number of *mala prohibita* crimes has greatly expanded. For example, statutes have been enacted to prohibit driving under the influence of alcohol or drugs, copyright infringement, and the manufacture, distribution, and possession of illegal drugs. Statutes have been created to control cybercrimes, including theft of information, creation of computer viruses to cause mischief or damage data, copying software, downloading of copyright-protected music or movies, and identity theft.

Felonies, Misdemeanors, and Infractions

U.S. criminal law distinguishes between felonies, misdemeanors, and infractions and assigns punishments accordingly.

The most serious crimes, called **felonies**, result in a more severe punishment. In most states, felonies carry maximum sentences of death or imprisonment for a term greater than one year in a state prison and typically carry higher fines than misdemeanors. A felony conviction also may result in the loss of certain rights, such as the loss of a person's right to vote, hold public office, carry a gun, or be licensed in certain professions.

Crimes classified as **misdemeanors** carry less severe punishments than are meted out for felonies. Typically, the maximum incarceration sentence is one year or less in a local jail and a smaller fine than would be incurred in a felony.

The third category of crimes, called **infractions**, is composed of petty offenses. These involve violations of city or county ordinances and include such offenses as illegal parking, jaywalking, cruising, and violations of noise ordinances. Infractions are generally not punishable by incarceration; rather, fines or community service may be imposed.

TABLE 2-1 Examples of Contemporary *Mala in Se* and *Mala Prohibita* Crimes

Mala in Se	*Mala Prohibita*
Murder	Prostitution
Rape	Gambling
Robbery	Vagrancy (loitering)
Larceny	Panhandling
Arson	Fraud
Burglary	Public intoxication
Aggravated assault	Public nudity
Incest	Trespassing
	Possession of drug paraphernalia
	Copyright infringement
	Illegal possession of weapon
	Disorderly conduct

Elements of a Crime

As a legal definition, crime also includes what is known as the ***corpus*** (literally, "body of the crime"), which refers to the facts, or foundation, of the crime that must be established in a court of law. These elements include *actus reus* (criminal act), *mens rea* (criminal intent), and the concurrence of these two concepts.

Actus Reus

In his novel *1984*, George Orwell described a society in which both thoughts and acts were restrained and regulated by the Think Pol, or thought police.[7] Through constant surveillance, the Think Pol were able to monitor and then punish any expression of prohibited thoughts. U.S. law, however, generally limits criminal responsibility to ***actus reus***—an actual act, the planning or attempt to act in violation of the law, or the specific omission to act when the law requires action. The written or oral expression of certain thoughts, such as making threats or intimidating remarks to a witness, may also be viewed as *actus reus* and, therefore, may be prohibited by criminal law.

Mens Rea

According to an old Latin maxim, an act does not make a person guilty unless the mind is guilty. In other words, a defendant is not criminally liable for conduct unless ***mens rea*** (criminal intent) was present at the time of the act. For a crime to exist, the person must intend for his or her action to have a particular consequence that is a violation of the law. The mere fact that a person engages in conduct in violation of law is not sufficient to prove criminal liability; rather, the defendant must also intend to commit the crime. As former Supreme Court Justice Oliver Wendell Holmes once noted, "Even a dog distinguishes between being stumbled over and being kicked."[8]

However, **strict liability laws**, in which there is liability without culpability, are an exception. Strict liability laws provide for criminal liability without requiring intent; in other words, a person may be held criminally responsible even though he or she had no intent to produce the harm. For example, bartenders have been held criminally liable for the intoxication of patrons and hosts of parties have been held criminally liable for the intoxication of their guests who are later involved in fatal accidents. The fact that neither the bartender nor the host had any intention to cause the intoxication or the subsequent accident is neither a required element of proof nor a valid defense. Penalties for strict liability violations typically involve fines rather than jail time.

Different degrees of criminal intent exist, and there are even some exceptions to the requirement that intent be present. In an attempt to create greater legal uniformity among the states, the American Law Institute wrote a Model Penal Code in 1962. It identifies levels of criminal responsibility, or culpability, reflecting differing degrees of intent to act: The person must have "acted (1) purposely, (2) knowingly, (3) recklessly, or (4) negligently, as the law may require, with respect to each material element of the offense."[9]

- *Purposely* means to act with conscious deliberation, planning, or anticipation to engage in some conduct that will result in specific harm.
- A person acts *knowingly* when he or she is aware that the conduct is prohibited or will produce a forbidden result.
- Acting *recklessly* involves conscious disregard of a known risk, although there is no conscious intent to cause the harm (such as speeding and unintentionally causing an automobile accident).
- *Negligent* conduct creates a risk of harm when an individual is unaware, but should have been aware. In other words, to be negligent, a person must engage in conduct

that a reasonable person would not engage in, or an individual must fail to act (an omission) in the manner in which a reasonable person would act under the same or similar circumstances.

Concurrence of *Actus Reus* and *Mens Rea*

For an act to be considered criminal, both the act (*actus reus*) prohibited by criminal law and the intent (*mens rea*) prohibited by the criminal law must be present before the crime is completed. It is not sufficient for an act to be defined as a crime if the person has only the guilty mind but commits no act. Nor is it sufficient for a person to have acted without criminal intent, with the exception noted earlier for strict liability offenses.

Concurrence may exist even if the act and the intent do not coincide as the offender intended. Suppose Jim aimed a gun at Brian and shot with the intent to kill him, but missed, hitting and killing John instead. Jim is still liable for murder under the doctrine of transferred intent. The intent to kill, in other words, is transferred from Jim to John. If the bullet missed both Brian and John but instead hit an electrical transformer and caused a fire, Jim would not be responsible for the crime of arson, because he did not intend to commit this specific act, though he may still be held responsible for reckless behavior.

Defenses and Responsibility

Society and criminal law have long recognized that certain actions may be justified or excused, such that the offender does not bear legal liability for the act. Sometimes these justifications and excuses, which are called defenses, are based on the mental state of the person at the time the act was committed. At other times, circumstances beyond the individual's control may come into play that may negate criminal liability. Both justifications and excuses are affirmative defenses; that is, the defendant must prove that his or her act was justified or excused.

John Hinckley, Jr.'s shooting of President Ronald Reagan in 1981 was seen by millions of people as they watched the television news, yet Hinckley's successful defense of "not guilty by reason of insanity" prevented him from being convicted for the crime. In this case, the defendant did not deny engaging in the action: Hinckley did shoot Reagan. Nevertheless, his defense of insanity successfully allowed him to avoid being held criminally responsible for the assault.

Justifications

Justifications are based on a defendant admitting responsibility but arguing that, under the circumstances, he or she did what was right.

Self-Defense

Defendants who raise the claim of **self-defense** as a justification for avoiding criminal responsibility argue that they acted in a lawful manner to defend themselves, others, or their property, or to prevent a crime. Most states permit a person to use as much force as is reasonably necessary for such protection. The individual must also have an honest and reasonable belief that he or she is in immediate danger from unlawful use of force by another person. The degree of force used in one's self-defense must be limited to a reasonable response to the threat: A person should meet force only with like force. Thus a person who is attacked by an unarmed assailant should not respond with a weapon.

According to the Model Penal Code, deadly force may be used only in response to a belief that there is imminent threat of death, serious bodily harm, kidnapping, or rape. It may *not* be used if the defendant provoked the offender to use force. Some jurisdictions also require that when a safe escape route from a house is available, a person must retreat

The majority of domestic violence victims are women, and this abuse may have varied and significant effects.

instead of using deadly force. Thus, if a person has an opportunity to retreat safely from the person posing the threat, deadly force would not be justified as self-defense. This retreat rule has several exceptions, such as cases of battered woman syndrome.

Necessity

Necessity, as a defense, represents the dilemma of choosing between two evils. A person may violate the law out of necessity when he or she believes that the act, which is a violation of law, is required to avoid a greater evil. According to the Model Penal Code, conduct that a person "believes to be necessary to avoid a harm or evil to himself or to another is justifiable, provided that the harm or evil sought to be avoided by such conduct is greater than that sought to be prevented by the law defining the offense charged."[10] For example, breaking into a mountain cabin to secure shelter or food during a snowstorm or into a home to use the telephone to report an emergency may establish thc defense of necessity and thereby negate the crime of breaking and entering. In either case, the individual must intend to avoid a greater harm than the crime charged to justify the act.

Kobe Bryant and his accuser had starkly different assessments of their sexual relationship, which resulted in a civil settlement.

Consent

The defense of consent arises when a defendant claims the victim consented to the act. Certain common law offenses, such as theft and rape, require a clear demonstration that the victim did not give consent. For example, if the owner of an automobile voluntarily consented to a neighbor taking her car, then the neighbor has not committed motor vehicle theft.

During the summer of 2003, professional basketball star Kobe Bryant was charged with raping a 19-year-old female hotel employee while he was staying at a Colorado resort. Bryant admitted he had sex with the woman but claimed that she had consented. Shortly after the charges were filed, Bryant stated, "Nothing that happened June 30 was against the will of the woman who now falsely accuses me." The rape charge was eventually dismissed. Afterward, Bryant stated, "Although I truly believe this encounter between us was consensual, I recognize that she did not and does not view this incident the same way I did. After months of reviewing [evidence submitted at] discovery, listening to her attorney, and even her testimony in person, I now understand how she feels that she did not consent to this encounter." The woman then filed a civil law suit against Bryant; the

Headline Crime — Carrying Guns on Campus

More than 11,000 students have joined the Facebook group Students for Concealed Carry on Campus to call attention to the need for greater personal safety on campus after the Virginia Tech shootings in 2007. According to one student, "The only way to stop a person with a gun is with another gun." A student at Washington State University said, "School is the only place I'm not allowed to carry my weapon."

Utah is the only state that allows permit holders to carry guns on campus. However, 12 states are currently considering legislation that would make it legal for people to carry guns, if they have concealed-weapons permits, at public universities. State legislatures in Alabama, Arizona, Georgia, Indiana, Kentucky, Michigan, Ohio, South Carolina, South Dakota, Tennessee, Virginia, and Washington are at some point in the process of changing state laws to enable students, faculty, and staff to carry a concealed weapon while on campus.

Source: Marisol Bello, "12 States Debate Guns on Campus," *USA Today,* February 15, 2008, p. 3A.

FOCUS ON CRIMINAL JUSTICE

The Battered Woman Syndrome and Deadly Force

Nancy Seaman, a 52-year-old elementary school teacher, may have suffered from *battered woman syndrome* after enduring years of alleged physical abuse by her husband, Robert. At her trial, Nancy admitted to killing her husband with a hatchet, but claimed it was an act of self-defense initiated during one of his attacks soon after she asked him for a divorce. She testified that when she told Robert she wanted a divorce, he became furious, cut her with a knife, chased her into the garage, forced her to the ground, and repeatedly kicked her. According to Nancy, she grabbed the closest object she could find—a hatchet—and drove it into her husband's skull. She then stabbed and beat him to ensure he was dead.

Prosecutors told another story. They claimed the act was premeditated and that Nancy purchased the ax and took great care to conceal the crime scene. Surveillance video from a hardware store showed Nancy stealing a hatchet identical to the one used in the murder. Two days later, she returned it using the receipt from the purchase of the hatchet used in the murder, perhaps in an attempt to erase the purchase from her credit card record. Prosecutors said that Nancy slammed the hatchet into Robert's skull more than a dozen times, dragged his body into the garage, and then stabbed him 21 times, severing his jugular vein and voice box. The next morning, she stopped to purchase a tarp, bottles of bleach, and latex gloves to clean up the mess.

Other testimony also appeared to contradict Nancy's account. When police first arrived at the couple's home, Nancy claimed Robert's death was an accident. A co-worker said he had overheard Nancy talking with another teacher at school about poisoning her husband. After five hours of deliberation, the jury found Nancy guilty of first-degree murder, rejecting her claim of self-defense. She was subsequently sentenced to life in prison.

According to criminologist Cynthia Gillespie, laws regulating deadly force have been created by men based on a code of "manly" behavior that expects a person to be fearless and confront an attacker directly. Such laws do not consider the woman's assessment that she cannot escape further injury as long as the abuser is alive.

Victims of battered woman syndrome are often unable to leave their abusers, even when circumstances appear to permit their escape. Over time, a battered woman may lose all hope of controlling her husband's or boyfriend's violence. Many such women succumb to learned helplessness: They become emotionally dependent on their abusive partners and learn to be passive as a result of beatings when they tried to assert themselves. In addition, some women do not leave because no safe refuge exists where an enraged partner cannot find them or their children. Abusive husbands often threaten to harm or take custody of the children if the woman leaves. Even with the increase in numbers of shelters for abused women, shelters must turn away more women than they serve.

Sources: Mike Martindale, "Seaman Gets Life in Prison," available at http://www.detnews.com/2005/metro/0501/25/B01-68930.htm, accessed June 28, 2008; "Teacher Claims Self-Defense in Husband's Ax-Murder," *Courttv*, March 30, 2005, available at http://www.courttv.com/trials/seaman/background_ctv.html, accessed June 28, 2008; Cynthia Gillespie, *Justifiable Homicide: Battered Women, Self-Defense, and the Law* (Columbus, OH: Ohio State University Press, 1989).

suit was settled out of court, and terms of the settlement were not released.[11] Such lawsuits are based on civil law, which is a body of private law that settles disputes between two or more parties to a dispute.

Excuses

Excuses are based on a defendant admitting that what he or she did was wrong but arguing that, under the circumstances, he or she was not responsible for the criminal act.

Insanity

Probably no other legal defense has resulted in more public scrutiny and debate than the insanity defense. In reality, insanity pleas are very rare. The insanity defense is raised in less than 1 percent of all criminal cases, and only in 25 percent of those cases is the person found not guilty because of insanity.[12] Even so, many people are concerned when a clearly dangerous person avoids incarceration and punishment after being found legally insane at the time the crime was committed. It is important to recognize that people who are released from criminal charges owing to insanity do not go free, but instead are sent to mental hospitals until they are considered sane. Only then are they released back into the community.

The insanity defense is based on a legal concept, rather than a medical or psychiatric definition of insanity. Legally, "insanity" refers to a person's state of mind at the time he or she committed the crime charged, though actual legal definitions of insanity have been—and continue to be—rather vague. In the past, concepts such as madness, irresistible impulse, states of unsound mind or weak-mindedness, and mental illness, disease, defect, or disorder have all been used to inform the law.[13]

The M'Naghten Rule

The **M'Naghten rule**, which is also known as the "right from wrong" test, is based on an English case that was decided in 1843. Until recently, it was the most widely accepted standard of insanity in the United States. Daniel M'Naghten, a Scottish woodcutter, believed that the English Prime Minister, Sir Robert Peel II, was persecuting him. In an attempt to assassinate Peel, M'Naghten mistakenly shot and killed Peel's assistant. At the trial, the court instructed the jury that

> [To] establish a defense on the ground of insanity, it must be clearly proved that, at the time of the committing of the act, the party accused was labouring under such a defect of reason from disease of the mind as not to know the nature and quality of the act he was doing; or, if he did know it, that he did not know he was doing what was wrong.[14]

M'Naghten was tried and found not guilty by reason of insanity.

Under the M'Naghten rule, the defendant is presumed to be sane and must prove that he or she suffered from a "disease of the mind" and, therefore, lacked a sufficient degree of reason to distinguish between right and wrong. This test of insanity has been criticized on several grounds:

- "Disease of the mind" is not clearly defined.
- Too much stress is placed on the requirement of knowing.
- It is unclear how a person must know that an act is wrong.
- Some people may be insane but still able to distinguish right from wrong.

Subsequent rules have sought to overcome these weaknesses in the M'Naghten rule.

Irresistible Impulse Test

In 1897, the U.S. federal courts and a number of the states added the **irresistible impulse test** to supplement the M'Naghten rule. According to this test, defendants may be found not guilty by reason of insanity if they can prove that a mental disease caused loss of self-control over their conduct. This test arose from an 1886 Alabama Supreme Court decision in *Parsons v. State*, which held that it may be possible for a person to know that the action was wrong but nevertheless to be so overcome by emotion that he or she temporarily lost self-control or the ability to reason to a degree sufficient to prevent the act.[15] In revising the M'Naghten rule, the irresistible impulse test allowed defendants to raise the insanity defense and plead that, although they knew that what they were doing was wrong, they were unable to control their behavior.

Durham Rule

The **Durham rule**, which states that "an accused [person] is not criminally responsible if his unlawful act was the product of mental disease or mental defect," was formulated in *Durham v. United States* in 1954.[16] According to the Durham rule, a mental condition may be either a disease (a condition capable of improving or deteriorating) or a defect (a condition not considered capable of improving or deteriorating). Further, the Durham rule states that a defect could be congenital, the result of injury, or the residual effect of either physical or mental disease. Under the Durham test, the prosecutor must prove beyond a reasonable doubt that the defendant was not acting as a result of mental illness, but the jury determines whether the act was a *product* of such disease or defect.

The Substantial Capacity Test

The Durham rule, like its predecessors, was soon criticized. Specifically, critics argued that it provided no useful definition of "mental disease or defect." In 1962, the American Law Institute offered a new test for insanity in its Model Penal Code. Known as the **substantial capacity test** or Model Penal Code Test, it includes the following provisions:

1. A person is not responsible for criminal conduct if, due to mental disease or defect, he or she lacks the substantial capacity to appreciate the criminality (wrongfulness) of his or her conduct or to conform to the requirements of law.
2. The terms "mental disease or defect" do not include an abnormality manifested only by repeated criminal or antisocial conduct.[17]

The substantial capacity test is broader than the M'Naghten rule because it substitutes the notion of "appreciate" for "know," thereby eliminating the M'Naghten requirement that a person be able to fully distinguish right from wrong. In other words, a defendant may know the difference between right and wrong yet not be able to appreciate the significance of that difference. The substantial capacity test absolves from criminal responsibility a person who knows what he or she is doing, but is driven to act by delusions, fears, or compulsions.[18] Like the Durham rule, the substantial capacity test places the burden of proof beyond a reasonable doubt on the prosecutor.

In 1972, in *United States v. Brawner*, the federal courts rejected the Durham rule and adopted a modified version of the substantial capacity test.[19] By 1982, it was being used in 24 states, the District of Columbia, and the federal courts.

Insanity Defense Reform Act of 1984

Until 1981, the substantial capacity test dominated federal and state practice. Matters changed after March 30, 1981, when John Hinckley, Jr., shot and wounded President Reagan. At his trial, experts testified that Hinckley was psychotic and had been suffering from delusions. A little more than a year after the shooting, the jury returned a verdict of "not guilty by reason of insanity" for Hinckley.

As a result of widespread criticism over Hinckley's acquittal, Congress restricted the use of the insanity defense in federal cases, and a number of states quickly followed suit. The Insanity Defense Reform Act of 1984, passed as part of the larger Comprehensive Crime Control Act of 1984, states:

> It is an affirmative defense to a prosecution under any Federal statute that, at the time of the commission of the acts constituting the offense, the defendant, as a result of a severe mental disease or defect, was unable to appreciate the nature and quality of the wrongfulness of his [or her] acts . . . The defendant has the burden of proving the defense of insanity by clear and convincing evidence.[20]

A significant part of the Insanity Defense Reform Act is the shifting of the burden of proof from the prosecution to the defense and the limitations placed on the role of experts. The defense now has the burden to prove, through the presentation of clear and convincing evidence, that the defendant lacked capacity. Furthermore, expert witnesses who testify about the mental state or condition of a defendant are prohibited from giving an opinion or drawing an inference as to whether the mental state of the defendant constituted an element of the crime. Rather, such conclusions are to be drawn solely by the judge or the jury.

Guilty, but Mentally Ill

At least 10 states have adopted statutes permitting a defense of **guilty, but mentally ill** (GBMI), or "guilty, but insane" (GBI—a variation on GBMI). This verdict, which is a supplement to the traditional defense of insanity, allows a jury to find the accused guilty and impose a punishment of subsequent incarceration. It also requires prison authorities to provide psychiatric treatment to the convicted offender during the specified period of confinement (see TABLE 2-2).

Supporters of GBMI and GBI statutes argue that these laws will reduce the number of determinations of not guilty by reason of insanity and, consequently, hold more people criminally responsible for their actions. In addition, they claim that such statutes will increase protection for the public by ensuring that offenders are subject to both incarceration and treatment.[21]

Headline Crime — Guilty, but Mentally Ill

Guilty, but mentally ill (GBMI) convictions are probably more common than acquittals based on successful insanity defenses. The following recent cases illustrate the variety of situations in which GBMI convictions are obtained.

- On June 26, 2006, Nader Ali was found guilty, but mentally ill of first-degree murder in the beating death of 25-year-old Lea Sullivan and was sentenced to life in prison. Both parties were Harvard graduates and classmates at Jefferson Medical College. Witnesses testified that Ali waited for Sullivan to exit a grocery store and then attacked her with a baseball bat. Ali was diagnosed with severe bipolar disorder, psychosis, and schizophrenia.
- Billy Paul Cobb was found guilty, but mentally ill on March 7, 2007. Cobb pleaded guilty to child molestation, aggravated child molestation, three counts of enticing a child for indecent purposes, and three counts of interference with custody. In late December 2005, Cobb was arrested for taking three girls, ages 11, 12, and 13, across state lines, where he performed an act of sodomy on one of the girls. A psychologist testifying on Cobb's behalf stated that Cobb showed signs of paranoid schizophrenia, heard voices, and suffered from dementia because of previous closed head injuries. As a result of the plea agreement, Cobb was sentenced to 12 years in prison and three years of probation.
- A judge found Cynthia Lord, age 45, guilty, but mentally ill in the murder of her three sons, ages 16, 18, and 19, whom she feared had become evil clones or robots. Each boy died from a single gunshot wound to the head. According to the judge, Lord suffered from a severe, disabling mental illness. The three first-degree murder convictions mean that Lord could spend as many as 99 years in a psychiatric institution. If at some point she is found mentally stable, she will be transferred to a correctional institution.
- On October 26, 2007, Jeanette Sliwinski, age 25, was found guilty, but mentally ill on three charges of reckless homicide. Sliwinski claimed that she had been trying to commit suicide when she intentionally crashed her Mustang into a Honda Civic at a speed of 87 miles per hour. Three Chicago musicians—Michael Dahquist, 39; John Glick, 35; and Douglas Meis, 29—were stopped at a light when Sliwinski's car crashed into them and were killed. Sliwinski's attorney claimed that she had been suffering from depression and was driven into madness when her psychiatrists failed her. She faces a maximum of 10 years in prison, where she will receive treatment while serving her sentence.

Sources: Daniel Wagner, "Alleged Murderer Can Stand Trial," *The Harvard Crimson*, available at http://www.thecrimson.com/article.aspx?ref=505346, accessed October 10, 2008; "Nader Ali Found Guilty in Classmate's Murder," available at http://abclocal.go.com/wpvi/story?section=local&id=4306503, accessed July 19, 2008; Pearce Adams, "Accused Child Molester Takes Plea Offer of Guilty, but Mentally Ill," available at http://www.independentmail.com/news/2007/mar/07/accused-child-molester-takes-plea-offer-guilty-men/, accessed July 19, 2008; Associated Press, "Mother Found Guilty, but Mentally Ill in Shooting Deaths of 3 Sons," available at http://www.foxnews.com/story/0,2933,272372,00.html, accessed July 19, 2008; Deborah Horan, Susan Kuczka, and Andrew Wang, "Suicidal Driver Guilty, But Ill," available at www.chicagotribune.com/chi-sliwinski_weboct27,0,4908242.story, accessed July 29, 2008.

TABLE 2-2 Insanity Rules for the 50 States and District of Columbia

State	Insanity Defense Rule	Location of Burden of Proof	Allows GBMI and GBI Verdicts
Alabama	M'Naghten rule	Defendant	No
Alaska	M'Naghten rule	Defendant	Yes
Arizona	M'Naghten rule	Defendant	Yes
Arkansas	Model Penal Code	Defendant	No
California	M'Naghten rule	Defendant	No
Colorado	M'Naghten rule; irresistible impulse test	State	No
Connecticut	Model Penal Code	Defendant	No
Delaware	Model Penal Code	Defendant	No
District of Columbia	Model Penal Code	Defendant	No
Florida	M'Naghten rule	State	No
Georgia	M'Naghten rule	Defendant	Yes
Hawaii	Model Penal Code	State	No
Idaho	Insanity defense abolished		Yes
Illinois	Model Penal Code	Defendant	No
Indiana	Model Penal Code	State	Yes
Iowa	M'Naghten rule	Defendant	No
Kansas	M'Naghten rule	State	No
Kentucky	Model Penal Code	Defendant	No
Louisiana	M'Naghten rule	Defendant	No
Maine	Model Penal Code	Defendant	No
Maryland	Model Penal Code	Defendant	No
Massachusetts	Model Penal Code	State	No
Michigan	Model Penal Code	Defendant	No
Minnesota	M'Naghten rule	Defendant	No
Mississippi	M'Naghten rule	State	No
Missouri	M'Naghten rule	Defendant	No
Montana	Insanity defense abolished		Yes
Nebraska	M'Naghten rule	Defendant	No
Nevada	M'Naghten rule		Yes
New Hampshire	Durham rule	Defendant	No
New Jersey	M'Naghten rule	Defendant	No
New Mexico	M'Naghten rule; irresistible impulse test	State	
New York	Model Penal Code	Defendant	No
North Carolina	M'Naghten rule	Defendant	No
North Dakota	Model Penal Code	State	No
Ohio	M'Naghten rule	Defendant	No
Oklahoma	M'Naghten rule	State	No
Oregon	Model Penal Code	Defendant	Yes
Pennsylvania	M'Naghten rule	State	Yes
Rhode Island	Model Penal Code	Defendant	No
South Carolina	M'Naghten rule	Defendant	No
South Dakota	M'Naghten rule	Defendant	No
Tennessee	Model Penal Code	State	No
Texas	M'Naghten rule; irresistible impulse test	Defendant	No
Utah	Insanity defense abolished		Yes
Vermont	Model Penal Code	State	No
Virginia	M'Naghten rule; irresistible impulse test	Defendant	No
Washington	M'Naghten rule	Defendant	No
West Virginia	Model Penal Code	State	No
Wisconsin	Model Penal Code	Defendant	No
Wyoming	Model Penal Code	Defendant	No

Source: The Defense of Insanity: Standards and Procedures, State Court Organization, 2004 (Washington, DC: U.S. Department of Justice Statistics, 2006), Table 35.

Intoxication

The defense of intoxication is based on the claim that the defender had diminished control over himself or herself owing to the influence of alcohol, narcotics, or drugs and, therefore, lacked criminal intent. According to the Model Penal Code, the defense of intoxication should not be used unless it negates an element in the crime, such as criminal intent.

The courts recognize a difference between involuntary intoxication and voluntary intoxication. Involuntary intoxication that results from mistake, deceit of others, or duress (for example, if a drug was unknowingly put in the person's drink, or if liquor was forcibly poured down the person's throat) will excuse the defendant from responsibility for criminal action that resulted from the intoxication.

Voluntary intoxication is generally not a defense, but it may be presented in an effort to mitigate the seriousness of the crime. A person charged with committing premeditated murder while voluntarily intoxicated, for example, may be able to have the charge reduced to the less serious charge of homicide. In 2005 in Lawrence, Kansas, Jason Dillon, who was charged with murdering his girlfriend's three-year-old daughter, cited "voluntary intoxication" as a factor in his crime. Dillon claimed that he had consumed 16 beers the night before he babysat the young girl and was incapable of acting intentionally. Dillon did not dispute that he struck the girl on the head more than a dozen times after she refused to help pick up laundry and told him she didn't want him to be her daddy anymore. As a result of a plea bargain, Dillon was convicted of second-degree murder rather than first-degree murder as initially charged; he was sentenced to a reduced term of 16½ years in prison.[22]

Entrapment

The defense of **entrapment** is an excuse for criminal actions based on the claim that the defendant was encouraged or enticed by agents of the state to engage in an act that he or she would not have committed otherwise. The courts have generally held that it is permissible for law enforcement agents to solicit information from informants, use undercover officers, and even place electronic monitoring devices on informants or officers to record conversations regarding criminal behavior. It is not, however, considered legitimate for police to encourage or coerce individuals to commit crimes when they had no previous predisposition to commit such acts. Government agents may not "originate a criminal design, implant in an innocent person's mind the disposition to commit a criminal act, and then induce commission of the crime so that the Government may prosecute."[23]

For an entrapment defense to be valid, two related elements must be present:

1. Government inducement of the crime
2. The defendant's lack of predisposition to engage in the criminal conduct[24]

Predisposition is generally considered to be the more important of these two elements. Thus entrapment may not have occurred if the government induces a person who is predisposed to commit such an act.

In recent years, many state and federal law enforcement agencies have conducted "sting" operations that are designed to trap people who are engaged in crime or predisposed to commit crimes. Such operations often involve law enforcement agents posing as prostitutes, drug buyers, buyers of stolen auto parts, and people attempting to bribe government officials. Do such activities create an illegal inducement to commit crime? In *Sherman v. United States*, the U.S. Supreme Court held that "to determine whether entrapment has been established, a line must be drawn between the unwary innocent and the trap for the unwary criminal."[25] Entrapment occurs when government activity in the criminal enterprise crosses this line.

The line suggested by the Supreme Court, however, is often ambiguous. The use of deceit by the police to create a circumstance in which a person then commits a crime does not necessarily constitute entrapment. In *United States v. Russell*, the Court held that

> [T]here are circumstances when the use of deceit is the only practicable law enforcement technique available. It is only when the government's deception actually implants the criminal design in the mind of the defendant that the defense of entrapment comes into play.[26]

Duress

The defense of duress presents the claim that the defendant is a victim, rather than a criminal. For example, if someone holds a gun to a person's head, threatening to shoot unless he or she steals money, the resulting theft would be considered an action under duress, and the thief should not be held criminally responsible for complying with the demand to steal. The Model Penal Code's provision on duress states that

> [It] is an affirmative defense that the actor engaged in the conduct charged to constitute an offense because he was coerced to do so by the use of, or a threat to use, unlawful force against his person or the person of another, which a person of reasonable firmness in his situation would have been unable to resist.[27]

This defense is *not* applicable to people who intentionally, recklessly, or negligently place themselves in situations in which it is probable that they will be subject to duress. For example, a person who, in the course of escaping from prison, commits a kidnapping to avoid being caught cannot claim duress as a defense against the charge of kidnapping.

Mistake

Everyone has probably heard the expression, "Ignorance of the law is no excuse." But what does it mean? Although we may be familiar with many laws, must we be aware of all the laws? Must we know exactly what they prohibit and under what circumstances?

Ignorance of what the law requires or prohibits generally does not excuse a person from committing a crime, but, under some circumstances, ignorance has been accepted as a defense. A federal court of appeals held in 1989 that "Under the proper circumstances . . . a good faith misunderstanding of the law may negate willfulness."[28] Mistake, as a criminal defense, takes two forms: mistake of law and mistake of fact.

Mistake of law occurs when the defendant does not know a law exists; only in rare cases is it a legitimate defense. Such a case might exist when a new law is passed but not published so as to give the public adequate notice of it. Mistake of fact occurs when a person unknowingly violates the law because he or she believes some fact to be true when it is not. In other words, had the facts been as a defendant believed them to be, the defendant's action would not have been a crime. For example, a woman who is charged with the crime of bigamy may have believed that her divorce was final before she remarried when, in fact, it was not. Mistake of fact is often raised as a defense by people who are charged with selling alcohol to a minor or with committing statutory rape. In such cases, defendants may have been led to believe that the minor was older than he or she claimed because the claim appeared consistent with the minor's appearance.

Exemptions

In some situations, a defendant may raise the defense that he or she is legally exempt from criminal responsibility. Unlike the defenses discussed earlier, legal exemptions are not based on the question of the defendant's mental capacity or culpability for committing the crime. Rather, they are seen as concessions to the defendant for the greater good of the public welfare.[29]

Double Jeopardy

The Fifth Amendment to the Constitution states that "no person shall be subject for the same offense to be twice put in jeopardy of life or limb." This protection against **double jeopardy** is not intended to provide protection for guilty defendants, but rather is meant to prevent the state from repeatedly prosecuting a person for the same charge until a conviction is finally achieved.[30] Jeopardy in a bench trial (a case tried before a judge rather than a jury) attaches (i.e., becomes activated) when the first witness is sworn in. In jury trials, some jurisdictions consider a defendant to be in jeopardy once the jury is selected, though a few define it at the point of indictment, when criminal charges are filed.

Double jeopardy does not apply when a court proceeding is ruled a mistrial on the motion of the defense or when a jury is unable to agree on a verdict and the judge declares a mistrial. In both circumstances, the prosecutor may retry the case. Also, if upon conviction a defendant appeals to a higher court and has the conviction reversed, he or she may be retried on the original charge.

Statute of Limitations

Under common law, there was no limit to the amount of time that could pass between a criminal act and the state's prosecution of that crime. More recently, however, the states and the federal government have enacted **statutes of limitations** establishing the maximum time allowed between the act and its prosecution by the state for most crimes. Thus in some cases a defendant may raise the defense that the statute of limitations for the crime has expired, which requires a dismissal of the charges.

Statutes of limitations vary by jurisdiction and are generally longer for more serious offenses. For instance, murder has no statute of limitations, whereas in many states burglary carries a five-year limitation. Misdemeanors have a two-year limitation period in most jurisdictions. The statute of limitations may, however, be interrupted if the defendant leaves the state. For example, if a person who is charged with assault leaves the state for a period of two years, an additional two years would be added to the statutory limit of five years.

First-grader Kayla Rolland was shot and killed by her classmate, Dedrick Owens, after a playground dispute.

Age

On March 8, 2000, six-year-old Kayla Rolland was shot in the neck in her first-grade classroom with a .32-caliber pistol and died a half hour later. Her killer, Dedrick Owens, was also six years old. He had gotten into a quarrel with Kayla on the playground the day before. Dedrick had found the loaded pistol in his home and brought it to school tucked in his pants. After shooting Kayla, Dedrick ran into a nearby bathroom and tossed the gun into a trashcan. Because of his age, the court determined that Dedrick could not be held criminally responsible for Kayla's death.[31]

Although not considered either a justification or an excuse for a criminal act, a person's age may establish a defense against criminal prosecution. Under early English common law, children younger than age 7 were considered incapable of forming criminal intent and, therefore, could not be convicted of crimes. Children between the ages of 7 and 14 were considered to have limited criminal responsibility, and children older than age 14 were presumed to have the capacity to form criminal intent and could be criminally prosecuted. With the creation of the juvenile court system in the United States at the end of the nineteenth century, most youths between ages 7 and 17 who were charged with crimes were processed through the more informal proceedings of that court.

Due Process and the Rights of the Accused

Due process, which is established in procedural criminal law, ensures the constitutional guarantees of a fair application of the rules and procedures in criminal proceedings, beginning with the investigation of crimes and continuing through an individual's arrest, prosecution, and punishment. Unfortunately, there is not always agreement over the concept of due process, its specific applications, or even who is eligible to claim the rights associated with the guarantees of due process.

When a person is arrested, the immediate concern typically focuses on whether he or she committed the crime. How does a court of law make this determination? The police might threaten or coerce the suspect to extract a confession, and some people might confess to crimes they did not commit to avoid further mistreatment. Evidence might also be presented to establish the individual's guilt even though that evidence was obtained by devious or unethical means (for example, searching a person's private property without a search warrant). The accused might be held in jail without bail and denied access to an attorney while the government builds a convincing case. Although convictions might be obtained in such instances, such procedures would offend the public's sense of fairness related to the criminal process.

The principles of procedural fairness in criminal cases are designed to reduce the likelihood of erroneous convictions. Criminal procedures that produce convictions of large numbers of innocent defendants would be patently unfair. The evolution of procedural safeguards against unfair prosecution is based on a relative assessment of the interests at stake in a criminal trial. According to law professor Thomas Grey, "While it is important as a matter of public policy (or even of abstract justice) to punish the guilty, it is a very great and concrete injustice to punish the innocent."[32] In U.S. criminal law, procedural safeguards have been established in the Fourth, Fifth, Sixth, Eighth, and Fourteenth Amendments to the U.S. Constitution to prevent that problem from occurring.

The Bill of Rights

The first 10 amendments, known as the **Bill of Rights**, were added to the Constitution on December 15, 1791—only three years after the Constitution had been ratified by the states. The framers of the Constitution had intended it to provide citizens with protections against a possible future dictatorship by establishing a clear separation of powers between the three branches of government (executive, legislative, and judicial). All too soon, they realized that the individual rights of citizens were not adequately protected against possible intrusions and violations by the newly formed federal government. To correct this deficiency, they added a series of amendments to the Constitution. Four of these amendments enumerate the rights of citizens in criminal proceedings (see Appendix A).

The Fourth Amendment

The Fourth Amendment protects citizens against unreasonable governmental invasion of their privacy. This amendment means that agents of the government may not arbitrarily or indiscriminately stop and search people on the street or in their vehicles, search their homes or other property, or confiscate materials without legal justification. Such justification must be based on sufficient probable cause to convince a judicial magistrate to issue a search warrant specifically describing who or what is to be searched and what is to be seized. Any evidence seized as a result of searches in violation of the Fourth Amendment cannot be used in a subsequent criminal prosecution.

The Fifth Amendment

The Fifth Amendment contains four separate procedural protections:

1. A person may not face criminal prosecution unless the government has first issued an indictment stating the charges against the person.
2. No person may be tried twice for the same offense (double jeopardy).
3. The government may not compel a defendant to testify against himself or herself (this provision includes protection against self-incrimination during questioning and the right to refuse to testify during a criminal trial).

4. No person may be deprived of due process, which means that people should be treated fairly by the government in criminal prosecutions.

The Sixth Amendment

The Sixth Amendment was designed to ensure a fair trial for defendants. Toward this end, it established six specific rights:

1. Speedy and public trial
2. Trial by an impartial jury (which has been interpreted by the courts to mean a jury of one's peers)
3. Notification of the nature and cause of the charges
4. Opportunity to confront witnesses called by the prosecution
5. Ability to present witnesses on the defendant's own behalf
6. Assistance of an attorney in presenting the defendant's defense

The Eighth Amendment

The Eighth Amendment simply states, "Excessive bail shall not be required, nor excessive fines imposed, nor cruel and unusual punishments inflicted." Although this amendment does not guarantee a defendant the constitutional right to be released on bail while awaiting trial, it does prohibit the imposition of excessive bail.

The Fourteenth Amendment

For nearly 80 years after the adoption of the Bill of Rights, the federal government and the various states interpreted the rights enumerated in these amendments to apply only to cases involving disputes between citizens and the federal government: The protections did not extend to citizens prosecuted by the states. (Actually, many state constitutions included these same rights, but if they were violated, the federal courts were not empowered to intervene.) On July 28, 1868, the Fourteenth Amendment to the Constitution was ratified. It was eventually interpreted to mean that the Bill of Rights did, indeed, apply to all citizens and that the states must ensure these rights.

Early court interpretations of the Fourteenth Amendment emphasized that its fundamental principle was "an impartial equality of rights"[33] and that its "plain and manifest intention was to make all the citizens of the United States equal before the law."[34] These initial decisions did not interpret the amendment to necessarily apply the Bill of Rights to the states. For example, in 1884, in ***Hurtado v. California***,[35] the Supreme Court held that the Fifth Amendment's guarantee of a grand jury indictment in criminal proceedings applied only to federal trials, not those conducted by the state.

It was not until the early decades of the twentieth century that the due process clause of the Fourteenth Amendment, which guaranteed that no state shall "deprive any person of life, liberty, or property, without due process of the law," began to specifically incorporate the Bill of Rights. This move ultimately made the rights described in these amendments applicable to the states.

During the 1960s, Chief Justice Earl Warren presided over a great expansion of due process rights for those accused of crimes.

Incorporation of the Bill of Rights

The process of incorporation of the Bill of Rights occurred only gradually and reflected a major split on the Supreme Court. In 1947, in *Adamson v. California*, Justice Hugo Black strongly called for total **incorporation**, arguing that the authors of the Fourteenth Amendment originally intended the Bill of Rights to place limits on state action.[36] At the time, Black's position was in the minority on the Court. The majority opinion, led by Justice Felix Frankfurter, held that, although the concept of due process incorporated fundamental values—one of which was fairness—it was left to judges to objectively and dispassionately discover and apply these values to any petitioner's claim of injustice. Therefore, according to Frankfurter, the due process clause only *selectively* incorporated those provisions necessary to fundamental fairness. In a series of cases, the fundamental values protecting the First Amendment freedoms of speech, religion, and assembly were held to be binding on the states, but the Fifth Amendment's protection against double jeopardy was not.[37]

In 1953, when Earl Warren was appointed Chief Justice of the Supreme Court, a liberal majority was formed on the Court. It rapidly expanded the application of the due process clause to the states. Over the next two decades, the Warren Court handed down numerous decisions establishing individual and civil rights, and clearly moved the Court from its fundamental fairness position to one of absolute compliance.

WRAPPING IT UP

Chapter Highlights

- Laws are formalized rules that reflect a body of principles prescribing or limiting people's actions. The laws collectively known as criminal law are generally divided into the subcategories of substantive law and procedural law. Together, they provide the framework for the criminal justice system.
- Most criminal law in the United States has its origins in English common law. One of the most important contributions from common law was *stare decisis* (the doctrine of precedent).
- Crimes have generally been conceptually divided between those considered to be *mala in se* (inherently wrong or evil acts) and those considered to be *mala prohibita* (acts that are wrong because they are prohibited by a criminal statute). Criminal codes further distinguish crimes as felonies, misdemeanors, and infractions.
- For an act to be defined as a crime, a number of elements must be present: *actus reus* (criminal act), *mens rea* (criminal intent), and the concurrence of these two concepts.
- In certain circumstances, an individual might engage in an act defined as a crime, yet not be held criminally responsible for that action. These circumstances involve legal justifications and excuses, or defenses that negate a person's criminal responsibility.
- Although the insanity defense is successfully raised in less than 1 percent of all criminal cases, it remains very controversial. The federal government and many of the states have revised their insanity statutes in recent years, and several have developed "guilty, but mentally ill" statutes to supplement other insanity defenses.
- Procedural criminal law establishes protections for individuals against unfair prosecution. These safeguards are found in the Fourth, Fifth, Sixth, and Eighth Amendments contained in the Bill of Rights.
- The constitutional protections found in the Bill of Rights were initially interpreted to apply only in federal prosecutions. It was not until the ratification of the Fourteenth Amendment, which occurred nearly 80 years after the adoption of the Bill of Rights, that they began to be applied to the states as well.

Words to Know

actus reus Guilty act; a required material element of a crime.

Bill of Rights First 10 amendments to the U.S. Constitution.

case law Law that emerges when a court modifies how a law in a particular case is applied.

civil law A body of private law that settles disputes between two or more parties in a dispute.

common law Case decisions by judges in England that established a body of law common to the entire nation.

corpus The body of the crime; the material elements of the crime that must be established in a court of law.

crime An intentional act or omission to act, neither justified nor excused, that is in violation of criminal law and punished by the state.

double jeopardy Trying a person for the same crime more than once; it is prohibited by the Fifth Amendment.

Durham rule An insanity test that determines whether a defendant's act was a product of a mental disease or defect.

entrapment The claim that a defendant was encouraged or enticed by agents of the state to engage in a criminal act.

excuses Claims based on a defendant admitting that what he or she did was wrong but arguing that, under the circumstances, he or she was not responsible for the criminal act.

felony A serious crime, such as robbery or embezzlement, that is punishable by a prison term of more than one year or by death.

guilty, but mentally ill (GBMI) A substitute for traditional insanity defenses, which allows the jury to find the defendant guilty and requires that the prisoner receive psychiatric treatment during his or her confinement. Also called guilty but insane (GBI).

Hurtado v. California U.S. Supreme Court decision that the Fifth Amendment guarantee of a grand jury indictment applied only to federal—not state—trials, and that not all constitutional amendments were applicable to the states.

incorporation The legal interpretation by the U. S. Supreme Court in which the Fourteenth Amendment applied the Bill of Rights to the states.

infraction A violation of a city or county ordinance, such as cruising or noise violations.

irresistible impulse test An insanity test that determines whether a defendant, as a result of a mental disease, temporarily lost self-control or the ability to reason sufficiently to prevent the crime.

justification Defense wherein a defendant admits responsibility but argues that, under the circumstances, what he or she did was right.

laws Formalized rules that prescribe or limit actions.

mala in se Behaviors, such as murder or rape, that are considered inherently wrong or evil.

mala prohibita Behaviors, such as prostitution and gambling, that are considered wrong because they have been prohibited by criminal statutes, rather than because they are evil in themselves.

mens rea Guilty mind, or having criminal intent; a required material element of most crimes.

misdemeanor A crime that is less serious than a felony, such as petty theft or possession of a small amount of marijuana, and that is punishable by less than one year in prison.

M'Naghten rule Insanity defense claim that because of a defect of reason from a disease of the mind, the defendant was unable to distinguish right from wrong.

procedural criminal law A body of law that specifies how crimes are to be investigated and prosecuted.

self-defense Claim that a defendant acted in a lawful manner to defend himself or herself, others, or property, or to prevent a crime.

stare decisis Literally, "to stand by the decision"; a policy of the courts to interpret and apply law according to precedents set in earlier cases.

statute Legislation contained in written legal codes.

statute of limitations The maximum time period that can pass between a criminal act and its prosecution.

strict liability laws Laws that provide for criminal liability without requiring either general or specific intent.

substantial capacity test An insanity test that determines whether the defendant lacked sufficient capacity to appreciate the wrongfulness of his or her conduct.

substantive criminal law A body of law that identifies behaviors harmful to society and specifies their punishments.

Think and Discuss

1. Do you think that it is reasonable for a crime victim to be able to file a civil suit against an offender? Why or why not?
2. Why is *mens rea* (criminal intent) such an important element to establish in a criminal case? Should parents be held criminally liable for the gang-related activities of their children?
3. Should the insanity defense be allowed? Should all states adopt "guilty, but mentally ill" or "guilty, but insane" statutes? Why or why not?
4. Why should there be any statutes of limitation in the criminal law? Should persons who commit crimes always face eventual possible prosecution for their acts?
5. Are the guarantees of due process for people accused of crimes reasonable? Do they make it more difficult to deal with the crime problem? Why are they so important to protect?

Notes

1. Aristotle, *The Politics*, Book VII, trans. Carnes Lord (Chicago: University of Chicago Press, 1994), p. 4.
2. Charles Thomas and Donna Bishop, *Criminal Law: Understanding Basic Principles* (Newbury Park, CA: Sage, 1987), p. 25.
3. P. S. Atiyah and Robert Summers, *Form and Substance in Anglo-American Law: A Comparative Study in Legal Reasoning, Legal Theory and Legal Institutions* (Oxford, UK: Oxford University Press, 1987), p. 97.
4. *Robinson v. California*, 370 U.S. 660 (1962).
5. U.S. Department of Justice, *Report to the Nation on Crime and Justice*, 2nd ed. (Washington, DC: Bureau of Justice Statistics, 1988), p. 16.
6. John Hewitt, "'Gardeners Shape a New Future for Delinquents," *China Reconstructs*, August 1987, pp. 29–31.
7. George Orwell, *1984* (New York: Penguin, 1981).
8. O. W. Holmes, *The Common Law* (Boston: Little, Brown, and Co., 1881), p. 3.
9. American Law Institute, *Model Penal Code, Proposed Official Draft*, Section 2.02 (1) (Philadelphia: American Law Institute, 1962).

10. American Law Institute, note 8, Section 3.02.1.

11. "Kobe Bryant Charged with Sexual Assault," available at http://www.nytimes.com/2006/08/07/us/07shoot.html, accessed June 28, 2008; http://www.courttv.com/trials/bryant/071804_ctv.html; "Judge Dismisses Kobe Bryant Rape Case," available at http://www.courttv.com/trials/bryant/090104_ctv.html, accessed June 28, 2008; Patrick O'Driscoll, "Kobe Bryant, Accuser Settle Her Civil Lawsuit," *USA Today*, March 2, 2005, available at http://www.usatoday.com/sports/basketball/nba/2005-03-02-bryant-settles_x.htm, accessed June 28, 2008.

12. Henry Steadman and Jeraldine Braff, "Defendants Not Guilty by Reason of Insanity," John Mohanan and Henry Steadman (Eds.), *Mentally Disordered Offenders* (New York: Plenum, 1983), pp. 200–237; John Martin, "The Insanity Defense: A Closer Look," *The Washington Post*, February 27, 1998, available at http://www.washingtonpost.com/wp-srv/local/longterm/aron/qa227.htm, accessed June 28, 2008; Associated Press, "Texas Lawmakers Studying State's Insanity Defense," January 4, 2005, available at http://www.demaction.org/dia/organizations/ncadp/news.jsp?key=1080&t=, accessed June 28, 2008.

13. Rita Simon and David Aaronson, *The Insanity Defense* (New York: Praeger, 1988).

14. *M'Naghten's Case*, 8 Eng. Rep. 718 (H.I. 1843).

15. *Parsons v. State*, 81 Alabama 577 (1886).

16. *Durham v. United States*, 214 F.2d 862 (D.C. Cir. 1954).

17. American Law Institute, note 9, Section 4.01.

18. Irving Kaufman, "The Insanity Plea on Trial," *The New York Times Magazine*, August 8, 1982, p. 18.

19. *United States v. Brawner*, 471 F.2d 969 (1972).

20. U.S. Congress, *The Comprehensive Crime Control Act of 1984*, P.L. 98-473 (Washington, DC: U.S. Congress, 1984).

21. John Klofas and Janette Yandrasits, "'Guilty But Mentally Ill' and the Jury Trial: A Case Study," *Criminal Law Bulletin* 24:425 (1988).

22. Eric Weslander, "Dillon Plans 'Intoxication Defense,'" *Lawrence Journal-World*, November 2, 2005, available at http://www2.ljworld.com/news/2005/nov/02/dillon_plans_intoxication_defense/?city_local, accessed June 28, 2008; Eric Weslander, "Child's Killer Expresses Regret as He's Given 16-Year Term," *Lawrence Journal-World*, March 4, 2006, available at http://www2.ljworld.com/news/2006/mar/04/childs_killer_expresses_regret_hes_given_16year_te/, accessed June 28, 2008.

23. *Jacobson v. United States*, 503 U.S. 540, 548 (1992).

24. *Mathews v. United States*, 485 U.S. 58, 63 (1988).

25. *Sherman v. United States*, 356 U.S. 369 (1958).

26. *United States v. Russell*, 411 U.S. 423 (1973).

27. American Law Institute, note 9, Section 2.09.1.

28. *United States v. Cheek*, 498 U.S. 192 (1994).

29. David Jones, *Crime and Criminal Responsibility* (Chicago: Nelson-Hall, 1978), pp. 67–68.

30. Jones, note 29, p. 68.

31. Christy McDonald and Chris Pavelich, "First-Grader Shot Dead at School," March 8, 2000, available at http://www.ABC-NEWS.com/2000/3/8, accessed June 28, 2008.

32. Thomas Grey, "Procedural Fairness and Substantive Rights," in J. Roland Pennock and John Chapman (Eds.), *Due Process* (New York: New York University Press, 1977), p. 185.

33. *State v. Hairston and Williams*, 63 N.C. 439 (1869).

34. *State v. Gibson*, 36 Ind. 393 (1871).

35. *Hurtado v. California*, 110 U.S. 516 (1884).

36. *Adamson v. California*, 332 U.S. 46 (1947).

37. *Palko v. Connecticut*, 302 U.S. 319 (1937).

CHAPTER

The Nature and Causes of Crime

OBJECTIVES

1 Know the strengths and weaknesses of the Uniform Crime Reports (UCR) and the National Crime Victimization Survey (NCVS).

2 Understand how self-report studies add to our knowledge of criminality.

3 Be familiar with the "dark figure of crime" and know how it affects crime statistics.

4 Know the age, gender, race, and ethnicity of the most likely persons to be criminal offenders or crime victims.

5 Distinguish between choice, trait, and sociological theories.

6 Explain the social policy applications of the theories.

PROFILES IN CRIME AND JUSTICE

Cassia Spohn
Professor of Criminal Justice
Arizona State University

I followed a rather indirect route to criminal justice. Throughout high school and college, I assumed that I would pursue a career in journalism. Later, at the University of Nebraska–Lincoln, I majored in journalism and political science, envisioning myself as a political reporter for a big-city newspaper or a national news magazine. After spending the summer following graduation from college writing about engagements, weddings, and symphony debutantes for the *Lincoln Journal-Star*, I decided to consider other options. I weighed the merits of law school and graduate school, and eventually decided to pursue a PhD in political science. I obtained my PhD in 1978 and spent the next eight years with a joint appointment in a political science department and an academic program for bright but economically disadvantaged students at the University of Nebraska at Omaha (UNO). Then, in 1986, the tides turned and I joined the Department of Criminal Justice at UNO, where I was a faculty member for 20 years, chair of the graduate program for 13 years, and department chair for one year. In 2006, I left UNO to accept the position as director of graduate programs in the School of Criminology and Criminal Justice at Arizona State University.

My route into criminal justice notwithstanding, the research that I have conducted over the past 30 years has been firmly grounded in issues of justice and fairness in the criminal justice system. My research generally revolves around issues related to criminal justice case-processing decisions, especially judges' sentencing decisions and prosecutors' charging decisions. One strand of my research focuses on the effects of the offender's race, ethnicity, gender, and age on sentencing decisions; another explores the influence of victim characteristics on charging decisions in sexual assault cases. I would like to think that my research has added to what we know about the treatment of those who either find themselves in the arms of the law or are victimized by a violent crime such as sexual assault. I hope that over time my work will influence criminal justice policies and practices.

One of the most rewarding aspects of my job is the opportunity to interact with undergraduate and graduate students who are concerned about the issues that spark my interest and stimulate my research. My experiences mentoring graduate students have been particularly satisfying. Helping these intellectually curious students to develop their theoretical and methodological expertise and collaborating with them on research projects and publications have been extremely rewarding.

Introduction

Historically, crime has been difficult to measure and crime data have always been problematic to count. Years ago the economist Sir Josiah Stamp suggested a reason for why crime statistics are dubious when he observed that they "come in the first instance from the village watchman, who just puts down what he damn pleases."[1] Even today, criminologists agree that public information about crime is not very accurate. This inaccuracy arises in part because crime is both context- and time-specific. Behavior is evaluated differently depending on where and when it occurs. For example, in 1992, chewing gum was illegal in Singapore. This ban has since been relaxed, but not entirely removed. Singaporeans today may purchase chewing gum only in a pharmacy and must submit their names and ID card numbers.[2] By constrast, governments in the United Kingdom and other European countries are now fining persons who spit chewing gum on the street. Another problem

AROUND THE GLOBE

Chewing Gum Crime

Governments in the United Kingdom and other European countries are cracking down with on-the-spot fines of $75 for people who spit their chewing gum onto the street. This "crime" costs taxpayers millions of dollars annually in clean-up expenses for sidewalks covered with wads of chewing gum. Ireland, in an effort to clean up the streets of Dublin, now fines gum litterbugs $160. In the United Kingdom, about 80 percent of major streets have gum spots, and the government spends about $15 million per year to remove wads of gum from its sidewalks.

Just about every major city in Europe has grappled with the sticky situation, and an entire industry has evolved around gum removal. The Dutch-developed GumBusters machine uses steam and a nontoxic solvent to remove gum at sites such as Barcelona's Las Ramblas pedestrian mall and Amsterdam's Schiphol airport. Launched in 2000, GumBusters International earns about $10 million in business annually cleaning walkways covered with the sticky remains of abandoned wads of chewing gum in Europe, the United States, Australia, and Japan.

Sources: Cesar Soriano, "Europe Tries to Eradicate Gum Crime," *USA Today*, July 25, 2006, p. 7A; Preston City Council, "We'd Hate to Burst Your Bubble, but . . . ," August 14, 2007, available at http://www.preston.gov.uk/News.asp?id=SX9452-A780C883, accessed August 18, 2008.

with crime data is that some people commit crimes at relatively high levels but are never caught, while others may be arrested when committing their first offense.

Thus arrest records do not always reflect a person's *actual* involvement in crime. To ease these problems, criminologists have developed multiple yardsticks that, when taken together, provide a respectable approximation of the extent and nature of criminality.

Two of the principal measures of crime are **official crime statistics**, which are based on the aggregate records of offenders and offenses processed by police, courts, and corrections agencies; and **unofficial crime statistics**, which are produced by people and agencies outside of the criminal justice system. The majority of criminal statistics comes from one of three sources: the Uniform Crime Reports, which are produced by the Federal Bureau of Investigation (FBI), the National Crime Victimization Survey (NCVS), which is produced by the U.S. Bureau of Justice Statistics, and one unofficial measure—self-report surveys.

Uniform Crime Reports

One of the earliest national measures of crime was the **Uniform Crime Reports** (UCR).[3] Since its inception in 1929, the UCR has collected statistics from local and state law enforcement agencies on Part I offenses, also known as **Crime Index** offenses, which are the violent crimes of murder and non-negligent manslaughter, forcible rape, robbery, and aggravated assault, and the property crimes of burglary, larceny-theft, motor vehicle theft, and arson (which was added in 1979) (see TABLE 3–1). In addition to covering crimes known to the police, the UCR provides information on (1) number of arrests and (2) characteristics of persons arrested, including the suspects' age, race, and sex. Today, the UCR represents a nationwide, cooperative effort of more than 17,000 law enforcement agencies (about 95 percent of all U.S. policing agencies) that *voluntarily* report data on crime to the FBI. The data submitted to the FBI are published annually in a report titled *Crime in the United States*.

TABLE 3-1 UCR Serious Criminal Offenses

Beginning in 2004, the UCR no longer reported a Crime Index; rather, it now simply provides data on the number of people arrested and crimes known to the law enforcement agencies for the following eight categories of serious violent and property crimes.

Serious Violent Crimes
Murder and non-negligent manslaughter is the willful killing of one person by another.
Forcible rape is the carnal knowledge of a female forcibly and against her will.
Robbery is the taking or attempting to take anything of value from the care, custody, or control of a person or persons by force or threat of force or violence and/or by putting the victim in fear.
Aggravated assault is the unlawful attack by one person upon another for the purpose of inflicting severe or aggravated bodily injury.
Serious Property Crimes
Burglary is the unlawful entry into a structure to commit a felony or theft.
Larceny–theft is the unlawful taking, carrying, leading, or riding away of property from the possession or constructive possession of others.
Motor vehicle theft is the theft or attempted theft of a motor vehicle.
Arson is any willful or malicious burning or attempt to burn, with or without intent to defraud, a dwelling house, public building, motor vehicle or aircraft, or the personal property of another.

Source: Federal Bureau of Investigation, *Crime in the United States, 2007* (Washington, DC: U.S. Department of Justice, 2008).

Problems with UCR Data

While UCR data are an improvement over the village watchmen's haphazard guesses, there are still several criticisms about the data's accuracy.

The UCR reports only crimes known to the police. Because a large percentage of crime victims do not report their experiences to a law enforcement agency, the data reported to the FBI *underestimate* the number of crimes committed (**incidence**) and the number of persons committing crimes (**prevalence**). There exists, in other words, a large gap between the *actual* amount of crimes committed and crimes reported. The **dark figure of crime** is the term criminologists use to describe the amount of unreported or undiscovered crime.[4]

The UCR reports on only the most serious crime incident. The information reported in the UCR is based on the **hierarchy rule**, which means that for a single crime incident in which multiple offenses were committed, only the most serious offense is reported. (Arson is an exception and is always reported to the FBI.) Thus, if an offender robs and murders a victim, and then steals his or her car, only the murder is reported to the FBI.

The UCR does not collect all the relevant data. The UCR collects crime details about the victim, the offender, and the circumstance *only* for homicide cases. The types of weapons used are gathered only for murder, robbery, and aggravated assault. Weapons used in forcible rape are not reported, and data for rapes include only female victims. (Male victims of forcible rape are recorded as aggravated assault.)

The UCR tells us more about police behavior than it does about criminality. Some law enforcement agencies falsify the reports they submit to the FBI. Once a citizen reports a crime, police must make an official record for the crime to be counted in the UCR. Sometimes law enforcement officers do not complete a crime report. For example, in Atlanta, it was found that crimes reported to police were not recorded for a number of years to help the city land the 1996 Olympics and boost tourism. In 2002, it was discovered that more than 22,000 police reports were never submitted to the FBI. In those reports were more than 4000 violent offenses that were committed but were never counted.[5]

In spite of these criticisms, the UCR is the most widely used source of national estimates of the nature and extent of criminality. Inaccuracies in UCR data are believed to be consistent over time and provide reasonably accurate estimates of crime trends.[6]

Reforming the UCR

Recognizing the need for more detailed crime statistics, law enforcement leaders called for a thorough evaluative analysis that would modernize the UCR program. These studies led to the creation and implementation in 1982 of the National Incident-Based Reporting System (NIBRS).[7]

The NIBRS currently is a component of the UCR program and is expected to replace the UCR. The NIBRS differs from the UCR in several significant ways (see TABLE 3–2). For example, the NIBRS collects data on each single incident and arrest. When a crime becomes known to the police, information is then gathered on the following categories: the crime incident, the victim, the nature of the property, and characteristics of the arrested suspect. A total of 53 data elements are recorded for crimes in 22 categories.

Data produced by the NIBRS are already benefiting law enforcement agencies. Having access to such comprehensive crime data, local police agencies today are making more effective arguments for acquiring and efficiently allocating resources needed to respond to crime.[8] Although only about 36 percent of all law enforcement agencies (approximately 6500 agencies) are currently reporting data to the NIBRS, it is expected that over the next few years the number of participating agencies will increase dramatically.[9]

In addition to the NIBRS, another important change to the UCR took place in 2004 when the FBI discontinued using the Crime Index. The purpose of the Crime Index was to show whether overall serious crime in the United States was increasing or decreasing. It was arguable whether it was achieving this goal. Now, efforts are under way to construct a "new" Crime Index. Until this work is completed, the FBI will report only the number of serious violent and serious property crimes known to police in its annual publication, *Crime in the United States*.[10]

National Crime Victimization Survey

A **victimization survey** asks crime victims about their crime experiences. The first victimization survey appeared in the late 1960s, partly in response to the inability of the UCR to provide accurate estimates of the dark figure of crime. Like the NIBRS, victim

TABLE 3–2 Differences Between UCR and NIBRS Data

	UCR	NIBRS
Offenses reported	Part I offenses (8 crimes)	Group A offenses (22 crimes)
Rape	Female victims only	Male and female victims
Attempted versus completed offenses	Does not differentiate	Does differentiate
Multiple-offense crime incidents	Hierarchy rule: reports only the most serious offense	All offenses are reported
Weapons	Recorded only for cases of murder, robbery, and aggravated assault	All weapons data are recorded
Crime categories	Crimes against persons (e.g., murder, rape, and aggravated assault)	Crimes against persons
	Crimes against property (e.g., robbery, burglary, and larceny-theft)	Crimes against property
		Crimes against society (e.g., drug or narcotic offenses)

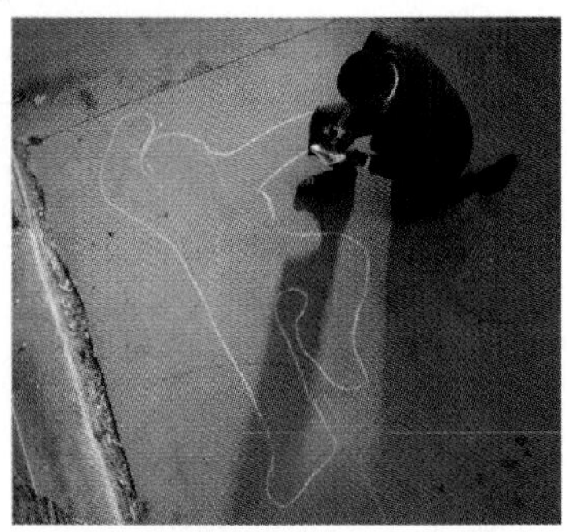

Murder is not measured by the NCVS because the victim obviously cannot be interviewed.

surveys gather specific information about such crime characteristics as when and where the crime occurred, whether a weapon was used, and whether there was any known relationship between victim and offender.[11]

In 1972, the U.S. Bureau of Justice Statistics launched the National Crime Survey, renamed the **National Crime Victimization Survey (NCVS)** in 1990, which is the most comprehensive and systematic survey of victims in the United States.[12] The NCVS produces data on both personal and household crimes. The crimes it measures include the personal crimes of assault, rape, and sexual assault and the household crimes of burglary, motor vehicle theft, and theft. These seven offenses form the **crimes of interest**, selected because victims are more likely to report them to police and victims are usually able to recall them when questioned about them. Murder is not measured by the NCVS because the victim obviously cannot be interviewed.

In addition to providing a better estimate of the dark figure of crime, NCVS data:

- Help criminologists understand why so many victims do not report crime incidents to police.
- Demonstrate that variations in crime reporting depend greatly on the type of offense, crime situation factors, the characteristics of the victim (for example, the victim's race, sex, and social class), and the nature of the victim–offender relationship.
- Allow criminologists to establish theoretical explanations for how crime often results from the social interactions between victims and offenders.[13]

Problems with NCVS Data

The NCVS is limited in scope. Obviously, the small number of crimes of interest is a problem because they represent only a small fraction of all crimes committed. The majority of crimes committed involve alcohol and illegal drugs, and many robberies, burglaries, and crimes committed against commercial establishments such as bars, businesses, and factories are not included in the NCVS.[14] By excluding these and other crimes, such as computer hacking, insider trading, and public order crimes (e.g., driving under the influence of alcohol or drugs, illegal gambling, and prostitution), the NCVS provides data on only a small subset of crime incidents.

Interview data may be unreliable. Because respondents do not have to meet legal or evidentiary standards to report crimes committed against them, NCVS data may overreport crimes that law enforcement would have considered unfounded and excluded from UCR data.

Additionally, because the NCVS is based on answers people give to questions regarding past and sometimes troublesome events, subjects may experience some of the following phenomena:

- *Memory errors*—difficulty recalling details about the event.
- *Telescoping*—difficulty remembering the time of the crime. It may feel as though the event occurred more recently than it did because the incident remains vivid in the interviewee's memory.
- *Errors of deception*—difficulty reporting events that are embarrassing, unpleasant, or self-incriminating. (It is also possible that people fabricate crime incidents.)
- *Sampling error*—difficulty including populations outside of ordinary households and resolving discrepancies between sample estimates of behavior and the actual amount of behavior. For instance, because the sampling unit in the NCVS is households, homeless persons, who are at greater risk of victimization, are excluded from the sample.[15]

Changes have recently been made to the NCVS to increase the likelihood of respondents recalling events accurately. Some of the changes made include having interviewers ask respondents questions and give them cues to help them possibly recall a crime incident.

Acclaim for the NCVS

Even though much more crime is reported by victims than the amount of crime reported to police, the trends reported in NCVS data and UCR data are very similar. For instance, when Janet Lauritsen and Robin Schaum compared UCR and NCVS data for robbery, burglary, and aggravated assault in Chicago, Los Angeles, and New York from 1980 to 1998, they found that for burglary and robbery, UCR crime rates were generally similar to NCVS estimates. Some discrepancies were noted between UCR and NCVS data for aggravated assault, but the differences reported were not statistically significant.[16] In other words, the UCR and NCVS data tell roughly the same story about these three serious crimes. Indeed, for more than 30 years, criminologists have found that UCR and victimization data generally reach similar conclusions regarding the nature of criminality.[17]

Self-Report Surveys

In a **self-report survey**, criminologists ask persons to identify their own criminality during a specific time period, such as during the prior year. For more than 60 years, criminologists have conducted self-report surveys and have consistently found that 85 to 90 percent of persons have committed behavior that could have led to arrest had they been caught.[18]

The most comprehensive self-reported survey is the **National Youth Survey** (NYS).[19] This survey began in 1976. At that time, 1725 adolescents between the ages of 11 and 17, as well as one of their parents, were interviewed. Participants were chosen by a scientific method designed to select individuals who were representative of the national population. More than 30 years later, the survey is still going. Its name has been changed to the *National Youth Survey: Family Study* because the original participants who were once 11–17 are now 43–49 years old. This study has followed these same individuals over time to look at their changing attitudes, beliefs, and behaviors about topics such as career goals, involvement with community and family, attitudes about violence, drugs, and social values.[20]

Problems with Self-Report Surveys

Self-report survey data are not always reliable. When people are asked to report to strangers their illegal acts, they may lie about their criminal involvement. In addition, many people forget, misunderstand, or distort their participation in crime. Typically the most active criminals do not participate in self-report surveys because they are not likely to reveal themselves or their activities to strangers.[21]

Self-report studies often exclude serious chronic offenders. Because most self-report surveys sample high-school or college student populations, it is not surprising that only a small amount of serious crime is detected using this method. These concerns have led criminologists to develop methods to validate the findings from self-report studies. Findings from studies using validity checks have provided general support of the self-report method. In a comprehensive review of the reliability and validity of self-reports, Michael Hindelang and his colleagues concluded that the difficulties of self-report instruments are surmountable and the self-report method is not fundamentally flawed.[22] Like the UCR and the NCVS, self-report studies provide criminologists with a variety of data for use in making generalizations about the nature and extent of crime in the United States.

Self-report studies typically discover trivial events. Studies often find an abundance of respondents stealing a small sum of money, using fake identification, occasionally smok-

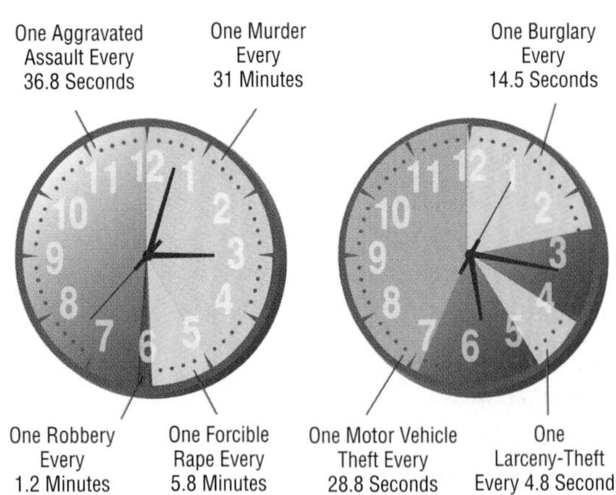

FIGURE 3-1 U.S. Crime Clock

Source: Federal Bureau of Investigation, *Crime in the United States, 2007* (Washington, DC: U.S. Department of Justice, 2008).

ing marijuana, and having premarital sex prior to age 18 (a crime in some states). These crimes do not help criminologists better understand or construct policies to address the problem of crime.[23]

Acclaim for Self-Report Surveys

Self-report surveys provide criminologists with much information about crime. For example, it is now widely accepted that more than 90 percent of all juveniles have committed at least one criminal act.[24] The surveys have also added to our awareness of the real extent of the dark figure of crime, being somewhere between 4 and 10 times greater than that reported in the UCR. Finally, self-report research provides clear evidence of ethnic, gender, and race bias in the official processing of suspects.[25]

Crime Statistics for the United States

There is no perfect measure of crime. Each method of producing crime data has both strengths and weaknesses. The best single source of data for estimating serious violent and property crimes is the UCR, which provides an indication of annual, 5-year, and 10-year trends in murder rates and circumstances. Reasonable estimates of less serious crimes can be derived from victimization surveys and self-report studies, although self-report studies are best for estimating drug offenses. When the data from the various sources are merged, they provide criminologists with a much better understanding of the nature and extent of crime than any one of them does alone.

More than 300 million people live in the United States, and the U.S. population is projected to increase in the coming decades. In the United States, a serious violent crime is committed every 22 seconds and a serious property crime is committed every 3 seconds (see FIGURE 3-1).[26] In 2007, more than 1 million serious violent crimes and more than 10 million serious property crimes were reported to law enforcement agencies.[27] These figures represent a very conservative estimate of the amount of crime committed because a lot of crime is not reported to law enforcement agencies. NCVS data published in the same year (2007) found that Americans age 12 and older reported being the victims of 14 million property crimes, 3.3 million violent crimes, and nearly 200,000 personal thefts.[28] Yet, between 1991 and 2007, the overall crime rate in the United States dropped by more than 35 percent, and the crime rates for serious violent and serious property crime during this period also declined (see FIGURE 3-2).[29]

There are several possible explanations for the lower crime rate in recent decades, including the controversial idea that legalized abortion may have played a significant role.[30] Other explanations for the dramatic decrease in crime during the past decade include changes in the following areas:

- *The economy.* The lower crime rate may be tied to the economy. During a recession, fewer crimes may occur because unemployed parents are more likely to stay home and supervise their children. In times of economic expansion, the economy might provide people with legitimate opportunities to earn money, making crime a less desirable option.
- *Prisons.* It is likely that incarcerating a greater number of offenders for longer periods of time will reduce crime rates. For example, the incarceration rate per 100,000 persons increased 350 percent from 139 in 1980 to 501 in 2006. The crime rate dropped by more than 36 percent during this same period.[31]
- *Policing.* Strengthened policing efforts may have led to a reduction in crime. In recent years, law enforcement has implemented more effective crime-controlling

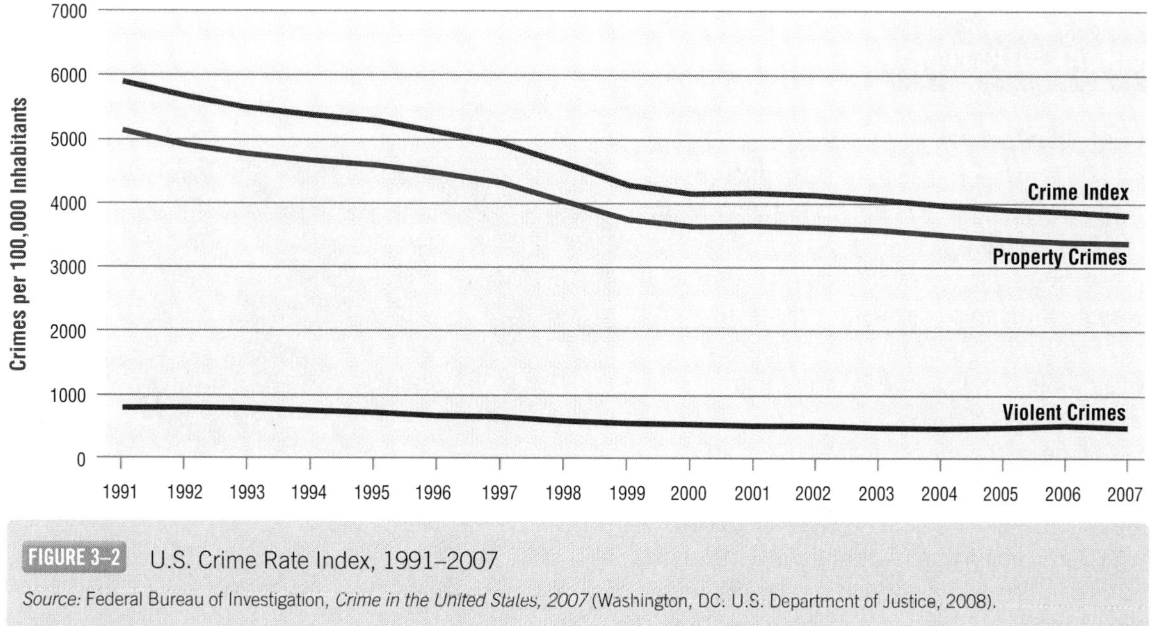

FIGURE 3-2 U.S. Crime Rate Index, 1991–2007

Source: Federal Bureau of Investigation, *Crime in the United States, 2007* (Washington, DC: U.S. Department of Justice, 2008).

strategies, such as community-oriented policing, and assigned a larger number of officers to the streets to fight crime.

- *Age.* Changes in crime rates are closely related to changes in the age distribution of the population. Males between the ages of 20 and 39 are the most likely to commit crimes. When young males account for a smaller portion of the total population, it would seem to follow that there will be less crime.[32]

Despite these correlated trends, criminologists do not know with certainty why the crime rate has fallen, although the violent crime rate ticked slightly upward in 2006 and 2007.[33] Most likely, the general decline in crime is the work of several factors entangled in complex and as yet unknown ways.

In 2007, nearly 2 million juveniles were arrested for committing either serious violent or serious property crimes.

Criminal Offenders

Data from the UCR, NCVS, and self-report studies have provided criminologists with an abundance of information about criminal offenders. Collectively, these sources show that 60 percent of persons arrested are between the ages of 19 and 39, even though this group represents only 28 percent of the U.S. population. With regard to race, about 13 percent of the population is African American, but African Americans are arrested for 37 percent of serious violent crimes and 28 percent of serious property crimes. While approximately 49 percent of the population is male, men are arrested for 82 percent of serious violent crimes and 68 percent of serious property crimes. Pulling the data together, the persons most likely to be arrested for both serious violent and serious property crimes are African American males between the ages of 19 and 39.[34]

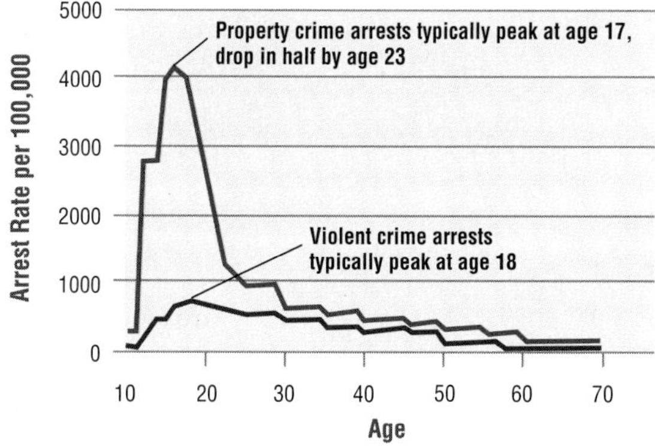

FIGURE 3-3 Age–Crime Curve

Source: Federal Bureau of Investigation, *Crime in the United States, 2006* (Washington, DC: U.S. Department of Justice, 2007).

Offenders by Age

Age and crime are closely related. The **age–crime curve** (see FIGURE 3-3) illustrates that crime rates increase during preadolescence, peak in late adolescence, and then decline steadily thereafter.[35] The high point of the curve is different for violent offenses and property offenses. Seri-

FOCUS ON CRIMINAL JUSTICE

The Criminal Unborn

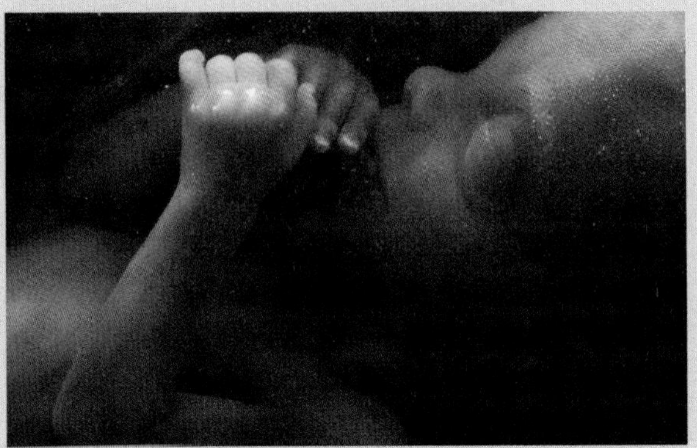

Between 1991 and 2007, the percentage of persons arrested for Crime Index offenses declined by about 35 percent. Many explanations for the decline have been offered, including the economy, population changes, aggressive police practices, and increased incarceration of chronic offenders. One of the most controversial explanations is suggested by John Donohue III and Steven Levitt: They attribute the decrease in crime to the 1973 *Roe v. Wade* decision that legalized abortion.

Donohue and Levitt present evidence that legalized abortion is primarily responsible for lower crime rates. The relationship between legalized abortion and crime is straightforward: A steep rise in abortions after 1973 has meant that many persons who would have been prone to criminal activity in the 1990s when crime began to decline were never born. There are two reasons for this relationship:

1. Abortion shrinks the number of people who reach the age where they are most prone to commit crimes.
2. Abortion is not random. Teenagers, unmarried women, the poor, and African Americans are more likely than others to have abortions; they are also more likely to have children who are "at risk" for committing crimes later in life.

Similarly, women with unwanted pregnancies are less likely to be good parents and may harm their fetuses during pregnancy by drinking alcohol and taking drugs that increase the likelihood of future criminality.

Donohue and Levitt present three strands of evidence to support each claim:

1. The precipitous drop in crime across the United States coincides with the period in which the generation affected by *Roe v. Wade* would have reached the peak of its criminal activity.
2. The five states that legalized abortion in 1970, three years before *Roe v. Wade*, were the first to experience the drop in crime.
3. States with high abortion rates from 1973 to 1976 have seen the largest decrease in crime since 1985, even after controlling for incarceration rates, racial composition, and income.

Donohue and Levitt conclude that the current crime rate in the United States would be 10 to 20 percent higher if abortion had not been legalized. They estimate that legalized abortion may account for as much as 50 percent of the recent drop in crime. In terms of costs of crime, they believe that legalized abortion has saved Americans more than $30 billion annually.

Sources: Federal Bureau of Investigation, *Crime in the United States, 2007* (Washington, DC: U.S. Department of Justice, 2008); Steven Levitt and Stephen Dubner, "Freakonomics: Opinion," *The New York Times* Blog, available at http://freakonomics.blogs.nytimes.com/, accessed April 12, 2008; Steven Levitt and Stephen Dubner, *Freakonomics*, rev. ed. (New York: Harper, 2006); John Donohue and Steven Levitt, "The Impact of Legalized Abortion on Crime," *Quarterly Journal of Economics* 116:379–420 (2001).

ous violent crime arrests peak at age 18 and then decline; property crime arrests hit their highest point at age 16 and then decrease.

Juveniles (persons younger than age 18) account for approximately 26 percent (about 80 million people) of the population and, in 2006, were arrested for 16 percent of serious violent crimes and 26 percent of serious property crimes. Between 1997 and 2006, overall, serious juvenile violent crime decreased by 20 percent. In the same period, arrests of juveniles for serious property crimes dropped sharply by 44 percent.[36]

The age–crime curve also shows that older persons commit fewer crimes, something criminologists call the **aging-out phenomenon**, as reductions in strength, energy, and mobility with age make it more difficult to commit crime. Other reasons why crime decreases with age have been attributed to personality changes, increased awareness of the cost of crime, decreased importance of peer influences, and lower testosterone levels linked with decreases in male aggression. Some people, however, do not age out of crime. These chronic offenders start offending at a very young age and continue to commit crime throughout their lives. Unfortunately, many chronic juvenile offenders become adult criminals who cannot be rehabilitated.[37]

Kenneth Lay, who was the CEO of the Enron Corporation, one of the largest companies in the U.S., was convicted of conspiring to inflate the energy company's stock price and misleading investors and employees who lost billions of dollars in its 2001 bankruptcy. Lay, who was to spend the rest of his life in prison, died of a heart attack before he could be sentenced.

Offenders by Socioeconomic Status

When most Americans think of crime, they think of street crime, which includes acts of personal violence and crimes against property. These perceptions of crime are reinforced by the news media, whose stories typically emphasize street crimes and magnify people's fears about their personal safety and belongings. The UCR and NCVS also stress street crimes, but white-collar crime, which is "a crime committed by a person of respectability and high social status in the course of his or her occupation," is also harmful to society.[38] Examples of white-collar crime include ATM fraud, cellular phone fraud, computer fraud, counterfeiting, credit card fraud, embezzlement, forgery, identity theft, illegal dumping of toxic waste, insider stock market trading, telemarketing fraud, and welfare fraud.

Over the years there have been countless incidents of white-collar crime.[39] The actual monetary cost of white-collar crime is unknown because very little information on this topic is available. The best source of data on white-collar crime is the NIBRS, which suggests that more than 6 million people are victims of white-collar crime in the United States each year. The FBI has estimated the annual monetary cost of white-collar crime in the United States to be greater than $300 billion.[40]

Crime Victims

There are no victimless crimes; criminal behavior always has consequences, although the cost of crime may not be immediate or the consequences may be hidden for many months and years. The study of the characteristics of crime victims and why certain people are more likely than others to become victims of crime is called **victimology**. Crime victims play an important role in the operation of the criminal justice system. Although police depend on victims to report crimes and to act as complainants and prosecutors, defense attorneys, judges, and juries rely on them as witnesses. Interest in studying crime victimization was limited until 1967 when the President's Commission on Law Enforcement and Administration of Justice, in a special task force report, declared that crime victims had been neglected.[41] Since then, more than 3000 state and federal laws have been passed to aid crime victims, and many states have added victims' rights amendments to their state constitutions (see FIGURE 3–4).

There are no victimless crimes. Behavior always produces consequences. Sometimes the consequences are immediate; other times they remain hidden for years.

Children

Children of all ages are vulnerable to becoming crime victims. Often the offenders are family members and acquaintances. Some juveniles are the victims of abuse and neglect at the hands of their caregivers. Child victimization and abuse have been linked with problem behaviors later in life, such as teen pregnancy, alcohol and drug abuse, and criminality.[42]

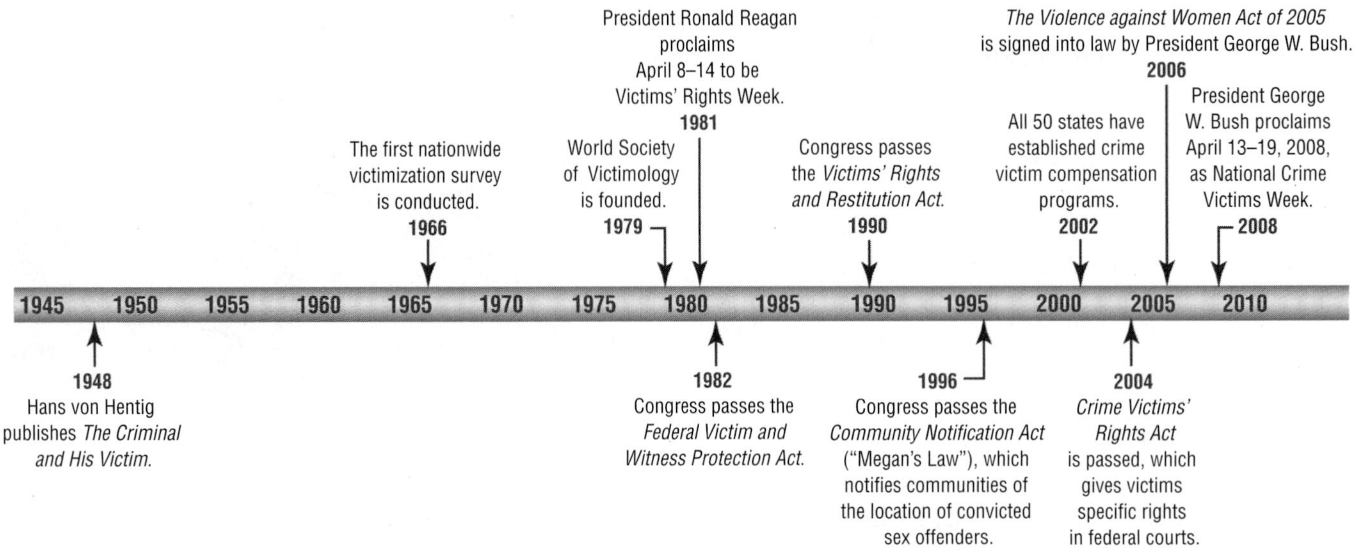

FIGURE 3-4 Victimology Timeline

Source: The National Center for Victims of Crime, available at www.ncgc.org/ncvc/main.aspx, accessed October 16, 2008.

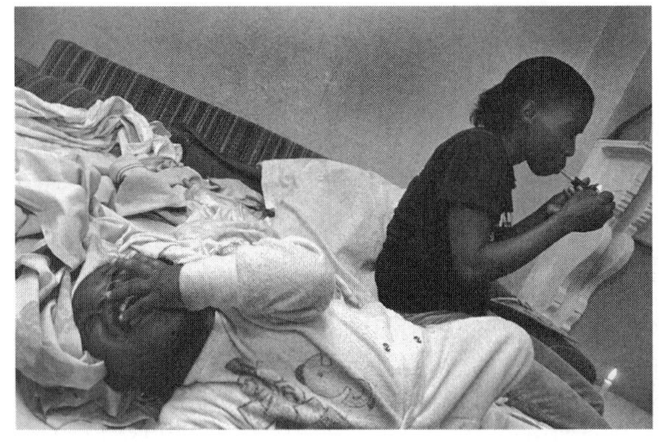

The long-term consequences of child maltreatment are severe and often include substance abuse and crime.

One of the most common forms of child victimization is child maltreatment, which is an act or an omission to act by a parent or other caregiver that causes harm or serious risk of harm to a child. Child maltreatment may take one of several forms, including physical abuse, sexual abuse, neglect, or emotional abuse. Each year, approximately 3 million cases of child maltreatment are referred to child protective service agencies. Almost 6 million children were included in these referrals. Of these cases about one-third are confirmed, which means that roughly 1 million children are victims of maltreatment each year. Moreover, experts estimate that the actual number of incidents of abuse and neglect is three times greater than what is reported.[43]

Senior Citizens

There are approximately 36 million senior citizens (persons age 65 and older) in the United States, accounting for about 12 percent of the population. These persons generally experience victimizations at much lower rates than younger groups of people. Seniors experience nonfatal violent crime at a rate that is 5 percent of that of young persons (only 4 per 1000 persons 65 and older). Households headed by seniors experience property crimes at a rate about 25 percent of that for households headed by persons younger than age 25. At the same time, seniors are disproportionately victimized by thefts of their purses and wallets, which accounts for 20 percent of personal crimes against seniors.[44]

Intimate Partner Violence Victims

One characteristic many victims share is that they run the risk of **intimate partner violence** (IPV)—violent victimization by intimates, including current or former spouses, boyfriends, girlfriends, or romantic partners. IPV includes violent acts such as murder, rape, sexual assault, robbery, aggravated assault, and simple assault. Data released in 2007 reported that less than 1 percent of households experienced IPV. While this number appears to be low, framed in another way, IPV occurs in 1 in 320 homes every year.[45] Roughly 1 million violent crimes are committed against intimates each year. Women are five times more likely than men to be victims of IPV; each year on average, more than 570,000 women are injured by intimates.[46] African American, young, divorced or separated women, as well as those with low incomes, living in rental housing, and living in an urban area are most likely to be victimized. Among men, those who are young, African American, divorced or separated, or living in rented housing are the most likely victims of IPV.[47]

Hate Crime Victims

Crimes of hatred and prejudice are a sad fact of American history. The term "hate crime" did not become part of the nation's vocabulary until the 1980s, when emerging hate groups like the Skinheads launched a wave of bias-related crime. Today, a **hate crime** (or bias crime) is defined as a crime in which an offender chooses a victim based on a specific characteristic, and evidence is provided that hate or personal disapproval of this characteristic prompted the offender to commit the crime.

The Southern Poverty Law Center has estimated that 888 hate groups were operating in the United States in 2007, up 5 percent from 844 hate groups in 2006. The hate groups with the largest number of chapters operating in the United States are the Neo-Nazis, Ku Klux Klan, White Nationalists, Neo-Confederates, Black Separatists, and Racist Skinheads. At least 90 other organizations are categorized as "General Hate" groups, which are anti-gay and anti-immigrant and favor Holocaust denial and racist music.[48]

Headline Crime: The Beating of Billy Ray Johnson

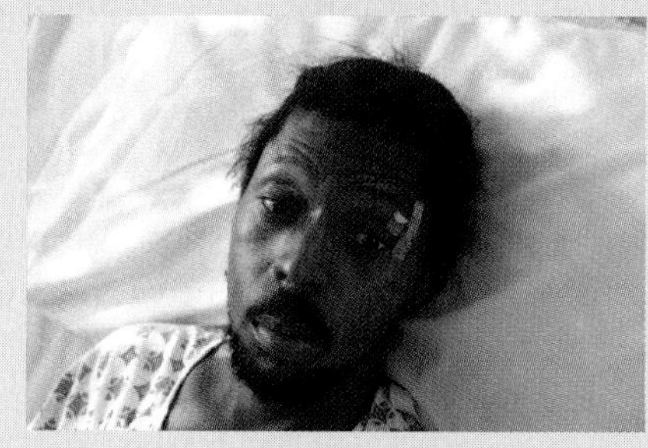

Even though thousands of hate crimes are reported annually, some hate crimes are so atrocious that they capture the attention of a nation. One such incident took place on the night of September 27, 2003, in Linden, Texas.

On that night, Billy Ray Johnson, a 42-year-old, mentally disabled African American, was brought to a "pasture party" where more than a dozen young white partygoers were having a bonfire. They got Johnson drunk, humiliated him, and jeered at him with racial epithets. When Johnson started to get angry, one of the men, Colt Amox, punched him, knocking Johnson to the ground. For nearly an hour, Johnson lay unconscious, bleeding from the head, as the group debated what to do. Eventually, they loaded Johnson into the back of pickup truck and drove two miles down a rural back road (rather than one mile to the nearest hospital) where they dropped Johnson onto a pile of stinging fire ants near a mound of rotten rubber at a used tire dumpsite.

The beating left Johnson severely injured with irreversible brain damage. Today he lives in a nursing home where he drools and soils himself. His speech has been severely impaired, and he has trouble swallowing food and walking unassisted.

Four men were arrested for the assault. One of those arrested defended his actions by claiming that Johnson aggressively charged toward him. The all-white jury acquitted two of the defendants of serious felony charges, instead convicting them on less serious charges, with a recommended sentence of probation. The men were fined and sentenced to both imprisonment and probation, though none served more than 60 days in jail.

The Southern Poverty Law Center filed a civil suit against the four men, alleging that the defendants were liable for assault and negligence and sought compensatory damages to help pay for Johnson's care. On April 22, 2007, a jury awarded Johnson $9 million in damages.

Sources: "Billy Ray Johnson Trial Set for April 17, 2007," Southern Poverty Law Center, available at http://www.splcenter.org/news/item.jsp?aid=246, accessed August 3, 2008; "Why I'm Angry—Billy Ray Johnson," *Angry Black Women,* http://theangryblackwoman.wordpress.com/2007/03/07/why-im-angry-billy-ray-johnson/, accessed August 3, 2008; Pamela Colloff, "The Beating of Billy Ray Johnson," *Texas Monthly,* February 2007, available at http://www.texasmonthly.com/2007-02-01/index.php, accessed August 12, 2008; Andre Coe, "'Good Ole Boys': Weapons of Black Destruction," available at http://www.blackpressusa.com/news/Article.asp?SID=3&Title=National+News&NewsID=4552, accessed August 12, 2008.

Following passage of the *Hate Crime Statistics Act of 1990*, the FBI has gathered and published statistics on hate crime every year since 1992.[49] These data illustrate that the most likely motivation for a hate crime is the victim's race. Other factors about the victim may also motivate an offender, such as the victim's sexual orientation, ethnicity, religion, or disability. The most frequently committed hate crimes are verbal threats or intimidation, simple assaults, vandalism, and aggravated assault. The most likely victims of hate crimes are males, whites, and persons 30–49 years old.

Causes of Crime

Armed with information about how criminologists measure crime and who are the most likely criminal offenders and crime victims, you are probably curious to know *why* people commit crime. To explain why people commit crime, criminologists have developed **theories**, or integrated sets of ideas that explain when and why people commit crime. Different theories explain crime in different ways and often lead to different social policy recommendations for its prevention.

There are three types of crime theories:

- **Choice theories** insist that people have free will, are rational and intelligent, and make informed decisions to commit crimes based on whether they believe they will benefit from doing so.
- **Trait theories** blame crime on biological and psychological factors over which individuals have little—if any—control, such as low intelligence and personality disorders.
- **Sociological theories** attribute crime to social factors external to the individual, focusing on how the environment in which the person lives affects his or her behavior.

Choice Theories

Choice theories are derived from the classical and neoclassical schools of criminology, which were particularly popular in the eighteenth and nineteenth centuries. Choice theories state that the decision to commit (or refrain from) crime is an exercise of free will based on the offender's efforts to maximize pleasure and minimize pain.

Classical School

The founding father of the **classical school** was Cesare Beccaria, who developed his ideas about crime and punishment at a time when European systems of criminal justice displayed callous indifference toward human rights. People were held accountable and punished for crimes against religion (including blasphemy and witchcraft) as well as for crimes against the state. Offenders would be punished without explanation, and anyone could be taken to jail for any variety of reasons.[50] These conditions inspired Beccaria to write an essay titled *On Crimes and Punishments*, in which he laid out the framework for a new system of justice—a system emphasizing consistency, rationality, and humanity.[51]

Did Debra LaFave, a Tampa, Florida, teacher exercise her free will when she had sex with her 14-year-old student?

In spite of its good intentions, the classical school ultimately failed owing to its rigidity. In the end Beccaria's ideas did not explain *why* people committed crime—only that they did. Classical theory held that people were equally responsible for their behavior; those who committed similar crimes received comparable punishments, regardless of the reason why crime was committed. The classical school, in other words, focused on the criminal act, not on the actor. Of course, in reality, people are quite different. People who are insane, incompetent, or still children may not be as responsible for their behavior and criminally culpable as normative adults. This idea that people are different from one another led to the formation of the neoclassical school.

Neoclassical School

The **neoclassical school** built on the works of the classical school by focusing on the role of the criminal justice system in preventing crime. While the founders of the neoclassical school were sympathetic to what the classical school had hoped to achieve, they also recognized that crime may be influenced by factors that are beyond the offender's control.

Mitigating circumstances, such as age or mental disease, affect the choices that people make and influence a person's ability to form criminal intent (*mens rea*). The introduction of mitigating circumstances at criminal trials led to the notion of *individual justice*—the idea that criminal law must take into consideration the significant differences among people and the unique circumstances under which the crimes they commit occur. Individual justice led to a number of important developments in the operation of criminal justice systems, including the introduction of the insanity defense and the inclusion of expert witnesses.[52]

Rational Choice Theory

Rational choice theory, developed by Ronald Clarke and Derek Cornish, explores the reasoning process of criminals and suggests that offenders are rational people who make calculated choices before they commit a criminal act.[53] According to this theory, offenders collect, process, and evaluate information about the crime; they weigh the costs and benefits of the crime before they make the decision to commit it. Offenders then use the same calculated process to decide where to commit crime, who to target, and how to execute the crime.

Routine Activities Theory

Expanding on rational choice theory, Lawrence Cohen and Marcus Felson constructed **routine activities theory**, which argues that for crime to occur, three elements must converge:

- Motivated offenders
- Suitable targets
- An absence of people to deter the would-be offender

In other words, crime increases when motivated offenders focus on vulnerable targets (e.g., keys in the car ignition), with few people (e.g., bystanders, police) available to protect them.[54]

Two objections have been raised to the routine activities theory. First, it does not identify those factors that would motivate someone to commit a crime in the first place; the theory incorrectly assumes that people are inclined to commit crime when opportunities arise (some people are and others are not). Second, the theory overlooks factors that cause the criminalization of some behavior (e.g., smoking marijuana) and the legalization of equally harmful behavior (e.g., drinking alcohol).[55]

Lifestyle Theory

Michael Hindelang, Michael Gottfredson, and James Garofalo have proposed **lifestyle theory**, which is closely related to routine activities theory, to explain why some people are more likely than others to be crime victims.[56] Hindelang and his colleagues suggest that people become crime victims because of the situations in which they put themselves (for example, spending time alone on dimly lit streets at night with no bystanders). Lifestyle theory proposes that the more time people spend away from home, the greater their risk of being victimized due to their increased visibility and accessibility. Additionally, when they are out, their cars and homes may be left unattended and, therefore, are likely to be victimized.

People are more likely to be crime victims because of situations they put themselves in.

Social Policy Implications of Choice Theories

Crime control legislation based on classical and neoclassical theories is designed to increase the certainty, severity, and swiftness of punishment. These measures include the following activities:

- Implementing cell-phone tracking surveillance
- Establishing three-strikes sentencing and truth-in-sentencing
- Hiring more police officers
- Making it physically more difficult to commit crimes (e.g., locks on steering wheels of motor vehicles)
- Increasing the perceived risk of crime (e.g., electronic merchandise tags or garments in department stores)
- Reducing anticipated rewards of crime (e.g., requiring a personal identification code to operate a stereo in a motor vehicle)[57]

Trait Theories

Trait theories offer a different way of thinking about crime and criminals. These theories are rooted in biology and psychology and claim offenders commit crimes because of certain traits, characteristics, or deficits they possess.

Biological Theories

The individual justice of the neoclassical school formed the foundation for a new explanation of crime, one that blamed criminality on individual characteristics that were in place *before* the act was committed. This new way of thinking about crime was called *scientific determinism* and relied on the application of the scientific method to explain crime, which became the centerpiece of the positive school of criminology. The **positive school** of criminology was based on the work of French sociologist August Comte, who described how as a society progressed, people embraced more of a rational and scientific point of view of the world. Scholars who adopted this position called themselves positivists and used factual information to test hypotheses.[58]

The first criminologist to apply positivism to the study of crime was Cesare Lombroso. He believed criminals were **atavistic beings**—that is, throwbacks to an earlier, more primitive stage of human development. Because they were not as highly evolved, criminals possessed **stigmata** or distinctive physical features, such as an asymmetrical face or large and protruding ears, that distinguished them from ordinary people. Lombroso did test his theory and produced evidence in support of it that led him to conclude that through no fault of their own, criminals were incapable of obeying the complex rules and regulations of modern society and should be placed in restrictive institutions, like prisons.[59]

Following Lombroso's landmark studies, others reexamined his data and found mixed support for his findings.[60] For a variety of reasons, not the least of which had to do with the eugenics movement in the United States and Nazi Germany during the early twentieth century, this line of research was largely abandoned. However, in recent years the link between biology and crime has been resurrected and some very impressive studies have been published. Today, biological theories of crime have one of three broad areas of focus: genetic factors, neurological factors, or environmental factors.

Genetic Factors

Criminality may be partially inherited. One way of determining whether heredity plays a role in criminality is by studying twins. **Monozygotic twins** (MZ), or identical twins, have identical DNA and come from a single fertilized egg. By contrast, **dizygotic twins** (DZ), or fraternal twins, come from two separate eggs fertilized at the same time; DZ twins are no more alike genetically than nontwin siblings. If there is a genetic factor in criminality, the behavior of MZ twins should be more alike than DZ twins. This similarity is called *concordance*. For instance, if one twin is involved in crime and the other twin also commits crime, there is concordance with respect to crime. Conversely, if one twin is criminal and the other twin is not, this is called *discordance*. Research investigating the amount of concordance for criminality among twins generally has found that criminal concordance is much higher for MZ twins than for DZ twins, which supports the idea of a link between heredity and crime.[61]

Monozygotic (identical) twins share the same DNA. Studies of MZ twins have shed light on the genetic underpinnings of behavior. While identical twins have the same DNA, however, all people share more than 99 percent of the same DNA.

A second way of evaluating the association between heredity and crime is by studying adoptees. Adopted children usually have little or no contact with their biological parents. Therefore, to the extent that the behavior of adopted children and their biological parents is similar, an argument can be made that genes influence behavior. In one of the largest studies of adoptees, Sarnoff Mednick and his colleagues matched the court convictions of more than 14,000 adoptees with the court convictions of their biological parents and adoptive parents. They found that the criminality of the child was more strongly related to the criminality of the biological parents.[62] Other studies of adoptees have since reported similar findings.[63]

Neurological Factors

One of the most consistently documented biological correlates of crime is an underaroused system marked by a low resting heart rate. Research has found a low resting heart rate more frequently among chronic and violent criminals. For example, when David Farrington examined the predictors of violence using 48 sociological, psychological, and biological independent variables, he found that low resting heart rate was the strongest and most consistent predictor of crime.[64]

A growing body of literature confirms that criminality is tied to differences in brain structure, which affects an individual's ability to exercise self-control (frontal lobe) and respond to environmental changes (temporal lobe). The brains of some people produce more or fewer chemicals than they need. A brain, for example, that produces too little *serotonin* may cause a behavioral condition, *attention-deficit/hyperactivity disorder* (ADHD), that has been coupled with impulsivity, aggression, and violent offending.[65]

Environmental Factors

Behavior is under the control of the brain. Even though the brain directs people's activities in everyday life, the activities themselves shape how the brain processes information throughout life. The environment, in other words, contributes to both the brain's contents and its wiring. Two environmental conditions—parental cigarette smoking and chemical toxins—are known to cause serious biological damage to the brain and create risk factors for criminality.[66]

Good, strong evidence shows that mothers who smoke while pregnant, fathers who smoke around pregnant women, and parents who smoke around their children are placing the fetus and children in harm's way. Nancy Day and her colleagues studied the effects of prenatal nicotine exposure on preschoolers' behavior and produced several distressing findings. They discovered that children whose mothers smoked while pregnant were more likely to be emotionally unstable, physically aggressive, and socially immature, and to have oppositional defiant disorder.[67] Similar conclusions have been reached by Patricia Brennan and her colleagues in their research on the long-term effects of maternal smoking during pregnancy. Controlling for a variety of predictors of crime, they found that children whose mothers smoked while pregnant with them were much more likely to participate in criminal behavior into adulthood.[68]

Few people blame crime on environmental toxins and chemicals. While chemicals do not *cause* people to commit crime, they indirectly affect behavior by interfering with the ability of the brain to perceive and react to the environment. One toxin that adversely affects brain functioning and causes changes in behavior is *lead*. Lead can get into the body in many different ways. A pregnant woman, for instance, may transmit lead to her child. Some people ingest lead by playing with toys, by inhaling dust particles traveling in the air or, in the case of children, by eating sweet-tasting lead-based paints peeled or chipped from walls and candy wrappers.[69]

Once lead enters the body, it makes its way into the bloodstream, then into soft body tissues (which include the brain and kidneys), and finally into hard tissues (bones and teeth).[70] Lead damages an individual's internal organs and causes brain and nerve damage that results in intelligence and behavioral problems, particularly in children. Lead poisoning has also been tied to criminality. Herbert Needleman and his colleagues have found children with high levels of bone lead tend to be more aggressive, self-report more criminal behavior, and exhibit more attention difficulties.[71]

Psychological Theories

Some criminologists blame crime on psychological flaws found inside of individual offenders. Many criminals grew up in dysfunctional families and lived in conflict with their parents, neighbors, peers, classmates, and teachers. The conflict they have experienced throughout their lives is a "red flag" to criminologists, who believe they may have mental deficiencies that cause them to "act out" and commit crime. However, psychologists disagree on why people are criminal.

Three popular crime theories based on psychology are psychoanalytic theory, behavioral theory, and social learning theory.

Psychoanalytic Theory

According to **psychoanalytic theory**, unconscious mental processes that develop in early childhood control the personality. This idea originated with the Austrian physician Sigmund Freud, who suggested that the personality consists of three components: *id*, *ego*, and *superego*.[72]

The **id** is present at birth and consists of blind, unreasoning, instinctual desires and motives; it represents basic biological and psychological drives and does not differentiate between fantasy and reality. The id is antisocial and knows no rules, boundaries, or limitations. If the id is left unchecked, it will destroy the person.

The **ego** grows from the id and represents the problem-solving dimension of the personality. The ego is able to differentiate reality from fantasy and teaches people to delay gratification because acting on impulse will only get them into trouble.

The **superego** emerges from the ego. It represents the moral code, norms, and values the person has acquired. The superego is responsible for feelings of guilt and shame.

In mentally healthy people the three parts of the personality work together. It is when the parts are in conflict that a person may turn to crime. In some people, for instance, the superego is underdeveloped. If the superego is too weak to curb the impulses and drives of the id, the person's behavior becomes a direct expression of the id—for example, "If you want something, steal it." Another possibility is that an individual may have an *overdeveloped superego*. When this occurs, impulses and urges of the id may elicit strong disapproval from the superego. This ongoing conflict causes the ego to experience guilt and anxiety. Because the ego knows that punishment must follow crime, the ego will lead the person to commit a crime. To minimize guilt and make sure he or she is punished, the ego will then unconsciously leave clues at the crime scene.[73]

Behavioral Theory

In **behavioral theory**, the behavior of people is seen as a consequence of their interactions throughout their lifetime. Psychologist B. F. Skinner theorized that people learn conformity and deviance from the *punishments* and *reinforcements* they receive in response to their behavior. Put differently, the environment shapes the behavior of people. People identify those aspects of their environment they find pleasing and those that are painful. Their behavior, therefore, is the result of the consequences it produces, so people will repeat behavior that is rewarding and discontinue behavior that is punishing.[74]

Social Learning Theory

An alternative way of thinking about crime is found in **social learning theory**, which was developed by Albert Bandura. He suggested that people learn by modeling and imitating others.[75] People may learn to be aggressive, for instance, by seeing parents argue, watching friends fight, viewing television, listening to violent music lyrics, and playing violent video games.

For example, recently in Greeley, Colorado, a teenage girl and her boyfriend were charged with beating her seven-year-old half-sister to death while imitating the video game "Mortal Kombat." It is alleged that the teens kicked, karate-chopped, and body-slammed the little girl while imitating the video game. The young child died of blunt-force injuries. The autopsy showed she had a broken wrist, more than 20 bruises, swelling in the brain, and bleeding in her neck muscles and under her spine.[76] It seems as though what some people learn from frequent and intensive playing of violent video games is that aggression may produce a desired outcome.

Sadly, if Bandura is correct, people learn aggression and commit violent crimes from what they see in the media. More concretely, media violence—whether it is in film, music, video games, or television—likely contributes to criminality.[77]

Some experts disagree with this conclusion. In *Grand Theft Childhood*, Lawrence Kutner and Cheryl Olson argue that video games in the "Grand Theft Auto" series, launched in 1997, have social benefits. They believe the games are a social tool for boys who use them to interact, build friendships, and learn problem-solving skills.[78]

Social Policy Applications of Biological and Psychological Theories

Social policies resulting from *biological theories* include recommendations that society must invest more money in prenatal and postnatal care for women, provide closer monitoring of young children during their most crucial developmental years, offer paid maternal leave, and make available nutritional programs for pregnant women, newborns, and young children. Although biologists do not believe that any of these programs alone will be a cure for internal deficiencies, taken collectively they may help to prevent future criminality. In addition, some biologists recommend that offenders receive pharmaco-

Headline Crime

Should Video Games Be Censored?

Researchers have shown that playing violent video games are linked to antisocial behavior.

In 2008, a new online video game stirred controversy across the nation. In the game, players shoot presidential candidates with paintballs. The game allowed the players to stalk then-candidates Barack Obama, Hillary Clinton, John McCain, Mitt Romney, John Edwards, and Rudy Giuliani through the White House with a high-powered rifle.

While paintballs are nonlethal, concern mounted regarding the game's impact on children. Some adults feared that the game was equivalent to "planting a seed in the mind of adolescents and young adults." Is there a point where video games "cross the line" and should be censored for the protection of the morality of society and of innocent people? Or should no game be censored regardless of its content?

Source: "Only in America," *The Week*, February 1:4 (2008).

logical treatments, such as medication for persons diagnosed with biological disorders like ADHD. The idea behind prescribing drugs to offenders—and specifically to young children—is that early intervention in their lives may help to promote factors that insulate them from crime, minimize or erase the risk factors that contribute to crime, and equalize the life chances for them to develop into healthy, prosocial adults. Finally, some biologists believe that some individuals pose a serious risk to public safety because their internal deficiencies cannot be controlled with drug therapy and, therefore, must be incarcerated. If offenders cannot control their biological predisposition to commit crimes on their own, public safety mandates that when the cause of the behavior is known, it must be neutralized.

Psychological theories, in contrast, begin with the view that individual differences predispose some people to commit crime. These differences may arise from personality characteristics or social interactions. Consequently, psychoanalytic theory, for example, argues that offenders need counseling to help them understand how destructive thinking has adversely affected their lives and has caused mental or emotional disturbance. Behavioral and social learning theories propose very different policies to prevent crime because they blame crime on individuals' interactions with their environments. Policies derived from these theories emphasize teaching people different ways to respond to their environment through techniques such as behavior modification. For instance, in **aversion therapy**, the individual learns to connect unwanted behavior with punishment. Alcohol offenders, for instance, receive treatment where they are required to ingest a drug that causes nausea or vomiting if they drink alcohol. If the theory is correct, these offenders will connect drinking with an unpleasant experience and will stop drinking to avoid the ill effect.

Sociological Theories

In the 1920s, criminologists began to look beyond individual-focused theories about crime, and sociological theories emerged. These theories suggested that the causes of crime were located *outside* the offender. Rather than blaming criminality on some biological or psychological flaw of the person, sociologists blamed crime on social factors found in people's environments, including their neighborhoods, schools, and family.

Cultural Deviance Theory

The first sociological explanation of crime was published in the 1920s and focused on the influence of the neighborhood in which an individual lives on that person's behavior. In **cultural deviance theory**, criminality is blamed on social and economic factors located within a neighborhood. In other words, crime is seen as a function of how a neighborhood is structured.[79] If this theory is correct, it would be expected that in more affluent neighborhoods the crime rate will be lower. These neighborhoods provide more consistency in values and norms and are in a better position to meet the needs of the children who are closely supervised by parents. In low-income neighborhoods characterized by *social disorganization*, crime rates will be higher because residents are more likely to have conflicting values and norms. In more socially disorganized neighborhoods, children do not receive the support or supervision they need to encourage them to obey the law. Through a process of **cultural transmission**, criminal values are transmitted from one generation to the next.

The transmission of values begins early in the life of a child. In Colorado, for instance, recently police received a call regarding a public disturbance. Upon further investigation they discovered a couple was fighting over which street gang their four-year-old son should join. The child's mother, who was African American, had her heart set on her toddler joining the Crips organization, while the little boy's father (who was Latino) wanted his son to become a member of the largely Latino Westside Ballers.[80]

Cultural values are transmitted from generation to generation, for example, from father to son.

Differential Association Theory

Differential association theory aims to explain both individual criminality and group crime by identifying those conditions that need to be present for crime to take place (and that must be absent when there is no crime). This theory tells us that criminal behavior is learned in interactions with family, friends, and other intimates through verbal and nonverbal communication.[81] From these interactions people acquire the techniques of committing crime, along with the attitudes, drives, motives, and rationalizations needed to do so. The longer, earlier, more intensely, and more often someone is exposed to attitudes about criminality (either positive or negative), the more likely it is that he or she will be influenced toward or away from committing crime.

Strain Theory

Strain theory faults American culture for teaching *all* of its members to strive for economic success (the American dream), while restricting some individuals' access to legitimate means to achieve that success. This theory blames crime on a lack of integration between cultural goals (what people are told they should want) and institutionalized means (allowable ways to achieve success within the social structure). When goals and ways to achievc those goals are not aligned, social norms break down, creating a condition called **anomie** in which people feel alienated and uncertain about society's expectations and are less able to control their behavior.[82]

According to this theory, crime is a normal response to a social condition that limits the opportunities for some members of society to obtain the economic success that all members try to achieve. For instance, one cultural goal in the United States is acquisition of money. The socially approved ways to acquire money are through training, education, career advancement, and hard work. Under this rubric, it is easy to see that some people confront fewer barriers on the path to success than others who are born in less advantaged circumstances.

The strain between means and goals is always present. Individuals adapt to this strain in one of five ways (see TABLE 3-3):

1. *Conformity*—buying into the system, accepting both cultural goals and the means approved to achieve those goals
2. *Innovation*—deviating from socially acceptable ways to achieve cultural goals
3. *Ritualism*—abandoning accepted cultural goals and accepting the status quo
4. *Retreatism*—withdrawing from society altogether
5. *Rebellion*—refusing to accept socially accepted goals or ways to achieve those goals

Strain theorists believe that people are inherently good and commit crime only out of desperation. If policymakers could find a way to eliminate those conditions that produce strain, crime could be eliminated.

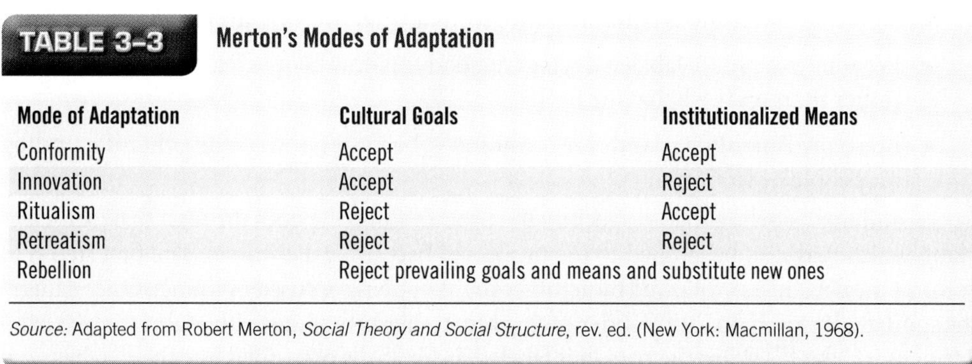

TABLE 3-3 Merton's Modes of Adaptation

Mode of Adaptation	Cultural Goals	Institutionalized Means
Conformity	Accept	Accept
Innovation	Accept	Reject
Ritualism	Reject	Accept
Retreatism	Reject	Reject
Rebellion	Reject prevailing goals and means and substitute new ones	

Source: Adapted from Robert Merton, *Social Theory and Social Structure*, rev. ed. (New York: Macmillan, 1968).

There are negative consequences of homelessness, including increased risks of crime and victimization.

Social Control Theory

Social control theory, in contrast to strain theory, argues that people are, by their very nature, amoral (without morals) and will break the law unless obstacles are thrown in their paths. Crime is expected behavior, according to this theory, which is why social control theorists are curious about why people do *not* commit crime, not why they commit crime. The theory claims that crime is something all people will engage in if there are no controls on their behavior.[83]

Controls are attitudes implanted quite effectively in most people, but less so in individuals who have a weak **social bond**, or connection to society. The bond consists of four components: attachment, belief, commitment, and involvement. The best predictor of criminality is a child's *attachment* to parents, schools, and peers—the primary agents of socialization. The second component of the bond, *belief*, refers to how strongly someone believes in the moral validity of law. *Commitment*, unlike attachment, is about success, achievement, and ambition, rather than respect, admiration, and identification. Finally, the theory proposes that *involvement* in conventional activities helps to prevent participation in crime by keeping people busy with conventional activities, such as involvement in recreational programs or after-school clubs.

Each component of the bond forms its own continuum. When the continua are merged, they provide a gauge of how strongly someone is tied to society. The stronger the bond to society, the less likely it is that someone will commit crime.

Self-Control Theory

Self-control theory argues that people are self-gratifying and pleasure seeking. According to this theory, individuals commit crime because they are unable to regulate their behavior owing to low self-control.[84] Some people are more impulsive, insensitive, and short-sighted; these risk takers have a low tolerance for frustration, making them more likely to engage in criminal behavior. In contrast, people with high self-control are less likely to commit crime.

The amount of self-control someone has is a product of early childhood rearing; post-childhood experiences have little effect on self-control. Parents who monitor the behavior of their children, supervise them closely, recognize unacceptable behavior, and administer punishment are, therefore, more likely to have children who have the self-control necessary to resist easy gratification and the desire to commit crime.

Labeling Theory

Labeling theory examines the role of societal reactions in shaping behavior; in other words, it focuses on why some people and behaviors are considered criminal and others are not.

Labeling theory reached the height of its popularity in the 1960s when it was believed that:

- Deviants and nondeviants are more similar than they are different.
- Whether people are labeled deviant depends on how people react to their behavior, rather than on the behavior itself.
- Behavior is neither moral nor immoral; it becomes one or the other depending on people's reaction to it.[85]

In addition, labeling theory specifies the process someone goes through to become deviant, which may also be applied to the process of becoming a criminal. The first step is to commit the deviant act, followed by getting caught or being accused of the act. Once caught, the spotlight is placed on the offender, giving him or her new status with a label (i.e., "skank," "drug user," "thief"). After the person is labeled, he or she is presumed by others to be more likely to commit other deviant behaviors. The negative label or stigma is, therefore, generalized to the whole person, such that someone who is accused of one type of deviance (i.e., being a "ho") is expected to commit other types of deviance (i.e., stealing).

When the label is successfully applied, being a deviant becomes the person's **master status** (what others think about him or her when they first meet). The final step in the process is for the deviant to join an organized group (e.g., delinquent or criminal gang) where members learn to rationalize their deviant activities so they may continue to commit crime without experiencing feelings of remorse, guilt, or shame.

Conflict Theory

Conflict theory views society in terms of inequalities in power and influence. This theory is grounded in the writings of Karl Marx and Friedrich Engels, who argued that in industrialized societies, the economic interests of those who own the means of production (the bourgeoisie) and those who sell their labor (the proletariat) are incompatible. The ensuing class conflict produces conditions ripe for criminality.[86] The bourgeoisie also exert control over all aspects of social life, including the production of ideas, which means they control the creation of the criminal law. Their beliefs form the basis for both law and its enforcement, which become important tools to protect their economic interests. Crime is the product of a disheartened working class that is trying to get ahead and thinking only of their personal needs.[87]

Developmental Theories

Developmental theories have recently gained popularity for their emphasis on treating behavior as constantly changing, evolving from demands, opportunities, interests, and events that people experience as they grow older. These theories focus on the offenders' early childhood and the way these experiences influence the onset of their participation in crime at later stages in life over the course of their **criminal career**. At the core of developmental theories is the idea that human development does not end either in childhood or during adolescence, but rather is a continuous process that stretches across the life cycle. These theorists look beyond what happened in the lives of people immediately before they got into trouble and instead assess what has been going on in their lives during all the years preceding their involvement in criminal activity.[88]

Social Policy Applications of Sociological Theories

Sociological theories point to a variety of external factors as the causes of crime. Crime prevention policies based on these theories are designed to change the relationship between criminal offenders and society.

Policies based on cultural deviance theory, for instance, try to find a way to alter the landscape of a neighborhood to make it easier to mainstream people—that is, to bring them into the larger society. One large-scale community program is the Chicago Area Project (CAP), started in 1931, which mobilizes residents living in neighborhoods with high crime rates by focusing on direct service, advocacy, and community involvement. Community residents work with CAP officials to keep children out of trouble, help children when they do get into trouble, and keep the neighborhood clean.[89]

Strain theorists promote policies that will reduce crime by creating new opportunities for disadvantaged people. Opportunities for offenders to "go straight" and be successful in the legitimate world should reduce the need to commit crime. Several far-reaching prevention programs based on strain theory were implemented in the 1960s. The best known is probably Project Head Start, which is a comprehensive child development program serving the needs of children from birth to age five. It still operates today: More than 1 million children are currently enrolled in Head Start programs throughout the nation.[90]

The purpose of social policies derived from social control theory is to strengthen the bond between children and their parents, other adults, schools, and the community by involving young people in prosocial activities. The Police Athletic League (PAL) is one example of this kind of effort. It offers youth a positive experience with police and provides at-risk children with guidance, discipline, and the inculcation of values from adults who serve as mentors, along with educational support, increased awareness of career options, and assistance for setting prosocial goals.[91]

Programs designed on principles of self-control theory will touch a child's life at a very young age, such as early childhood intervention programs that assist single parents with what child care might do. Other programs that have been successful include ones with a parent-training curriculum that helps to strengthen parents' monitoring and disciplinary skills and build confidence in their parenting abilities.[92]

Labeling theory sees the best strategies for reducing crime as being to ignore minor acts of deviance, react informally to crime by diverting people from the formal criminal justice system, and bring the offender, victim, and community together to restore justice. Formal intervention should be a last resort, and diversion programs should be used whenever possible.[93]

Conflict theory has had a negligible impact on crime policy. The theory is too radical for state and federal governments to implement, as it calls for sweeping changes to the social and economic organization of society (e.g., such as eliminating inherited wealth). Nevertheless, conflict theory has led to productive discussions about the consequences of structural inequalities, such as the variable prison sentences for possessing crack versus powder cocaine, efforts to eliminate overt discrimination within the criminal and juvenile justice systems, and, more generally, state legislation.

Developmental theories have been implemented in many ways, most of which focus on prevention programs for at-risk people of various ages. For younger children, programs will often be geared toward strengthening family ties and engaging in effective communication. For youths in high school, programs may be designed to address issues such as drug use, gang involvement, peer pressure, teen pregnancy, and other concerns of at-risk children. Later intervention strategies will focus on teaching people how to make an effective transition to the job market and avoiding dysfunctional personal relationships.

Headline Crime

In 2008, the state of Kentucky considered a proposal introduced by State Representative Charles Siler to make Kentucky Fried Chicken the official picnic food of the state. According to Siler, the purpose of the bill was to honor the late Colonel Harland Sanders, who created a signature blend of herbs and spices that made Kentucky famous for its fried chicken.

Not all agreed with Siler's efforts. Bruce Friedrich of People for the Ethical Treatment of Animals (PETA) argued vehemently that it was wrong to honor fried chicken because it amounted to an endorsement of animal cruelty. If the Kentucky legislature passed Siler's proposed legislation, PETA recommended that it should also "change Kentucky's state bird from the cardinal to the debeaked, crippled, scalded, diseased, dead chicken." The resolution did not pass in the Kentucky House of Representatives.

Sources: "Only in America," *The Week*, February 22:4 (2008); "PETA Opposes Tribute to Fried Chicken," *The Boston Globe*, February 9, 2008, available at http://www.boston.com/news/odd/articles/2008/02/09/peta_opposes_tribute_to_fried_chicken/, accessed April 20, 2008.

WRAPPING IT UP

Chapter Highlights

- The Uniform Crime Reports (UCR) include data on crimes known to the police, number of arrests, and persons arrested.
- The National Crime Victimization Survey (NCVS) asks people directly whether they have been victims of a crime during the past year.
- Self-report studies ask people directly about which crimes they have committed in a recent period of time during the past year.
- The "dark figure of crime" is the gap between the actual amount of crime committed and the number of crimes reported to police.
- Classical and neoclassical theories claim that criminals are rational and intelligent and choose to commit crime. Crime may be prevented if the pain of punishment is greater than the pleasure the offender receives from committing the crime.
- Biological theories suggest that criminals are inherently different from noncriminals. Social policies based on these theories may focus on investing more money in prenatal and postnatal programs, offering paid parental leave, and medicating offenders to reduce aggression, for example.
- Psychological theories, such as psychoanalytic theory, behavioral theory, and social learning theory, recommend the use of counseling and behavior modification strategies as tools for preventing crime.
- Sociological theories blame crime on external forces. Crime can be prevented by improving the community, eliminating social and structural obstacles to achievement, strengthening the bond people have to society, and improving parenting practices.

Words to Know

age–crime curve A curve showing that crime rates increase during preadolescence, peak in late adolescence, and steadily decline thereafter.

aging-out phenomenon Older persons commit fewer crimes in part because reductions in strength, energy, and mobility with age make it more difficult to commit crime.

anomie A social condition where the norms of society have broken down and cannot control the behavior of its members.

atavistic beings Individuals who are throwbacks to an earlier, more primitive stage of human development, and more closely resemble their ape-like ancestors in traits, abilities, and dispositions.

aversion therapy Therapy in which people are taught to connect unwanted behavior with punishment.

behavioral theory Theory that views behavior as a product of interactions people have with others throughout their lifetime.

choice theories Theories that assume people have free will, are rational and intelligent, and make informed decisions to commit crimes based on whether they believe they will benefit from doing so.

classical school A school of thought that holds criminals are rational, intelligent people who have free will and the ability to make choices.

conflict theory Theory that blames crime on inequalities in power.

Crime Index A statistical indicator consisting of eight offenses that was used by the FBI to gauge the amount of crime reported to the police. It was discontinued in 2004.

crimes of interest The seven offenses in the National Crime Victimization Survey, which asks people whether they have been victims of these crimes during the past year.

criminal career The progression of criminality over time or over the life-course.

cultural deviance theory Theory that proposes crime is the product of social and economic factors located within a neighborhood.

cultural transmission The process through which criminal values are transmitted from one generation to the next.

dark figure of crime A term used by criminologists to describe the amount of unreported or undiscovered crime; it calls into question the reliability of Uniform Crime Reports data.

developmental theory Theory that focuses on the offenders' early childhood and the way these experiences influence the onset of their participation in crime at later stages in life.

differential association theory Theory that proposes that through interaction with others, people learn the attitudes, values, techniques, and motives for criminal behavior.

dizygotic twins Twins who do not share the same set of genes (DZ twins).

ego Component of the personality that represents problem-solving dimensions.

hate crime A crime in which an offender chooses a victim based on a specific characteristic, and evidence is provided that hate or personal disapproval of this characteristic prompted the offender to commit the crime.

hierarchy rule A rule dictating that only the most serious crime in a multiple-offenses incident will be recorded in the Uniform Crime Reports.

id Component of the personality that is present at birth, and consists of blind, unreasoning, instinctual desires and motives.

incidence The number of crimes committed in a specific time period.

intimate partner violence Violent victimization by intimates, including current or former spouses, boyfriends, girlfriends, or romantic partners.

labeling theory Theory that examines the role of societal reactions in shaping a person's behavior.

lifestyle theory Theory suggesting that people become victims because of the situations in which they put themselves.

master status The status bestowed on an individual and perceived by others as a first impression.

mitigating circumstances Factors such as age or mental disease that influence the choices people make and affect a person's ability to form criminal intent.

monozygotic twins Twins who share the same set of genes (MZ twins).

National Crime Victimization Survey (NCVS) An annual survey of criminal victimization in the United States conducted by the U.S. Bureau of Justice Statistics.

National Youth Survey (NYS) A comprehensive, nationwide self-report study of 1700 youths who have reported their illegal behaviors each year for more than 30 years.

neoclassical school A school of thought that considers mitigating factors when deciding culpability for criminal behavior, such as the offender's age and whether he or she has a mental disease.

official crime statistics Statistics based on the aggregate records of offenders and offenses processed by police, courts, corrections agencies, and the U.S. Department of Justice.

positive school A school of thought that blames criminality on factors that are present before a crime is actually committed.

prevalence The number of offenders committing crime during a specific time period.

psychoanalytic theory Theory that unconscious mental processes developed in early childhood control the personality.

rational choice theory Theory suggesting that offenders are rational people who make calculated choices to commit crimes.

self-control theory Theory claiming that people who seek pleasure are self-gratifying, and commit crimes owing to their low self-control.

self-report survey A survey that asks offenders to self-report their criminal activity during a specific time period.

social bond A measure of how strongly people are connected to society.

social control theory Theory that holds people are amoral and will break the law unless obstacles are thrown in their path.

social learning theory Theory that suggests children learn by modeling and imitating others.

sociological theories Theories that attribute crime to a variety of social factors external to the individual, focusing on how the environment in which the person lives affects his or her behavior.

stigmata Atavistic beings who possess unique, distinguishing features, such as large and protruding ears.

strain theory Theory that proposes a lack of integration between cultural goals and institutionalized means causes crime.

superego Component of the personality that develops from the ego and comprises the moral code, norms, and values the person has acquired.

theories Integrated sets of ideas that explain when and why people commit crime.

trait theories Theories that argue offenders commit crimes because of traits, characteristics, deficits, or psychopathologies they possess.

Uniform Crime Reports (UCR) An annual publication from the Federal Bureau of Investigation that presents data on crimes reported to the police, number of arrests, and number of persons arrested.

unofficial crime statistics Crime statistics produced by people and agencies outside the criminal justice system, such as college professors and private organizations.

victimization survey A method of producing crime data in which people are asked about their experiences as crime victims.

victimology The study of the characteristics of crime victims and the reasons why certain people are more likely than others to become victims of crime.

Think and Discuss

1. Of what value are the UCR, NCVS, and self-report studies? What are their strengths and weaknesses?
2. If you could use only one source of crime data on which to develop policies, would you choose the UCR, NCVS, or self-report surveys?
3. What is the relationship between theory and crime control policies?
4. Are people rational when they commit crime? What evidence supports your position?
5. Is crime learned in the same way other behaviors are learned? If so, what are the implications of this idea for parenting and for a community's responsibility for crime?
6. According to labeling theory, crime is a social construct. If this is true, should society assign labels to criminals in attempt to control crime?
7. What are the inherent flaws of conflict theories of crime? Are state legislatures likely to adopt their basic ideas? If not, of what value are such theories?

Notes

1. Sir Josiah Stamp, *Some Economic Matters in Modern Life* (London: King and Sons, 1929), pp. 258–259.
2. R. W. Apple, Jr., "Asian Journey; Snacker's Paradise: Devouring Singapore's Endless Supper," *The New York Times*, September 10, 2003, available at http://query.nytimes.com/gst/fullpage.html?sec=travel&res=9C01E0DF153BF933A2575AC0A9659C8B63&fta=y, accessed October 4, 2008.
3. The discussion of the UCR is from Federal Bureau of Investigation, *Crime in the United States, 2007* (Washington, DC: U.S. Department of Justice, 2008).
4. Wesley Skogan, "Dimensions of the Dark Figure of Unreported Crime," *Crime & Delinquency* 23:41–50 (1977); Adolphe Quetelet, *Research on the Propensity for Crime at Different Ages* (Cincinnati: Ander-

son, 1831/1984); Adolphe Quetelet, *Treatise on Man and the Development of His Faculties* (Edinburgh, Scotland: S.W. and R. Chambers, 1842).

5. Samuel Walker and Charles Katz, *The Police in America*, 4th ed. (New York: McGraw-Hill, 2002).
6. Walter Gove, Michael Hughes, and Michael Geerken, "Are Uniform Crime Reports a Valid Indicator of the Index Crimes? An Affirmative Answer with Minor Qualifications," *Criminology* 23:451–501 (1985); Gary LaFree and Kriss Drass, "The Effect of Changes in Intraracial Income Inequality and Educational Attainment on Changes in Arrest Rates for African Americans and Whites, 1957 to 1990," *American Sociological Review* 61:614–634 (1996).
7. Federal Bureau of Investigation, *Developments in the National Incident-Based Reporting System* (Washington, DC: U.S. Department of Justice, 2004).
8. Federal Bureau of Investigation, *Crime Reporting in the Age of Technology* (Washington, DC: U.S. Department of Justice, 1999)
9. Federal Bureau of Investigation, notes 3 and 8.
10. Federal Bureau of Investigation, note 3.
11. Patsy Klaus, *Crime and the Nation's Households, 2005* (Washington, DC: U.S. Department of Justice, 2007).
12. Robert O'Brien, *Crime and Victimization Data* (Beverly Hills, CA: Sage, 1985); Michael Rand and Shannon Catalano, *Criminal Victimization, 2006* (Washington, DC: U.S. Department of Justice, 2007); David Cantor and James Lynch, "Self-Report Measures of Crime and Criminal Victimization," in *Criminal Justice 2000*, edited by U.S. Department of Justice, Volume 4 (Washington, DC: National Institute of Justice, 2000), pp. 85–138.
13. L. Edward Wells and Joseph Rankin, "Juvenile Victimization," *Journal of Research in Crime and Delinquency* 32:287–307 (1995).
14. Anthony Walsh and Lee Ellis, *Criminology* (Thousand Oaks, CA: Sage, 2007); Albert Biderman and James Lynch, *Understanding Crime Incidence Statistics* (New York: Springer-Verlag, 1991).
15. Wesley Skogan, *Issues in the Measurement of Victimization* (Washington, DC: U.S. Department of Justice, 1981).
16. Janet Lauritsen and Robin Schaum, *Crime and Victimization in the Three Largest Metropolitan Areas, 1980–1998* (Washington, DC: U. S. Department of Justice, 2005).
17. Alfred Blumstein, Jacqueline Cohen, and Richard Rosenfeld, "Trend and Deviation in Crime Rates: A Comparison of UCR and NCS Data for Burglary and Robbery," *Criminology* 29:237–264 (1991); Michael Hindelang, "The Uniform Crime Reports Revisited," *Journal of Criminal Justice* 2:1–17 (1974); David MacDowall and Colin Loftin, "Comparing the UCR and NCS Over Time," *Criminology* 30:125–132 (1992); Steven Messner, "The 'Dark Figure' and Composite Indexes of Crime: Some Empirical Explorations of Alternative Data Sources," *Journal of Criminal Justice* 12:435–444 (1984).
18. Austin Porterfield, *Youth in Trouble* (Austin, TX: Leo Potishman Foundation, 1946); James Wallerstein and J. C. Wyle, "Our Law-Abiding Lawbreakers," *Federal Probation* 25:107–112 (1947); James F. Short, Jr., "A Report on the Incidence of Criminal Behavior, Arrests and Convictions in Selected Groups," *Research Studies of the State College of Washington* 22:110–118 (1954); James F. Short, Jr., and F. Ivan Nye, "Extent of Unrecorded Juvenile Delinquency," *Journal of Criminal Law, Criminology, and Police Science* 49:296–302 (1958); Maynard Erickson and LaMar Empey, "Court Records, Undetected Delinquency and Decision-Making," *Journal of Criminal Law, Criminology, and Police Science* 54:456–469 (1963); Jay Williams and Martin Gold, "From Delinquent Behavior to Official Delinquency," *Social Problems* 20:209–229 (1972).
19. Suzanne Ageton and Delbert Elliott, *The Incidence of Delinquent Behavior in a National Probability Sample* (Boulder, CO: Behavioral Research Institute, 1978); Delbert Elliott and Suzanne Ageton, "Reconciling Race and Class Differences in Self-Reported and Official Estimates of Delinquency," *American Sociological Review* 45:95–110 (1980).
20. Available at http://www.colorado.edu/ibs/NYSFS/, accessed August 21, 2008.

21. Steven Levitt and Stephen Dubner, *Freakonomics*, rev. ed. (New York: HarperCollins, 2006); Porterfield, note 18; Erickson and Empey, note 18; Williams and Gold, note 18.

22. Michael Hindelang, Travis Hirschi, and Joseph Weis, *Measuring Delinquency* (Beverly Hills, CA: Sage, 1981), p. 114.

23. Walsh and Ellis, note 14.

24. Wallerstein and Wyle, note 18; Short, note 18; Short and Nye, note 18; Erickson and Empey, note 18; Williams and Gold, note 18.

25. William Chambliss and Richard Nagasawa, "On the Validity of Official Statistics," *Journal of Research in Crime and Delinquency* 6:71–77 (1969); Leroy Gould, "Who Defines Delinquency," *Social Problems* 16:325–336 (1969); Michael Leiber, "Comparison of Juvenile Court Outcomes for Native Americans, African Americans, and Whites," *Justice Quarterly* 11:257–279 (1994).

26. Federal Bureau of Investigation, note 3.

27. Federal Bureau of Investigation, note 3.

28. Patsy Klaus, *Crime and the Nation's Households, 2005* (Washington, DC: U.S. Department of Justice, 2007).

29. Federal Bureau of Investigation, note 3.

30. Levitt and Dubner, note 21.

31. William Sabol, Heather Couture, and Paige Harrison, *Prisoners in 2006* (Washington, DC: U.S. Department of Justice, 2007).

32. Gordon Witkin, "The Crime Bust," *U.S. News & World Report*, May 25, 1998, pp. 28–40.

33. Federal Bureau of Investigation, note 3.

34. Federal Bureau of Investigation, note 3.

35. Quetelet, note 4, *Research on the Propensity for Crime at Different Ages*; Daniel Nagin, David Farrington, and Terrie Moffitt, "Life-Course Trajectories of Different Types of Offenders," *Criminology* 33:111–139 (1995); David Farrington, "Age and Crime," in Michael Tonry and Norval Morris (Eds.), *Crime and Justice*, Volume 7 (Chicago: University of Chicago Press, 1983), pp. 189–250; Travis Hirschi and Michael Gottfredson, "Age and the Explanation of Crime," *American Journal of Sociology* 89:552–584 (1983).

36. Federal Bureau of Investigation, note 3.

37. Matt DeLisi, *Criminal Careers in Society* (Thousand Oaks, CA: Sage, 2005).

38. Edwin Sutherland, *White Collar Crime* (New York: Dryden, 1949), p. 9.

39. CNNMoney.com, "Stewart Convicted on All Charges," available at http://money.cnn.com/2004/03/05/news/companies/martha_verdict/, accessed July 24, 2008; Brooke Masters, "WorldCom's Ebbers Convicted," *The Washington Post*, March 16, 2005, p. A01; Gregg Farrell, "Trial Judge Vacates Conviction of Late Enron Founder Lay," *USA Today*, October 18, 2006, p. 3A; Roben Farzad, "Jail Term for 2 at Top of Adelphia," *The New York Times*, June 21, 2005, p. C1; Andrew Ross Sorkin and Jennifer Bayot, "Ex-Tyco Officers Get 8 to 25 Years," *The New York Times*, September 20, 2005, p. A1; Susan Haigh, "Cendant Official Must Pay Back $3.27 Billion," *The Washington Post*, August 4, 2005, p. D03.

40. Cynthia Barnett, *The Measurement of White-Collar Crime Using Uniform Crime Reporting* (UCR) Data (Washington, DC: U.S. Department of Justice, 2003).

41. President's Commission on Law Enforcement and the Administration of Justice, *Task Force on Assessment* (Washington, DC: U.S. Government Printing Office, 1967), p. 80.

42. Howard Snyder and Melissa Sickmund, *Juvenile Offenders and Victims: 2006 National Report* (Washington, DC: U.S. Department of Justice, 2006).

43. Childhelp—Prevention and Treatment of Child Abuse, "National Child Abuse Statistics, 2006," available at http://www.childhelp.org/resources/learning-center/statistics, accessed July 24, 2008; National Center for Injury Prevention and Control, *Child Maltreatment: Fact Sheet, 2006* (Atlanta: Centers for Disease Control and Prevention, 2006); Lisa Jones, "Child Maltreatment Trends in the 1990s," *Child*

Maltreatment 11:107–120 (2006).

44. Patsy Klaus, *Crimes against Persons Age 65 or Older, 1993–2002* (Washington, DC: U.S. Department of Justice, 2005).

45. Klaus, note 28.

46. National Center for Injury Prevention and Control, *Intimate Partner Violence: Fact Sheet, 2006* (Atlanta: Centers for Disease Control and Prevention, 2006).

47. Callie Rennison and Sarah Welchans, *Intimate Partner Violence* (Washington, DC: U.S. Department of Justice, 2000).

48. "Hate Groups Active in 2007," *Intelligence Report*, Spring, Issue 129 (Montgomery, AL: Southern Poverty Law Center, 2008), pp. 52–69.

49. Federal Bureau of Investigation, note 3; Caroline Wolf Harlow, *Hate Crime Reported by Victims and Police* (Washington, DC: U.S. Department of Justice, 2005).

50. Leon Radzinowicz, *Ideology and Crime* (New York: Columbia University Press, 1966); "Why Did Josh Kill?" *CBS News*, June 12, 2000, available at www.cbsnews.com/stories/1999/10/07/48hours/main65411.shtml, accessed July 23, 2008.

51. Cesare Beccaria, *On Crimes and Punishments* (Indianapolis: Bobbs-Merrill, 1764/1963).

52. Walsh and Ellis, note 14.

53. Ronald Clarke and Derek Cornish, "Modeling Offender Decisions: A Framework for Research and Policy," in Michael Tonry and Norval Morris (Eds.), *Crime and Justice*, Volume 6 (Chicago: University of Chicago Press, 1985), pp. 145–167.

54. Lawrence Cohen and Marcus Felson, "Social Change and Crime Rate Trends: A Routine Activity Approach," *American Sociological Review* 44:588–609 (1979); Marcus Felson, *Crime and Everyday Life*, 4th ed. (Thousand Oaks, CA: Sage, 2007).

55. Clarke and Cornish, note 53.

56. Michael Hindelang, Michael Gottfredson, and James Garofalo, *Victims of Personal Crime* (Cambridge, MA: Ballinger, 1978).

57. Walsh and Ellis, note 14.

58. Harriet Martineau, *The Positive Philosophy of August Comte* (Whitefish, MT: Kessinger, 1855/2003).

59. Cesare Lombroso, *On Criminal Man* (Milan, Italy: Hoepli, 1876); Marvin Wolfgang, "Pioneers in Criminology: Cesare Lombroso," *Journal of Criminal Law, Criminology, and Police Science* 52:361–369 (1961).

60. Charles Goring, *The English Convict* (London: His Majesty's Stationary Office, 1913); Ernest Hooton, *The American Criminal* (Westport, CT: Greenwood Press, 1939/1969).

61. David Rowe, *Biology and Crime* (Los Angeles: Roxbury, 2002); David Rowe, *The Limits of Family Influence* (New York: Guilford Press, 1995); Sarnoff Mednick, W. Gabrielli, and Barry Hutchings, "Genetic Factors in the Etiology of Criminal Behavior," in Eugene McLaughlin, John Muncie, and Gordon Witkin (Eds.), *Criminological Perspectives*, 2nd ed. (Thousand Oaks, CA: Sage, 2003), pp. 67–80.

62. Sarnoff Mednick and Karl Christiansen, *Biosocial Basis of Criminal Behavior* (New York: Gardner Press, 1977).

63. Michael Bohman, C. Robert Cloninger, Soren Siguardson, and Anne-Liss von Knorring, "Predisposition to Petty Criminalistics in Swedish Adoptees," *Archives of General Psychiatry* 39:1233–1241 (1982); R. R. Crowe, "The Adopted Offspring of Women Criminal Offenders," *Archives of General Psychiatry* 27:600–603 (1972); David Rowe, "Genetic and Cultural Explanations of Adolescent Risk Taking and Problem Behavior," in Robert Ketterlinus and Michael Lamb (Eds.), *Adolescent Problem Behavior* (Mahwah, NJ: Lawrence Erlbaum Associates, 1994), pp. 109–126.

64. David Farrington, "The Relationship between Low Resting Heart Rate and Violence," in Adrian Raine, Patricia Brennan, David Farrington, and Sarnoff Mednick (Eds.), *Biosocial Bases of Violence* (New York:

Plenum, 1997), pp. 89–106.

65. Michael Reiff, Sherill Tippins, and Anthony Letourveau, *ADHD* (Elk Grove, IL: American Academy of Pediatrics, 2004); Travis Pratt et al., "The Relationship of ADHD to Crime and Delinquency," *International Journal of Police Science and Management* 4:344–360 (2002).

66. Ronald Burns and Michael Lynch, *Environment Crime: A Sourcebook* (New York: LFB Scholarly Publishing, 2004); Diana Fishbein, *Biobehavioral Perspectives in Criminology* (Belmont, CA: Wadsworth, 2001.

67. Nancy Day, Gale Richardson, Lidush Goldschmidt, and Marie Cornelius, "Effects of Prenatal Tobacco Exposure on Preschoolers' Behavior," *Journal of Developmental and Behavioral Pediatrics* 21:180–188 (2000); Marie Cornelius, Christopher Ryan, Nancy Day, Lidush Goldschmidt, and Jennifer Willford, "Prenatal Tobacco Effects on Neuropsychological Outcomes among Preadolescents," *Journal of Developmental and Behavioral Pediatrics* 22:217–225 (2001).

68. Patricia Brennan, Emily Grekin, and Sarnoff Mednick, "Maternal Smoking during Pregnancy and Adult Male Criminal Outcomes," *Archives of General Psychiatry* 56:215–219 (1999).

69. Mark Opler, Alan Brown, Joseph Grziano, Manisha Desal, Wei Zheng, Catherine Schaefer, Pamela Factor-Litvak, and Ezra Susser, "Prenatal Lead Exposure, Aminolevulinic Acid, and Schizophrenia," *Environmental Health Perspectives* 112:548–552 (2004); "Report: CA Ignored Poison Candy," *CBSNews.com*, April 25, 2004; "Lead-Wrapped Lollipop Poses Health Hazard," *The Denver Post*, April 27, 2001, p. 15A.

70. Karen Florini, George Krumbhaar, and Ellen Silbergeld, *Legacy of Lead* (Washington, DC: Environmental Defense Fund, 1990); Herbert Needleman, *Human Lead Exposure* (Boca Raton, FL: CRC Press, 1991).

71. Herbert Needleman and David Ballinger, *Prenatal Exposure to Toxicants* (Baltimore: Johns Hopkins University Press, 1994).

72. Sigmund Freud, *The Standard Edition of the Complete Psychological Works of Sigmund Freud* (London: Hogarth Press, 1925).

73. Sigmund Freud, *The Interpretation of Dreams* (New York: Avon, 1910/1980); Sigmund Freud, *The Ego and the Id* (New York: W. W. Norton, 1923/1962); Franz Alexander and William Healy, *Roots of Crime* (New York: Knopf, 1935); August Aichhorn, *Wayward Youth* (New York: Viking Press, 1936); Fritz Redl and David Wineman, *Children Who Hate* (New York: Free Press, 1951).

74. B. F. Skinner, *The Behavior of Organisms* (New York: Appleton, 1938); B. F. Skinner, "Are Theories of Learning Necessary?", *Psychological Review* 57:211–220 (1950); B. F. Skinner, *Science and Human Behavior* (New York: Macmillan, 1953); C. Ray Jeffery, "Criminal Behavior and Learning Theory," *Journal of Criminal Law, Criminology, and Police Science* 56:294–300 (1965); Robert Burgess and Ronald Akers, "A Differential Association–Reinforcement Theory of Criminal Behavior," *Social Problems* 14:128–147 (1966).

75. Albert Bandura, *Social Learning Theory* (Englewood Cliffs, NJ: Prentice Hall, 1977).

76. "Teens Charged in 7-Year-Old Sister's 'Mortal Kombat' Death," *Rocky Mountain News*, December 20, 2007, available at http://www.rockymountainnews.com/news/2007/Dec/20/teens-held-girls-mortal-kombat-death/, accessed July 26, 2008.

77. Craig Anderson, Douglas Gentile, and Katherine Buckley, *Violent Video Game Effects on Children and Adolescents* (New York: Oxford University Press, 2007).

78. Lawrence Kutner and Cheryl Olson, *Grand Theft Childhood* (New York: Simon & Schuster, 2008); Wendy Koch, "Video Game's Release Under Fire," *USA Today*, April 25, 2008, p. 1A.

79. Clifford Shaw and Henry McKay, *Juvenile Delinquency in Urban Areas* (Chicago: University of Chicago Press, 1942); Clifford Shaw and Henry McKay, *Juvenile Delinquency in Urban Areas*, rev. ed. (Chicago: University of Chicago Press, 1969).

80. "Only in America," *The Week*, April 25, 2008, p. 6.

81. Edwin Sutherland, *Principles of Criminology*, 4th ed. (Philadelphia: Lippincott, 1947).

82. Robert Merton, "Social Structure and Anomie," *American Sociological Review* 3:672–682 (1938); Robert Merton, *Social Theory and Social Structure*, rev. ed. (New York: Macmillan, 1968).

83. Travis Hirschi, *Causes of Delinquency* (Berkeley, CA: University of California Press, 1969).

84. Michael Gottfredson and Travis Hirschi, *A General Theory of Crime* (Stanford, CA: Stanford University Press, 1990).

85. Frank Tannenbaum, *Crime and the Community* (New York: Columbia University Press, 1938); Edwin Lemert, *Social Pathology* (New York: McGraw-Hill, 1951); Howard Becker, *Outsiders* (New York: Free Press, 1963).

86. Karl Marx and Friedrich Engels, *Capital* (New York: International Publishers, 1867/1967).

87. Willem Bonger, *Criminality and Economic Conditions* (New York: Agathon Press, 1916/1967).

88. David Farrington and Henry Pontell, *Developmental and Life Course Theories of Offending* (Englewood Cliffs, NJ: Prentice-Hall, 2007); Terence Thornberry, Marvin Krohn, Alan Lizotte, Carolyn Smith, and Kimberly Tobin, *Gangs and Delinquency in Developmental Perspective* (New York: Cambridge University Prcss, 2003).

89. Available at Chicago Area Project, http://www.chicagoareaproject.org/, accessed July 28, 2008.

90. Office of Head Start (Washington, DC: U.S. Department of Health and Human Services, 2007), available at http://www.acf.hhs.gov/programs/hsb/, accessed July 28, 2008.

91. Available at National Association of Police Athletic League Activities, available at http://www.nationalpal.org/, accessed July 29, 2008.

92. Carolyn Webster-Stratton, *The Incredible Years Training Series* (Washington, DC: Office of Juvenile Justice and Delinquency Prevention, 2000).

93. Edwin Schur, *Radical Nonintervention* (Englewood Cliffs, NJ: Prentice-Hall, 1973).

Police are the frontline of crime control. They are the first to respond to calls for help, and they play an important role in keeping society safe by investigating crimes, making arrests, patrolling the streets, and managing traffic. Police may also be the most controversial component of the criminal justice system. This controversy is not surprising, given their complex responsibilities in a diverse, democratic society.

Chapter 4 reviews the history of American policing and discusses modern policing and practices. The chapter also reviews various police systems of the twenty-first century, including local, state, and federal law enforcement agencies, as well as private security firms. It concludes with a brief look at how police departments today are structured to perform many different duties.

Chapter 5 reviews the legal constraints placed on police as they carry out their duties. Chapter 6 discusses an array of critical issues facing police today, such as discretion, use of force, corruption, and the delicate balance between social order and individual liberty within the boundaries of the law as prescribed by the Constitution and the U.S. Supreme Court.

PART

The Police

Customer Parking ONLY
NORTHERN FURNITURE CO.
ENTRANCE ON 8th STREET
12B
12B
12B
12B
POLICE

CHAPTER

Police History and Organization

OBJECTIVES

1. Understand the origins of policing in the United States, including the various systems that formed the foundation of modern policing.
2. Explain the purposes and goals of community policing and intelligence-led policing.
3. Identify the functions of local, state, and federal law enforcement agencies.
4. Describe the role of private security, its members, and their powers and limitations.
5. Understand the strengths and weaknesses of the formal structure of law enforcement agencies.
6. Know how the informal structure of policing may influence police practices and operations.
7. Explain how law enforcement agencies provide services to civilians.
8. Grasp the process of criminal investigations and the duties of police during investigations.
9. Describe the central role of police in traffic enforcement and their important service functions.

PROFILES IN CRIME AND JUSTICE

Clyde L. Cronkhite
Retired Chief of Police
Santa Ana, California
Professor of Law Enforcement and Justice Administration
Western Illinois University

Being a police chief is one of the most satisfying, yet challenging occupations. Police administration is at the very heart of the American way of governing and the American way of life. Those who oversee police agencies are charged with responsibilities important to public quality of life. They are responsible for providing to all people "justice" and "domestic tranquility" as set forth in the Preamble to the U.S. Constitution. But they are also responsible for satisfying the needs of their employees.

After serving in all police ranks—from patrol officer to deputy chief—in the Los Angeles Police Department, I accepted a position in the private sector as Director of Security for a multibillion-dollar financial institution. Even though the position was rewarding, I found I missed public service. I missed the satisfaction one gets from servicing the public as a member of the law enforcement profession—the satisfaction one gains from knowing he or she is providing an important contribution to our communities. Consequently, I applied for and was selected to be Police Chief of Santa Ana, California.

As a police chief, I found the duties to be much like those of a chief executive officer (CEO) in the private sector. You have a board of directors (the city council, police commission), shareholders (the public), and your employees. The salaries of police chiefs are certainly not comparable to the salaries of many CEOs in the private sector. However, the average salary today for a police chief is typically between $100,000 and $150,000, with those responsible for large police agencies making in the vicinity of $300,000.

In comparison with a private-business CEO, the police chief's tenure rests upon "three pillars of support." The first pillar consists of the elected officials to whom the chief reports. The second pillar consists of the community members. The third pillar represents the employees. Maintaining the support of all three is paramount to a police chief's success. Police chiefs sometimes have to make decisions that are not popular with one or more of these entities, which means making sure the others are supportive is critical. When police chiefs lose support from any two of the pillars, they will likely find themselves out of a job.

The leadership qualities of a successful police chief have changed over the past 50 years. Today's police chiefs (often serving with 4- to 5-year contracts and without civil service protections) are less vocal and more willing to give credit to their elected officials for the successes of their agencies. One important quality of today's police chiefs is empathy—empathy and understanding as it relates to those "three pillars of support." Another is an unyielding commitment to protecting the rights of *all* people. Given today's mission of maintaining public trust through community policing while facing the new task of providing for homeland security, being a police chief is truly a challenging, yet satisfying position—a position very important in preserving the American way of life.

Introduction

To fully understand policing today, it is necessary to first examine it within its historical context. Studying police history provides valuable insights into modern police organization and procedures. Likewise, familiarity with police history informs modern policing problems, such as the use of excessive force and corruption, and also provides assistance in grappling with these issues.[1] Knowing the problems of the past may help police avoid repeating the mistakes that were made.

American Policing

The history of American policing begins with the colonists bringing the *parish-constable police system* they knew in England with them to monitor the many widely scattered villages that evolved into America's first towns and cities.[2] Under this system, one man from each parish (or county) served a one-year term as constable on a rotating basis. This model had several key components:

- *Watch and ward system.* Constables had the authority to draft any male citizen into positions as night watchmen. These guards protected town gates and arrested law violators, putting them in jail and turning them over to the constable.
- *Hue and cry system.* When a watchman confronted more resistance than he could handle, he delivered a loud call for help (the "hue and cry"). Upon hearing the call, the men of the town were required by law to stop what they were doing and lend assistance. Anyone who did not join in this effort could be arrested for aiding and abetting the criminal.
- *Weapons ordinance.* Semiannual inspections ensured that all male town residents owned and maintained a short, broad-bladed saber to protect themselves.
- *Curfew.* At a set time determined by the constable, the city's gates were locked to keep out wanderers and other unsavory characters from entering the township.

In the beginning, this system worked well. However, as towns became more populated and their economies prospered, the nature of crime became more serious. With this change, policing became more time-consuming, dangerous, and less attractive. Many citizens began finding ways to avoid their policing obligation, which forced cities to pass ordinances that imposed fines on individuals who abandoned their responsibility; these ordinances and fines proved to be ineffective, however.

1700s: Origins of Organized Policing in America

Once the threat of a fine proved to be an ineffective way of coaxing citizens into fulfilling their police duties, the responsibility of law enforcement shifted from *all* male citizens to only those men who could not afford to hire others to take their place. City managers soon realized that public ownership of policing did not work and that what was needed was a salaried, full-time police force.[3]

Philadelphia was the first city to move in this direction when, in 1749, it passed two pieces of legislation: one law permitting constables to hire as many guards as they needed and a second law that established a tax to pay them. Other cities soon followed Philadelphia's lead. Unfortunately, city managers immediately realized that this new approach to policing was also ineffective because cities could not find enough capable men for the job. Police work had become increasingly unsafe, and the pay was still too low to attract highly qualified persons. As a result, some officers increased their paltry salaries by accepting bribes from gambling houses and prostitution rings.[4]

1800s: Growth, Brutality, and Corruption

The stage was set for new police reforms when, in the nineteenth century, the United States experienced rapid population growth. Government officials became fearful of the possible ramifications of the rapidly increasing number of foreign immigrants, many of whom were poor, spoke and dressed differently, and appeared to have different cultural values. Immigrants were also believed to be a factor in the growing crime problem that resulted from the increasing number of poor people languishing on the streets. These factors resulted in various policing reforms. One of the most notable reforms was the

Police systems of the political era were characterized by corruption and brutality.

August Vollmer is widely considered the founder of the professional American police department.

creation of police departments with paid, full-time, uniformed officers. By 1860, these departments had become a fixture in the largest U.S. cities.

Despite all the reforms, the newly created police organizations were plagued with many problems as the nineteenth century came to a close. The "new" police received a small salary and, like some of their predecessors, a number of officers supplemented their incomes by accepting bribes by "turning a blind eye" toward illegal activities. In response to many of these flaws, the early years of the twentieth century were characterized by a series of reform efforts designed to change how police did their jobs.

Early 1900s: Development of Organizations and Technology

One early police reformer was Theodore Roosevelt, who served as Police Commissioner in New York City from 1895 to 1897, before becoming the 26th President of the United States. When Roosevelt became commissioner, the New York Police Department (NYPD) was one of the most corrupt police agencies in the nation. Bringing his iron will to the office, Roosevelt instantly changed how the department was run. He started by establishing new disciplinary rules, requiring officers to arm themselves with .32-caliber pistols and insisting that officers take annual physical exams. Roosevelt also received national press attention for his "midnight rambles" where he searched for police officers not at their posts. He also ordered all police officers to report for target practice, thus establishing the first Police Academy in the United States. By the time he had finished reforming the NYPD, Roosevelt had appointed 1600 new officers based on their physical and mental qualifications, rather than their political affiliations, and created opportunities within the department for women as well as racial and ethnic minorities.[5]

In the following years, Roosevelt's ideas were expanded upon by August Vollmer, Chief of Police in Berkeley, California, from 1905 to 1932. Vollmer was responsible for bringing more change to the police profession than any other single individual. Some of the reforms he implemented included the following measures:

- Installation of the first basic police records system
- Conducting the first scientific investigation of a crime utilizing the analysis of blood, fibers, and soil
- Establishing a police school based on law and evidence procedures
- Organizing the first motorcycle and automobile patrols
- Forming the first School of Criminology at the University of California at Berkeley
- Requiring officers to have a college degree
- Using intelligence testing to select police recruits
- Introducing the polygraph
- Establishing one of the first fingerprint analysis centers[6]

Vollmer thought that police departments needed to become more efficient to protect the public, and his reforms were introduced with that end in mind.

It was also during Vollmer's era that advances in technology increased the proficiency of police. For example, the first police patrol car hit the streets prior to World War I; by the end of the 1920s, patrol vehicles were being used by nearly all police departments in the United States. With the addition of telephones and two-way radios, citizen reports to police increased and response times quickened dramatically.[7]

An unintended consequence of the changes and improvements inspired by the reform agenda was that the public expected more from the police than they had in the past. This included the expectations that the police would achieve faster response times to calls for service and that they would make more arrests, thus bringing a reduction in crime. These high expectations led to difficult times for police in the 1960s, as police were increasingly unable to deliver on what citizens believed they had implicitly promised.

Violence erupted in the streets of Los Angeles soon after four LAPD officers were acquitted of assault and brutality in the beating of Rodney King.

Mid-twentieth Century: Responses to Increasing Crime Rates

The decade of the 1960s was a period of intense conflict between the police and the public, particularly in terms of clashes between police and both civil rights demonstrators and antiwar activists. Police responded to these challenges by implementing reforms, such as sending specialized riot units to suppress incidents of public disorder and having police chiefs address citizen concerns and media.[8]

However, when put into action, these and other reforms failed to calm the complaints of an increasingly disgruntled public. Crime rates soared (see FIGURE 4-1) and fear of crime increased. Racial and ethnic minorities loudly protested perceived police mistreatment and discrimination, and protesters challenged the legitimacy of the police. Additionally, the national media publicized riots and police responses to them. All of this occurred in the midst of a struggling economy that forced local governments to slash police budgets.[9] Ultimately, as both the police and the public watched crime rates jump considerably, they discovered that the changes made in the reform era did not reduce crime (see Chapter 1).

Late Twentieth Century: The Quiet Revolution

The reforms implemented in the 1960s and 1970s achieved, at best, only modest success. Perhaps the greatest change to police strategies came from recommendations made by federal commissions charged with studying police problems. The new recommendations emphasized the importance of police officers taking time to talk with and listen

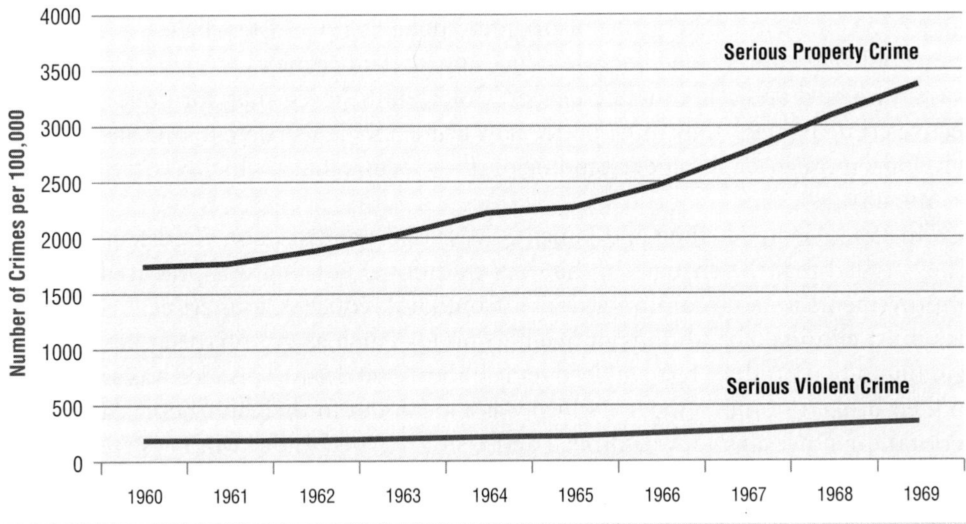

FIGURE 4-1 U.S. Crime Rates, 1960–1969

Source: Federal Bureau of Investigation, *Crime in the United States, 2007* (Washington, DC: U.S. Department of Justice, 2008).

Headline Crime

Police Communication with Diverse Populations

In Los Angeles dozens of languages are spoken, which often causes problems for law enforcement officers when they are communicating with citizens. To help remedy the problem, today many LAPD officers carry a new hand-held device called the *Phraselator*, which has eased the communication gap. To operate the *Phraselator*, the officer selects a language—Korean, for example—and speaks a phrase—such as "medical assistance"—into the microphone. A speaker in the patrol vehicle then announces a preprogrammed Korean phrase, "If you require medical assistance, please approach the nearest officer." LAPD Police Captain Dennis Kato believes that "when it comes to crowd control, natural disasters, or medical emergencies, it [the *Phraselator*] can be a lifesaver."

Sources: "It Wasn't All Bad," *The Week*, February 15, 2008, p. 4; Richard Winston, "LAPD Finds a Way to Connect," *Los Angeles Times*, January 16, 2008, available at http://www.latimes.com/news/local/la-me-translate16jan16,0,6435263.story?coll=la-home-center, accessed October 4, 2008.

Community policing strengthens the bond between law enforcement and the public, with a focus on solving problems and community empowerment rather than strict enforcement of the law.

to victims, witnesses, and other members of crime-plagued communities—an idea that led to the emergence of the community policing movement.

Community policing includes the understanding that police cannot control crime alone and need help from citizens to prevent crime. At the core of community policing is good, strong police–community relations.[10] The community policing model requires police to become involved in an array of community activities, including these:

- Neighborhood Watch programs
- Mini- and storefront-police stations
- Police-sponsored athletic leagues
- Citizen auxiliary police[11]

The roots of community policing can be traced to an essay written in 1979 by criminologist Herman Goldstein, who argued that police officers should handle not only the most obvious, superficial manifestations of a problem, but also the problem itself—an approach Goldstein called "problem-oriented" policing.[12] Goldstein believed that traditional policing efforts failed because police approached crime as though each incident was an isolated and self-contained event. Goldstein believed that, for police to be effective crime fighters, they must notice how crime incidents relate to one another and develop a more in-depth understanding of those factors that are highly correlated with criminality.

In 1982, George Kelling and James Q. Wilson expanded upon Goldstein's work.[13] They argued that the changes in the ways traditional policing was practiced, such as improvements in radio communications, would not reduce serious crime. Instead, police must eliminate conditions in neighborhoods (such as graffiti, drug dealing, and gambling) that produce fear and lead to neighborhood decay. This idea was articulated in their **broken windows theory**, which was a metaphor for neighborhood signs of deterioration: Once a window is broken and is not repaired, other windows are likely to be broken. Similarly, when a "social window" is broken and not repaired (e.g., roadside litter), other social windows will be broken (e.g., vandalism). The broken windows theory insists that small signs of public disorder set in motion a downward spiral of deterioration, neighborhood decline, and increasing crime. Interestingly, evidence for this theory is mounting as a result of the subprime loan crisis being experienced across the nation. Researchers Dan Immergluck and Geoff Smith found that in one neighborhood a 1 percent increase in foreclosure rates contributed to a 2.33 percent increase in violent crime.

In real terms, in a city such as Chicago, for example, where the average neighborhood has 900 homes with mortgages, 38 violent crimes, and 22 foreclosures per year, just one more foreclosure would result in four more violent crimes.[14]

The principle behind community policing is to prevent these social windows from being broken in the first place by paying attention to the overall quality of life in a neighborhood, not just the serious crime. Both physical incivilities, such as trash and graffiti, and social incivilities, such as gamblers in alleys and drunks in public areas, greatly diminish the quality of life in an area. Through face-to-face communications with the neighborhood's residents, police officers are able to identify the sources of incivility and then work with residents to eliminate them.[15]

The Twenty-First Century: Intelligence-Led Policing

Prior to the terrorist attacks on the United States on September 11, 2001, many law enforcement agencies on the federal, state, and local levels routinely employed intelligence and intelligence gathering. However, the attack of September 11 resulted in an increase in the intelligence-gathering activities of many law enforcement agencies, particularly with the creation of the U.S. Department of Homeland Security, which was established by the Homeland Security Act of 2002.[16] This agency has provided significant financial assistance to state and local police agencies to form special intelligence units, which are the foundation of **intelligence-led policing**. Intelligence-led policing includes the following features:

- Police intelligence units that identify security threats from terrorists groups, extremists, and gangs
- Federal guidelines for police conduct
- Advances in police computing and network systems

Intelligence-led policing is a newly emerging model of policing driven by computer databases, intelligence gathering, and analysis. Whereas in the past only big-city police departments had the resources to maintain intelligence units to target drug smugglers and organized crime, today law enforcement agencies of all sizes are developing these capabilities.

Police Systems

There is no monolithic or national police system in the United States. Instead, the U.S. police system consists of the many local, state, and federal law enforcement agencies that enforce the criminal law. While not uniform in structure, three general ideas guide how they operate and distinguish them from police systems in many other countries. In the United States:

1. *Police have limited authority.* Police must follow specific rules and regulations to protect individual liberties.
2. *There is local police control.* Some countries in Asia, Europe, the Middle East, and South America have centralized national police forces. By contrast, in the United States it is usually (but not always) the responsibility of cities and counties to provide citizens with police protection. An exception to this general rule can be found in Pennsylvania, and some other states, where *state* police agencies are the primary law enforcement agency in certain political jurisdictions that have no law enforcement. In these areas, the state truly is the political entity that provides citizens with police protection. There also is "home rule" in the United States, which gives cities and counties the right of self-government within certain parameters.

Headline Crime: Baggy Pants

Throughout the United States, an increasing number of city leaders are proposing outlawing the wearing of low-slung or "baggy" pants. The movement is being fueled by a growing number of lawmakers who contend that sloppy dress by America's teens is related to delinquency, poor learning, and crime. The underwear-exposing style, inspired by oversized, no-belt prison uniforms, has become a criminal offense in some communities. In Opa-locka, Florida, a suburb of Miami, city leaders have proposed an ordinance to ban wearing sagging pants in city parks, the library, and other municipal buildings. Violators would be evicted from city property. In other states, city leaders have introduced new indecency statutes. Bans on sagging pants have been adopted in Hawkinsville, Georgia, and six Louisiana parishes, including Alexandria and Shreveport. Other cities, including Atlanta, Baltimore, Charlotte, and Dallas, are also considering ordinances banning baggy pants. Wearing baggy pants could invoke a penalty as much as a $500 fine or six months in jail. Critics of the ordinances include the American Civil Liberties Union, which contends that dress, including baggy pants, is a form of free speech and as such is protected by the First Amendment.

Sources: "The Fashion Police," *Neatoday* 26:17 (2008); Laura Parker, "Cities Snapping Over Baggy Pants," *USA Today*, October 15, 2007, p. 3A.

Local law enforcement officers are involved in a variety of duties, including traffic control, arresting criminal suspects, crowd control, criminal investigations, and much more.

3. *Agencies are decentralized and fragmented.* Instead of having a single, national police force, the United States supports nearly 18,000 separate law enforcement agencies that are loosely coordinated, with much duplication or overlap among them.[17]

Each type of police force, regardless of its level, has a **jurisdiction**, which is the territory or body of law it controls. U.S. police agencies employ more than 1 million people and have a total operating budget of nearly $48 billion.[18] Nearly 700,000 persons employed by law enforcement are **sworn officers**, who are men and women empowered to arrest suspects, serve warrants, carry weapons, and use force.[19] The overall "police–population ratio" is about 2.5 sworn officers per 1000 citizens,[20] although the actual ratio varies widely across different cities. Washington, DC, for instance, has 6.6 officers per 1000 population, whereas the police–population ratio in San Francisco is 1.6. Research has not found any statistically significant relationship between the police–population ratio and the crime rate.[21]

Local Police

There are more than 17,000 local law enforcement agencies in the United States. This number includes city, county, and special-jurisdiction agencies, such as campus police, park rangers, and transit police.[22] Most local police agencies are very small and homogeneous, employing fewer than 25 sworn officers and serving fewer than 10,000 residents.[23] However, some local departments are very large. The New York City police department, the nation's largest, employs 36,000 or more uniformed officers.[24]

Regardless of the size of the department, local police officers perform similar duties. They control traffic, patrol streets, and investigate crimes. Officers in some departments also handle animal control, operate search-and-rescue missions, provide emergency medical care, and control crowds at entertainment events such as NFL games or rock concerts. In big-city departments, special units handle counterterrorism and community problems such as drunk driving, missing children, victim assistance, and gang violence. Local police also assist in meeting the needs of special populations, including persons with HIV/AIDS, the homeless, victims of domestic violence, and abused or neglected children.

A principal difference between past and present local police departments is their racial, ethnic, and gender composition. Although these departments were once the near-exclusive domain of whites, today racial and ethnic minorities account for 24 percent of full-time sworn officers in local departments, up from 15 percent in 1987; women represent 12 percent of officers, up from 8 percent in 1987.[25] Yet, in many departments in large cities, African Americans and Latinos are still underrepresented relative to their proportion of the general population (see TABLE 4–1).

In city police departments, the police chief is usually appointed by the city council or mayor. Such a department's jurisdiction is limited by statute to the geographic boundaries of the city. By contrast, all states are divided into districts called *counties* (*parishes* in Louisiana and *boroughs* in Alaska). The chief law enforcement officer of a county is the **sheriff**, who is an elected official, except in Rhode Island (where the sheriff is appointed by the governor) and Hawaii (where the sheriff is appointed by the Department of Health). The sheriff's department investigates crimes, operates jails, processes court orders, provides security for county courts, and collects county fees and property taxes.

The largest sheriff's department serves Los Angeles County, which has 10 million residents. This department employs more than 8200 officers.[26] However, most of the nation's 3000 sheriff's departments are small, with two-thirds employing fewer than 25 sworn officers and 71 percent serving fewer than 50,000 residents.[27]

TABLE 4–1 Ratio of Minority Officers to Minority Residents in 25 Large City Police Departments

City	Officer–Resident Ratio	
	African American	Latino
1. New York City	0.50	0.66
2. Los Angeles	1.21	0.71
3. Chicago	0.70	0.49
4. Houston	0.77	0.48
5. Philadelphia	0.80	0.66
6. Phoenix	0.40	0.35
7. San Diego	0.61	0.63
8. Dallas	0.56	0.38
9. San Antonio	0.70	0.71
10. Las Vegas	0.48	0.33
11. Detroit	0.77	0.60
12. San Jose, California	1.60	0.75
13. Honolulu	0.67	0.39
14. San Francisco	1.24	0.96
15. Indianapolis	0.69	0.18
16. Jacksonville	0.67	0.29
17. Columbus	0.59	0.12
18. Austin	1.07	0.54
19. Baltimore	0.60	0.94
20. Memphis	0.72	0.63
21. Charlotte	0.64	0.23
22. Milwaukee	0.57	0.80
23. Boston	0.95	0.42
24. Washington, DC	1.11	0.63
25. Nashville	0.72	0.94

Source: Bureau of Justice Statistics Sepcial Report by Brian Reaves and Matthew Hickman, *Police Departments in Large Cities, 1990–2000* (Washington, DC: U.S. Department of Justice, 2002), p. 11.

The U.S. highway system is the main jurisdiction of state police departments.

The duties of sheriff deputies, particularly in many of the southern and western states, often are much more demanding than those of city police. The countywide jurisdiction, for instance, may pose special obstacles because of its large geographical size and often small population compared to that of municipalities. A deputy may need to drive 100 or more miles to respond to a citizen's call for assistance. This requirement poses special problems for deputies, because they are more likely than city police officers to ride alone and backup units may not be readily available in an emergency. Given the people they serve, deputies are also more likely to confront armed citizens than city police because per capita gun ownership is higher in rural areas than it is in either suburban or urban areas.[28] However, even though gun ownership is higher in rural areas, it is also true that illegal gun ownership is higher in cities and the will to utilize those weapons against the police may be more likely.

Interestingly, the role of the sheriff in some northern states is very different. In many of these states, the sheriff is only a figurehead. He or she is an elected official, whose department is primarily responsible for providing security in the county courthouse, serving bench warrants, and transporting prisoners. In some states, the sheriff and his or her deputies have no true law enforcement powers. They do not investigate crimes, in some states they cannot by law make traffic stops, and they are prevented from participating in the use of electronic surveillance. Therefore, a caveat to the statement in the preceding paragraph that the role of sheriff is much more demanding than that of city police is necessary. In states that have not adopted a strong sheriff model, the role of sheriff is not as demanding as the job of some other law enforcement officers. As an example, in Pennsylvania, the state police are responsible for primary police services in any area that does not have its own police department. In these areas it is the state police trooper (not the sheriff) who covers vast areas, with backups often being miles and precious minutes away.

Special-jurisdiction police typically safeguard transportation systems and facilities. A total of 130 special police departments serve transportation-related jurisdictions, such as mass-transit systems, airports, bridges, tunnels, and port facilities. These agencies collectively employ approximately 9100 full-time sworn officers. The largest, the Port Authority of New York–New Jersey, employed 1607 officers in 2004, 25 percent more than in 2000. The Port Authority Police protects LaGuardia, Kennedy, and Newark Airports; the Lincoln and Holland Tunnels; the George Washington and Staten Island Bridges; the PATH train system; the Port Authority Bus Terminal; and the Port Newark and Port Elizabeth Marine Terminals. Many of the nation's largest transit systems have their own dedicated police forces. The five largest are in the New York, Washington, DC, Atlanta, Philadelphia, and Boston metropolitan areas. Collectively, the 10 largest transit police departments employed 20 percent more sworn personnel in 2004 than in 2000.[29]

State Police

There are 49 state police agencies in the United States (Hawaii does not have a state police agency).[30] State police agencies have statewide authority to conduct criminal investigations, enforce traffic laws, investigate traffic accidents, respond to calls for service, and provide law enforcement assistance to any police agency that requests it. Often, but not always, state police perform functions outside of the county sheriff's jurisdiction, such as enforcing traffic laws on state highways and interstate expressways. They also protect state capital buildings and the governor, train officers for local jurisdictions that are too small to operate their own training facilities, and provide local police access to state crime laboratories as needed.

TABLE 4-2 Federal Law Enforcement Agencies Employing 500 or More Officers

Agency	Number of Officers
U.S. Customs Service and Border Protection	27,705
Federal Bureau of Prisons	15,214
Federal Bureau of Investigation	12,242
Immigration and Naturalization Service	10,399
U.S. Secret Service	4,769
Drug Enforcement Administration	4,400
U.S. Federal Probation Office	4,126
U.S. Marshals Service	3,233
U.S. Postal Inspection Service	2,976
Internal Revenue Service	2,777
Veterans Health Administration	2,423
Bureau of Alcohol, Tobacco, and Firearms	2,373
National Park Service	2,148
U.S. Capitol Police	1,535
Bureau of Diplomatic Security	825
U.S. Fish and Wildlife Service	708
USDA Forest Service	600

Source: Bureau of Justice Statistics by Brian Reaves, *Federal Law Enforcement Officers, 2004* (Washington, DC: U.S. Department of Justice, 2006).

Federal Law Enforcement Officers

Federal law enforcement agents enforce national laws. Their work includes controlling illegal immigration, investigating counterfeiting, policing airports, and protecting the President and other members of federal institutions. Federal law enforcement agents may also investigate crimes that are not local to just one state—for example, kidnapping, narcotics trafficking, and Internet and mail fraud. In addition, they enforce the law in federal buildings (e.g., the U.S. Mint, the U.S. Capitol) and national parks (e.g., Yellowstone National Park). There are 65 federal law enforcement agencies that employ more than 100,000 agents, all of whom are authorized to make arrests and carry firearms (see TABLE 4-2).[31] The total annual budget of these agencies is roughly $4 billion.[32]

Following the terrorist attacks on the United States on September 11, 2001, federal law enforcement agencies experienced a massive reorganization. Today the best-known federal law enforcement agency is the Department of Homeland Security (DHS). The creation of the DHS represents the most significant transformation of the U.S. government in more than half a century, realigning the current government policing activities into a single department whose primary mission is to protect the United States. The DHS is divided into several divisions. The criminal justice agencies that are now part of the DHS have the following functions:

- U.S. Customs and Border Protection (CBP) is the unified border agency within the DHS that combined the inspectional work forces and broad border authorities of U.S. Customs, U.S. Immigration, Animal and Plant Health Inspection Service, U.S. Border Patrol, and the Federal Emergency Management Agency (FEMA).[33]
- Immigration and Customs Enforcement (ICE) is the largest investigative branch of the DHS and was created by combining the law enforcement arms of the former Immigration and Naturalization Service (INS) and the former U.S. Customs Service. Before September 11, 2001, immigration and customs authorities were not widely recognized as an effective counterterrorism tool in the United States. ICE changed this perception by creating a host of new systems to better address

FOCUS ON CRIMINAL JUSTICE

U.S. Park Police Understaffed

U.S. Park Police guard national monuments and parks across the nation. Today, in the time of greatest need, the U.S. Park Police force is severely understaffed, which is an especially serious development at a time of heightened terrorism. Because there are too few officers, the U.S. Park Police are not able to adequately protect national monuments, such as the Statue of Liberty and the Washington Monument. In fact, the security is so lax that recently a large suitcase was left unattended for more than five minutes at the Washington Monument before it was discovered by Park Police. The problem Park Police face is that since the terrorist attacks of September 11, 2001, the number of U.S. Park Police officers has decreased to about one-half of what the number was before September 11, while their responsibilities have increased to include antiterrorism duties, even as the U.S. Park Police budget has been decreased.

Sources: "National Monuments Undefended," *The Week*, February 18, 2008, p. 6; "Park Police Understaffed," *The Week*, March 7, 2008, p. 4.

national security threats, detect potential terrorist activities in the United States, effectively enforce immigration and customs laws, and protect against terrorist attacks. ICE does so by targeting illegal immigrants; the people, money, and materials that support terrorism; and other criminal activities.[34]

- The U.S. Secret Service protects the President and Vice President, their families, heads of state, and other designated individuals; investigates threats against these persons; protects the White House, Vice President's residence, foreign missions, and other buildings within Washington, DC; and plans and implements security designs for designated National Special Security Events. In addition, it investigates violations of laws relating to counterfeiting of obligations and securities of the United States; financial crimes that include access device fraud, financial institution fraud, identity theft, computer fraud; and computer-based attacks on the U.S. financial, banking, and telecommunications infrastructure.[35]

Two of the most widely known federal law enforcement agencies are the U.S. Marshal's Service and the Federal Bureau of Investigation.

U.S. Marshals

The oldest federal police agency is the U.S. Marshals Service, which was established by the Judiciary Act of 1789. Marshals occupy a unique position in law enforcement: They are the enforcement arm of the federal courts, are involved in every federal policing program, and have the broadest authority and jurisdiction of all federal officers. Among the duties of marshals are to

- Protect federal judicial officials, which includes judges, attorneys, and jurors
- Arrest persons who commit federal crimes
- Arrest fugitives
- Operate the Witness Security Program
- Provide prison services to approximately 53,000 inmates in 1300 federal prisons each day[36]

Federal Bureau of Investigation

Established in 1908, the Federal Bureau of Investigation (FBI) is the principal investigative arm of the U.S. Department of Justice.[37] The FBI has a threefold mission:

- To defend the United States against terrorist and foreign intelligence threats
- To uphold and enforce the criminal laws of the United States
- To provide leadership and law enforcement assistance to federal, state, municipal, and international agencies

This mission is performed by the agency's more than 30,000 employees, including special agents and support professionals, such as intelligence analysts, language specialists, scientists, and information technology specialists. The FBI has the authority and responsibility to investigate specific crimes assigned to it but primarily focuses on counterterrorism, cybercrime, white-collar crime, organized crime, major thefts, and violent crime. The FBI is also authorized to provide other law enforcement agencies with support, including fingerprint identification, laboratory examinations, and police training.

Private security guards provide services to individuals and a variety of small businesses, and large corporations. Private security guards do not have arrest powers.

Some of the other federal policing agencies include the U.S. Postal Inspectors, U.S. Forest Service, U.S. Fish and Wildlife Service, National Park Service, U.S. Park Police, Bureau of Prisons, Federal Trade Commission, Indian Affairs, and Amtrak.

Private Security Guards

In the United States, *private security guards* also assist local policing efforts. Private security guards are not sworn law enforcement officers and do not have the power of arrest. These officers do not provide police services, but rather provide security services to individuals, small businesses, and large corporations, including amusement parks, healthcare facilities, hotel and resort complexes, industrial plants, museums, office buildings, professional sports teams, restaurants, schools, and shopping malls. Private security guards perform a variety of duties, including these:

- Installing and servicing burglar alarms
- Transporting valuable commodities
- Patrolling buildings or parks
- Providing protection at schools
- Monitoring public transportation systems

Today, private security in the United States is a $12 billion annual industry, employing approximately 2 million people in roughly 90,000 private security firms.[38] There are nearly three private security officers for every one sworn law enforcement officer in the United States.[39] One of the largest employers, the Sears Roebuck Company, employs about 6000 security guards; by comparison, the Denver Police Department has only 1500 sworn police officers.[40]

Police Organization

Police have two primary functions: to fight crime and to maintain order. As crime fighters, they are law enforcers. When police are maintaining order, they are providing civilians with services and keeping the peace.[41] Police agencies are organized to efficiently and effectively carry out these functions. The formal structure of large departments resembles a semi-military structure in that it establishes relationships among department members and clarifies the responsibilities of each position (see FIGURE 4-2).

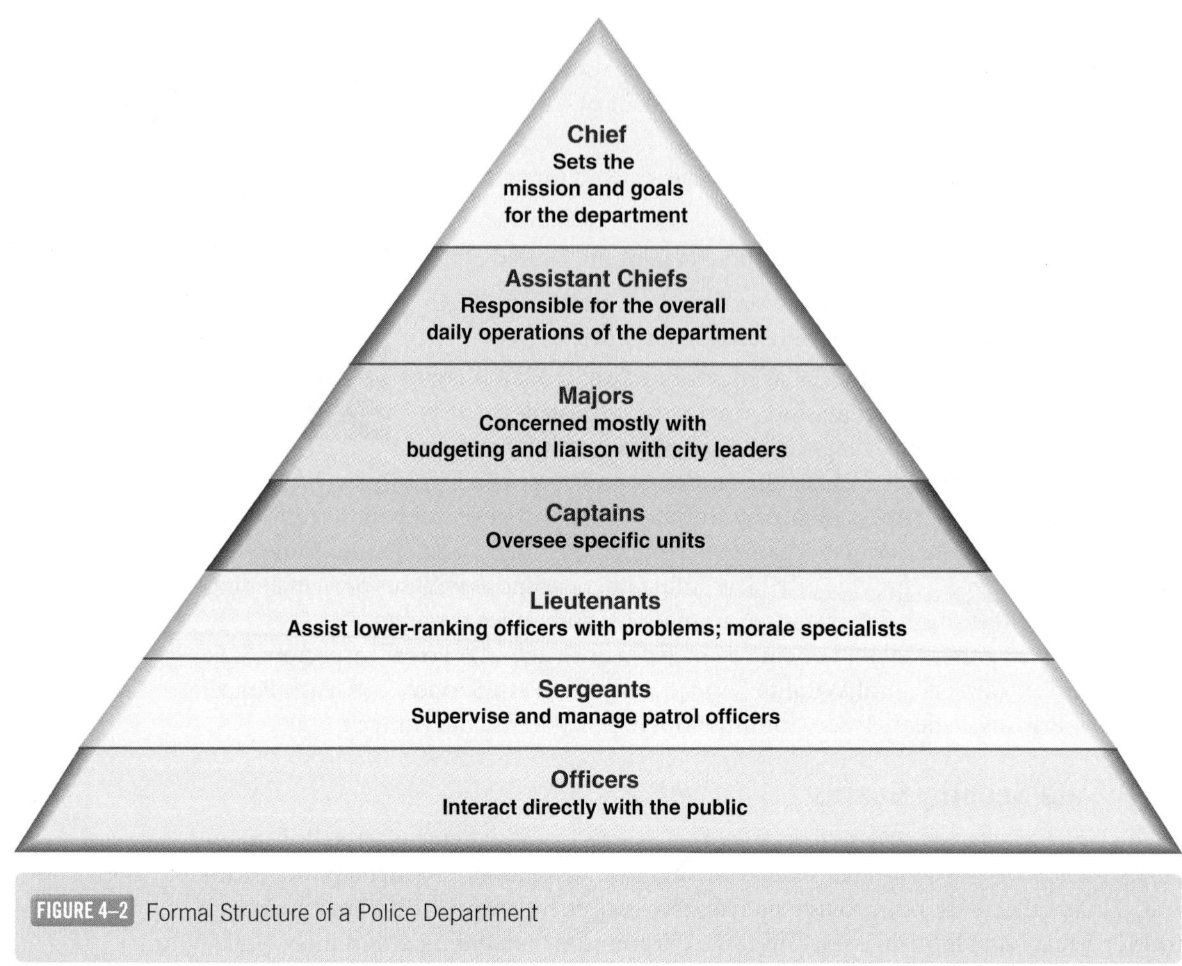

FIGURE 4–2 Formal Structure of a Police Department

Police work also involves an underlying, informal structure, which represents the unofficial relations that exist among officers. These relations affect police operations and the ways in which police perform their duties of patrol, criminal investigations, traffic enforcement, and community services. It is important for police agencies to strike a balance between the official rules and the informal structure as they go about trying to achieve departmental goals and carry out their law-related functions.

Formal Structure of Police Organizations

A police department is a **bureaucracy**, which is a type of organization that operates on strict rules, close supervision, and reliance on authority. This organizational model includes the following components:[42]

- Chain of command
- Delegation of authority
- Specialization
- Rules and regulations
- Limited rewards
- Competency

Chain of Command

A **chain of command**, or hierarchy of authority, identifies who communicates with and gives orders to whom. In police departments, this chain establishes the working relation-

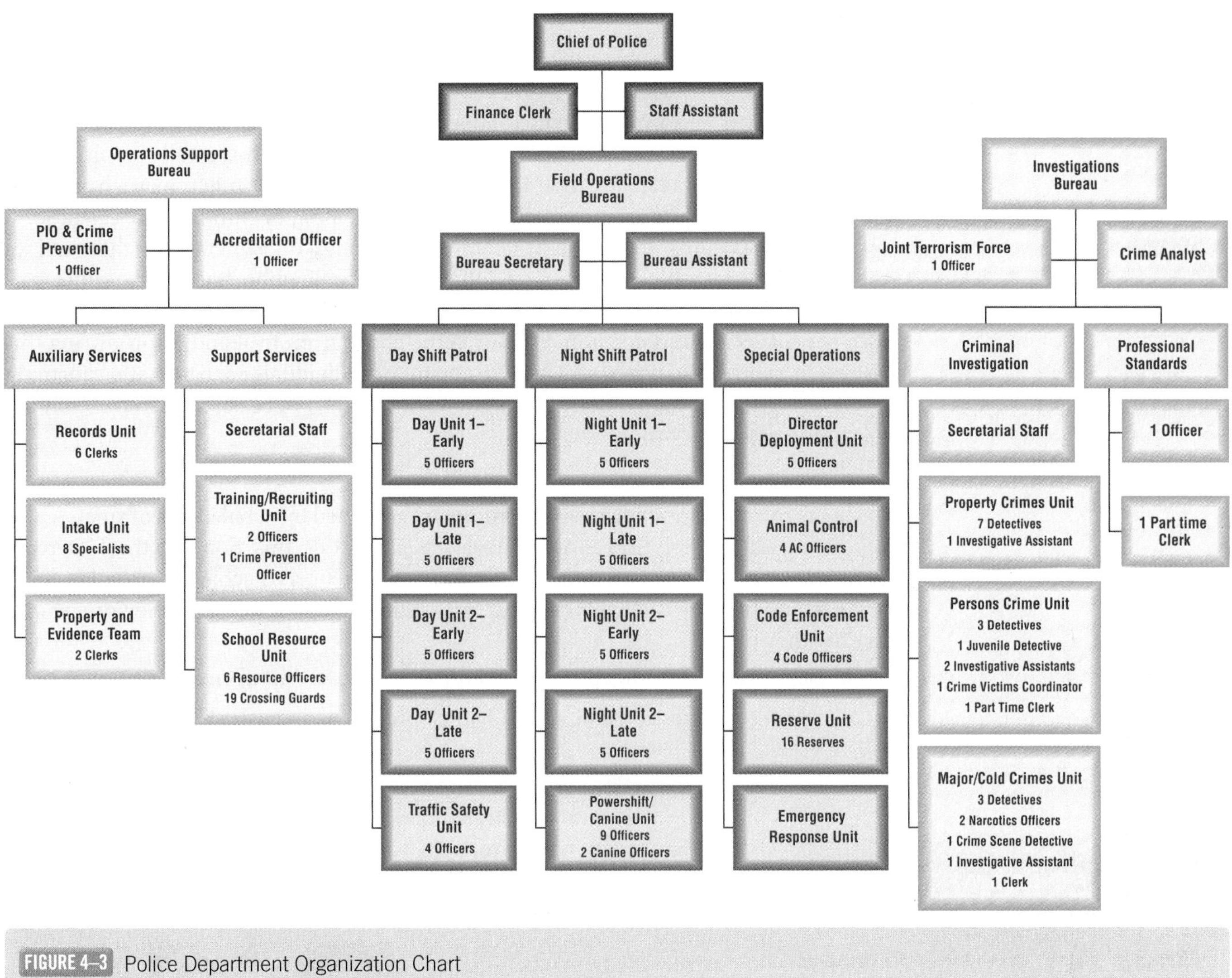

FIGURE 4-3 Police Department Organization Chart

ships among the different ranks. The purpose of the chain of command is to make the lines of authority clear and precise. Sergeants, for example, know they have less authority than lieutenants but more authority than corporals, who in turn have more authority than patrol officers. The complexity of a department's chain is linked to its size (e.g., number of employees). In a small department, the bureaucratic structure is less complex than it is in large agencies. Regardless of the department's size, all police departments have an organization chart (see FIGURE 4-3). The chart identifies how information will flow inside the department and makes it clear who is responsible for what specific tasks and operations.

Delegation of Authority

The practice of passing decision-making responsibilities through a chain of command is called **delegation of authority**. Police chiefs delegate authority to assistant chiefs, who in turn pass authority to captains, and so forth down the line. Authority is delegated because chiefs cannot monitor every situation or make every decision on their own. In the most efficient organizations, the department leaders will share management of the various responsibilities.

Specialization

No one person has the time or the skills to perform all of the duties associated with running a police department. Big-city police agencies, for example, often focus or concentrate their efforts on specific activities. **Specialization** requires an agency to concentrate its resources on a narrow area of knowledge, skill, or activity. It typically involves a law enforcement agency adapting itself to perform some particular function, such as forming a special unit on domestic violence, gang suppression, or homicide investigations. Specialization is similar to the department implementing a **division of labor** that outlines and assigns tasks to officers, such as patrolling a specific neighborhood, controlling traffic at an event, or updating the media about an ongoing criminal investigation. Usually both specialization and division of labor come about from trial and error; during this process, it may be discovered that certain groups of individuals are better at performing specific assignments than others. Through specialization, police departments usually are able to increase their productivity.

Rules and Regulations

Police organizations and internal operations are governed by detailed sets of rules. A rule in policing is a proscription about behavior (i.e., must do this, don't do that). Department rules govern behavior and specific courses of action to achieve particular goals. For instance, in some agencies the department rule manual states that when officers are on duty they must:

- Be neat and clean in appearance, and wear standard uniforms
- Avoid cigarettes, alcohol, and vulgar or profane language

FOCUS ON CRIMINAL JUSTICE

Body Art on the Squad

Tattoos are becoming popular among young adults, and even among law enforcement officers. Today, an increasing number of police agencies across the United States are crafting stricter policies regarding just how much body art is acceptable for their officers. Departments are concerned that "tattooed" officers do not present a professional image to the public and that the tattoos themselves do not comply with the grooming standards of the profession.

Police agencies differ in terms of what they regard as an excessive tattoo. Some agencies disqualify applicants with any body art; other departments allow tattoos that may cover 25 percent or less of an arm or a leg. For example, in Baltimore, no tattoos are permitted; in Kentucky, applicants with visible tattoos are rejected; in Los Angeles, police must cover tattoos with skin-colored patches or clothing; in San Diego, officers must hide any markings that cover 30 percent or more of exposed body parts; and in Houston, police must wear clothing to cover all tattoos.

In Hartford, Connecticut, police officers have challenged their department's rules on tattoos. These officers argued that their tattoos were protected under the First Amendment, specifically as part of their right to free speech. A ruling in 2006 by a U.S. Appeals Court disagreed, stating that police officer tattoos do not enjoy First Amendment protection and can be subject to department rules.

Source: Matt Reed, "Tattoos: Official Blots on Reputations?" *USA Today*, July 23, 2007, p. 3A.

- Not engage in political or religious arguments
- Be obedient and loyal to the department at all times

Rules contribute to maintaining order and keeping the peace by portraying to the public a positive image of police officers and police agencies.

The formal rules in police departments are clear, widely understood, and intended to be fairly applied. Having clear-cut rules and regulations reduces ambiguity, decreases internal conflicts, and increases the likelihood that work will be completed satisfactorily and on time. The responsibilities and authority for each role in the police agency are plainly spelled out in the department policy manual. During a criminal investigation, for instance, patrol officers—who usually are the first members of the department to reach the crime scene—complete the preliminary inquiry. Later, detectives arrive and interrogate suspects. Both the patrol officers and the detective on the scene know when and where the responsibility of one party ends and the responsibility of the other party begins.

Limited Rewards

Most police officers begin and end their careers as patrol officers. Promotion opportunities in police agencies are limited for several reasons:

- Civil service regulations mandate that officers serve for a specific number of years in a particular rank before they become eligible for promotion.
- Promotional exams are given at irregular intervals because department promotions depend more on the financial well-being of a city than on the needs of the police agency.
- Promotions are based on a formal testing process that usually consists of an oral interview and written exams that may favor applicants with more privileged educational backgrounds.

While it was once true that there were limited opportunities for employment and promotion of women and racial and ethic minority members in law enforcement agencies, this is no longer the case. Most law enforcement agencies have voluntarily leveled the playing field; others were instructed to do so by the courts. Today in many instances the hiring and promotion rates for women and racial and ethnic minorities exceed those for white males. While personal interviews in some law enforcement agencies sometimes give white males an advantage, the conditions for promotion for women and racial and ethnic minorities are much better today than they were only a short time ago.[43]

Competency

In bureaucracies, personnel are hired and promoted based on their knowledge, skills, and capacity to perform the job. Collectively, these capabilities are called **competency**. Competency is made apparent by evidence that reflects the desired abilities or skills of employees, such as qualifications, test scores on promotional exams, and field performance. Ascribed attributes, such as gender, ethnicity, and race, should not influence hiring, promotion, or retention decisions in a bureaucracy—but sometimes they do.

Informal Structure of Police Organizations

The foundation of the informal structure of police departments is a **police subculture**, which is the collective set of beliefs, values, and patterns of behavior that separate officers from the public and police administrators. Subcultures are not unique to police work; they are found in both legitimate and illegal lines of work ranging from lawyers and physicians to criminal gangs and auto thieves. The police subculture has a strict code of conduct that teaches police officers to adhere to the following expectations:

- Take care of their partner(s)
- Never back down

- Do not interfere in another officer's sector or work area
- Do not snitch on another officer[44]

Like many other subcultures, the police subculture enforces a "code of silence," ensuring that what goes on "behind closed doors" stays private. A 1950s study by William Westley discovered that police often believe that the public is their enemy.[45] This perception pushes officers to turn to fellow members of the department for support, a tendency that is strengthened by officers' strong commitment to secrecy. To shield themselves from outsiders, police officers may go to great lengths to protect one another, which could include covering up improper behavior and lying to supervisors.

The idea that a strong, unified, and influential police subculture exists has been challenged over the past several decades. Some criminologists contend that while police have slightly different attitudes and beliefs than the public, these differences are unimportant.[46]

For instance, Eugene Paoline, who studied big-city police agencies, concluded that the notion of a police subculture has been highly overestimated.[47] In fact, in nearly all law enforcement agencies today, the power wielded by the police subculture is much less than it was years ago. Today's law enforcement agencies are more professional, and law enforcement officers are more professional and are more concerned with legal considerations and self-preservation than adhering to any particular code of conduct. This does not mean that in some law enforcement agencies there does not exist rogue officers; they are still present, but there are fewer today than in the recent past.

Working Personality

Criminologist Jerome Skolnick hypothesized that police develop a **working personality** to deal with the danger and authority inherent in their job. Over time, through their interactions with the public and police administrators, officers become more authoritarian and suspicious than they were before they entered the police academy. Police also learn to carefully protect their authoritative position, which often means establishing a disdain for the rights of criminals and a high suspicion of the stereotypical criminal—poor, young, and minority males—to the point where "every hostile glance directed at the passing patrolman is read as a sign of possible guilt."[48]

Operational Styles

Political scientist James Q. Wilson has constructed a typology to represent common operational styles of policing. Wilson found that police departments (not officers) develop

Headline Crime

Breaking the "Code of Silence"

In 1951, William Westley identified the strong solidarity that exists among police officers. Through his research he discovered that police viewed themselves as "brothers" who under no circumstances would "rat out" one of their own.

As time passed and as the ethnic, racial, and sex composition of law enforcement agencies changed, however, the power of the brotherhood, or the "wall of silence," also diminished. For example, in Milwaukee in 2007, the beatings by police officers of Frank Jude, Jr., and Lovell Harris triggered massive outrage across the city after a state trial ended with the jury acquitting the three police officers who were involved. Following the state trial, Milwaukee police officers came forward, breaking the "code of silence," and spoke to federal officers about what happened on that night. A subsequent federal investigation led to plea agreements with the three officers, each of whom received a sentence of 15 or more years in prison for his role in the beatings.

Source: Kevin Johnson, "Busting the 'Code of Silence'," *USA Today*, December 18, 2007, p. 3A.

one of three **operational styles** that alter the behavior of the department's officers when they are reacting to misdemeanor crimes and noncrime incidents:[49]

- *Legalistic departments* adopt a zero-tolerance approach to serious crime. In these departments, administrators believe arrest deters crime. For minor infractions, police may not always arrest the perpetrators, but they will almost always use the threat of arrest to maintain order.
- *Watchmen departments* resolve disputes and community problems informally before they resort to making an arrest. They believe arrests exacerbate an already tenuous relationship between police and the public.
- *Service departments* emphasize helping the public and are not overly concerned with enforcing the law for minor violations. Rather than making arrests, officers are more likely to refer offenders to neighborhood treatment agencies for guidance and assistance. Taking formal action against someone who has committed a minor crime is a last resort.

The operational style of a department and its officers derives from a city's political culture, climate, financial resources, and organization.[50] However, it is likely that the operational styles identified by Wilson do not exist in all departments. In her study of the Dallas Police Department, criminologist Ellen Hochstedler was unable to find either the department or its officers having developed a particular type of operational style; instead, she concluded, police work is too unpredictable and complicated for either the organization or its officers to utilize one specific style consistently.[51]

Police Operations

Police operations describe the services that police agencies provide to civilians and how these services are delivered. The public expects more from the police than the police can deliver.[52] Police agencies and their officers are always "a day late and a dime short." Yet, they do their best to meet the varied and complex demands placed on them. After all, they are one of few public agencies available 24 hours a day, 7 days a week, 365 days a year. They provide citizens with a 9-1-1 telephone number to call during emergencies and use automobiles with flashing lights and sirens to offer rapid response to citizen complaints.

Police Patrol

Despite common misconceptions, police on average spend only 25 percent of their time enforcing the law (see FIGURE 4-4).[53] Police spend most of their time on patrol—that is, moving through assigned areas by foot or vehicle to deter crime, apprehend criminals committing crimes in progress, assist citizens who find themselves in dangerous situations, maintain order, enforce regulations, and manage traffic.

Historically, police patrolled their beats on foot. Beginning in the 1930s, police expanded the use of automobile patrol because officers in cars could cover a greater area in less time. This type of patrol also made officers less accessible to the public and, therefore, less likely to be tempted by corrupting influences. In addition to foot and automobile patrols, police today use a variety of other methods of patrolling their beats, including bicycles, horses, motorcycles, snowmobiles, watercrafts, and Segways (a two-wheeled stand-up personal transportation device).

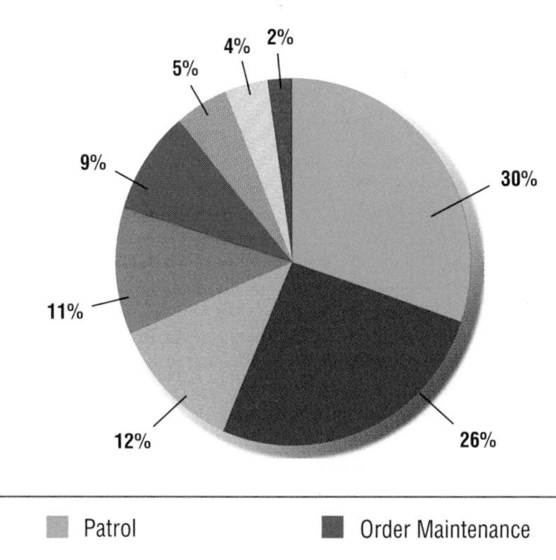

FIGURE 4-4 Police Responsibilities

Adapted from Jack Green and Carl Klockars, "What Police Do," in Stephen Mastrofki (ed.). *Thinking about Police,* 2nd ed. (New York: Mcgraw-Hill, 1991) pp. 273–284.

More than 150 law enforcement agencies worldwide use Segways for a variety of purposes, such as parking enforcement, patrol, providing crowd control, event security, and in community policing activities. What makes the Segway ideal for police work is its ability to transverse all terrain, including bike paths, gravel, and sand.

Foot Patrol

Today, only about 6 percent of all patrol officers work their beats on foot. The reason is that generally foot patrol is inefficient and not cost-effective in modern-day policing. An officer on foot is no match for a fleeing suspect in a vehicle. However, on the positive side, foot patrol has several advantages over other types of patrol. Foremost is that it reduces the public's fear of crime, improves community relations, and increases morale and job satisfaction among police.[54] Foot patrol also provides police with the opportunity to produce "new" information that may help them solve future crimes. Additionally, foot patrol allows officers to establish long-term, face-to-face relationships with citizens; this rapport can later help police when they try to solve crimes, as officers may be able to call upon citizens for assistance.

Research evaluating the effectiveness of foot patrol has found that it generally produces positive results.[55] If a department has the resources to utilize both foot and automobile patrol, then the positives far outweigh the negatives. Unfortunately, most law enforcement agencies today do not find themselves in the position of having an abundance of resources. While foot patrol may be more likely to reduce citizens' fear of crime, its widespread implementation is too costly for most cities.

Automobile Patrol

Today, motor vehicles are the most widely used method of patrol, for of the following reasons:

- Police can respond to calls more quickly
- Police can patrol a larger physical area, even patrolling more than one beat
- Cars protect officers from inclement weather
- Cars provide police with a shield from bullets and thrown objects
- Officers in cars may be fully equipped with a radio, first-aid kit, report forms, weapons, a dog, and other necessary tools and supplies
- Cars can be used to confine and transport criminals

Today, patrol vehicles have been enhanced by technology including the *global positioning system* (GPS), a satellite-based radio navigation system developed and operated by the U.S. Department of Defense. GPS makes it easier for police to track suspects and determine the whereabouts of undercover surveillance officers during emergency situations and search-and-rescue missions. In addition, in rare instances prosecutors have asked judges to place GPS tracking devices on criminal suspects who have been released on bail to ensure they do not disappear before trial.[56]

Police Patrol Strategies

It is common for a police agency to assign more than 60 percent of its personnel to patrol work.[57] Most officers are assigned a particular geographic area, called a **beat**. The entire collection of beats in a specific geographic area is called a **precinct**. These are generic terms, and in some departments other terminology is used to describe the geographic area patrolled by police agencies. As an example, in Philadelphia the geographic areas patrolled are called "districts" and the Pennsylvania State Police call the areas they patrol "zones." Nevertheless, in small departments, usually one precinct serves as the department's headquarters or station house for the entire agency. Regardless of their size, police departments generally adopt one of two patrolling strategies: preventive patrol or directed patrol.

Preventive Patrol

Preventive patrol was introduced in the 1950s by Orland W. Wilson, who was then superintendent of the Chicago Police Department. Wilson believed that if the police established an omnipresence in a neighborhood by driving conspicuously marked cars randomly through the city's streets, giving special attention to **hot spots of crime** (i.e., areas with high crime rates), they would deter criminal activity and alleviate the public's fears.[58]

This idea dominated police patrol operations for two decades, until 1972. In that year George Kelling and his associates launched the Kansas City Prevention Experiment, in which they gathered crime data from 15 patrol beats, each of which they had assigned to one of three levels of patrol:

1. *Reactive beats:* Police did not patrol and only responded to citizen calls for service
2. *Proactive beats:* Police regularly patrolled in vehicles at a higher rate than usual (two or three cars per beat)
3. *Control beats:* Police patrolled at regular rates (one car per beat)

Kelling and his colleagues found that increasing or decreasing patrol activity in an area had no measurable impact on crime rates, citizens' fear of crime, public attitudes toward police effectiveness, police response time, or the number of traffic accidents.[59] Follow-up studies in Houston, New York, San Diego, and Syracuse produced similar results. Criminologists concluded that preventive patrol made about as much sense as firemen driving their trucks around city streets looking for fires to put out.[60] Taken collectively, these findings caused police administrators to conclude that "random patrol produced random results" and prompted them to reevaluate police operations.[61]

Directed Patrol

The Kansas City Prevention Experiment changed the way police administrators viewed the effectiveness of patrol. Initially, they responded to the study's findings by developing alternative methods of patrol. One strategy introduced was *directed patrol*, in which police patrol is focused on high-crime areas. Another strategy involved the application of *geographic information systems* (GIS)—that is, systems for capturing, storing, analyzing, and managing data and associated attributes that are spatially referenced to the Earth. With this technology, police are able to see a visual map of the times, offenses, and places where crime most frequently occurs. Armed with this knowledge, police dispatchers know the best time to saturate the neighborhoods with officers, making them highly visible, and to establish decoy units to catch potential offenders, conduct sting operations, and assign special units to track offenders.[62] Even so, this tactic may not produce the desired outcome, as in many instances saturation of an area with police merely drives drug dealers, for example, to another area of the city.

When thinking about crime mapping, it is best to think of it as being only a means to identify where crimes and criminal activity occur. Usually this practice identifies a crackhouse, prostitution ring, illegal gambling site, or gang hangout, for example. If a crime has not occurred in the past at a crackhouse, for instance, then it will not show up on the department's crime map.

Advocates of directed patrol contend that crime decreases when departments aggressively enforce the law by being vigilant and intrusive, and by adopting a "zero tolerance" stance, which is a full-scale strategic attack on all crimes and disorder in a city. In particular, this approach focuses on the enforcement of "quality of life" offenses such as drinking alcoholic beverages in the street, urinating in public, panhandling, playing loud radios, graffiti, and disorderly conduct. By quickly addressing and correcting these minor problems, presumably a message is being sent to the public that more serious crime will not be tolerated.[63] Research supports these claims. In an analysis of 171 cities,

Robert Sampson and Jacqueline Cohen found that aggressive policing reduced both the incidence (the number of offenses committed) and the prevalence (the number of people committing the crime) of robbery.[64] Other studies have reported that directed patrol has substantially reduced crime rates when it targeted a specific crime in a particular location, such as firearms-related crimes in areas with high rates of violent crime.[65]

Whether a strategy of directed patrol is effective depends in part on *response time* (how long it takes for an officer to arrive at the scene) and *reporting time* (the amount of time that passes between when a crime was committed and when the police are called). Reducing response time has been found to only slightly increase the likelihood of arrest for serious crimes, because most crimes are reported to police after the offender has left the scene. If a crime is not reported within 60 seconds of being committed, police generally cannot respond quickly enough to apprehend the suspect.[66] For *involvement* crimes—that is, crimes in which an offender directly confronts the victim (such as a sexual assault or mugging)—a fast response time has a greater effect.

To help reduce reporting time, the 9-1-1 telephone dispatch system was developed in Alabama in 1973. Unfortunately, it has not had a large effect in decreasing reporting time, making a difference of only about 10 seconds. In some instances, the 9-1-1 system has actually increased reporting time because some citizens—particularly elders—may delay contacting authorities for fear of using the system in an improper situation and angering the police.[67]

Criminal Investigations

During a *criminal investigation*, a goal of the police investigator is to obtain enough evidence to establish probable cause to make an arrest in an investigation. Typically investigators cannot uncover sufficient evidence to hand over to a prosecutor to prove beyond a reasonable doubt that the suspect committed the crime. An examination of crime clearance rates, for instance, shows this to be the case; on average, only 20 percent of all crimes committed are cleared, although the rate is higher for some crimes than others (see TABLE 4-3). In 2007, for example, the crime clearance rate for murder was 61 percent, while for burglary and motor vehicle theft it was less than 13 percent.[68] Although police are only moderately successful at producing evidence leading to convictions,

TABLE 4-3 Crime Clearance Rates, 2007

Offense Known to Police	Crime Clearance Rate
Murder and nonnegligent manslaughter	61.2
Forcible rape	40.0
Robbery	25.9
Aggravated assault	54.1
Violent Crime	**44.5**
Burglary	12.4
Larceny–theft	18.6
Motor vehicle theft	12.6
Arson	18.0
Property Crime	**16.5**
Total Clearance Rate	**20.0**

Source: Federal Bureau of Investigation, *Crime in the United States, 2007* (Washington, DC: U.S. Department of Justice, 2008).

emerging innovations, such as *iris scans* (see page 112), may generate stronger evidence for prosecutors to take to trial.

When responding to a call, the first officer on the scene conducts a preliminary investigation that may include arresting a suspect, assisting victims, securing the crime scene, collecting physical evidence, and writing an initial report. If the crime cannot be solved immediately, a detective is assigned to the case for a follow-up investigation.[69]

The *detective division* includes investigative officers and, depending on the size of the department, may have forensic laboratories or specialized units that focus on specific types of crimes (i.e., homicide, narcotics). Because crime labs are expensive to operate and maintain, only federal and state governments and big-city police departments have forensic labs; smaller agencies typically send their forensic evidence to state-run or regional crime centers for analysis.

The job of the detective is more specialized than that of the patrol officer and typically includes the following responsibilities:

- Interviewing suspects, witnesses, and informants
- Discussing the case with patrol officers, their peers, and supervisors
- Searching crime scenes for physical evidence
- Attending autopsies
- Reviewing state and federal computer databases for clues

Despite how the popular media portray crime investigations, detective work is often tedious, routine, mundane, and boring. Detectives spend most of their day writing reports and examining computer files, and they solve only a very small percentage of all crimes they investigate.[70] The majority of cases that are solved rely on information from the interrogation of suspects and witnesses or information provided by informants (often insiders within criminal gangs) rather than on key evidence discovered by detectives. Occasionally detectives solve crimes by gathering forensic evidence, which includes fingerprints, DNA analysis, bloodstains, footprints, tire tracks, and the presence of narcotics. This evidence is sent to crime laboratories, where it is analyzed by scientific experts called **criminalists** or forensic scientists.[71]

An alternative to DNA testing that will soon be used in law enforcement identifications of humans is a forensic tool that uses antibody profiles rather than DNA to identify criminal offenders. The test, called *AbP ID*, can produce reliable results within a few hours and can be conducted by police officers at the crime scene, rather than a technician in a laboratory. The antibody test is not a replacement for DNA testing, but rather is a tool for law enforcement agents to use at a crime scene to sort out victims and suspects, which speeds up the process compared to having to submit samples to a crime lab. The *AbP ID* is an aid for criminal investigators in determining which criminal suspects should undergo more extensive and costly DNA testing. The *AbP ID* test has the following advantages over a DNA test:

- It does not require expensive equipment or highly skilled personnel to administer
- Training on how to use the test is relatively simple
- The test results do not have to be sent to a crime lab
- The test does not require large evidence samples

The *AbP ID* test is a tool for getting a case to move faster toward a final legal resolution. For example, an AbP ID test using semen, saliva, and perspiration can return reliable human identifications in only five hours. Test kits will be made available to law enforcement agencies beginning in 2009.[72]

Headline Crime — Solving Crime Using Iris Scans

An increasing number of law enforcement agencies are using iris scans to identify sex offenders, runaways, and abducted children. Departments in 27 states are taking digital pictures of eyes and storing the information in a database where they later can search for a missing person or identify someone who uses a fake name. Experts believe that iris scans will someday be as common as fingerprinting is today. Iris scans are also much more effective. A central database can make matches within seconds, whereas matches for fingerprints take weeks and DNA matches take months. The most common use of iris scans today is as part of the war on terror: Airports are beginning to use the scans to expedite security checks.

A scan is produced with a camera that uses infrared light to record the iris's minute ridges and valleys. The camera can detect 235 unique details and differentiate between right and left eyes and eyes of identical twins. By contrast, a fingerprint provides an investigator with about 70 details. In addition, an individual's iris is not affected by age, Lasik eye surgery, or disease, whereas a fingerprint can be changed. Critics of the new technology worry that iris scans are too intrusive and violate personal privacy.

Source: Wendy Koch, "Iris Scans Let Law Enforcement Keep Eye on Criminals," *USA Today*, December 5, 2007, p. 1A.

Traffic Enforcement

Traffic enforcement includes all traffic safety functions, including law enforcement, accident investigation, impoundment of abandoned or stolen vehicles, and roadside sobriety checkpoints. In 2007, 41,059 people died in traffic crashes in the United States, which was the lowest number of traffic deaths in more than a decade. Of those deaths, 12,998 were alcohol-related fatalities.[73] To thwart drunken driving, more states are adopting laws requiring first-time offenders to equip their vehicles with high-tech devices that prevent operation by intoxicated people. Today, for instance, Arizona, Illinois, Louisiana, Nebraska, New Mexico, and Washington require alcohol-ignition interlocks for anyone convicted of drunken driving. Other states, including California, Colorado, and Hawaii, also are considering interlocks for first offenders.[74]

Law enforcement officers have passing drivers pull over to a checkpoint and ask whether they have been drinking. The officers sniff for alcohol fumes and marijuana smoke.

Even though enforcing traffic laws consumes a large amount of time and resources, it can be an effective tool for reducing criminal activity, capturing fugitives, and recovering stolen property. Routine traffic enforcement stops have led to significant arrests and apprehensions for other offenses, such as when Oklahoma State Trooper Charles Hanger stopped Timothy McVeigh for having no license plate on his vehicle, following his bombing of the Alfred P. Murrah Federal Building in Oklahoma City.

Community Services

As society changes, so do the services the police provide. The *service function* has been an important part of police work for more than 100 years. Typical services include:

- Rendering first aid
- Rescuing animals
- Giving tourists information
- Providing roadside assistance
- Finding lost pets

AROUND THE GLOBE

Ballet and Traffic Control in Romania

In Timisoara, Romania, 20 police officers are taking dance classes from a ballet company to help them direct traffic. The police agency believes that learning dance will help the officers to make their signals clearer and become more noticeable to drivers. As one of the ballet instructors who helped to convince police administrators that teaching the officers to dance was a good idea put it, "Why shouldn't policemen be pleasant and well guided when they pull drivers over?" "Instead of having robots guiding the traffic, we can have very graceful agents doing the same thing." Police leaders agreed, and now police officers are taking ballet lessons.

Source: "It Wasn't All That Bad," *The Week*, March 7, 2008, p. 2.

- Checking door locks on vacationers' homes
- Opening doors for people locked out of their vehicles

Police deliver these services to citizens as part of an overall crime-fighting strategy. Officers provide services to build goodwill with the public, who in turn may be more motivated to help police solve crimes by providing information.

James Q. Wilson disagrees with this line of reasoning. He suggests that police should not provide services, which he believes drain scarce resources, fail to be cost-effective, and help only a few individuals. Instead, Wilson argues, private industry should assume this responsibility.[75] It is interesting that even proponents of community policing find merit in Wilson's position. One possible reason why advocates of community policing agree with Wilson is that providing services does drain scarce resources. It also is true that asking officers to provide services along with everything else they do may be asking too much and results in poor job performance on all counts. Yet, it is difficult to predict the impact a reduction of police services would have on community relations. Police agencies across the United States are trying to strike a balance between two positions: They want to streamline the services they offer while offering the services the public wants.

WRAPPING IT UP

Chapter Highlights

- The U.S. police system is based on English models, which evolved from volunteer citizens serving as night watchmen.
- In community policing, police officers work in partnership with neighborhood residents to prevent and respond to crime.
- Intelligence-led policing uses information centers or hubs to coordinate intelligence reports from national, state, and local agencies for more effective crime fighting.
- Law enforcement agencies in the United States work at the local, state, and federal levels. In addition to these public agencies, private security agencies serve both the public and private sectors.
- Police departments have both formal and informal structures that guide the activities of their members.
- The law enforcement function of policing consists of three major activities: patrol, crime investigation, and traffic enforcement.
- Police provide the public with services, including rendering first aid, rescuing animals, and giving tourists information.

Words to Know

beat The largest geographic area that a patrol unit can patrol effectively; an assigned area for police patrol.

broken windows theory A theory that proposes small signs of public disorder set in motion a downward spiral of deterioration, neighborhood decline, and increasing crime.

bureaucracy A model of organization in which strict and precise rules are used as a way of effectively achieving organizational goals.

chain of command A hierarchical system of authority that prescribes who communicates with (and give orders to) whom.

community policing A policing model that was popular in the 1990s, in which police and citizens unite to fight crime.

competency A list of factors that reflect abilities or skills, including qualifications, test scores on promotional exams, and field performance.

criminalists Scientists who work in crime laboratories and examine forensic evidence, which includes fingerprints, DNA analysis, bloodstains, footprints, tire tracks, and the presence of narcotics.

delegation of authority Decision making made through a chain of command in a bureaucracy.

division of labor A system of assigning duties for the routine jobs completed in bureaucracies.

hot spots of crime Locations characterized by high rates of crime.

intelligence-led policing A crime-fighting strategy driven by computer databases, intelligence gathering, and analysis.

jurisdiction The territory over which a law enforcement agency has authority.

operational style Within law enforcement agencies, common patterns or styles of policing emerge.

police subculture Beliefs, values, and patterns of behavior that separate officers from police administrators and the public.

precinct The entire collection of police beats in a specific geographic area.

sheriff The principal law enforcement officer in a county.

specialization The practice of dividing work among employees so that the work will be completed more effectively and efficiently.

sworn officers Officers who are empowered to arrest suspects, serve warrants, carry weapons, and use force.

traffic enforcement Police duties related to highway and traffic safety and accident investigations.

working personality A term that distinguishes an officer's off-the-job persona from his or her on-the-job behavior.

Think and Discuss

1. The United States does not have a centralized national police force, but instead has many separate police agencies. Is this the best approach for controlling crime?
2. The introduction of new technology changed policing in the early part of the twentieth century. What are some of the new technologies being used in the twenty-first century that are once again transforming the U.S. system of policing?
3. Private security officers may not be well trained or always have the best interests of the community in mind. Knowing that, should private agents be permitted to take citizens into custody and detain them?
4. Traditional hiring and promotional practices in police departments have been criticized because they limit opportunities for racial and ethnic minorities and for women. Should quota systems be used to create diversity in police departments?
5. Given the large number of traffic fatalities that occur each year, should a larger percentage of the police budget be allocated to traffic law enforcement and taken from the crime-fighting and service functions?

Notes

1. Eric Monkkonen, *Policing in Urban America, 1860–1920* (Cambridge, UK: Cambridge University Press, 1981); Wilbur Miller, *Cops and Bobbies*, 2nd ed. (Columbus, OH: Ohio State University Press, 1999).
2. Craig Uchida, "The Development of the American Police," in Roger Dunham and Geoffrey Alpert (Eds.), *Critical Issues in Policing*, 5th ed. (Prospect Heights, IL: Waveland Press, 2005), pp. 20–30.

3. Herbert Johnson, *History of Criminal Justice* (Cincinnati: Anderson, 1988); Roger Lane, *Policing the City* (Cambridge, MA: Harvard University Press, 1967); Samuel Walker and Charles Katz, *The Police in America*, 6th ed. (New York: McGraw-Hill, 2008).

4. Andrew Harris, *Policing the City* (Columbus, OH: Ohio State University Press, 2004); Robert Fogelson, *Big-City Police* (Cambridge, MA: Harvard University Press, 1977); Johnson, note 3.

5. The New York City Police Museum, "Leadership of the City of New York Police Department, 1845–1901," available at http://www.nycpolicemuseum.org/html/tour/leadr1845.htm, accessed August 5, 2008; H. W. Brands, *T.R.: The Last Romantic* (New York: Basic Books, 1998); H. Paul Jeffers, *Commissioner Roosevelt* (New York: John Wiley, 1996); Jay Stuart Berman, *Police Administration and Progressive Reform: Theodore Roosevelt as Police Commissioner of New York* (Westport, CT: Greenwood Press, 1987); see also "Timeline of Theodore Roosevelt," available at http://www.theodoreroosevelt.org/life/timeline.htm, accessed August 4, 2008.

6. August Vollmer, *The Police and Modern Society* (Berkeley: University of California Press, 1936); Gene Carte and Elaine Carte, *Police Reform in the United States* (Berkeley: University of California Press, 1975); Walker and Katz, note 3.

7. Walker and Katz, note 3.

8. Uchida, note 2; Walker and Katz, note 3.

9. Fogelson, note 4; Johnson, note 3.

10. Herman Goldstein, "The New Policing," paper presented at the National Institute of Justice Conference on Community Policing, 1993, p. 5.

11. Jerome Skolnick and David Bayley, *Community Policing* (Washington, DC: U.S. Department of Justice, 1988).

12. Herman Goldstein, "Improving Policing: A Problem-Oriented Approach," *Crime & Delinquency* 25:236–258 (1979).

13. George Kelling and James Q. Wilson, "Broken Windows: The Police and Neighborhood Safety," *Atlantic Monthly* 249:29–38 (1982).

14. Dan Immergluck and Geoff Smith, "The Impact of Single-Family Mortgage Foreclosures on Neighborhood Crime," *Housing Studies* 21:851–866 (2006); see also J. Michael Collins, "Promises and Pitfalls," available at http://www.chicagofed.org/cedric/files/2005_conf_discussant_session1_collins.pdf, accessed August 17, 2008.

15. Samuel Walker, *The Police in America*, 2nd ed. (New York: McGraw-Hill, 1992).

16. David Kaplan, "Spies Among Us," *U.S. News & World Report* 8:40–49 (2006).

17. Walker and Katz, note 3.

18. Brian Reaves, *Census of State and Local Law Enforcement Agencies, 2004* (Washington, DC: U.S. Department of Justice, 2007); Brian Reaves, *Federal Law Enforcement Officers, 2004* (Washington, DC: U.S. Department of Justice, 2006); Brian Reaves and Andrew Goldberg, *Campus Law Enforcement Agencies, 1995* (Washington, DC: U.S. Department of Justice, 1996); Bureau of Justice Statistics, *Justice Expenditure and Employment Extracts, 2005* (Washington, DC: U.S. Department of Justice, 2007), available at http://www.ojp.gov/bjs/eande.htm#selected, accessed August 18, 2008.

19. Reaves, *Census of State and Local Law Enforcement Agencies, 2004*, note 18.

20. Matthew Hickman and Brian Reaves, *Local Police Departments, 2003* (Washington, DC: U.S. Department of Justice, 2006).

21. Hickman and Reaves, note 20.

22. Brian Reeves and Matthew Hickman, *Police Departments in Large Cities, 1990–2000* (Washington, DC: U.S. Department of Justice, 2002).

23. Hickman and Reaves, note 20.

24. New York City Police Department, available at http://www.nyc.gov/html/nypd/html/faq/faq_police.shtml#1, accessed August 6, 2008.

25. Hickman and Reaves, note 20.

26. Reaves, *Census of State and Local Law Enforcement Agencies, 2004*, note 18.

27. Matthew Hickman and Brian Reaves, *Sheriffs' Offices, 2003* (Washington, DC: U.S. Department of Justice, 2006); see also http://www.sheriffs.org/, accessed August 15, 2008.

28. "More Gun Ownership Statistics, April 23, 2007," available at http://www.halfsigma.com/2007/04/more_gun_owners.html, accessed August 17, 2008; Lee Brown, "The Role of Sheriff," in Alvin Cohn (Ed.), *The Future of Policing* (Beverly Hills, CA: Sage, 1978), pp. 227–247; Dana Brammer, *A Study of the Office of the Sheriff in the United States* (Mississippi State, MS: University of Mississippi Press, 1968).

29. Reaves, note 18.

30. Hickman and Reaves, note 27.

31. Hickman and Reaves, note 27.

32. Brian Reaves, *Federal Law Enforcement Officers, 2004*, note 18.

33. United States Customs and Border Protection, available at http://www.cbp.gov, accessed August 3, 2008.

34. United States Citizenship and Immigration Services, available at http://www.uscis.gov, accessed October 23, 2008.

35. United States Secret Service, available at http://www.secretservice.gov/, accessed August 5, 2008.

36. U.S. Marshals Service, available at http://www.usdoj.gov/marshals/, accessed October 25, 2008; James Chenowith, *Down Darkness Wide* (Frederick, MD: Publish America, 2004); Robin Langley Sommer, *A History of U.S. Marshals* (Philadelphia: Running Press, 1993); see also http://www.usmarshals.gov/falcon/facts/general-facts-usms.pdf, accessed August 7, 2008.

37. Federal Bureau of Investigation, available at http://www.fbi.gov/, accessed August 7, 2008.

38. U.S. Department of Justice, *National Policy Summit: Building Private Security/Public Policing Partnerships to Prevent and Respond to Terrorism and Public Disorder* (Washington, DC: International Association of Chiefs of Police, 2004).

39. Elizabeth Joh, "The Paradox of Private Policing," *Journal of Criminal Law and Criminology* 95:49–131 (2004).

40. Brian Frost, "The Privatization and Civilianization of Policing," in Charles Friel et al. (Eds.), *Criminal Justice 2000: Boundary Changes in Criminal Justice* (Washington, DC: National Institute of Justice, 2000), pp. 19–79, available at http://www.independent.org/newsroom/article.asp?id=389, accessed August 7, 2008; Hickman and Reaves, note 20, p. 2.

41. Jack Green and Carl Klockars, "What Police Do," in Carl Klockars and Stephen Mastrofski (Eds.), *Police Contemporary Readings*, 2nd ed. (New York: McGraw-Hill, 1991), pp. 273–284.

42. Max Weber, *The Theory of Social and Economic Organization*, translated by Talcott Parsons (New York: Free Press, 1947).

43. Geoffrey Alpert, Roger Dunham, and Meghan Stroshine, *Policing: Continuity and Change* (Long Grove, IL: Waveland Press, 2006).

44. Elizabeth Reuss-Ianni, *Two Cultures of Policing* (New Brunswick, NJ: Transaction Books, 1982).

45. William Westley, "Violence and the Police," *American Journal of Sociology* 59:34–41 (1953); William Westley, *The Police: A Sociological Study of Law, Custom, and Morality*, Ph.D. dissertation, University of Chicago, 1951; William Westley, *Violence and the Police* (Cambridge, MA: MIT Press, 1971).

46. Steve Herbert, "Police Subculture Revisited," *Criminology* 36:343–369 (1998).

47. Eugene Paoline, *Rethinking Police Subculture* (New York: LFB: Scholarly Publishing, 2001).

48. Jerome Skolnick, *Justice without Trial*, 3rd ed. (New York: Macmillan, 1994).

49. James Q. Wilson, *Varieties of Police Behavior* (Cambridge, MA: Harvard University Press, 1968).

50. Gad Barzical, *Communities and Law* (Ann Arbor, MI: University of Michigan Press, 2003); William Lyons, *The Politics of Community Policing* (Ann Arbor, MI: University of Michigan Press, 1999); Charles Bonjean, *Community Politics* (New York: Free Press, 1971).

51. Ellen Hochstedler, "Testing Types: A Review and Test of Police Types," *Journal of Criminal Justice* 9:451–466 (1981).

52. Carl Klockars, *The Idea of Policing* (Beverly Hills, CA: Sage, 1985), pp. 15–16.

53. Elaine Cumming, Ian Cumming, and Laura Edell, "Policeman as Philosopher, Friend, and Guide," *Social Problems* 12:276–286 (1965); Dorothy Guyot, *Policing as Though People Mattered* (Philadelphia: Temple University Press, 1991); Thomas Bercal, "Calls for Police Assistance," *American Behavioral Scientist* 13:681–691 (1970); Stephen Mastrofski, "The Police and Non-crime Services," in Gordon Whitaker and Charles Phillips (Eds.), *Evaluating Performance of Criminal Justice Agencies* (Beverly Hills, CA: Sage, 1983), pp. 33–62; Albert Reiss, Jr., *The Police and the Public* (New Haven, CT: Yale University Press, 1971); Green and Klockars, note 41.

54. Lawrence Sherman, "Police Crackdowns," *NIJ Reports* (Washington, DC: National Institute of Justice, 1990).

55. The Police Foundation, *The Newark Foot Patrol Experiment* (Washington, DC: The Police Foundation, 1981); Robert Trojanowicz, *An Evaluation of the Neighborhood Foot Patrol Program in Flint, Michigan* (East Lansing, MI: Michigan State University Press, 1982); Robert Trojanowicz and Dennis Banas, *The Impact of Foot Patrol on Black and White Perceptions of Policing* (East Lansing, MI: Michigan State University Press, 1985).

56. Christine Reid, "Prosecutors Want GPS Device on Midyette," *Boulder Daily Camera*, January 9, 2008, pp. 1A, 6A; Donna Rogers, "GPS Gains a Stronger Position," *Law Enforcement Technology*, June 2001, pp. 64–68.

57. Hickman and Reaves, note 20.

58. Orlando W. Wilson, *Police Administration*, 3rd ed. (New York: McGraw-Hill, 1977).

59. George Kelling, Tony Pate, Duane Dieckman, and Charles Brown, *The Kansas City Preventive Patrol Experiment* (Washington, DC: The Police Foundation, 1974).

60. Carl Klockars, *Thinking about Police* (New York: McGraw-Hill, 1983).

61. Henry Wrobleski and Karen Hess, *Introduction to Law Enforcement and Criminal Justice*, 8th ed. (Belmont, CA: Thomson Learning, 2006).

62. Herman Goldstein, *Problem-Oriented Policing* (Philadelphia: Temple University Press, 1990); Anthony Braga, *Problem-Oriented Policing and Crime Prevention* (Monsey, NY: Willow Tree Press, 2002).

63. James Q. Wilson and Barbara Boland, "The Effect of Police on Crime," *Law and Society Review* 12:367–387 (1978); New York City Police Department, *Frequently Asked Questions*, available at http://www.nyc.gov/html/nypd/html/faq/faq_police.shtml#2, accessed August 7, 2008.

64. Robert Sampson and Jacqueline Cohen, "Deterrent Effects of Police on Crime," *Law and Society Review* 22:163–190 (1988).

65. Edmund McGarrell, Steven Chermak, Alexander Weiss, and Jeremy Wilson, "Reducing Firearms Violence Through Directed Patrol," *Criminology and Public Policy* 1:119–148 (2001); Michael Scott, *The Benefits and Consequences of Police Crackdowns* (Washington, DC: U.S. Department of Justice, 2003).

66. William Spelman and Dale Brown, *Calling the Police* (Darby, PA: Diane, 1984).

67. Spelman and Brown, note 66.

68. Federal Bureau of Investigation, *Crime in the United States, 2007* (Washington, DC: U.S. Department of Justice, 2008).

69. James Poland, "Detectives," pages 140–143 in William Bailey (Ed.), *The Encyclopedia of Police Science* (New York: Garland, 1995), p. 142.

70. Goldstein, note 10; Goldstein, note 12; Goldstein, note 62.

71. Michael Baden and Marion Roach, *Dead Reckoning: The New Science of Catching Killers* (New York: Simon & Schuster, 2001); Stuart Kind and Michael Overman, *Science Against Crime* (New York: Doubleday, 1972); Joe Nickell and John Fischer, *Crime Science: Methods of Forensic Detection* (Lexington, KY: University Press of Kentucky, 1999).

72. Charles Montaldo, "Antibody Profiling a New Law Enforcement Tool," available at http://www.cnn.com/2008/TECH/science/04/29/Antibody.profiling.asp/index.html, accessed August 7, 2008.

73. National Highway Traffic Safety Administration, *Traffic Safety Facts, 2007* (Washington, DC: National Highway Traffic Safety Administration, 2008).

74. Larry Copeland, "Intoxicated Drivers Face Lockouts," *USA Today*, April 15, 2008, p. 1A.

75. Wilson, note 49.

CHAPTER

5

Police and the Law

OBJECTIVES

1 Understand what constitutes a legal search and seizure.
2 Know the exclusionary rule, its significance, and its importance.
3 Identify the exceptions that allow warrantless searches and seizures.
4 Outline the process of arrest, including obtaining an arrest warrant.
5 Explain the *Miranda* warning and the controversy that surrounds it.
6 Describe the rules that police must follow during booking, line-up, interrogation, and confession.

PROFILES IN CRIME AND JUSTICE

Kim Budreau

Sergeant, Medford Police Department
Medford, Oregon

When I chose to enter the field of law enforcement, my motives were driven by my inspiration to help others. Whether the call is responding to an emergency with a life-changing, split-second decision to be made or just being a set of ears for someone who is alone, elderly, or in need, I learned and experienced that I can make a difference. This is a career that offers a plethora of challenges and rewards.

The most exciting thing about my job is the day-to-day activities. One day you could be running from one felony hot call to another hot call, and the next day you may spend most of your time dealing with a sexual assault victim. The calls for service are often unique to the day of the week and time of the day. Weekend night shifts provide for frequent in-progress disturbances, many of which will involve alcohol. Weekday nights often involve domestic disputes, while day shifts entail investigating crimes that are "cold." While these are generalities, you just never know what the next call is going be. This, of course, is specific to my community, Medford, Oregon. Officers in metropolitan areas may be dealing with a variety of day-to-day tasks, but the training and professionalism of my department are a major reason I have built my career here and not transferred to a larger city.

This is a career where you can truly make a difference in someone's life just about every day you're at work. Whether it's a victim or a suspect, your decisions and actions matter. While helping those who need assistance is always rewarding, some of my most satisfying moments involve arresting a person or persons for a serious crime. Holding people accountable, securing the streets and community, and having a victim know that the person or persons who hurt them are locked up make a difference for everyone. I also find it gratifying when I know I've helped an individual make a difficult decision. Making any part of life a little easier and being a big support mechanism for those who do not have a support structure such as family or friends to be there for them attract me to this line of work.

Success in this profession is grounded in having integrity, high moral values, and lots of common sense. This is a profession where you will have to use all three of these characteristics on a daily basis. Also, understanding how to talk to people from all walks of life is one of the best skills a police officer can possess. Police officers play many roles. Depending on the situation, they can be counselors, parents, enforcers, mediators, or even referees, so good communication is vital for success. It can actually mean life or death in certain situations.

Understanding that you can be the person whom they are so happy just arrived as well as the last person whom they wanted to see is an important piece of information for every officer. I would also add that the team approach in policing is very rewarding. The officers you come in contact with and work close to on a daily basis can also be the ones who save your life. Building trust and understanding their strengths and weaknesses develop a stronger department and better workplace.

I started as an Explorer when I was 17 years old. By the age of 19, I was a community service officer. Once I turned 21, I applied for a full-time sworn position and was hired. After 12 years as a sworn officer, I am proud to be the first female sergeant at the Medford Police Department. I feel I am well on my way to fulfilling my career goals as a law enforcement professional.

Introduction

Criminal investigations are one of many functions that police perform. Criminal investigations focus on the gathering of evidence and interrogation of suspects. To perform these functions, police have been granted a range of powers, including the right to stop, frisk, question, and detain suspects, as well as the ability to search and seize their property. Importantly, however, the Constitution places formal limitations on the rights of police in these realms. Indeed, police may be held accountable for violating a suspect's constitutional rights. Such forms of accountability may include being reprimanded by superiors, being reassigned to a less desirable position, being suspended without pay, being subject to a civil lawsuit, or, in the most egregious cases, being criminally prosecuted.

Among these possibilities, the fear of civil lawsuits is often of greatest concern for agencies and individual officers. As you recall from the beating of Rodney King discussed in Chapter 1, after the four accused officers were acquitted of criminal charges, King filed a $15 million civil lawsuit against them and a separate lawsuit against the city of Los Angeles for $3.8 million. In separate trials, King won the case against the city and was awarded $3.8 million, but lost the case against the individual officers.[1]

Pursuant to the Constitution, all individuals in the United States receive a variety of rights. The most important of these rights are as follows:

- The Fourth Amendment: People cannot be searched or have their property seized in ways that are inconsistent with the law.
- The Fifth Amendment: People cannot be forced to say anything that would help convict them of a crime (this is commonly referred to as the right against self-incrimination).
- The Sixth Amendment: People accused of crimes may have counsel appointed for their defense, if they are unable to afford counsel.
- The Fourteenth Amendment: States cannot violate the aforementioned rights.

This chapter will explore the profound implications that these rights have on the operations of law enforcement agencies and their officers.

Search and Seizure

In accordance with suspects' constitutional rights, police must have either reasonable suspicion or probable cause before initiating an action against a suspect.

Reasonable suspicion is based on the totality of the circumstances and exists when a person is suspected of imminent illegal behavior or has previously broken the law.[2] It is the basis for an investigatory or *Terry stop* (discussed later in the chapter) and requires less evidence than *probable cause*, the legal requirement for arrests and warrants. Reasonable suspicion is evaluated using the "reasonable person" or "reasonable officer" standard. Under this standard, one must ask whether under the circumstances a reasonable officer could believe that a person has been, is, or is about to be, engaged in criminal activity. Such suspicion must be more than a mere hunch. On the basis of a reasonable suspicion for their safety, officers may frisk suspects for weapons; however, on this basis alone, officers do not have the attendant right to search a suspect for contraband. Importantly, a compilation of particular facts, even if each is individually innocuous, may form the basis for an officer's reasonable suspicion.

In contrast to reasonable suspicion, **probable cause** requires that officers have a reasonable ground for "belief of *guilt*." Importantly, "[t]he probable cause standard is incapable of precise definition or quantification into percentages because it deals with probabilities and depends on the totality of the circumstances."[3] Nevertheless, it is important to keep in mind that the probable cause standard is a "practical, nontechnical conception that deals with the factual and practical considerations of everyday life on which reasonable and prudent men, not legal technicians, act."[4] Once probable cause has been established, police may search for additional evidence and seize (take into police custody) objects relating to the crime. Additionally, citizens may be legally seized—held in police **custody** at a crime scene and restricted from leaving.

To comply with the Fourth Amendment's prohibition against unreasonable searches and seizures, police must receive voluntary consent before engaging in a search and seizure of any propery.[5] If permission is not granted by the property owner or other authorized third party, or if police do not request such permission, they must obtain a **search warrant**—a written order that grants permission for search and seizure, outlines the specific location of a certain property or person(s) relating to a crime, and requires that police account for the results of their search to a judicial officer.

To obtain a warrant, police must present to a judicial officer an **affidavit of probable cause**, which is a document that lists evidence regarding a crime and asserts there is additional evidence of that crime in a certain location that needs to be searched. The affidavit of probable cause does not have to include evidence against a suspect. For example, an officer may be investigating a homicide and looking for a murder weapon in a certain location, yet have no suspect. The officer would need a search warrant for the weapon but would not have to present evidence against a particular suspect. When deciding whether a search warrant should be issued, the judicial officer evaluates all of the available information. Indeed, in accordance with the **totality-of-the-circumstances rule**, the judicial officer makes a judgment based on all information outlined in the affidavit and, then based on this evidence, determines whether there is a good probability that the police will find what they are looking for at the proposed location.

The Exclusionary Rule

The **exclusionary rule** prohibits the introduction of illegally obtained evidence, including confessions, into a criminal trial. The U.S. Supreme Court formally established the exclusionary rule in 1914 in ***Weeks v. United States***.[6] The Court's ruling in *Weeks* had a monumental impact on the rules governing the admissibility of illegally obtained evidence. However, *Weeks'* impact was limited to federal officers. That is, its ruling did not extend to the practices of state or municipal officers.

A consequence of this limitation was the development of the **silver platter doctrine**. Pursuant to this idea, state officers would hand over "on a silver platter" illegally obtained evidence that could then be used in federal trials, so long as federal agents had no role in obtaining the evidence. The Supreme Court put an end to this practice in 1960 in *Elkins v. United States*.[7] Thus federal officers may no longer rely on state officers to do their "dirty work."

Although *Elkins* ended the silver platter doctrine, it was not until 1961, in ***Mapp v. Ohio***, that the Court extended the exclusionary rule to the states.[8] Nevertheless, since *Mapp*, the Court has recognized several exceptions to the exclusionary rule. In 1965, the Court held that *Mapp* did not apply retroactively—in other words, the decision could not be used to throw out previously decided cases.[9] In 1984, the Court ruled in *Nix v. Williams* that evidence obtained illegally, but that would have eventually been discovered during the course of a normal investigation by lawful means, is admissible. This exception is known as the **inevitable discovery rule**.[10] In addition to the inevitable discovery rule, in 1984 the Court established the **good faith exception** in ***United States v. Leon***. The good faith exception allows evidence collected illegally to be admitted at trial if the police had good reason to believe that their actions were legal.[11] In 2006, in *Hudson v. Michigan*, the Supreme Court decided that the exclusionary rule did not apply to violations of the **knock-and-announce rule**. The knock-and-announce rule required that police announce their presence and wait about 20 seconds before entering a home.

FOCUS ON CRIMINAL JUSTICE

Mapp v. Ohio

On May 23, 1957, three police officers arrived at the residence of Dollree Mapp, having received information that a suspect in a recent bombing would be found at her home. The police were also told by an informant that Mapp was concealing a large amount of gambling paraphernalia. The officers knocked on Mapp's door and demanded they be allowed in the home, but Mapp, after telephoning her attorney, refused to admit the officers without a search warrant. The officers advised their headquarters of the situation and undertook surveillance of the home.

Three hours later, the officers again sought entrance into Mapp's home. When Mapp did not come to the door immediately, the police forcibly opened the door and entered. Mapp demanded to see the search warrant, and an officer held up a piece of paper that he claimed to be a warrant. Mapp grabbed the paper and placed it in her bosom. A struggle ensued in which the officers recovered the piece of paper and handcuffed Mapp, claiming she had resisted their official rescue of the "warrant" from her person. Thereafter, the officers forcibly took Mapp upstairs to her bedroom while they thoroughly searched Mapp's home and personal belongings.

Police found neither the bombing suspect nor the gambling paraphernalia, but they did find some pornographic materials, which were illegal under Ohio law at that time. Based on this evidence, the officers arrested Mapp and charged her with possessing "lewd and lascivious books, pictures, and photographs." At trial, the prosecution did not produce a search warrant, nor was the failure to produce one ever explained or accounted for. The trial court determined that there was "considerable doubt as to whether there ever was any warrant for the search of [Mapp's] home." In spite of this doubt, Mapp was convicted.

On appeal, the U.S. Supreme Court held that in conducting such a search, police violated Mapp's rights under the Fourth Amendment. Perhaps most importantly, the Supreme Court's ruling extended the application of the exclusionary rule to state criminal cases and therefore held that any evidence found during the illegal search was inadmissible.

Source: Mapp v. Ohio, 367 U.S. 643 (1961).

After the Court's decision in *Hudson*, any evidence police obtain in violation of this rule has been determined to be admissible at trial.[12] Finally, in 2008, the U.S. Supreme Court ruled that evidence seized in a police search that violates state law is admissible at trial if the search was "reasonable" under the Constitution.[13]

In 2006, the Supreme Court held in *Hudson v. Michigan* that no-knock searches of homes were constitutional.

"One Arm's Length" Rule

When the police make an arrest, they are permitted, without a warrant, to search the suspect as well as the immediate area (colloquially referred to as "one arm's length") that the suspect occupies. This rule places limits on warrantless searches while ensuring officer safety.

The "one arm's length" rule was established in 1969 in ***Chimel v. California***.[14] In *Chimel*, three police officers arrived at the home of Ted Chimel in Santa Ana, California, with a warrant for his arrest in connection with the burglary of a coin shop. Police knocked on the door, identified themselves to Chimel's wife, and asked if they could come inside. She let the officers in, where they waited for Chimel to return from work. When Chimel entered the house, one of the officers handed him the arrest warrant and asked if he could look around. Chimel refused, but the officers nevertheless searched the premises without permission or a search warrant. During their search, the officers seized numerous items, including some coins that were admitted as evidence in Chimel's trial and led to his conviction.

Headline Crime

Virginia v. Moore (2008)

In a unanimous opinion, the U.S. Supreme Court held that evidence seized in a police search that violates state law may be admissible at trial if the search was reasonable under the Constitution. Specifically, in *Virginia v. Moore* the Court reversed a ruling of the Virginia Supreme Court that threw out the conviction against David Lee Moore. Police had arrested Moore for driving with a suspended license, rather than issuing a summons, which is required for such an offense under Virginia law. A search incident to Moore's arrest yielded a quantity of crack cocaine, and Moore was subsequently tried on drug charges. Moore moved to suppress the evidence obtained during the search incident to his arrest on the grounds that because his arrest violated Virginia law, the subsequent search violated his Fourth Amendment rights. The trial denied Moore's motion to suppress, and Moore was convicted.

The case eventually reached the Virginia Supreme Court, which ruled the opposite way: Because the officers violated Virginia law when they arrested Moore, the search incident to Moore's arrest violated the Fourth Amendment. The U.S. Supreme Court disagreed. According to the Court, police *did not* violate the Fourth Amendment when they made the arrest because, although the arrest may have violated state law, it was nevertheless based on probable cause. Importantly, the Court concluded that whenever an arrest is based on probable cause, it is sufficient for Fourth Amendment purposes even if that arrest violated state law. The Court reasoned that reaching the opposite conclusion would have the effect of causing the Fourth Amendment to needlessly differ from state to state.

Sources: Virginia v. Moore, U.S. 553 U.S. --- (2008); "High Court Ruling Backs Police Searches," *USA Today,* April 24, 2008, p. 3A.

On appeal, the Supreme Court reversed Chimel's conviction, ruling that the officers' search was unconstitutional. Justice Stewart explained, "[w]hen an arrest is made, it is reasonable for the arresting officer to search the person arrested in order to remove any weapons that the latter might seek to use in order to resist arrest or affect his escape. Otherwise, the officer's safety might well be endangered, and the arrest itself frustrated. In addition, it is entirely reasonable for the arresting officer to search for and seize any evidence on the arrestee's person in order to prevent its concealment or destruction. And the area into which an arrestee might reach in order to grab a weapon or evidentiary items must, of course, be governed by a like rule."[15]

Under a *Terry Stop,* if a police officer has reasonable suspicion that the suspect has committed a crime, the officer may frisk the suspect for weapons. Searches must comply with the Fourth Amendment requirements.

In 1981, in the case of *New York v. Belton*, the Court applied *Chimel* in the context of automobile searches.[16] According to the Court, because articles "inside the relatively narrow compass of the passenger compartment of an automobile are in fact generally, even if not inevitably, within the area into which an arrestee might reach in order to grab a weapon or evidentiary item," when an officer "has made a lawful custodial arrest of the occupant of an automobile, he may, as a contemporaneous incident of that arrest, search the passenger compartment of that automobile [and] may also examine the contents of any containers found within the passenger compartment." This holding was reaffirmed by the Court in 2004 in *Thornton v. United States*, as the Court recognized the "need for a clear rule, readily understood by police officers and not depending on differing estimates of what items were or were not within reach of an arrestee at any particular moment."[17]

Stop and Frisk

In 1968, in ***Terry v. Ohio***, the Supreme Court considered what constitutes a legal stop by a police officer.[18] In considering this issue, the Court concluded that for a stop to be legal, it must be based on an officer's reasonable suspicion that the individual being stopped has committed, is committing, or is about to commit a crime.

Headline Crime — Must You Tell the Police Your Name?

Do you have to tell the police your name? The simple answer is *yes*. The U.S. Supreme Court answered this question in *Hiibel v. Sixth Judicial District Court of Nevada*. The officer had been called to the scene by a bystander who observed the driver of a pick-up truck hitting a female passenger. Patrol deputy Lee Dove asked the driver several times to identify himself, but he remained silent. Officer Dove then arrested the driver, placed him in handcuffs, and brought him to jail. At trial, Officer Dove testified that because the defendant, now identified as Hiibel, had possibly committed a crime (assaulting the female passenger), he made an arrest. Hiibel was convicted of resisting a police officer.

Hiibel appealed his conviction on the grounds that the Nevada statute requiring someone stopped under reasonable suspicion by a law enforcement to identify him or herself violates the Fourth Amendment of the U.S. Constitution. In a 4–3 opinion, the state court ruled that it is constitutional to arrest a person for exercising his or her right to remain silent by refusing to identify him or herself to a law enforcement officer. The Supreme Court of Nevada upheld the statute, arguing that any intrusion on privacy caused by the statute was outweighed by the benefits to officers and community safety, as well as the public interest in requiring individuals to identify themselves to officers when reasonable suspicion existing is overwhelming. The case was then appealed to the U.S. Supreme Court. In a 7–2 vote, the Court also upheld the statute and affirmed Hiibel's conviction.

Sources: Hiibel v. Sixth Judicial District Court of Nevada, 542 U.S. 177; "Do You Have to Tell Police Your Name? Supreme Court Will Decide," *USA Today*, March 22, 2004, available at http://www.usatoday.com/news/washington/2004-03-22-scotus-police x.htm, accessed August 7, 2008.

If an officer observes behavior that leads him or her to conclude that criminal activity may be in progress and that the suspect is armed and dangerous, the officer may stop, frisk, and question the suspect after identifying him- or herself as a police officer. If, in doing so, the officer has reasonable fear for his or her own safety or that of others, the Supreme Court has ruled that the officer may conduct a "carefully limited search of the outer clothing of such persons in an attempt to discover weapons . . . Such a search is a reasonable search under the Fourth Amendment, and any weapons seized may properly be introduced in evidence against the person from whom they were taken."[19]

The **stop-and-frisk rule**, however, does not apply in all cases. Before frisking a suspect, police must first establish "reasonable suspicion" to justify an investigative search and seizure. These suspicions should be established by considering the totality of the circumstances.[20] An airport narcotics agent, for instance, may identify drug couriers by considering the presence or absence of the following characteristics:

- Whether the suspect traveled from a source city of drugs
- Whether the suspect carried little or no baggage
- Whether the suspect appeared nervous
- Whether the suspect purchased his or her airline ticket with cash
- Whether the suspect made telephone calls at the airport[21]

Importantly, even when police lack reasonable suspicion, they may engage a person in conversation and ask questions, as long as the person feels free to leave.[22]

Motor Vehicle Searches

Police may conduct a warrantless search of a motor vehicle as long as they have established probable cause to believe it is involved in illegal activity. The landmark decision

The Carroll doctrine permits the police to search vehicles without warrants as long as they have probable cause.

governing motor vehicle searches was handed down in 1925, during the Prohibition era, in *Carroll v. United States*.[23] George Carroll, a well-known bootlegger, was stopped by officers, who searched his car and discovered alcohol. Pursuant to this discovery, Carroll was arrested and convicted of transporting liquor for sale, a violation of federal law and the Eighteenth Amendment. Because the liquor had been seized by federal agents acting without a search warrant, Carroll appealed his conviction to the Supreme Court. The Court upheld Carroll's conviction. The Court's ruling established the **Carroll doctrine**, which permits the warrantless search of vehicles whenever police have probable cause for assuming the vehicle is involved in illegal activities.

How exhaustive such a search may be has evolved through a series of related cases:

- *United States v. Ross* (1982): Police may search "every part of a vehicle that might contain the object of the search" if they have probable cause.[24]
- *California v. Acevedo* (1991): Police may search "an automobile and *any container* found within it when they have probable cause to believe contraband or evidence will be found."[25]
- *Illinois v. Caballes* (2005): Police may use a drug-sniffing dog around the outside of a vehicle during a routine traffic stop, even when police have no grounds on which to suspect illegal activity.[26] However, once the dog indicates the likely presence of drugs, then the officer has probable cause to search further.

In *Delaware v. Prouse* (1976), the Court ruled that police may not randomly stop vehicles.[27] However, an exception to this rule is roadside sobriety checkpoints, which the Court held are constitutional in *Michigan Department of State Police v. Sitz* (1990).[28] The Court based this decision on the fact that such stops represent only a minor intrusion that is easily counterbalanced by the public interest.

Plain View Doctrine

The **plain view doctrine**, which was established in the 1968 case of *Harris v. United States*, states that when police inadvertently discover evidence (such as contraband, stolen property, or weapons) in a place where they have a legal right to be, they have a right to seize it.[29] However, the U.S. Supreme Court has also ruled that when police lack probable cause, they may not move an object to gain a better view of things that might otherwise remain hidden.

Open Field Searches

Open field searches are becoming increasingly popular and have played an important role in the government's war on drugs. The issue raised in open field searches is whether police should be allowed to fly over or enter private land without a search warrant and seize illegal substances, such as marijuana plants. The Supreme Court has ruled repeatedly that such searches are legal in *Hester v. United States* (1924), *Oliver v. United States* (1984), and *Florida v. Riley* (1989).[30]

The warrantless search of open fields is permissible and serves as a police tool in the war on drugs.

Consent Searches

Police may conduct a warrantless search if consent is given voluntarily and the person giving the consent has the legal ability to do so—for instance, if he or she is the owner of the property to be searched. However, someone cannot voluntarily give police permission to search their neighbor's property. When acting pursuant to a **consent search**, police have no constitutional obligation to inform the suspect that he or she may deny them permission to engage in the search.[31] However, when voluntary consent is obtained through deception, the evidence police seize during the search will not be admissible in court.

Florida v. Bostick (1991)

In *Florida v. Bostick*, the Court ruled that police may board buses, trains, and planes and ask passengers to consent to being searched, without a warrant or probable cause.[32] In the case, two armed officers, wearing their badges and insignia, boarded a bus bound for Atlanta during a stopover in Fort Lauderdale. Once on board, and without reason for suspicion, the officers randomly selected Terrance Bostick and asked to inspect his ticket and identification. Bostick complied, and the officers found nothing unusual about his papers. They then told Bostick they were narcotics officers who were in search of illegal drugs. They asked Bostick if they could search his luggage. Police found one pound of cocaine, and Bostick was arrested and charged with drug trafficking.

At Bostick's trial, his attorney moved to suppress the cocaine as evidence on the ground that it had been obtained by an illegal seizure, thus violating Bostick's Fourth Amendment rights. The trial court denied the motion, and Bostick was convicted. The case eventually reached the U.S. Supreme Court, which held that in evaluating the "whole picture" (totality of the circumstances), Bostick had not been "seized" at the time he voluntarily consented to the search and, therefore, the evidence had not been illegally obtained.

Georgia v. Randolph (2006)

In *Georgia v. Randolph*, the Supreme Court ruled that police may not enter a home to conduct a search if one resident gives permission but another resident who is present does not.[33] In this case, Janet Randolph called police to report a domestic disturbance and asked police to come to the home she shared with her husband, Scott Randolph. Upon their arrival, police asked the couple if they could search the home. Scott objected, but Janet consented. She then led police to their bedroom, where cocaine was found. Police used the cocaine to charge Scott with drug possession. While the Supreme Court had previously ruled that cohabitants were allowed to give consent to search, in *Randolph* it held that this decision did not apply if another cohabitant was present and objected, except when there is evidence of abuse or other circumstances that may require immediate entry by police.[34]

Abandoned Property Searches

The Supreme Court has consistently held that police can conduct warrantless searches of **abandoned property**, which is property that is intentionally left behind or placed in a situation in which others may reasonably take it into their possession. For example, in *California v. Greenwood*,[35] the Court ruled that garbage disposed of in a public place where others might have access to it constitutes abandoned property. Specifically, in this case, a police officer received information that Billy Greenwood was selling illegal drugs. The officer acted on the tip by conducting surveillance of Greenwood's home, during which she observed behavior consistent with drug trafficking. The officer then asked Greenwood's regular trash collector to pick up the plastic garbage bags that Greenwood had left on the curb in front of his house and give the bags to her without mixing their contents with garbage from the other homes. After receiving the garbage bags, the officer searched them and found items suggesting narcotics use. Thereafter, the officer applied for and received a warrant to search Greenwood's residence, where she found cocaine and hashish.

At trial, the lower court dismissed the charges against Greenwood, asserting that the warrantless search of Greenwood's garbage violated his right to privacy under the Fourth Amendment. The Supreme Court, however, reversed this decision and charges were reinstated.[36] In short, the Court held that because Greenwood left his garbage in a public place, he had no reasonable expectation of privacy. However, had Greenwood placed his garbage on his back porch, then legally he still would have an expectation of privacy, even though the garbage was outside of his home.

Border Searches

Individuals entering the United States have been subject to warrantless searches for many years. Such searches are designed to seize illegal drugs and control illegal immigration. The Supreme Court has historically placed limits on border searches by prohibiting border agents from stopping motor vehicles for the sole purpose of seizing illegal aliens.[37] In recent decades, however, increased public concern over the number of illegal immigrants entering the United States has influenced Court rulings. For instance, in *United States v. Martinez-Fuerte* (1976), the Court held that police did not need probable cause to stop cars and to question passengers at fixed checkpoints.[38]

Electronic Surveillance

In 1928, the U.S. Supreme Court in *Olmstead v. United States* ruled that electronic eavesdropping did not constitute a violation of an individual's constitutional rights. The *Olmstead* decision was severely criticized by civil libertarians, and Congress responded by passing the Federal Communications Act in 1934. This Act declared that no person who is not authorized by the sender shall intercept any communication, or divulge or publish the existence, contents, substance, purpose, effect, or meaning of such intercepted communication to any person.[39]

Further restrictions were placed on wiretapping in 1967. In *Katz v. United States*, federal agents believed that the defendant, Charles Katz, was using a pay phone to transmit gambling information.[40] The agents placed a listening device outside a public telephone booth and secured information sufficient to convict Katz. The Supreme Court later overturned Katz's conviction on the ground that the Fourth Amendment protects people's privacy, regardless of the place of their offense. The ruling in *Katz*, however, did not entirely prohibit electronic surveillance.

In 1968, Congress passed the Omnibus Crime Control and Safe Streets Act, which included a provision on electronic surveillance. The Act established that the federal use of wiretaps and other electronic eavesdropping equipment is legal, so long as officers have previously obtained a warrant.

U.S. Border Patrol officers do not need probable cause to stop cars and question passengers at fixed checkpoints, such as border crossings.

Kyllo v. United States (2001) tested the legality of this Act.[41] Police believed that Danny Kyllo was growing marijuana in his home and used a thermal imaging device to scan the area. The scan revealed that the roof and sidewall of Kyllo's garage were hotter than normal, which police suspected was due to the presence of the high-intensity lighting required to grow marijuana indoors. Police requested and received a warrant to search Kyllo's home. During this search, they found marijuana and arrested Kyllo on federal drug charges. Kyllo unsuccessfully moved to suppress the evidence and eventually appealed his conviction to the U.S. Supreme Court. The Court ruled that such surveillance by the government—even without physical intrusion—qualifies as an unreasonable search under the Fourth Amendment and requires a warrant.

As a side note, states may also utilize electronic surveillance. The Omnibus Crime Control and Safe Streets Act regulates the action of only federal agencies. All states have their own electronic surveillance laws that control state and local law enforcement agencies' use of electronic surveillance. Nevertheless, any such actions may still be subject to Fourth Amendment challenges.

Headline Crime — Tracking Cell Phones

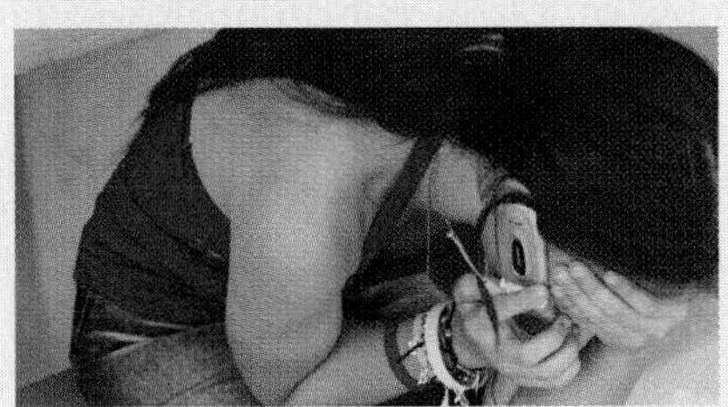

An emerging issue related to electronic surveillance in the United States (and throughout the world) is whether the government, without probable cause, may track suspects using cell phones. On several occasions, U.S. courts have received requests from the U.S. Department of Justice (DOJ) for permission to track suspects without showing probable cause. In all but one instance, judges have denied the DOJ's motions, stating that the government did not have the authority to track cell phone locations without a warrant. In a recent case dealing with this issue, Judge Gabriel Gorenstein of the U.S. District Court for the Southern District of New York ruled in the government's favor, stating that the USA Patriot Act and the 1986 Electronic Communications Privacy Act permitted such tracking. According to Judge Gorenstein, a cell phone user who chooses to voluntarily transmit a signal to a cell phone provider assumes the risk that the provider may reveal cell-site information to police.

Cell phone tracking is a source of significant controversy. On the one hand, proponents of tracking view it as an effective tool for law enforcement, because it saves police significant time when searching for a suspect by allowing them to rely on cell phone technology to determine a suspect's general whereabouts. On the other hand, critics contend that the practice of real-time tracking constitutes a violation of the Fourth Amendment.

The issue of whether police may use cell phones to track criminal suspects has yet to be ultimately resolved. At some point, the government will undoubtedly present evidence in a criminal trial obtained through cell phone tracking without having shown probable cause. No doubt, the defendant will challenge the admissibility of such evidence. When this happens, not only may the case reach the Supreme Court, but it may also place increased pressure on Congress to revisit and redefine current wiretapping statutes.

Sources: Teresa Baldas, "Feds' Cell Phone Tracking Divides the Courts," *The National Law Journal*, January 19, 2006, pp. 1–3; Matt Richtell, "Live Tracking of Mobile Phones Prompts Court Fights on Privacy," *The New York Times*, December 10, 2005, pp. A1–A2; Daniel Wise, "U.S. Wind Bid to Collect Cell Tower Location Data," *New York Law Journal*, December 23, 2005, available at http://www.law.com/jsp/article.jsp?id=1135245911048, accessed August 7, 2008; Gorenstein Opinion, 405 F.Supp. 2d 435 (2005).

Arrest

Once police have either established probable cause or directly observed a crime, they may make an arrest. An **arrest** occurs when police physically take a suspect into custody based on the belief that the suspect has committed a criminal offense.

Arrest Warrant

When police have established probable cause to make an arrest, but not yet taken the suspect into custody, they apply to a judicial officer for an **arrest warrant**. An arrest warrant is a written court order instructing the police to arrest a specific person for a specific crime. It will be granted if the police can demonstrate probable cause. A faulty arrest warrant, however, can create issues of legal liability.

Police Liability

When applying for an arrest warrant, police must be certain that the affidavit establishes probable cause. If it does not, the arresting officer may be held civilly liable if an arrest is made without probable cause. If a plaintiff pursues such a case against an officer, the plaintiff has the burden to prove the officer deprived him or her of a constitutional right. Police officers involved in such cases often rely on a good faith defense, which stems from the Supreme Court's decision in *United States v. Leon*.[42] To invoke the good faith defense, the accused officer must prove the following:

- The officer believed in good faith that his or her actions were lawful
- The officer believed the legality of his or her conduct was reasonable when measured against some objective standard

In more extreme cases, police officers may be held *criminally liable* for such violations if the prosecution proves that the officer willfully violated an individual's constitutional rights.[43] Police officers have only limited immunity from civil and criminal prosecution, so they must be informed about constitutional rights and the decisions interpreting them.[44]

Judicial Liability

In contrast to police officers, who have only limited immunity from civil actions and criminal prosecutions, judicial officers have absolute immunity because they must rely on the information given to them—and that information can sometimes be faulty.[45] If a judge or magistrate signs a search warrant when no probable cause exists, the trial judge will in all likelihood determine the arrest was invalid and dismiss the case. However, the defendant cannot file a civil suit against the judge who originally issued the search warrant.

Warrantless Arrests

Most arrests that police make are without a warrant. Indeed, they often make decisions to arrest on the scene during their interactions with suspects. Police may make a **warrantless arrest** in the following circumstances:

- Police observe a felony in progress
- Police have knowledge that a felony has been committed and have probable cause to believe that the crime was committed by a particular suspect
- The law of the particular jurisdiction permits police to make arrests without warrants[46]

In general, police do not need to delay an arrest because they lack a warrant.[47] If warrants were always required before an arrest could be made, many suspects would escape while a warrant was being secured. However, pursuant to most state laws, officers may not make a warrantless arrest for a misdemeanor offense unless it is committed in their presence, a limitation known as the **in-presence requirement**.

One exception to the ability of officers to make warrantless arrests occurs when officers want to enter a suspect's home. In *Payton v. New York* (1980), the Supreme Court held that an arrest warrant is a prerequisite to valid entry into a home in all nonemergency situations.[48] Whether a "situation" constitutes an emergency is determined by the seriousness of the offense. For instance, in *Minnesota v. Olson* (1990), the Court ruled that police acted properly when they entered the home of a fleeing armed robber and executed an arrest.[49]

Miranda Warning

Technically speaking, when suspects are arrested, with or without a warrant, police do not have to give them the ***Miranda*** **warning**. There are two legal triggers to informing someone of their constitutional rights under *Miranda*. One is that the person is in *physical custody*—that is, feels that he or she does not have the right to disengage from the officer (e.g., is unable to leave the scene). The second is *interrogation*. Legally persons could be arrested and never informed of their *Miranda* rights if they were not going to be interrogated.

In 1966, in its ruling in ***Miranda v. Arizona***, the U.S. Supreme Court ordered that police create an environment that would produce only *voluntary* confessions. The result of this case—the *Miranda* warning—is well known:

> You have the right to remain silent; anything you say can and will be used against you in a court of law. You have the right to the presence of an attorney; if you cannot afford an attorney, one will be appointed for you prior to any questioning.[50]

This decision came as a result of a case involving an assault against Patricia Ann Weir, who was then age 18. In 1963, Weir was walking to a bus in downtown Phoenix, Arizona, when she was abducted by a man who shoved her into his car, tied her hands and ankles, drove her to a location somewhere outside the city, and raped her.[51] Weir was then driven to a street near her home and let out of the car. Immediately afterward, Weir called the police to report the crime.

Ernesto Miranda abducted Patricia Ann Weir, kidnapped, and raped her. The police who arrested and interrogated Miranda did not advise him of his right to counsel during questioning. The U.S. Supreme Court ruled that police had violated Miranda's Fifth and Sixth Amendment rights.

Shortly after the incident, police arrested Ernesto Miranda, who voluntarily agreed to speak with police about the incident and willingly participated in a line-up in which Weir identified him as the man who raped her. Miranda, age 23, was an eighth-grade dropout who had a police record dating back nearly a decade. He had been previously diagnosed by psychiatrists as being seriously mentally disabled and having pronounced sexual fantasies. Police asked Miranda to write a confession, which he did, stating he was guilty, describing his crime, acknowledging that his confession was voluntary, and agreed that he had full knowledge of his legal rights. Police then charged Miranda with kidnapping and rape.

At trial, Miranda's court-appointed attorney, Alvin Moore, questioned the officers at length about their interrogation. The officers admitted that during the two-hour interrogation, neither of them had advised Miranda of his right to have counsel present during questioning (a right that had been established two years earlier in *Escobedo v. Illinois*).[52] Additionally, during interrogation and prior to the line-up, two officers misled Miranda when they told him that Weir had already identified him as her attacker.

In spite of these violations, and over Moore's objection, the trial judge ruled that Miranda's written confession could be admitted into evidence. Miranda was found guilty and sentenced to 20–30 years in prison for his crime. The Arizona Supreme Court upheld Miranda's conviction. Eventually, the case reached the U.S. Supreme Court, where Miranda's new attorney, John Flynn, argued that Miranda had been manipulated into confessing as a result of his poor education and lack of knowledge regarding his rights.

On June 13, 1966, the Supreme Court announced its decision. In a narrow 5-to-4 ruling, Chief Justice Earl Warren, writing for the majority, asserted that officers had violated Miranda's Fifth Amendment right to protection from self-incrimination and his Sixth Amendment right to counsel. Today, as a result of this decision, police are required to give a person who is taken into custody a *Miranda* warning if they wish to question the person and use the person's answers as evidence at trial.

Although the Supreme Court overturned Miranda's conviction, it did not nullify the indictment that had been brought against him. Instead, in 1967, Miranda was retried, and again found guilty of raping and kidnapping Weir after his common-law wife, Twila Hoffman, testified that Miranda had confessed to her that he had committed the crimes.[53] Miranda was sentenced to 11 years in prison and was paroled after serving one-third of his sentence. (In a twist of fate, four years after being paroled, Miranda was stabbed to death in a bar fight; when his assailant was arrested, police officers read him his *Miranda* rights.[54])

While some experts hailed the *Miranda* decision as long overdue, others criticized it. For instance, Justice John Marshall Harlan dissented from the majority opinion, denouncing it as "dangerous experimentation" at a time when the "high crime rate is of growing concern."[55] Similarly, the reaction of the police to the *Miranda* outcome was generally negative. Most officers thought the ruling would interfere with their efforts to protect society, believing that if suspects were informed of their rights, they would not confess.

In *Miranda*, the Court noted that, in addition to informing suspects of their constitutional rights, police may not use interrogation procedures that intimidate the suspect. The Court defined custodial interrogation as any "questioning initiated by law enforcement officers after a person has been taken into custody" and established procedural safeguards for its conduct:

> Prior to any questioning, the person must be warned that he has the right to remain silent, that any statement he does make may be used as evidence against him, and that he has a right to the presence of an attorney, either retained or appointed. The defendant may waive effectuation of these rights, provided the waiver is made voluntarily, knowingly, and intelligently. If, however, he indicates in any manner and at any stage of the process that he wishes to consult with an attorney before speaking, there can be no questioning. Likewise, if the individual is alone and indicates in any manner that he does not wish to be interrogated, the police may not question him. The mere fact that he may have answered some questions on his own does not deprive him of the right to refrain from answering any further inquiries until he has consulted with an attorney and thereafter consents to be questioned.[56]

This statement formed the basis for the *Miranda* warning, but several subsequent cases have more clearly defined its parameters.

Brewer v. Williams (1977)

Ten-year-old Pamela Powers was abducted, raped, and strangled on Christmas Eve, 1968, in Des Moines, Iowa.[57] Two days later, Robert Williams surrendered to police in Davenport, Iowa, in relation to the crime. Police booked Williams and read him the required *Miranda* warning.

Thereafter, the Davenport police telephoned their counterparts in Des Moines to inform them that Williams had surrendered and was in custody. Williams' attorney was at the Des Moines police headquarters when Williams called and spoke with him on the telephone. In the presence of the Des Moines chief of police and Detective Leaming, the attorney advised Williams that Des Moines police officers would drive to Davenport to pick him up, that the officers would not interrogate him, and that Williams was not to talk to the officers about Pamela Powers until after consulting with his lawyer.

While transporting Williams from Davenport to Des Moines, a detective appealed to Williams' religious inclinations. The detective noted that Williams was the only person who knew where the body was buried, stated that they would be driving right by the area where she was last seen, and asked if they could stop and locate the body because "the parents of this little girl should be entitled to a Christian burial." Soon after the detective finished the speech, Williams directed the officers to where he had buried the body.

Williams was indicted and convicted of first-degree murder. The U.S. Supreme Court, however, eventually overturned his conviction on three grounds:

1. The detectives' questioning of Williams was improper because Williams' attorney was not present
2. The officers used psychological coercion
3. The detectives were explicitly instructed not to interrogate Williams without his attorney present

Edwards v. Arizona (1981)

On January 19, 1976, Robert Edwards was arrested and charged with robbery, burglary, and first-degree murder. Upon his arrest, he was informed of his *Miranda* rights. Nevertheless, Edwards indicated he was willing to talk with the police, so he was questioned until he said he wanted an attorney. The next day, detectives came to the jail and said they wanted to again speak with Edwards. The officers again informed him of his *Miranda* rights and subsequently obtained a confession.

At trial, Edwards' attorney moved to suppress Edwards's confession. The motion was denied, and Edwards was convicted. The case eventually reached the U.S. Supreme Court, which held that once an accused individual has invoked his or her right to have counsel present during custodial interrogation, a valid waiver of that right cannot be established by showing only that the suspect responded to police-initiated interrogation after being again advised of his or her rights. Rather, if at any point a suspect requests the presence of counsel, police cannot resume questioning the suspect until counsel has been made available to the suspect. An exception to this general rule exists if the suspect initiates the communications. In this circumstance, officers may proceed in questioning the suspect.[58]

During questioning, a suspect's request for an attorney must be stated clearly. Officers may continue questioning until a suspect clearly makes a request for an attorney. For example, in *Davis v. United States*, the suspect, Robert Davis, stated to investigators, "Maybe I should talk to a lawyer." At that point, the investigators asked Davis outright whether he wanted a lawyer. Davis replied, "No, I'm not asking for a lawyer," and the interrogation continued. The court ruled that based on these facts, Davis' rights were not violated, as police are not required to seek clarification of ambiguous statements.[59]

New York v. Quarles (1984)

In *New York v. Quarles*, the Supreme Court established a public safety exception to *Miranda*.[60] In this case, the police officers pursued a rape suspect after being notified of the crime by the alleged victim. They found the suspect, Charles Quarles, in a supermarket, frisked him, and found an empty shoulder holster. Upon seeing the empty holster, an officer asked Quarles, prior to reading him his *Miranda* rights, where his gun was. After Quarles responded, the officer formally arrested Quarles and then read him his *Miranda* rights. When the case reached the Supreme Court, the Court focused on whether Quarles' statement about the gun should be suppressed because the officer had not yet read Quarles his *Miranda* rights. The Court ruled that the statement should not be suppressed, as based on the fact that there was a "public safety" exception to the requirement that officers read Quarles his *Miranda* rights. Accordingly, no constitutional violation had occurred.

Arizona v. Roberson (1988)

Are self-incriminating statements admissible if a suspect makes them while being interrogated a second time about an unrelated offense? Ronald Roberson was arrested at the scene of a burglary and, after being advised of his *Miranda* rights, requested counsel. Three days later, when Roberson was still in custody and still had not spoken with an attorney, a second police officer, who was unaware that Roberson had previously requested assistance of counsel, advised Roberson of his *Miranda* rights and asked him about a second burglary. During that round of questioning, Roberson made incriminating statements about both crimes.

At trial, citing the Court's ruling in *Edwards v. Arizona* (discussed earlier in this section), the trial judge suppressed Roberson's incriminating statements, reasoning that once a suspect has invoked his or her right to counsel, the suspect may not be interrogated a second time unless counsel has been provided to the suspect or the suspect has initiated the conversation. On this basis, the trial judge determined that even though the second instance of questioning regarded a separate, unrelated crime, both sets of confessions should be suppressed because counsel was not present at the time of Roberson's statements.

The photo line-up is a staple of crime dramas and a way to use eyewitness identification.

Eventually the case reached the Supreme Court. The Court affirmed the trial court's decision, reasoning that failure on the part of the police to honor Roberson's initial request could not be justified because another police officer was unaware that Roberson had requested assistance of counsel.[61] The *Roberson* decision was later affirmed in *Minnick v. Mississippi* (1990). In that case, the Supreme Court held that where an accused person had requested and been provided counsel, reinitiation of interrogation in which the accused was compelled to attend without counsel was impermissible.[62] More recently the Supreme Court held in *Dickerson v. United States* that the requirement of a *Miranda* warning is constitutional in nature and, therefore, may not be overruled by a legislative act.[63]

Booking

Once arrested, a suspect is taken to a police station and booked. **Booking** is the process of officially recording the name of the person arrested, the place and time of the arrest, the reason for the arrest, and the name of the arresting authority. The suspect is photographed and fingerprinted, and samples of his or her handwriting, voice, and blood may be taken. After booking, the suspect will be held in police custody until his or her initial appearance before a judicial officer. It is at this time that the charges are read, the suspect is informed of his or her rights, and bail is set.[64]

Line-Ups

After booking, a suspect may be required to participate in a line-up.[65] A **line-up** is a pretrial identification procedure in which several people are shown to a victim or witness of a crime. This individual is then asked whether he or she believes any of the people in the line-up committed the crime. Suspects have a constitutional right to have counsel present during a line-up.[66]

Although police cannot suggest to a victim or witness that one of the people in the line-up is the suspect, they can ask each person in the line-up to speak words that were allegedly spoken at the crime scene.[67] If police suggest to the victim or witness that one of the people in the line-up is the suspect, the suspect's right to due process as guaranteed by the Fifth and Fourteenth Amendments has been violated.

Thus it is important that during a line-up, the police do not say or do anything that might lead or encourage the victim or witness to identify the suspect.

Interrogation and Confession

Interrogation is the stage in the pretrial process when police ask the suspect questions to obtain information the suspect might not otherwise willingly disclose. An interrogation can take place anywhere and at any time, before arrest or after arrest, before booking or after booking. It is not unusual for an interrogation to take place before the suspect is placed in a line-up, and the interrogation may continue until well after a line-up is conducted. During the course of an interrogation, officers may obtain a confession. A **confession** is a voluntary declaration by someone who has committed a crime in which that person admits his or her involvement in the offense.

Interrogations may be emotionally charged, and police may become upset during the course of such events. In the past, police sometimes used physical force to extract a confession. Today, if force is used to obtain a confession, the confession will be suppressed.[68]

Over one hundred years ago, in 1884, the Supreme Court established the parameters for an **involuntary confession** in ***Hopt v. Utah***. There, the court held that a confession cannot be precipitated by a promise, threat, fear, or torture.[69] The Court's ruling in *Hopt* was limited to the inadmissibility of involuntary confessions at the federal level. Twelve years later, in *Wilson v. United States*, the Supreme Court broadened its *Hopt* decision, asserting that a court must broadly review the circumstances surrounding a confession before deciding whether it was voluntary.[70] As with the *Hopt* decision, however, *Wilson* applied only to federal cases.

In 1936, in ***Brown v. Mississippi***, the Supreme Court extended to the state level its previous holdings regarding involuntary confessions.[71] *Brown* involved three African American men—Yank Ellington, Ed Brown, and Henry Shields—who were arrested for the murder of a white man, Raymond Stewart. The only evidence against the suspects was their confessions, which was enough to convict them and to sustain death sentences. The defendants' case reached the Supreme Court, where their convictions were overturned. The Court ruled that the suspects' confessions had been extorted only after the suspects had endured brutal treatment, which included whipping, and therefore the confessions were inadmissible. *Brown* raised several important questions about the nature and extent of confessions.

What Is a Coerced Confession?

In *Chambers v. Florida*, four males were convicted of murder on the basis of confessions obtained several days after their arrests.[72] The Supreme Court ruled that such a long delay, coupled with constant interrogation, constituted a form of psychological coercion that, in all likelihood, produced involuntary confessions. Since *Chambers*, the Court has consistently ruled that coercion can be either mental or physical.[73] Police cannot, for instance, deliberately make suspects uncomfortable during an interrogation by not letting them sit, rest, or use a toilet. In general, courts determine the admissibility of a confession by examining the totality of the circumstances surrounding the arrest and subsequent interrogation.

Can Delay Constitute Coercion?

In 1943, in *McNabb v. United States*, the Supreme Court ruled there can be no unnecessary delay between arrest and arraignment.[74] In *McNabb*, a confession obtained after almost 36 hours of continuous interrogation was judged to be "inherently coercive" and, therefore, was not allowed to be presented at trial. In 1957, in *Mallory v. United States*, the Court broadened *McNabb* when it reversed the conviction of an alleged rapist who confessed after an 18-hour delay.[75]

In 1968, Congress passed the Omnibus Crime Control and Safe Streets Act, which abolished the *McNabb–Mallory* rule and created a new guideline: The admissibility of a confession will be based on the voluntary nature of the confession, and delay in arraignment will be one factor that will be considered in determining whether the confession was "voluntary."[76]

Do Suspects Have a Right to Counsel During Interrogation?

In the 1963 case of ***Gideon v. Wainwright***, the Supreme Court handed down a far-reaching decision when it ruled that *any* person who is charged with a felony has the right to counsel.[77] The Court expanded this ruling in *Argersinger v. Hamlin*, when it decided

FOCUS ON CRIMINAL JUSTICE

Escobedo v. Illinois (1964)

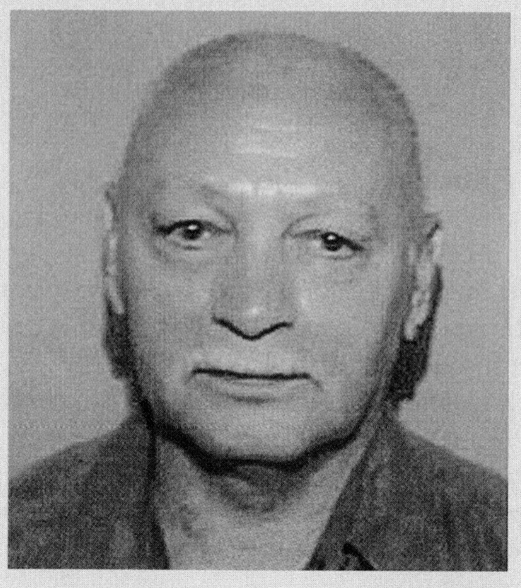

On the night of January 19, 1960, Danny Escobedo's brother-in-law, Manuel Valtierra, was fatally shot. Escobedo was arrested the next morning without a warrant and interrogated by the police. He made no statement and was subsequently released.

On January 30, Benedict DiGerlando, who was then in police custody, told police that Escobedo had fired the fatal shots that killed Valtierra. Escobedo was arrested later that day. While transporting Escobedo to the police station, one of the arresting officers told Escobedo that DiGerlando had named him as the killer. Police also told Escobedo that they had a pretty tight case against him and that he might as well confess. Escobedo replied, "I am sorry, but I would like to have advice from my lawyer."

When Escobedo's attorney, Warren Wolfson, arrived at the police station, police would not let him talk with Escobedo as they continued their interrogation. Throughout the interrogation, Escobedo repeatedly asked to consult with his attorney. Each time, his request was denied. Escobedo eventually confessed, and he was convicted of murder.

Escobedo's case was later reviewed by the Supreme Court. In a 6-to-3 decision, the Court vacated Escobedo's conviction on the ground that the accused must be permitted to consult with attorneys before or during interrogation.

Interestingly, Escobedo was arrested in 2001 outside of Mexico City, Mexico, on a federal probation violation and an Illinois warrant in connection with a 1983 stabbing death. Escobedo had been listed by the U.S. Marshals Service as one of its 15 most-wanted fugitives prior to his arrest.

Sources: Escobedo v. Illinois, 378 U.S. 478 (1964); NationMaster.com, available at http://www.nationmaster.com/encyclopedia/Danny-Escobedo, accessed October 20, 2008.

that accused persons also have the right to counsel in misdemeanor cases if they face the possibility of incarceration.[78]

In *Gideon*, the Court did not explicitly state at what point in the process a suspect becomes entitled to an attorney. Nevertheless, that issue was later decided in 1964 in ***Escobedo v. Illinois***, where the Court ruled that suspects accused of a felony may request that an attorney be present during police interrogation.[79]

WRAPPING IT UP

Chapter Highlights

- Police are expected to investigate crimes according to established procedural laws governing what they may and may not do to produce evidence. These laws are designed to protect suspects from abuses of their constitutional rights.
- Police must have either reasonable suspicion or probable cause before initiating an action against a suspect.
- If police believe a suspect committed a crime, but the suspect is not yet in custody, police must demonstrate probable cause in their application for an arrest warrant from a judicial officer.
- To obtain a search warrant, police must present to a judicial officer an affidavit of probable cause. This document lists evidence regarding a crime and asserts there is additional evidence of the crime that will be found in the location to be searched.
- The exclusionary rule excludes from trial any evidence or confessions that have been unlawfully obtained. It prohibits police from using the fruits of illegal searches and seizures, although exceptions to the rule do exist.
- Once suspects are arrested, they are held in police custody until their first appearance before a judicial officer. At that time, charges are read, they are informed of their rights, and bail is set.
- Suspects have a legal right to have their attorney present during a line-up or interrogation.
- During interrogations, police may not use coercion or any other unlawful means to obtain a confession.

Words to Know

abandoned property Property that is intentionally left behind or placed in a situation where others may reasonably take it into their possession.

affidavit of probable cause A document that lists evidence regarding a crime and asserts there is additional evidence of that crime in a certain location that needs to be searched.

arrest Action where police physically take a suspect into custody on the grounds that there is probable cause to believe the suspect has committed a criminal offense.

arrest warrant A written court order instructing the police to arrest a specific person for a specific crime.

booking The process of officially recording the name of the arrested individual, the place and time of the arrest, the reason for the arrest, and the name of the arresting authority.

Brown v. Mississippi Supreme Court case that established involuntary confessions as inadmissible in state criminal prosecutions.

Carroll doctrine Doctrine that permits the warrantless search of a vehicle whenever police have a reasonable basis for believing the vehicle is involved in a crime.

Chimel v. California Supreme Court case that established the "one arm's length" rule, which allows police without a warrant to search suspects and, to a limited extent, the immediate area they occupy.

confession A voluntary declaration by someone who has committed a crime in which the suspect admits his or her involvement in the offense.

consent search A legal, warrantless search conducted after a person gives expressed consent to police.

custody Assumed legal control of a person or object.

Escobedo v. Illinois Supreme Court case that established suspects accused of felonies may request an attorney during questioning.

exclusionary rule Rule generally prohibiting the introduction of illegally obtained evidence or confessions into a trial.

Gideon v. Wainwright Supreme Court ruling that state courts, under the Sixth Amendment of the Constitution, must provide legal counsel in criminal cases for defendants who cannot afford an attorney.

good faith exception Rule that allows for evidence collected in violation of a suspect's rights under the Fourth Amendment to be admitted at trial if the police had good reason to believe their actions were legal.

Hopt v. Utah Supreme Court case that established guidelines for involuntary confessions.

inevitable discovery rule Rule that if illegally obtained evidence would have eventually been discovered by lawful means, it is admissible regardless of how it was originally discovered.

in-presence requirement Police may not make a warrantless arrest for a misdemeanor offense unless the offense is committed in their presence.

interrogation A method used by police during an interview with a suspect to obtain information the suspect might not otherwise disclose.

involuntary confession A confession precipitated by promise, threat, fear, torture, or another external factor such as mental illness.

knock-and-announce rule Rule that requires police to announce their presence and wait approximately 20 seconds before entering a home.

line-up A pretrial identification procedure where several people are shown to a victim or to a witness of a crime, who is then asked if any of those individuals committed the crime.

Mapp v. Ohio Supreme Court ruling that expanded the exclusionary rule to the states.

Miranda v. Arizona Supreme Court case that ruled criminal suspects must be informed of their right to consult with an attorney and their right against self-incrimination prior to questioning by police.

***Miranda* warning** A warning that police must recite at the time of a suspect's arrest, informing the suspect of his or her constitutional right to remain silent and have an attorney present during questioning.

plain view doctrine Standard that allows police to seize evidence that they discover in places where they have a legal right to be.

probable cause A set of facts and circumstances that would lead a reasonable person to believe that a crime had been committed and that the accused committed it.

reasonable suspicion Arises when a reasonable officer could believe that a person has been, is, or is about to be, engaged in criminal activity.

search warrant A written order instructing police to examine a specific location for certain property or persons relating to a crime, to seize the property or persons if found, and to account for the results of the search to the judicial officer who issued the warrant.

silver platter doctrine Doctrine that permitted state officers to hand over "on a silver platter" evidence that had been illegally obtained for use at federal trials.

stop-and-frisk rule Rule that police may stop, question, and frisk individuals who are engaged in suspicious behavior.

Terry v. Ohio Supreme Court case in which the Court determined that police investigating suspicious behavior could stop, briefly detain, and frisk a person on a street, without having to meet the Fourth Amendment's probable cause requirement.

totality-of-the-circumstances rule Rule that requires a judge to evaluate all available information when deciding whether to issue a search warrant.

United States v. Leon Supreme Court case that established the good faith exception to the exclusionary rule, under which evidence that is produced in good faith and later discovered to be obtained illegally may still be admissible.

warrantless arrest An arrest without a warrant, which may be performed when an officer has probable cause to believe that a felony has been or is being committed.

Weeks v. United States Supreme Court case that applied the exclusionary rule in federal cases.

Think and Discuss

1. Should police be allowed to stop citizens randomly and search for evidence?
2. Are warrantless searches necessary? Are there situations where a warrantless search should be permitted?
3. When should third parties be permitted to give police consent to search the residence of another person? What relationship should exist between the person who gives consent and the suspect?
4. Does the *Miranda* warning impede crime prevention? Why or why not?
5. How does the release of guilty offenders because of legal "technicalities" affect your view of the criminal justice system?

Notes

1. Seth Mydans, "Punitive Damages Denied in Beating of Rodney King," *The New York Times*, June 2, 1994, available at http://query.nytimes.com/gst/fullpage.html?res=980CE5D911BF931A35755CO A962958260, accessed August 6, 2008.
2. *Ornelas v. United States*, 517 U.S. 690 (1996).
3. *Maryland v. Pringle*, 540 U.S. 366 (2003).

4. *Maryland v. Pringle*, note 3; *Ornelas v. United States*, note 2.
5. *Payton v. New York*, 445 U.S. 573 (1980); William Cohen, *Constitutional Law*, 12th ed. (Belmont, CA: Foundation Press, 2005).
6. *Weeks v. United States*, 232 U.S. 383 (1914).
7. *Elkins v. United States*, 364 U.S. 206 (1960).
8. *Mapp v. Ohio*, 367 U.S. 643 (1961).
9. *Linkletter v. Walker*, 381 U.S. 618 (1965).
10. *Nix v. Williams*, 467 U.S. 431 (1984).
11. *United States v. Leon*, 468 U.S. 897 (1984), see also the companion case, *Massachusetts v. Sheppard*, 468 U.S. 981 (1984).
12. *Hudson v. Michigan*, 547 U.S. 1096 (2006).
13. *Virginia v. Moore*, 553 U.S. --- (2008).
14. *Chimel v. California*, 395 U.S. 752 (1969).
15. *Chimel v. California*, note 14.
16. *New York v. Belton*, 453 U.S. 454 (1981).
17. *Thorton v. United States*, 514 U.S. 615 (2004).
18. *Terry v. Ohio*, 392 U.S. 1 (1968).
19. *Terry v. Ohio*, note 18.
20. *United States v. Sokolow*, 490 U.S. 1 (1989).
21. Morgan Cloud, "Search and Seizure by the Numbers," *Boston University Law Review* 65:843–921 (1985); Gerald Robin, "Inquisitive Cops, Investigative Stops, and Drug Courier Hops," *Journal of Contemporary Criminal Justice* 9:41–49 (1993).
22. *Florida v. Royer*, 460 U.S. 491 (1983).
23. *Carroll v. United States*, 267 U.S. 132 (1925).
24. *United States v. Ross*, 456 U.S. 798 (1982).
25. *California v. Acevedo*, 500 U.S. 565 (1991).
26. *Illinois v. Cabelles*, 543 U.S. 405 (2005).
27. *Delaware v. Prouse*, 440 U.S. 648 (1978).
28. *Michigan Department of State Police v. Sitz*, 496 U.S. 444 (1990).
29. *Harris v. United States*, 390 U.S. 234 (1968).
30. *Hester v. United States*, 265 U.S. 57 (1924); *Oliver v. United States*, 466 U.S. 170 (1984); *Florida v. Riley*, 488 U.S. 445 (1989).
31. *Schneckloth v. Bustamonte*, 412 U.S. 218 (1973).
32. *Florida v. Bostick*, 501 U.S. 429 (1991).
33. *Georgia v. Randolph*, 547 U.S. 103 (2006).
34. *Illinois v. Rodriguez*, 497 U.S. 177 (1990); *United States v. Matlock*, 415 U.S. 164 (1974).
35. *California v. Greenwood*, 486 U.S. 35 (1988).
36. *California v. Greenwood*, note 35.
37. *Almeida-Sanchez v. United States*, 413 U.S. 266 (1973); *United States v. Brignoni-Ponce*, 422 U.S. 873 (1975); *United States v. Ortiz*, 422 U.S. 891 (1975).
38. *United States v. Martinez-Fuerte*, 428 U.S. 543 (1976).
39. *Olmstead v. United States*, 277 U.S. 438 (1928).
40. *Katz v. United States*, 389 U.S. 347 (1967).
41. *Kyllo v. United States*, 533 U.S. 27 (2001).

42. *United States v. Leon*, note 11.
43. *Screws v. United States*, 325 U.S. 91 (1945).
44. *Malley v. Briggs*, 475 U.S. 335 (1986).
45. *Heimbach v. Village of Lyons*, 597 F2d 344 (2d Cir 1979); *Stump v. Sparkman*, 435 U.S. 349 (1978); *Pierson v. Ray*, 386 U.S. 547 (1967).
46. Cohen, note 5.
47. *United States v. Watson*, 423 U.S. 411 (1976); *United States v. Santana*, 427 U.S. 38 (1976).
48. *Payton v. New York*, note 5.
49. *Minnesota v. Olson*, 495 U.S. 91 (1990).
50. *Miranda v. Arizona*, 384 U.S. 436 (1966).
51. *State v. Miranda*, 401 P.2nd 721 (1965).
52. *Escobedo v. Illinois*, 378 U.S. 478 (1964).
53. David Davies, "Second Rape Conviction for *Miranda*," *The Arizona Republic*, February 25, 1967, pp. 1A, 4A; Liva Baker, *Miranda: Crime, Law and Politics* (New York: Atheneum, 1983).
54. Baker, note 53.
55. Fred Graham, "High Court Puts New Curb on Powers of the Police to Interrogate Suspects," *The New York Times*, June 14, 1966, p. A1.
56. *Miranda v. Arizona*, note 50.
57. *Brewer v. Williams*, 430 U.S. 387 (1977).
58. *Edwards v. Arizona*, 451 U.S. 477 (1981).
59. *Davis v. United States*, 114 S. Ct. 2350 (1994).
60. *New York v. Quarles*, 467 U.S. 649 (1984).
61. *Arizona v. Roberson*, 486 U.S. 675 (1988).
62. *Minnick v. Mississippi*, 498 U.S. 146 (1990).
63. *Dickerson v. United States*, 530 U.S. 428 (2000).
64. *Schmerber v. California*, 384 U.S. 757 (1966); *United States v. Dionisio*, 410 U.S. 1 (1973); *United States v. Mara*, 410 U.S. 19 (1973); *Gilbert v. California*, 388 U.S. 263 (1967); *United States v. Wade*, 388 U.S. 218 (1967); *United States v. Euge*, 444 U.S. 707 (1980).
65. *United States v. Wade*, note 64.
66. *Kirby v. Illinois*, 406 U.S. 682 (1972).
67. *Simmons v. United States*, 390 U.S. 377 (1968); *Neil v. Biggers*, 409 U.S. 188 (1972).
68. "Beating Nullifies Conviction," *The Seattle Times*, July 6, 1991, pp. A1, 12.
69. *Hopt v. Utah*, 110 U.S. 574 (1884).
70. *Wilson v. United States*, 162 U.S. 613 (1896).
71. *Brown v. Mississippi*, 297 U.S. 278 (1936).
72. *Chambers v. Florida*, 309 U.S. 227 (1940).
73. *Blackburn v. Alabama*, 361 U.S. 199 (1960).
74. *McNabb v. United States*, 318 U.S. 332 (1943).
75. *Mallory v. United States*, 354 U.S. 449 (1957).
76. Leonard Levy, Kenneth Karst, and Dennis Mahoney, *Encyclopedia of the American Constitution*, 2nd ed. (New York: Macmillan Reference Books, 2000).
77. *Gideon v. Wainwright*, 372 U.S. 335 (1963).
78. *Argersinger v. Hamlin*, 407 U.S. 25 (1972).
79. *Escobedo v. Illinois*, note 52.

PARISH PLAZA
100TH ANNIVERSARY
BY
LLEY OFM CAP
P. OF BOSTON
ER 6 2005

CHAPTER

Critical Issues in Policing

OBJECTIVES

1 Understand the purpose and consequences of police discretion.

2 Know the legal and extralegal factors that influence police decisions to make an arrest.

3 Explain the history of police corruption.

4 Grasp the research on police brutality and use of excessive force.

5 Understand federal and state laws and policies regulating high-speed chases.

6 Know factors that exacerbate police stress.

7 Understand how stress affects the performance of police officers and law enforcement agencies.

8 Describe the history of women and minorities in policing and the unique problems that these groups face.

PROFILES IN CRIME AND JUSTICE

Lorenzo M. Boyd

Former Deputy Sheriff
Suffolk County Massachusetts
Assistant Professor of Criminal Justice
Fayetteville State University

While growing up in inner-city Boston in the 1970s, I saw firsthand the tumultuous relationship between the police and the community. I never was able to buy into the proverbial "officer-friendly" ideal that many others did. But in spite of that, I had a true fascination with law enforcement. In Boston, there were multiple local, state, and county agencies from which to choose. While most of these departments seemed singularly focused, the County Sheriff's Department appeared to have a multilevel vision and would likely yield the most wide-reaching experience. Knowing that the main divisions of the criminal justice system are law enforcement, courts, and corrections, I believed that the County Sheriff's Department would be the best way to explore each. In January 1988, I was deputized and my quest to understand the criminal justice system was more fully under way.

After being deputized, my first assignment was running an inmate-housing unit in the county jail. This experience was the first real exposure that I had to the correctional system. Custody is where new deputies get to decide if they have what it takes to work for the county. When you walk into a secure facility and that big metal door slams behind you, it is sobering to know that you are locked in with the same offenders you read about in the morning papers or saw on the evening news. My first assignment was in the homicide unit in the county jail. To work there, you need to be firm, but fair, and always watch your back. This is by far the hardest part of being a deputy sheriff. You have to cut your teeth in the jail before you can move into other responsibilities in a sheriff's department. For the deputies who never get assignments outside of the jail, many liken it to doing a 20-year sentence, 8 hours at a time. The one constant shared by inmates and deputies in jails across the country is that both are trying to get out of the jail and onto the streets with the same amount of eagerness.

Many sheriffs' deputies get promoted to the street after only a few years working in jails. Being on the street can mean many things. It could mean patrol, warrant management, motorcycles, or the transportation of inmates. Although these are very different assignments, the main issue is a sense of freedom, not being confined to the jails. After several years working in the jail, I remember the overwhelming sense of relief when I finally hit the street. The assignment didn't matter—what mattered was not being in the jail. Patrol is the glory assignment for deputies. Although most deputies have a certain cop mentality, it is when you are on patrol that you feel most connected to the role and identity of law enforcement. Because state police departments are often understaffed and many city departments are overtaxed, it is the sheriff's department that patrols and handles many calls in suburban and rural areas. Of course, these responsibilities also bring new levels of both danger and awareness.

Many jurisdictions also use sheriff's deputies as security in county courts. Being a court officer is a mixed bag: You get to be out of the jail, but you are also off the streets. The hours can be long and often boring, but the work is extremely necessary. Court duty can lull you into a false sense of security, but at a moment's notice you may have to spring into action to protect the occupants in a courtroom and quell any disturbances. Like many other assignments, being a court officer is a thankless job, yet one that is embraced by many deputies. After a decade and a half as a sheriff's deputy, I have come to believe that deputies are the backbone of the entire criminal justice system, and that deputies enjoy the best of all possible criminal justice worlds.

Introduction

Police officers work in one of the most dangerous professions.[1] On a daily basis they may confront violent or angry people, and occasionally they may be assaulted or killed in the line of duty (see FIGURE 6–1).[2] From 1998 to 2007, 549 officers were feloniously killed in the United States (see FIGURE 6–2).[3] On June 26, 2008, their job was made more difficult when the U.S. Supreme Court ruled in *District of Columbia v. Heller* that Americans have a right to own guns for self-defense and hunting.[4]

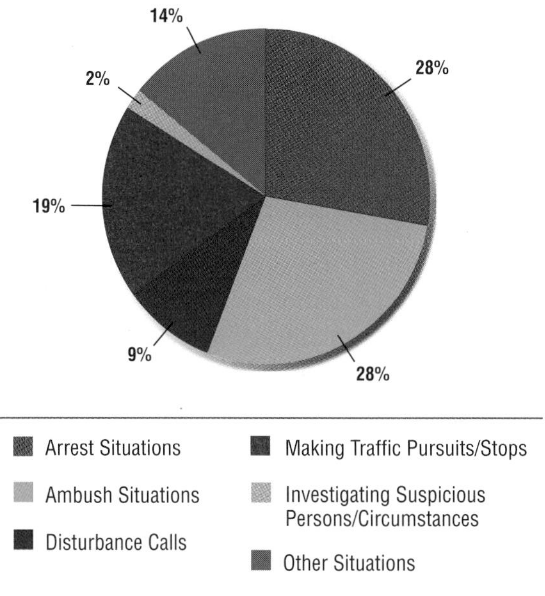

FIGURE 6–1 Percentage of Police Officers Feloniously Killed or Assaulted in Different Situations, 2007

Source: Federal Bureau of Investigation, *Law Enforcement Officers Killed and Assaulted, 2007* (Washington, DC: U.S. Department of Justice, 2008).

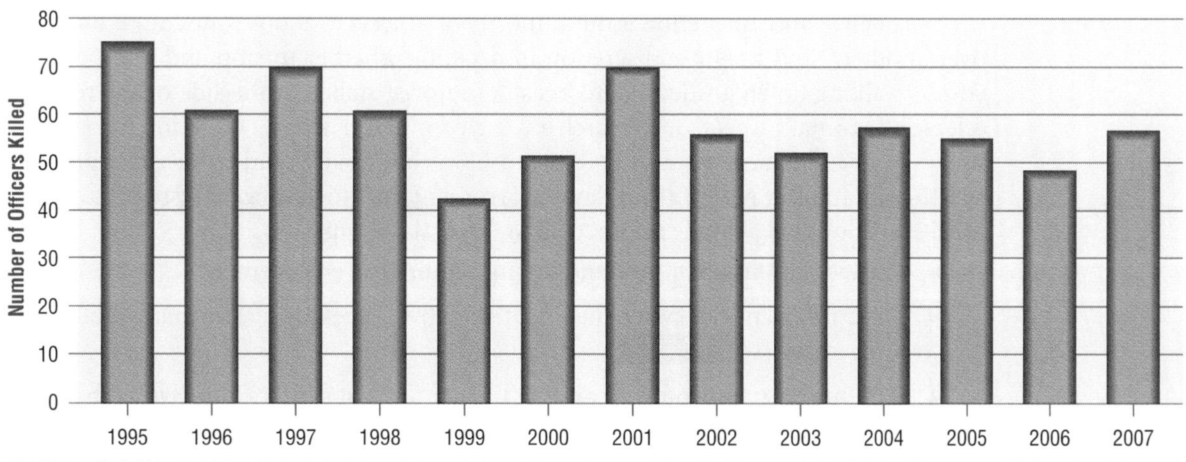

FIGURE 6–2 Law Enforcement Officers Feloniously Killed, 1995–2007

Source: Federal Bureau of Investigation, *Law Enforcement Officers Killed and Assaulted, 2007* (Washington, DC: U.S. Department of Justice, 2008).

Headline Crime — *District of Columbia v. Heller*

On June 26, 2008, the U.S. Supreme Court ruled in *District of Columbia v. Heller* that Americans have a right to own guns for self-defense and hunting. Dick Heller, a 66-year-old, armed security guard, sued the District of Columbia after it rejected his application to keep a handgun at his home for protection. In a 5–4 decision, the Court's ruling struck down the District of Columbia's 32-year-old ban on handguns, stating that the ban was incompatible with the scope of the Second Amendment.

The Second Amendment states: "A well-regulated militia, being necessary to the security of a free state, the right of the people to keep and bear arms, shall not be infringed." In *Heller*, the issue before the Court was whether the Second Amendment permits an individual to own guns no matter what, or whether the right to own guns is tied to service in a state militia. As a result of the Court's ruling, the National Rifle Association said they would file lawsuits in Chicago, San Francisco, and other jurisdictions challenging the laws they have in place restricting ownership of handguns.

Sources: District of Columbia v. Heller, 554 U.S. --- (2008); "Supreme Court Says Americans Have Right to Guns," available at http://www.comcast.net/articles/news-general/20080626/Scotus.Guns/, accessed August 26, 2008.

That said, on every shift, officers must make difficult decisions about how to handle suspects and when to exercise discretion in stressful situations such as in high-speed chases and cases that require the use of deadly force. Sometimes they cross the line and apply unnecessary or inappropriate force against citizens. In addition to the issues of stress, deadly force, and brutality, police departments constantly face challenges in the form of corruption.

Police Discretion

At the heart of policing is discretion. When deciding whether to use discretion, police officers typically ask themselves three questions:

1. Should I intervene?
2. What should I do?
3. How should I do it?

These are difficult questions to answer, particularly when he or she must make a critical, split-second decision about how the law should be applied.

Formally, **police discretion** is the authority of officers to choose one course of action over another. They may use discretion in deciding whether to stop and question two youths walking down a sidewalk, to assist a motorist stalled at the side of the road, to release a criminal suspect, or to search a vehicle for illegal drugs. Discretion is so widely used by police because it is not possible to have rules that would cover every possible specific situation. A policy of **full law enforcement**, in which officers respond formally to all suspicious behavior, is impractical for several reasons:

- Most violations are minor and do not require full enforcement.
- The criminal justice system has insufficient resources to react formally to all violations of law (see TABLE 6–1).
- Full enforcement would mean that the majority of officers' time would be spent completing paperwork and testifying in court, not policing the streets.
- Even well-defined legal statutes are sometimes vague and open to interpretation.
- Full enforcement would create an extraordinary strain between the police and the public, reducing citizen cooperation and possibly increasing crime.

TABLE 6-1 Average Ratio of Police Officers per 1000 Residents

Population Served	Number of Officers per 1000 Residents
All sizes	2.5
250,000 or more	2.5
100,000–249,999	1.9
50,000–99,999	1.8
25,000–49,999	1.8
10,000–24,999	2.0
2500–9999	2.2
1000–2499	2.6

Source: Adapted from Matthew Hickman, and Brian Reaves, *Local Police Departments, 2003* (Washington, DC: U.S. Department of Justice, 2006).

Because full enforcement is not a realistic approach in policing, agencies practice **selective law enforcement**, in which officers will under-enforce some laws and over-enforce other laws. In Denver, for instance, possession of less than one ounce of marijuana is an under-enforced law, whereas laws prohibiting driving impaired or speeding in a school zone are strictly enforced. While on its face selective law enforcement is a practical approach for policing, it also brings its own challenges. Selective enforcement has historically proven to be problematic for three reasons:

1. It is inherently unfair that police respond differently to similar situations.
2. Officers may abuse their power, targeting specific individuals or populations.
3. Selective enforcement may lead to favoritism and corruption, with those empowered to choose being able to help their friends, take bribes, and threaten parties from whom they desire favors.

Despite these concerns, discretion is an essential component of policing. Selective enforcement may certainly be warranted for minor offenses. For instance, in some circumstances, a warning may be equally effective as an arrest at preventing future violations without draining the government's legal resources.

In particular, discretionary authority is used by police when making decisions to arrest suspects. Only about 13 percent of encounters between police and suspects result in arrests.[5] In an ideal world, police might use only legal criteria to make their arrest decisions. In reality, studies have found that extralegal factors such as sex, race, and socioeconomic class influence police decisions as well (see TABLE 6-2).

Legal Factors

Seriousness of the Offense

People who engage in more serious crimes are more likely to be arrested than are those who commit minor offenses.[6] A suspect is also more likely to be arrested if he or she possesses a weapon.[7] In addition, crimes that are perceived by police as sophisticated, premeditated, or malicious more often result in arrest.[8]

Prior Arrest Record

Police are more likely to arrest persons who have previously been arrested. For example, juveniles with five or more previous arrests account for more than 66 percent of juvenile arrests, whereas first-time offenders account for only 7 percent of those taken into custody.[9] This factor is more likely to become an issue when the decision about whether to formally process a suspect is made at the police station rather than on the street, although

TABLE 6-2 Factors Influencing the Decision to Arrest

Legal Factors
Offense Seriousness: People who commit more serious offenses are more likely to be arrested.
Prior Arrest Record: Police are more likely to arrest persons with a prior arrest record.
Presence of Evidence: When police have strong evidence, they are more likely to arrest the suspect.
Suspicious Behavior: Police are more likely to arrest people who engage in behavior that is out of place in the specific circumstances (e.g., wearing a heavy coat in hot and humid weather).
Extralegal Factors
Race and Ethnicity: Research has produced mixed results regarding the relationship between race and arrest.
Attitude and Disrespect: Suspects who are disrespectful of police are more likely to be arrested.
Sex: Research on the relationship between sex and arrest has been mixed.
Social Class: Police generally treat poor and wealthy persons similarly for comparable offenses.
Demeanor: Persons who show a hostile demeanor are more likely to be arrested.
Characteristics of Police Officers: Younger, less educated, and African American police officers are the most likely to arrest suspects.
Organization of Police Departments: The social organization of the police agency has only a small effect on the arrest decision.

studies have shown in general that police consider having a prior record as confirmation of the suspect's involvement in criminality.[10] Whether there exists a relationship between prior arrest record and arrest decisions is arguable. In many instances, arrests are made before police know anything about a suspect's criminal background. It could be that people with prior arrests might commit more crimes and, therefore, are more likely to get arrested again.

Presence of Evidence

Police have sufficient evidence to link a suspect to a crime in approximately 75 percent of police–citizen contacts, and nearly 20 percent of these cases result in an arrest. In contrast, when no situational evidence is available, only 0.5 percent of cases result in arrest.[11] Suspects are significantly more likely to be arrested when more evidence is present—for example, when an officer hears a suspect confess, hears others talking about the suspect's involvement in the crime, observes physical evidence, or personally sees the suspect commit the act.[12]

Suspicious Behavior

Merely acting suspicious does not provide a legal justification for an arrest. Yet, a police officer's decision to stop and possibly arrest a suspect often begins when the officer has reasonable suspicion—for example, when observing someone engaging in "out-of-the-ordinary" behavior, such as wearing a long coat while shopping in a department store during the heat of the summer or driving a car very slowly in a neighborhood known for drug sales.

The presence of physical evidence of a crime significantly increases the likelihood of arrest.

Extralegal Factors

Extralegal factors are elements of a police–citizen encounter or characteristics of a suspect or of the officer that have nothing to do with the actual crime, but may influence the decision-making process. Factors such as race, ethnicity, sex, social class, and demeanor may all affect an officer's perception of a suspect. The decision to arrest, which is usually based on probable cause that a crime was committed and the person committed the crime, may also be influenced by behavioral cues such as the person's appearance, the location, or the time the suspect is observed.

Race

African American police officers act more harshly toward African American citizens than do white officers.

Extensive research on the relationship between race and police discretion has produced mixed findings. Most research shows that police decision making is affected by the race and ethnicity of a suspect for comparable offenses.[13] Proportionally, police arrest more African Americans than whites (see Chapter 3).[14] A variety of explanations have been suggested for this disparity:

- Law enforcement agencies receive a disproportionate number of calls for assistance from African American neighborhoods and, therefore, assign more vehicles to patrol those neighborhoods, which results in more opportunities to observe persons engaging in crimes.[15]
- Police stop and question African Americans at higher rates, and record these encounters, which increases the likelihood that arrests will be made.[16]
- Police perceive African Americans as being more likely to engage in serious crimes than whites.[17]
- African Americans commit a disproportionate amount of serious criminal behavior.[18]

At least one study found that police treat minorities more leniently than they treat whites, although the majority of African Americans continue to believe that they are personally harassed by the police, that police surveillance is discriminatory, and that clear racial differences exist in terms of who police officers watch and stop.[19] The vast amount of research on police–citizen encounters does support claims of racial bias by police. Evidence of police suspiciousness of minorities by police frequently produces hostile feelings among African Americans toward police. As a consequence, African Americans are more likely to interact with police in a more antagonistic or disrespectful manner than whites, which may in turn produce a greater likelihood of arrest.[20]

Sex

Research has shown that police officers are more suspicious of males than of females. In fact, one study found that more than 84 percent of police officers agreed with the statement that "If two or more males are together, they are probably committing a [criminal] act."[21] Males generally commit much more serious crimes more often than females, and men are significantly more likely to be arrested than women (see Chapter 3).[22]

Some studies report that women are treated more leniently in the criminal justice system than men, although other studies have not confirmed this finding.[23] For example, researchers have found evidence to support the following assertions:

- Police generally treat female suspects more leniently, but they are more likely to arrest females than males for sex offenses.[24]
- Police treat females with greater compassion, even when the case is serious.[25]
- Although females who commit serious felonies are less likely to be arrested than men, they are more likely than men to be arrested for less serious crimes.[26]
- Police officers adopt a more paternalistic and punitive attitude toward young females in an attempt to deter them from engaging in further inappropriate sex-role violations.[27]
- Females who violate middle-class expectations of traditional female roles do not receive more lenient treatment by police.[28]

Social Class

Most research has found that the police treat people similarly for comparable offenses regardless of the suspects' social standing, although the seriousness of offending varies

The attitude and demeanor of the suspect may influence the decision of a law enforcement officer to issue a ticket, take a suspect into custody, and, possibly, make an arrest.

between classes.[29] Researchers report that suspects police encounter in lower-class neighborhoods are more likely to be arrested than persons stopped in middle- or upper-class areas.[30] This difference may, in part, reflect two facts: (1) lower-income persons are more likely to be repeat offenders and (2) persons from lower-class neighborhoods account for a larger proportion of petty offenses that generally result in high arrest rates.[31] In addition, police allocation of resources (patrolling activities) is influenced by neighborhood-level social class. Although individual officers may respond to suspicious behavior consistently across classes, police may be more likely to observe suspicious behavior in neighborhoods characterized by lower socioeconomic status, simply because they tend to have a greater presence in those communities in the first place owing to the larger number of calls from the public reporting crimes.

Social class also plays a role in police arrests of juveniles. That is, juveniles from middle- and upper-class families are often treated more leniently (perhaps their families have more resources to help minimize their involvement with the juvenile justice system), whereas parents of lower-class youths more frequently look to the police and probation officers to help them control their children.[32]

Demeanor

Theoretically, for law enforcement officers to make an arrest, they must have probable cause based on evidence that a crime was committed and the person probably committed that crime. Research, however, has found that extralegal factors, such as the suspect's race, sex, and socioeconomic class, may influence (even though they should not) the arrest decision. In fact, the attitude or demeanor of the suspect typically affects the arrest decision-making process.[33] Studies repeatedly show that the arrest decision is based on character cues present in police–citizen encounters, such as the suspect's age, demeanor, dress, and race. In fact, the individual's demeanor is one of the most important predictors of arrest decisions in 50 to 60 percent of the cases.[34] An arrest is a more likely outcome for individuals who disrespect police.[35] A suspect who is hostile is nearly three times more likely to be arrested than one who is friendly.[36]

When police are initially trying to establish a relationship with a suspect, they may interpret his or her demeanor as evidence of acceptance or rejection of their attempt to build trust. Such failure to display an appropriate attitude (i.e., deference to authority, contriteness, politeness) is often viewed by officers as a violation of that trust and, therefore, is more likely to lead to an arrest.[37] Noncompliance or verbal resistance in front of other officers further increases the likelihood of arrest. At least one study has reported that suspects who are hostile toward an officer in the presence of other police are four times more likely to be arrested than friendly suspects.[38]

Police may also treat citizens with disrespect, though this kind of unprovoked behavior is relatively rare. Disrespectful behavior by police varies widely based on the suspect's age. It has been found that police are three times more likely to be disrespectful to teenagers than to senior citizens.[39] Studies have also shown that a suspect's race also may elicit disrespect from some police officers. Most interestingly, minority suspects experienced disrespect less often than whites.[40]

Additional Extralegal Factors

Characteristics of the police officers themselves may also affect the arrest decision:[41]

- Younger officers are more likely to arrest suspects than older officers.[42]
- College-educated officers are less likely to make arrests than officers with no college education.[43]

- African American officers generally adopt a more aggressive patrol style and make proportionally more arrests than white officers, especially among African American citizens.[44]
- Female and male police officers arrest suspects at about the same rate.[45]

In addition to these personal characteristics, aspects of the social organization within an officer's own police department may affect the arrest decisions that he or she makes. For example, James Q. Wilson found that three factors related to how a police agency is structured influence the way officers treat suspects:[46]

- Department organization
- Strength of connections to the local community
- Formal and informal organizational norms

Wilson reported that in bureaucratized agencies characterized by direct supervision of officers, police are expected to apply a strict interpretation of department rules when dealing with suspects. In contrast, police officers in more fraternal agencies without systematic rules that guide decision making use personal judgments to make arrest decisions, which are then affected by individual and situational differences.

Wilson's study suggests that a combination of centralized management and close supervision creates situations where officers in the field are more likely to follow department policy. Other studies have demonstrated that departments with greater bureaucratic control are also more likely to have policies emphasizing counsel and release dispositions, which results in higher rates of counseling and releasing of suspects. By contrast, in departments characterized by low bureaucratic control, an emphasis on following department policies has little effect on disposition rates.[47] However, contrary to Wilson's assertion, when criminologist Robin Engel and her colleagues examined the effect of close supervision on arrest decisions in a recent study, they reported that management styles of police supervisors had little or no impact on the decision to arrest.[48]

Regulating Police Discretion

Police discretion is a double-edged sword. Justice is not being evenly applied to all members of society, and so some citizens may be denied due process of law or given preferential treatment.[49] As a result, police administrators develop safeguards through written rules and technology to help regulate police discretion.

Written rules are the most widely used method for controlling discretion. These rules provide police officers with guidelines about which actions they may take in specific situations. Nearly every municipal and county law enforcement agency today has specific regulations for controlling the following issues:

- When force may be used and to what extent
- How and when to participate in high-speed chases
- How to handle special populations (e.g., juveniles, mentally ill persons, and the homeless)
- How many hours per week police may work
- Which types of employment police may accept outside of their regular shift hours[50]

In addition to written rules, police administrators may rely on technological developments to track officers while they are on duty. For example, the Automatic Vehicle Locator (AVL) system uses a Global Positioning System (GPS) device to monitor patrol cars. With an AVL system, a police dispatcher can pinpoint the longitude, latitude, ground speed, and course direction of every patrol vehicle in operation at a given time; the dispatcher can also route the vehicle to a particular location if necessary. The AVL

Headline Crime

Cop Moonlights as Prostitute

A New Zealand policewoman who was moonlighting as a prostitute was censured by the Auckland Police Department. Prostitution is legal in New Zealand, and police officers are permitted to take approved second jobs, but the Auckland police department decided that prostitution was unauthorized for officers, even when they are working undercover. The officer had moonlighted as a prostitute only for a short time to make some extra money before her concealed activity was uncovered, though neither her name nor her rank were made public.

The officer was allowed to keep her day job as a police officer but was told that she would have to give up her job as a prostitute. When asked about the officer's activity in the sex trade industry, New Zealand Police Minister Annette King said it would be inappropriate for her to comment because the matter was an internal police employment issue.

Source: "Lady Cop Goes Undercover . . . Um . . . *Really* Undercover," *FoxNews.com*, July 20, 2006, available at http://www.foxnews.com/story/0,2933,204774,00.html, accessed August 5, 2008.

system provides dispatchers with real-life snapshots of the locations of police vehicles so that they can advise citizens as to when an officer will arrive. This system also reduces police response time because the dispatcher can direct the closest patrol vehicle in the area to the scene. With this approach, administrators are able to more closely monitor officer activities.[51]

Police Corruption

As with any position of power, there is always the potential for **corruption** within police departments—that is, the misuse of authority by officers for the benefit of themselves or others. There are innumerable ways for an officer to become involved in corruption: Some seek out opportunities for economic gain, some are tempted as they observe other officers engaging in corrupt activities, and some find themselves becoming corrupt as a result of bad decisions involving deals made with criminals. Some corrupt activities are benign, whereas others are much more serious.

Criminologists such as Julian Roebuck and Tom Barker have developed typologies of police corruption that group such actions into conceptual categories in increasing order of seriousness.[52] These categories are as follows:

- *Corruption of authority.* The most common form of corruption occurs when an officer accepts a small gratuity for services, such as a free meal for being at a restaurant while in uniform.[53]
- *Kickbacks.* An officer may receive goods or services for referring business to individuals or companies.
- *Opportunistic theft.* Officers may take advantage of situations they are in—for example, stealing from intoxicated citizens.[54]
- *Shakedowns.* An officer may extort money from a citizen with a threat to enforce a law if the officer is not paid, or an officer may offer to accept a bribe in return for ignoring an offense.[55]
- *Protection of illegal activities.* Officers may systematically accept bribes for protecting ongoing criminal activity, thereby allowing individuals and businesses to commit crimes, such as those committed in drug operations.[56]
- *"Fixing" charges.* Police sometimes undermine criminal investigations or proceedings—for example, "fixing" a traffic ticket by failing to show up to testify in court against the defendant.

- *Direct criminal activities.* Some police commit crimes against persons or property, such as forcing a prostitute to engage in sex or using their patrol vehicles to transport drugs for dealers.[57]
- *Internal payoffs.* Officers may barter, buy, and sell favors to other officers, such as falsifying scores on promotional exams.[58]
- *"Flaking" or "pudding."* An officer may place a firearm at a crime scene to give the impression that a suspect who was shot and killed by police was armed so as to justify the shooting.[59]

In addition, **noble cause corruption** is a type of corruption that some police and civilians promote because they believe it is justified—that is, because it serves the greater public good. For example, some officers and citizens believe that police should be permitted to beat confessions out of known murderers or to fabricate evidence against known child rapists so that they will be convicted and be put behind bars.[60]

Department Corruption

Entire departments also may be corrupt. Corrupt departments range from those where there are only a few dishonest officers to those characterized by pervasive organized corruption.

When police supervisors are asked about corruption, many will admit that a few corrupt officers accept bribes and sometimes commit crimes. Few will admit to the existence of small groups of corrupt officers who work together in a manner similar to a criminal gang. On the agency level, criminal activity may be widespread but unorganized (i.e., officers regularly take advantage of situations without coordination or discussion among other officers), or it may be organized into a complex system of corruption replete with payoffs, theft, and extortion.

Investigating Police Corruption

If widespread corruption is discovered, city managers or mayors may form a commission to investigate the breadth and depth of the illegal activities. The most important commissions to investigate police corruption in the United States to date have been the Chicago Crime Commission, the Wickersham Commission, the Knapp Commission, and the Mollen Commission.

Begun in 1919 to combat organized crime, the *Chicago Crime Commission* was the first of these watchdog groups to be formed, and it continues to operate today. The purpose of the Commission is to keep a watchful eye on organized crime throughout Chicago. Today, the Commission's efforts focus on monitoring the city's criminal justice system primarily for carelessness, corruption, and leniency. The Commission is also a strong proponent of a more efficient criminal justice system in Chicago and promotes deterrence through severe punishment.[61]

In 1929, President Herbert Hoover appointed George Wickersham to head the *Wickersham Commission*, which was charged with identifying the causes of crime, recommending social policies for preventing it, and examining the failure by federal, state, and local police to enforce Prohibition, which had been established by the Eighteenth Amendment in 1920.[62] In their report, the members of the Commission documented innumerable instances of police participating in bribery, entrapment, coercion of witnesses, fabrication of evidence, and illegal wiretapping. Curiously, the Commission recommended to President Hoover that Prohibition should not be repealed. Its recommendations on that front were ignored, however, and in 1933 Congress passed the Twenty-First Amendment repealing Prohibition, with state ratification conventions quickly endorsing the amendment.

The *Knapp Commission* was formed in April 1970 by Mayor John Lindsay to investigate police corruption inside the New York City Police Department (NYPD). Its roots

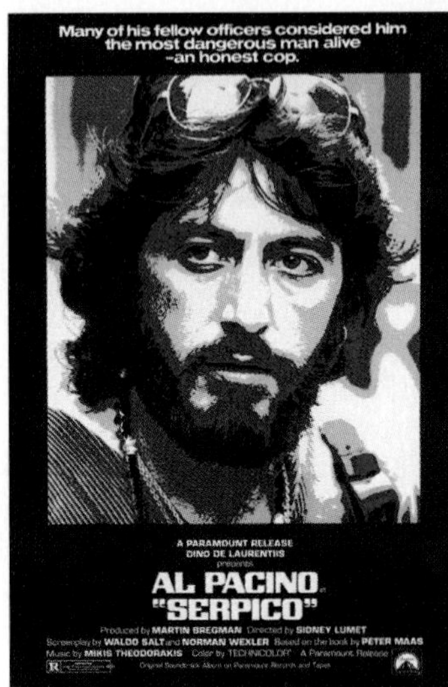

Immortalized by Al Pacino in the film *Serpico*, Frank Serpico blew the lid off corruption in the NYPD.

can be traced to the publicity generated by the public revelations of police corruption made by patrol officer Frank Serpico and Sergeant David Durk. Following an exhaustive review of hundreds of documents and countless interviews with officers and supervisors, the Knapp Commission issued its final report in 1973. It identified two types of corrupt police officers: **grass-eaters** (those who accept bribes when offered) and **meat-eaters** (those who aggressively misuse their power for personal gain). It was the conclusion of the Knapp Commission that the majority of corrupt police officers were in the former category.[63]

In 1992, Mayor David Dinkins appointed former judge Milton Mollen to head a commission to once again investigate corruption in the NYPD. The *Mollen Commission* issued its final report in 1994, concluding that the corruption it uncovered in the NYPD was different from what the Knapp Commission had found just two decades earlier. Corruption in the 1970s was largely a matter of accommodation: criminals and police officers giving and taking bribes, and buying and selling protection. In other words, corruption was consensual. By the 1990s, however, corruption had become characterized by brutality, theft, abuse of authority, and active police criminality. Corruption within the NYPD was not merely widespread, but well organized and allowed to persist by Internal Affairs investigators and high-level police officials who turned a blind eye to its presence. The Mollen Commission charged that virtually all of the corruption it unearthed involved groups ("crews") of officers who protected and assisted one another's criminal activities. On average, each of these "crews" consisted of 8 to 12 officers, who operated with set rules and used a group name. They worked in flexible networks, planning and coordinating their criminal raids with the help of intelligence, communications, and special equipment from their departments.[64]

Reasons for Police Corruption

There are many explanations for police corruption, including:

- *Limited accountability.* Police are often under minimal supervision and, therefore, are not held accountable for many of their actions.
- *Officer secrecy.* The police subculture isolates officers from the public, creating a "blue wall of silence" that prevents police from "snitching" on one another or discussing police business with outsiders.
- *Managerial secrecy.* Supervisors are not exempt from the police subculture and often buy into the "code of silence." As a consequence, they may hesitate to investigate charges of corruption due to group loyalty.

Studies have shown that certain characteristics help explain the predictability of police corruption:

- *Pre-employment history.* Officers whose life histories include records of arrest, traffic violations, and failure in other jobs are more likely than others to become involved in corruption.
- *Education.* Officers who hold associate or higher degrees are less likely to be terminated due to criminal involvement.
- *Training.* Officers who do well at the police academy's recruit training program are less likely than marginal recruits to eventually be terminated due to corruption.
- *Diversity.* Agencies with more racial and ethnic diversity among officers tend to have less corruption.[65]

The message to police administrators is clear: To minimize corruption, police agencies must hire officers with clean histories and strong educations. Once hired, officers must be well trained and closely supervised to make certain that minor problems with the department's internal disciplinary system do not escalate into career-ending misconduct.[66] Police supervisors must admit when corruption exists and confront the problem. Furthermore, they must recognize that corruption often begins at the top and drifts downward through the ranks, so police managers must lead by example. Sincere and candid administrators establish the parameters for what is considered acceptable behavior, which strongly affects the recruitment and promotion processes.

Police Brutality

Police brutality is the unlawful use of force. It consists of excessive force and all "unnecessary force" used by police. Use of excessive force by a police officer is a crime.

The use of excessive force by police officers is an unfortunate but constant aspect of policing history. As early as 1931, an investigative commission found the widespread, systematic using coerced confessions with force, violence, and psychological threats as well as many incidents of excessive force during street encounters with suspects.[67] Even today, the Human Rights Watch Organization estimates that thousands of incidents of police use of excessive force take place each year, only a fraction of which are reported and even fewer are formally investigated.[68]

A commission formed after the 1991 assault of Rodney King by members of the Los Angeles Police Department (LAPD) found that 5 percent of all officers accounted for more than 20 percent of allegations of excessive force, and 28 percent of officers agreed that prejudice may have led to the use of excessive force in these situations.[69] This finding is supported by further research indicating that victims of excessive force are usually younger, lower class, minority, and male.[70] Additionally, victims of excessive force tend to be under the influence of alcohol or drugs.[71] Other victims of police brutality are suspected of committing violent crimes.[72] The officers charged with using excessive force in such incidents are usually less-experienced males.[73]

These findings led the commission to recommend specific steps be taken to identify "violence-prone" officers before they act out.[74] One way to reduce police brutality is by creating a more balanced approach to address citizen complaints of excessive use of force by bringing such complaints to independent review boards. As long as police continue to investigate themselves, suspicions of undisclosed corruption and brutality will inevitably persist. Approaches to remedy this situation include more effective disciplinary procedures, refined police selection criteria, more thorough police training on appropriate use of force, and instruction on alternative methods to maintain control when a suspect is resisting arrest.[75] Unfortunately, these remedies have not significantly reduced police use of excessive force. Data from the U.S. Department of Justice indicate that from 2001 to 2007, alleged brutality by law enforcement officers increased by 25 percent.[76]

Deadly Force

When police find themselves in dangerous and volatile situations, they must act quickly. Officers do not have time to call supervisors and ask what they should do. When an explosive situation presents itself, combined with the possibility that the officer may be prosecuted if he or she makes the wrong decision, the officer is in a risky position.[77] Should the officer choose to use too little force, the officer may endanger both his or her life and the lives of other officers and innocent bystanders. When too much force is used, suspects may be killed or seriously injured, and the officer may face public condemnation, discipline by the department, and possibly prosecution.[78]

The most severe action an officer can take against a citizen is deadly force. The standards regulating deadly force have changed considerably over the years. The colonial ap-

Headline Crime

New Orleans Police Assault Citizen

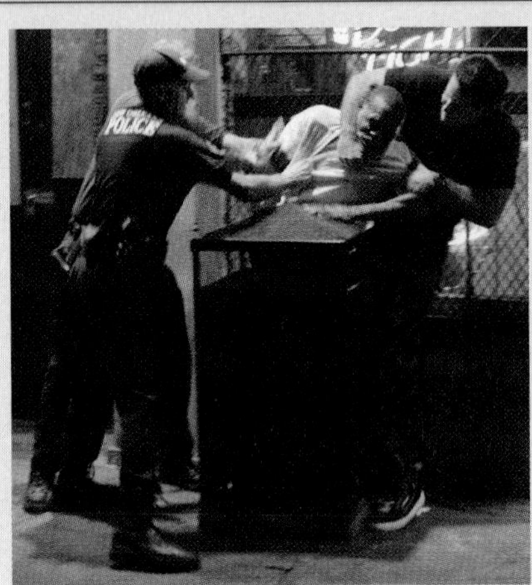

In 2006, Robert Davis was allegedly assaulted by New Orleans Police officers.

One night in New Orleans' famed French Quarter, a 64-year-old retired school teacher named Robert Davis was out for a walk when he encountered a police officer on horseback. What exactly happened next is unclear. According to Davis' attorney, two other officers approached and made some rude remarks to Davis, who responded by saying, "I think that was unprofessional." As Davis turned to walk across the street, he claims that one of the officers struck him from behind.

What is known is that after this brief encounter, officers hit Davis at least four times on the head and dragged him to the ground. One officer kneed Davis and punched him twice. The entire incident was caught on camera by a television news crew covering the aftermath of Hurricane Katrina. The video ended with Davis lying on a sidewalk with his head and shirt soaked in blood. Police charged him with public intoxication, resisting arrest, battery on a police officer, and public intimidation. Besides the concerns about police brutality, this violent incident also raised civil rights issues: Davis is African American, and the three officers are white.

Two officers involved in the attack, Robert Evangelist and Lance Schilling, were fired. Evangelist was charged with false imprisonment and second-degree battery but was eventually acquitted. Charges against the third officer, Stewart Smith, were dismissed. Davis pleaded "not guilty" to municipal charges of public intoxication, resisting arrest, battery on a police officer, and public intimidation; all charges against Davis were later dropped. On June 11, 2007, Schilling was found dead from a self-inflicted gunshot only one month before his trial was to begin.

Sources: Mary Foster, "New Orleans Officers Indicted in Beating," *Sacbee*, March 30, 2006, available at www.sacbee.com/24hour/special_reports/katrina/story/3244298p-12001341c.html, accessed August 7, 2008; "Victim of Police Beating Says He Was Sober," *Associated Press*, October 10, 2005, available at http://www.msnbc.msn.com/id/9645260/, accessed August 7, 2008; Cyndi Nguyen, "A Former NOPD Officer Accused in a Videotaped Beating Takes His Own Life," available at http://abc26.trb.com/news/wgno_071207suicide,0,2503818.story?coll=wgno-news-1, accessed August 24, 2007; "Judge Acquits New Orleans Cop in Videotaped Beating," available at http:www.cnn.com/2007/US/law/07/24/nola.beating.ap/index.html, accessed August 7, 2008.

proach to deadly force mirrored its English predecessor: the **fleeing felon doctrine**, which stated that if an individual suspected of committing a felony fled, a police officer was permitted to use deadly force to stop the suspect.[79] However, in 1985, the U.S. Supreme Court ruled in *Tennessee v. Garner* that the fleeing felon doctrine was unconstitutional. In this case, police shot 15-year-old Edward Garner in the back as he ran from a house. The Court stated, "When the suspect poses no immediate threat to the officer and no threat to others, the harm resulting from failing to apprehend him does not justify the use of deadly force to do so."[80]

A new standard for the use of deadly force, the **defense of life standard**, essentially says that officers may use deadly force only in defense of their own lives or another's life. For police, the impact of the *Garner* ruling has been profound. The decision in *Garner* opened the door for all use of force by police to be looked at from the "reasonableness standard"—that is, "What would a reasonable person do in the same situation?" In response to the *Garner* outcome, police departments across the nation have quietly expanded the Supreme Court's ruling by implementing a **preservation of life policy**, which mandates that officers use every other means possible to maintain order before turning to deadly force.

Police in Springdale, Arkansas, for example, recently introduced a graduated use of force scale for their officers.[81] Today in Springdale an officer is instructed to take the following steps when confronting a dangerous suspect:

FOCUS ON CRIMINAL JUSTICE

Tennessee v. Garner

In 1974, two Memphis police officers were dispatched to answer a call from a woman about a prowler. When they arrived on the scene, they saw a woman standing outside on her porch gesturing toward the adjacent house. She told the officers that she heard glass shattering and that someone was breaking in next door. One of the officers went behind the house, while the other officer radioed for backup. While looking outside, one of the officers heard a door slam and saw someone running across the backyard. With the aid of a flashlight, the officer reported that he saw no signs of a weapon and was reasonably sure that the suspect was unarmed. The officer yelled at the man—Edward Garner—to halt. Instead, Garner attempted to climb over a fence. When he did, the officer shot him. Garner died from the gunshot wounds. Police later found that Garner had stolen 10 dollars and a purse.

At that time, Tennessee statute instructed police to shoot to kill fleeing felons rather than risk their possible escape. The U.S. Supreme Court ruled that the fleeing felon law was unconstitutional, arguing that deadly force is a seizure and that seizures must conform to the reasonableness requirement of the Fourth Amendment. Because Garner had posed no immediate threat to the officer or to others, the legal force used to apprehend him did not justify the resulting harm.

Source: Tennessee v. Garner, 471 U.S. 1 (1985).

1. Identify himself or herself as a police officer
2. Give the suspect a verbal command to terminate his or her activities
3. Use (in order) soft hand restraints, chemical spray or stun gun, physical restraints, or a baton
4. Rely on deadly force as a last resort

The policy used in Springdale parallels many of the newer standards being implemented in police agencies across the United States.

Even with policies like these, which seek to reduce the use of deadly force, between 2002 and 2007 police justifiably killed more than 2200 citizens, or an average of more than 360 people each year (FIGURE 6–3).[82] If an officer contributes to the unnecessary death of a citizen because of his or her reckless behavior, the officer may be held criminally liable and be prosecuted. Research has shown that the most likely victim of deadly force is an unarmed, African American male between the ages of 17 and 30, who is out at night in a public location, with some connection to an armed robbery.[83] In fact, racial and ethnic minorities are killed by police in disproportionate numbers.[84] Research on deadly force has also uncovered the following relationships:

- Use of deadly force corresponds with neighborhood crime rates
- African American officers are more likely than white officers to use deadly force
- Male officers are more likely to use deadly force than female officers[85]

In reality, very few police–citizen contacts end with the use of lethal force. Of the more than 45.3 million police–citizen contacts that occur annually in the United States, only about 1.5 percent of citizens report police use of force. Nearly all force used against citizens is nonlethal. The most frequently used forms of force by police include these measures:

- Pushing or grabbing
- Kicking or hitting
- Pointing a gun
- Threatening to use force

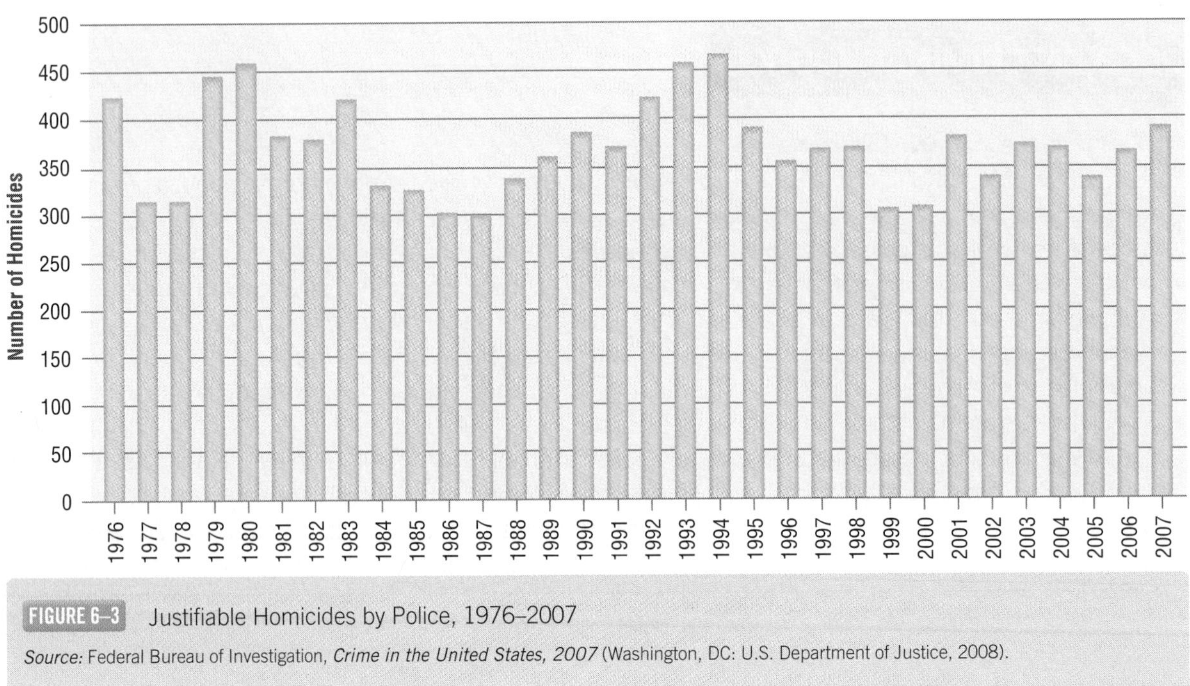

FIGURE 6-3 Justifiable Homicides by Police, 1976–2007

Source: Federal Bureau of Investigation, *Crime in the United States, 2007* (Washington, DC: U.S. Department of Justice, 2008).

Data from a 2005 study by the U.S. Department of Justices indicate that nonlethal force is used on more than 650,000 people per year.[86]

Because of risks to public safety, many police departments have developed more conservative policies regarding high-speed chases.

High-Speed Chases

Nearly as many citizens are killed as a result of high-speed chases as from police shootings.[87] Fleeing suspects and innocent bystanders are not the only ones at risk during high-speed pursuits; sometimes a police officer is killed or seriously injured during a chase.[88] A high-speed chase becomes dangerous very quickly. In 50 percent of such pursuits, a collision is likely to occur within the first two minutes, and 70 percent of all high-speed chase collisions take place within the first six minutes.

To decrease the danger associated with high-speed chases, officers in some departments today are trained in defensive driving tactics. Nevertheless, the most effective method for reducing fatalities is for the officer to terminate the chase. In a study of 146 jailed suspects who had been involved as drivers in high-speed chases, more than 70 percent of them said they would have slowed down if police had stopped chasing them.[89]

Training alone will not prevent high-speed chases; department policy is equally important. Most departments are formalizing procedures and enforcing written policies regarding when police may participate in a pursuit of a fleeing suspect (see TABLE 6-3 for the policies of some police departments). Ninety-four percent of local police departments, including all of those serving 25,000 or more residents, have a written policy governing high-speed chases. Sixty-one percent of departments, employing 82 percent of all officers in the United States, have a restrictive pursuit driving policy—one that restricts pursuits according to specific criteria such as type of offense or maximum speed. Twenty-five percent of departments, employing about 13 percent of police officers in the United States, have a judgmental pursuit policy—one that leaves pursuit decisions to the officer's discretion. Only 6 percent of departments, employing 3 percent of all officers nationwide, have a policy that discourages high-speed chases.[90]

TABLE 6-3 Circumstances in Which Officers May Engage in a High-Speed Chase

	Suspect's Offense			
	Traffic Violation	Misdemeanor	Nonviolent Felony	Violent Felony
Police Agency				
Colorado Springs	Yes	Yes	Yes	Yes
Detroit	No	No	Yes	Yes
Los Angeles	No	Yes	Yes	Yes
New Orleans	No	No	No	No
Oakland	No	No	Yes	Yes
San Francisco	No	No	No	Yes
San Jose	No	No	Yes	Yes
Philadelphia	No	No	No	Yes
Phoenix	No	No	No	Yes

Source: Gabe Cabrera, *Police Pursuit Policies in Other Jurisdictions* (San Francisco: San Francisco City Government, 2004), available at www.sfgov.org/site/bdsupvrs_page.asp?id=24020, accessed August 4, 2008.

There are no federal guidelines regulating police chases, but lack of guidelines is typically not problematic. Federal law enforcement agencies seldom get involved in high-speed chases, as they are primarily the result of an encounter with a uniformed officer in a marked police vehicle, something federal agencies do not have.

The decision to chase is initially made by the department and executed by officers using the following criteria:

- Severity of the offending infraction
- Speed of travel
- Number of pedestrians and vehicles on the street
- Weather conditions
- Whether the suspect is known and could be apprehended at a later time
- Whether the benefits of apprehending the suspect outweigh the risks of endangering officers, the public, and the suspect[91]

Occasionally, high-speed chases end in death or serious injury, and police may be held accountable. The courts have awarded third parties (e.g., passengers) injured in high-speed chases monetary settlements. For example, in *Travis v. City of Mesquite*, the court determined that the officer did not calculate the risk involved in the chase and was liable for damages.[92] However, the U.S. Supreme Court has ruled that police officers and departments cannot be held liable when suspects are injured in high-speed chases as long as they had no intention of physically harming the suspect or worsening the suspect's potential criminal charges. Bystanders, by contrast, may file lawsuits for damages against the officer and the department if it can be shown that the officer did not drive responsibly.[93]

Policing is among the most stressful occupations.

Police Stress

Stress frequently interferes with police officers performing their jobs to the best of their ability. **Stress** is an upsetting condition that occurs in response to adverse external influences and is capable of affecting an individual's physical health. Stress often leads

TABLE 6-4 Leading Causes of Police Stress

1. Handling child abuse/neglect cases
2. Killing an innocent person
3. Disagreement with department policies
4. The killing of a fellow police officer
5. Domestic violence
6. Terrorism
7. Lack of support from supervisors
8. Controlling riots
9. Disrespect by the public
10. Shift work

Source: Adapted from Heith Copes (ed.), *Policing and Stress* (Upper Saddle River, NJ: Prentice-Hall, 2005).

to an increased heart rate, a rise in blood pressure, muscular tension, irritability, and depression.[94]

Officers experience stress for a variety of reasons. In addition to individual characteristics, the most common sources of police stress are difficult decisions, conflict with supervisors, frustration with the courts, and criticism from the public (see TABLE 6-4).

During the course of performing their duties, officers regularly experience role conflict and role ambiguity. They are expected to maintain order and provide citizens with services while enforcing the law. They often find themselves having to be a counselor, law enforcer, public servant, and social worker all at the same time. In these situations officers are supposed to follow strict policies and procedures, yet the situations themselves often are ambiguous and not a simple "black-and-white" decision. Volatile situations force officers into a difficult position: They may need to make split-second decisions for their own safety and the safety of others without knowing whether their decisions will be supported by their supervisiors.[95]

It is not unusual for police to believe they are not supported by their supervisors and their department. In fact, the most common source of stress for officers comes from supervisors who may either overwhelm or under-support officers, providing them with too much paperwork and not enough structure. Other supervisors may apply discipline and enforce rules inconsistently, adding to officers' uncertainty.[96] The courts may also be seen as unsupportive, issuing rulings that are viewed as too lenient on offenders and too restrictive on procedural issues (such as rules governing the admissibility of evidence at criminal trials). As a consequence, police may view the courts as making their job more dangerous than it already is and be resentful of their actions.

Officers also frequently complain they are treated unfairly by the media and the public. Police may think reporters distort the truth to meet publication deadlines, do not understand the complexity of the cases they are reporting on, or simply fail to report the facts. Police may also believe that the public does not support them, instead preferring to challenge what police do and how they perform their jobs.[97] Citizens may submit complaints to the mayor's office, police chiefs, and newspapers criticizing speed traps, slow response times, busy 9-1-1 numbers, or—even worse—police discrimination and brutality. These actions reinforce a feeling among police that they are "damned if they do, and damned if they don't." This belief further alienates police from the public, builds solidarity among police, and contributes to police stress.

In addition to these factors, stress levels are strongly affected by the officer's individual personality and background characteristics, such as amount of experience, level of education, and assigned duties. For example, being assigned for a long period of time to a neighborhood with a high crime rate will likely produce more stress for an officer than if he or she is assigned to patrol an affluent neighborhood. Additionally, officers with more education and training tend to handle stress better than other officers.[98]

When officers experience stress, it can produce emotional, psychological, and physical problems. Studies have shown that officer stress may lead to a variety of extremely negative consequences:

- Poor job performance
- Absenteeism
- Corruption
- Alcoholism
- Heart disease
- Divorce
- Child abuse/neglect[99]

Critics of these studies complain that the studies are based on small samples that cannot be generalized and that the causal order between stress and these outcomes is difficult to establish; in other words, these destructive consequences may, in fact, be precursors to stress.[100] Additionally, critics of these studies suggest that police may simply do a poor job of managing their stress, such that the maladaptive coping strategies contribute to increased stress levels and negative outcomes.

Women and Minorities in Policing

Women have worked in policing for more than 100 years, but were not assigned to regular uniformed street patrol until 1967.[101] Lola Baldwin, the first female police officer in the United States, was hired by the Portland (Oregon) Police Department in 1905 to shelter women and children from the unruly crowds and seedy characters that would be roaming the streets when the city anticipated a large influx of people due to a large event (the Lewis and Clark Exposition).[102] The first regularly commissioned police woman was Alice Stebbins-Wells, who was hired in 1910 by the Los Angeles Police Department. By 1925, women were employed in more than 145 police departments across the United States.[103]

During the next 40 years, the hiring of female officers stalled and the status of women who were working in police departments changed very little from what it was at the turn of the twentieth century: working only with children, caring for prisoners, and performing secretarial duties. In 1940, only 141 of the 417 largest cities employed any females. Then, in 1967, the President's Commission on Law Enforcement and the Administration of Justice released a ground-breaking report that stated women should perform the same duties in policing as men.[104] As a result of this recommendation, women were hired by police forces throughout the country, opening new opportunities for women in the profession.[105]

Since the 1960s, police departments around the country have made great strides in recruiting larger numbers of women and minorities. Today, more than 11 percent of all police officers nationwide are females (more than 50,000 officers), although they account for nearly 13 percent of all sworn officers in large agencies (those with more than 100 sworn officers).[106] Even though more women are being hired, they still tend to hit a "glass ceiling" in terms of promotion: Only a few female officers advance beyond the rank of patrol officer over the course of their careers.

Studies have shown that female police are equally as effective as their male counterparts. They consistently perform as well as men, generally use the same techniques to gain and keep control, and are no more likely than male officers to display or use a weapon.[107]

Studies have found that female police officers are as effective as male officers, when it comes to applying and enforcing the law.

In response to domestic violence incidents, female officers have been found to respond more effectively than their male counterparts.[108] Yet women in the force face several unique problems, such as trying to balance pregnancy with regular work assignments.

Women are not the only ones entering the police force in great numbers; there are also more African Americans and Latinos in policing today than at any other time in the history. The first African American officers were hired in 1861 in Washington, DC, and the first Latino officer was hired in 1896 in New York City. Since then, their numbers have climbed significantly. By 1900, approximately 3 percent of all U.S. police officers were African Americans, most of whom worked in northern metropolitan areas. The percentage of African American officers held steady until after World War II. In the post-war era, there has been a steady increase in African Americans' numbers on police forces relative to their share of the U.S. population.[109] In 2004, approximately 12 percent of all law enforcement officers nationwide were African Americans (totaling 54,000 officers), representing an increase of more than 1500 officers since 2000, and the number of African American officers is now roughly equivalent to their proportion of the U.S. population.[110] In contrast, Latinos account for about 14 percent of the U.S. population but only 9 percent of police officers, although they—like African Americans and women—are making gains in the profession (see FIGURE 6-4).[111]

In part, the increase in minority officers is a result of lawsuits filed by African Americans and Latinos charging police agencies with racial and ethnic discrimination regarding the entrance requirements and promotion examinations. The U.S. Supreme Court decisions in *Griggs v. Duke Power Company* and *Albemarle Paper Co. v. Moody*, for example, supported their claims of discriminatory practices, and today law enforcement agencies are deemed to be in violation of federal law if their hiring practices are discovered to be unfair.[112] The decisions in these two cases make it clear that police agencies must be able to demonstrate that their entrance requirements for hiring and promotion are job related, bias free, fairly administered, and properly graded.

The Equal Employment Opportunity Act of 1972 laid the groundwork for the establishment of affirmative action programs and quota systems for hiring and promotion of police officers. In 1987, in *United States v. Paradise*, the U.S. Supreme Court questioned the use of promotion quotas by the Alabama State Police and required the state to promote one African American officer for each white officer promoted until 25 percent of the top

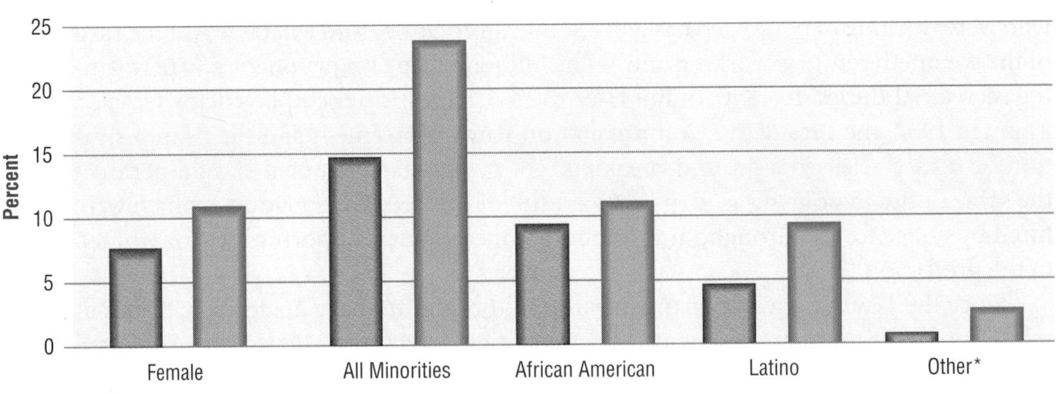

FIGURE 6-4 Female and Minority Local Police Officers

Source: Matthew Hickman and Brian A. Reaves, ***Local Police Departments, 2003*** (Washington, DC: U.S. Department of Justice, 2006).

ranks were occupied by African Americans.[113] Critics of this ruling contend that quotas that tie employment decisions to race or ethnicity violate the Civil Rights Act of 1964. They also believe that lowering standards to achieve a targeted quota creates resentment among employees and jeopardizes the ability of law enforcement to serve and protect citizens. Conversely, proponents of quotas see these measures as an obligatory remedy for past wrongs. They also contend there is no evidence to show that department standards are lowered when an affirmative action plan is in place.

For police to do their jobs effectively and safely, they must be able to communicate with the people they protect and serve. In particular, they need to immediately understand the complaint of a victim or the information being provided by a witness to a crime. A recent U.S. Census report noted that approximately 20 percent of all U.S. residents speak a language other than English at home and approximately 10 percent qualify as limited English proficient (LEP). For example, 26 percent of all Spanish speakers, 30 percent of all Chinese speakers, and 28 percent of all Vietnamese speakers report that they speak English "not well" or "not at all."[114] For police officers, the task of communicating and building trust with these new residents can be immense and presents an enormous challenge for law enforcement agencies committed to developing community policing in neighborhoods throughout their city.

WRAPPING IT UP

Chapter Highlights

- The exercise of police discretion is central to officers carrying out their duties. This decision is influenced by several important factors, including legal considerations and characteristics of the suspect.
- A major problem in policing is corruption—that is, the misuse of authority by an officer in a manner designed to obtain some sort of personal gain. Corruption among officers ranges from receiving or demanding minor items from businesses during the course of their duties, to extorting cash from suspects, accepting bribes, and engaging in perjury and premeditated theft.
- Police are among the few public servants authorized to use force, but sometimes their use of force is excessive. Police brutality refers to instances when officers use unlawful, unnecessary, or extreme force with suspects.
- The automobile is a police officer's most deadly weapon. More than 350 citizens are killed annually as a result of high-speed chases—even more are killed from police shootings.
- Stress is inherent in police work. Sources of police stress include rotating shift assignments, fear and danger, limited opportunities for career growth and development, and inadequate rewards.
- The number of women and minorities in policing is increasing every year, but these groups are still underrepresented at the supervisory ranks and face unique challenges in police work.

Words to Know

corruption Misuse of authority by officers for the benefit of themselves or others.

defense of life standard Policy mandating that officers may use deadly force only in defense of their own lives or another's life.

fleeing felon doctrine Law (prior to 1985) stating that an officer could use deadly force to stop a felony suspect from fleeing.

full law enforcement Law enforcement approach in which officers respond formally to all suspicious behavior.

noble cause corruption A type of corruption that some police and civilians believe is justified because it serves the greater public good.

grass-eaters Police who accept bribes when offered.

meat-eaters Police who aggressively misuse their power for personal gain.

police brutality The unlawful use of force.

police discretion Authority of police to choose between alternative courses of action.

preservation of life policy Policy mandating that police use every other means possible to maintain order before turning to deadly force.

selective law enforcement Law enforcement approach in which officers under-enforce some laws and over-enforce others.

stress A condition that occurs in response to adverse external influences and is capable of affecting an individual's physical health.

Tennessee v. Garner U.S. Supreme Court ruling that eliminated the "shoot a fleeing felon" policy and replaced it with a defense of life standard.

Think and Discuss

1. Should there be limits on police use of discretion? How can officers exercise discretion and treat all civilians in a fair and impartial manner?
2. Is it possible to regulate police corruption? If you were a police administrator, which policies would you put in place to control police corruption?
3. Under which conditions should police use force? When does force become excessive? When is it reasonable for police to use deadly force?
4. Should police participate in high-speed chases? Is the benefit of potentially capturing an offender worth the potential costs of such a chase?
5. Should female and male officers perform the same duties? Does more attention need to be devoted to the recruitment and promotion of racial and ethnic minorities in policing?

Notes

1. Francis Cullen, Bruce Link, Lawrence Travis, and Terrence Lemming, "Paradox in Policing," *Journal of Police Science and Administration* 11:457–462 (1983); Federal Bureau of Investigation, *Uniform Crime Reports, 2007* (Washington, DC: U.S. Department of Justice, 2008); William Westley, "Violence and the Police," *American Journal of Sociology* 59:34–41 (1953).
2. Federal Bureau of Investigation, note 1.
3. Federal Bureau of Investigation, note 1.
4. *District of Columbia v. Heller*, 554 U.S. --- (2008); Matthew Hickman and Brian Reaves, *Local Police Departments, 2003* (Washington, DC: U.S. Department of Justice, 2006).
5. Stephanie Myers, *Police Encounters with Juvenile Suspects: Explaining the Use of Authority and Provision of Support* (Washington, DC: National Institute of Justice, 1999).
6. Robert Terry, "Discrimination in the Handling of Juvenile Offenders by Social-Control Agencies," *Journal of Research in Crime and Delinquency* 4:218–230 (1967); Donald Black and Albert Reiss, "Police Control of Juveniles," *American Sociological Review* 35:63–77 (1970).
7. Myers, note 5.
8. Nathan Goldman, *The Differential Selection of Juvenile Offenders for Court Appearance* (New York: National Council on Crime and Delinquency, 1963).
9. Terry, note 6.
10. Ronald Farrell and Lynn Swigert, "Prior Offense Record as a Self-fulfilling Prophecy," *Law and Society Review* 12:437–453 (1978).
11. Black and Reiss, note 6; Irving Piliavin and Scott Briar, "Police Encounters with Juveniles," *American Journal of Sociology* 70:206–214 (1964).
12. Kenneth Novak, James Frank, Brad Smith, and Robin Engel, "Revisiting the Decision to Arrest: Comparing Beat and Community Officers," *Crime & Delinquency* 48:70–98 (2002).
13. Black and Reiss, note 6.
14. Federal Bureau of Investigation, note 1.

15. Samuel Walker, Cassia Spohn, and Miriam DeLone, *The Color of Justice*, 4th ed. (Belmont, CA: Wadsworth, 2006).

16. John Boydstun, *San Diego Field Interrogation* (Washington, DC: The Police Foundation, 1975); Robert Sampson, "Effects of Socioeconomic Context on Official Reaction to Juvenile Delinquency," *American Sociological Review* 51:876–885 (1986).

17. Black and Reiss, note 6.

18. Federal Bureau of Investigation, note 1.

19. Sandra Lee Browning, Francis Cullen, Liqun Cao, Renee Kopache, and Thomas Stevenson, "Race and Getting Hassled by the Police," *Police Studies* 17:1–11 (1994); Matt DeLisi and Bob Regoli, "Race, Conventional Crime, and Criminal Justice," *Journal of Criminal Justice* 27:549–558 (1999).

20. Carl Werthman and Irving Piliavin, "Gang Members and the Police," in David Bordua (Ed.), *The Police* (New York: John Wiley & Sons, 1967), pp. 56–98.

21. Terrence Allen, "Taking a Juvenile into Custody: Situational Factors That Influence Police Officers' Decisions," *Journal of Sociology and Social Welfare* 32:121–129 (2005).

22. Federal Bureau of Investigation, note 1.

23. Novak et al., note 12; Joan McCord, Cathy Widom, and Nancy Crowell, *Juvenile Crime/Juvenile Justice* (Washington, DC: National Academy Press, 2001), p. 245.

24. Thomas Monahan, "Police Dispositions of Juvenile Offenders," *Phylon* 31:91–107 (1970).

25. Delbert Elliott and Harwin Voss, *Delinquency and Dropout* (Lexington, MA: Lexington Books, 1974).

26. Gail Armstrong, "Females under the Law: Protected but Unequal," *Crime & Delinquency* 23:109–120 (1977); Meda Chesney-Lind, "Judicial Paternalism and the Female Status Offender," *Crime & Delinquency* 23:121–130 (1970); Ruth Horowitz and Ann Pottieger, "Gender Bias in Juvenile Justice Handling of Seriously Crime-Involved Youth," *Journal of Research in Crime and Delinquency* 28:75–100 (1991).

27. Christy Visher, "Gender, Police Arrest Decisions, and Notions of Chivalry," *Criminology* 21:5–28 (1983).

28. Visher, note 27, pp. 22–23.

29. Paul Tracy, *Decision Making in Juvenile Justice* (New York: Praeger, 2002); Christopher Uggen, "Class, Gender, and Arrest," *Criminology* 38:835–862 (2000); Robert Sampson, "Effects of Socioeconomic Context of Official Reaction to Juvenile Delinquency," *American Sociological Review* 51:876–885 (1986).

30. Douglas Smith and Christy Visher, "Street-Level Justice," *Social Problems* 29:167–177 (1981); Stephen Mastrofski, Robert Worden, and Jeffrey Snipes, "Law Enforcement in a Time of Community Policing," *Criminology* 33:539–563 (1995); Ronet Bachman, "Victims' Perceptions of Initial Police Responses to Robbery and Aggravated Assault," *Journal of Quantitative Criminology* 12:363–390 (1996); David Huizinga and Delbert Elliott, "Juvenile Offenders," *Crime & Delinquency* 33:206–223 (1987).

31. George Bodine, "Factors Related to Police Dispositions of Juvenile Offenders," paper presented at the annual meeting of the American Sociological Association, Montreal, 1964.

32. Sampson, note 29.

33. Robert Brown, "Black, White, and Unequal: Examining Situational Determinants of Arrest Decisions from Police–Suspect Encounters," *Criminal Justice Studies* 18:51–68 (2005).

34. Werthman and Piliavin, note 20.

35. Richard Lundman, "Demeanor and Arrest: Additional Evidence from Previously Unpublished Data," *Journal of Research in Crime and Delinquency* 33:306–323 (1996); Robert Worden and Robin Shepard, "Demeanor, Crime, and Police Behavior: A Reexamination of the Police Services Study Data," *Criminology* 34:83–105 (1996); Robert Worden, Robin Shepard, and Stephen Mastrofski, "On the Meaning and Measurement of Suspects' Demeanor toward the Police: A Comment on 'Demeanor and Arrest,'" *Journal of Research in Crime and Delinquency* 33:324–332 (1996).

36. Novak et al., note 12.

37. Aaron Cicourel, *The Social Organization of Juvenile Justice* (New York: John Wiley & Sons, 1976).

38. Robin Engel, James Sobol, and Robert Worden, "Further Exploration of the Demeanor Hypothesis: The Interaction Effects of Suspects' Characteristics and Demeanor on Police Behavior," *Justice Quarterly*

17:249 (2000).

39. Stephen Mastrofski, Michael Reisig, and John McCluskey, "Police Disrespect toward the Public: An Encounter-Based Analysis," *Criminology* 40:519–551 (2002); Michael Reisig, John McCluskey, Stephen Mastrofski, and William Terrill, "Suspect Disrespect toward the Police," *Justice Quarterly* 21:241–268 (2004).
40. Mastrofski et al., note 39, p. 534.
41. Theodore Ferdinand, "Police Attitudes and Police Organization," *Police Studies* 3:46–60 (1980).
42. Lonn Lanza-Kaduce and Richard Greenleaf, "Age and Race Deference Reversals," *Journal of Research in Crime and Delinquency* 37:221–236 (2000); Charles Crawford and Ronald Burns, "Resisting Arrest," *Police Practice and Research* 3:105–117 (2002).
43. Douglas Smith and Jody Klein, "Police Control of Interpersonal Disputes," *Social Problems* 31:468–481 (1984).
44. Robert Friedrich, "Police Use of Force," *Annals of the American Academy of Political and Social Science*, 452:82–97 (1980).
45. Bodine, note 31.
46. James Q. Wilson, *Varieties of Police Behavior* (Cambridge, MA: Harvard University Press, 1968).
47. Richard Sundeen, "Police Professionalization and Community Attachments and Diversion of Juveniles from the Justice System," *Criminology* 11:570–580 (1974).
48. Robin Engel, "The Effects of Supervisory Styles on Patrol Officer Behavior," *Police Quarterly* 3:283 (2000).
49. Samuel Walker and Charles Katz, *The Police in America*, 6th ed. (New York: McGraw-Hill, 2008).
50. Hickman and Reaves, note 4; Westley Jennings and Edward Hudak, "Police Response to Persons with Mental Illness," in Roger Dunham and Geoffrey Alpert (Eds.), *Critical Issues in Policing*, 5th ed. (Long Grove, IL: Waveland Press, 2005), pp. 115–128.
51. Brad Brewer, "AVL/GPS for Front Line Policing," *Law and Order* 55:46–54 (2007); Peter Manning, "Information Technologies and the Police," in Michael Tonry and Norval Morris (Eds.), *Modern Policing* (Chicago: University of Chicago Press, 1993), pp. 349–399.
52. Julian Roebuck and Thomas Barker, "A Typology of Police Corruption," *Social Problems* 21:423–437 (1974).
53. William DeLeon-Granados and William Wells, "Do You Want Extra Coverage with Those Fries?" *Police Quarterly* 1:71–85 (1998).
54. James Spradley, *You Owe Yourself a Drunk* (Prospect Heights, IL: Waveland Press, 1970).
55. Samuel Walker and Dawn Irlbeck, *Driving while Female* (Omaha: University of Nebraska, 2002).
56. Geoffrey Alpert, Roger Dunham, and Meghan Stroshine, *Policing* (Long Grove, IL: Waveland Press, 2006).
57. Milton Mollen, *Commission to Investigate Allegations of Police Corruption and the Anti-corruption Procedures of the Police Department* (New York: Mollen Commission, 1994).
58. W. Doherty, "Ex-sergeant Says He Aided Bid to Sell Exam," *The Boston Globe*, February 26, 1987, p. 61.
59. Maurice Punch, *Conduct Unbecoming* (London: Tavistock, 1985).
60. John Kleinig, "Rethinking Noble Cause Corruption," *International Journal of Police Science and Management* 4:287–314 (2002).
61. "Chicago Crime Commission," available at http://www.chicagocrimecommission.org/ADD, accessed August 6, 2008.
62. George Wickersham, *Enforcement of Prohibition* (Washington, DC: U.S. Government Printing Office, 1931).
63. Knapp Commission, *The Knapp Commission Report on Police Corruption* (New York: George Braziller, 1973).
64. Mollen, note 57, p. 2.

65. James Fyfe and Robert Kane, *Bad Cops: A Study of Career-Ending Misconduct among New York City Police* (Washington, DC: U.S. Department of Justice, 2006).

66. Fyfe and Kane, note 65.

67. Wickersham, note 62.

68. Allyson Collins, *Shielded from Justice* (New York: Human Rights Watch, 1998).

69. Independent Commission on the Los Angeles Police Department, *Report of the Independent Commission on the Los Angeles Police Department* (Los Angeles: Independent Commission of the Los Angeles Police Department, 1991).

70. William Terrill and Stephen Mastrofski, "Situational and Officer-Based Determinants of Police Coercion," *Justice Quarterly* 19:215–248 (2002); Joel Garner and Christopher Maxwell, *Understanding the Use of Force by and against the Police in Six Jurisdictions* (Washington, DC: U.S. Department of Justice, 2002).

71. Alpert et al., note 56.

72. Terrill and Mastrofski, note 70; Garner and Maxwell, note 70.

73. Terrill and Mastrofski, note 70; National Center for Women and Policing, *Men, Women, and Police Excessive Force* (Los Angeles: National Center for Women and Policing, 2002).

74. Independent Commission on the Los Angeles Police Department, note 69; Victor Kappeler, *Critical Issues in Police Civil Liability*, 4th ed. (Long Grove, IL: Waveland Press, 2006).

75. Kappeler, note 74.

76. Kevin Johnson, "Police Brutality Cases Up 25%; Union Worried over Dip in Hiring Standards," *USA Today*, December 18, 2007, p. 1A.

77. Federal Bureau of Investigation, *Supplementary Homicide Reports, 1976–2004* (Washington, DC: Bureau of Justice Statistics, 2006).

78. William Geller and Hans Toch, *Police Violence* (New Haven, CT: Yale University Press, 2005); William Geller and Kevin Karales, *Shootings of and by Chicago Police* (Chicago: Law Enforcement Study Group, 1981), p. 56.

79. Eric Weslander, "Child's Killer Expresses Regret as He's Given 16-Year Term," available at http://www2.ljworld.com/news/2006/mar/04/childs_killer_expresses_regret_hes_given_16year_te/, accessed August 3, 2008.

80. *Tennessee v. Garner*, 471 U.S. 1 (1985).

81. Steve Caraway, "Agencies Set Own Deadly Force Policy," *The Morning News* (Springdale, AR), March 9, 2006, p. 6A.

82. Federal Bureau of Investigation, note 1.

83. James Fyfe, "Police Use of Deadly Force," *Justice Quarterly* 5:165–205 (1988); William Geller, *Deadly Force* (Washington, DC: Police Executive Research Forum, 1992); Catherine Milton, Jeanne Halleck, James Lardner, and Garry Albrecht, *Police Use of Deadly Force* (Washington, DC: The Police Foundation, 1977).

84. Jodi Brown and Patrick Langan, *Policing and Homicide, 1976–98: Justifiable Homicide by Police, Police Officers Murdered by Felons* (Washington, DC: U.S. Department of Justice, 2001).

85. Fyfe, note 83; Geller and Karales, note 78; Sean Grennan, "Findings on the Role of Officer Gender in Violent Encounters with Citizens," *Journal of Police Science and Administration* 15:78–85 (1987).

86. Matthew Durose, Erica Schmitt, and Patrick Langan, *Contacts between Police and the Public* (Washington, DC: U.S. Department of Justice, 2005).

87. Federal Bureau of Investigation, note 1; Mark Sherman, "High Speed Chase Reaches Supreme Court," *USA Today*, available at http://www.usatoday.com/news/washington/judicial/2007-02-24-police-chase-case_x.htm, accessed August 7, 2008.

88. Alpert et al., note 56; Geoffrey Alpert and Lorie Fridell, *Police Vehicles and Firearms* (Prospect Heights, IL: Waveland Press, 1992).

89. John Hill, "High-Speed Police Pursuits," *FBI Law Enforcement Bulletin*, July 2002, pp. 1–5.

90. Gabe Cabrera, *Police Pursuit Policies in Other Jurisdictions* (San Francisco: City of San Francisco Government, 2004).

91. Cabrera, note 90.

92. *Travis v. City of Mesquite*, 830 S.W.2d 94 (1992).

93. *Sacramento v. Lewis*, 523 U.S. 833 (1998); *Indianapolis v. Garman*, 49S00-0602-CV-55 (2006); Kevin Corcoran, "Bystanders Can Sue Police over Chases," *The Indianapolis Star*, June 15, 2006, p. 1A; Kappeler, note 76; *Scott v. Harris*, 127 S.Ct. 1769 (2007).

94. Kent Kerley, "The Costs of Protecting and Serving," in Heith Copes (Ed.), *Policing and Stress* (Upper Saddle River, NJ: Prentice Hall, 2005), pp. 73–86.

95. Vivian Lord, *Changes in Social Support Sources of New Law Enforcement Officers*, doctoral dissertation, North Carolina State University (Raleigh, NC: North Carolina State University, 1992).

96. John Crank and Michael Caldero, "The Production of Occupational Stress in Medium-Sized Police Agencies," *Journal of Criminal Justice* 19:339–349 (1991).

97. Cara Donlon-Cotton, "How Dangerous Is That Reporter?" *Law and Order* 55:20–22 (2007); Kenneth Dowler and Valerie Zawilski, "Public Perceptions of Police Misconduct and Discrimination: Examining the Impact of Media Consumption," *Journal of Criminal Justice* 35:193–203 (2007).

98. Kerley, note 94.

99. Dennis Stevens, "Police Officer Stress," *Law and Order* 47(9):77–81 (1999); Copes, note 94.

100. Victor Kappeler and Gary Potter, *The Mythology of the Criminal Justice System*, 4th ed. (Prospect Heights, IL: Waveland Press, 2004).

101. Alissa Pollitz Worden, "The Attitudes of Women and Men in Policing," *Criminology* 31:203–242 (1993).

102. Gloria Myers, *A Municipal Mother* (Corvallis, OR: Oregon State University Press, 1995).

103. Phil Clements, *Policing a Diverse Society*, 2nd ed. (New York: Oxford University Press, 2008); Sandra Wells and Betty Alt, *Police Women* (New York: Praeger, 2005); Penny Harrington, "History of Women in Policing," available at http://www.pennyharrington.com/herstory.htm, accessed August 5, 2008.

104. President's Commission on Law Enforcement and Administration of Justice, *The Challenge of Crime in a Free Society* (Washington, DC: U.S. Government Printing Office, 1967).

105. President's Commission, note 104.

106. Federal Bureau of Investigation, note 1.

107. Alissa Worden, "The Attitudes of Women and Men in Policing," *Criminology* 31:203–242 (1993); Joyce Sichel, *Women on Patrol* (Washington, DC: U.S. Government Printing Office, 1978).

108. Robert Homant and Daniel Kennedy, "Police Perceptions of Spouse Abuse: A Comparison of Male and Female Officers," *Journal of Criminal Justice* 13:29–47 (1985).

109. Roger Able, *The Black Shields* (Bloomington, IN: AuthorHouse, 2006); National Black Police Association, available at http://www.blackpolice.org/, accessed August 6, 2008; Jack Kuykendall and David Burns, "The Black Officer," *Journal of Contemporary Criminal Justice* 1:103–113 (1980).

110. Hickman and Reaves, note 4.

111. Hickman and Reaves, note 4.

112. *Griggs v. Duke Power Company*, 401 U.S. 424 (1971); *Albemarle Paper Co. v. Moody*, 422 U.S. 405 (1975).

113. *United States v. Paradise*, 480 U.S. 149 (1987).

114. U.S. Department of Justice, "Department of Justice Sends Limited English Proficiency Guidance to the *Federal Register* That Will Help Reduce Language Barriers," available at http://www.usdoj.gov/opa/pr/2002/April/02_crt_218.htm, accessed August 5, 2008.

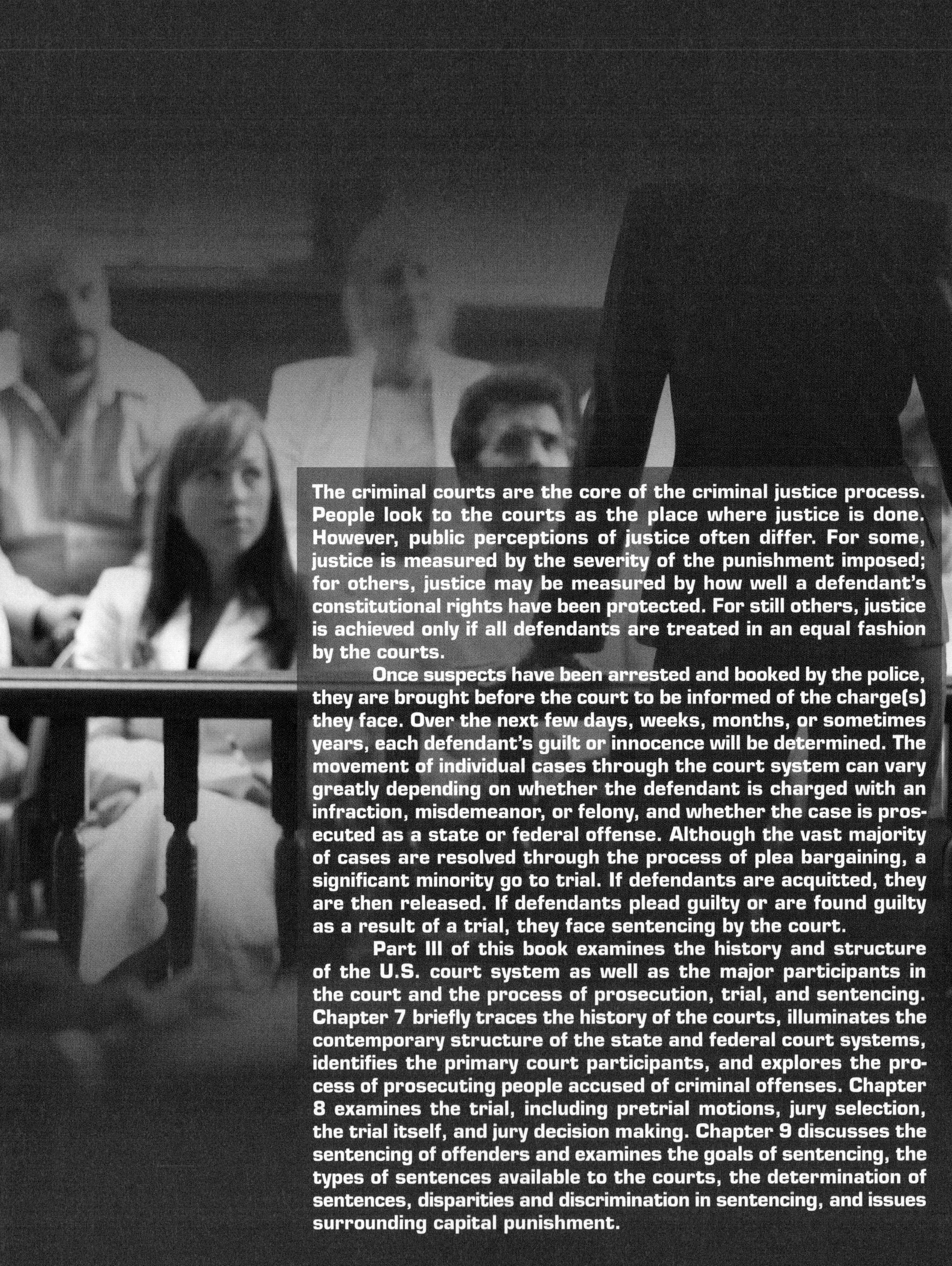

The criminal courts are the core of the criminal justice process. People look to the courts as the place where justice is done. However, public perceptions of justice often differ. For some, justice is measured by the severity of the punishment imposed; for others, justice may be measured by how well a defendant's constitutional rights have been protected. For still others, justice is achieved only if all defendants are treated in an equal fashion by the courts.

Once suspects have been arrested and booked by the police, they are brought before the court to be informed of the charge(s) they face. Over the next few days, weeks, months, or sometimes years, each defendant's guilt or innocence will be determined. The movement of individual cases through the court system can vary greatly depending on whether the defendant is charged with an infraction, misdemeanor, or felony, and whether the case is prosecuted as a state or federal offense. Although the vast majority of cases are resolved through the process of plea bargaining, a significant minority go to trial. If defendants are acquitted, they are then released. If defendants plead guilty or are found guilty as a result of a trial, they face sentencing by the court.

Part III of this book examines the history and structure of the U.S. court system as well as the major participants in the court and the process of prosecution, trial, and sentencing. Chapter 7 briefly traces the history of the courts, illuminates the contemporary structure of the state and federal court systems, identifies the primary court participants, and explores the process of prosecuting people accused of criminal offenses. Chapter 8 examines the trial, including pretrial motions, jury selection, the trial itself, and jury decision making. Chapter 9 discusses the sentencing of offenders and examines the goals of sentencing, the types of sentences available to the courts, the determination of sentences, disparities and discrimination in sentencing, and issues surrounding capital punishment.

PART

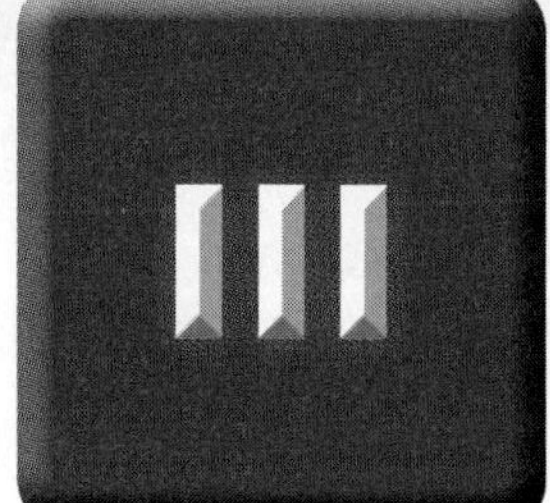

Courts

THE TRUE ADMINIST

CHAPTER

7

The Criminal Courts: Structure and Process

OBJECTIVES

1 Understand the similarities and differences between federal courts and state and local courts.
2 Comprehend the functions and responsibilities of the various courts at each level.
3 Know the roles and responsibilities of the major court participants, including judges, prosecutors, and defense attorneys.
4 Understand the nature and function of the initial appearance.
5 Know the reasons behind pretrial release, alternatives to money bail, and justifications for the use of preventive detention.
6 Know the major factors considered by prosecutors in selecting or dismissing charges.
7 Distinguish between the types of pleas, understand the nature of plea bargaining, and elucidate the advantages and disadvantages of bargained justice.

PROFILES IN CRIME AND JUSTICE

Diana Reynolds Clayton

Assistant Professor of Criminal Justice
Rogers State University

Pride. Responsibility. Fear. These are a few of the emotions I felt when acting as either an Assistant District Attorney or an Assistant Attorney General. I felt such pride that I was chosen to protect society by holding those persons accountable for violating the criminal law. It was my responsibility to represent the state by my actions and my decisions. My actions would forever change the lives of the individuals involved.

An appellate judge once described a "prosecutor with a pen" as the most powerful person in the criminal justice system. I didn't realize at the time how accurate those words were. The prosecutor is the person who makes the decision to charge or not charge an individual with a crime. The prosecutor alone decides which crime to charge, whether to offer a plea bargain, and how to set the terms of that plea bargain. No one can enter or progress through the criminal justice system except as determined by the prosecutor. Even if a defendant is later acquitted, the actions of the prosecutor determine whether he or she will have to spend large sums of money to post bail or spend months in jail, to accept a plea bargain and immediately become a felon, or to endure the scrutiny of a public trial in the hope of an acquittal. These are the types of decisions routinely made by a prosecutor.

State prosecutors generally have greater latitude over more aspects of the criminal case and operate in a less formal courtroom environment than do federal prosecutors because of the more specific procedures manifest in the federal system. State prosecutors have much heavier caseloads, and their salaries are typically lower than those of prosecutors at the federal level. However, federal prosecutors often handle more complicated crimes involving criminal enterprises, national security, or interstate commerce.

Whether acting at the state or federal level, most prosecutors embrace their responsibilities as conscientious professionals, some do their jobs as a mere exercise of the authority that comes with the office, and a few, unfortunately, act with a sense of indifference. One need simply read the decisions of appellate courts or review the statistics about the causes of wrongful convictions to grasp the full magnitude of prosecutorial decisions.

I became a prosecutor after a district attorney heard me make a presentation at a juvenile justice conference and then offered me a job. Although I had been working in the public sector for several years, at the time I did not fully comprehend the nature of the career change I was making. I thrived as a prosecutor. I loved researching the law, crafting an argument to capture the essence of the crime for the jury, and engaging in the creative problem solving that is part of the fundamental nature of justice when the consequences match the criminal act.

Introduction

The modern system of U.S. courts incorporates both federal and state or local courts. This system is the product of many years of gradual development. This chapter examines the structure and process of the criminal courts, the key actors in the courts, and the pretrial processing of those accused of crimes.

History of the American Court System

English common law and the English court system were the primary role models for the beginnings of the American court system. Colonial courts performed a variety of functions, ranging from legislative and executive activities, such as the determination of tax assessments, to more traditional activities associated with the judicial branch.[1] These courts were relatively simple, with most of the judicial personnel being local influential citizens who were appointed to their positions by the colonial governor. **Justice of the Peace (JP) courts** were established at the local county level; they were typically administered by a person with some degree of status or recognition within the community rather than by someone with formal legal training.

The American Revolution and Creation of State Courts

When the American Revolution took place, the royal colonial courts were closed down and then reestablished as state courts by the new state assemblies. Most state courts were

FOCUS ON CRIMINAL JUSTICE

The Foreign Intelligence Surveillance Court

The Foreign Intelligence Surveillance Court was created in 1978 by the Foreign Intelligence Surveillance Act (FISA). This court consists of 11 district court judges from seven of the U.S. judicial circuits, each of whom serves a term of seven years. No fewer than three of the judges are required to reside within 20 miles of the District of Columbia.

The court meets every two weeks to secretly review applications by the Department of Justice and grant orders approving electronic surveillance, including wiretaps, telephone record traces, and physical searches anywhere within the United States. Normally search warrants and requests for wiretaps from local law enforcement need the approval of a judge after those personnel have demonstrated there is probable cause a crime has been committed or is being planned. The warrant must be specific and, in case of a search warrant, the target of the search must be notified. Warrantless searches are very narrowly circumscribed. The FISA court operates differently from local courts, however. Because it involves issues of foreign intelligence, law enforcement agents need to simply identify the target as a foreign power or its agent, whether the person is a U.S. citizen or not. Between 1978 and 2004, the court approved nearly 19,000 warrants and rejected only five. All documents pertaining to the cases brought to the Foreign Intelligence Surveillance Court are classified, and targeted individuals are unable to challenge any evidence used in the requests for warrants.

The passage of the Patriot Act in 2001 and subsequent investigations of suspected terrorist activities, both within the United States and abroad, have led to questions about the FISA court and its operation. In 2006, controversy arose when some of the secret activities of the court became publicly known. Sometime after the September 11, 2001, terrorist attacks, President George W. Bush issued a secret order to permit the National Security Agency to monitor emails and telephone conversations between persons in the United States and suspected terrorists overseas. Critics believed that this warrantless surveillance may have been used to obtain additional wiretap warrants from the FISA court. While some members of Congress demanded an investigation into the warrantless wiretaps, the Bush administration defended it as being constitutional. Because the FISA court operates in secrecy, both congressional and media interest in its operations is necessarily limited.

On August 17, 2006, U.S. District Judge Anna Taylor, acting for the 6th Circuit, ruled that the eavesdropping program was unconstitutional, stating that it violates citizens' rights to free speech and privacy. Less than two months later, however, a unanimous ruling by a three-judge panel of the 6th Circuit ruled that the Bush administration could continue the warrantless surveillance program while the administration appeals Judge Taylor's decision. In 2008, Congress amended the FISA Act that allows the government to spy on emails, phone calls, Web surfing, and other communications without warrants. The law also includes immunity from privacy lawsuits for telecommunication companies such as AT&T and Verizon who participated in illegal spying by the government.

Sources: Carol Leonnig, "Secret Court's Judges Were Warned about NSA Spy Data," *The Washington Post*, February 9, 2006, p. A1; Elizabeth Bazan, *The Foreign Intelligence Surveillance Act: An Overview of the Statutory Framework and Recent Judicial Decisions* (Washington, DC: Library of Congress, 2004); *The Foreign Intelligence Surveillance Act*, P.L. 95-511, Title I, § 103, 50 U.S.C. § 1803 (1978); Dan Eggen and Dafina Linzer, "Judge Rules Against Wiretaps," *The Washington Post*, August 18, 2006, p. A01; David Ashenfelter, "Eavesdropping Will Continue During Appeal: Ruling Against Spying Is on Hold," *Detroit Free Press*, October 5, 2006; Dan Eggen and Paul Kane, "Surveillance Bill Offers Protection to Telecom Firms," *The Washington Post*, June 20, 2008, p. A1.

assigned general trial jurisdiction over both criminal and civil matters, and each state created at least one court of appeals.

To protect themselves from the possibility of having their rights trampled on by the new federal government, members of Congress added a Bill of Rights in 1791 as the first 10 amendments to the U.S. Constitution. Because the states had already implemented many of these safeguards, Congress intended the Bill of Rights to protect citizens from abuses by the federal government alone; abuses of citizens by the states were to be regulated by state protections.

Creation of the Federal Court System

The Judiciary Act of 1789, which was created by the First United States Congress, laid out the basic structure of the federal court system. Four federal circuit courts were established, along with 13 federal district courts. The circuit courts were assigned general trial jurisdiction and the responsibility to hear appeals from the lower district courts. Separate federal circuit courts of appeal were created in 1891. Two decades later, the trial functions of the circuit and district courts were combined under the aegis of U.S. District Courts. Today, there are 94 District Courts, 12 regional U.S. Courts of Appeal, and a single U.S. Court of Appeals for the Federal Circuit.

Article III of the U.S. Constitution states that the ultimate judicial power of the government is to be placed in a supreme court. In addition, it gives Congress the right to create more federal courts and provides for the lifetime tenure of federal judges, thus protecting them from political pressures and possible capricious attempts by Congress to remove judges who make unpopular decisions.

In 1803, in ***Marbury v. Madison***, the U.S. Supreme Court established the principle of judicial review—the power of the Supreme Court to review and determine the constitutionality of acts of Congress and orders by the executive branch.[2] In 1810, the Supreme Court extended this principle to acts by the states in *Fletcher v. Peck*.[3] During the 35 years that John Marshall was Chief Justice, the Court handed down decisions overturning more than a dozen state laws, ruling that they were in conflict with the Constitution.[4]

State Court Systems

Although the general structures of the court systems of the 50 states are very similar, some differences between them are apparent.[5] For example, Illinois has a very simplified court structure that features only three tiers: 22 circuit courts with general jurisdiction (the authority to hear both criminal and civil cases), 5 intermediate district appellate courts, and a supreme court. By comparison, Texas has a much more complex structure. Its system includes nearly 2200 courts of limited jurisdiction (divided into county courts, probate courts, county courts at law, municipal courts, and Justice of the Peace courts), 410 district courts, 10 criminal district courts with general jurisdiction, 14 intermediate courts of appeals, a supreme court to hear civil cases, and a last-resort court of criminal appeals.

Limited Jurisdiction

Courts of limited jurisdiction, often referred to as lower or inferior courts, are the most numerous of the various state courts and handle much heavier caseloads than do general trial courts. They include city courts, Justice of the Peace courts, juvenile courts, police courts, and traffic courts. The vast majority of cases handled by limited jurisdiction courts deal with traffic offenses. Cases involving minor misdemeanors, civil and domestic disputes, juvenile offenses, and local ordinance violations account for most of the remaining filings.

In many jurisdictions, the lower courts handle the defendant's initial appearance in a criminal case—that is, the reading of charges, the setting of bail in felony cases, and the determination of the need for a court-appointed attorney. If the offense is a misdemeanor or violation of a local ordinance, the case may be dealt with immediately by the defendant entering a plea of guilty, by the presiding judge making a determination of guilt, or by the judge dismissing the case. In felony cases, if the defendant's initial appearance is in a lower court, the case is then transferred to a general trial court.

General Jurisdiction

General trial courts, or **courts of general jurisdiction**, go under many different names but are most commonly known as superior courts, circuit courts, district courts, or courts of common pleas. These trial courts have the power to hear virtually any criminal or civil case as a court of first instance. They are often formally divided into criminal, civil, probate, juvenile, and domestic or family courts. In criminal cases, such courts typically hear felony cases.

Appellate Jurisdiction

A defendant may appeal the decision of a general trial court in a criminal case to an appellate court. Thirty-eight states have intermediate or first-level courts of appeal. These intermediate appellate courts are positioned between the general trial courts and the state court of last resort or supreme court. Unlike the general trial courts, which may retry a case after a decision made by a lower court, appellate courts do not retry cases, nor may they consider evidence not presented in the original trial. Instead, they examine the transcript of the case, read written briefs submitted by attorneys for both sides, and hear oral arguments. Generally, the decision of the appellate court is final. However, if the case involves a constitutional issue unresolved by the appellate court, it may then be appealed to the state's Supreme Court.

Courts of Last Resort

Courts of last resort are the final appellate courts within the state court system. In most states, the court of last resort is referred to as the State Supreme Court. Appealed criminal cases may reach the supreme court either by proceeding there directly from trial court or by going through intermediate appellate courts. Only certain kinds of cases (depending on state mandates) may be appealed directly to the supreme court, such as cases in which the death penalty was imposed at sentencing or in which a speedy hearing is otherwise required.

The Federal Court System

The Constitution calls for a supreme court and "such inferior Courts as the Congress may from time to time ordain and establish." The contemporary structure of the U.S. federal court system includes lower trial courts, appellate courts, and a court of last resort in addition to a few special federal judicial entities outside the federal court system (see FIGURE 7–1).

U.S. Magistrate Judges

In 1968, Congress passed the Federal Magistrates Act, which provided for the appointment of judicial officers for each federal district court by federal district court judges. Full-time magistrate judges are appointed for eight-year terms, whereas part-time magistrate judges are appointed for only four years. Either type of magistrate may be reappointed. Magistrates do not have all the powers of a judge, but rather generally handle criminal

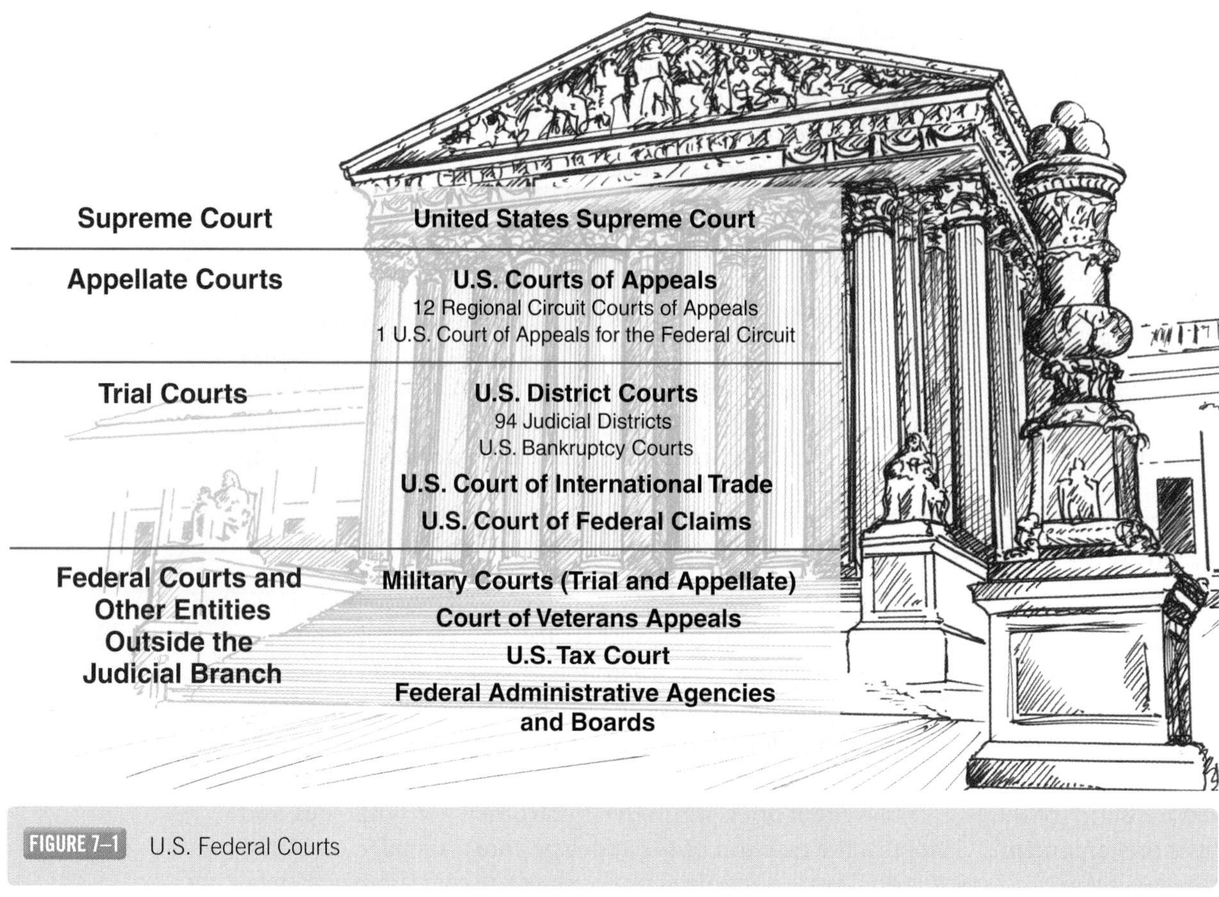

FIGURE 7–1 U.S. Federal Courts

misdemeanor cases, such as failure to pay child support obligations and possession of a firearm after being convicted of a "qualifying" domestic violence offense. In criminal cases, magistrates conduct pretrial hearings and, if both sides agree, try misdemeanors.

U.S. District Courts

The federal system includes a single level of general trial courts—the 94 U.S. District Courts. Each state has at least one district, as do the District of Columbia, the Commonwealth of Puerto Rico, Guam, the Virgin Islands, and the Northern Mariana Islands; California, New York, and Texas have four districts each.

U.S. District Courts have jurisdiction in all cases involving federal law or disputes over treaties. In addition to civil suits and criminal cases, these courts hear cases dealing with job discrimination and violations of equal opportunity, citizenship matters, environmental protection, and educational discrimination. U.S. District Courts also have concurrent jurisdiction with state trial courts in certain criminal matters (for example, bank robbery and kidnapping, which violate both state and federal laws) and civil disputes between people of different states where damages exceed a designated amount.

U.S. Courts of Appeals

The middle tier of the federal court system consists of 13 U.S. Courts of Appeals, including 11 numbered circuits based on geographic regions and containing three or more states, one court for the District of Columbia, and a separate Court of Appeals for the Federal Circuit (see FIGURE 7–2).

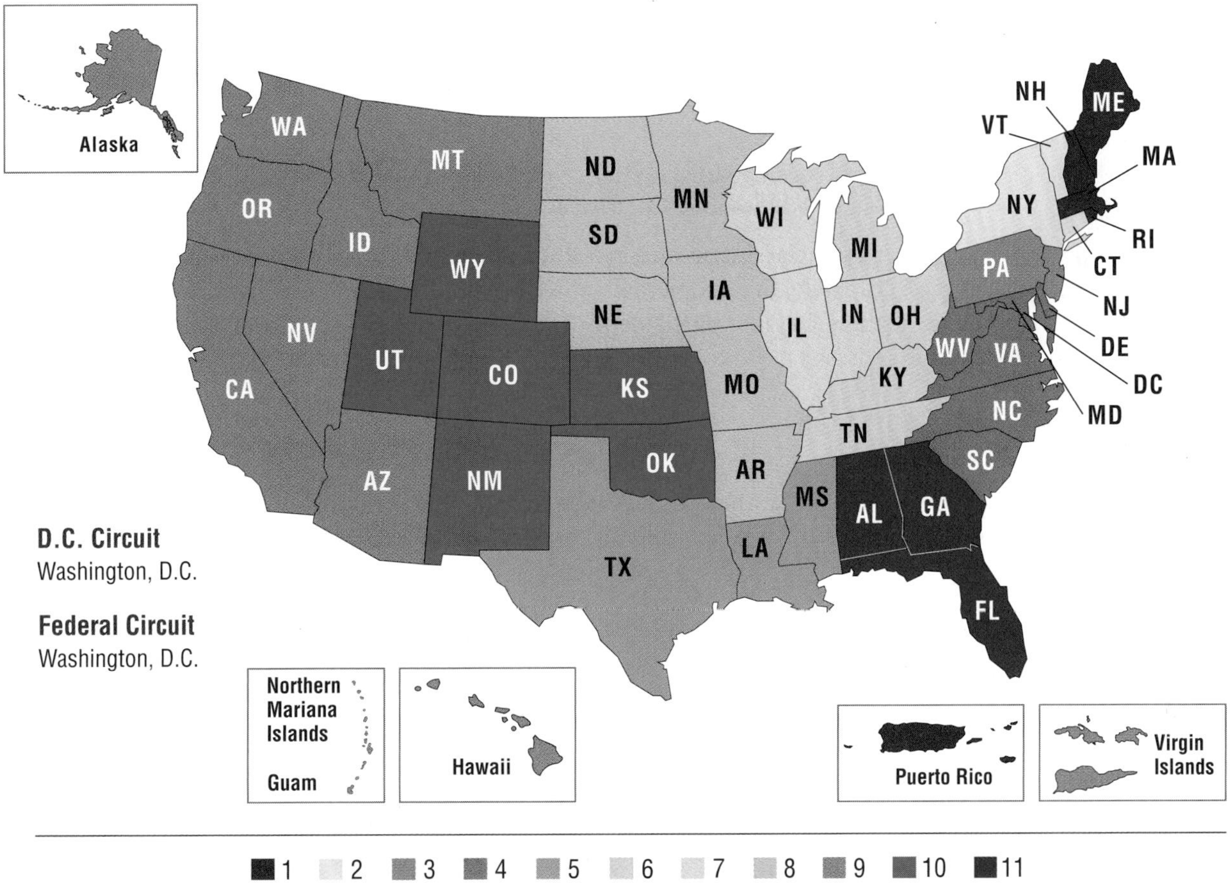

Alaska

WA OR CA ID NV MT WY UT CO AZ NM ND SD NE KS OK TX MN IA MO AR LA WI IL MS MI IN KY TN AL OH GA FL WV VA NC SC PA NY VT NH ME MA RI CT NJ DE DC MD

D.C. Circuit
Washington, D.C.

Federal Circuit
Washington, D.C.

Northern Mariana Islands
Guam

Hawaii

Puerto Rico

Virgin Islands

1 2 3 4 5 6 7 8 9 10 11

FIGURE 7–2 Federal Judicial Circuits

U.S. Supreme Court

The nine Justices of the U.S. Supreme Court are the final arbiters of questions dealing with interpretation of the U.S. Constitution.

Like the various state supreme courts, the **U.S. Supreme Court** is the court of last resort for the federal system. In addition to its power of judicial review over Congressional legislation and acts by the executive branch, its jurisdiction extends to all cases in which a substantial federal question is involved. In other words, the Supreme Court is empowered to review any federal appellate court decision or any decision from a state supreme court in which the decision raises an issue related to federal law. The final arbitrator in cases of state law would be the appropriate state supreme court.

A case reaches the U.S. Supreme Court following an appeal from the party who wants it to review a decision of a federal or state court. To do so, the dissatisfied party files a petition asking that the case be heard by the Supreme Court. This initial petition to the Supreme Court requests that it issue a **writ of certiorari**, or an order to the lower court to certify the court record and send it up to the higher court. The order includes a request to provide

- The lower court's decision
- A statement of the federal legal question(s) involved in the decision
- A statement of the reasons why the Supreme Court should review the case

Brian Nichols killed four people during his escape from the courtroom where he was on trial for rape.

If the Supreme Court grants the writ, the case is scheduled for the filing of briefs and for oral argument. If it denies the request for a writ, the decision by the lower court stands. When its decision is published, the Court's ruling on a case becomes a precedent for the lower courts.

Court Participants

Courts and judicial systems are merely the structures in which the quest for justice takes place. Ultimately, the people who work in these structures define the nature of what happens there. Regular participants in the court give life and meaning to concepts such as "due process" and "law and order."

Court Staff

Although the court participants who receive nearly all of the media attention are the judges, prosecutors, and defense attorneys (each of whom will be discussed shortly), the daily operation of a court relies on the activities of its staff.

Administrators

Larger court systems typically have court administrators. They are responsible for maintaining the court's budget; hiring personnel; overseeing case flow, space, and office equipment; managing the jury system in the court; creating and maintaining uniform court record systems; managing public relations, general information, and research; and serving as liaisons with other people in the judicial or local government system.

Clerks

The clerk performs the daily clerical work of the court. Nearly everything that goes before the judge must pass through the clerk first. Prosecutors and defense attorneys bring to the clerk motions, pleadings, and other matters to be acted upon by the judge. In addition, clerks are responsible for keeping court records, maintaining evidence submitted to the court, issuing subpoenas for jury duty, administering the jury selection system, and maintaining the court docket and calendar.

Bailiffs

The bailiff is responsible for maintaining security and order within the courtroom and judge's chamber. In addition, bailiffs are responsible for keeping custody of defendants, court summons, and witnesses as well as looking after the needs of jurors during trial proceedings.

Reporters

Court reporters are responsible for the official recording of the proceedings as well as any depositions taken outside the courtroom. A deposition is the testimony of a witness taken under oath outside the court through oral questioning or written interrogation.

Judges

To members of the public, judges are the most easily distinguished participants in the court system. They are highly visible, because they sit positioned above the center of the courtroom in their symbolic black robes.

Role and Responsibilities of Judges

The judicial role in criminal cases begins even before a suspect is arrested and continues past the sentencing decision. Judges in general trial courts are responsible for a variety of tasks, including the following:

- Determining whether there is probable cause to issue search or arrest warrants
- Determining whether there is sufficient cause to hold a suspect for prosecution

Judges are the centerpiece in the judicial process, from signing search warrants to sentencing convicted offenders.

- Determining whether a defendant should be released on bail and, if so, how much bail is required
- Ruling on pretrial motions submitted to the court by prosecutors and defense attorneys
- Deciding whether to accept plea agreements
- Deciding on the admissibility of evidence and testimony
- Deciding whether there is sufficient evidence for a jury to make a decision or whether the case should be dismissed
- Deciding on an appropriate sentence
- Determining whether a request for a reduction in the defendant's sentence is warranted
- Deciding whether to grant requests from prisoners for early release

Selection of Judges

Judges for the state courts are selected through one of three methods:

- Merit selection, with appointment by the chief executive from a certified list of qualified candidates, which is typically prepared by a state judicial merit committee
- Direct appointment by the governor or election by the legislature
- Popular election

The process of selecting judges for the federal courts is quite different. All federal judges—with the exception of Federal Magistrates, who are appointed by U.S. District Court judges—are nominated by the President of the United States and then confirmed by the U.S. Senate. Federal judges, unlike state and local judges, have lifetime appoint-

Headline Crime — Oklahoma Judge Behind Bars

District Judge Donald Thompson was indicted on four felony counts of indecent exposure based on allegations that he had exposed himself at least 15 times to the court recorder and repeatedly used a sexual device known as a penis pump for masturbation during trials between 2001 and 2003. Thompson had spent nearly 23 years on the bench before retiring in 2004, following an investigation into his violations of the code of judicial ethics.

At his trial, a witness testified that Thompson used a penis pump almost daily during a murder trial in which a man was charged with murdering a young child. An audiotape of the trial included frequent whooshing sounds similar to air being pumped or released from a blood pressure cuff. A police officer testified that while he was testifying on the stand in a murder trial in 2003, he noticed a piece of plastic tubing disappear under the judge's robe. During the lunch break, he and another officer took photographs of the pump under the desk. Thompson denied using the pump entirely, insisting that it had been given to him as a gag gift by a longtime friend. However, investigators found semen stains on the judge's chair and surrounding carpet, as well as on his judicial robes. The jury found Thompson guilty, and he was sentenced to four years in prison.

Sources: "Oklahoma Judge Accused of Using Sexual Device in Court," *USA Today*, June 25, 2004, available at http://www.usatoday.com/news/nation/2004-06-25-judge-conduct_x.htm, accessed August 16, 2008; "Penis Pump Judge Gets 4-Year Jail Term," *USA Today*, August 18, 2006, available at htttp://www.usatoday.com/news/nation/2006-08-18-judge-sentenced_x.htm, accessed August 16, 2008.

ments, whereas judges at the state and local levels must be reelected to retain their positions on the bench. Sometimes judges are removed from office not because they fail to get reelected, but because they engage in improper behavior.

Prosecutors

In the adversarial system, prosecutors represent the state. Although they are expected to win cases, there is a presumption that they will be fair and impartial in the pursuit of justice. Prosecutors work with the police and sheriffs' departments, as well as with staff investigators, to build cases that can be won. Although prosecutors are responsible for obtaining convictions in cases brought before the court, they have an ethical duty not to prosecute people who they believe are probably innocent.

Role and Responsibilities of Prosecutors

The primary responsibilities of the prosecutor are to decide which cases are to be prosecuted, to evaluate evidence, to determine which charges are most likely to end in convictions, and then to prosecute the case before the court. In addition, the prosecutor often acts as a legal advisor to the police, giving advice about law enforcement practices that will withstand court challenges, ensuring appropriate gathering of evidence, and interviewing witnesses.

After police officers make arrests and take suspects into custody, the prosecutor must decide whether the case should proceed. Prosecutors may decide to decline prosecution, to dismiss the case at any point, to negotiate and accept a plea of guilty, or to go ahead with the prosecution.

Defense Attorneys

Although defense attorneys are the kind of lawyer most often portrayed on television, they account for only a small share of the approximately 950,000 lawyers practicing in the United States today (the total number of U.S. lawyers has increased approximately 150 percent since 1970).[6] Relatively few attorneys in the United States specialize in criminal law. Those who do are likely to be full-time public defenders assigned by the court to represent indigent defendants. Private attorneys who handle criminal cases typically derive most of their income from their general law practice, which often deals with civil disputes such as divorces, wills, and estate planning.

Role and Responsibilities of Defense Attorneys

The role of the defense attorney is very narrowly defined. He or she acts as the advocate for the accused and is obligated to use every lawful means to protect the interests of the defendant in court. If possible, this outcome includes achieving an acquittal of the charges or, if the defendant is convicted, minimizing the punishment. It is the defense attorney's responsibility to probe and test every bit of evidence presented by the state to ensure that the defendant is not convicted unless the prosecution can prove the defendant guilty beyond a reasonable doubt.[7]

The Right to Counsel

The Sixth Amendment to the Constitution states, "In all criminal prosecutions, the accused shall enjoy the right . . . to have the assistance of counsel for his defense." However, just when and under what circumstances counsel must be provided was not made clear.

Until the early part of the twentieth century, the Sixth Amendment was generally interpreted to mean that a defendant had a right to an attorney if he or she could not afford to hire one. During the last six decades, however, the Supreme Court's rulings in a series of cases have clarified its position on a defendant's right to counsel (see TABLE 7–1).

TABLE 7-1 Summary of Cases Regarding a Defendant's Right to Counsel

Case	Ruling
Powell v. Alabama (1932)	An indigent person who is accused of a capital offense in a state court is entitled to counsel provided by the state.
Johnson v. Zerbst (1938)	Defendants in federal cases must be provided with counsel if they cannot afford to hire an attorney.
Betts v. Brady (1942)	States are not obligated to provide free counsel to indigent defendants in *every serious case.*
Gideon v. Wainwright (1963)	Any indigent person charged with a felony has a right to an attorney at the state's expense.
Argersinger v. Hamlin (1972)	An indigent defendant in a misdemeanor case has the right to a state-provided attorney if the penalty includes the possibility of incarceration.
Scott v. Illinois (1979)	Indigent defendants in misdemeanor cases do not have a right to free counsel in cases punishable only by fines.

In its first ruling on this issue in 1932 (*Powell v. Alabama*), the Court held that only an indigent person accused of a capital offense in a state court is entitled to counsel provided by the state.[8] Six years later, the Court ruled that the Sixth Amendment required that defendants in federal cases be provided with attorneys if they could not afford to hire one.[9] In 1942, the Court held that states were not obligated to provide free counsel to indigent defendants in *every serious case.*[10] The Court reversed this position in 1963 when, in ***Gideon v. Wainwright***,[11] it held that any indigent person charged with a felony has a right to an attorney at the state's expense. In 1972, in *Argersinger v. Hamlin*, the Court extended the right to counsel for indigent defendants to misdemeanor cases if the penalty included the possibility of incarceration.[12] In 1979, the Court made it clear, in *Scott v. Illinois*, that the *Argersinger* decision was not meant to include cases punishable *only* by fines.[13]

Representing Indigent Defendants

Three primary systems are used to provide counsel for indigent defendants: contract systems, assigned counsel systems, and public defender systems. Many jurisdictions use a combination of all three.

Approximately 42 percent of the largest 100 U.S. counties use *contract systems*, in which a private attorney, local bar association, or law firm is contracted to provide legal representation for indigent defendants.[14] Fees are paid to contract attorneys on a flat rate and are typically inadequate for the attorney to mount an effective defense. Consequently, the motivation to spend the necessary time and effort is minimal.

In *assigned counsel systems*, which are used in 89 percent of the largest 100 counties, private attorneys whose names appear on a list of volunteers are assigned to represent indigents on a case-by-case basis. Often, these attorneys are younger and less experienced and receive only minimal compensation to defend clients.

Public defender systems are used in 90 percent of the nation's largest 100 counties.[15] Most public defenders are appointed to serve on a full-time basis by either a general trial court judge or county officials, although many maintain small private practices on the side. Public defenders complain that they work hard yet receive little respect for their efforts, from either their clients or the court. Most public defenders are underpaid and overwhelmed with heavy caseloads. Many manage to spend only 30 minutes conferring with a client before his or her court appearance.

Initial Appearance

The **initial appearance** is the stage at which an accused is informed of the charges and of three constitutionally guaranteed rights: the right to counsel, the right to remain silent, and the right to reasonable bail. In misdemeanor cases, a defendant may choose to plead guilty at the initial appearance and face immediate sentencing. Felony charges are handled differently, as defendants are rarely permitted to enter pleas and consequently are not sentenced at this time.

Timing of the Initial Appearance

Both the states and the federal government have established guidelines that regulate the timing of the initial appearances of defendants. These guidelines are designed to protect the rights of citizens so that the government cannot let people languish in jail without knowing why, conduct secret interrogations, or coerce people into making confessions. These guidelines are often inconsistent, however, and the various levels of governments have not agreed on exceptions to the rules or the consequences for their violation.

The 48-Hour Rule

In 1975, the Supreme Court ruled in *Gerstein v. Pugh* that defendants must be brought before a judge or magistrate "promptly after arrest."[16] However, this decision did not include a specific time frame. In 1991, in *Riverside County, California v. McLaughlin*, the Court ruled that the notion of "promptly," which was the guiding statement in *Gerstein*, did not mean "immediately upon completion of booking the defendant."[17] The Court held that the criminal justice system requires some degree of flexibility and that 48 hours provides that needed flexibility. This ruling defined the **48-hour rule**, which allows delays of as much as 48 hours before the defendant's initial appearance.

Pretrial Release

The belief that a person who is accused of a crime has a right to **pretrial release** (that is, being released from custody while awaiting judicial action) has been long and widely held in the United States. Generally, pretrial release has involved the posting of bail by the defendant. The Eighth Amendment states that "excessive bail shall not be required." However, this amendment merely prohibits *excessive* bail; it does not *guarantee* a defendant the right to pretrial release.[18] Even so, the majority of people who are arrested—even for felony offenses—are eventually released before trial or final adjudication by the court. Not all felony defendants are equally likely to be released, however. For example, between 1990 and 2004 in state cases in the United States' 75 largest counties, 64 percent of those charged with assault, 44 percent of those charged with robbery, and 19 percent charged with murder were released before trial (see FIGURE 7–3). The percentage of federal felony defendants released prior to case disposition also varies by offense—from 11 percent for robbery defendants, to 65 percent for defendants charged with forgery, to 94 percent of those charged with gambling-related crimes.[19]

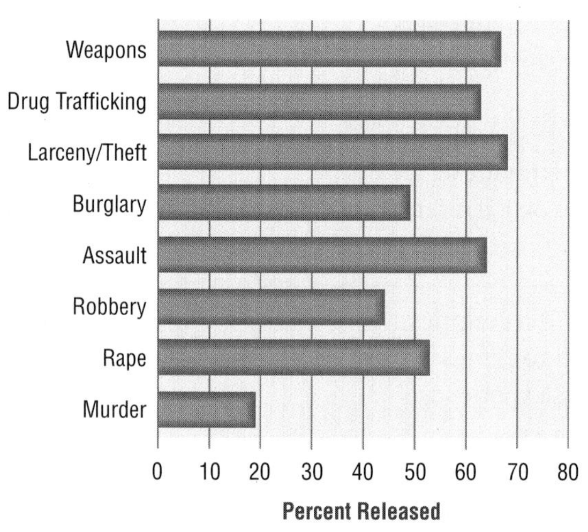

FIGURE 7–3 Pretrial Release in the 75 Largest Counties in the United States, 1999–2004

Source: Thomas Cohen and Brian Reaves, *Pretrial Release of Felony Defendants in State Courts* (Washington, DC: U.S. Department of Justice, 2007), p. 6.

The Purpose Behind Bail

Historically, it has been believed that providing for pretrial release would do less harm to the defendant and his or her family than might occur by keeping the defendant in custody. Pretrial release has typically involved setting some bail amount that was large enough to ensure that the defendant would appear at subsequent hearings. This compulsion to appear was to be accomplished by having the defendant deposit a monetary bond upon booking or at the initial appearance. If the accused is able to post the full bail amount, he or she is released. Many defendants, because they are unable to post the full amount of the bail, turn to a **bail bondsman** for assistance. For a fee of 10 to 15 percent of the full bond, the bondsman will guarantee payment to the court of the full fee.

Bias in Pretrial Release

For many defendants, nearly any bail amount is unaffordable. As a consequence, these individuals may wait in jail for weeks or months while the wheels of justice turn. The poor and minorities suffer disproportionately from a loss of freedom before trial because they often lack the resources needed to gain their pretrial release by posting bail. A substantial body of evidence indicates that race, ethnicity, and even gender all bias bail decisions. Studies that have examined the patterns of pretrial release in the United States' 75 largest counties as well as in smaller, more rural counties, for example, have consistently found that African Americans and Latinos are more likely to be denied bail

Headline Crime: Bail Bonds and Bounty Hunters

Bail bondsmen post bail for persons accused of crimes for a fee, typically 10 to 15 percent of the bail amount determined by the court. The use of commercial bail bondsmen is a uniquely American innovation for ensuring that defendants show up for required court dates. Few countries use this system, as it dominates the pretrial release systems of only the United States and the Philippines. Most other countries use one of a number of approaches—either keeping defendants in jail until trial, asking defendants to promise to show up, or making failure to appear a separate crime.

Critics of commercial bail bonds, including the American Bar Association and the National District Attorneys Association, claim that the bail bond system discriminates against poor and middle-class defendants, while doing nothing to promote public safety. Four states—Illinois, Kentucky, Oregon, and Wisconsin—have abolished the use of commercial bail bonds. In these states, defendants either pay a deposit directly to the court, are released on their own recognizance, or simply promise to appear.

Because bail bondsmen put up their own guarantees for the full amount of bail with the court, they choose their clients carefully and are quick to pursue defendants who skip or fail to appear in court. Bondsmen themselves or persons specifically hired by the bond company typically hunt down defendants. However, in a number of states, bond enforcement agents, commonly known as bounty hunters, are given greater powers than bondsmen to pursue skippers. Bounty hunters may break into homes, take defendants into custody without search warrants and temporarily imprison them, and even take them across state lines without being required to enter an extradition process.

Advocates of commercial bail bonds and related methods for tracking down defendants who fail to appear in court point to the success of the system. They note that there is no cost to the state to ensure the appearance of defendants or to track them down if they flee. Moreover, defendants who rely on the bail bond system appear significantly more likely to appear in court than those released on other forms of supervision. As one Florida bail bondsman noted, his failure rate is less than 1 percent.

Source: Adam Liptak, "Illegal Globally, Bail for Profit Remains in U.S.," available at www.nytimes.com/2008/01/29/us/29bail.html, accessed January 29, 2008.

Defendants who are unable to post bond and remain in jail typically face increased legal problems.

than white defendants in felony cases. In addition, Latinos are more disadvantaged than African Americans in terms of both the likelihood of their pretrial release and the dollar amount required for release. Moreover, in addition to race and ethnicity, defendants with weak community ties (local residence and employment status) are less likely to be released prior to trial.[20]

Alternatives to Monetary Bail

Partly because of public perceptions of inequities in the use of bail, and perhaps even more because of severe jail overcrowding, a number of alternatives to monetary bail have been created. One of the most widely used alternatives is **release on recognizance** (ROR)—that is, a personal promise to appear at trial. Other measures include the following:

- *Conditional release.* Defendants promise to meet stated conditions that extend beyond simply promising to appear in court. Such conditions might include agreeing to maintain one's residence or employment status, remain in the jurisdiction, adhere to a curfew, report to a third party or designated release program, or participate in a drug or alcohol treatment program.
- *Unsecured bail.* No payment is required at the time of release. However, if the defendant fails to appear at required hearings, he or she becomes liable to pay the full amount.
- *Property bail.* The defendant may post evidence of real property, such as a car title, as an alternative to paying cash bail.
- *Court deposit bail.* The defendant may deposit a certain percentage of the bail amount with the court (usually 10 to 15 percent). When the defendant fulfills his or her appearance requirements, the deposit is returned. Some courts subtract a small administrative fee from this deposit.[21]

The successful use of these alternatives to the traditional posting of monetary bail gave support for the passage of the **Bail Reform Act of 1966.**[22] This legislation presumed that defendants were to be considered for ROR or conditional release unless the prosecution could show strong evidence supporting the need for monetary bail.

In an attempt to reduce the apparent race, ethnicity, and class bias in pretrial release, **bail guidelines** were developed for use in a number of courts. Using a two-dimensional grid that plots the severity of the offense against the defendant's personal characteristics (such as his or her courtroom demeanor, any physical or mental health concerns, other current or outstanding warrants, and the possibility of a mandatory sentence in the current case), the court determines whether the defendant should receive ROR or conditional release or pay a money bail.[23]

Preventive Detention

Another concern—the need to protect society from the additional commission of crimes by dangerous offenders awaiting trial—led the U.S. Congress to pass the **Bail Reform Act of 1984.**[24] This legislation extended the opportunity for ROR for suspects in many federal cases by mandating that defendants should not be kept in custody simply because they could not afford money bail. At the same time, it provided for the preventive detention of defendants who are charged with particularly serious crimes and thus are perceived to be high risks for committing further crimes or absconding before trial. Temporary **preventive detention** without bail is permitted if a defendant is on pretrial release for another offense, is on probation, is out on parole, or if the judicial officer finds that no conditions or combination of conditions will reasonably ensure the appearance of the person as required and the safety of any other person and the community. The burden of rebuttal is forced on the defendant; that is, the defendant must convince the court that he or she is not a risk.

Does the presumption of future dangerousness and denial of pretrial release deny the accused of his or her due process rights by imposing punishment before the person faces trial? This question was considered by the Supreme Court in 1987 in ***United States v. Salerno***,[25] when the Court in a 6-to-3 decision, ruled that the preventive detention provisions of the Bail Reform Act of 1984 were constitutional.

The Grand Jury

It is not unusual to pick up a newspaper and read that a grand jury recently indicted someone for a crime, investigated corruption in a governmental office, or declared that a public agency such as a housing authority or a prison was in violation of government regulations. The grand jury of today comprises a body of citizens who are called by a prosecutor to investigate the conduct of public officials and agencies and criminal activity in general and to determine whether a crime has been committed.

The grand jury meets in relative secrecy to keep their targets of investigation from knowing who and what are being investigated. While the existence of specific hearings may be known, the public, the media, family and friends, and often even attorneys for witnesses are prohibited from attending grand jury sessions.

Former mob henchman Sammy "The Bull" Gravano received immunity and was not prosecuted for 19 homicides he committed.

Witnesses, including target witnesses (i.e., those suspected of wrongdoing), have no right to present evidence on their own behalf or to cross-examine other witnesses. In most states and in the federal system, they do not have the right to have an attorney present and may generally not raise objections.[26] Jurors may ask questions of witnesses, but typically allow the prosecutor to set the stage and establish the direction of the questioning. The exclusionary rule, which prohibits illegally obtained evidence from being presented in court proceedings, does not apply in grand jury hearings.[27] Although such evidence may not be used directly in a later criminal trial, the testimony is recorded and may be used at trial to impeach the witness's statement. For example, if a targeted witness admits to a grand jury that he or she committed a particular crime but later at trial denies doing so, the earlier testimony may be submitted to show the inconsistency of the person's statements.

Once they hear all of the testimony, the members of the grand jury retire to deliberate and vote to determine whether there is a sufficient basis for believing that the crime was committed by the targeted witness. Unlike trial juries, grand juries are not required to make this determination beyond a reasonable doubt. Rather, they need to determine simply whether there is probable cause to believe that the person is guilty. Based on such a determination, the grand jury then issues a bill of indictment, which is called a **true bill**.

The Prosecutor's Decision to Prosecute

Prosecutors do not necessarily file identical charges in similar kinds of cases, nor do they choose to prosecute all cases brought to them by the police. Samuel Walker has suggested that the differential treatment of cases is similar to the structure of a wedding cake (see FIGURE 7–4). Each layer is composed of cases that are perceived as being more or less important than those in the surrounding layers and are consequently given differential treatment by the courts as well as differential attention by the media and the public.[28]

FIGURE 7–4 The Criminal Justice "Wedding Cake"

Source: Adapted from Samuel Walker, *Sense and Nonsense About Crime and Drugs: A Policy Guide*, 6th ed. (Belmont, CA: Thomson/Wadsworth, 2006), p. 36.

- *Celebrated cases.* These relatively rare cases receive the greatest attention from the criminal justice system and the media. They are likely to involve wealthy or well-known people as victims or offenders and highly publicized trials involving high-profile defense attorneys and prosecutors. Through the media, these cases reinforce the public perception that the criminal justice system handles all cases similarly; in reality, few cases go to trial, and few involve high-profile private defense attorneys.
- *Heavy-duty felonies.* These cases include serious felonies such as murder, rape, robbery, and burglary—crimes that often are violent, involve strangers, and are committed by offenders with lengthy criminal records. They are generally given higher priority than less serious cases and typically result in more severe sentences for convicted offenders.
- *Lightweight felonies.* These cases are considered less serious felonies. Offenders typically are younger, have no prior criminal records, and are more likely to have some prior relationship with their victims. Because they are viewed as less serious, these cases have a lower priority for prosecution and typically result in plea bargains and quick dispositions.
- *Misdemeanors.* Misdemeanors (which account for nearly 90 percent of all criminal cases) make up nearly all cases in this layer. They include disturbing the peace, shoplifting, public intoxication, prostitution, and minor drug offenses. In these cases, guilty pleas are common and trials are rare. Convicted offenders generally receive sentences of fines, probation, restitution, or short jail terms.

Preliminary Hearings

The purpose of the **preliminary hearing** is to determine probable cause. That is, the prosecutor must produce sufficient evidence to show the judge that the facts and circumstances would lead a reasonable person to believe that a crime was committed and that the defendant committed it. If the evidence indicates that the defendant is probably guilty, the prosecutor files an *information* stating the charges and the accused is bound over for trial. If the judge believes that the evidence submitted by the prosecutor is not sufficient, however, the charge or charges are dismissed and the defendant is released.

The preliminary hearing goes beyond the mere investigation of charges. The following critical actions are taken during preliminary hearings:

- Review of the charges
- Review of bail for possible reduction
- Initial presentation of witnesses
- Cross-examination of witnesses
- Discovery (the right of the defense to be informed of the basic facts and evidence that the state will introduce at trial)

A defendant may waive his or her right to a preliminary hearing if the judge determines that the decision was made knowingly and intelligently. Defendants in about 50 percent of all cases waive their right to the preliminary hearing at the initial appearance.[29] This course is typically taken when the charging complaint stating probable cause is supported by affidavits (sworn signed statements of fact) and the defense believes that there would be no advantage to the defendant's participation in a preliminary hearing.

FOCUS ON CRIMINAL JUSTICE

Prosecuting Terrorists

In 2002, federal prosecutors filed terrorism-related charges against more than 1200 individuals. This number represents only about two thirds of all terrorism cases referred to prosecutors, however. Among the most notable terrorism-related cases were the prosecutions of the 1992 World Trade Center bombers, Oklahoma City bombers Timothy McVeigh and Terry Nichols, and the bombers of the U.S. embassies in Kenya and Tanzania, and the plea bargain convictions of John Walker Lindh (the "American Taliban"), Richard Reid (the "shoe bomber"), and the Lackawanna Six (an alleged terrorist "sleeper cell" in New York state).

Between 2001 and 2003, 45 states amended or created more than 60 new antiterrorism laws, although the primary responsibility for prosecuting such cases lies with the federal Department of Justice. The new and existing statutes generally fall within one of the following categories:

- Laws that criminalize precursor crimes (i.e., identity theft, money laundering, sale of illegal drugs)
- Laws dealing with threats, hoaxes, and false reports of terrorist activities
- Laws designed to punish specific incidents of terrorism
- Laws enhancing the ability of agencies to investigate and prosecute acts of terrorism

One of the more controversial laws is the federal material support statute, 18 U.S.C. 2339B, which states that it is unlawful to "knowingly provide material support or resources to a foreign terrorist organization." This statute has been on the books since 1996, but it was not used until 2002. Since then, at least 20 criminal cases have been filed in which material support was one of the charges. One of the most notable cases involved the Lackawanna Six. These six American Yemenis traveled from New York to Kandahar, Pakistan, where they listened to lectures on jihad and justifications for suicide bombings. They then traveled to the Al Farooq training camp, where they received training in firearms and more specialized skills such as mountain climbing; they also met with Osama bin Laden. Eventually, after returning to the United States, the six were arrested and federal prosecutors charged them with providing material support to Al Qaeda. All of the defendants pled guilty and were sentenced to prison for terms of seven to 10 years.

Approximately 90 percent of all federal criminal prosecutions are resolved through plea bargains, but this is not the case for prosecutions of alleged terrorists. Between 1996 and 2002, fewer than 40 percent of alleged terrorist defendants were convicted as a result of plea bargains. Perhaps terrorists are unwilling to plead guilty because they want to use the trial as an opportunity to express their ideology and air their grievances. Or perhaps prosecutors refuse to offer "acceptable" bargains to defendants or they, like the defendants, wish to use these trials (which will likely draw national attention) as stages to gain political attention.

Sources: Ravi Satkalmi, "Material Support: The United States v. the Lackawanna Six," *Studies in Conflict and Terrorism* 28:193–199 (2005); M. Elaine Nugent, James Johnson, Brad Bartholomew, and Delene Bromirski, *Local Prosecutors' Response to Terrorism* (Alexandria, VA: American Prosecutors Research Institute, 2005); Nora Demleitner, "How Many Terrorists Are There? The Escalation in So-called Terrorism Prosecution," *Federal Sentencing Reporter* 16:38–42 (2003); Brent Smith and Kelly Damphousse, *American Terrorism Study: Patterns of Behavior, Investigation, and Prosecution of American Terrorists, Final Report* (Fayetteville, AR: Terrorism Research Center, University of Arkansas, 2002).

Format of Preliminary Hearings

In some ways, the preliminary hearing resembles a mini-trial, although no jury is involved at this stage. The case is presented before a judge, who evaluates the evidence and initial testimony to determine whether probable cause exists to hold the defendant for trial. Because the burden of proof is on the prosecutor, he or she must present evidence and call witnesses to support the state's case. As in grand jury investigations, because the prosecutor must prove only that there is probable cause—not that the defendant is guilty beyond a reasonable doubt—the prosecutor is not likely to call all witnesses or present all available evidence at this hearing.

As in a trial, the defendant has the right to be represented by counsel during a preliminary hearing, to cross-examine witnesses for the state, and to challenge any evidence submitted by the prosecutor. The defense may also call witnesses to testify, although this practice is very uncommon because it enables the prosecutor to examine those witnesses and exposes the defense's strategy to the state.

Discovery

Perhaps the greatest advantage to a defendant during the preliminary hearing is the initial opportunity for **discovery**, or the legal motion that allows the defense to discover the basis for the prosecutor's case. The defense can find out which theories or evidence will be used in trying the case, is given access to statements and physical evidence, and is informed which witnesses will be called. Discovery is often viewed as providing a level playing field for both parties in the adversarial system and as helping the defendant make an informed judgment as to which plea to enter.

Entering Pleas

Jurisdictions vary in their organization and the sequence of judicial procedures for dealing with people charged with crimes. One of these variations is the time at which a defendant may enter a **plea**—the individual's response to a criminal charge. In misdemeanor cases, a person may enter a plea at the initial appearance in response to the first reading of the criminal charge. In felony cases, following either a filing of an information by the prosecutor or a grand jury indictment, the suspect enters a plea at an **arraignment**.

Guilty Plea

A **guilty plea** is an admission of guilt to the crime as charged.[30] A guilty plea must be made in open court, and the judge must inform the defendant of the nature of the charge or charges, the mandatory minimum sentence (if any), and other consequences of such a plea. Defendants must also be informed that to plead guilty means that they waive their rights to avoid self-incrimination, have a trial by jury, and confront their accusers.

Nolo Contendere Plea

A plea of ***nolo contendere*** (literally, "no contest") means that the defendant neither admits nor denies the charge. It is similar to a guilty plea in that the defendant is still subject to any sentence imposed by the court; unlike a guilty plea, however, a *nolo contendere* plea may not be used later against a defendant in any civil suit based on the same act. For instance, in an assault or rape case in which the evidence is overwhelming, the defendant may plead *nolo contendere* to save the expense of the criminal trial and to avoid creating an official record of admission of guilt that may be used as evidence in a later civil suit brought by the victim or the victim's family.

Not Guilty Plea

Very few people who are accused of felonies initially plead guilty or *nolo contendere* and then move directly to sentencing. Instead, most initially plead not guilty, and then later plead guilty after negotiating a plea bargain. Although many minor misdemeanor cases handled in the lower courts are resolved through guilty pleas, the standard plea in felony cases is not guilty. When a defendant refuses to enter any plea (stands mute), is obviously incompetent, or is not represented by counsel, the judge will enter a plea of not guilty on his or her behalf. After a not guilty plea is entered, a trial date is set. In some jurisdictions, if a not guilty plea is entered at the initial appearance, the case must be sent on either to a grand jury or to a preliminary hearing before a trial date is set.

Arraignment is an important legal step because approximately 95 percent of criminal cases reach a disposition without going to trial.

Plea of Not Guilty by Reason of Insanity

A defendant may choose to enter a plea of not guilty by reason of insanity. In this situation, the defendant does not deny committing the crime but does deny that he or she is criminally responsible because of insanity at the time of the offense. The federal courts and many states require that a defendant who intends to enter this plea do so in a pretrial motion (a written or oral request to the judge before the beginning of the trial) to allow the government time to have a psychiatrist examine the defendant. Contrary to public perceptions, pleas of not guilty by reason of insanity are rarely entered (in fewer than 5 percent of all criminal cases); when such a plea is entered, it is even more rarely successful (fewer than 1 percent of those pleas entered).[31]

Plea Bargaining

Plea bargaining, sometimes referred to as plea negotiation, continues to be one of the most controversial and misunderstood facets of the U.S. criminal justice system. Plea bargaining is an interactive process that involves the prosecutor and the defense, who attempt to arrive at a mutually satisfactory disposition of a case without going to trial. In some jurisdictions, it requires the approval of the victim, and in *all* jurisdictions it requires the approval of the judge. In contrast to the popular conception based on fictional courtroom dramas, approximately 95 percent of all criminal cases resulting in convictions in state courts are disposed of by guilty pleas, while only 2 percent are resolved by jury trials and 3 percent by bench trials.[32] Defendants in federal criminal cases are also overwhelmingly more likely to enter guilty pleas rather than go to trial (see FIGURE 7–5).

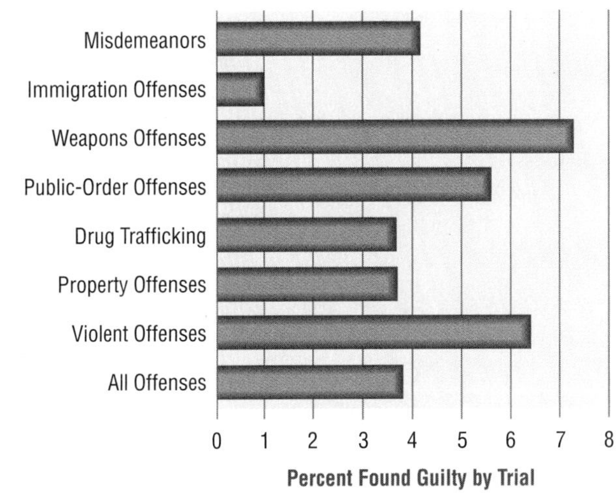

FIGURE 7–5 Percentage of Convicted Defendants in Federal District Courts Found Guilty by Trial

Source: Bureau of Justice Statistics, *Federal Criminal Case Processing, 2004* (Washington, DC: U.S. Department of Justice, 2006), Table 4.2.

Types of Plea Bargains

There are four general types of plea bargains:

1. Reducing the seriousness of the charge
2. Reducing the number of charges or counts
3. Reducing the sentence
4. No recommendation regarding sentence

Reducing the Seriousness of the Charge

Reducing the seriousness of the charge involves pleading guilty to a charge that is less serious than the initial charge. Such a plea bargain most often occurs when a prosecutor determines that a conviction on the original charge is unlikely or when he or she wishes to use the reduction in charge to entice the defendant to plead guilty to the lesser charge.

Reducing the Number of Charges or Counts

Defendants often face a number of different charges or counts stemming from a single criminal event. In many jurisdictions, the sole purpose behind this pattern of charging is to overwhelm the defendant with a sense of futility in fighting all of the charges or counts. In addition, defendants are likely to consider the accumulation of sentences that might occur if they are convicted on each charge. Consequently, either side may suggest dropping some of the charges or counts in exchange for a guilty plea.

Reducing the Sentence

A third form of plea bargaining occurs when the defendant enters a plea of guilty to the charge in exchange for the prosecutor's agreement to support a reduced sentence. This agreement may involve a lengthy prison sentence rather than the death penalty, a shorter rather than longer prison sentence, or probation rather than prison.

No Recommendation Regarding Sentence

Sometimes, the best a defendant can hope for is an agreement that the prosecutor will stand mute at sentencing or not make a sentence recommendation at all in exchange for the guilty plea. Under this kind of plea agreement, when a judge asks for the prosecutor's recommendation, the prosecutor states that he or she will make no recommendation, and the defense is then allowed to present its case for leniency without objection.

Who Wins with Bargained Justice?

Plea bargaining may allow all parties to benefit from a negotiated plea. Defendants are most likely to benefit directly from plea bargains: They spend less time in custody, incur fewer costs (such as loss of income and attorney expenses), and are likely to receive more lenient sentences.[33]

One of the most significant benefits of plea bargaining for prosecutors is the increased predictability they offer. Trials produce uncertainty, and the longer a case takes, the greater the uncertainty and the likelihood that a defendant will be acquitted. Through plea bargains, prosecutors increase their confidence that people they believe are probably guilty will be convicted.[34] Likewise, defense attorneys benefit from plea bargains to the extent they gain the appreciation of clients who receive lighter sentences. And, like prosecutors, they are able to spend more time on cases that must go to trial.

Who Loses with Bargained Justice?

Although defendants stand to win through plea bargains, they may also be the first to lose under such agreements. Most notably, defendants give up a number of constitutionally protected due process rights as part of a plea bargain. Innocent defendants may be enticed or coerced into pleading guilty to a minor charge to avoid the costs of a larger defense or the possibility of a severe punishment.

Victims of crime may also lose in plea bargains. In many jurisdictions, they are not involved in any stage of the negotiation process and are told of the outcome only after it has been finalized. Victims frequently perceive plea bargains as failing to punish the offender appropriately for the *actual* crime committed.

WRAPPING IT UP

Chapter Highlights

- After the American Revolution, each of the new states created its own independent court system. Congress established the basic structure of the federal court system in the Judiciary Act of 1789.
- Although there are many variations in the general state court structures, all of them make similar distinctions between the courts according to their basic jurisdiction. State-level courts generally include courts of limited jurisdiction, courts of general jurisdiction, intermediate appellate courts, and courts of last resort.
- The federal court system parallels the structure of the state courts and includes U.S. Magistrates, U.S. District Courts, U.S. Courts of Appeals, and the U.S. Supreme Court.
- The criminal courts employ a number of people who are collectively responsible for scheduling cases, maintaining order, recording the actions of the courts, and administering budgets and managing personnel.
- The judge is the most central figure in the court. He or she performs a wide range of duties, from issuing warrants, to deciding whether to accept plea agreements, to determining appropriate sentences.
- Prosecutors decide which cases to prosecute, which charges will be filed, and whether to negotiate a plea bargain. In addition, they frequently make recommendations regarding bail and sentences and may speak in support of (or in opposition to) an inmate's parole at parole hearings.
- The primary role of defense attorneys is to protect the interests of their clients and to present the best possible case before the court. The Sixth Amendment guarantees that a criminal defendant shall have the right to counsel, although the courts have only recently held that this right extends to defendants in both state and federal courts who are charged with either a felony or a misdemeanor.
- At the initial appearance, defendants are informed of the charge(s) against them and their right to counsel, right to remain silent, and right to reasonable bail.
- The Eighth Amendment prohibits the setting of excessive bail. During the past few decades, a number of alternatives to monetary bail have been created to allow less affluent defendants to be released from custody.
- The grand jury is composed of citizens who are called by a prosecutor to investigate the conduct of public officials and agencies and criminal activity in general and to determine whether a crime has been committed.
- The prosecutor's charging discretion includes options ranging from the decision to drop the case to the decision to file additional charges. A number of factors influence the charging decision, such as the suspect's prior record, characteristics of the victim, chances of obtaining a conviction, and visibility and seriousness of the charge(s).

- The preliminary hearing is an opportunity to present the outlines of the state's case to determine whether to continue prosecution. It is also the first opportunity for the defense to discover the strength of the prosecution's case.
- Once arrested and charged, a suspect is asked to enter a plea. In some jurisdictions, the plea is entered at the initial appearance when the charges are read; in other jurisdictions, it is entered later, at the preliminary hearing or the arraignment.
- Nearly 95 percent of criminal cases are resolved by guilty pleas. Although many defendants initially plead guilty (especially in misdemeanor cases), many others negotiate a plea bargain.

Words to Know

48-hour rule Supreme Court ruling in *Riverside County, California v. McLaughlin*, that a defendant must be brought before a magistrate within 48 hours of his or her arrest.

arraignment Hearing at which felony defendants are informed of the charges and their rights and given an opportunity to enter a plea.

bail Money or a cash bond deposited with the court or bail bondsman allowing the defendant to be released on the assurance that he or she will appear in court at the proper time.

bail bondsman Person who guarantees court payment of the full bail amount if the defendant fails to appear.

bail guidelines Use of a grid to plot a defendant's personal and offense characteristics to determine probability of appearance.

Bail Reform Act of 1966 Act providing for release on recognizance (ROR) in noncapital federal cases when it is likely that the defendant will appear in court at required hearings.

Bail Reform Act of 1984 Act extending the opportunity for release on recognizance (ROR) in many federal cases but also providing for preventive detention without bail of dangerous suspects.

Bill of Rights First 10 amendments to the U.S. Constitution.

courts of general jurisdiction Courts with the authority to hear virtually any criminal or civil case.

courts of last resort In most states and in the federal court system, the final appellate court.

courts of limited jurisdiction Courts usually referred to as the lower or inferior courts, which are limited to hearing only specific kinds of cases.

discovery Legal motion to reveal to the defense the basis of the prosecutor's case.

Gideon v. Wainwright The U.S. Supreme Court ruling that gave every person charged with a felony the right to an attorney.

grand jury A group of citizens who are called upon to investigate the conduct of public officials and agencies and criminal activity in general and to determine whether probable cause exists to issue indictments.

guilty plea Admission of guilt to the crime charged.

initial appearance Defendant's first appearance in court, at which the charge is read, bail is set, and the defendant is informed of his or her rights.

judicial review The power of the U.S. Supreme Court to review and determine the constitutionality of acts of Congress and orders by the executive branch.

Judiciary Act of 1789 Act created by the First Congress establishing the basic structure of the federal court system.

Justice of the Peace (JP) courts Courts first established in the American colonies to hear minor criminal cases.

Marbury v. Madison U.S. Supreme Court case that established the principle of judicial review.

nolo contendere Plea of no contest; essentially the same as a guilty plea except that the defendant neither admits nor denies the charge.

not guilty by reason of insanity plea Plea in which the defendant does not deny committing the crime but claims that he or she was insane at the time of the offense and, therefore, is not criminally responsible.

not guilty plea Plea denying guilt.

plea Defendant's response to a criminal charge.

plea bargaining Negotiation between a prosecutor and a defense attorney in which they seek to arrive at a mutually satisfactory disposition of a case without going to trial.

preliminary hearing Early hearing to review charges, set bail, present witnesses, and determine probable cause.

pretrial release Release of a defendant from custody while he or she is awaiting trial.

preventive detention Practice of holding a defendant in custody without bail if he or she is deemed likely to abscond or commit further offenses if released.

release on recognizance (ROR) Personal promise by the defendant to appear in court; does not require a monetary bail.

true bill Indictment issued by a grand jury charging a person with a crime; similar to a prosecutor's filing of an information.

U.S. Supreme Court Highest appellate court in the U.S. judicial system; it reviews cases appealed from federal and state court systems that deal with constitutional issues.

United States v. Salerno U.S. Supreme Court ruling that the preventive detention provisions of the Bail Reform Act of 1984 were constitutional.

writ of certiorari Order by the U.S. Supreme Court to a lower court to send up a certified record of the lower court decision to be reviewed.

Think and Discuss

1. Should judges be appointed to the bench for life? Why or why not?
2. The U.S. Supreme Court has stated that defendants should be brought before a magistrate within 48 hours of being arrested. Is this a reasonable time period?

3. In *United States v. Salerno*, the Supreme Court ruled that the preventive detention of dangerous defendants was constitutional. Do you agree or disagree with this decision?
4. Which factors should be considered by a prosecutor when deciding which charge or charges to file against a defendant? Which factors should not enter into this decision?
5. Should plea bargaining be abolished? Why or why not?

Notes

1. Herbert Johnson, *History of Criminal Justice* (Cincinnati: Anderson, 1988), pp. 82–84.
2. *Marbury v. Madison*, 1 Cr. 137 (1803).
3. *Fletcher v. Peck*, 6 Cr. 87 (1810).
4. Robert Carp and Ronald Stidham, *The Federal Courts* (Washington, DC: Congressional Quarterly, 1985).
5. Lynn Langton and Thomas Cohen, *State Court Organization, 1987–2004* (Washington, DC: U.S. Department of Justice, 2007).
6. American Bar Association, *Fall 2007 Enrollment Statistics* (Chicago: American Bar Association, 2008).
7. Rodney Uphoff, "The Criminal Defense Lawyer: Zealous Advocate, Double Agent, or Beleaguered Dealer?" *Criminal Law Bulletin*, September–October 1992, p. 420.
8. *Powell v. Alabama*, 287 U.S. 45 (1932).
9. *Johnson v. Zerbst*, 304 U.S. 458 (1938).
10. *Betts v. Brady*, 316 U.S. 455 (1942).
11. *Gideon v. Wainwright*, 372 U.S. 335 (1963).
12. *Argersinger v. Hamlin*, 407 U.S. 25 (1972).
13. *Scott v. Illinois*, 440 U.S. 367 (1979).
14. Carol DeFrances and Marika Litras, *Indigent Defense Services in Large Counties, 1999* (Washington, DC: U.S. Department of Justice, 2000).
15. Jill Smolowe, "The Trials of the Public Defender," *Time*, March 29, 1993, p. 50.
16. *Gerstein v. Pugh*, 420 U.S. 103 (1975).
17. *Riverside County, California v. McLaughlin*, 500 U.S. 44 (1991).
18. *United States v. Salerno*, 481 U.S. 739 (1987).
19. Bureau of Justice Statistics, *Compendium of Federal Justice Statistics, 2004* (Washington, DC: U.S. Department of Justice, 2006), Table 3.1.
20. Traci Schlesinger, "Racial and Ethnic Disparity in Pretrial Criminal Processing," *Justice Quarterly* 22:170–193 (2005); K. B. Turner and James Johnson, "A Comparison of Bail Amounts for Hispanics, Whites, and African Americans: A Single County Analysis," *American Journal of Criminal Justice* 30:35–56 (2005); Stephen Demuth, "Racial and Ethnic Differences in Pretrial Release Decisions and Outcomes: A Comparison of Hispanic, Black, and White Felony Arrests," *Criminology* 41:873–908 (2003); Cassia Spohn, *Offender Race and Case Outcomes: Do Crime Seriousness and Strength of Evidence Matter? Final Activities Report* (Omaha, NE: University of Nebraska Press, 2000); Stephen Demuth and Darrell Steffensmeier, "The Impact of Gender and Race-Ethnicity in the Pretrial Release Process," *Social Problems* 51:222–242 (2004).

21. Andy Hall, *Pretrial Release Program Options* (Washington, DC: National Institute of Justice, 1984), pp. 32–33.

22. Pub. Law 89-465, 89th Cong. S. 1357, 80 Stat. 214.

23. John Goldkamp and Michael Gottfredson, *Judicial Guidelines for Bail: The Philadelphia Experiment* (Washington, DC: U.S. Department of Justice, 1984); John Goldkamp and Michael White, *Restoring Accountability in Pretrial Release: The Philadelphia Pretrial Release Supervision Experiments, Final Report* (Philadelphia: Crime and Justice Research Institute, 2001).

24. *Comprehensive Crime Control Act of 1984*, Public Law 98-473, October 12, 1984.

25. *United States v. Salerno*, note 18.

26. Niki Kuckes, "The Useful, Dangerous Fiction of Grand Jury Independence," *American Criminal Law Review* 41:1–66 (2004).

27. *United States v. Calandra*, 414 U.S. 338 (1974).

28. Samuel Walker, *Sense and Nonsense about Crime: A Policy Guide*, 6th ed. (Monterey, CA: Brooks/Cole, 2005), pp. 22–27.

29. Ronald Carlson, *Criminal Justice Procedure*, 4th ed. (Cincinnati: Anderson, 1991), p. 65.

30. *Boykin v. Alabama*, 395 U.S. 238 (1969).

31. Henry Steadman and Jeraldine Braff, "Defendants Not Guilty by Reason of Insanity," in John Mohanan and Henry Steadman (Eds.), *Mentally Disordered Offenders* (New York: Plenum, 1983).

32. Matthew Durose and Patrick Langan, *Felony Sentences in State Courts, 2004* (Washington, DC: U.S. Department of Justice, 2007), p. 1.

33. Anthony Walsh, "Standing Trial Versus Copping a Plea: Is There a Penalty?" *Journal of Contemporary Criminal Justice* 6:226–236 (1990).

34. Scott Baker and Claudio Mezzetti, "Prosecutorial Resources, Plea Bargaining, and the Decision to Go to Trial," *Journal of Law, Economics, and Organization* 17:149–167 (2001); William McDonald, *Plea Bargaining: Critical Issues and Common Practices* (Washington, DC: U.S. Government Printing Office, 1985); Celesta Albonetti, "Criminality, Prosecutorial Screening, and Uncertainty: Toward a Theory of Discretionary Decision Making in Felony Case Processing," *Criminology* 24:623–644 (1986).

CHAPTER

The Trial

OBJECTIVES

1 Identify the nature and functions of the various pretrial motions.

2 Know the procedures and constitutional issues surrounding a defendant's right to a speedy, public, and fair trial.

3 Grasp the advantages and disadvantages of both bench and jury trials.

4 Understand the nature of the contemporary jury system.

5 Recognize the basic procedural steps of a trial and understand the importance of the concepts of innocence and reasonable doubt.

6 Explain the dynamics of jury deliberations and describe how verdicts are reached.

PROFILES IN CRIME AND JUSTICE

Jeffrey S. Cohen
Attorney at Law
Office of the Alternate Public Defender
County of Los Angeles

I decided to practice criminal law while I was an associate, practicing at a small civil rights litigation firm in Los Angeles. It was a heavy motion practice, and like most lawyers, I was spending most of the day at a desk, behind a computer screen. I soon realized that what I enjoyed most was arguing the discovery motions at court hearings. It didn't take me long to learn that most good civil cases settle before trial, and if I really wanted to be in the courtroom, I needed to get into criminal law.

My favorite part of my job is the constant excitement of being in court every day. When I'm in trial, there's the adrenaline rush of getting to persuade a jury that my client's version of events is more plausible than the prosecution's. And when I'm not in trial, I'm preparing for trial: investigating the facts of a case, interviewing witnesses, and writing motions to protect my clients' rights. It's not the job for everyone—you have to be passionate and *com*passionate—otherwise, it is easy to become jaded and uncaring.

Another reason that working in an office like mine is so exciting is because we protect people's constitutional rights and force the government to meet its burden of proof. Part of trying a case means opening jurors' eyes to their own stereotypes and penchant for snap judgments, and ensuring that the Constitution's presumption of innocence isn't an empty promise.

There are certain characteristics that are absolutely critical for the job. A good criminal defense attorney is smart, patient, articulate, and quick on his or her feet. Naturally, a successful trial attorney also needs good "people skills," because our clients' fate often depends on our ability to connect with a jury. Another important characteristic is confidence. It's very important to be able to stand up to a judge who is bullying your client. Between the police, district attorneys, and everyone else in the courtroom, what we say is often the only thing that stands between our clients and a very long prison sentence, or worse.

Introduction

The first national live, televised criminal trial aired in the United States in 1991. It involved the trial of William Kennedy Smith, a nephew of Senator Edward Kennedy, who was charged with the rape of Patricia Bowman. Before then, the public relied on news accounts or brief taped footage of testimony to learn about the events at a trial. Now, the public was able to watch the jury selection process, presentation of evidence, cross-examination, instructions to the jury, and reading of the verdict.

Smith's trial did not resemble the highly dramatized events aired in television programs such as *Law and Order* and in films such as *The Firm*, *To Kill a Mockingbird*, *The Verdict*, and *American Tragedy*. These fictionalized trials presented a much more polished—and ultimately less realistic—process than occurred in actual trials. With the goal of entertainment and excitement, these programs and films exaggerate the questioning of witnesses and their testimony, the introduction of surprise witnesses at the last moment, and the ability of defense attorneys to outwit prosecutors.[1] Prior to the Smith trial, the public's beliefs about the trial process had been based on such fictionalized presentations and were far from the reality of what actually occurs as defendants go through the stages of a trial from pretrial motions to jury selection, trial, and, for many, appeal of conviction (see FIGURE 8–1).

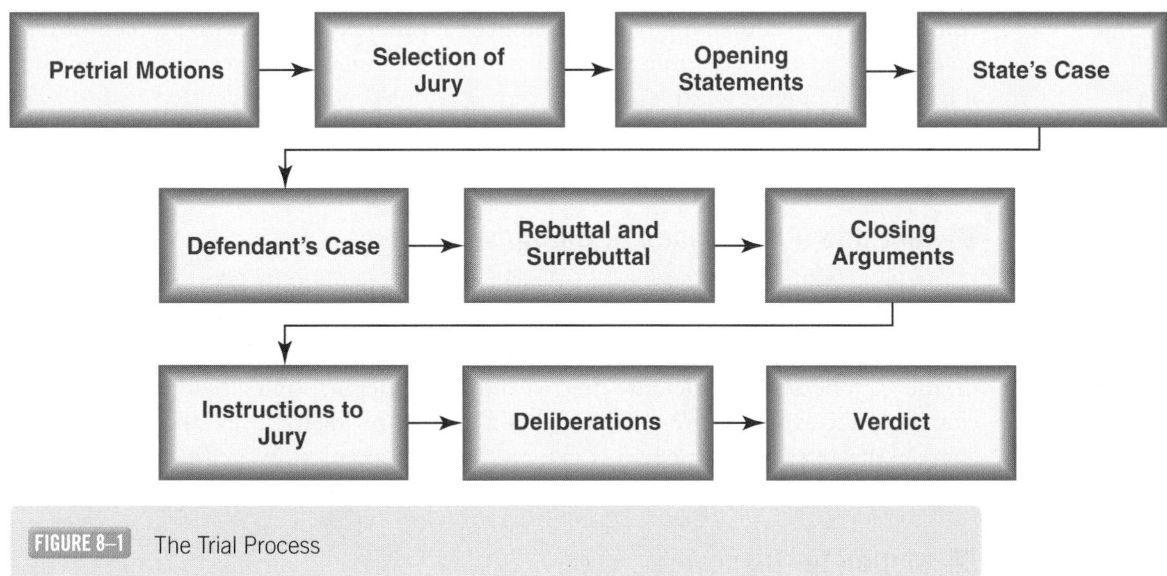

FIGURE 8–1 The Trial Process

Pretrial Motions

Although the vast majority of cases are resolved by the plea bargaining process, some defendants choose to have their cases decided through a trial. Once a case has been set for trial, the prosecutor may reevaluate the strength of the case based on the outcome of various pretrial motions raised by the defense. **Pretrial motions** are written or oral requests to the judge to make a ruling or to order that action be taken in favor of the applicant. By definition, they are made before any opening statements or presentation of evidence and usually even before jury selection, although the timing of these motions varies widely among the states.

William Kennedy Smith's 1991 rape case was the first live, nationally televised trial in the United States.

Motion for Dismissal of Charges

A motion to dismiss is often one of the first motions made by the defense before trial and is based on the defense's claim that the indictment is not sufficient to justify a trial. The prosecutor may also file a motion to dismiss the case by entering a *nolle prosequi* (a Latin term meaning that the prosecutor "will not further prosecute" the case). The reasons that prosecutors cite to dismiss cases vary but often result from a discovery that the original allegation is unfounded, that evidence produced by the police was unlawfully obtained, or that critical witnesses are no longer available.

Motion for Change of Venue

Typically, criminal cases are tried in the county (or, in federal cases, the district) in which the crime was committed. Sometimes, however, the defense may move for a change of venue if there has been excessive pretrial publicity about the case or if there is reason to believe that substantial prejudice exists that would deny the defendant a fair trial, as when the judge ordered a change of venue in the Scott Peterson murder case. If the trial judge agrees to this motion, the trial is moved to another county or district. The prosecution frequently objects to motions for a change of venue because of the difficulty and expense in transporting staff and witnesses to another city.

Motion for Severance of Defendants

When two or more defendants are jointly charged with the same offense, most states require they be tried together. The savings in time and money from conducting a single trial are obvious, and, in many cases, a joint trial generally presents no problems to the defendants. On some occasions, a defendant may file a motion for severance of defendants if it is in his or her best interest to do so. For example, evidence presented against a co-defendant may not apply to the defendant, and the jury may have difficulty in keeping the cases separate in their minds.

Motion for Severance of Charges

Sometimes, multiple charges are filed against one defendant. It is to the prosecutor's advantage to try the defendant on all of these charges at the same time: It saves time and effort, and the collective weight of the charges may have a greater negative impact on the jury. Because the defense may wish to use different strategies to deal with each charge, and to avoid the prejudicial effect on the jury owing to the existence of multiple charges, the defense may file a motion for a *severance of charges* in such a case, requesting a separate trial for each charge.

Motion for Discovery

In jurisdictions that do not allow discovery at the preliminary hearing or in cases where the defendant was indicted by a grand jury, it is critical for the defense to file a pretrial motion for discovery to request access to evidence and the list of witnesses who the prosecutor plans to present at trial.

Motion for a Bill of Particulars

Similar to a motion for discovery, a motion for a *bill of particulars* asks for a written statement from the prosecutor revealing the details of the charge(s), including the time, place, manner, and means of commission of the crime. Having this information allows the defense to prepare a more accurate defense, set limits on the evidence that the prosecutor may present at trial, avoid surprise claims of criminal acts, and establish the basis for a claim of double jeopardy if the defendant has already been tried for the same crime.

Motion for Suppression of Evidence

The *exclusionary rule* prohibits the introduction at trial of any evidence obtained illegally. Through motions for discovery, the defense may become aware of evidence that the prosecutor plans to introduce. If the defense believes that this evidence was unlawfully acquired, it may file a motion to suppress the evidence. In response to such a motion, the court may hold an evidentiary or suppression hearing to determine whether the evidence has been tainted by any illegal search or seizure.

Motion of Intention to Provide an Alibi

The use of an alibi defense typically requires the filing of a pretrial motion indicating the intent to use this defense. A motion of intention to provide an **alibi** (an assertion that the defendant was somewhere else at the time the crime was committed) states that the defendant's attorney plans to present a defense based on this notion. The motion must place the defendant in a location different from the crime scene at the time of the crime in such a way that it would have been impossible for him or her to be the guilty party.

Motion for Determination of Competency

If the defense counsel questions his or her client's sanity while preparing for trial or at any time during the trial, the attorney should file a motion for *determination of competency*. A defendant who lacks the capacity to understand the charge or the possible penalties

Headline Crime

Successful Use of an Alibi in the Robert Blake Murder Trial

Bonny Bakley, wife of actor Robert Blake, was shot in the head as she waited in the car outside an Italian restaurant where she and her husband had just finished dinner. Blake told authorities that he had returned to the restaurant to retrieve a revolver he had accidentally left behind after it had fallen under the table. Blake maintained that he was inside the restaurant at the time his wife was shot. Despite Blake's claim of innocence, the 71-year-old star of the 1970s television show *Baretta* was tried for first-degree solicitation for murder. After nearly 35 hours of deliberation, the jury acquitted Blake, indicating a lack of sufficient evidence to convict beyond a reasonable doubt, even though no witnesses had testified to seeing him return to his table in the restaurant.

Source: "Actor Robert Blake Acquitted of His Wife's Murder," available at http://www.courttv.com/trials/blake/031605_verdict_ctv.html, accessed January 3, 2008.

if convicted, to assist or confer with counsel, or to understand the nature of the court proceedings is considered not competent to stand trial.[2]

A competency hearing is not designed to establish the defendant's guilt or innocence, but rather to determine his or her present mental competence. If the defendant is found not competent to stand trial, he or she is ordered to be confined to a mental institution until judged by the staff at the institution to be competent.

Motion for Continuance

One of the most frequently filed pretrial motions is the *motion for continuance*, or postponement or adjournment of the trial until a later date. This kind of request is typically filed by the defense. Why would the defense choose to delay a trial, especially if the defendant is confined in jail during this process? The defense is likely to claim the need to prepare for the trial, but requests for a continuance are often part of a defense strategy to wear down victims and to allow for the possibility that prosecution witnesses may move away, be unable to be located, forget details of the crime, or die by the time the trial begins. In addition, when the trial is delayed, public outrage over a particularly heinous crime may have subsided by the time the trial gets underway.

The Right to a Speedy, Public, and Fair Trial

The Sixth Amendment to the Constitution states that "In all criminal prosecutions, the accused shall enjoy the right to a speedy and public trial, by an impartial jury." This statement raises several issues: How soon after a person is arrested must a trial be held? How much access to pretrial hearings and the trial itself should the public have? How do we ensure that the jury is untainted by prejudice?

The Right to a Speedy Trial

Few people would argue with the proposition that "Justice delayed is justice denied." The plight of a defendant who languishes in jail for months while the state prepares its case is clearly objectionable. Nevertheless, many defendants must wait a long time to

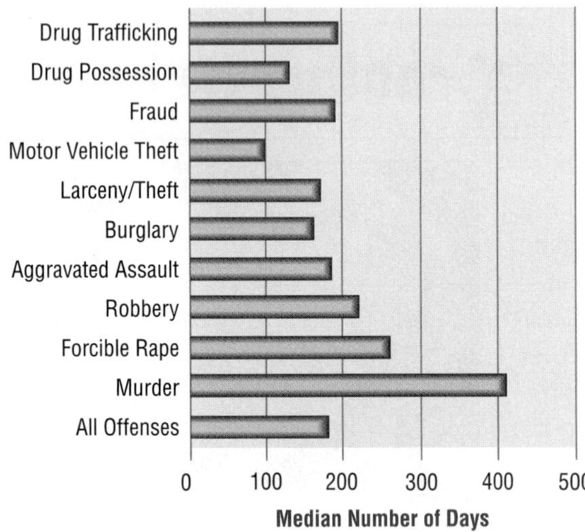

FIGURE 8–2 Median Number of Days from Arrest to Sentencing

Source: Matthew Durose and Patrick Langan, *Felony Sentences in State Courts*, 2002 (Washington, DC: U.S. Department of Justice, 2004).

have their day in court. How long they wait from arrest to sentencing varies greatly across jurisdictions and even from court to court within particular jurisdictions. However, the greatest influence on case processing is the seriousness of the charge. For example, for cases involving motor vehicle theft, the median number of days between arrest and sentencing is only 99; by comparison, it is 222 days for robbery and 412 days for murder (see FIGURE 8–2).

Defining the Limits of a Speedy Trial

The Sixth Amendment does not mean that a defendant may demand an immediate trial following his or her arrest. Both the prosecutor and the defendant have a right to prepare their cases before the trial begins. In attempting to define the meaning of "speedy trial," both federal and state governments have established rules limiting the time between arrest and trial. For example, in Illinois, the defendant must be brought to trial within 120 days if in custody or within 160 days if he or she is free on bond. By comparison, a defendant in California must be brought to trial within 60 days for either a felony or a misdemeanor, and in federal cases the trial must begin within 70 days. If the prosecutor exceeds that limit, the defendant may file a motion to have the charge dismissed.

In *Barker v. Wingo*,[3] the U.S. Supreme Court held that a defendant's right to a speedy trial is not necessarily infringed upon by prosecutorial requests for continuances; rather, such decisions should be made on a case-by-case basis. If the defense files a motion for continuance, it is considered a waiver of the right to a speedy trial. If neither the defendant nor the defense counsel has done anything to cause the delay, and the trial has not begun within the designated number of days, the judge may dismiss the case.

The Courts, the Public, and the Press

The Sixth Amendment to the Constitution also guarantees defendants the right to a public trial. This right was established to ensure that people who were accused of crimes were treated fairly by the government by allowing the public full access to information regarding the proceedings. The Constitution does not tell us what makes a trial "public," how many people must be allowed to view a trial, or how they might view it, nor does it say whether a defendant may waive this right and request a private trial. Furthermore, there has been extensive debate over the conflict between the press's First Amendment right to report information about a case, the defendant's Sixth Amendment right to an impartial jury, and the right of victims and witnesses to privacy, as implied by the Fourth Amendment.

Over the years, a common-sense definition of a public trial has come to mean one that the public is free to attend, and the limit on the number of people allowed or required has been determined by the size of normal courtrooms. Other questions have not been so easily resolved.

The Public's Right to Attend

A number of U.S. Supreme Court decisions have addressed the question of just how open trials must be. In *Gannett Co., Inc. v. DePasquale*, the Court held that the public and press could be barred from pretrial hearings.[4] Because many pretrial hearings involve sensitive matters such as determining the admissibility of evidence, access of the public and press to these hearings could pose special risks of unfairness. In 1986, the Supreme Court ruled that the press and public should not be excluded from the jury selection stage of the trial, even though the decision of the lower court in question was based on a desire to protect the privacy of potential jurors and to promote their candor during questioning.[5]

Despite several accusations and financial settlements with alleged victims, Michael Jackson has never been convicted of child molestation.

Freedom of the Press and Pretrial Publicity

In 2004, Santa Barbara County Superior Court Judge Rodney Melville issued a blanket gag order that prohibited singer Michael Jackson, his accuser, and attorneys on both sides from publicly commenting on Jackson's child molestation case. Representatives of the media and Jackson's attorneys appealed to the California Supreme Court to have the gag order lifted, but the judge refused to drop the order.

Judges in high-profile cases have frequently issued gag orders to prohibit the reporting of highly inflammatory information based on comments from attorneys outside the court or testimony during a trial. Until recently, the U.S. Supreme Court had not clearly defined the limits of gag orders designed to prevent extensive or prejudicial pretrial publicity that could deny a defendant a fair trial. In 1976, in *Nebraska Press Association v. Stuart*, the Supreme Court finally set forth guidelines for the use of prior restraint by lower trial courts.[6] The Court held that prior restraint should be used only when absolutely necessary and only when the court can show all of the following:

- There is a clear threat to the fairness of trial
- Such a threat is posed by the actual publicity to be restrained
- No less restrictive alternatives are available

Some evidence suggests that general pretrial publicity may, indeed, influence jurors. As they consider the testimony at hand, jurors may remember what they have heard about similar but unrelated cases and may draw upon this knowledge to evaluate the case before them.[7] For example, jurors who have seen news coverage of rape cases and heard defendants' claims that the victims consented to have sex may apply their understanding of those cases to the case they are hearing, thereby influencing their evaluation of the testimony.

Cameras in the Courtroom

Prior to 1977, if the news media wished to report on a criminal trial, they had to assign a reporter to attend the trial, take notes and perhaps make drawings, and then write the news story. Newspapers, radio, and television could then report the story. That situation changed in 1977, when television cameras were first admitted into the Florida courts on a regular basis. Since then, all 50 states have developed rules permitting cameras into their courts under certain circumstances.

In 1977, Florida pioneered the use of cameras in the courtroom when it passed a new law that presumed news media have the right to present live or taped coverage of trials unless the court finds compelling reasons to ban such a broadcast. However, rules permitting cameras in the courts have not been uniformly accepted by the states. Congress is currently considering legislation that would permit cameras in all federal courts, including the Supreme Court. In addition, the U.S. Court of Military Appeals has permitted television coverage of a number of important cases since 1989.

Bench Trial Versus Jury Trial

One of the more critical decisions a defendant must make along the path to trial is whether to ask for a trial by jury. Of all criminal defendants convicted at trial, about 40 percent are convicted by juries; the other 60 percent are tried and convicted before the judge alone in a **bench trial**.[8]

There are several reasons why a defendant might choose to waive his or her right to a jury trial and request to a trial before a judge:

- The crime may be so heinous that it could generate a greater emotional reaction in jurors, who are generally less familiar with such crimes than are judges.
- A defendant's unusual appearance may create a bias in the minds of jurors.
- Excessive media coverage of the crime may make it difficult to ensure a fair and impartial jury.
- The case may be too complex for a jury to understand.
- Attorney fees may be lower because a bench trial generally involves less total attorney time than a jury trial.[9]

Trial by Jury

The right to a jury trial is found only in the handful of countries with criminal justice systems operating under common law procedures, such as the United Kingdom, Canada, and Australia. Today, the United States accounts for nearly 80 percent of all jury trials that take place around the world.[10]

Constitutional Right to a Trial by Jury

The Sixth Amendment guarantees not only the right to a jury trial, but also the right to a trial by an impartial jury. However, early Supreme Court interpretations of this provision limited those rights to federal cases. In 1937, the Court held in *Palko v. Connecticut*,[11] that only those rights "so rooted in the traditions and conscience of our people as to be ranked as fundamental"[12] and considered essential to the "principle of justice" were to be applied to the states through the due process clause of the Fourteenth Amendment. Jury trials were not deemed to be a fundamental right.

In 1968, the Court held that jury trials were fundamental to the criminal justice process "to prevent oppression by the government." Any serious crime that would qualify for a jury trial in federal court entitles a defendant the right to jury trial in state court.[13] In 1989, however, the Supreme Court held that defendants do not have the right to jury trial in minor criminal cases that carry punishments of less than six months in prison or jail.[14] Furthermore, the right to a jury trial is not considered a fundamental right in juvenile proceedings.[15]

Size of the Jury

Most states and the federal courts use 12-person juries. However, the Sixth Amendment does not establish a required size for juries. In 1970, the Supreme Court ruled on the constitutionality of juries with fewer than 12 people.[16] The justices held that the number 12 was only a "historical accident, unnecessary to effect the purposes of the jury system and wholly without significance." They determined that juries should be "large enough to promote group deliberations and . . . to provide a fair possibility for obtaining a representative cross section of the community."

Jury duty is one of the primary ways that citizens engage in civic activities.

The size of juries is determined by each state, and juries with as few as six people have been held to be constitutional, except in death penalty cases. To reaffirm the Supreme Court's belief that at least six people were needed to achieve reasonable deliberations, in 1978 the Court, in *Ballew v. Georgia*, struck down a conviction by a five-person jury.[17]

Jury Selection

While the Sixth Amendment guarantees trial by an impartial jury, neither the prosecutor nor the defense really desires a fully impartial jury. That is, each party generally attempts to select people who they believe will favor their side. The complex jury selection process is designed to eliminate certain people from serving while retaining others. Both the prosecutor and the defense attorney, and sometimes the judge, ask questions of potential jurors. Once a sufficient number of jurors are found acceptable by both sides, the jury is established.

Eligibility for Serving on Juries

There are few requirements for jury service. Minor variations exist among the states, but the basic qualifications are the same. A prospective juror must meet the following requirements:

- United States citizenship
- Eighteen years of age or older
- Minimum residence in the jurisdiction in which the trial is being held (generally one year, but may be one month in some states)
- Possession of natural faculties (be able to see, hear, talk, feel, and smell and be relatively mobile) to be able to evaluate evidence
- Ordinary intelligence
- Knowledge of the English language sufficient to understand the proceedings and communicate with the other jurors

State rules for excluding people from serving on juries vary. Generally, people excluded have been convicted of a felony or illegal act while in public office or those who have served on a jury during the preceding year.

Many jurisdictions also exempt people from jury duty because of their occupation or duties they perform within the community. For example, attorneys, clergy members, teachers, physicians, firefighters, law enforcement and correctional officers, military personnel, many public officials, caregivers of young children, and those with proven hardship are generally exempt from jury service, although they may serve if they wish to do so.

Selection Process

The selection of people to serve on a jury involves a number of steps (see FIGURE 8-3). The first step is the construction of a master list, called the **jury pool**, which contains approximately 1000 names of citizens randomly selected from the community. In an attempt to ensure the broadest inclusion of people, most communities cull jury pools from several sources, such as voter and welfare lists, property tax rolls, lists of licensed drivers, telephone directories, and even utility records.

Each person in the jury pool receives a questionnaire that asks basic questions about residency, occupation, ability to understand English, prior felony convictions, and physical impairments that might automatically exclude the person from jury duty. In addition, the questionnaire is designed to elicit information about the respon-

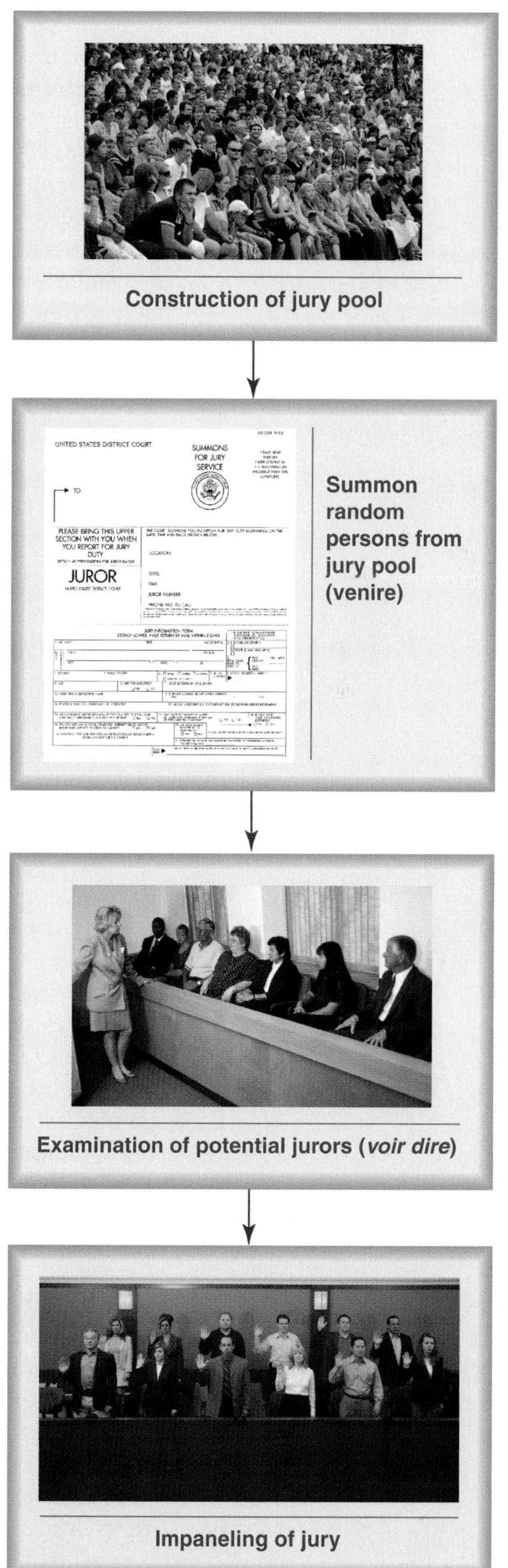

FIGURE 8-3 The Process of Jury Selection

dent's possible biases in a criminal trial, such as prior jury duty, involvement in lawsuits, or familiarity with police officers in the community.

The second step is to randomly select a group of people from the jury pool to establish the jury panel, called the venire. The **venire** (from a Latin word, meaning "to come") is composed of people who are sent a summons (a legal document notifying them to report for jury duty). The number of potential jurors summoned is usually determined by the expected difficulty in obtaining a qualified jury. These people then become the panel from which the final jury is selected.

Unfortunately, not all potential jurors show up for jury selection. In many jurisdictions, as few as 40 percent of the venire report to the courthouse.[18] Many people fail to show up because they do not want to take the time or effort to participate. Consequently, it is not unusual for juries to have disproportionate numbers of homemakers with grown children, retirees, and the unemployed.

Once assembled in the courtroom, the venire is sworn in and the *voir dire* begins. The ***voir dire*** (derived from the French words, meaning "to speak the truth") is a preliminary examination of potential jurors. It seeks to answer two questions:

1. Is this person qualified to serve on the jury?
2. Is he or she capable of making a determination of guilt or innocence without prejudice?

During the *voir dire*, the prosecutor, the defense counsel, and often the judge ask questions to elicit information about the person's familiarity with the case and possible biases that might affect his or her judgment and willingness to listen impartially to all the evidence before making a decision. There are a few limits on the kind of questions that may be asked during this process, however. For example, potential jurors may not be asked specific questions about their sexual orientation or their religious affiliation and beliefs.

After the *voir dire*, prosecutors, defense attorneys, or the judge may excuse people from jury duty using one of two methods—challenge for cause or peremptory challenge.

Challenge for Cause

A **challenge for cause** is a call by the prosecutor or the defense to dismiss a person from a jury panel for a legitimate cause. Any number of people may be challenged for cause and dismissed from the panel. For example, if a prospective juror has vision or hearing problems that could interfere with observing or understanding the proceedings; if he or she indicates an existing bias toward one of the parties in the case; if the individual is worried about a sick family member; or if the person has knowledge of the defendant, witnesses, or attorneys involved in the case, then, with the agreement of the judge, that person may be excused.

Peremptory Challenge

Peremptory challenges allow attorneys to eliminate people from the jury who they believe are not likely to be sympathetic to their arguments. Because both the prosecutor and the defense attorney may challenge a limited number of prospective jurors without giving any reasons for doing so, the use of peremptory challenges has become a controversial part of the jury selection process.

Inasmuch as the process of excusing people based on personal characteristics or views introduces a form of bias into the jury and may deny a defendant or the state a representative jury,[19] government statutes limit the number of peremptory challenges allowed to each side. The minimum in felony cases is usually three, but both sides may be allowed as many as 20 in highly publicized murder cases or cases in which several defendants are being tried together.

When a sufficient number of jurors (usually 12) and one or two alternates have been accepted by the defense and prosecution, they are impaneled—that is, sworn in.

Bias in Jury Selection

Can a person be excused from serving on a jury simply because of his or her race or gender? Does a defendant have a right to a jury composed of people with particular racial, ethnic, or gender characteristics? Must the jury be a cross section of the community? The Supreme Court has tried to answer these questions. In 1947, the Court ruled as follows:

> There is no constitutional right to a jury drawn from a group of uneducated and unintelligent persons. Nor is there any right to a jury chosen solely from those at the lower end of the economic and social scale. But there is a constitutional right to a jury drawn from a group which represents a cross section of the community.[20]

The requirement of a representative cross section of the community is met only if there is no systematic exclusion of any particular group of people. Of course, owing to peremptory challenges, when no reason for the challenge is given, it may be difficult to determine whether a particular race or gender is being deliberately excluded from the jury.

Race

In 1986, the Supreme Court held, in *Batson v. Kentucky*, that the Fourteenth Amendment's equal protection clause "forbids the prosecutor to challenge potential jurors solely on account of their race or on the presumption that black jurors as a group will be unable impartially to consider the State's case against a black defendant."[21] Excluding members of a certain racial group would deny the defendant the right to be tried by an impartial jury representative of a cross section of the local community. In 1991, the Supreme Court in *Hernandez v. New York*,[22] extended the *Batson* rule to the ethnicity of defendants.

Gender

In 1994, in *J.E.B. v. Alabama*, the U.S. Supreme Court ruled that peremptory challenges based on gender were unconstitutional.[23] The Court, in a 6–3 decision, held that "gender, like race, is an unconstitutional proxy for juror competence and impartiality." The justices ruled that:

> Intentional discrimination on the basis of gender by state actors violates the Equal Protection Clause, particularly where, as here, the discrimination serves to ratify and perpetuate invidious, archaic, and overbroad stereotypes about the relative abilities of men and women.

Religion

Even though jurors may not be asked specific questions about their religious affiliation or beliefs during the *voir dire* process, indirect indicators or responses during questioning may provide information about the religion of potential jurors. The constitutionality of using peremptory challenges based on a potential juror's religion has not yet been resolved. For example, Connecticut has recently prohibited religion-based peremptory challenges. In contrast, a Texas appellate court has held that *Batson* does not apply to such challenges.[24] Finally, a Florida appellate court may have opened the door to prohibiting religion-based challenges in that state based on the "free exercise of religion" protection in the First Amendment to the U.S. Constitution.[25]

Scientific Jury Selection

In an attempt to make effective decisions about potential jurors, many attorneys are turning to psychological and sociological studies designed to correlate background characteristics, personality profiles, courtroom behaviors, body language, and facial expressions with particular biases. Such studies include community surveys conducted before a trial to identify characteristics of people who are more inclined to be sympathetic toward either the prosecution or the defense. People on the venire exhibiting those characteristics are more likely to be either challenged or accepted as attorneys try to build a favorable jury.

The Trial

Jury trials account for only 5 percent of criminal prosecutions today. Most trials are rather routine and highly regulated in terms of procedure, and are typically completed in a matter of hours or days. Only the most complex and celebrated cases take a week or more to conclude. TABLE 8–1 shows the average length of jury trials.

Opening Statements

Once the jury has been sworn in and seated and the formal charges against the defendant have been read, the prosecutor presents an **opening statement** to the jury. (The prosecutor goes first because it is the state's burden to prove the defendant's guilt.) The length of the statement depends on the complexity of the case, but its purpose is always to provide a factual outline of the case the prosecutor intends to prove. The opening statement may include a restatement of the charges, a general overview of why the prosecutor believes the defendant is guilty, and a brief listing of the witnesses the prosecutor intends to call and what each will testify to.

Nothing said by the prosecutor in the opening statements may be considered by the jury as evidence or facts in the case. Rather, it is commentary designed to help jurors follow the case as it develops. Prosecutors are not allowed to make statements considered inflammatory or prejudicial against the defendant, such as commenting on evidence already known to be inadmissible.

The defense is then given an opportunity to make its opening statement. Often, the defense may choose to delay its opening statement until after the prosecution's case has been fully presented. In any event, the defense will usually stress during this statement that the prosecutor must prove his or her case beyond a reasonable doubt, given the presumption of innocence.

TABLE 8–1 Average Length of Jury Trials

Court	Average Time[a]
Elizabeth, New Jersey	6:20
Paterson, New Jersey	7:24
Golden, Colorado	8:10
Monterey, California	9:27
Denver, Colorado	10:50
Jersey City, New Jersey	12:09
Marin County, California	17:44
Oakland, California	23:16

[a]In hours and minutes. Does not include jury deliberation time.

Source: Adapted from Dale Anne Sipes, *On Trial: The Length of Civil and Criminal Trials* (Williamsburg, VA: National Center for State Courts, 1988), p. 17.

Presentation of Evidence

Evidence is presented by witnesses, not by the attorneys. The prosecutor and the defense attorney call various witnesses to present different kinds of evidence. Ideally, each witness will present evidence that lays a foundation for the evidence offered by subsequent witnesses.

Types of Evidence

All evidence submitted must be relevant, competent, and material. That is, it must relate directly to the issue at hand and to the material elements of the crime, and it must be provided by someone considered competent or qualified to testify. Although there is often overlap, most evidence falls into one of the following categories:

- Real evidence includes physical objects such as fingerprints, clothing, weapons, stolen property, documents, confiscated drugs, and genetic material. Sometimes, the original real evidence is not convenient to present to the jury, so photographs or reconstructions may be used.
- Testimonial evidence includes the testimony of witnesses who are qualified to speak about specific real evidence. For example, an expert witness such as a forensic chemist may be called to testify to the fact that drugs confiscated by the police are what they are purported to be.
- Direct evidence is provided by eyewitnesses to the crime about what they directly observed.
- Circumstantial evidence requires that the jury draw a reasonable inference from the testimony. A witness may testify that he or she heard a scream followed by a gunshot coming from a victim's apartment; moments later, the witness saw the defendant leave the apartment. Although the witness did not directly observe the shooting, absent any other suspects in the apartment, it is reasonable to infer that the defendant was involved in the crime.
- Hearsay evidence includes testimony based on something that the witness does not have direct knowledge of but has heard or been told. Generally, hearsay evidence is considered inadmissible. For example, if Chris were to testify, "Jennifer told me that Bill sold Tiffiny a kilo of marijuana," it would be considered hearsay evidence because Chris had no direct knowledge of the alleged sale. However, several exceptions to this rule exist:
    1. *Dying declarations.* Because it is assumed that dying people will not lie when they believe themselves close to death, such testimony may be admitted for the jury's consideration.
    2. *Statements made by victims of child abuse.* Such statements made to a caseworker, teacher, or doctor may be admitted.
    3. *Admission of a criminal act by the defendant to a witness.* Because both the witness and the defendant are in court and the defendant may rebut the statement, it may be admitted as evidence.

The Prosecution's Case

The prosecutor presents the state's case through a succession of witnesses and introduction of evidence. Questioning is usually straightforward, with each witness being asked to discuss what he or she knows to be the facts of the case. The defense attorney may object to a question on several grounds:

- The question is irrelevant (immaterial) or incompetent (not admissible).
- The question calls for speculation on the part of the witness (only expert witnesses may offer opinions).

FOCUS ON CRIMINAL JUSTICE

Real Evidence: Fingerprints and DNA

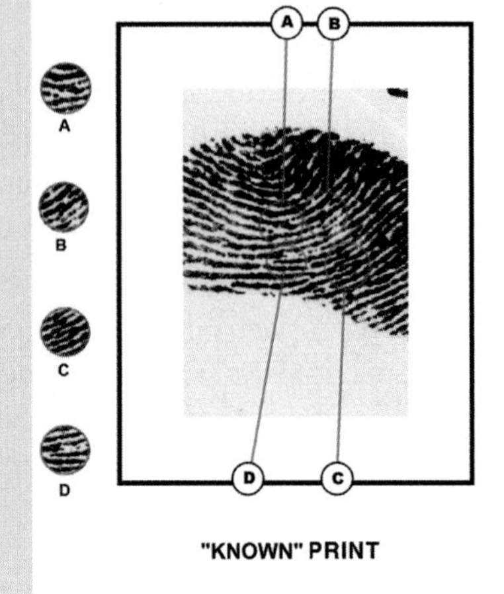

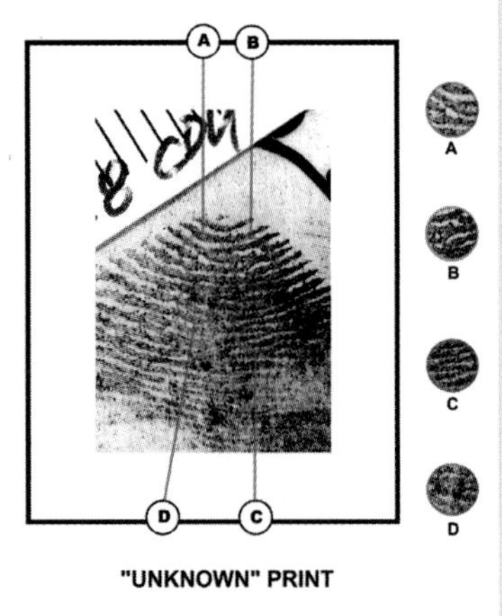

Rick Jackson was arrested in Upper Darby, Pennsylvania, for a gruesome murder and told that the police had solid evidence against him—photographs of his bloody fingerprints taken from the crime scene. Even though experts agreed that the fingerprints were a match, Jackson insisted that they couldn't be his. He was found guilty and sentenced to a life sentence without possibility of parole. Two years later, other fingerprint experts testified that the prosecution had been wrong and that the prints, in fact, did not belong to Jackson. He was released after spending two years in prison.

While fingerprints have long been considered the "gold standard" of identification at trial and frequently are the key evidence used to obtain convictions, their reliability is increasingly being questioned, especially with the growing refinement of DNA technologies. DNA samples are often retrieved from crime scenes and used by prosecutors in minor property crimes. These samples may consist of small amounts of blood on broken glass in burglaries, sweat on a hat or mask, or skin cells left behind on a drinking glass, cigarette butt, chewing gum, or food. All of these materials are real evidence and are admissible in court.

The DNA of property offenders collected at crime scenes is matched against the nearly 2 million DNA samples contained in the Combined DNA Index System (CODIS) maintained by the Federal Bureau of Investigation (FBI). The CODIS database includes both state and federal DNA samples collected from convicted felons, prison inmates, and adults and juveniles charged with serious crimes. One such DNA match helped to solve a "cold case" involving the homicide of an 11-year-old girl murdered in 1986 in Fort Worth, Texas, as well as 9 rapes and 22 homicides in Kansas City, Missouri. However, DNA samples have also been used to establish that individuals were wrongfully convicted when reexamination of their cases revealed mishandling of evidence.

Experts claim that a DNA match is conclusive evidence because less than one in 200 million matches is likely to be faulty. Nearly all states now admit DNA

- The prosecutor is leading the witness's response (presenting the desired response in the question itself).

The judge either sustains (consents to) or overrules the objection. If the objection is sustained, the question must be rephrased or replaced; if it is overruled, the witness is asked to answer the question.

When the prosecutor is finished questioning a witness, the defense may cross-examine the witness but may cover only those issues raised in the prosecutor's direct examination. The **cross-examination** is designed to discredit the witness by identifying inconsistencies or contradictions in his or her testimony. If the defense attorney believes the witness was telling the truth and any further questioning might strengthen the state's case, he or she may waive the right to cross-examine the witness.

Once cross-examination is complete, the prosecutor may ask additional questions through redirect examination. The purpose of redirect examination is to clarify any issue brought out in response to questions posed by the defense. If the prosecutor chooses to redirect, the defense is given a final opportunity to ask clarifying questions based on the

evidence at trial, although the specific standards for analysis and testing vary. Both prosecutors and defense attorneys look for DNA evidence to strengthen their cases.

As DNA evidence gains popularity, fingerprint evidence has developed a more questionable reputation. In 2002, a federal judge, in *United States v. Plaza*, first ruled that fingerprint evidence is unreliable and declared that he would no longer allow fingerprint experts to testify with certainty that prints from a defendant match or do not match those found at a crime scene. Two months later, the same judge overruled himself, stating that the methodology used by the FBI is generally accepted and reliable enough to be presented to juries.

The debate about the reliability of fingerprint matches continues. Matches identified when known or rolled (sometimes called "inked") prints—those fingerprints obtained from individuals by inking fingers and purposefully rolling fingertips onto paper—are compared to other known prints are generally considered valid. There is much less certainty about matches made by comparing known prints to latent prints—those obtained from surfaces of objects at the crime scene. Latent prints are typically invisible under normal viewing conditions and are rendered visible only with the help of special technologies, such as the use of powders or other chemicals. Unfortunately, latent prints are generally incomplete, representing only a little more than 20 percent of the average size of a known print, and are frequently smudged or distorted. Comparisons of latent prints to known prints are considered subjective and subject to error. Indeed, there is currently no agreed-upon standard in the United States regarding exactly how many points in prints are required to declare a match. Fingerprint examiners in Sweden require 7 points to declare a match, while Australia requires 12 and Brazil requires 30.

Many critics argue that testimony regarding fingerprint analysis is only opinion, with little or no empirical research proving the reliability of known-to-latent print matches. The use of computer fingerprint databases produces only a narrowed-down list of possible matches; fingerprint examiners then must visually—and subjectively—make the comparison and draw conclusions. When DNA evidence is not available, fingerprints are still important evidence and will continue to have a role at trial.

Sources: Lesley Stahl, "Fingerprints: Infallible Evidence?" *CBS News 60 Minutes*, June 6, 2004, Available at http://cbsnews.com/stories/2003/07/16/60minutes/563607.html, accessed July 16, 2008; Office of Justice Programs, *DNA in "Minor" Crimes Yields Major Benefits in Public Safety* (Washington, DC: U.S. Department of Justice, 2004); Donna Lyons, "Capturing DNA's Crime Fighting Potential," *State Legislatures* 32:16–18 (2006); Lisa Kreeger and Danielle Weiss, *Forensic DNA Fundamentals for the Prosecutor* (Alexandria, VA: American Prosecutors Research Institute, 2003); *United States v. Plaza*, Eastern District of Pennsylvania, No. 98-362 (2002); Tamara Lawson, "Can Fingerprints Lie?: Re-weighing Fingerprint Evidence in Criminal Jury Trials," *American Journal of Criminal Law* 31:1–67 (2003); Sandy Zabell, "Fingerprint Evidence," *Journal of Law and Policy* 13:143–179 (2005).

redirect examination through recross-examination. Thus each side has a maximum of two opportunities to question a witness.

Once the prosecutor has presented the state's evidence, the prosecution rests. At this point, the defense may ask for a **judgment of acquittal**, claiming that the state failed to establish that a crime was committed or that the defendant committed it. In most states, if the judge believes that the prosecutor has not established a sufficient case, he or she can take the case out of the hands of the jury and enter a directed verdict—a judgment of acquittal—which bars any further prosecution of the defendant on the crime charged. In some states, a directed verdict means that the judge directs the jury to return a not guilty verdict; however, a few states allow the jury to disregard the instruction and return a guilty verdict.

The Defense's Case

In the United States, a defendant is innocent until proven guilty. Thus the prosecution must prove its case to win a conviction. The defense is not required to present any case

Headline Crime — Questionable Expert Testimony

Expert witnesses testifying about real evidence are assumed to provide honest and accurate descriptions of the evidence being presented to juries. Sometimes, however, the testimony may be far from accurate, whether intentionally misleading or not. For example, the expert testimony of a dentist who was considered to be an authority on forensic odontology (bite mark evidence) has been called into question. At least two recent murder convictions were obtained in part on the strength of his testimony. In 1995, the dentist testified that bite marks on a three-year-old girl were, without question, made by the defendant; the defendant was subsequently convicted of rape and murder. Three years earlier, the dentist testified in another case involving rape and murder and again tied bite marks to the defendant. However, a confession by a third man to both killings and DNA analysis connecting that defendant to one of the rapes has led to an investigation of more than 100 cases involving the dentist's testimony.

In the first case, the dentist had testified that bite marks on the victim's arm were made by the defendant. However, in 2007 a panel of experts examining the case concluded that the marks were not human bites, but rather were likely the result of insects and crawfish nibbling on the corpse, natural decomposition, and marks made when the body was pulled out of the pond where it had been found. The panel also stated that the bite marks the dentist had testified to in the earlier case were only scrapes, not bites at all.

The Innocence Project's panel of experts from the United States, Canada, and England believe that forensic odontology is a solid science in cases where it is applied properly. However, they believe that in these two cases, and perhaps dozens of other cases, it was not applied properly.

Source: "Bite Mark Evidence Disputed in Murder Cases," available at www.cnn.com/2008/CRIME/02/29/bite.ap/index.html, accessed March 1, 2008.

at all, although this is rarely done. If the defense does decide to present its case, it calls its own witnesses to testify on the defendant's behalf after the prosecution rests.

The defendant is not required to testify. This right is protected by the Fifth Amendment, which states that no one "shall be compelled in any criminal case to be a witness against himself." There are many reasons why a defendant might decline to testify, such as a prior criminal record or the desire not to give the jury a bad impression. In any event, a prosecutor may not comment on the refusal of a defendant to testify.[26]

In most cases, the defense attempts to present sufficient evidence to cast doubt on the prosecutor's case, thereby creating reasonable doubt about guilt in the minds of the jurors.

Rebuttal and Surrebuttal

Once the defense has completed its case and the cross-examination and redirection of defense witnesses are complete, the prosecutor may present additional evidence in a **rebuttal** to issues raised in the defense's case. Witnesses called by the prosecutor may then be questioned by the defense and additional new evidence presented in **surrebuttal**.

Closing Arguments

After the defense rests its case, both sides present their summation, also called **closing arguments**. This statement gives each side an opportunity to review and summarize the facts of the case, highlight the significant weaknesses in the opposing case, and, if necessary, make an emotional appeal to the jury in a final attempt to win them to their side.

Typically, the prosecution presents its closing argument first, arguing that guilt has been established and emphasizing to the jury the wrongness of the crime, the impact of the crime on the victim, and the jury's responsibility to return a guilty verdict. The defense then presents its closing argument, in which it summarizes facts presented in direct and cross-examination, and likely argues that it is the prosecutor's responsibility to prove the guilt of the defendant. After the defense makes its closing argument, the prosecution is allowed to make a final rebuttal.

Judicial Instruction

The judge's instructions, or **charge to the jury**, provide the members of the jury with guidelines for making their decision. Most states have developed standard jury instructions covering the issues of standards of proof, the responsibility of the state to prove guilt, the rights of the defendant, the elements of the crime that must be proven, possible verdicts, restrictions on communicating with others during jury deliberations, and

FOCUS ON CRIMINAL JUSTICE

The Judge's Instructions to the Jury

After reading a statement of the formal charges against the defendant, the judge defines the charge(s) according to state (or federal) statute and indicates the elements that must be proven to the jury. The judge then delivers instructions regarding the finding of guilt or innocence.

The following instructions deal with the issues of reasonable doubt and weighing of evidence in a typical felony case. While university students may find these instructions easy to understand, they are likely to be difficult for many average citizens serving on juries to fully comprehend. According to the Flesch-Kincaid Grade Level scale, the instructions are written at the 12th-grade level.

> If you are convinced beyond a reasonable doubt that the defendant is guilty of the offense charged, or one of the lesser included offenses, but have a reasonable doubt as to which of such offenses he is guilty, then it is your duty to resolve such doubt in the defendant's favor, and you can only convict him of the least serious offense.
>
> The defendant is presumed innocent until proven guilty beyond a reasonable doubt, and this presumption prevails until the conclusion of the trial, and you should weigh the evidence in the light of this presumption of innocence and it should be your endeavor to reconcile all the evidence with this presumption of innocence if you can, but if this cannot be done, and the evidence so strongly tends to establish the guilt of the defendant as to remove all reasonable doubt of the guilt of such defendant from the mind of each juror, then it is the duty of the jury to convict. A "reasonable doubt" is a fair, actual, and logical doubt that arises in your mind after an impartial consideration of all of the evidence and circumstances in the case. It should be doubt based upon reason and common sense and not a doubt based upon imagination or speculation.
>
> If, after considering all of the evidence, you have reached such a firm belief in the guilt of the defendant that you would feel safe to act upon that conviction, without hesitation, in a matter of the highest concern and importance to you, when you are not required to act at all, then you will have reached that degree of certainty which excludes reasonable doubt and authorizes conviction.
>
> If, after careful consideration of all the evidence in this case, you are left with two different theories: one consistent with the defendant's innocence, and the other with his guilt, both reasonable; and you are not able to choose between the two, you must find the defendant not guilty.
>
> You are the exclusive judges of the evidence, the credibility of the witnesses and of the weight to be given to the testimony of each of them. In considering the testimony of any witness, you may take into account his or her ability and opportunity to observe; the manner and conduct of the witness while testifying; any interest, bias, or prejudice the witness may have; any relationship with other witnesses or interested parties; and the reasonableness of the testimony of the witness considered in the light of all the evidence in the case.
>
> In considering this case you will no doubt meet with conflicts in the evidence. It is a matter of common knowledge that witnesses to an event rarely see or hear all the circumstances alike. Whenever you meet with such conflicts, reconcile them, if you can, on the assumption that each witness has testified truthfully. If you cannot so reconcile the conflicts, it is for you to determine what you will believe and what you will not believe.

suggestions for determining the credibility of witnesses. In addition, the judge may give special instructions regarding the nature of the offense and any lesser included charges. Often, the prosecutor and the defense attorney will confer with the judge before the charging of the jury to discuss additional instructions that they wish to include.

Many studies suggest that a large percentage of jurors do not understand the judicial instructions.[27] Other studies suggest that jurors who receive standard instructions comprehend their responsibilities no better than jurors who receive no instructions at all—both groups appear to make similar decisions and to raise similar questions of the judge after beginning to deliberate.[28]

The Presumption of Innocence and Reasonable Doubt

One of the most important instructions a judge gives to jury members is to remind them that a defendant is considered innocent and that the state must prove its case beyond a reasonable doubt. The **presumption of innocence** means that a person is presumed to be innocent until the state proves beyond a reasonable doubt that he or she is guilty of the crime charged. This is the principle under which the process of determining guilt operates.

Many people believe that because there was probable cause to arrest and charge a suspect, the suspect must be guilty. In reality, probable cause means only that there are reasonable grounds to believe the accused committed certain acts. A fine line exists between the grounds necessary to make an arrest and those necessary to convict.

The requirement that the accused be judged guilty beyond a **reasonable doubt** means that the jury (or the judge in the case of a bench trial) must find the evidence entirely convincing and must be satisfied beyond a moral certainty of the defendant's guilt to convict him or her. Fanciful or imagined doubt, or doubt that arises in the face of the unpleasant task of convicting or acquitting a defendant, is not sufficient. This standard does not require that the case be proved beyond *all* doubt—a situation generally unlikely given human nature.

This requirement of proof beyond a reasonable doubt protects defendants from being convicted of crimes when the case against them is not very strong. In essence, the Supreme Court has held that it is better to let a guilty person go free as a result of less than adequate proof than to convict an innocent person solely on the basis of the probability of guilt. When much of the evidence presented against a defendant is circumstantial, or when testimony by both prosecution and defense witnesses appears reasonable and yet contradictory, it is better for the jury to err on the side of setting the defendant free than to send him or her to prison.

Jury Deliberations

After hearing the judge's instructions, the jury retires to the jury room to begin deliberations. If the case has generated much public attention or deliberations are likely to take some time, the judge may request that members of the jury be sequestered (segregated from all outside contact). In some highly publicized trials, juries have been sequestered from the point at which they were impaneled. The jury members are kept together for the duration of their deliberations, sometimes receiving temporary housing and meals, to protect them from outside influences. In most cases, such precautions are not needed and jurors simply take an oath to stay together during breaks and to refrain from talking to others about the case.

The jury selects a jury foreperson to act as the leader. It is this juror's responsibility to conduct the voting, to communicate with the judge regarding requests for clarification or additional instructions, and to read the verdict once it has been made. Generally, before the members of the jury begin deliberating, they take a straw vote (an unofficial vote) to get a sense of how each person feels about the case. With few exceptions, the initial vote is indicative of the final vote.[29] Mock jury experiments confirm these findings, showing that jurors reversed the vote only 6 percent of the time.[30]

Hung Jury

Because a jury generally must reach a unanimous verdict, if the jury is split (even if it is 11 to 1) and no verdict can be reached, it is considered a **hung jury**. Hung juries do not occur frequently; the National Center for State Courts reports the average hung jury rate in state courts is only 6.2 percent (although it ranges from less than 1 percent to nearly 15 percent, depending on the jurisdiction). The average hung jury rate in the federal courts is much lower, averaging only 2.5 percent.[31]

Disagreement often exists among jurors at the early stages of deliberations. Indeed, it is not unusual for the judge to call the jury back to the courtroom if deliberations have taken more than a few days (or longer in complex cases) to ask whether the foreperson believes that a verdict can be reached. However, the judge may not intervene to push the jury for a verdict. Because a hung jury is considered by law to be a legitimate outcome in a trial, any attempt to put undue pressure on the jury to reach a verdict is viewed as inappropriate. It is considered coercive and improper for judges to emphasize the expense and inconvenience that will result from a retrial or to require a jury to continue deliberations for more than 24 hours without sleep.[32]

If only a few jurors are dissenting from the majority's position, the judge may instruct the jury to continue deliberations. After this step, if the jury again reports that it cannot reach a verdict and that further deliberation would be futile, the judge may once more instruct them to continue. Generally speaking, the longer a judge keeps the jury deliberating, the more likely it becomes that the jury will reach a verdict.[33]

In some jurisdictions, the judge may give the jury *Allen* instructions, which are designed to push them to reach a verdict. Such instructions are based on the 1896 Supreme Court decision in *Allen v. United States*.[34] The judge may lecture dissenting jurors about the importance of listening to other jurors' opinions and considering whether the doubt in his or her own mind is reasonable. The purpose of such instructions is to encourage a compromise that will allow the jury to arrive at a verdict.

Judgment or Verdict

The federal courts and most states require unanimous verdicts. Two states allow for non-unanimous decisions in non-death-penalty felony cases: Louisiana allows convictions to be based on agreement of 10 of 12 jurors for less serious felonies, and Oregon accepts an agreement of 10 of 12 jurors in all felony cases except for murder. The U.S. Supreme Court has held that such verdicts are constitutional.[35]

Upon arriving at a verdict, the jury returns to the courtroom. The jury foreperson gives the signed verdict to the bailiff, who then gives it to the judge. The judge glances at the verdict and gives it to the court clerk, who reads it to the court. Next, the judge asks the prosecutor or the defense attorney whether they would like the jury polled; if so requested, the judge asks each juror to state his or her vote on the verdict. Sometimes jurors feel pressured to go along with the majority, even though they may believe the defendant is innocent. If a juror states that he or she did not really agree with the verdict, the judge will send the jury back to the jury room to deliberate again in an attempt to reach a unanimous verdict.

Appeal of the Verdict

If the verdict is "not guilty," the defendant is acquitted and released. The state may not appeal a verdict of not guilty because the Fifth Amendment guarantees that no person "shall be subject for the same offense to be twice put in jeopardy of life or limb." This prohibition against **double jeopardy** means that once a person has been tried and acquitted of a criminal charge, he or she may not be recharged and retried for the same offense. By contrast, if the verdict is "guilty," the defendant has the right to appeal. He or she may or may not be released on bail while awaiting the outcome of that appeal.

An appeal of the verdict is a request to the state appellate court to correct mistakes or injustices that occurred in the trial process, such as a judge's error in permitting certain evidence to be introduced, misconduct by the prosecutor, or jury tampering. The U.S. Supreme Court has held that indigent defendants have the right to be represented by counsel on appeal.[36] This right is limited to the defendant's first appeal only. The Court has also held that a defendant loses the right to counsel in a first appeal if he or she delays in filing the appeal with the court.

The issues raised in an appeal must be based on objections raised by the defense in pretrial motions or at the time of the trial, such as a motion for a change of venue or a motion to suppress evidence. With two exceptions, issues not raised in pretrial motions or during the trial may not be considered. Issues that are the result of plain error and those that affect substantial rights of the defendant may be appealed—for example, a claim that the court lacked legal jurisdiction to hear the case is grounds for an appeal. An appeal may also be based on the claim that the defendant's attorney was incompetent.

Appeals are sometimes rejected because they are based on **harmless error**—an error, defect, irregularity, or variance that does not affect substantial rights of the defendant. Harmless errors include the following:

- Technical errors having no bearing on the outcome of the trial
- Errors corrected during trial (for example, when testimony was allowed but then ordered stricken and the jury admonished to ignore it)
- Errors resulting in a ruling in the appellant's favor
- Situations in which the appeals court believes that even without the error, the appealing party would not have won at trial

Very few appeals result in an overturned conviction; most produce only minor modifications, leaving the conviction itself undisturbed.[37] Nevertheless, if the appellate court finds that a significant error did occur, it may reverse the conviction, thereby setting aside the guilty verdict and sending the case back to the trial court. If the conviction is reversed, the prosecutor may appeal the decision of the appellate court.

Contrary to widely held perceptions, few criminals are eventually set free as a result of errors in the original trial. Approximately half of all offenders who are retried after appeal are convicted again.[38]

Other Post-conviction Remedies

Once a defendant has exhausted all appeals through the state appellate courts and is incarcerated, he or she may still seek post-conviction relief by filing a petition for a writ of habeas corpus with the Federal Courts of Appeals or directly with the U.S. Supreme Court. A petition of **habeas corpus** asks the federal court to release the defendant from an alleged illegal imprisonment or confinement by the state.

Habeas corpus petitions differ from appeals in several ways. For example, they may be filed only by people who are actually confined, and they must raise constitutional issues rather than issues of error. They may be broader in scope than appeals; for example, an inmate may claim that the current conditions in his or her prison constitute cruel and unusual punishment. Since the 1960s, courts have granted writs of habeas corpus in several instances:

- To release defendants on bail when the bail amount was considered excessive
- To release inmates from prison when the sentence was considered excessive

- To overturn capital punishment sentences
- To release inmates who claimed their attorneys did not provide competent counsel

In 1963, in *Fay v. Noia*, the Supreme Court required federal courts to consider habeas corpus petitions even from inmates who had failed for some reason to appeal their case properly in the state courts, as long as the inmate had not deliberately bypassed the state's appeal process and the allegation of newly discovered evidence was not irrelevant, frivolous, or incredible.[39] By the early 1990s, with nearly 10,000 habeas corpus petitions being filed annually and the justices having a decidedly more conservative bent, the Supreme Court placed severe restrictions on the conditions under which federal courts would hear such petitions. Today, only a small fraction of petitions are granted. Most petitions are viewed as frivolous, and federal judges dismiss the majority of them without a hearing.

One of the first attempts to reduce the burden placed on federal courts by habeas corpus petitions came in 1991, in *Coleman v. Thompson*.[40] In this case, the defendant's lawyer filed the habeas corpus petition with the Virginia Supreme Court three days after the 30-day time limit had expired. The Virginia court held that, although there was "no doubt an inadvertent error . . . the petitioner must bear the risk of attorney error" and barred any further review in the federal courts. The next year, in *Keeney v. Tamayo-Reyes*,[41] the U.S. Supreme Court ruled that the federal courts are not obligated to grant a hearing on a state prisoner's challenge to his or her conviction, even if the prisoner can show that the defense attorney did not properly present crucial facts in a state court appeal. In 1993, in *Herrera v. Collins*, the U.S. Supreme Court ruled that a Texas court's rejection of a defendant's late claim of innocence based on new evidence did not necessarily violate the petitioner's right to due process.[42] Texas, as well as several other states, requires that such a claim be filed within 30 days; other states allow up to a few years for such an appeal, and nine states have no time limit for filings based on new evidence.

The implications of these decisions are far-reaching, affecting the lives of inmates who may have been incorrectly convicted. At the same time that the Supreme Court has tightened the reins on the numerous frivolous petitions from prisoners, it has also significantly reduced the rights of prisoners to post-conviction relief from judicial errors and wrongful imprisonment.

WRAPPING IT UP

Chapter Highlights

- Few events draw more public attention than a criminal trial. As an alternative to the less public plea bargaining method of obtaining justice, the trial epitomizes the adversarial process in which the prosecution and the defense present evidence and arguments in their attempts to convince a jury of their side of a case.
- The prosecutor and the defense attorney typically submit pretrial motions to the judge before the beginning of the trial. Some of these motions must be decided before the start of the trial, but the judge may choose to rule on other motions, such as those to suppress evidence, later during the trial when the evidence is actually submitted.
- The Sixth Amendment guarantees defendants the right to a speedy, public, and fair trial. State time guidelines differ widely, but the federal Speedy Trial Act of 1974 requires that charges be filed within 30 days of a suspect's arrest and that the trial begin within 70 days of the filing of charges.
- Approximately 40 percent of all cases that go to trial are tried before juries. The remaining 60 percent involve bench trials.
- Defendants charged with either a felony or a misdemeanor are entitled to a trial by jury. Most states, as well as the federal government, use juries composed of 12 people, although juries with as few as six members have been deemed constitutional except in death penalty cases.
- The prosecutor and the defense attorney ask questions during the *voir dire* to determine which people will make the best jurors.
- During the trial, the prosecution and the defense alternate in presenting evidence, questioning the evidence introduced by the opposing side, and then submitting the evidence to the jury. After both sides present their closing arguments, the judge gives his or her charge (instructions) to the jury.
- After receiving its charge, the jury retires to the jury room to begin deliberations. The federal courts and most states require unanimous verdicts, although the Supreme Court has held that non-unanimous verdicts are constitutional in non-death-penalty cases. A jury that cannot arrive at a verdict is called a hung jury.
- If the verdict is not guilty, the defendant is acquitted and released and may not be retried on the same charge (double jeopardy). The defendant may appeal a guilty verdict to an appropriate appellate court based on objections raised by the defense in pretrial motions or at trial.
- Defendants who have exhausted the appeal process and are incarcerated may still seek post-conviction relief by filing a writ of habeas corpus. The Supreme Court has restricted the grounds on which such petitions may be filed.

Words to Know

alibi Assertion that the defendant was somewhere else at the time the crime was committed.

bench trial Trial before a judge alone; an alternative to a jury trial.

challenge for cause Challenge by the prosecutor or the defense to dismiss a person from a jury panel for a legitimate cause.

charge to the jury Judge's instructions to the jury, which are intended to guide the jury's deliberations.

circumstantial evidence Testimony by a witness that requires jurors to draw a reasonable inference.

closing arguments The final presentation of arguments to the jury.

cross-examination Questioning of a witness by counsel after questions have been asked by the opposing counsel.

direct evidence Testimony by an eyewitness to the crime.

double jeopardy Once a person has been tried and acquitted of a criminal charge, he or she may not be recharged and retried for the same offense.

habeas corpus A judicial order to bring a person immediately before the court to determine the legality of his or her detention.

harmless error An error, defect, irregularity, or variance that does not affect substantial rights of the defendant.

hearsay evidence Testimony involving information the witness was told but has no direct knowledge of.

hung jury A jury that is deadlocked and cannot reach a verdict. As a result, the judge may declare a mistrial.

judgment of acquittal A defense motion for dismissal of a case based on the claim that the prosecution failed to establish that a crime was committed or that the defendant committed it.

jury pool The master list of community members who are eligible to be called for jury duty.

opening statement The initial presentation of the outline of the prosecution's and the defense's cases to the jury.

peremptory challenge A challenge by the defense or the prosecution to excuse a person from a jury panel without having to give a reason.

presumption of innocence The notion that a person is presumed to be innocent unless proved guilty beyond a reasonable doubt.

pretrial motion A written or oral request to a judge for a ruling or action before the beginning of trial.

real evidence Physical evidence introduced at the trial.

reasonable doubt The requirement that the jury (or the judge in the case of a bench trial) must find the evidence entirely convincing and must be satisfied beyond a moral certainty of the defendant's guilt before returning a conviction.

rebuttal The presentation of additional witnesses and evidence by the prosecutor in response to issues raised in the defense's presentation of witnesses.

surrebuttal Questioning by the defense of witnesses who were presented by the prosecutor during rebuttal.

testimonial evidence Sworn testimony of witnesses who are qualified to speak about specific real evidence.

venire A group of people who are selected from the jury pool and notified to report for jury duty.

voir dire Preliminary examination by the prosecution and defense of potential jurors.

Think and Discuss

1. Should the defense or the prosecution be limited in the number of continuances requested? Why?
2. Should the public and the press be allowed to attend criminal trials? Why or why not?
3. How much control should the court exercise over the media in reporting of trials?
4. What are the benefits of peremptory challenges of potential jurors? Why do some critics argue they should be abolished?
5. Should all jury verdicts be unanimous? Why or why not?

Notes

1. Donna Burchfield, "Appearance v. Reality: 'L.A. Law,'" *Phi Kappa Phi Journal* (Fall 1991), p. 20.
2. *Dusky v. United States*, 362 U.S. 402 (1960).
3. *Barker v. Wingo*, 407 U.S. 514 (1972).
4. *Gannett Co., Inc. v. DePasquale*, 443 U.S. 368 (1979).
5. *Press Enterprise Co. v. Superior Court of California*, 478 U.S. 1 (1986).
6. *Nebraska Press Association v. Stuart*, 427 U.S. 539 (1976).
7. Edith Greene, "Media Effects on Jurors," *Law and Human Behavior* 14:442 (1990).
8. Brian Ostrom, Shauna Strickland, and Paula Hannaford-Agor, *Court Statistics Project* (Williamsburg, VA: National Center for State Courts, 2004).
9. Orville Richardson, "Jury or Bench Trial? Considerations," *Trial* 19:58–63 (1983); Harry Kalven and Hans Zeisel, *The American Jury* (Boston: Little, Brown, 1966), pp. 56–60.
10. Valerie Hans and Neil Vidmar, *Judging the Jury* (New York: Plenum, 1986), p. 109.
11. *Palko v. Connecticut*, 302 U.S. 319 (1937).
12. *Snyder v. Massachusetts*, 291 U.S. 97 (1934).
13. *Duncan v. Louisiana*, 391 U.S. 145 (1968).
14. *Blanton v. North Las Vegas*, 489 U.S. 538 (1989).
15. *McKeiver v. Pennsylvania*, 403 U.S. 528 (1971).
16. *Williams v. Florida*, 399 U.S. 78 (1970).
17. *Ballew v. Georgia*, 435 U.S. 223 (1978).

18. Robert Boatright, "Why Citizens Don't Respond to Jury Summonses and What Courts Can Do about It," *Judicature* 82:156–163 (1999); Nancy King, "Juror Delinquency in Criminal Trials in America, 1796–1996," *Michigan Law Review* 94:2673–2715 (1996); James Levine, *Juries and Politics* (Pacific Grove, CA: Brooks/Cole, 1992).

19. Amanda L. Kutz, "A Jury of One's Peers: Virginia's Restoration of Rights Process and Its Disproportionate Effect on the African American Community," *William and Mary Law Review* 46:2109–2162 (2005); Marvin Steinberg, "The Case for Eliminating Peremptory Challenges," *Criminal Law Bulletin* 27:216–229 (1991).

20. *Fay v. New York*, 332 U.S. 261 (1947).

21. *Batson v. Kentucky*, 476 U.S. 79 (1986).

22. *Hernandez v. New York*, 500 U.S. 352 (1991).

23. *J.E.B. v. Alabama*, 511 U.S. 127 (1994).

24. Thomas Scheffey, "Connecticut Outlaws Religion-Based Juror Challenges," *Connecticut Law Tribune*, April 5, 1999; *Casarez v. State*, 913 S.W.2d 468 (Tex. Crim. App. 1995).

25. Kelly Kuljol, "Where Did Florida Go Wrong? Why Religion-Based Peremptory Challenges Withstand Constitutional Scrutiny," *Stetson Law Review* 32:171–203 (2002).

26. *Griffin v. California*, 380 U.S. 609 (1965).

27. Amiram Elwork, Bruce Sales, and James Alfini, "Juridic Decisions: In Ignorance of the Law or in Light of It?" *Law and Human Behavior* 1:163–178 (1977); R. Reid Hastie, Steven Penrod, and Nancy Pennington, *Inside the Jury* (Clark, NJ: Lawbook Exchange, 2002); David Strawn and Raymond Buchanan, "Jury Confusion: A Threat to Justice," *Judicature* 59:478–483 (1976); Laurence Severance, Edith Greene, and Elizabeth Loftus, "Toward Criminal Jury Instructions That Jurors Can Understand," *Journal of Criminal Law and Criminology* 75:198–233 (1984).

28. Amiram Elwork, Bruce Sales, and James Alfini, *Making Jury Instructions Understandable* (Charlottesville, VA: Michie, 1982); Walter Steele, Jr. and Elizabeth Thornburg, "Jury Instructions: A Persistent Failure to Communicate," *Judicature* 74:249–254 (1991).

29. Kalven and Zeisel, note 9, p. 488.

30. Sarah Tanford and Steven Penrod, "Jury Deliberations: Discussion Content and Influence Processes in Jury Decision Making," *Journal of Applied Social Psychology* 16:322–347 (1986).

31. Paula Hannaford-Agor, Valerie Hans, Nicole Mott, and Thomas Munsterman, *Are Hung Juries a Problem?* (Williamsburg, VA: National Center for State Courts, 2002).

32. Bennett Gershman, "Judicial Misconduct during Jury Deliberations," *Criminal Law Bulletin* 27:291–314 (1991).

33. Levine, note 18, p. 164.

34. *Allen v. United States*, 164 U.S. 492 (1896).

35. *Johnson v. Louisiana*, 406 U.S. 356 (1972); *Apodaca v. Oregon*, 406 U.S. 404 (1972).

36. *Douglas v. California*, 372 U.S. 353 (1963).

37. Joy Chapper and Roger Hanson, "Understanding Reversible Error in Criminal Appeals," *State Court Journal* 14:16–18, 24 (1990); David Neubauer, "Winners and Losers Before the Louisiana Supreme Court: The Case of Criminal Appeals," *Justice Quarterly* 8:85–106 (1991).

38. Robert Roper and Albert Melone, "Does Procedural Due Process Make a Difference? A Study of Second Trials," *Judicature* 65:136–141 (1981).

39. *Fay v. Noia*, 372 U.S. 391 (1963).

40. *Coleman v. Thompson*, 501 U.S. 722 (1991).

41. *Keeney v. Tamayo-Reyes*, 504 U.S. 1 (1992).

42. *Herrera v. Collins*, 506 U.S. 390 (1993).

SALT

CHAPTER

Sentencing

OBJECTIVES

1. Know the goals and objectives of sentencing.
2. Understand the concept of proportionality in sentencing and describe how the Supreme Court has applied this concept in its review of sentencing cases.
3. Identify the various types of sentences, including intermediate, indeterminate, determinate, and mandatory sentences, and elucidate the reasons behind "get tough" reforms such as habitual offender statutes.
4. Be aware of the process of arriving at a sentence and the potential problems of disparities and discrimination in sentencing.
5. Describe the current status of the death penalty, the Supreme Court's rulings on capital punishment, and the arguments put forth in support and against the death penalty.
6. Grasp the process for appellate review of sentences.

PROFILES IN CRIME AND JUSTICE

Pablo Cortes
Chief Judge
Wyoming District Court
Wyoming, Michigan

After serving as a State Assistant Prosecutor for 10 years I received, a judicial appointment to the 62A District Court, located in Wyoming, Michigan. I felt being a judge would allow me to both broaden my legal capabilities and to become more involved in various aspects of community development.

Michigan District Courts have jurisdiction over small claims matters, landlord–tenant cases, civil cases involving $25,000 or less, all misdemeanor and city ordinance violations, and felony cases through the preliminary examination stage. District Courts often interact directly with the individuals involved in particular matters rather than with attorneys representing clients. Working with regular citizens, who may not be conversant with the law or judicial rules and procedures, requires that I adapt and adjust my approach to ensure that all parties understand the process. This close contact I enjoy with our citizens permits me to identify and understand changing economic, social, and criminal trends within our community and, ideally, to then make a positive difference within the mechanisms and confines of the law.

Much of my time is spent working with prosecutors, law enforcement, victim advocates, and defense attorneys as cases move through the criminal process, as well as helping individuals or corporations settle their civil disputes. Each of these activities provides great feelings of satisfaction and accomplishment. The consequences for individuals who come before me in court frequently involve loss of liberty, eviction from homes, or financial hardships. Imposing these consequences is rarely easy, but, unfortunately, all too often necessary. Therefore, to avoid errors and unwarranted consequences, it is critical for District Court judges to do all they can to become educated about all relevant areas under their jurisdiction and to exercise patience and discretion, always keeping the principles of fundamental fairness and justice in mind.

Introduction

A number of theories have been put forth regarding ways to deal with offenders and the goals of sentencing. According to James Q. Wilson, "Wicked people exist. Nothing avails except to set them apart from innocent people."[1] If he is right, then the best way to deal with people who are convicted of serious crimes may be to set them apart from "good" people through imprisonment. Wilson's position represents a commonly held belief: Criminals are basically bad people who must be held accountable for their crimes and face incapacitation (incarceration) to prevent them from committing future crimes. If the rate of imprisonment is viewed as an indicator of the amount of punishment in a society, then the United States certainly punishes a substantial portion of its population every year. Even so, crime remains widespread in this country.

An alternative view, which was held by seventeenth-century English philosopher Thomas Hobbes, suggests that society should punish offenders solely to achieve future goodness in people. Hobbes argued that "in revenges and punishments men ought not to look at the greatness of evil past, but at the greatness of the good to follow."[2] That is, sentencing should be imposed solely to deter offenders (past, present, and future) from committing crimes.

The history of sentencing reflects a variety of reasons for imposing sanctions, some of which are contradictory:

- Retribution
- Deterrence

- Incapacitation
- Rehabilitation
- Proportionality

These goals are not mutually exclusive; indeed, they often overlap. For example, the wish to express moral outrage over a crime and extract a degree of revenge (retribution) by sentencing the offender to life in prison may correspond with the desire that the harsh sentence will be viewed by others as a warning not to commit similar crimes (deterrence).

Gary Ridgway, the most prolific serial killer in U.S. history, pled guilty to 48 counts of first-degree murder to avoid a death sentence.

Retribution

Retribution reflects society's moral outrage or disapproval of a crime. It is a moral statement that the act was fundamentally wrong and must be punished. Here the focus is on the crime rather than on the individual who committed it; there is virtually no concern with deterring future crime or changing the individual through punishment or rehabilitation. Furthermore, retribution calls for sentences to be proportionate to the crime and, therefore, is designed to balance the harm caused by the crime.

Retribution serves as not only a just punishment for the offender, but also a means of deterring those who might consider committing criminal acts. Through punishment, offenders receive their "just desserts," and potential offenders are made aware of the consequences of crime. As a result, the total misery produced by punishing the few who commit crimes is outweighed by the total greater reduction in misery that would be created by the failure to punish. According to Andrew von Hirsch, through retributive punishment, "Fewer innocent persons will be victimized by crimes, while those less deserving—the victimizers—will be made to suffer instead."[3]

Deterrence

The writings of utilitarian philosophers in Europe during the seventeenth and eighteenth centuries gave rise to **deterrence** theories. These philosophers believed that people are rational beings with free will who prefer pleasure over pain; therefore, people weigh the benefits and costs of future actions before deciding to act. Utilitarians such as Cesare Beccaria and Jeremy Bentham suggested that people choose crime when they believe that the benefits resulting from the criminal behavior will exceed its costs.[4] This theory viewed punishment as justified as a means to deter (prevent) people from committing crime. According to utilitarian theory, punishment should be designed to achieve the greatest good or to do the least harm to those who are affected. Although support for deterrence theory declined during the late nineteenth and early twentieth centuries, it has reemerged to become the dominant justification for punishment in the late twentieth and early twenty-first centuries.

Specific deterrence is aimed at individual offenders. According to this theory, criminals are punished for past crimes in an effort to make them afraid (or unable, in the case of the death penalty) to commit new crimes. **General deterrence**, by contrast, aims to dissuade *potential* offenders through the punishment of convicted criminals. That is, if people are made aware of the punishments received by criminals, then they may consider the likely consequences of crime and ultimately be deterred from engaging in criminal activity.

Incapacitation

Incapacitation is the removal of offenders from the community through imprisonment or banishment (e.g., deportation). Offenders who commit crimes while in prison can be further incapacitated by being placed in solitary confinement. Although banishment has

FOCUS ON CRIMINAL JUSTICE

They May Not Be Cruel, but Are They Unusual Punishments?

Although the Eighth Amendment prohibits cruel and unusual punishment, the Supreme Court has yet to rule on what constitutes an "unusual" punishment. As local judges search for effective means to punish offenders and to achieve a degree of retribution, they sometimes arrive at sentences that many people might consider unusual and often humiliating. During the past few years, the following sentences have been imposed:

- An Ohio judge ordered a man to spend two hours on a city sidewalk next to a 350-pound pig and a sign reading, "This is not a police officer," for disorderly conduct in a confrontation in which he called a police officer a pig (amid several other obscenities).
- A Nebraska judge ordered a woman who was convicted of making a false accusation of rape to apologize in half-page advertisements in four newspapers and 10 spot announcements on two radio stations.
- A Kansas judge ordered a man who admitted to molesting a boy to post signs around his house reading "A Sex Offender Lives Here" and to place a decal on his car reading "Sex Offender in This Car."
- An Illinois judge ordered a woman to quit smoking for a year or face imprisonment for stealing cigarettes.
- A Tennessee woman who was convicted of molesting her sons agreed to be sterilized as an alternative to going to prison.
- A Wisconsin judge ordered a woman who had stolen money from her employer to donate her family's season tickets to Green Bay Packers games to the Make-a-Wish Foundation.

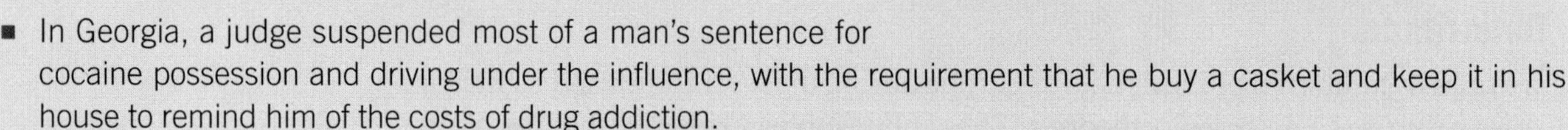

- In Georgia, a judge suspended most of a man's sentence for cocaine possession and driving under the influence, with the requirement that he buy a casket and keep it in his house to remind him of the costs of drug addiction.

- In New Mexico, men convicted of domestic abuse were required to attend meditation classes with scented candles and herbal teas.

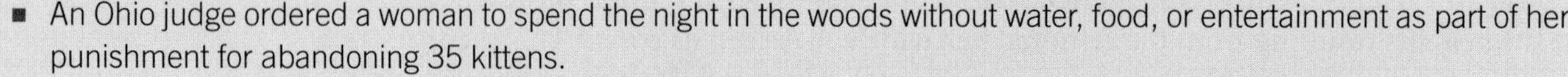

- An Ohio judge ordered a woman to spend the night in the woods without water, food, or entertainment as part of her punishment for abandoning 35 kittens.

Sources: "Pigheadedness Lands Man in Pigpen," available at http://www.courttv.com/news/scm/scm_021402.html, accessed January 21, 2008; "Sex Offender Ordered by Judge to Post Signs," available at www.foxnews.com/story/0,2933,341268,00.html, accessed May 1, 2008; "Smoking Deal: Judge Snuffs Shoplifter's Habit," *Arizona Republic*, January 17, 1991, p. A13; "Sentence for Lie on Rape Charge Creates Debate," *The New York Times*, July 7, 1990, p. 8; "Woman Who Molested Sons Agrees to Sterilization," *The New York Times*, January 31, 1993, p. A13; "Shame on You," *The Washington Post*, September 18, 2005, p. B3; "Woman Ordered to Spend Night in Woods for Abandoning Kittens," *ABC News*, available at http://abcnews.go.com/GMA/LegalCenter/story?id=1322751, accessed August 17, 2008.

been practiced throughout the ages, the incapacitation of offenders through imprisonment did not become popular until the nineteenth century.

Incapacitation is a form of specific deterrence in that it is designed to prevent individual offenders from committing future crimes. However, criminologists David Greenberg and Stephan Van Dine suggest that increasing the average prison sentence or making prison terms mandatory for all people who are convicted of felonies would have little overall effect on reducing serious crime, because much crime goes unreported and only a small percentage of reported crime results in arrest and conviction.[5] Conversely, some studies suggest that the selective incapacitation of repeat offenders who are convicted of serious crimes would have a much greater impact. Because a small number of offenders are responsible for a large proportion of all serious crimes, imposing mandatory sentences or longer prison terms on those high-rate offenders could significantly alter crime patterns.[6]

Given the great difficulties in achieving true rehabilitation, prisoners often have difficulty reintegrating into mainstream society.

Rehabilitation

Rehabilitation—reforming an offender to become a productive member of society through treatment, education, or counseling—was the dominant philosophical orientation guiding sentencing practices in the United States from the 1940s through the 1970s. During this period, most state legislatures included statements in their sentencing laws that established rehabilitation as the primary goal of punishment.

This theory holds that the causes of crime are located within individuals or in their immediate social environments. Once these causes are identified, appropriate treatment can change the internal make-up of offenders or alter the way they respond to their environment. In this way, the offender can be successfully reintegrated into the community. From a rehabilitative perspective, punishments should be designed to help the offender change his or her behavior.

A flurry of evaluations of rehabilitation programs conducted during the 1960s and 1970s questioned the effectiveness of the rehabilitative approach in corrections. The general consensus from these studies was that—at best—only some forms of treatments work for some types of offenders in some settings and there was little reason to be enthusiastic about future rehabilitation efforts.[7] The rehabilitation movement was set back by these reports, although more recent studies have provided support to those who advocate rehabilitation over strict punishment.

Proportionality

As with all aspects of criminal justice, one of the goals of sentencing is fairness, which is often interpreted as proportionality—making the punishment fit the crime. But how do we determine which kind of punishment is appropriate or how much punishment is proportional to a particular offense?

While capital punishment has largely been reserved for those convicted of first-degree or felony murder, a few states hoped to apply the death penalty to sex offenders who were convicted of raping young children. However, in 2008 the U.S. Supreme Court held that such punishment was disproportionate, and thus, unconstitutional.[8]

The U.S. Supreme Court ultimately determines whether these kinds of sentencing guidelines are proportional. For example, in 1910, in *Weems v. United States*,[9] the Court ruled that a sentence involving 12 years at hard labor while wearing leg irons, a heavy fine, and loss of all political rights during imprisonment for falsifying official records of the U.S. Coast Guard violated the defendant's Eighth Amendment protection against cruel and unusual punishment. The Court held that what constitutes cruel and unusual punishment is not static and stated that what may have been an acceptable sentence at one point in time may be considered too severe at another point in time. Nearly five decades later, the Court, in *Trop v. Dulles*,[10] further clarified this point by noting that an interpretation of "cruel and unusual" must draw its meaning from the evolving standards of decency that reflect a maturing society.

Types of Sentences

Sentences today are primarily linked to particular offenses and are specified by the criminal codes established by the state and federal governments. Judges typically have a wide range of sentencing options available to them as they seek to determine the most appropriate sentence for an offender. To help ensure proportionality, the kinds and lengths of sentences that may be imposed for misdemeanors differ from the punishments for felonies, reflecting the greater severity of the latter crimes. Misdemeanors typically do not carry prison terms of a year or longer, and the death penalty is unlikely to be imposed in criminal cases that do not involve homicide or a very limited number of other extremely serious offenses (i.e., treason).

Intermediate Sentences

Incarceration and probation are common sentences for people who are convicted of felonies and major misdemeanors. Prison overcrowding and excessively large probation caseloads, however, have recently led to the creation of a wider range of intermediate sentencing options, including the following punishments:

- Intermittent incarceration allows offenders to serve relatively short sentences in jail on specified days. For example, a 30-day sentence could be served over a period of 15 successive weekends. The advantage to offenders is that they are able to retain their jobs or stay involved with their families.
- Intensive probation supervision is intended to ensure frequent and close contact between probation officers and offenders. When they have small caseloads, probation officers are able to give greater attention to offenders assigned to house arrest, electronic monitoring, drug or alcohol treatment, or psychological counseling.
- Fines, which are probably the most widely used form of sanction by lower courts, have been used as punishments for traffic offenses, local ordinance violations, and misdemeanors. The inability of poor defendants to pay even modest fines and the minimal impact of fines on wealthier offenders may be partly responsible for the limited use of fines in felony cases.[11]
- Community service requires offenders to make reparation to the community. Typically, it involves contributing less than 100 hours of time to a local government agency or volunteer organization.
- Restitution generally takes one of two forms: direct financial payment to victims to compensate them for their losses or indirect restitution by payment into a victim-assistance program.
- In forfeiture, offenders give up property that they obtained through criminal activity. The federal Drug Enforcement Administration (DEA) has used forfeiture extensively in its war on drugs. It is not always necessary for a person to be convicted of criminal activity to have property forfeited; in some states, simply being charged with a crime may result in confiscation of property believed to be connected to the offense.

Intermediate punishments are rarely used alone because each, by itself, is generally considered by the courts to be an insufficient sanction. More often, several such punishments or the combination of an intermediate punishment and either probation or a short term of incarceration is imposed.

Indeterminate Prison Sentences

An **indeterminate sentence** establishes a minimum and a maximum number of years to be served. The actual time for release is determined by a parole board after the offender has served a portion of the minimum sentence. For example, a burglar might receive a 2- to 5-year sentence and a robber might receive a 10- to 20-year sentence. Although states vary in terms of the number of years that must be served before an offender can be considered for parole, at least one-third of the minimum term is the typical point at which parole becomes available.

Determinate or Structured Prison Sentences

Determinate sentences, which feature fixed terms of imprisonment, emerged as a result of the sentencing reform movement in the early 1970s. Reformers argued that rehabilitation did not work and that indeterminate sentences led to gross disparities and unfairness.[12] Determinate sentencing systems built upon retributive and deterrence theories of punishment were advocated as better options, with the following goals:

- To eliminate the disparities created by the sentencing discretion of judges
- To create a system of relatively uniform sentences for offenders convicted of similar crimes and with similar records
- To redistribute time served in prison (so that less serious offenders spent less time in prison and more serious felons spent more time) without significantly increasing the total person-years served or the associated costs of incarceration[13]

The determinate sentencing systems that were developed over the past two decades have generally taken one of two forms: presumptive sentencing or sentencing guidelines.

Presumptive Sentencing

Presumptive sentencing relies on a range of minimum and maximum terms of incarceration that have been established by a legislature for particular categories or classes of crimes, with the judge determining the specific number of years to be served within this range. If aggravating or mitigating factors exist, the judge may depart from the presumptive sentence by adding or subtracting time, within certain limits (see TABLE 9-1). Any departure from the presumptive sentence typically requires the judge to submit a written explanation for the decision.

TABLE 9-1 Aggravating and Mitigating Factors

Aggravating Factors
The offender has a criminal history.
The offender has recently violated the terms of his or her probation or parole.
A reduced or suspended sentence would make the crime appear less serious than it is.
The victim is older than age 65 or is mentally or physically infirm.
The offender is in need of correctional or rehabilitative treatment that can best be provided by commitment to a penal facility.
Mitigating Factors
The circumstances of the crime are unlikely to recur.
The offender acted under strong provocation.
The victim of the crime induced or facilitated the offense.
The crime did not cause or threaten serious harm to people or property.
Grounds exist to justify or excuse the crime.
The offender has no prior criminal record or has led a law-abiding life for a substantial period of time before committing the crime.
The character and attitude of the offender indicate that he or she is not likely to commit another crime.
The offender has made or will make restitution to the victim.
The offender is likely to respond affirmatively to probation or short-term imprisonment.

Source: Todd Clear, John Hewitt, and Robert Regoli, "Discretion and the Determinate Sentence: Its Distribution, Control, and Effect on Time Served," *Crime & Delinquency* 24:428–445 (1978).

Sentencing Guidelines

Alternatives to presumptive sentencing schemes, known as **sentencing guidelines**, were developed to limit judges' discretion, which many people believed resulted in widely disparate sentences for similar offenders. Like presumptive sentences, sentencing guidelines were intended to deemphasize rehabilitation as a primary goal in sentencing.

Guidelines direct the judge to arrive at a sentence by weighing the criminal history of an offender against the severity of the current offense. Using these guidelines, judges are allowed to exercise some degree of discretion by selecting a specific number of months within a specified range. As in other presumptive sentencing systems, judges must write a statement explaining any departures from sentencing guidelines.

In 2004, in *Blakely v. Washington*,[14] the U.S. Supreme Court ruled that the state of Washington's guidelines were unconstitutional because they violated a defendant's Sixth Amendment protections. In this case, Ralph Blakely pleaded guilty to the kidnapping of his estranged wife. The facts admitted in his plea supported a maximum sentence of 53 months. At his sentencing, the judge rejected the prosecutor's recommendation based on the guidelines and instead imposed a sentence of 90 months, justifying the sentence on the grounds that Blakely had acted with "deliberate cruelty." The Supreme Court held that "the facts supporting the petitioner's exceptional sentence were neither admitted by petitioner nor found by a jury," meaning that the sentence violated Blakely's Sixth Amendment right to trial by jury and to be found guilty beyond a reasonable doubt.

One year later, in *United States v. Booker*,[15] the Supreme Court ruled that the federal sentencing guidelines were unconstitutional and reduced them to an advisory status. Although the federal guidelines are not prescriptive, judges continue to use them as a starting point in deciding a sentence and must provide a written justification for any departure from the guidelines.

Federal sentencing statutes have long been criticized for the significantly more severe penalties they impose for selling crack cocaine compared to powdered cocaine. For example, under the federal sentencing guidelines, selling five grams of crack can warrant the same prison sentence as selling 500 grams of powdered cocaine. In December 2007, the U.S. Supreme Court held that federal district judges have the discretion to hand down "reasonably" shorter sentences for crack offenses, thereby eliminating the discrepancy. The next day the U.S. Sentencing Commission voted to allow the sentences of federal inmates incarcerated for the sale of crack to be reviewed for reduction. More than 19,000 federal inmates will become eligible to request reductions in their sentences as a result of this ruling.[16]

Mandatory Sentences

Many states have established **mandatory sentences**, requiring imprisonment of offenders who are convicted of certain types of serious crimes. Mandatory sentences prohibit judges from suspending prison sentences and placing offenders on probation. For example, some states have gun laws mandating prison sentences for persons who are convicted of using firearms in the commission of crimes, and a number of states and the federal government have adopted mandatory minimum sentences for certain violent crimes and drug offenses.[17] Some critics believe that much of the national increase in both incarceration rates and sentence length is attributable to such laws.[18]

Habitual Offender Statutes

In the past few years, a number of states have passed habitual or persistent offender legislation, also known as **three-strikes laws** (as in "Three strikes and you're out"). Most of these statutes require lengthy prison sentences or even life in prison without parole for offenders who are convicted of a third violent felony, although some states do not require any of the felonies to be violent crimes. Currently, 25 states and the federal government have three-strikes laws. Some states, such as Georgia, have passed even tougher laws mandating life-without-parole sentences for offenders who are convicted twice of certain violent crimes, such as murder, armed robbery, kidnapping, and rape.[19]

Three-strikes laws may have some unintended consequences. Recent studies have found a positive association between such laws and homicide rates; that is, homicide rates have actually increased after the passage of the laws.[20] In addition, three-strikes laws have disproportionately harsh effects on African Americans. In their study of the impact of California's three-strikes laws, Franklin Zimring and his colleagues report that African Americans, who make up less than 10 percent of the state's population, account for nearly two-thirds of third-strike eligible arrests.[21] Moreover, African Americans account for slightly more than 30 percent of the state prison population but fully 44 percent of inmates serving three-strikes sentences.[22]

The effectiveness of three-strikes laws has been hotly debated. Some politicians have even advocated two-strikes laws that would impose life imprisonment after a person commits a second serious felony.

Truth in Sentencing

The wave of sentencing reforms implemented during the past two decades also included legislation to establish a much closer correspondence between judicially imposed sentences and the actual time offenders serve in prison. A number of states have moved to create **truth-in-sentencing** laws, which require that offenders—and especially violent offenders—serve at least 85 percent of their sentences. Most research suggests that, as a consequence of TIS laws, there is now a more truthful relationship between the imposed sentence and the time actually served.[23]

Concurrent and Consecutive Sentences

Offenders are often convicted on more than one charge. In such a case, the judge must first determine the appropriate prison sentence for each conviction charge. Then, whether in an indeterminate or determinate sentencing system, the judge must decide whether to impose these sentences concurrently or consecutively. **Concurrent sentences** are served at the same time. That is, a person with two convictions, each carrying a 10-year sentence, would serve the sentences together and still be eligible for release in 10 years, assuming he or she served the full maximum term. **Consecutive sentences**, by contrast, require that the offender serve one sentence before the next. Thus, an offender who is facing two 10-year prison sentences might not be released until the full 20 years have been served.

Arriving at an Appropriate Sentence

Despite determinate sentencing reforms in many jurisdictions, sentencing remains a difficult decision for judges. They must consider three interrelated questions:

- What are the appropriate goals of sentencing, and how should they be weighed in light of the facts of the case?
- How can the goals of sentencing be achieved under the circumstances of the case?
- Which specific sentence is justified given the facts of the case?[24]

Judges seek to answer these questions as they try to determine the most appropriate sentence for a given case, using any sentencing guidelines or case-specific information contained in the presentence investigation report.

The Presentence Investigation Report

The **presentence investigation (PSI)**, which is widely believed to be the cornerstone of the sentencing decision, is a comprehensive report on the background of the offender, the offense, and any other information that the judge considers relevant to deciding an appropriate sentence, including aggravating and mitigating circumstances. The PSI report helps the court understand the nature of the crime within the context of the offender's life. In jurisdictions relying on sentencing guidelines, such individualized considerations are viewed as less relevant and consequently have less impact on the sentence that is ultimately imposed.

The PSI report is based on interviews with the offender, family members, employers, and friends, as well as reviews of police reports and victim statements concerning the crime. It includes information about the offender's background, such as his or her educational, employment, medical, sexual, and military history; past juvenile and adult criminal records; evidence of alcohol and drug use; and any psychological or psychiatric evaluations. It may also include a sentence recommendation from a probation officer, although this practice varies by jurisdiction and even among judges within local court systems.

The Sentencing Hearing

Sentencing in felony cases usually occurs at a **sentencing hearing**, which is often scheduled three to six weeks after the defendant's conviction (except in lower court sentencing of minor misdemeanors and ordinance violations, where offenders may be sentenced immediately upon conviction). At this hearing, the offender has an opportunity to deny, explain, or add to information contained in the PSI report. In addition, the prosecutor may submit a written statement or make an oral recommendation regarding the sentence. In many plea agreements, the prosecutor may agree to support a reduced sentence or concurrent sentences, or to make no recommendation about the sentence. Judges typically make the final sentencing decisions in felony cases, whereas juries must make the sentencing decision in capital cases.

Until 2002, juries in six states (Arkansas, Kentucky, Missouri, Oklahoma, Texas, and Virginia) decided sentences in all felony cases except those involving the death penalty.

The sentencing of offenders who are convicted of capital crimes where the death penalty may be imposed requires a **bifurcated trial**, which includes a separate jury hearing after a guilty verdict to determine the offender's penalty. At sentencing, the jury considers mitigating and aggravating circumstances and then recommends either the death penalty or a prison sentence.

The Role of the Victim in Sentencing

Many jurisdictions allow victims to prepare written or oral **victim impact statements (VIS)** to be given to the court during the plea bargaining stage or at the sentencing hearing.[25] The VIS details the impact of the crime on the victim (including financial, social, physical, and psychological effects) and describes the victim's feelings about the crime, the offender, and the proposed sentence.

Criminologist Anthony Walsh has examined the role of the VIS in 417 sexual assault cases in a metropolitan Ohio county.[26] Ohio law provides that in all felony cases involving victims, a VIS may be included as part of the proceedings. Nevertheless, Walsh found only slightly more than half of the victims submitted a VIS and only 6 percent spoke at the sentencing hearing. He concluded that the VIS had little influence on the judge's choice between probation and prison. Although he found greater overall agreement than disagreement between the victim recommendation and the imposed sentence, Walsh noted that the outcome was primarily explained by legal constraints rather than by the VIS.

At least one recent study did find that the VIS could have a significant effect on jury sentencing decisions. Bryan Myers and Jack Arbuthnot presented two separate mock juries with trial transcripts of a murder case. One of the juries read the VIS of the grandmother of the murder victim; the other jury did not. Two thirds of the jurors who read the VIS voted to impose the death penalty compared to less than one third of those jurors who had not read the VIS.[27]

Disparity and Discrimination in Sentencing

The use of indeterminate sentencing demands sensitivity to the differences between offenders. Believing in the rehabilitative ideal, judges attempt to fit the sentence to the unique characteristics and circumstances in each case. Little attention is paid to the possibility that extralegal factors—such as the offender's race, ethnicity, gender, socioeconomic status, age, or even victim characteristics—might produce unintentional disparities in sentencing or cause judges to consciously or unconsciously discriminate against particular groups of defendants. By contrast, determinant sentencing systems—and especially sentencing guidelines—reduce but do not eliminate disparities in sentencing, although the range of differences is more limited. For the most part, while limiting the sentencing discretion of judges, these systems simply shift discretion to prosecutors.

Sentencing disparities occur when similar cases are sentenced differently.[28] Disparities are statistical differences in sentencing that reflect some characteristic of interest, such as the race or ethnicity of the offender. Disparities may or may not reflect intentional or unintentional bias or discriminatory sentencing practices; they simply indicate that differences in sentences appear to be related to certain case-related factors. When judges are allowed to have some degree of discretion in making their sentencing decisions, they may take into consideration a wide variety of case factors relating to the offense and the offender.[29]

Sentencing discrimination exists when illegitimate, morally objectionable, or extralegal factors are taken into account in the sentencing decision. Discrimination often leads to disparities in sentences based on extralegal factors. It occurs when a judge sentences certain offenders to prison or to longer terms while sentencing other offenders convicted of similar offenses and with prior records to probation or shorter sentences solely on the basis of the defendant's race, socioeconomic status, age, or gender, or the characteristics of the victim.

Most studies of sentencing disparity and discrimination have examined the effects of four extralegal factors tied to the offender: race/ethnicity, gender, socioeconomic status, and age. These factors are important because they appear to be related to decisions made at nearly every stage in the criminal justice process.

Race and Ethnicity

In 2008, African Americans accounted for 38 percent of all inmates in U.S. prisons and jails even though they represented only 13 percent of the U.S. population. Latinos accounted for an additional 19 percent of inmates, and whites made up another 37 percent.[30] Compared to whites, African Americans are more likely to receive prison sentences instead of jail or probation regardless of the offense of which they are convicted. It is not clear whether these disparities are a reflection of racial discrimination, factors unrelated to race, or more subtle institutional racism.

Many studies find only a small—if not entirely absent—effect of race and ethnicity on the decision to incarcerate or the length of prison sentence. Generally, race and ethnicity appear to play minor roles compared to other legally relevant factors such as the offense committed and the offender's prior record.[31]

In truth, race may have a more complicated and less obvious impact on sentencing. For example, James Gibson, in his study of sentencing patterns in Atlanta, found that African American and white defendants received similar sentences, even when controlling for the effect of the current offense and the offender's prior record. When Gibson examined the sentencing patterns of individual judges, however, he found that the race of the defendant was a factor in the decisions of some judges. Some judges were clearly biased against African Americans, some judges were biased in favor of African Americans, and other judges appeared not to consider race at all.[32]

Kathleen Daly and Michael Tonry note that while most sentencing studies do not find statistical advantages for whites at sentencing, such findings are likely to reflect institutional discrimination masking the real effects of race and ethnicity.[33] For example, African Americans are more likely to be held in jail awaiting trial and to have court-appointed attorneys. Perhaps, as Cassia Spohn suggests, African Americans are more likely than whites to be involved in more ambiguous or borderline cases where the seriousness of crime, the strength of the evidence, and the defendant's degree of culpability are less clear. In such instances, ambiguity tends to increase judicial discretion and enhance the potential for extralegal factors, such as race, to enter into the sentencing decision.[34]

Darrell Steffensmeier and Stephen Demuth report that while federal judges hand out similar sentences for similar defendants convicted of the same offenses, those defendants who have been convicted of more serious offenses, have more extensive prior records, and have been convicted at trial (rather than pleading guilty) are significantly more likely both to be sentenced to prison and to receive longer sentences. Steffensmeier and Demuth also found evidence that Latino defendants are sentenced somewhat more harshly than white defendants, while African Americans fall in between the two extremes, possibly due to differences in the seriousness of the offenses committed and the offenders' prior records.[35]

Gender

Women are less likely than men to be arrested, denied bail, or prosecuted. As they go through the criminal justice process, women find increasing leniency at every stage. They account for only 7 percent of all offenders held in local, state, and federal correctional institutions in 2007,[36] and they are less likely to be sentenced to prison and more likely to be sentenced to jail or probation than males who commit similar offenses.

Generally, even when the severity of the offense, prior record, and other legally relevant factors are held constant, women are still treated more leniently at sentencing than men. In a study of murder cases in the 75 largest counties in the United States, women convicted of murder were found to be treated more leniently than men who committed the same offense.[37] More than 50 percent of the men who were convicted of murder were given life sentences, compared with only 42 percent of the women; 13 percent of the men were sentenced to death, but none of the women received this punishment. Women who were convicted of murder also received shorter sentences than men: Half of the men received a sentence of 17 years or less, whereas half of the women received sentences of 8 years or less. Finally, analysis of sentencing under Pennsylvania guidelines reports that males are less likely than females to receive downward departures in sentence length and more likely to receive upward departures.[38]

What might explain these differences? One factor, according to Daly and Tonry, relates to differences in defendants' ties and responsibilities to others, especially within family relationships.[39] Having ties and responsibilities in the day-to-day care of others is often cited as a mitigating circumstance at sentencing.[40] Although men with dependents receive less severe sentences than men without dependents, women—especially married ones with dependents—receive more lenient sentences overall.[41]

Another factor related to gender-linked stereotyped beliefs in the greater potential for women to be reformed. Moreover, according to Daly and Tonry, "court officials assume that women are more easily deterred than men and that women will make greater efforts to reform themselves."[42]

Socioeconomic Status

Because poor defendants are less likely to be able to post bail and afford their own counsel, concern exists that they may be at a disadvantage in sentencing. Some research suggests defendants who remain in custody while awaiting trial or who have court-appointed counsel are more likely to be sentenced to prison and to receive longer sentences.[43]

The actual relationship between socioeconomic status and sentence severity may be obscured because many studies fail to consider the seriousness of the current offense and the prior conviction record of the defendant. Criminologists John Hagan, Ted Chiricos, and Gordon Waldo found no difference in three Southeastern states in sentences for defendants based on their economic status in a study of more than 10,000 inmates.[44]

Age

Research on sentencing patterns in Kentucky, Tennessee, and Virginia found that elderly offenders (older than age 60) were more likely to receive probation or shorter incarceration sentences than younger people who were convicted of the same or similar crimes.[45] This difference may stem partly from the fact that jails and prisons are not well-suited for the elderly. In addition, a recent study of departures from Pennsylvania's sentencing guidelines found that younger defendants are more likely to have upward departures from the recommended sentences and less likely to have downward departures than older defendants.[46]

Capital Punishment

Between 1930 and 2007, more than 4900 executions were carried out in the United States. Excluding the 10 years between 1968 and 1977, when there was a moratorium on executions because of legal challenges brought before the Supreme Court, an average of 104 executions took place each year. Fully 1099 persons were executed between 1977 and 2007, or an average of slightly fewer than 38 per year. Executions peaked in 1999, when 98 persons were put to death (see FIGURE 9–1).[47]

Supreme Court Decisions

In its 1972 landmark decision in ***Furman v. Georgia***,[48] the Supreme Court ruled 5 to 4 that the death penalty, as it was applied, was unconstitutional, thereby overturning death penalty statutes in 37 states. The *Furman* case actually consisted of three unrelated cases, each involving an African American defendant. In all three cases, the defendants had been sentenced to death by a jury that was allowed complete discretion in the decision to impose a sentence of imprisonment or execution. The Court argued that the death penalty was being imposed in an arbitrary, infrequent, and discriminatory manner and held that it was unconstitutional for juries to exercise total discretion in imposing the sentence of death. The *Furman* decision suggested that states might rewrite statutes to reduce inequities in the application of the death penalty by removing judicial and jury discretion in sentencing. It was also suggested that this goal might be achieved by specifying mandatory death sentences for all capital crimes or by developing statutes that guide the decision making of judges and juries.

During the next few years, 35 states developed new capital punishment statutes. In 1976, the Supreme Court handed down a critical decision in ***Gregg v. Georgia***.[49] Troy

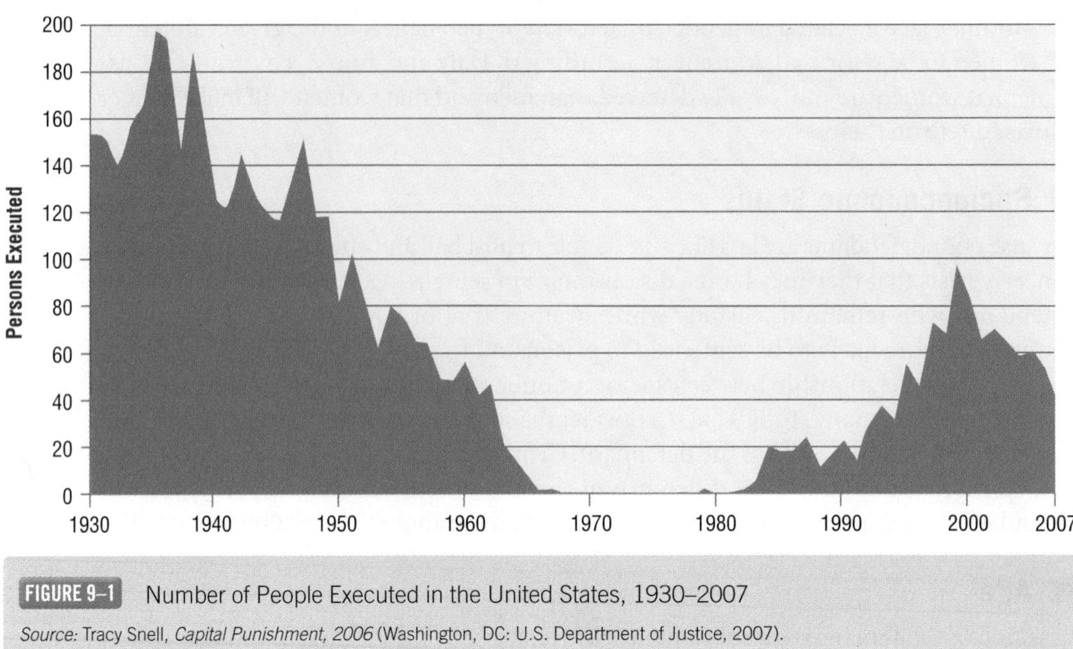

FIGURE 9–1 Number of People Executed in the United States, 1930–2007

Source: Tracy Snell, *Capital Punishment, 2006* (Washington, DC: U.S. Department of Justice, 2007).

Gregg had been convicted of robbing and murdering two men. After he was found guilty by the trial jury, a penalty hearing was held before the same jury, where aggravating and mitigating circumstances surrounding the case were presented. The judge carefully instructed the jury that the sentence of death would not be authorized unless the jury found beyond a reasonable doubt that one of several specific aggravating circumstances listed in the death penalty statute was present. The jury determined that two of the circumstances were present and returned a sentence of death. The Supreme Court, in a 7-to-2 decision, upheld Gregg's sentence, ruling that the Georgia statute providing for a bifurcated process and consideration of aggravating and mitigating circumstances was constitutional.

In 1977, the Supreme Court overturned a lower court's death sentence for rape in *Coker v. Georgia*.[50] In this case, the Court held that "a sentence of death is grossly disproportionate and excessive punishment for the crime of rape and is therefore forbidden by the Eighth Amendment as cruel and unusual punishment." However, the Court did not stipulate whether other non-homicide offenses may be prohibited from punishment by the death penalty, although this issue was taken up by the Court in 2008 when it heard arguments over whether states should be allowed to execute persons convicted of child rape in *Kennedy v. Louisiana*. Patrick Kennedy was sentenced to death for the rape of his eight-year-old stepdaughter. Although the rape was horrific, the majority of the Supreme Court held that executing a person for raping a child was unconstitutional because it violated the defendant's right against cruel and unusual punishment.[51]

One of the more controversial death penalty cases since the *Furman* decision in 1972 was *McCleskey v. Kemp*, which the Supreme Court ruled on in 1986.[52] In a 5-to-4 decision, the Court rejected the claim by the defendant that the imposition of the death penalty had been influenced by racial considerations and was, therefore, unconstitutional. Warren McCleskey, an African American, had been convicted of two counts of armed robbery and the murder of a white police officer. Despite the introduction of extensive social science research demonstrating that African American offenders convicted of killing white victims were significantly more likely to receive a death sentence than were whites who killed whites, the Court held that there was no evidence to suggest that racial discrimination entered into the sentencing decision in McCleskey's case.

Headline Crime

Supreme Court Prohibits Execution of Child Rapists

On March 2, 1998, Patrick Kennedy, age 43, brutally raped his eight-year-old stepdaughter. An expert in pediatric forensic medicine testified at Kennedy's trial that this sexual assault was the most severe he had encountered in his career. The little girl suffered a laceration to the left wall of the vagina that separated her cervix from the back of her vagina, causing her rectum to protrude into the vaginal structure. Her entire perineum was torn from the rear rim of the vagina to the anus.

Kennedy claimed that his step daughter had been attacked by two neighborhood boys, who had raped her in the yard and ridden away on a blue bike. No evidence of blood was found in the yard, and the blue bike had flat tires and cobwebs on the handles. However, blood was found under the girl's mattress; a colleague of Kennedy's testified that he called him early in the morning to ask how to get blood out of a carpet, and a cousin and goddaughter of Kennedy's ex-wife testified that he had sexually abused her three times when she was eight years old and that the last time involved sexual intercourse. The jury found Kennedy guilty of violating Louisiana's law that made the rape of a child younger than age 12 a capital offense, and he was sentenced to death.

On June 25, 2008, the U.S. Supreme Court, in a 5-to-4 ruling, held that it is unconstitutional to execute someone who rapes a young child but does not kill the victim. Justice Anthony Kennedy wrote that the harm caused a child who is raped is "grave," but "cannot be quantified in the same way as death of the victim." According to the Court, the Eighth Amendment's Cruel and Unusual Punishment Clause draws its "meaning from the evolving standards of decency that mark the progress of a maturing society. . . . Capital punishment must be limited to those offenders who commit 'a narrow category of the most serious crimes' and whose extreme culpability makes them 'the most deserving of execution.'" The Court went on to state that there is "a national consensus against capital punishment for the crime of child rape."

Justice Alito, joined in his dissent by Chief Justice Roberts and Justices Scalia and Thomas, wrote that the Court's "sweeping conclusion" categorically prohibits the imposition of the death penalty for the crime of raping a child "no matter how young the child, no matter how many times the child is raped, no matter how many children the perpetrator rapes, no matter how sadistic the crime, no matter how much physical or psychological trauma is inflicted, and no matter how heinous the perpetrator's prior criminal record may be." Justice Alito went on to add, "it is the judgment of the Louisiana lawmakers and those in an increasing number of other states that these harms justify the death penalty."

The claim by the majority in the Court's controversial decision that there is a national consensus against executing child rapists was countered by Justice Alito, who wrote that there is no evidence of such a consensus and that "the Court is willing to block the potential emergence of a national consensus in favor of permitting the death penalty for child rape because, in the end, what matters is the Court's 'own judgment' regarding 'the acceptability of the death penalty.'"

Some angry politicians vowed to continue finding ways to legislatively condemn child rapists to death. Republican Governor Bobby Jindal called the ruling "incredibly absurd . . . a clear abuse of judicial authority [and added that] state officials will evaluate ways to amend our statute to maintain death as a penalty for this horrific crime." Democratic Senator (and president-elect) Barack Obama was quoted as saying that "there should be no blanket prohibition of the death penalty for the rape of children if states want to apply it in those cases."

Sources: Kennedy v. Louisiana, No. 07-343, (2008); Robert Barnes, "Supreme Court Rejects Death Penalty in Child Rape Cases," available at http://washingtonpost.com//wp-dyn/content/article/2008/06/25/AR2008062500638.html, accessed June 26, 2008; Associated Press, "Unbowed, Politicians Vow to Execute Child Rapists," available at http://apnews.excite.com/article/20080626/D91HLG9G0.html, accessed June 26, 2008.

The Supreme Court has also ruled on whether a mentally retarded person can be executed. In 1989, in *Penry v. Lynaugh*,[53] it held that a mentally retarded person may be sentenced to death. The Court noted there was little consensus among the states to bar the execution of mentally retarded offenders and that only two states prohibited such executions at the time. Thirteen years later, in 2002, the Court reversed its decision allowing mentally retarded persons to be executed. In ***Atkins v. Virginia***,[54] the Court held that much had changed since the ruling in *Penry*. According to the Court, "a significant number of states have [now] concluded that death is not a suitable punishment for a mentally retarded criminal," and that to execute such a person would be a violation of the Eighth Amendment's prohibition of cruel and unusual punishment.

In 1991, in *Payne v. Tennessee*,[55] the Supreme Court overturned two prior decisions that prevented the prosecutor from introducing evidence about the murder victim's character and the impact of the crime on the victim's family.[56] Chief Justice William Rehnquist, in writing the 6-to-3 decision that upheld the conviction of a Tennessee murderer, stated that barring victim impact statements in cases involving the death penalty "unfairly weighted the scales in a capital trial" in favor of the defendant, who is allowed to present all possible mitigating evidence about the crime and his or her own life circumstances.[57]

Finally, in 2005 in ***Roper v. Simmons***,[58] the Supreme Court overturned its 1989 decision in *Stanford v. Kentucky*,[59] which allowed the execution of persons who were age 16 or 17 at the time they committed their crimes. In *Roper*, the Court held that the execution of a person younger than age 18 is disproportionate punishment under the Eighth Amendment and, therefore, is cruel and unusual punishment.

The Death Penalty Today

Today, 37 states and the federal government have statutes authorizing the death penalty. In 2007, New Jersey repealed its capital punishment statute, becoming the first state to do so since 1976.[60] However, since 1977, executions have been carried out in only 32 states. Five states—Florida, Missouri, Oklahoma, Texas, and Virginia—accounted for 65 percent of all executions since 1977, with Texas performing more than one third of all executions in the United States during that period.[61] In 2007, Texas accounted for 26 of the nation's 42 executions, or 62 percent.[62] Given that nearly 3300 people are currently on death row, the potential for large numbers of executions in the future remains very high.

In 2006, 3228 prisoners were under a sentence of death in the United States. The majority of them were white, had never been married, had less than a high school education, and were overwhelmingly male (see TABLE 9-2). Of the 1057 prisoners executed between 1977 and 2007, 64 percent were white, 34 percent were African American, and 2 percent were Latino. During this period, only 11 women were executed, accounting for only 1 percent of all executions.[63]

Headline Crime: Repeal of Death Penalty in New Jersey Takes "Megan's Law" Killer off Death Row

On December 17, 2007, New Jersey Governor Jon Corzine signed legislation that abolished the death penalty after a state sentencing commission decided that capital punishment was not an effective deterrent to violent crime. Among the eight men on death row whose death sentences were commuted to life in prison was Jesse Timmendequas, a convicted child rapist who, after an earlier release from prison, beat, raped, and murdered seven-year-old Megan Kanka, whose death gave rise to "Megan's Law." Another death row inmate spared by the legislative decision was Ambrose Harris, who had kidnapped, raped, and murdered 22-year-old Kristen Huggins. Governor Corzine signed the bill abolishing the death penalty exactly 15 years to the date after the murder of Huggins.

Sources: Chris Marcum, "'Megan's Law' Killer Jesse Timmendequas' Death Penalty Sentence Reduced to Life in Prison," available at http://www.associatedcontent.com/article/495361/megans_law_killer_jesse_timmendequas.html, accessed January 2, 2008; "'Megan's Law' Killer Escapes Death Under N.J. Execution Ban," available at http://www.cnn.com/2007/POLITICS/12/17/death.penalty/index.html, accessed January 2, 2008.

TABLE 9-2 Demographic Profile of Prisoners Under Sentence of Death, 2006

Characteristic	Year-End 2006	2006 New Admissions
Total number under sentence of death	3228	115
Sex		
Male	98.3%	95.7%
Female	1.7%	4.3%
Race		
White	55.8%	62.6%
African American	41.9%	36.5%
Other	2.3%	0.9%
Ethnicity		
Latino	11.1%	11.5%
Non-Latino	76.1%	88.5%
Median Age	**27 years (at time of arrest)**	
Education		
Eighth grade or less	13.9%	11.7%
Ninth to eleventh grade	37.0%	40.3%
Twelfth grade	40.0%	40.3%
Any college	9.0%	7.8%
Median education	Eleventh grade	Eleventh grade
Marital Status		
Married	21.7%	17.7%
Divorced/separated	20.6%	22.9%
Widowed	3.0%	3.1%
Never married	54.8%	56.3%

Source: Tracy Snell, *Capital Punishment, 2006—Statistical Tables* (Washington, DC: U.S. Department of Justice, 2007).

Methods of Execution

Several methods of execution are used in the United States, including lethal injection, electrocution, lethal gas, hanging, and firing squad (see TABLE 9-3). Since 1977, 84 percent of all executions have been by lethal injection; indeed, all of the executions in 2007 used this method. Today 36 states use lethal injection as the exclusive or primary method of execution. Seventeen states authorize the use of more than one method; in such a case, the condemned prisoner is generally given the choice of method. The method of execution for federal prisoners is exclusively lethal injection.

Although the popularity of lethal injection may reflect public perceptions that it is more humane, legal challenges to this method of execution have recently come before the U.S. Supreme Court. In 2006, the Court heard an appeal by Clarence Hill, a Florida inmate who was convicted of murdering a police officer in 1982. Hill's appeal claimed that the three chemicals used in the lethal injection process would cause unnecessary pain in the execution and that the risk of inflicting unnecessary and wanton infliction of pain is contrary to contemporary standards of decency, thus constituting cruel and unusual punishment. During questioning, Justice Antonin Scalia noted that "lethal injection is much less painful than hanging, which has sometimes resulted in decapitation or slow

TABLE 9-3 Method of Execution, by State, 2006

Lethal Injection	Electrocution	Lethal Gas	Hanging	Firing Squad
Alabama	Alabama	Arizona	Delaware	Idaho
Arizona	Arkansas	California	New Hampshire	Oklahoma
Arkansas	Florida	Missouri	Washington	Utah
California	Kentucky	Wyoming		
Colorado	Nebraska			
Connecticut	Oklahoma			
Delaware	South Carolina			
Florida	Tennessee			
Georgia	Virginia			
Idaho				
Illinois				
Indiana				
Kansas				
Kentucky				
Louisiana				
Maryland				
Mississippi				
Missouri				
Montana				
Nevada				
New Hampshire				
New Mexico				
New York				
North Carolina				
Ohio				
Oklahoma				
Oregon				
Pennsylvania				
South Carolina				
South Dakota				
Tennessee				
Texas				
Utah				
Virginia				
Washington				
Wyoming				

Source: Tracy Snell, *Capital Punishment, 2006—Statistical Tables* (Washington, DC: U.S. Department of Justice, 2007).

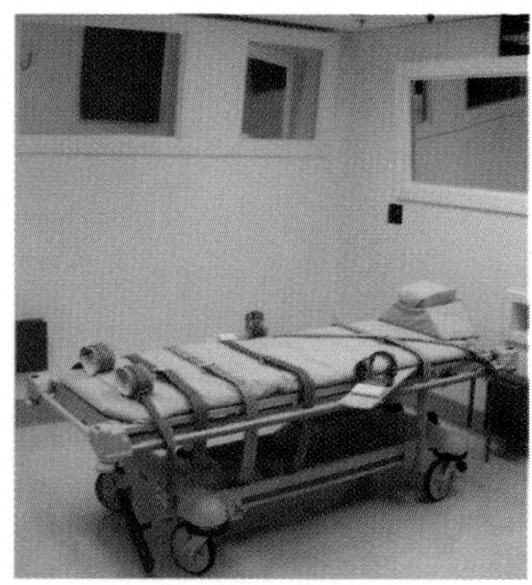
A number of states proceeded with executions after the U.S. Supreme Court held that lethal injection was not cruel and unusual punishment.

strangulation."[64] The Court denied Hill's stay and he was executed on September 21, 2006, by lethal injection.

On April 16, 2008, the Supreme Court, in *Baze v. Rees*, ruled that the three-drug "cocktail" used by Kentucky for lethal injection executions, which is essentially the same as that used by the federal government and 34 other states, does not violate the Eighth Amendment's prohibition of cruel and unusual punishment.[65] Chief Justice Roberts wrote, "Simply because an execution method may result in pain, either by accident or as an inescapable consequence of death, does not establish the sort of 'objectively intolerable risk of harm' that qualifies as cruel and unusual." Justice Scalia added that a method of execution would violate the ban on cruel and unusual punishment "only if it is deliberately designed to inflict pain."[66]

The Capital Punishment Debate

Arguments for Capital Punishment

Contemporary arguments in support of capital punishment have largely focused on the deterrent impact of the penalty and the need to express moral condemnation of heinous crimes. Advocates of capital punishment are quick to point out its specific deterrent effect. According to James Q. Wilson, "Whatever else may be said about the death penalty, it is certain that it incapacitates."[67] In other words, people who are executed do not kill again. Advocates also argue that the death penalty carries a strong general deterrent: The very threat of the death penalty is thought to deter potential killers. For the death penalty to deter murder, however, the potential offender must know of the penalty's application and believe that the certainty of its application is sufficient to make the possibility of incurring it an unacceptable risk.

A large number of studies appear to support the general deterrence hypothesis. Economist Isaac Ehrlich's analysis of homicide between 1934 and 1969 led him to conclude that an additional execution per year would prevent seven or eight other murders annually.[68] When Steven Layson examined homicides and executions from 1936 to 1977, he concluded that 18 murders are prevented by each execution. Paul Zimmerman's analysis of executions and subsequent homicides between 1978 and 1997 found that each execution deters 14 murders per year on average.[69] Finally, in a study by Hashem Dezhbakhsh and his colleagues of data from 2054 U.S. counties between 1977 and 1996 they found that the murder rate was significantly reduced by both death sentences and executions and that, on average, each execution produced 18 fewer murders.[70]

Another justification for capital punishment rests on the principle of retribution. Retribution may involve a base desire for revenge, or it may represent a general statement by society that the most extreme crimes must be dealt with by the most extreme punishment. Society's moral outrage at murder requires that the act be condemned by an equally severe response.

In the United States, broad public support for the death penalty persists. Since the mid-1970s, between 60 percent and 70 percent of Americans surveyed have maintained that they favor the death penalty for a person convicted of murder (see FIGURE 9-2).

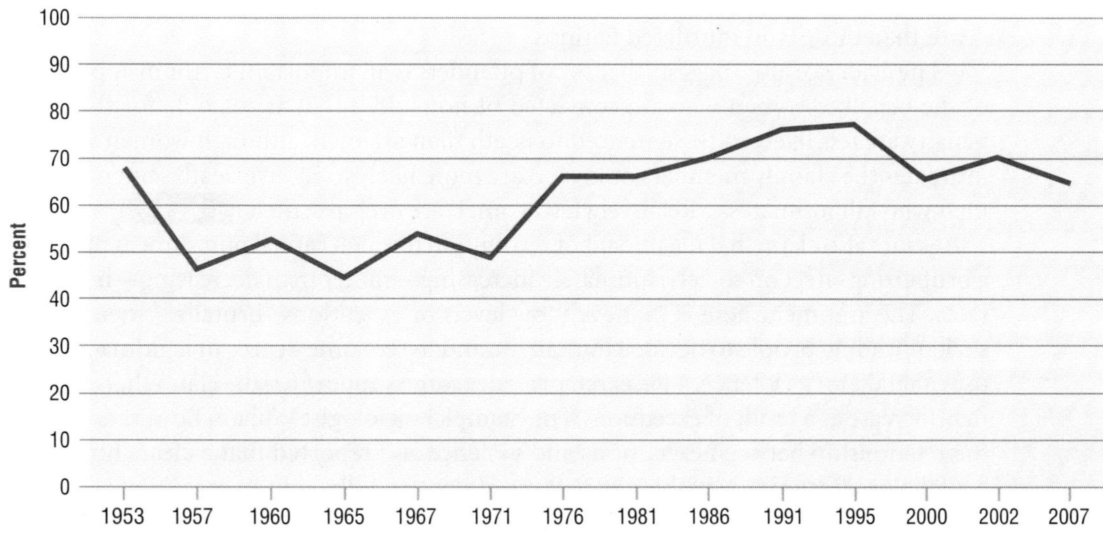

FIGURE 9-2 Public Support for the Death Penalty in the United States, 1953–2007

Source: Gallup Organization, *The Gallup Poll*, available at http://www.gallup.com/poll/1606/death-penalty.aspx, accessed November 5, 2008.

Currently, approximately 65 percent of American adults support the death penalty, while only 31 percent oppose it. Although the majority of both men and women support the penalty, there is a large gap between whites and African Americans on this issue: 70 percent of whites support the death penalty, compared to only 56 percent of African Americans.[71] Support declines, however, if people are asked if they would still support capital punishment if there was a viable alternative, such as life in prison without parole. When given such a choice, support for the death penalty drops to about 52 percent. Americans also are less supportive of capital punishment if the defendant is mentally retarded or mentally ill, female, or younger than age 18.[72]

Arguments against Capital Punishment

In 2007, more than 10,000 people were arrested for homicide and non-negligent manslaughter.[73] During the same year, 110 offenders received the death penalty, but only 42 were executed. Although a large number of people who were arrested for murder did not commit death-eligible homicides (crimes that by law may carry the death penalty), it is clear that throughout the criminal justice process, decisions are made that result in very few prosecutions on death-eligible charges and even fewer death sentences.

Critics of capital punishment point to apparent discrimination in the application of the death penalty. They argue that many prosecutors are more likely to select homicide cases for prosecution that have African American defendants and white victims, that juries are more likely to convict African Americans, and that death sentences are disproportionately imposed on minority defendants. The races of both offender and victim appear to be significant factors in this selective process. A number of studies have shown that African Americans who are charged with the murder of whites have a much greater risk of receiving a death sentence[74] and are less likely to have their death sentences commuted to a lesser sentence than whites who kill African Americans or people who are involved in intraracial killings.[75]

Studies have shown that, regardless of the race of offender, the race of the victim alone appears to have a significant effect on death sentencing.[76] When Glenn Pierce and Michael Radelet examined all homicides and related death sentences in California from 1990 through 1999, they found that convicted murderers were significantly more likely to receive the death penalty if their victims were white.[77] Those who murdered whites were more than three times more likely to be sentenced to death than were those who murdered African Americans and more than four times more likely to be sentenced to death than those who murdered Latinos.

The evidence also suggests that sex of offenders is an important factor in application of the penalty. Women who are convicted of homicides that are eligible for the death penalty are less likely to be sentenced to death than are men, although women who kill intimates (i.e., family members or lovers) are more likely to receive death sentences than men who kill intimates.[78] Relatively few women are ever executed (TABLE 9–4).

Critics also claim that the pursuit of retribution through capital punishment produces a brutalizing effect on society, ultimately increasing—rather than decreasing—homicide rates. The argument here is that even low levels of executions "brutalize" members of society, leading people to devalue human life and to see some degree of legitimacy in the use of retaliatory violence.[79] Research provides some support for the claim that violence may increase as a result of executions. For example, sociologist William Bowers examined the relationship between executions and violence and reported that a clear short-term brutalizing effect occurs within the first month or two following an execution.[80] Bowers believes that a small number of people existing in a state of emotional turmoil are ready to kill and are pushed over the edge by the message they perceive from executions—namely, that it is appropriate to kill those who betray, disgrace, or dishonor them.

Opponents of the death penalty also point out that the criminal justice system is not infallible. Truly innocent people are sometimes arrested and even convicted of crimes they

TABLE 9-4 **Executions of Women Are Rare**

Only 2 percent of all persons executed in the United States since 1608 have been women, and only 11 women have been executed since 1977.

Name	State	Date
Velma Barfield	North Carolina	November 2, 1984
Karla Faye Tucker	Texas	February 3, 1998
Judy Buenoano	Florida	March 30, 1998
Betty Lou Beets	Texas	February 24, 2000
Christina Riggs	Arkansas	May 2, 2000
Wanda Allen	Oklahoma	January 11, 2001
Marilyn Plantz	Oklahoma	May 1, 2001
Lois Smith	Oklahoma	December 4, 2001
Lynda Block	Alabama	May 10, 2002
Aileen Wuornos	Florida	October 9, 2002
Frances Newton	Texas	September 14, 2005

Source: Raymond Paternoster, Robert Brame, and Sarah Bacon, *The Death Penalty: America's Experience with Capital Punishment* (New York: Oxford University Press, 2008), p. 208.

did not commit. Often, such errors are corrected on appeal, but no appeal is possible once the defendant has been executed. In 2000, Illinois Governor George Ryan suspended executions and then in 2003, he commuted the death sentences of all inmates on death row, arguing that the possibility of a death-row inmate being innocent was simply too great.[81]

Although we cannot be certain that a truly innocent person has been executed in recent decades, strong evidence exists that a number of persons on death row were not guilty of the crimes that resulted in their death sentences. According to the Innocence Project (a national litigation and public policy organization), 200 persons have been exonerated by DNA evidence in the United States since the Innocence Project began its work in 1994.[82] While most of the 200 exonerations did not involve death-row inmates, at least 13 inmates facing execution have been exonerated on the basis of DNA tests, and more than 60 have been exonerated largely on the basis of either new evidence establishing the prisoner's innocence or the exclusion at retrial of inappropriately admitted evidence from the initial trial. Quite possibly the discovery of these false convictions was a result of the much greater attention given to the review of death penalty cases after convictions. Alternatively, false convictions may be more likely to occur in capital murder

Headline Crime

Naming Executioners

Five death-row inmates in Missouri filed suit in federal court to require that executioners be identified. The lawsuit claims that the state's procedure for screening persons who will participate in executions is defective. A state law prohibits anyone, including the news media, from knowingly disclosing the identity of a current or former execution team member, and makes it possible for anyone so identified to seek civil damages.

The current case comes after a newspaper reported that a nurse on the execution team had once been accused of stalking and damaging the property of a man involved with his estranged wife. The inmates claim that the nurse's criminal record raises questions about his "temperament and suitability" to be a member of an execution team.

Source: www.cnn.com/2008/CRIME/01/21/secret.executioners.ap/index.html, accessed August 25, 2008.

cases because there is greater room for error—the victims are dead and unavailable as witnesses, there is an incentive for the real killers to frame others to avoid punishment, police face enormous pressure to clear murders, and prosecutors want to obtain a conviction and help bring closure to the victim's family.[83]

Appeal of Sentence

Unlike the post-conviction appeal of errors that may have occurred in a trial (discussed in Chapter 8), appellate review of sentencing is more restricted.

Grounds for Appellate Review of Sentence

Five types of sentences typically lead to an appeal:

- Sentences that are in violation of the Eighth Amendment prohibition against cruel and unusual punishment
- Sentences that are disproportionate to the seriousness of the offense
- Sentences based on an abuse of discretionary power by the sentencing judge
- Sentences that fall outside statutory sentencing guidelines
- Sentences imposed by a court not having jurisdictional authority to impose the sentence

All cases that meet one or more of these criteria may be appealed to a higher court and follow the same process of appeal.

The Appeal Process

As in general post-conviction appeals, a notice of appeal of a sentence must be filed with the court (usually within 30 to 90 days following the defendant's conviction). Following the filing of the notice, the defendant must file a written brief identifying the error in sentencing. The state is then required to respond by filing a brief in the case, and the appellate court schedules both briefs for review. If the appellate court believes that an error was made, the case will be returned to the lower court for resentencing.

Since the *Furman v. Georgia* decision, all death penalty sentences have been required to undergo automatic review by an intermediate appellate court or the state court of last resort. Death sentences also may be appealed directly to the Supreme Court through a petition by the offender for a writ of habeas corpus.

Recent decisions by the Supreme Court restricting habeas corpus petitions by prisoners included those filed by inmates under death sentences. For example, in *McCleskey v. Kemp*,[84] Warren McCleskey's first petition for a writ of habeas corpus was accepted by the Court and resulted in the 1986 decision discussed previously. Five days before his scheduled execution in July 1987, McCleskey appealed a second time, this time claiming that his Sixth Amendment right to counsel had been violated after it was discovered that prosecutors had planted an informant in an adjoining cell. The trial judge stayed McCleskey's execution and ordered a new trial. Later, a federal appeals court reinstated McCleskey's conviction on the grounds that the defendant should have raised the informant issue in his first appeal, despite the fact that neither McCleskey nor his lawyers had any way of knowing about the existence of the informant. Once again, McCleskey petitioned for a writ of habeas corpus from the Supreme Court. The Court, in *McCleskey v. Zant*, held that McCleskey had no legitimate excuse for failing to bring up his claim.[85] Reflecting the Court's growing irritation with seemingly endless numbers of habeas corpus petitions by prisoners, Justice Anthony Kennedy, in writing the 6-to-3 majority opinion, stated, "Perpetual disrespect for the finality of convictions disparages the entire criminal justice system." Now, after exhausting state appeals, most prisoners are allowed only one appeal in the federal courts.

WRAPPING IT UP

Chapter Highlights

- There are five general goals in sentencing: retribution, deterrence, incapacitation, rehabilitation, and proportionality.
- Intermediate sentences offer alternatives to the traditional sentences of imprisonment and probation. They include intermittent sentences, intensive probation, fines, community service, restitution, and forfeiture.
- Indeterminate prison sentences have been largely replaced by determinate sentencing systems, including presumptive sentencing, sentencing guidelines, mandatory sentences, and three-strikes laws, in an attempt to reduce the discretion of judges and make sentences more uniform.
- At the sentencing hearing, a judge reviews the presentence investigation (PSI) report, the offender is given an opportunity to speak and make a case for a lenient sentence, the prosecutor may make a recommendation regarding the sentence, and the victim is allowed to submit a victim impact statement or statement of opinion.
- The discretion permitted in the judge's sentencing decision in many jurisdictions often results in sentencing disparities (differences in sentences for people who are convicted of similar offenses). Sentencing discrimination may also occur when judges abuse their discretion and consider illegitimate, morally objectionable, or extralegal factors in determining sentences.
- Many proponents of capital punishment stress its deterrent effect; others support capital punishment as a form of retribution. Critics of the death penalty argue that it is discriminatory, has a brutalizing effect on society, fails to deter homicides more effectively than long-term imprisonment, and has resulted in innocent people being put to death.
- An offender may appeal what he or she considers to be an unjust or faulty sentence. If the appellate court finds that an error was made in sentencing, the case is returned to the lower court for resentencing.

Words to Know

Atkins v. Virginia Supreme Court ruling that the death sentence is not a suitable punishment for a mentally retarded criminal, and that to execute such a person would be a violation of the Eighth Amendment's prohibition of cruel and unusual punishment.

bifurcated trial Two-stage trial: the first stage determines guilt, and the second stage determines the sentence.

concurrent sentences Two or more prison sentences to be served at the same time.

consecutive sentences Two or more prison sentences to be served one after the other.

determinate sentence A prison sentence with a fixed term of imprisonment.

deterrence A punishment philosophy based on the belief that punishing offenders will deter crime.

Furman v. Georgia Supreme Court ruling that the death penalty, as applied at that time, was unconstitutional.

general deterrence Punishing offenders to discourage others from committing crimes.

Gregg v. Georgia Supreme Court ruling that the death penalty was constitutional under a state statute requiring the judge and the jury to consider both aggravating and mitigating circumstances.

incapacitation A punishment aimed at removing offenders from the community through imprisonment or banishment.

indeterminate sentence A prison sentence that identifies a minimum number and a maximum number of years to be served by the offender; the actual release date is set by a parole board or the institution.

mandatory sentence A requirement that an offender must be sentenced to prison.

presentence investigation (PSI) A comprehensive report including information on the offender's background and offense and any other information the judge desires to determine an appropriate sentence.

presumptive sentencing The use of ranges—that is, minimum number and maximum number of years of incarceration—to set punishments for types of particular crimes. The judge determines the number of years to be served from within this range.

proportionality A punishment philosophy based on the belief that the severity of the punishment should fit the seriousness of the crime.

rehabilitation A sentencing objective aimed at reforming an offender through treatment, education, or counseling.

retribution A punishment philosophy based on society's moral outrage or disapproval of a crime.

Roper v. Simmons Supreme Court ruling that the death penalty for anyone who was younger than age 18 at the time of a crime's commission is unconstitutional.

sentencing discrimination Differences in sentencing outcomes based on illegitimate, morally objectionable, or extralegal factors.

sentencing disparities Differences in sentencing outcomes in cases with similar case attributes.

sentencing guidelines Sentencing schemes that limit judicial discretion; the offender's criminal background and severity of current offense are weighed to determine the sentence.

sentencing hearing A court hearing to determine an appropriate sentence, which is typically scheduled within three to six weeks after the offender's conviction.

specific deterrence Punishing offenders to prevent them from committing new crimes.

three-strikes laws Laws that provide a mandatory sentence of incarceration for persons who are convicted of a third separate serious criminal offense.

truth-in-sentencing (TIS) Laws that require offenders, especially violent offenders, to serve at least 85 percent of their sentences.

victim impact statement (VIS) A statement informing the sentencing judge of the physical, financial, and emotional harm suffered by the crime victim or his or her family.

Think and Discuss

1. Which goals of punishment (retribution, deterrence, incapacitation, rehabilitation, or restorative justice) should guide sentencing?
2. To what extent should the background characteristics of offenders (i.e., family, education, prior military service) play a role in determining a sentence?
3. Do structured sentencing systems provide greater justice in sentencing? Why or why not?
4. Is the death penalty a positive factor or a negative factor in dealing with crime in society?
5. Are there crimes other than first-degree murder that might justify the use of the death penalty? If so, what are they?

Notes

1. James Q. Wilson, *Thinking about Crime*, revised edition (New York: Vintage Books, 1985), p. 260.
2. Thomas Hobbes, cited in Graeme Newman, *The Punishment Response* (Albany, NY: Harrow and Heston, 1985), p. 201.
3. Andrew von Hirsch, *Doing Justice: The Choice of Punishments* (New York: Hill and Wang, 1976), p. 54.
4. Cesare Beccaria, *On Crimes and Punishments*, trans. by Henry Paolucci (New York: Bobbs-Merrill, 1963); J. H. Burns and H. L. A. Hart (Eds.), *The Collected Works of Jeremy Bentham: An Introduction to the Principles of Morals and Legislation* (London: Athlone Press, 1970).
5. David Greenberg, "The Incapacitative Effect of Imprisonment: Some Estimates," *Law and Society Review* 9:541–580 (1975); Stephan Van Dine, Simon Dinitz, and John Conrad, "The Incapacitation of the Dangerous Offender: A Statistical Experiment," *Journal of Research in Crime and Delinquency* 14:22–34 (1977).
6. Steven Levitt, "Why Do Increased Arrest Rates Appear to Reduce Crime: Deterrence, Incapacitation, or Measurement Error?" *Economic Inquiry* 36:353–373 (1998); Don Gottfredson, *Effects of Judges' Sentencing Decisions on Decisions on Criminal Careers* (Washington, DC: National Institute of Justice, 1999).
7. Robert Martinson, "What Works? Questions and Answers about Prison Reform," *Public Interest* 35:22–54 (1974); Douglas Lipton, Robert Martinson, and Judith Wilks, *The Effectiveness of Correctional Treatment: A Survey of Evaluation Studies* (New York: Praeger, 1975); William Bailey, "Correctional Outcome: An Evaluation of 100 Reports," *Journal of Criminal Law, Criminology, and Police Science* 57:153–160 (1966); Hans Eysenck, "The Effects of Psychotherapy," *International Journal of Psychiatry* 1:99–144 (1965).

8. "State Senate Approves Change in Law," available at http://www.cnn.com/2006/LAW/04/20/child.rapists.ap/index.html, accessed January 4, 2008; *Kennedy v. Louisiana*, No. 07-343 (2008).
9. *Weems v. United States*, 217 U.S. 349 (1910).
10. *Trop v. Dulles*, 356 U.S. 86 (1958).
11. Sally Hillsman, Barry Mahoney, George Cole, and Bernard Auchter, *Fines as Criminal Sanctions* (Washington, DC: National Institute of Justice, 1987).
12. Todd Clear, John Hewitt, and Robert Regoli, "Discretion and the Determinate Sentence: Its Distribution, Control, and Effect on Time Served," *Crime & Delinquency* 24:428–445 (1978).
13. David Fogel, "... We Are the Living Proof ...," in *The Justice Model for Corrections* (Cincinnati: Anderson, 1975), p. 310.
14. *Blakely v. Washington*, 542 U.S. 296 (2004).
15. *United States v. Booker*, 543 U.S. 220 (2005).
16. Bill Mears, "Justices: Judges Can Slash Crack Sentences," available at http://www.cnn.com/2007/US/law/12/10/scotus.crack.cocaine/index.html, accessed August 1, 2008; Darryl Fears, "For Crack Offenders, Earlier Shot at Release," available at http://www.washingtonpost.com/wp-dyn/content/article/2007/12/11/AR2007121101655.html, accessed August 1, 2008.
17. Milton Heumann and Colin Loftin, "Mandatory Sentencing and the Abolition of Plea Bargaining: The Michigan Felony Firearm Statute," *Law and Society Review* 13:393–430 (1979); U.S. Department of Justice, "Mandatory Sentencing: The Experience of Two States," *Policy Briefs* (Washington, DC: U.S. Government Printing Office, 1982).
18. Barbara Meierhoefer, *The General Effect of Mandatory Minimum Prison Terms* (Washington, DC: Federal Judicial Center, 1992).
19. Larry Rohter, "In Wave of Anticrime Fervor, States Rush to Adopt Laws," *The New York Times*, May 10, 1994, p. A19.
20. Katherine Rosich and Kamala Kane, "Truth in Sentencing and State Sentencing Practices," *NIJ Journal* 252:18–21 (2005).
21. Massachusetts Sentencing Commission, *Survey of Sentencing Practices: Truth-in-Sentencing Reform in Massachusetts* (Boston: Massachusetts Sentencing Commission, 2000); William Sabol, Katherine Rosich, Kamala Kane, David Kirk, and Glenn Dubin, *The Influences of Truth-in-Sentencing Reforms on Changes in States' Sentencing Practices and Prison Populations* (Washington, DC: Urban Institute, 2002).
22. Tomislav Kovandzic, John Sloan, and Lynne Vieraitis, "'Striking Out' as Crime Reduction Policy: The Impact of 'Three Strikes' Laws on Crime Rates in U.S. Cities," *Justice Quarterly* 21:207–240 (2004); Tomislav Kovandzic, John Sloan, and Lynne Vieraitis, "Unintended Consequences of Politically Popular Sentencing Policy: The Homicide Promoting Effects of 'Three-Strikes' Laws in U.S. Cities," *Criminology and Public Policy* 1:399–424 (2002); Thomas Marvell and Carlisle Moody, "The Lethal Effects of Three Strikes Laws," *Journal of Legal Studies* 30:89–106 (2001); Franklin Zimring, Sam Kamin, and Gordon Hawkins, *Crime and Punishment in California* (Berkeley, CA: Institute of Governmental Studies Press, 1999).
23. Walter Dickey and Pam Hollenhorst, "Three-Strikes Laws: Five Years Later," *Corrections Management Quarterly* 3:1–19 (1999).
24. Austin Lovegrove, *Judicial Decision Making, Sentencing Policy, and Numerical Guidance* (London: Springer-Verlag, 1989).
25. Maureen McLeod, "Victim Participation at Sentencing," *Criminal Law Bulletin* 22:501–517 (1986).
26. Anthony Walsh, "Placebo Justice: Victim Recommendations and Offender Sentences in Sexual Assault Cases," *Journal of Criminal Law and Criminology* 77:1126–1141 (1986).
27. Bryan Myers and Jack Arbuthnot, "The Effects of Victim Impact Evidence on the Verdicts of Sentencing Judgments of Mock Jurors," *Journal of Offender Rehabilitation* 29:95–112 (1999).

28. Alfred Blumstein, Jacqueline Cohen, Susan Martin, and Michael Tonry, *Research on Sentencing: The Search for Reform*, Volume I (Washington, DC: National Academy Press, 1983), p. 8.

29. Lovegrove, note 24, p. 4.

30. William Sabol and Heather Couture, *Prison Inmates at Midyear 2007* (Washington, DC: U.S. Department of Justice, 2008), p. 7.

31. Gary Kleck, "Racial Discrimination in Sentencing: A Critical Evaluation of the Evidence with Additional Evidence on the Death Penalty," *American Sociological Review* 46:783–805 (1981); Martha Myers and Susette Talarico, *The Social Contexts of Criminal Sentencing* (New York: Springer-Verlag, 1987); Cassia Spohn, "The Sentencing Decisions of Black and White Judges: Expected and Unexpected Similarities," *Law and Society Review* 24:1197–1216 (1990); Stephen Klein, Joan Petersilia, and Susan Turner, "Race and Imprisonment Decisions in California," *Science* 247:812–816 (1990); John Dawson and Barbara Boland, *Murder in Large Urban Counties, 1988* (Washington, DC: U.S. Department of Justice, 1993).

32. James Gibson, "Race as a Determinant of Criminal Sentences: A Methodological Critique and a Case Study," *Law and Society Review* 12:455–478 (1978).

33. Kathleen Daly and Michael Tonry, "Gender, Race, and Sentencing," *Crime and Justice* 22:201–252 (1997).

34. Cassia Spohn, *Offender Race and Case Outcomes: Do Crime Seriousness and Strength of Evidence Matter? Final Activities Report Submitted to the National Institute of Justice* (Washington, DC: National Institute of Justice, 2000).

35. Darrell Steffensmeier and Stephen Demuth, "Ethnicity and Sentencing Outcomes in U.S. Federal Courts: Who Is Punished More Harshly?" *American Sociological Review* 65:705–729 (2000).

36. Sabol and Couture, note 30, p. 1.

37. Dawson and Boland, note 31.

38. Brian Johnson, "Racial and Ethnic Disparities in Sentencing Departures Across Modes of Sentencing," *Criminology* 41:449–490 (2003).

39. Daly and Tonry, note 33.

40. Roy Lotz and John Hewitt, "The Influence of Legally Irrelevant Factors on Felony Sentencing," *Sociological Inquiry* 47:39–48 (1977); John Hewitt, "The Effects of Individual Resources in Judicial Sentencing," *Review of Public Data Use* 5:30–51 (1977); Darrell Steffensmeier, John Kramer, and Cathy Streifel, "Gender and Imprisonment Decisions," *Criminology* 31:411–446 (1993).

41. Kathleen Daly, "Discrimination in the Criminal Courts: Family, Gender, and the Problem of Equal Treatment," *Social Forces* 66:154 (1987).

42. Daly and Tonry, note 33.

43. David Jacobs, "Inequality and the Legal Order: An Ecological Test of the Conflict Model," *Social Problems* 25:515–525 (1978); Alan Lizotte, "Extra-legal Factors in Chicago's Criminal Courts: Testing the Conflict Model of Criminal Justice," *Social Problems* 25:564–580 (1978).

44. Theodore Chiricos and Gordon Waldo, "Socioeconomic Status and Criminal Sentencing: An Empirical Assessment of a Conflict Proposition," *American Sociological Review* 40:753–772 (1975).

45. Gerri Turner and Dean Champion, "The Elderly Offender and Sentencing Leniency," *Journal of Offender Counseling, Services, and Rehabilitation* 13:125–140 (1988/1989).

46. Johnson, note 38.

47. Tracy Snell, *Capital Punishment, 2006—Statistical Tables* (Washington, DC: U.S. Department of Justice, 2007).

48. *Furman v. Georgia*, 408 U.S. 238 (1972).

49. *Gregg v. Georgia*, 428 U.S. 153 (1976).

50. *Coker v. Georgia*, 433 U.S. 584 (1977).

51. *Kennedy v. Louisiana*, note 8.

52. *McCleskey v. Kemp*, 481 U.S. 279 (1986).

53. *Penry v. Lynaugh*, 492 U.S. 302 (1989).

54. *Atkins v. Virginia*, 536 U.S. 304 (2002).

55. *Payne v. Tennessee*, 498 U.S. 1076 (1991).

56. *Booth v. Maryland*, 482 U.S. 496 (1987); *South Carolina v. Gathers*, 490 U.S. 805 (1989).

57. *Payne v. Tennessee*, note 55.

58. *Roper v. Simmons*, 543 U.S. 551 (2005).

59. *Stanford v. Kentucky*, 492 U.S. 361 (1989).

60. Jeremy Peters, "Death Penalty Repealed in New Jersey," available at http://www.nytimes.com/2007/12/17/nyregion/17cnd-jersey.html, accessed August 28, 2008; Keith Richburg, "N.J. Approves Abolition of Death Penalty; Corzine to Sign," available at http://www.washingtonpost.com/wp-dyn/content/article/2007/12/13/AR2007121301302.html, accessed January 1, 2008.

61. Snell, note 47.

62. Adam Liptak, "Executions Decline Elsewhere, but Texas Holds Steady," available at http://www.nytimes.com/2007/12/26/us/25cnd-death.html, accessed January 1, 2008.

63. Snell, note 47.

64. *Hill v. Florida*, No. SC06-2 (2006).

65. *Baze et al., v. Rees*, No. 07-5439 (2008).

66. *Baze et al., v. Rees*, note 65; See also Ron Word, "High Court to Hear Lethal Injection Case," *Mercury News*, April 23, 2006, p. A1; Bill Mears, "Justices: Does Lethal Injection Hurt?" available at http://www.cnn.com.2006/LAW/04/26/scotus.injection/index.html, accessed January 15, 2008.

67. Wilson, note 1, p. 178.

68. Isaac Ehrlich, "The Deterrent Effect of Capital Punishment: A Question of Life and Death," *American Economic Review* 65:397–417 (1976).

69. Paul Zimmerman, "State Executions, Deterrence, and the Incidence of Murder," *Journal of Applied Economics* 7:163–193 (2004).

70. Hashem Dezhbakhsh, Paul Rubin, and Joanna Shepherd, "Does Capital Punishment Have a Deterrent Effect? Evidence from Postmoratorium Panel Data," *American Law and Economics Review* 5:344–376 (2003).

71. Lydia Saad, "Racial Disagreement Over Death Penalty Has Varied Historically," available at http://www.gallup.com/poll/28243/Racial-Disagreement-Over-Death-Penalty-Has-Varied-Historically.aspx, accessed August 1, 2008.

72. Pamela Paul, "The Death Penalty," *American Demographics* 23:22–23 (2001).

73. Federal Bureau of Investigation, *Crime in the United States, 2007* (Washington, DC: U.S. Department of Justice, 2008).

74. Thomas Keil and Gennaro Vito, "Race and the Death Penalty in Kentucky Murder Trials: An Analysis of Post-*Gregg* Outcomes," *Justice Quarterly* 7:189–206 (1990); Samuel Gross and Robert Mauro, *Death and Discrimination: Racial Disparities in Capital Sentencing* (Boston: Northeastern University Press, 1989); Raymond Paternoster, "Prosecutorial Discretion in Requesting the Death Penalty: A Case of Victim-Based Racial Discrimination," *Law and Society Review* 18:437–478 (1984); Michael Radelet and Glenn Pierce, "Race and Prosecutorial Discretion in Homicide Cases," *Law and Society Review* 19:587–621 (1985); Hans Zeisel, "Race Bias in the Administration of the Death Penalty: The Florida Experience," *Harvard Law Review* 95:456–468 (1981); Kleck, note 30.

75. Marvin Wolfgang, Arlene Kelly, and Hans Nolde, "Comparison of the Executed and Commuted Among Admissions to Death Row," *Journal of Criminal Law and Criminology* 53:301–310 (1962).

76. David Baldus, Charles Pulaski, and George Woodworth, "Comparative Review of Death Sentences: An Empirical Study of the Georgia Experience," *Journal of Criminal Law and Criminology* 74:661–685 (1983); David Baldus and George Woodworth, "Race Discrimination in the Administration of the Death Penalty: An Overview of the Empirical Evidence with Special Emphasis on the Post-1990 Research," *Criminal Law Bulletin* 39:194–227 (2003).

77. Glenn Pierce and Michael Radelet, "The Impact of Legally Inappropriate Factors on Death Sentencing for California Homicides, 1990–1999," *Santa Clara Law Review* 46:1–47 (2005).

78. Elizabeth Rapaport, "The Death Penalty and Gender Discrimination," *Law and Society Review* 25:367–383 (1991); Dawson and Boland, note 31.

79. Joanna Shepherd, "Deterrence Versus Brutalization: Capital Punishment's Differing Impacts Among the States," *Michigan Law Review* 104:203–255 (2005); Carol Steiker, "No, Capital Punishment Is Not Morally Required: Deterrence, Deontology, and the Death Penalty," *Stanford Law Review* 58:751–790 (2005).

80. William Bowers, "The Effect of Executions Is Brutalization, Not Deterrence," in Kenneth Haas and James Inciardi (Eds.), *Challenging Capital Punishment: Legal and Social Science Approaches* (Newbury Park, CA: Sage, 1988), pp. 49–89. See also William Bowers and Glenn Pierce, "Deterrence or Brutalization? What Is the Effect of Executions?" *Crime & Delinquency* 26:453–484 (1980).

81. Michael Radelet and Marian Borg, "The Changing Nature of Death Penalty Debates," *Annual Review of Sociology* 26:43–61 (2000); John Donohue and Justin Wolfers, "Uses and Abuses of Empirical Evidence in the Death Penalty Debate," *Stanford Law Review* 58:791–846 (2005).

82. Richard Willing, "DNA to Clear 200th Person," *USA Today*, April 23, 2007, p. 1A.

83. Samuel Gross, Kristen Jacoby, Daniel Matheson, Nicholas Montgomery, and Sujata Patil, "Exonerations in the United States, 1989 through 2003," *Journal of Criminal Law and Criminology* 95:523–560 (2005).

84. *McCleskey v. Kemp*, note 52.

85. *McCleskey v. Zant*, 499 U.S. 467 (1991).

Once offenders have been convicted and sentenced, they enter the corrections segment of the criminal justice system. Corrections include those programs or institutions designed to punish, confine, or rehabilitate people convicted of crimes.

Part IV examines the history of U.S. corrections, the various reform movements responsible for its transformation, the structure of modern corrections and the contemporary prison, and the movement toward greater use of community corrections. The history of corrections, the birth (and rebirth) of the prison, and the structure of state and federal prison systems today are explored in Chapter 10. Chapter 11 examines the contemporary institution of the prison, the characteristics of prisoners, prison management, life in prison for male and female inmates, and the effects of the prisoners' rights movement. Chapter 12 looks at community corrections, into which the vast majority of people who commit crimes are placed.

PART

Corrections

Corrections History and Structure

OBJECTIVES

1 Understand the history and evolution of corrections in the United States.

2 Know the organization of U.S. prison systems and the various types and security levels available.

3 Grasp the unique nature of military prisons and facilities for the confinement of terrorists.

4 Become familiar with the history, operation, and characteristics of jail systems.

PROFILES IN CRIME AND JUSTICE

Art Beeler
Warden
Federal Correctional Complex
Butner, North Carolina

I found my way into corrections because I found myself without resources to go to law school. My mentor knew I was paying my way through school and that I needed the money so he set me up with a paid internship. So in a way, institutional corrections found me. At the end of the internship. I started as a Correctional Officer at the Federal Reformatory in Petersburg, Virginia, and have never looked back.

For the past 21 years, I have had the honor of serving as a warden at six different federal correctional institutions. As different as they all were, the one thing they had in common was good staff. Staff is the foundation of any institution. Leadership matters, but line staff keep the institution and public safe, provide care for the offender, and deal with all the bureaucracy along the way. Being warden of a prison is much like being a CEO of any major company. You deal with budget (or the lack of budget), personnel, discipline and cheerleading, and a large number of inmates, most of whom do not want to be where they are and a few who would kill you as soon as look at you.

The world of being a warden today is certainly different than when I first became one in 1987. The rules have become more complicated, and decision making is less autonomous. The close public scrutiny and "Monday-morning quarterbacking" have become intense. Even with these changes, it is still a job I enjoy most days. The days I do not enjoy are ones when I have to fire staff who are good people but who have made bad choices. I have no problem firing or arresting staff who are corrupt or abuse their power. The days I most enjoy are ones when staff I have helped along the way are promoted. Other good days are when an offender or ex-offender, who no one gave a snowball's chance of doing well, proves us wrong and succeeds on the outside.

When I talk to college classes, I advise students first to learn as much as they can about interpersonal communication, which includes the ability to talk with and listen to people. Second on my list is for students to improve their ability to write. You would not believe the number of bright people who cannot write. Third, students should learn Spanish (I wish I had). Fourth, develop some computer proficiency and ability to do data analysis—many employees have the proficiency part down pat, but lack the ability to analyze what the information says. Finally, you will need the moral strength to work in a negative environment. Prison is not a place where you will get warm fuzzies.

Introduction

In the United States, once offenders have been prosecuted, convicted, and sentenced, they enter the **correctional system**. This system consists of institutions such as jails, reformatories, and prisons and the correctional practices of parole, intermediate sanctions, and probation. It employs more than 700,000 people and has total costs of nearly $61 billion each year.[1]

Within the correctional system, three major settings focus on incarceration: jails, reformatories, and prisons. Although these terms are sometimes used interchangeably, they describe different types of facilities:

- **Jails** are used to confine people who are awaiting trial and people who have been sentenced to short-term incarceration (one year or less), typically those convicted of misdemeanors or petty offenses.
- **Reformatories** typically confine younger, first-time offenders between the ages of 16 and 30 who have been tried as adults and convicted of felonies.

- **Prisons** are used for long-term confinement (more than one year) for serious or repeat felony offenders.

The modern American corrections system differs significantly from its early form in the colonial period and reflects changes in how people perceive crime, criminals, and victims. When people's perceptions about these phenomena change, their reactions to them change as well. Thus it is not surprising that state and federal corrections have undergone numerous reforms that parallel changes in society's perceptions of crime.

Early American Prisons

In 1787, the Philadelphia Society for Alleviating the Miseries of Public Prisons was established to bring about changes in how offenders were treated. Led by social reformers Benjamin Rush and Benjamin Franklin, the Society sought to replace capital and corporal punishments with incarceration. It proposed the establishment of a prison program that would accomplish the following goals:

- Classify prisoners by gender and type of offense
- Provide labor for individual inmates to perform
- Include gardens to provide food and outdoor areas for recreation
- Classify convicts according to a judgment about the nature of the crime (whether it arose out of passion, habit, temptation, or mental illness)
- Impose indeterminate periods of confinement based on the convicts' reformative progress[2]

In 1790, the Pennsylvania state legislature established a wing of the Walnut Street Jail as a **penitentiary house**—that is, as a place of penitence and repentance for all "hardened and atrocious offenders."[3] However, overcrowding, lack of productive work for inmates, incompetent personnel, and public apathy ultimately led to the jail's closing in 1835.

The Pennsylvania Model

In the early nineteenth century, the Pennsylvania state legislature ordered the construction of the Eastern State Penitentiary in Philadelphia. Inmates were kept in isolation. Separation was built into the physical structure of the prison; inmates were confined in single cells where they ate, slept, prayed, and worked. **Separate confinement** had the following aims:

Eastern State Penitentiary was once the most luxurious prison in the United States.

- To provide opportunities for hard work and selective forms of suffering without vengeful treatment
- To prevent the prison from becoming a corrupting influence
- To allow time for reflection and repentance
- To provide punishing discipline by denying social contact
- To lessen the amount of time necessary to benefit from the penitential experience
- To ease the financial burden of imprisonment by minimizing the number of prison keepers required[4]

The Eastern prison (known as Cherry Hill because its site had once been a cherry orchard) became well established as one of the most famous prisons in the world. Cherry Hill looked like a square wheel with seven wings, each containing 76 cells, radiating from a central hub where prison officials were stationed. Each inmate was placed in a solitary cell with a private exercise yard, which the inmate was permitted to use one hour per day.

The Auburn system was seen as an advance in penology but was characterized by brutality.

To eliminate distractions, Cherry Hill prisoners spent their entire sentences in their cells, where they worked at handcrafts such as shoemaking, spinning, and weaving. Inmates wore blindfolds whenever they were taken to or from their cells and were not allowed to speak to each other. Even the guards who brought them food were not allowed to talk to them. Inmates were referred to only by numbers (rather than by their names) for the duration of their sentences. Visits with relatives were forbidden, and inmates were not allowed to receive mail.[5]

Despite their efforts and public expectations, complete isolation did more to damage the sanity and health of the inmates than it did to instill sorrow for wrongdoings.[6] The very modest prison labor carried out in individual cells and the requirement that all inmates were to be fed in their cells meant that the institution was also extremely costly.

The New York Model

The New York state legislature adopted a different strategy for handling criminals and ordered the construction of the Auburn Prison, which opened in 1829 in central New York. Rather than being a system of separate confinement, this prison followed a paramilitary program called the **congregate system** (or silent system). In this model, prisoners were isolated during the night but worked together during the day under a strict rule of silence.

The cells in the Auburn Prison were much smaller than those at Cherry Hill, and no light could penetrate them, which made them damp in the summer and cold in the winter. Some of the trademarks of early prisons—including black-and-white uniforms and lock-step marches—originated at the Auburn Prison in an effort to treat all prisoners equally, make supervision easier, and prevent conversation between inmates.[7]

Criticisms of the Two Models

Ultimately, neither the Pennsylvania model nor the New York model rehabilitated inmates very well. Critics of the Pennsylvania model held that these kinds of prisons were too expensive to build and operate and that separate confinement led to widespread insanity within the prison population. Opponents of the New York model argued that the system was too cruel and inhumane to affect people's lives in a positive way.[8] In the end, the New York model was more widely adopted in the United States for one principal reason: It reinforced the emerging industrial philosophy that allowed states to use convict labor to defray prison costs.[9]

Reformation of Penology

As the inmate population increased, prison reformers started to question the future of a prison system that had become overcrowded, understaffed, and financially floundering. As an alternative to large, sterile, forbidding prisons designed to isolate and punish offenders, a new treatment philosophy began to emerge—one built on the idea that offenders could be reformed when provided with the right incentives. This reformatory movement was initiated through the efforts of people such as Captain Alexander Maconochie in Australia, Sir Walter Crofton in Ireland, and Enoch Wines and Zebulon Brockway in the United States.[10]

The Mark System

For nearly two centuries, from 1597 until 1776, England had transported its worst criminals to the United States. The exact number of offenders England sent to America is unknown; estimates vary between 15,000 and 100,000.[11] The practice ended with the American Revolution, after which England began transporting its criminals to Australia.

In 1840, Captain Alexander Maconochie was placed in charge of one of the worst British penal colonies, located about 1000 miles off Australia's coast on Norfolk Island. This site was where twice-condemned criminals were sent—offenders who had committed felonies in England, been transported to Australia, and committed additional crimes there. In response to the brutal treatment that had been instituted on Norfolk Island before his arrival, Maconochie introduced humane reforms that would give prisoners some degree of hope for their future. He proposed the following changes, known as the **mark system**:

- Criminal sentences should not be for a specific period of time; rather, release would be based on the performance of a specified quantity of labor.
- The quantity of labor that prisoners must perform should be expressed in a number of marks that must be earned before their release.
- While in prison, inmates should earn everything they receive; all sustenance and indulgences should be added to their debts of mark.
- Prisoners would be required to work in groups of six or seven people, and the entire group should be held accountable for the behavior of each of its members.
- Prisoners, while still obliged to earn their daily tally of marks, should be given proprietary interest in their own labor and be subject to a less rigorous discipline so as to prepare them for release into society.[12]

The Irish System

Sir Walter Crofton of Ireland was impressed with Maconochie's idea of preparing convicts for their eventual return to society. He proposed a similar set of reforms in a program called the Irish system or indeterminate system, based on the idea "that criminals can be reformed, but only through employment in a free community where they are subjected to ordinary temptations."[13]

Under Crofton's plan, an inmate's release was based on sustained good behavior. Prisoners moved through a series of stages, where each stage was characterized by increasing freedom and responsibilities, and were ultimately placed in a work environment outside the prison as part of their conditional release. This program was referred to as a ticket-of-leave for inmates who agreed to live up to the conditions attached to their release and was the forerunner to our modern system of parole.

The Elmira Model

Based on what he saw in the Irish system, American reformer Enoch Wines believed that some criminals—specifically younger ones—could be successfully rehabilitated.[14] This idea was adopted as part of the National Prison Association's Declaration of Principles, a document consisting of 37 proposals advocating a philosophy of reformation that included the classification of inmates based on a mark system, indeterminate sentencing, and the cultivation of the inmate's self-respect. The first institution in the United States to implement this new ideology was the Elmira Reformatory, built in Elmira, New York.

In 1876, the Elmira Reformatory began receiving inmates between the ages of 10 and 30. Elmira was built much like the Auburn Prison, with inside cell blocks for solitary confinement at night and communal workshops. However, some of its cells were built with outside courtyards, similar to those at Cherry Hill. Inmates were subject to indeterminate sentencing, much like their counterparts in the Irish system. Prisoners received a maximum sentence but could win early release on parole if they exhibited good behavior. At entry, all prisoners were placed in the second grade. After six months of good conduct, they were promoted to the first grade. Another six months of continued good conduct entitled them to parole. Prisoners who misbehaved were demoted to the third level, where a month's good conduct was required to restore them to the second grade. Inmates who regularly misbehaved were obliged to serve their maximum sentence.

The enlightened concepts of the reformers gave way once more to a more control-oriented approach to corrections. At Elmira and elsewhere, custody reemerged as the primary goal and punishment as the method for controlling prisoners.[15]

Prisons for Women

More than 115,400 women, accounting for just over 7 percent of all prisoners, are currently confined in U.S. state and federal prisons,[16] and an additional 100,000 women are held in local jails.[17] Although new studies are beginning to shed light on the early treatment of women in prison, relatively little has been written about the imprisonment of women during the nineteenth century or the overall contributions of women to corrections. Some early lawmakers believed female prisoners threatened the social order by sinning and by removing the "moral constraints on men." They assumed that, by their nature, women were more chaste and virtuous than men. Consequently, it was thought that incarcerated women had fallen even further than men because it was assumed that they were initially more pure.[18]

Historically, female offenders were housed with male inmates, though today most are incarcerated in separate women's-only facilities.

Some early reformers viewed incarcerated women—and particularly prostitutes—as a "serious eugenic danger to society."[19] They feared that female criminals might produce defective offspring—a perceived threat to society that prompted some states to pass laws providing for the sterilization of female inmates. In addition to imprisonment, women were subject to harsh punishments, including whipping and death by hanging, because it was widely held that some women, due to some sort of inherent deficiency, could not be reformed.

Reform Efforts

American reformers lobbied for female wardens to govern female inmates, and in 1822, Maryland became the first state to hire a female jail keeper, Rachel Perijo. Nearly from the beginning, female offenders were confined in the same penitentiaries as men. Generally, women were placed in separate cells or a small wing of the facility. For example, the first women admitted to the Auburn Prison in 1825 were placed in the third-floor attic. As the number of female inmates increased, however, separate buildings were built at the prisons to house women. The Mount Pleasant Female Prison—the first facility exclusively devoted to female offenders—opened in 1835.[20]

Although women were separated from male offenders, they still endured many physical hardships. In 1843, Sing Sing penitentiary in New York, best known for the long-term incarceration of hardened male prisoners, included a small number of female inmates. This institution housed mothers with children, pregnant women, and other females in small, crowded, and unsanitary rooms, where they were often beaten for even minor rule violations.[21]

Most of the women incarcerated in reformatories were younger, white, and not considered dangerous; they were typically convicted of misdemeanors. African American females were segregated into separate cottages. Although a few reformatories emphasized outdoor labor, most offered little more than domestic training, and women were rewarded for maintaining a feminine appearance.[22]

By 1900, female prison administrators, in contrast to their counterparts in reformatories, were more concerned with prison management than with the inmates' moral condition. Moreover, the Great Depression of the 1930s had a dramatic effect on prison populations. Reformatories and prisons started receiving larger numbers of female felons, and as additional institutions were built, an increasing number of female administrators began to manage the institutions.

Rebirth of the Prison

By the early twentieth century, crime appeared to have reached epidemic proportions in the United States. Prison populations were swelling and demands for new prisons increased. As public support for the reformatory system declined, penologists blamed crime on bad people, not on bad laws; they saw criminals as defective people, rather than as the victims of an arbitrary and capricious criminal justice system. This line of thinking set the stage for the emergence of a new ideology that perceived prisoners as sick people who were in need of treatment. This philosophy exerted a profound influence on corrections, laying the groundwork for a new model with changes in prison design and operations. Prison reform came to mean the addition of libraries, recreation facilities, schools, and vocational programs.

Particularly interesting among these innovations were the vocational programs. Like the hard labor programs that preceded them, vocational programs were grounded in the idea that inmates needed to work. The new philosophy, however, emphasized the idea that inmates needed to work so they would be prepared with a trade and good work habits upon their release so they could find employment.

Prison Industry

The vocational programs developed as part of the reform movement meant that inmates learned skilled labor and could produce goods that were sold by the state to defray the costs of prison operations. Perhaps not surprisingly, these industrial prisons faced stiff opposition from private industry, which could not compete with the low cost of prison-made goods made possible by the low inmate wages. Responding to pressure from organized labor, between 1929 and 1940, Congress passed three federal statutes that brought an end to the industrial prison.

With the passage of the **Hawes–Cooper Act** in 1929, prison-made products became subject to the laws of the state to which they were being shipped. In 1935, Congress passed the **Ashurst–Sumners Act**, which prohibited the transportation of prison goods to any state whose laws forbade it. This act was later amended in 1940 to exclude almost all prison-made products from interstate commerce.

In 1979, Congress passed the **Percy Amendment**, which allowed states to sell prison-made goods across state lines as long as they complied with strict rules, such as making sure unions were consulted and preventing prison-based manufacturers from undercutting existing wage structures.[23] As a result of the Percy Amendment, prison industry rapidly expanded and engaged an increasing number of inmates in meaningful work experiences. Although some states continue to prohibit the sale of prison-made goods, most provide opportunities for private-sector employment of inmates. Some prison-made goods are even sold over the Internet to buyers around the world. Maryland, for example, has put its 182-page catalog of prison-made goods online (http://www.dpscs.state.nd.us/mce/products.shtml). The sale of these goods, which range from furniture to clothing, helps to offset the cost of incarceration and contributes funds to victim compensation and restitution programs.

FOCUS ON CRIMINAL JUSTICE

Made on the Inside to Be Worn on the Outside

In 1997, voters in Oregon passed Ballot Measure 49, which required the Oregon Department of Corrections to create inmate work programs to defray the costs of incarceration. Approximately 80 percent of an inmate's wages is held by the institution and applied toward the cost of room and board, victim restitution, child support, and taxes. The remaining 20 percent is invested in an inmate savings account, which becomes available to the inmate at the time of his or her release.

One result of Measure 49 was the creation of a line of clothing called Prison Blues, which is produced at the Eastern Oregon Correctional Facility in Pendleton, Oregon. Prisoners are paid the prevailing industry wages to produce a clothing line that includes blue jeans, denim jackets, sweatshirts, T-shirts, and yard coats.

Initially sold only through a limited number of retail stores, Prison Blues has expanded into markets in Asia and Europe via an arrangement with a catalog distributor and established an Internet-based store (www.prisonblues.com). In 2002, Rob Waibel, 20-time world champion in lumberjack sports competitions including tree climbing, axe throwing, log rolling, wood chopping, and cross-cut sawing, endorsed the Prison Blues brand; he wears the clothing as he competes. According to Waibel, "Prison Blues makes the toughest, U.S.A.-made work jean I have been able to find. In addition, it is a company with a purpose and objective I believe in."

Sources: "Prison Blues Launches Online Retail Store," available at http://www.Prisonblues.com, accessed August 17, 2008; Robert Goldfield, "Prison Blues Hoping to Find Favor in Germany," *Portland Business Journal* (April 13, 2001), available at http://portland.bizjournals.com/portland/stories/2001/04/16/newscolumn5.html, accessed August 31, 2008.

Work Release

Work release was authorized by the federal government through the Federal Prisoner Rehabilitation Act of 1965. This act permitted prisoners (usually those in minimum-security prisons) to work outside the institution during the day and return after work. Inmates in work-release programs typically are expected to contribute some portion of their wages for their room and board, but they also have greater access to drug or alcohol treatment programs in the community and are able to draw upon a wide variety of community resources to increase the likelihood of their success upon reentry into society.

Conjugal Visits

Conjugal visits—that is, private visits between inmates and their spouses intended to help them maintain interpersonal and sexual relationships and strengthen the family unit—became widely used in many states in the 1960s. In 1968, the California Correctional Institute at Tehachapi permitted inmates nearing parole a three-day-per-month family visitation pass that brought an inmate's spouse (and children, when appropriate) to an apartment within the prison compound. Generally, the inmate and his or her spouse and children stayed in the apartment until the visit was over. This community-based concept was endorsed by the National Advisory Commission on Criminal Justice Standards. Today, in part because of increased concerns with security, only six states—California, Connecticut, Mississippi, New Mexico, New York, and Washington—permit conjugal visits.[24]

Modern Prisons

On June 30, 2007, 1,595,034 men and women were incarcerated in state and federal prisons in the United States; an additional 780,581 were held in local jails. Between 2006 and

TABLE 10-1 **States with the Highest and Lowest Incarceration Rates**

State	Rate per 100,000 Population
States with the Highest Incarceration Rates	
Louisiana	857
Mississippi	723
Texas	682
Oklahoma	670
Alabama	611
U.S. Average	**509**
States with the Lowest Incarceration Rates	
Rhode Island	229
North Dakota	224
New Hampshire	212
Minnesota	190
Maine	133

Source: William Sabol and Heather Couture, *Prison and Jail Inmates at Midyear 2007* (Washington, DC: U.S. Department of Justice, 2008).

2007, the number of inmates held in state and federal prisons increased by 1.6 percent.[25] The prison incarceration rate in the United States is 509 inmates per 100,000 population, although there is substantial variation in rates of imprisonment among the states.[26] TABLE 10-1 compares the states with the highest and lowest total incarceration rates.

Prison Security Levels

The federal government and all state governments operate a system of correctional institutions. These institutions are classified according to their level of security—that is, the amount of security required to safely confine inmates with different levels of potential for violence or escape:

- Minimum
- Low
- Medium
- Maximum
- Super-maximum

Each security category has its own unique characteristics that determine the nature of the prison environment.

There are approximately 814 **minimum-security prisons** in operation around the country, including work camps and farms. These institutions do not have high walls or armed guards in towers, but often have fences around their perimeters. Most inmates in these institutions are serving relatively short sentences for less serious offenses such as property and drug crimes. Work furloughs and education programs are widely available, and inmates receive more privileges and are given more personal time for recreational activities than their counterparts in more secure prisons. This security level is designed for nondangerous, stable offenders, who are given the opportunity to avoid the stress and violence found in more secure facilities.

Low-security facilities, as established by the Federal Bureau of Prisons, operate between medium and minimum security levels. They typically house nonviolent offenders with drug or alcohol problems. Low-security facilities have double-fenced perimeters, mostly dormitory or cubicle housing, and strong work and program components.

In **medium-security prisons**, correctional officers typically are not armed and there are no high walls. In fact, many of the 522 medium-security prisons in operation today have been built using a campus design, allowing inmates to live in single rooms that have a window or in dormitory-style housing rather than in cells (which have three solid walls and an obtrusive steel security door). In these facilities, inmates are typically a mix of violent and property offenders serving less than life sentences. Medium-security prisons may give the impression that inmates are not under constant surveillance, but they are actually closely supervised by unobtrusive surveillance equipment such as hidden cameras.

Nationally, 332 **maximum-security prisons** collectively house more than 245,000 prisoners.[27] They are designed to prevent escape and to exert maximum control over inmates. Many resemble Auburn Prison, with high walls, watchtowers, and barbed wire or electronic fences to deter escape attempts. These fortress-like structures are home to many of society's most violent offenders. Inmate privacy is limited in these facilities, which include open bathrooms and showers; inmates may be subjected to full-body searches, especially after seeing visitors.

Some states and the federal government have recently constructed **super-maximum-security prisons**, where the most predatory or dangerous criminals are confined. Only 20 years ago, the only super-max prison was a federal facility located in Marion, Illinois. Today, there are at least 57 super-max institutions located in more than 40 states that serve a total inmate population of about 20,000, although these facilities remain somewhat controversial (see "Focus on Criminal Justice," p. 269).[28] According to the National Institute of Corrections, super-max prisons seek to provide maximum control over inmates who have exhibited violent or seriously disruptive behavior while incarcerated and are viewed as a security threat in standard correctional settings.[29] In super-maximum-security facilities, inmates are separated, their movement is restricted, and they have only limited direct access to staff and other inmates. These facilities are the most expensive institutions in the correctional system, sometimes having twice the per-inmate cost of maximum-security prisons.[30]

Prison Farms and Camps

A number of state correctional systems operate minimum-security prison farms and forestry camps. The inmates who are placed in these facilities are typically serving short sentences and are considered very-low-risk offenders. **Prison farms** produce much of the livestock, dairy products, and vegetables used to feed inmates in the state prisons. For example, the Bolduc Correctional Facility in Maine, which was built in the early 1930s, became one of the largest dairy and beef farms in the state; it currently produces potatoes and dried beans for Maine correctional facilities.[31]

Prison forestry camps, sometimes known as conservation camps, provide labor for the maintenance of state parks, tree planting and thinning, wildlife care, maintenance of fish hatcheries, and cleanup of roads and highways. Some camps, such as the South Fork Forest Camp in Oregon and Sugar Pine Conservation Camp in California, provide a labor source for fighting forest fires. These inmate crews are paid $1 per hour (which is significantly more than their standard pay while incarcerated in the camp) to provide emergency firefighting assistance as well as to respond to floods, search and rescues, and earthquakes.[32]

Boot Camps

Boot camps are highly structured and regimented correctional facilities where inmates undergo rigorous physical conditioning and discipline. Boot camps were established in

FOCUS ON CRIMINAL JUSTICE

Life in a Super-Max Prison

In most super-maximum-security prisons, inmates spend 23 hours a day locked in their 7 × 14 foot cells. A light remains on in the cell at all times, though it is sometimes dimmed. Cells have solid metal doors with metal strips along their sides and bottoms that prevent conversation or communication with other inmates. All meals are taken alone in the inmate's cell instead of in a common eating area.

Super-max inmates around the country experience additional security when they venture outside their cells. For example, at California's Pelican Bay State Prison, during the hour inmates are not in their cells, they are typically strip-searched, shackled, and then transported by guards to the exercise room or shower, where the chains are removed. To ensure the safety of the prison staff, contact between inmates and staff members is kept to a minimum. In some super-max prisons, inmates are not transported by guards to shower or exercise. Instead, an inmate is moved from one location to another by the use of intercoms, automatic doors, and surveillance cameras controlled by guards in a separate location. Some super-max prisons have been designed for constant monitoring of all inmates. At the Illinois Closed Maximum Security Correctional Center, for example, inmates are housed in a number of pods (similar to those in the new-generation jails, discussed later in this chapter), with 60 cells surrounding a central control station.

Most politicians and citizens are supportive of super-max prisons, believing that they provide the greatest safety for both inmates and staff. Critics argue that the near-total isolation of inmates such prisons enforce likely produces serious psychological and emotional problems. Inmates may begin to exhibit symptoms of psychiatric decomposition, depression, psychological withdrawal, and heightened anxiety, and some even lose touch with reality. Critics also charge that the extreme deprivations in super-max prisons may violate inmates' Eighth Amendment protection against cruel and unusual punishment.

Sources: Charles Pettigrew, "Technology and the Eighth Amendment: The Problem of Supermax Prisons," *North Carolina Journal of Law and Technology* 4:191–215 (2002); Robert Sheppard, Jeffrey Geiger, and George Welborn, "Closed Maximum Security: The Illinois Supermax," *Corrections Today* 58:84–87, 106 (1996); Terry Kupers, *Prison Madness: The Mental Health Crisis Behind Bars and What We Must Do about It* (San Francisco: Jossey-Bass, 1999); Hans Toch, "The Future of Supermax Confinement," *Prison Journal* 81:376–388 (2001).

27 states and the federal system in the early 1980s and quickly gained favor with politicians and the public looking for high-profile, "get-tough" responses to crime.

Initially a military-style, get-tough initiative, boot camps today stress educational and vocational training.

Offenders who are eligible for boot camps are generally young adults (younger than 30 years of age) serving their first prison term. They are typically given a choice of a boot camp or a traditional prison. If they elect the boot camp option, their sentence will be shorter (90 to 180 days), but what is expected of them will be very demanding. Offenders who successfully complete boot camp are released to community supervision. Inmates who fail boot camp (for example, those who drop out or break rules) are returned to traditional prisons, where they serve out their complete sentences.

Despite their growing popularity in the 1990s, at which point more than 7000 inmates were housed in approximately 75 adult state and federal boot camps around the nation, one third of the state-run camps had closed by 2000. The Federal Bureau of Prisons closed all of its boot camps in 2005.[33]

Military Prisons

The military penal system differs significantly from the state and federal systems. First, the military has its own criminal code, called the *Uniform Code of Military Justice*. Many of

Since April 28, 2002, Camp Delta in Guantanamo Bay, Cuba, has detained Al Qaeda and Taliban enemy combatants.

its rules are peculiar to the armed services. For example, civilians can quit their jobs and walk away, but military personnel who walk away from their jobs are court-marshaled. Similarly, civilians who disobey an order from their bosses may be fired, but they cannot be prosecuted. By contrast, military personnel who disobey a lawful order from a superior are usually prosecuted in a military court. If convicted, they are sentenced to a military prison.

The military prison system operates 59 facilities, which currently hold about 2400 inmates. The most common offense among military inmates is rape, followed by drug possession and trafficking. Only a relatively small percentage (about 12 percent) of the inmates have been convicted of desertion, malingering, being absent without leave (AWOL), or other specifically military offenses.[34]

The United States Disciplinary Barracks, located in a portion of Fort Leavenworth Prison in Kansas, is the only maximum-security prison operated by the Department of Defense. It houses nearly 1400 prisoners from all branches of the military. The Miramar Naval Consolidated Brig is designated for female personnel only.

The Navy also operates a unique set of correctional facilities aboard ships at sea to supplement its waterfront brigs at major naval bases. On any given day, approximately 150 sailors are confined in onboard brigs around the world.[35] The military also operates 11 overseas correctional Army and Air Force facilities; in 2002, these facilities confined 142 inmates.[36]

Camp Delta: A Prison for Terrorists

The Pentagon runs one of the most unusual prisons in the U.S. correctional system: **Camp Delta**, which is located at the Guantanamo Naval Base in Cuba and operated by U.S. Military Police. Shortly after the terrorist attacks on September 11, 2001, President George W. Bush issued a military order for the "Detention, Treatment, and Trial of Certain Non-citizens in the War against Terrorism." This order authorized the Secretary of Defense to detain any persons subject to the order. In early 2002, the first Al Qaeda and Taliban inmates from Afghanistan arrived at the temporary Guantanamo detention facility known as Camp X-Ray. A few months later, Camp Delta, a permanent facility for confinement of suspected terrorists, opened to hold more than 300 detainees.[37] According to camp officials, the detainees held at Camp Delta are viewed as very dangerous and have expressed a commitment to kill Americans and its allies if released. They are not classified as common criminals, but rather as "enemy combatants" detained because of their acts of war against the United States.[38]

Co-correctional Prisons

One approach to reducing some of the pains of imprisonment for U.S. inmates is reflected in the relatively small number of **co-correctional prisons** or "coed" prisons, where men and women are confined in the same institution. Until recently, men and women were often housed together in the same institutions, often even the same cells. The contemporary approach has been to create sexually integrated institutions, where inmates are housed separately but interact in normal institutional activities.

There are currently 21 co-correctional prisons located throughout the United States.[39] Most of these are small, minimum-security prisons, although there are some medium- and maximum-security coed institutions. In these prisons, inmates live in sexually segregated housing units—either in different buildings, in walled-off wings of buildings, or in separate cottages. During the day and evening hours, men and women come together in prison shops, educational or vocational programs, and recreational activities.

A major concern in coed prisons is how to regulate physical contact between inmates. The rules governing such contact vary greatly between institutions. In some prisons, all touching is prohibited; in others, inmates are allowed to hold hands or walk arm-in-arm.

Moreover, an increasing body of evidence suggests that male and female prisoners may not generally benefit equally from coed prisons. Criminologists John Smykla and Jimmy Williams report that while coed prisons increase economic, educational, vocational, and social opportunities for male prisoners, female inmates do not realize equivalent benefits from these arrangements.[40] Perhaps owing to the lack of significant advantages demonstrated by these prisons and to their opponents' preference for the get-tough approach to punishment, many co-correctional facilities have closed in recent years.[41]

The Federal Prison System

Although most of the penal institutions in the United States are operated by the various states, cities, and counties, the federal government has its own prison system that is operated by the U.S. Bureau of Prisons, a division of the Department of Justice. Today, more than 106 federal correctional institutions employ about 35,000 people across seven regional offices. The Federal Bureau of Prisons (BOP) operates numerous facilities, including the following:

- *U.S. penitentiaries.* The BOP currently operates six maximum-security U.S. penitentiaries. These institutions are designed to house male inmates who have been convicted of serious crimes and are serving long sentences.
- *Federal correctional institutions.* These 40 institutions are lower-security facilities designed to house male and female prisoners who are serving terms of two to five years in dormitory-style housing.
- *Metropolitan correctional centers.* There are six such centers, housing prisoners who are serving short sentences and offenders of any security level who are awaiting trial or sentencing.
- *Medical centers.* The BOP operates four regional medical centers for patients from any institution in the federal prison system who require medical, surgical, or psychiatric care.
- *Federal prison camps.* The 14 minimum-security federal prison camps are primarily work-oriented facilities for minor federal offenders. These camps use dormitory-style housing and are often located adjacent to larger institutions.
- *Federal detention center.* The single detention center, located in Oakdale, Louisiana, houses pretrial detainees or noncitizens convicted of crimes and awaiting deportation.

In total, more than 201,500 people are being held by the BOP. More than half are white, 93 percent are male, and the majority are incarcerated on drug offenses (see FIGURE 10-1).

Privatization of Correctional Services

Private prisons have become increasingly popular, largely as a response to the rapidly growing prison population. **Privatization** is a process in which state and federal governments contract with the private sector to help construct, finance, and operate correctional facilities for agreed-upon fees.

Since the early 1800s, five types of private prison labor systems have been dominant in the United States:

- *Contract labor system.* Private contractors provide prisons with machinery and raw materials in exchange for the inmate labor to produce finished products.
- *Piece-price system.* Contractors give raw materials to prisons, which use convict labor to produce finished products. Once the goods are manufactured, they are sold by the piece to the contractor, which resells them on the open market.

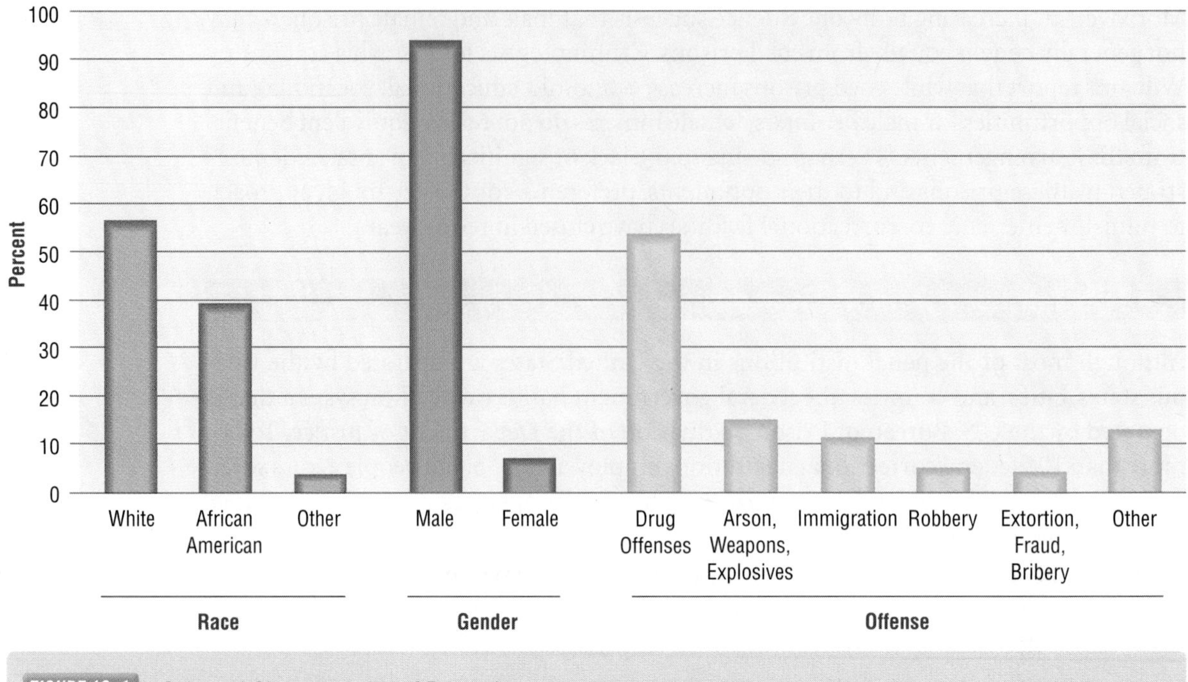

FIGURE 10–1 Selected Characteristics of Prison Inmates

Source: Federal Bureau of Prisons, available at http://www.bop.gov/about/facts.jsp#4, accessed November 7, 2008.

- *Lease system.* Contractors bid against one another to own the rights to inmate labor. Inmates work outside the prison facility, under the supervision of a private contractor, which is responsible for the inmates' food, shelter, and clothing.[42]
- *Public account system.* The state retains control of inmate labor and provides convicts with the machinery and raw materials to produce finished products. The state sells these products on the open market and uses the profits to defray the cost of prison operations.
- *State-use system.* Prison labor is used to produce goods for state-supported institutions (e.g., schools and hospitals).

Privatization continues to be a mainstay of penal philosophy. In the 1980s, with encouragement from President Ronald Reagan, who wanted to involve private enterprise in both state and federal government operations, privatization of prisons began to flourish.[43] Today, state and federal correction agencies contract with private companies that provide a wide range of services, including drug and psychiatric treatment; high school, college, and vocational education; physicians' services; staff ironing; and even the full operation of correctional facilities.[44]

Approximately 118,000 inmates (slightly more than 7 percent of the total U.S. prison population) are confined in more than 150 privately contracted prisons.[45] Nevertheless, privatization is a controversial issue.

Proponents of such prisons argue that private construction is faster and cheaper and that the resulting facilities are less expensive to operate. Costs can be kept down owing to these prisons' lower labor costs (e.g., through use of non-unionized workers and elimination of overtime and employee benefits), less bureaucratic red tape, ability to negotiate item costs, and bulk purchasing.[46] Private firms claim to show greater concern for quality and quantity, with less waste. Private management may also be better at transforming prisons into "factories within fences" to reduce inmate idleness. Research suggests that recidivism rates for inmates released from private prisons are at least as low as those for inmates released from state prisons, with the former individuals' new offenses generally being less serious.[47]

Critics, however, voice a variety of concerns about privatization. Foremost is the constitutionality of delegating the incarceration function to a private entity.[48] Opponents of privatization also argue that the apparent efficiency and cost-effectiveness of privatization will eventually produce less humane treatment for prisoners because private firms have no incentive to reduce overcrowding, as they are paid on a per-prisoner basis. Furthermore, a recent review of 33 cost evaluations comparing private and public prisons found "no overall significant pattern of cost savings for private over public prisons."[49]

Another concern is that personnel in privately owned prisons will be of the "rent-a-cop" variety—that is, poorly trained, unprofessional, undereducated, and willing to accept low wages. In addition, the liability costs of regulating private industry could possibly negate any real savings.[50] What would happen, for example, if a state or federal government contracted with a private agency to detain inmates, and a guard employed by the private contractor shot and killed an inmate who was trying to escape? Such an incident occurred in the 1980s, and a U.S. Court of Appeals ruled that the government could be held legally responsible for the inmate's safety in *Medina v. O'Neill*.[51] In 1997, the Supreme Court, in *Richardson v. McKnight*, held that individual correctional officers employed in private prisons do not have full immunity from civil suits brought by inmates, unlike officers in public prisons.[52] Four years later, in *Correctional Services Corporation v. Malesko*, the Court further defined the rights of inmates in private prisons when it ruled that although an inmate could not sue the prison itself in a civil rights claim, the inmate may file suit against the individual employee of the prison.[53]

Jail Systems

Jails confine the following types of individuals:

- Persons serving short sentences, typically less than one year
- Persons awaiting arraignment, trial, conviction, and sentencing
- Persons who are in violation of their probation or parole, or who absconded while out on bail
- Mentally ill persons and individuals awaiting movement to a mental health facility
- Persons who are in protective custody, in contempt of court, or in witness protection programs
- Federal or state inmates from overcrowded facilities

Colonial Jails

The earliest jails in America were built in the 1650s and typically consisted of a house-like structure with stocks, a pillory, and a whipping post. Colonial jails had only small rooms, where 20 or 30 people might be housed closely together with no heat. Inmates were required to buy their food from the jailer; destitute inmates were forced to rely on their families, friends, and the goodwill of others for assistance.

Modern Jails

The adage "The more things change, the more they stay the same" applies to modern jails: They have changed relatively little in the past 200 years. The majority of the nearly 3400 jails in the United States are located in rural areas.[54] Jails still serve the same basic functions they did in the colonial era: They detain people awaiting trial and provide short-term confinement for petty offenders. All jail inmates, whether they have been convicted

Headline Crime

Jail Webcams

In Phoenix, Arizona, Sheriff Joe Arpaio implemented a round-the-clock broadcast of his "Jail Cam." Four cameras feed live footage over the Internet of the intake, holding, and searching cells, as well as the hallway of the Maricopa County jail. The cameras provide views of inmates being searched, sleeping in small bunk beds or on the concrete floor, and generally milling about. According to Sheriff Arpaio, "We get people booked in for murder all the way down to prostitution. . . . When these johns are arrested, they can wave to their wives on the camera." He also noted that the webcasts are educational: "Kids can tune in and see what it's like in the jail. Maybe they'll learn something."

Although the "Jail Cam" website received between 3 and 10 million hits each day, critics believe the sheriff crossed over the fine line between education and exploitation. In 2001, inmates filed a lawsuit charging that the "Jail Cam" violated detainees' basic right to privacy, because detainees have only been arrested but not yet convicted. In 2004, the 9th Circuit Court of Appeals affirmed a lower court decision ruling against the use of the "Jail Cam." In its majority opinion, Judge Richard Paez wrote that the "Jail Cam" broadcasts amounted to little more than a "reality show" and went beyond what would be considered a reasonable deterrent to crime. According to Judge Paez,

> Exposure to millions of complete strangers, not to mention friends, loved ones, co-workers, and employers, as one is booked, fingerprinted, and generally processed as an arrestee, and as one sits, stands, or lies in a holding cell, constitutes a level of humiliation that almost anyone would regard as profoundly undesirable.

Sources: "'Jail Cam' Raises Hackles and a Lawsuit When Links to Porno Sites Are Discovered," *Village Voice*, June 6, 2001, p. 7; *Demery et al. v. Arpaio*, 378 F. 3d 1020 (2004).

or not, are housed together. In fact, 62 percent of all people being held in jail are awaiting trial. Jails are also a refuge for what criminologist John Irwin calls "rabble"—people society finds disreputable and disruptive (i.e., the uneducated, unemployed, chronic alcoholics, and homeless).[55]

On June 30, 2007, 780,581 people were being held in U.S. jails—nearly 2 percent more than in the previous year.[56] The average daily occupancy was 96 percent of the rated capacity of the nation's jails—up from 90 percent at mid-year 2001.[57] As with prison populations, the characteristics of jail inmates demonstrate a disproportionate number of minorities and males being held in local jails. Unlike prison inmates, however, nearly two thirds of the individuals in jails have not been convicted (see FIGURE 10–2).

Jails in urban areas are often overcrowded; by comparison, rural jails typically operate under capacity, but are generally older and poorly staffed.[58] Many jails, whether urban or rural, provide inmates with relatively little treatment, education, or recreation programs. These poor conditions can have serious consequences. For example, jail overcrowding has been found to contribute to violence, rape, and sickness. Some research indicates that prolonged exposure to overcrowding may reduce life expectancy.[59] Rural jails, which are poorly staffed compared to urban jails, have less supervision of inmates and report higher inmate homicide and suicide rates.[60] To combat this problem, many new, regional jails have been built to serve multiple counties.

New-Generation Jails

Historically, jail standards have been criticized by both the public and the private sectors as being unacceptably low in many jurisdictions. Responding in part to mounting public pressure, the federal government has stepped in to reform jail conditions. In 1974, three new federal Metropolitan Correctional Centers were opened in Chicago, New York, and San Diego. These federal jails were the first intentionally planned and designed to imple-

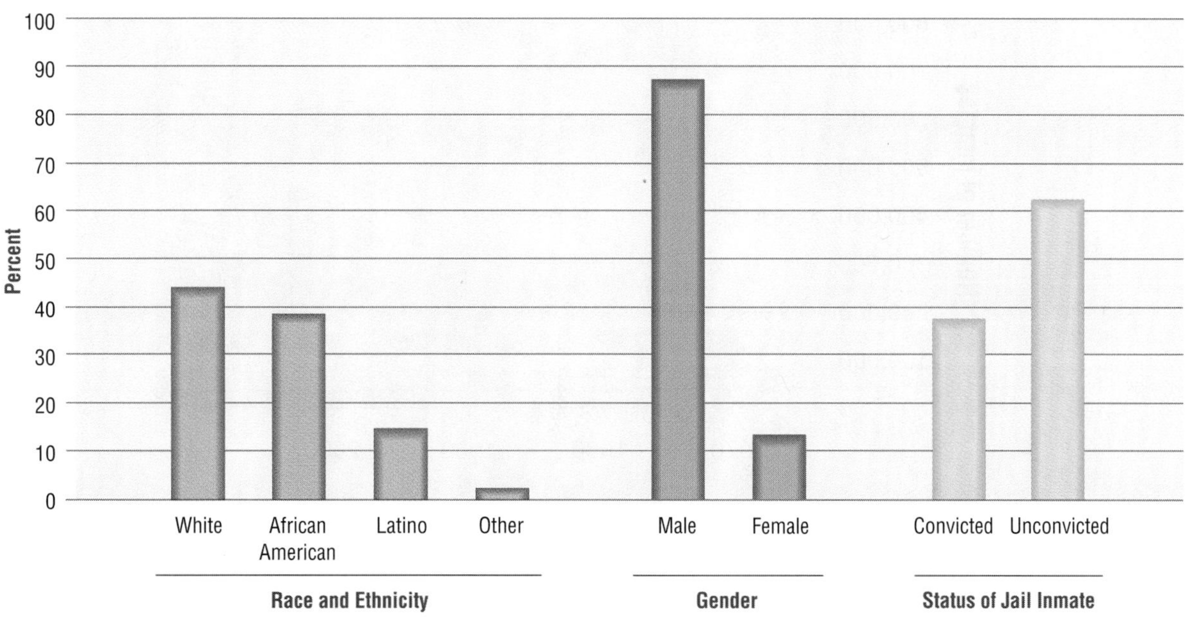

FIGURE 10–2 Selected Characteristics of Jail Inmates

Source: William Sabol, Todd Minton, and Paige Harrison, *Prison and Jail Inmates at Midyear 2006* (Washington, DC: U.S. Department of Justice, 2007).

ment a new approach to jail administration, known as functional unit management, a precursor to the current model of direct supervision.

Other changes to improve jail conditions have focused on jail design and inmate supervision. In older jails, cells are in rows, and staff members walk down a central corridor to observe the behavior of inmates through bars. In contrast, most new-generation jails are designed to increase staff interaction with inmates by placing the staff inside the inmate housing unit. This new layout increases direct surveillance so that staff can help actively change inmate behavior patterns rather than just reacting to them.[61]

New-generation jails are built on a podular design with small living units for each inmate situated around the perimeter of either a circle or triangle to permit staff to view all cells from the center.

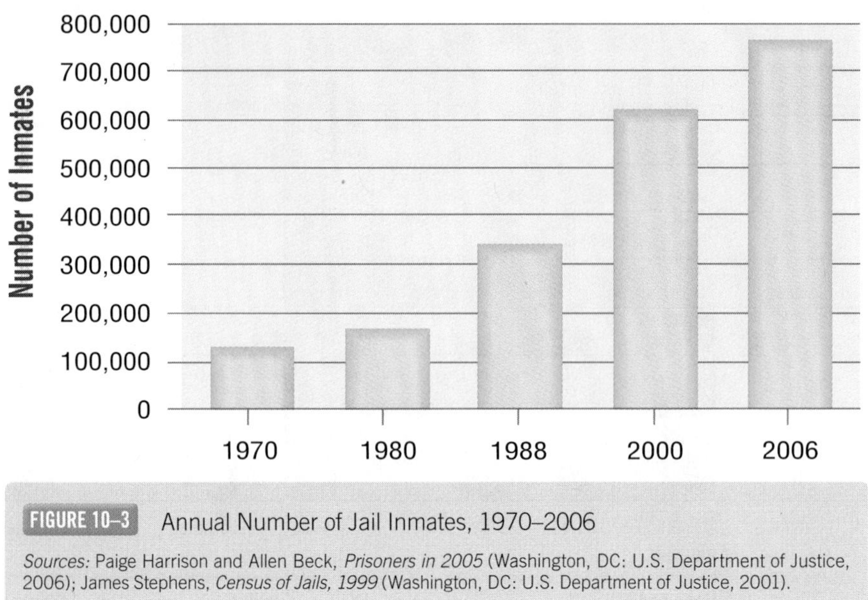

FIGURE 10–3 Annual Number of Jail Inmates, 1970–2006

Sources: Paige Harrison and Allen Beck, *Prisoners in 2005* (Washington, DC: U.S. Department of Justice, 2006); James Stephens, *Census of Jails, 1999* (Washington, DC: U.S. Department of Justice, 2001).

Research examining differences in staff and inmate attitudes in traditional and new-generation jails demonstrates the value of direct supervision. A number of studies looking at new-generation jails have reported that staff and inmates felt more positively about the overall jail environment, including living and working conditions, than did staff or inmates in traditional jails. They have also found that direct supervision reduced the number of inmate-on-inmate assaults and lowered the overall costs of operation.[62]

Direct supervision may also prevent inmate suicides. Males continue to be at much greater risk of committing suicide in jail, being approximately 56 percent more likely to commit suicide than female jail inmates. In addition, white jail inmates are about six times more likely to commit suicide than African American inmates and three times more likely to commit suicide than Latino inmates.[63]

Despite the variety of reform efforts over the decades, jails have experienced rapid population growth in recent years, with their populations growing by more than one third in less than a decade (see FIGURE 10–3).

WRAPPING IT UP

Chapter Highlights

- The first U.S. prisons were built after the American Revolution. Two competing models of prisons emerged: the Pennsylvania model, based on a philosophy of separate confinement, and the New York model, based on a congregate system.
- Between 1865 and 1900, correctional philosophy underwent a major shift, reflected in the reformatory movement. The Elmira Reformatory for younger, first-time offenders opened in 1876.
- The first correctional facility exclusively devoted to female offenders was established in 1835. Before that time, women were confined in houses of refuge, shelters, or local jails.
- Prisons are classified by their level of security: minimum-security prisons, low-security prisons, medium-security prisons, maximum-security prisons, and super-maximum-security prisons.
- The military penal system includes special facilities for confining offenders from each branch of the armed forces. In addition, the military is responsible for managing Camp Delta, a special prison for captured terrorists located at the Guantanamo Naval Base in Cuba.
- The Federal Bureau of Prisons operates U.S. penitentiaries, federal correctional institutions, metropolitan correctional centers, medical centers, minimum-security prison camps, and a federal detention center.
- Nearly 100,000 persons are incarcerated in the more than 150 privately contracted prisons in the United States. Although privatization is controversial, it does appear to cost less and often provides higher-quality services than public prisons.
- Jails have their origins in medieval England, where each county was ordered to establish a jail to confine offenders. Contemporary U.S. jails provide a combination of high security with greater treatment opportunities for those confined in them.

Words to Know

Ashurst–Sumners Act Legislation passed by Congress in 1935 and amended in 1940 that prohibited interstate transportation of prison goods.

boot camp A highly regimented correctional facility where inmates undergo extensive physical conditioning and discipline.

Camp Delta A facility at the Guantanamo Naval Base in Cuba that is used for the confinement of suspected terrorists.

co-correctional prison An institution where men and women are confined together.

congregate system A nineteenth-century model that held prisoners in isolation during the night, allowing them to work together during the day in silence. It was implemented at New York's Auburn Prison.

conjugal visit A private visit that some prison systems allow between inmates and their spouses to help them maintain sexual and interpersonal relationships.

correctional system Programs, services, and institutions designed to manage people accused or convicted of crimes.

Hawes–Cooper Act Legislation passed by Congress in 1929 requiring that prison products be subject to the laws of the state to which they were shipped.

jail An institution to hold pretrial detainees and people convicted of less serious crimes.

low-security prison An institution that operates between the medium and minimum security levels.

mark system System by which prisoners earned "marks" for good behavior to achieve an early release from prison.

maximum-security prison The most secure prison facility, having high walls, gun towers, and barbed wire or electronic fences.

medium-security prison A middle-level prison facility, which has more relaxed security measures and fewer inmates than a maximum-security prison.

minimum-security prison A prison facility with the lowest level of security that houses nondangerous, stable offenders.

new-generation jails Jails that are designed to increase staff interaction with inmates by placing the staff inside the inmate housing unit.

penitentiary house An eighteenth-century place of penitence for all convicted felons except those sentenced to death.

Percy Amendment Law that allowed states to sell prison-made goods across state lines as long as they complied with strict rules to ensure unions were consulted and to prevent manufacturers from undercutting existing wage structures.

prison An institution for the confinement of people who have been convicted of serious crimes.

prison farms Correctional institutions that produce much of the livestock, dairy products, and vegetables used to feed inmates in the state prisons.

prison forestry camps Correctional institutions that provide labor for the maintenance of state parks, tree planting and thinning, wildlife care, maintenance of fish hatcheries, and cleanup of roads and highways.

privatization A process in which state and federal governments contract with the private sector to help finance and manage correctional facilities.

reformatory A penal institution generally used to confine first-time offenders between the ages of 16 and 30.

separate confinement A nineteenth-century prison model that separated inmates. It was implemented in Pennsylvania's Western and Eastern penitentiaries.

super-maximum-security prison A prison where the most predatory and dangerous criminals are confined.

work release A program allowing the inmate to leave the institution during the day to work at a job.

Think and Discuss

1. Which system was probably better for prisoners—the Pennsylvania model or the New York model? Why?
2. Should inmates have the right to conjugal visits? Should such visits be limited to an inmate's spouse, or should they be expanded to include any intimate of the offender?
3. What kinds of issues do private business ventures in prison raise, and how might those issues be overcome?
4. Who benefits from confinement in co-correctional institutions? Should the use of these facilities be expanded?
5. Should prisons be privatized, or should the function of incarcerating and punishing offenders be the exclusive role of the state?

Notes

1. Bureau of Justice Statistics, "Expenditure and Employment Statistics," available at http://www.ojp.usdoj.gov/bjs/glance/exptyp.htm, accessed September 2, 2008.
2. Wayne Morse, "The Attorney General's Survey of Release Procedures," in George Killinger and Paul Cromwell, Jr. (Eds.), *Penology* (St. Paul, MN: West, 1973), p. 23.
3. Norman Johnston, "The World's Most Influential Prison: Success or Failure?" *The Prison Journal* 84:20S–40S (2004).
4. Thorsten Sellin, "The Origin of the Pennsylvania System of Prison Discipline," *The Prison Journal* 50:15–17 (1970).
5. Harry Elmer Barnes, *The Story of Punishment* (Boston: Stratford, 1930).
6. Larry Sullivan, *The Prison Reform Movement: Forlorn Hope* (Boston: Twayne Publishers, 1990), p. 13.
7. Margaret Wilson, *The Crime of Punishment* (New York: Harcourt Brace, 1931).
8. Harry Elmer Barnes and Negley Teeters, *New Horizons in Criminology*, 3rd ed. (Englewood Cliffs, NJ: Prentice Hall, 1959).
9. Gustav de Beaumont and Alexis de Tocqueville, *On the Penitentiary System in the United States and Its Application in France* (Carbondale, IL: Southern Illinois University Press, 1833/1964).
10. John Vincent Barry, "Captain Alexander Maconochie," *Victorian Historical Magazine*, June 27, 1957:5.
11. Wilson, note 7.
12. John Vincent Barry, "Alexander Maconochie," *Journal of Criminal Law, Criminology and Police Science* 47:145–161 (1956).
13. Barnes and Teeters, note 8, p. 423; see also Torsten Eriksson, *The Reformers*, trans. by Catherine Djurklou (New York: Elsevier, 1976), pp. 91–97.
14. *Twenty-Sixth Annual Report of the Executive Committee of the Prison Association of New York and Accompanying Documents for the Year 1870* (Albany, NY: State of New York, 1871).
15. Harry Elmer Barnes and Negley Teeters, *New Horizons in Criminology*, revised ed. (New York: Prentice Hall, 1942/1945), pp. 555–556.
16. William Sabol and Heather Couture, *Prison Inmates at Midyear 2007* (Washington, DC: U.S. Department of Justice, 2008).
17. William Sabol and Todd Minton, *Jail Inmates at Midyear 2007* (Washington, DC: U.S. Department of Justice, 2008).

18. Estelle Freedman, "Their Sisters' Keepers," *Feminist Studies* 2:77–95 (1974).

19. Richard Hofstadter, *The Age of Reform* (New York: Vintage Books, 1955); Philip Klein, *Prison Methods in New York State* (New York: Longmans Green, 1920).

20. Kay Harris, "Women's Imprisonment in the United States: A Historical Analysis of Female Offenders Through the Early 20th Century," *Corrections Today* 60:74–80 (1998).

21. Clarice Feinman, "An Historical Overview of the Treatment of Incarcerated Women," *The Prison Journal* 63:12–26 (1984).

22. Harris, note 20; Nicole Rafter, *Partial Justice: Women in State Prisons, 1800–1935* (Boston: Northeastern University Press, 1985); Sheryl Nicole Rafter, "Gender and Justice," in Lynne Goodstein and Doris MacKenzie (Eds.), *The American Prison* (New York: Plenum, 1989), pp. 89–109.

23. Public Law 96-157, 827, codified as 18 U.S. Code 1761(c).

24. *National Advisory Commission on Criminal Justice Standards and Goals, Standard 2.17, part 2c* (Washington, DC: U.S. Department of Justice, 1974).

25. Sabol and Couture, note 16.

26. Sabol and Couture, note 16.

27. James Stephan and Jennifer Karberg, *Census of State and Federal Correctional Facilities, 2000* (Washington, DC: U.S. Department of Justice, 2003).

28. Daniel Mears and Jamie Watson, "Toward a Fair and Balanced Assessment of Supermax Prisons," *Justice Quarterly* 23:232–270 (2006).

29. National Institute of Corrections, *Supermax Housing: A Survey of Current Practices* (Longmont, CO: National Institute of Corrections Information Center, 1997).

30. Jesenia Pizarro and Vanja Stenius, "Supermax Prisons: Their Rise, Current Practices, and Effects on Inmates," *The Prison Journal* 84:248–264 (2004).

31. Bulduc Correctional Facility, Maine Department of Corrections (2006), available at http://www.maine.gov/corrections/Facilities/bcf/index.htm, accessed May 28, 2008.

32. South Fork Forest Camp, Oregon Department of Corrections, available at http://www.oregon.gov/DOC/OPS/PRISON/sffc.shtml, accessed May 28, 2008; Sugar Pine Conservation Camp, California Department of Forestry and Fire Protection, available at http://www.fire.ca.gov/php/fire_er_consrvncamp.php, accessed May 28, 2008.

33. "Federal Prisons to Eliminate Boot Camps," *Corrections Today* 67:13 (2005).

34. David Haasenritter, "The Military Correctional System: An Overview," *Corrections Today* 65:58–61 (2003).

35. William Peck and Timothy Purcell, "U.S. Navy Corrections: Confining Sailors Both at Sea and on Land," *Corrections Today* 65:66–70 (2003).

36. Haasenritter, note 34.

37. John Crank and Patricia Gregor, *Counter-terrorism after 9/11: Justice, Security and Ethics Reconsidered* (Cincinnati: LexisNexis, 2005).

38. Josh White, "Three Detainees Commit Suicide at Guantanamo," *The Washington Post*, June 11, 2006, p. A01.

39. American Correctional Association, *2006 Directory: Adult and Juvenile Correctional Departments, Institutions, Agencies, and Probation and Parole Authorities* (Lanham, MD: American Correctional Association, 2006).

40. James Ross, Esther Heffernan, James Sevick, and Ford Johnson, "Characteristics of Co-correctional Institutions," in John Smykla (Ed.), *Coed Prison* (New York: Human Sciences Press, 1980), pp. 77–78; John Ortiz Smykla and Jimmy Williams, "Co-corrections in the United States of America, 1970–1990: Two Decades of Disadvantages for Women Prisoners," *Women and Criminal Justice* 8:61–76 (1996).

41. Dede Short, "Illinois Correctional Policy-Makers Initiate Historical Changes," *Corrections Today* 64:102–106 (2002).

42. J. C. Powell, *The American Siberia* (Chicago: H. J. Smith, 1891); "Prison Labor in 1936," *Monthly Labor Review* 47:251 (1938).

43. Philip Ethridge and James Marquart, "Private Prisons in Texas," *Justice Quarterly* 10:31–50 (1993).

44. Linda Calvert Hanson, "The Privatization of Corrections Movement," *Journal of Contemporary Criminal Justice* 7:1–28 (1991); see also Charles Thomas, "Does the Private Sector Have a Role in American Corrections?", paper presented at A Critical Look at Privatization conference, Indianapolis, IN, 1988; John Dilulio, Jr., *Private Prisons* (Washington, DC: U.S. Department of Justice, 1988); T. Don Hutto, "The Privatization of Prisons," in John Murphy and Jack Dison (Eds.), *Are Prisons Any Better?* (Newbury Park, CA: Sage, 1990), pp. 111–127.

45. Sabol and Minton, note 16.

46. Dina Perrone and Travis Pratt, "Comparing the Quality of Confinement and Cost-Effectiveness of Public Versus Private Prisons: What We Know, Why We Do Not Know More, and Where to Go from Here," *The Prison Journal* 83:301–322 (2003).

47. William Bales, Laura Bedard, Susan Quinn, David Ensley, and Glen Holley, "Recidivism of Public and Private State Prison Inmates in Florida," *Criminology and Public Policy* 4:57–82 (2005); Charles Thomas, "Recidivism and Public and Private State Prison Inmates in Florida: Issues and Unanswered Questions," *Criminology and Public Policy* 4:89–99 (2005).

48. Ira Robbins, *The Legal Dimensions of Private Incarceration* (Washington, DC: American Bar Association, 1988).

49. Travis Pratt and Jeff Maahs, "Are Private Prisons More Cost-Effective Than Public Prisons? A Meta-Analysis of Evaluation Research Studies," *Crime & Delinquency* 45:358–371 (1999).

50. Dilulio, note 44.

51. *Medina v. O'Neill*, 589 F. Supp. 1028 (1984).

52. *Richardson v. McKnight*, 521 U.S. 399 (1997).

53. *Correctional Services Corporation v. Malesko*, 534 U.S. 61 (2001).

54. Ralph Weisheit, David Falcone, and L. Edward Wells, *Rural Crime and Rural Policing: An Overview of Selected Issues* (Normal, IL: Rural Police Project, 1994).

55. John Irwin, *Jails* (Berkeley: University of California Press, 1985).

56. Sabol and Minton, note 17.

57. Sabol and Minton, note 17.

58. G. Larry Mays and Joel Thompson, "Mayberry Revisited: The Characteristics and Operations of America's Small Jails," *Justice Quarterly* 5:421–440 (1988).

59. Weisheit et al., note 54.

60. Paul Paulus, Garvin McCain, and Verne Cox, "Prison Standards: Some Pertinent Data on Crowding," *Federal Probation* 45:48–54 (1981).

61. Lois Spears and Don Taylor, "Coping with Our Jam-Packed Jails," *Corrections Today* 52:20 (1990).

62. Richard Wener, "Effectiveness of the Direct Supervision System of Correctional Design and Management: A Review of the Literature," *Criminal Justice and Behavior* 33:392–410 (2006); Linda Zupan, *Jails: Reform and the New Generation Philosophy* (Cincinnati: Anderson, 1991); Linda Zupan and Ben Menke, "Implementing Organizational Change: From Traditional to New Generation Jail Operations," *Policy Studies Review* 7:615–625 (1988); Linda Zupan and M. Stohr-Gillmore, "Doing Time in the New Generation Jail," *Policy Studies Review* 7:626–640 (1988).

63. Christopher Mumola, *Suicide and Homicide in State Prisons and Local Jails* (Washington, DC: U.S. Department of Justice, 2005).

CHAPTER 11

Prisons

OBJECTIVES

1. Comprehend the characteristics of persons currently confined in prison and understand how they have changed in recent years.
2. Become familiar with the variety of prison programs provided to inmates.
3. Understand how prisons are managed and how discipline is maintained.
4. Examine special prison populations and their needs.
5. Grasp the nature of prison life, the ways in which inmates adapt to prison, and the problems facing inmates and staff.
6. Know the current status of prisoner rights and discover how these rights evolved over time.

PROFILES IN CRIME AND JUSTICE

Judith Simon Garrett

Deputy Assistant Director
Division of Information, Policy, and Public Affairs
Federal Bureau of Prisons
Washington, DC

Like many others in the corrections profession, I chose this field, and prisons in particular, quite by accident. I took a job as a correctional officer at a medium-security men's prison in Michigan for one year in between college and law school. While that job was short term and was not the start of a continuous career in corrections, it did foster in me an interest in the corrections profession. I was most drawn to the opportunity to work with people, both staff and inmates, whose life experiences were very different from my own.

Today, as a senior manager working at the headquarters of the Federal Bureau of Prisons, my work is focused on ensuring that our agency has the resources and support it needs to continue to operate prisons that are safe, secure, humane, and efficient and that provide inmates with opportunities for self-improvement. Specifically, I oversee the research department, which has validated the effectiveness of our major inmate programs, both in reducing recidivism and in improving inmate behavior while in prison. This research has been critical to convince legislators and others of the need to support inmate programs including education, drug treatment, and prison industries. I also oversee the public affairs office, which responds to media inquiries and communicates with the public about significant issues regarding the operations of our agency. I oversee the operations of the office of legislative affairs, which ensures that our agency is well represented before the United States Congress. This is done by monitoring the introduction of bills to ensure that members of Congress are informed of the potential impact on our agency, and by responding to constituent-based inquiries as well as oversight requests and other congressional inquiries. Our staff members also develop testimony when we are asked to appear at a hearing and coordinate the preparation of myriad congressional reports.

I appreciate the opportunity to make a difference in the lives of others. Sometimes I have been able to affect the lives of inmates through the creation of policies or rules that apply throughout the agency and affect thousands of inmates. Finally, I enjoy developing written communications for staff, and inmates, on a wide variety of issues, ranging from cost-savings initiatives to the retroactive application of changes to the sentencing guidelines for crack cocaine. As a correctional officer, I felt that I was making a difference in the lives of the inmates I supervised by modeling prosocial values and behavior and by letting them know that their lives did matter. I also gained great satisfaction from being part of the "team" of corrections staff that relied on one another for our safety and security.

Corrections is a difficult profession because the personal qualities that attract people to the field may be the same qualities that lead to their downfall. Most staff members spend their day talking to people—both inmates and staff. Staff members who are the most effective are those who take a genuine interest in the lives of the inmates, encouraging them to take advantage of opportunities to improve their skills and their decision making. However, corrections staff working in institutions must never forget that inmates should not be relied upon to assist staff or protect staff.

Honesty, reliability, and consistency are critical skills for staff working in corrections, particularly staff who work with inmates. It is essential that staff behave as consistently as possible, from one day to the next, and that they be honest and straightforward with inmates, knowing of course that there are many issues that cannot be fully disclosed. It is also essential that staff be honest with one another and that staff be able to rely on one another to assist them in the myriad types of crises and emergencies that could occur on any given day.

Introduction

A female inmate at the federal women's prison at Alderson, West Virginia, once wrote:

> When I came through the gate, I said to myself: "This is a prison?" All the trees and flowers—I couldn't believe it. It looked like a college with the buildings, the trees, and all the flowers. But after you're here a while—and it don't take too long—you know it's a prison.[1]

This inmate's reaction to entering prison reflects the same misconceptions about prisons many people have today—that prisons are fortress-like structures with high stone walls, guard towers, and a foreboding sense of isolation and danger. Despite the trees and flowers, this facility was still a prison, and this inmate soon discovered it would confine her in close quarters with other convicted women, deprive her of privacy, and place restrictions on when and how often she could be visited by friends and relatives. This difference between the appearance and the reality of prisons illustrates the ambivalence of many Americans about what prison is and what it should be.

According to the Sentencing Project, nearly 10 percent of all state prisoners are serving a life sentence.

Certainly the early prisons, such as Auburn Prison in New York, were cold, dark fortresses where inmates were removed from society for extended periods of time. The bleakness of most prisons up to the early twentieth century reflected the widely held belief that prisoners should be confined in structures with few of the amenities of the outside world. This notion of **less eligibility** posited that prisoners should always live in conditions that were less desirable than even the worst conditions in free society.

Over the past 100 years, both changes in correctional philosophy and U.S. Supreme Court decisions concerning prisoners' constitutional rights have altered the general appearance of prisons and the conditions under which inmates are confined. Many prisons today have flowers and trees, and some have tennis courts and exercise facilities, high school and college classrooms, rooms for watching television (or even TV sets in cells), law libraries, state-of-the-art vocational training, and Internet access. Even so, they are still prisons: Their primary function is to house people who have been convicted of crimes.

Prisons and Prisoners

Sociologist Erving Goffman characterized prisons as **total institutions**, where "all aspects of life are conducted in the same place and under the same single authority."[2] All persons are treated alike, and activities are tightly scheduled, with the institution providing for all the basic needs within an environment closed off from the outside world. The large group of people within a total institution is divided into two subgroups: those who exercise control and those who are controlled. In prison, this means that all aspects of inmates' lives, from the time they awake each morning until they go to their cells at night, are governed by institutional rules enforced by prison staff. When inmates arrive at the prison, they are stripped of their personal clothing and possessions and given institutional clothes and a set of rules that govern how they will interact both with the staff and with other inmates. Their contact with the outside world is limited, and many normal social activities are curtailed. Phone calls and visits with family members are minimal, and most inmates are deprived of heterosexual contact.

Classification of Prisoners

Few inmates arrive at correctional institutions directly from the courts that sentenced them. Instead, they usually go from the court to a reception or diagnostic center for orientation and initial **classification**, where the type of custody and treatment appropriate to their needs is determined. In some correctional systems, the classification system sorts inmates according to their age, severity of offense or prior incarceration record, and work experience. Classification allows administrators to assign inmates to institutions or housing units appropriate to their security level, thereby separating more aggressive or violent inmates from those considered to be more vulnerable to assault or exploitation (e.g., because they are younger, more timid, or smaller) as well as members of rival gangs.[3]

The Changing Prison Population

Largely as a result of the federal government's drug-enforcement policies, the number of prisoners in the United States has skyrocketed in the past decade. At midyear 2007, 1,595,034 prisoners were incarcerated in state and federal prisons, an increase of about 370 percent since 1980 (see FIGURE 11-1).[4] The increasing number of prisoners has required both the states and the federal government to build new prisons and to employ more people to operate them.

As noted in Chapter 10, the nation's jails incarcerate another 780,000 persons, including those awaiting trial and presumed innocent as well as offenders serving short jail sentences for misdemeanors or waiting to be transferred to another court or to the state department of corrections. What this means is that nearly 2.4 million persons, or one out of every 100 adults, are in prison or jail in the United States.[5] When compared to other countries based on official statistics regarding incarceration rates, the United States ranks as the world's number one incarcerator. However, it is important to note that some countries do not count jail inmates and a few countries, such as China and North Korea, are believed to dramatically understate the number of people incarcerated and even the number of prisons used to house offenders, including political prisoners.[6]

The type of inmate in U.S. prisons has changed over the years: Prisons have become populated by younger and more violent offenders. As a result, correctional institutions have been forced to increase the sizes of their staffs. In 1958, state prisons employed one correctional officer for every 9 inmates, on average; in 2001, there was one officer for every 4.5 inmates.

Although most inmates in state and federal prisons are male (nearly 93 percent of the total prison population), the number of female inmates has increased at a much faster rate than the number of male inmates in recent years (a 4.5 percent increase for females versus a 3 percent increase for males).[7] As shown in TABLE 11-1, the majority of inmates are

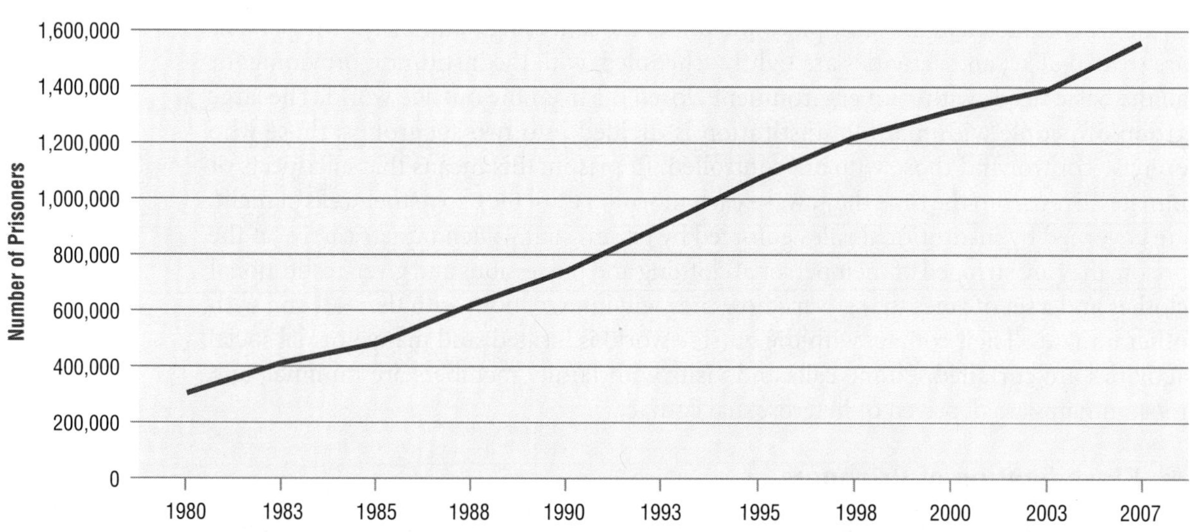

FIGURE 11-1 State and Federal Prison Populations

Sources: William Sabol, Heather Couture, and Paige Harrison, *Prisoners in 2006* (Washington, DC: U.S. Department of Justice, 2007); Bureau of Justice Statistics, National Prisoners Statistics—1 (Washington, DC: U.S. Department of Justice, 1994).

TABLE 11-1 Characteristics of State and Federal Prison Inmates

Characteristic	Percentage of Prison Inmates
Gender	
Females	7.2
Males	92.8
Race and Ethnicity	
White, non-Latino	40.0
African American	41.6
Latino	15.5
Other	2.9
Gender and Race	
Females	
White	47.6
African American	27.7
Latina	17.0
Other	7.7
Males	
White	34.2
African American	38.2
Latino	20.7
Other	6.9

Source: William Sabol, Heather Couture, and Paige Harrison, *Prisoners in 2006* (Washington, DC: U.S. Department of Justice, 2007).

members of racial and ethnic minorities. Approximately half of all state prison inmates were sentenced for violent crimes, and slightly more than half of all federal prisoners were sentenced for drug offenses.[8]

Prison Crowding

The growth in prison populations has resulted in greater crowding in most facilities. Federal prisons are currently at 134 percent of their rated capacity (the optimal number of beds for the facility), while state prisons are at 101 percent of their capacity.[9] Consequently, an increasing number of prisoners have to share living space. While many inmates are housed in single-person cells, most are forced to adjust to sharing a 6 foot by 9 foot cell; increasingly, many live in more open, but less secure, dormitories. Crowding, combined with the slumping economy, has led some states to consider freeing inmates to reduce prison populations and reduce costs (see "Headline Crime").

Prison Programs

It was not until the middle of the twentieth century that prisons began expanding beyond mere custody to include a variety of programs geared toward meeting both inmate and institutional needs. Today, with the exception of a few super-maximum-security institutions, nearly all prisons offer counseling, health and medical services, academic and vocational education, and prison industries.

The nature and extent of each kind of program vary among institutions, depending on the size of the institution, the state funding available, and the composition of the inmate population (i.e., prisoners' sex, age, security levels, or psychological and medical needs). Inmates are typically assigned to academic or work programs as a result of the

Headline Crime **Freeing Inmates**

The dramatic increase in the U.S. prison population has not only produced extreme crowding in many state prison systems, but also cut greatly into state budgets. In an attempt to reduce overcrowding and save money, a number of states are proposing to release tens of thousands of prisoners. Estimates are that such early releases in California and Kentucky alone would save those states $450 million. Among the proposals or new laws are these measures:

- Kentucky has approved legislation that will release 2000 inmates, although sex offenders and violent convicts would be exempt.
- Michigan is proposing to speed up the parole process for more than 3000 inmates who are seriously ill or were not convicted of violent or sexual offenses.
- Mississippi is considering early parole for inmates convicted of selling marijuana or prescription drugs.
- Plans in New Jersey, South Carolina, and Vermont include sending drug-addicted inmates to treatment programs outside the prison system.
- Rhode Island is considering a proposal that would deduct 12 days a month from an inmate's sentence for good behavior in prison. Certain categories of violent offenders will be eligible, but not inmates serving life sentences.

Source: Ray Henry, "States May Free Inmates to Save Millions," available at http://www.abcnews.go.com/US/wireStory?id=4582534, accessed April 29, 2008.

classification process or by request once they arrive at the institution. If prisoners participate in education or industry programs, they will receive a basic—albeit very low—wage. They may spend these earnings on incidentals such as candy and cigarettes, save them in their prison account, or send a portion home to their family. Some states require that a percentage of an inmate's pay be contributed to make restitution or be sent to a victim compensation program. Inmates who are assigned to work in private prison industries may earn significantly higher wages based on either federal minimum wage standards or the prevailing wages in the industry.[10]

Counseling

The past two decades have seen a dramatic decline in the emphasis on inmate counseling and rehabilitation. A number of studies published in the 1970s called into question the ability of prisons to achieve any significant rehabilitation of inmates. Although critics called for spending less money and effort on treatment, they were also quick to suggest placing a much greater emphasis on security and control in institutions. Some states went so far as to change the stated goal in their sentencing code from rehabilitation to punishment.

Even so, most prisons continue to provide some degree of counseling and treatment for inmates, with programs aimed at "the elimination of criminal behavior and the establishment of prosocial behavior, both during imprisonment and subsequent release."[11] Psychological treatments typically include a variety of individual counseling techniques:

- *Reality therapy*, in which the therapist attempts to improve the inmate's willingness or ability to behave more responsibly by focusing on the consequences of acting inappropriately
- *Group psychotherapy*, which involves bringing inmates into confrontational group interactions with other inmates as they discuss shared problems and call each other on their attempts to manipulate or rationalize their behaviors
- *Behavior therapy*, in which behavior modification techniques, such as rewards and punishments, are used to alter the behaviors of inmates

Health and Medical Services

Because most prisons are large institutions in which hundreds of inmates live in close quarters for years at a time, the normal medical and health concerns of prisoners become a major responsibility of the prison. In addition, inmates frequently bring with them a history of inadequate medical attention, poor diets, and drug and alcohol abuse. Unfortunately, the funding for most correctional institutions is not large enough to provide the same kinds of medical and health care to inmates that many civilians receive.

Every prison has some sort of medical and health services, but few institutions have anything close to state-of-the-art facilities and many do not employ a full-time physician. Typically, nurses and paraprofessionals meet the daily or routine needs of inmates; the prison contracts with the local medical community to provide weekly visits by doctors and dentists. Most prison hospitals are more like small clinics where inmates stay when ill, receive medication, and have cuts and broken bones treated. Inmates are transported to a community hospital for more serious injuries and illnesses or surgery.

Despite often checkered work histories, inmates are expected to have gainful employment upon release.

Academic and Vocational Education

Roughly two thirds of all inmates have not finished high school by the time they enter prison. Also, about one third of all men and more than half of all women in prison were not employed at the time of their arrest.[12] Their lack of basic educational and vocational skills may have contributed to the problems inmates faced in the outside world before coming to prison, and it merely exacerbates the difficulties they confront once they are released. As part of the rehabilitative goals of correctional institutions, therefore, academic and vocational education programs have become a standard part of the program services offered.

All federal prisons and roughly 90 percent of state prisons provide educational programs to their inmates. These programs include the following:

- Adult basic education
- Adult secondary education
- Special education
- College coursework
- Vocational education
- Study release

Secondary education programs designed to prepare inmates for the GED exam are the most common type of courses offered in prison. Next most common are basic classes in math and reading. Only 27 percent of state prisons offer college classes.[13]

Slightly less than one third of inmates in state and federal prisons participate in vocational education. These programs typically focus on developing skills in auto mechanics and body work, plumbing, welding, air-conditioner and small appliance repair, dental and optical technician training, computer programming, and carpentry and cabinet making.

Prison Industries

All institutions must be maintained, and prisons are no exception. Within the prison, the laundry must be done, lawns mowed, meals prepared, and plumbing and electrical systems serviced. Most of these tasks are performed by inmates. Nearly half of all state and federal inmates are assigned to maintaining facilities, and another 20 percent are assigned to prison industries such as farming, repair of office equipment, food processing, or the manufacturing of goods such as license plates, road signs, and prison clothing.[14]

Managing Prisons

Prisons are highly structured organizations. The organization of prisons varies depending on the emphasis placed on custody and security versus rehabilitation.[15] Institutions that emphasize custody and control are highly regimented, with relationships between staff and inmates being strictly regulated. Such institutions emphasize strict obedience to prison rules, and staff members spend much of their time supervising inmates. By contrast, institutions that emphasize rehabilitation are less highly regulated and may even encourage the development of informal relationships between staff and inmates in an attempt to reinforce the treatment goals of the prison. Most prisons operate with some combination of these organizational styles.

Prison Personnel

Each prison is managed as a hierarchy. At the top of this hierarchy is a warden or superintendent, followed by deputy wardens, and then an administrative staff.

- **Wardens** are primarily responsible for the overall operation of the prison; they report to the central office of the state Department of Corrections or Federal Bureau of Prisons. Deputy wardens are responsible for overseeing the various functions of the prison, such as custody, programs, and industry.
- **Line personnel** are employees who have direct contact with inmates and whose jobs are intended to achieve the custodial and rehabilitative goals of the prison. These employees include custody staff (guards), teachers, counselors, classification officers, medical personnel, and religious and recreational staff.
- **Staff personnel** provide support services to the line personnel and administrators. They include clerks, secretaries, training officers, and research, budget, and accounting personnel.

Approximately two thirds of all prison employees are correctional officers (see FIGURE 11-2). As a result of civil rights legislation and court decisions regarding affirmative action and equal opportunity hiring practices, the racial, ethnic, and gender composition of prison employees has changed dramatically in the past few decades. Before the 1980s, most prison employees were white males. Since then, however, women and minorities (especially Latinos) have been employed in increasing numbers.

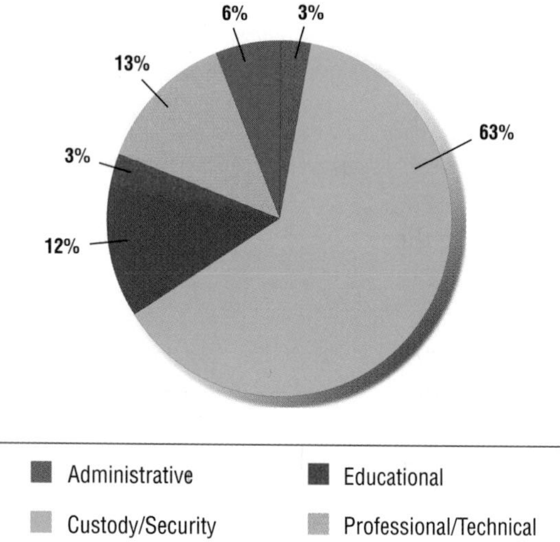

FIGURE 11-2 Job Classification of State Prison Employees

Adapted from James Stephan and Jennifer Karberg, *Census of State and Federal Correctional Facilities, 2000* (Washington, DC: U.S. Department of Justice, 2003), p. 13.

Custody Staff

Correctional officers (guards) have the most access to and potential influence over inmates. Their primary functions are to supervise inmates throughout the institution, conduct periodic counts of prisoners, search for contraband, patrol the grounds and the walls, and transport inmates to court hearings and to other institutions. They may also sit on disciplinary hearing committees and classification boards within the institution.

Gender-Related Issues

Until the 1970s, women were generally prohibited from working in the inner confines of men's prisons. Today, females account for 15 to 20 percent of all correctional officers. Some debate has arisen about women guarding men in all-male institutions, however, and there is a growing concern about men working as correctional officers in women's prisons.

Male Prisons

Correctional officers perform a thankless and dangerous job.

Female correctional officers in all-male prisons, like female police officers who have to deal disproportionately with male suspects, face a variety of special problems and barriers in their work. Because of their generally smaller size, lesser strength, and gender stereotypes, female officers are perceived by many prison administrators and male officers as being more vulnerable to inmate assaults or more likely to be conned or manipulated by inmates. In reality, this may not be the case: Research suggests that female officers are assaulted only 28 percent as often as male officers, and that male inmates generally accept female guards, find them easier to interact with, and believe that they are less likely to be punitive than male officers.[16]

Another issue is the potential violation of inmates' rights to privacy. Guards are often expected to supervise inmates in the shower and toilet areas; to conduct pat-down searches of inmates, including the genital area; and to occasionally conduct visual body cavity searches. In general, the courts have held that female officers' rights to equal employment override the privacy rights of inmates. For example, in 1985, in *Grummett v. Rushen*, a U.S. District Court held that the observation of male inmates in showers and cells by female guards was "infrequent and casual . . . or from a distance" and that no privacy rights had been violated.[17]

Female Prisons

Male correctional officers in female prisons raise a special issue. Lawsuits have been filed by female prisoners in a number of states over sexual harassment, abuse, and sexual assaults by male correctional officers. In 1997, Michigan was one of two states sued by the federal government over recurring sexual abuse of female inmates; in only a little more than 15 years, at least 30 male officers had been convicted of sexual assaults against female prisoners.[18] In 2007, Pennsylvania settled a lawsuit for $35,000 dating back to a claim filed in 1996 by Lisa Lambert, a convicted murderer. Lambert alleged that administrators did nothing to prevent multiple rapes and sexual assaults by correctional officers while she was serving a life sentence. She also alleged that she was videotaped during a strip search.[19]

Headline Crime

When Female Correctional Officers Have Sex with Male Inmates

In April 2006, two former female correctional officers were charged with having sex with a male inmate. Christine Roberge and Heather Bartosch were accused of having sexual relations with a male inmate in several locations at the Oakhill Prison on various occasions. Both officers were charged with second-degree sexual assault under a Wisconsin law making it a felony for officers to have sexual involvement with inmates. The law—which provides for a maximum penalty of 40 years in prison—applies equally to both male and female officers, arguing that no sex between an inmate and an officer can be consensual because the officer has significantly greater power and inmates have no power of coercion over officers.

Source: Lisa Schuetz, "Former Prison Guards Charged with Sex Assault," *Wisconsin State Journal*, April 5, 2006, p. A-1.

Maintaining Discipline

More than half of all inmates are charged with violating prison rules at least once per sentence, and at least one third commit multiple infractions. Most rule violators are charged with administrative infractions, followed by possession of contraband and violence without injury. Only about 10 percent are involved with incidents of injury, threat, or escape.[20]

A study of inmate self-reported rule-breaking in a federal correctional facility in Fort Worth, Texas, found that inmates admitted to many more rule violations than were reported and that guards reported very few of the violations they did observe.[21] In their desire to achieve a smoothly running shift, many guards attempted to gain inmate acquiescence with the carrot rather than the stick.[22]

The Disciplinary Process

Prison staff are bound by a variety of legal rules and judicial mandates set forth by the U.S. Supreme Court in 1974 in ***Wolff v. McDonnell***.[23] In *Wolff*, the Court rejected the right of inmates to counsel and to confront or cross-examine witnesses in disciplinary hearings, noting that to exercise such rights could threaten the security of the institution, although reprisals may be taken by accused inmates against staff members or inmates who brought the charges. It also held that administrators must follow these steps in the disciplinary process:

- Write and file an incident report
- Provide a formal hearing
- Give a written 24-hour notification of the charge(s) and supporting evidence
- Allow inmates to call witnesses on their own behalf unless it would jeopardize institutional safety
- Provide inmates with the assistance of a staff member or another inmate in presenting their defense if the inmate is illiterate or the issue is unusually complex

At a **disciplinary hearing**, the disciplinary committee informs the inmate of the charge and gives the inmate and the person who wrote the incident report an opportunity to testify regarding the incident. In addition, the inmate may present witnesses on his or her behalf, although inmates are not entitled to cross-examine witnesses. Most state correctional systems allow inmates to appeal disciplinary hearing decisions to the warden, to the superintendent of the institution, or to the commissioner of the state department of corrections.

Sanctions for Rule Violations

Rule violators generally face one of three forms of sanction: administrative segregation, loss of good time, and loss of privileges.

When in **administrative segregation**, an inmate is placed in a single-person cell in a high-security section of the institution for a specified period of time. Inmates placed in segregation usually spend 22 to 23 hours a day in their cells.[24] This punishment typically is applied in cases involving more serious rule violations, such as assault, but may also be used for inmates who are repeatedly insubordinate. Most states limit the amount of time an inmate may be in segregation to a maximum of 20 days.

Good time is the practice of reducing the days of an inmate's sentence for maintaining a record of good behavior; for participating in educational, vocational, or treatment programs; or for providing some sort of special service to the institution (such as assisting a guard who is in trouble). In some jurisdictions, for each good time day served, an inmate's sentence is reduced by one day; in other jurisdictions, an inmate may be required to earn seven good time days for each day to be reduced from his or her sentence. Inmates who earn the maximum amount of good time can dramatically reduce the total amount of time they serve in prison. Loss of good time may, therefore, extend the inmate's actual amount of time served.

Inmates who violate institutional rules may also face **loss of privileges**. Correctional institutions are places with few amenities, but inmates do have limited privileges. Because they are considered privileges, rather than guaranteed rights, these benefits can be taken away. For example, prisoners can lose privileges such as receiving visits, receiving or sending mail, participating in recreation, and having access to the commissary.

Managing Special Populations

While most inmates are capable of being managed with standard procedures in traditional institutional settings, some groups have special needs or present unique challenges for prison administrators.

Inmates with HIV/AIDS

HIV (human immunodeficiency virus) infection and AIDS (acquired immune deficiency syndrome) have become major concerns for today's prison administrators. Because many inmates have personal histories that include high-risk behavior (such as intravenous drug use and male homosexual activity), prison and public health officials are now taking a closer look at the rate of HIV/AIDS in prison populations. According to the Centers for Disease Control and Prevention (CDC), residents of prisons have the highest rate of HIV infection among all residents of public institutions. In 2006, 2 percent of state prison inmates and 1 percent of federal prison inmates tested positive for HIV. Of those nearly 22,000 inmates testing positive for HIV, 5422 inmates were confirmed as having AIDS. During the same year, 168 inmates in state prisons died from AIDS-related illnesses.[25]

Mentally Disordered Inmates

Many severely mentally disordered offenders are routinely sent to prison, as are much larger numbers of inmates who have less problematic mental or emotional problems. Surveys of state correctional departments have found that approximately 16 percent of inmates (nearly 300,000 individuals) are either mentally disordered or deficient.[26] Prisons frequently receive inmates with histories of mental disorders or institutionalization for mental health treatment. In addition, stress can exacerbate an inmate's mental disorder once he or she is confined to a prison.[27]

Special services for mentally disordered offenders are typically limited, and only about one fourth of disordered inmates see psychiatrists or other licensed therapists while in prison. Many of these inmates are housed in segregated units for the mentally disordered to provide protection for themselves or others, including staff and other inmates.[28] Because some mentally disordered inmates are unpredictably violent or aggressive, in 1990 the U.S. Supreme Court, in *Washington v. Harper*, agreed that such inmates could be forced to take antipsychotic drugs for their benefit or if they are a danger to themselves or others.[29]

The number of elderly inmates will increase in coming decades due to both demographic changes in the larger population and recent changes in sentencing policies.

Elderly Inmates

Older inmates are the fastest-growing population in state prisons. Today, approximately 76,000 prisoners are age 55 or older; this is double the number of older persons who were imprisoned just a decade earlier, and accounts for about 5 percent of all inmates.[30] According to the National Center of Institutions and Alternatives, elderly inmates cost two to three times more to incarcerate than younger inmates.[31]

One of the main reasons for the greater cost of caring for elderly inmates is the range of debilitating health conditions they bring into prison or acquire as a result of growing older in prison. Common conditions faced by these individuals include arthritis, hypertension, myocardial infarction (heart attack), and diabetes.[32]

Inmates with Disabilities

An estimated 10 percent of inmates in state prisons have some sort of disability, ranging from mental retardation and learning disabilities to drug dependency and a variety of physical disabilities.[33] Although prisons generally have programs or separate housing for inmates with certain disabilities, few prisons have kept pace with the needs of the physically disabled. For example, few prisons have made accommodations for inmates in wheelchairs, and it is rare for prisons to have elevators, ramps, special toilets, or handles or bars to assist physically disabled inmates while showering.

According to the Americans with Disabilities Act of 1990, all public accommodations are prohibited from discriminating against persons with physical disabilities, including prisoners. In 1998, the Supreme Court reaffirmed that prisons were public entities and that inmates with disabilities must be appropriately accommodated within the facilities and given reasonable access to most prison programs.[34]

Juvenile Offenders

Approximately 2639 persons under age 18 were in custody in adult prisons in 44 states at midyear 2006, with slightly more than 6800 being housed temporarily in adult jails. Juveniles accounted for slightly less than 0.2 percent of all inmates in state prisons.[35]

In most states, juvenile inmates are housed in correctional facilities as part of the general population. That is, they are assigned to the same cell blocks as adults and may even be placed in cells with adults. Of those states with juvenile inmates, only 13 maintain separate facilities or units for juvenile offenders.[36] Only six states (Arizona, Hawaii, Kentucky, Montana, Tennessee, and West Virginia) require separate housing for all inmates younger than age 18.

Female Offenders

Although their numbers are increasing, relatively few women are sentenced to prison. In 2007, slightly more than 115,000 women were under the jurisdiction of state and federal prisons, accounting for more than 7 percent of the total inmate population.[37] Those women who are incarcerated are more likely to be placed in smaller institutions, face a less formal and bureaucratic administration, receive greater freedom of movement within the institution, and face less violence or intimidation by other inmates than their male counterparts.

For many female inmates, family disruption is one of the many collateral consequence of imprisonment.

Most female inmates are young, are unmarried, have less than a high school education, and have children under age 18.[38] More than 29 percent of all women sentenced to prison in 2006 were drug offenders (see FIGURE 11-3).

Social Order of Women's Prisons

Female inmates, like their male counterparts, must make adjustments to prison life. Women in prison are generally in greater need of social support than are male inmates, however. Males tend either to be more anomic and isolated or to join prison gangs, whereas females are more likely to seek out companionship and social support through the development of interpersonal relationships with other inmates. Imprisoned women sometimes establish homosexual relationships, but more often platonic friendships, and they sometimes become members of surrogate families.[39] **Surrogate families**, often referred to as fictive families or *pseudofamilies*, involve a number of inmates coming together to establish a set of relationships based on traditional family roles. These kinship groups perform most of the normal functions of a family and provide stability, warmth, security, and social bonding for women seeking primary group relationships.[40]

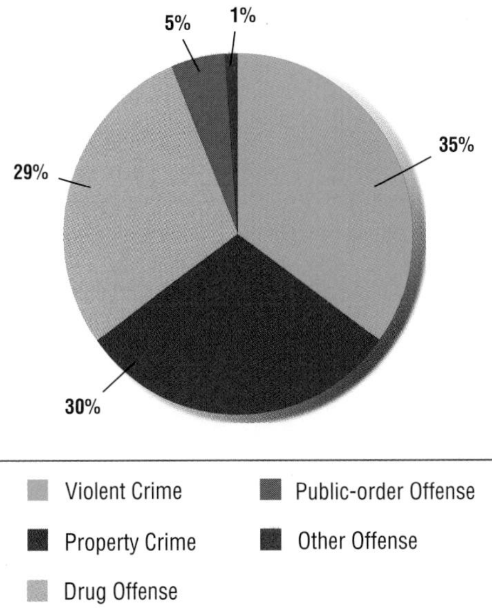

FIGURE 11–3 Most Serious Offense of New Female Commitments to Prison

Source: William Sabol, Heather Couture, and Paige Harrison, *Prisoners in 2006* (Washington, DC: U.S. Department of Justice, 2007).

Mothers in Prison

Nearly 80 percent of the women in prison have children, compared to only 60 percent of the men in prison. Between 60 and 70 percent of these women have one or more children younger than age 18.[41] Most of these inmate-mothers report that at least one of their dependent children lives with a grandparent, father, or other relative/friend; approximately 10 percent have children in foster care or in other institutions.[42]

The special pains of imprisonment for these women are often expressed in feelings of helplessness, guilt, and anxiety about their children's care, education, and health. In addition to the anguish of explaining to their children why they have been sent to prison and concerns about their well-being, inmate-mothers often fear the possibility of losing custody. Additionally, because most women's prisons are located some distance from inmates' homes, female inmates do not see their children often; more than half of all mothers in prison have no visits from their children during their incarceration.[43]

Ideally, pregnant inmates receive prenatal care from prison medical staff and are then transported to a local community hospital for the delivery. In some instances, however, inmates are offered little prenatal care and deliver the baby in the prison hospital. Most states require that baby and mother be separated soon after birth; arrangements are made for a custody hearing for placement of the child.[44] There are no consistent state policies regarding newborn infants and whether, and for how long, they are allowed to stay with their incarcerated mothers.

Inmate Subculture

Prison is a place that requires order, whether it is imposed by institutional staff or created informally by inmates. Many people believe that order is maintained by correctional officers backed up by authority and, sometimes, the barrel of a gun. In reality, the social order of prisons is largely a product of an informal subculture that inmates create to help them cope with their imprisonment. Although debate has arisen regarding the origins of the inmate subculture, scholars support one of two explanations for its development.

The first explanation, which is known as the **deprivation model**, views inmate behavior as a matter of adaptation to the unique demands and conditions of the prison environment and the inmate's response to the loss of amenities and freedoms such as possessions, dignity, autonomy, security, and heterosexual relationships. Because all inmates share these deprivations, or **pains of imprisonment**, they create bonds to help them cope.[45] The bonds form a social system that permits inmates to maintain self-esteem and a sense of dignity by rejecting the formal norms of the prison. The inmate social system is also responsible for maintaining an underground economy in which inmates are able to obtain and distribute valued and scarce items—both legal and illegal—such as cigarettes, snack food, magazines, shaving cream, drugs, alcohol, and sex. These items' availability and cost, which is often measured in packs of cigarettes, can vary according to the amount of attention the institution gives to controlling the economy. Many inmates seek out particular job assignments so they will have greater access to goods. These inmates then sell or trade the goods to other inmates.

The second model suggested as an explanation for the development of inmate subculture is the **importation model**. Proponents of this theory contend that inmates bring to prison their previously established values and patterns of behavior.[46] They adapt these beliefs, identities, and group allegiances from existing street subcultures to the prison context. In addition to a well-developed set of attitudes and values, many inmates may enter prison armed with a deep-seated hostility to authority, which causes them to reject the attitudes and opinions of prison staff and administration.[47]

Coping in Prison

The process by which inmates adjust to or become assimilated into the prison subculture is called **prisonization**.[48] Once in prison, inmates adjust to prison routines and the inmate subculture. Donald Clemmer suggests that individuals adapt to prison life by taking on the inmate role little by little and then remaining "cons" until release. However, Charles Tittle argues that prisoner socialization follows more of a bell-shaped curve in terms of individuals' adaptation to the prison subculture. He thinks most inmates are more likely to express pro-staff beliefs (including an acceptance of the legitimacy of institutional rules and emphasis on treatment and rehabilitation) during the first and last six months of their imprisonment, whereas inmates express much more pro-prisoner beliefs in the middle of their sentences.[49]

The Inmate Code

Criminologists Gresham Sykes and Sheldon Messinger described the **inmate code**, or system of informal norms regulating inmate behavior, which help to order relationships among inmates and between inmates and prison employees. The major tenets of the code include the following norms:

- *Don't exploit inmates.* This maxim demands that inmates do not break their word, steal from other inmates, or fail to pay their debts.
- *Don't lose your head.* Inmates are told to "play it cool" and "do their own time," meaning that they should not mess with other inmates.
- *Don't weaken.* The ideal inmate should be tough and never back down from a fight. This involves showing courage, strength, and integrity when faced with deprivations or threats from other inmates or guards.
- *Don't interfere with inmate interests.* Inmates should not be too curious about the activities or interests of other inmates; inmates should mind their own business; and should "Never rat on a con" or "put another inmate on the spot."
- *Don't be a sucker.* Inmates should always regard prison officials with suspicion and distrust. In any conflict between inmates and prison employees, the employees should always be considered in the wrong.[50]

The code is violated to some degree by most inmates. Those who adhere strictly to the code are considered to be "right guys" and are accorded a certain amount of esteem by other inmates. Those who blatantly violate the code suffer the consequences: ostracism, beatings, or even death. Many criminologists believe that this traditional inmate code has lost much of its influence over inmate behavior during recent decades, however, as a consequence of the increasing number of racial and ethnic prison gangs.

Prison Gangs

Latino gangs have developed a strong presence both inside and outside prison.

Gangs develop in prison for a variety of reasons, including solidarity, power, and self-preservation. One of the first sociological studies of the rise of prison gangs was conducted by James Jacobs at the Stateville Prison in Illinois.[51] Jacobs noted that the street gangs of Chicago, such as the Vice Lords, El-Rukns, Latin Kings, and Disciples, brought their organizational structure and ideologies along when members were sentenced to prison. The gangs placed the old inmate order in jeopardy as inmates began to relate to one another on the basis of group affiliation rather than as individuals. The sheer numbers and solidarity of the gangs also made it much more difficult for staff to manage or control individual inmates who were affiliated with gangs. Formal prison control weakened as established relations between inmates and staff were replaced by gang–staff relations, prison rackets were taken over by gangs, and gang leaders gained informal control over the distribution of prison jobs. New inmates belonging to Chicago gangs were met by gang associates as they entered prison, for example, and were quickly absorbed into the prison gang structure, thereby providing them with an immediate sense of identity and belonging.

Today, prison administrators around the country, as well as personnel within the Federal Bureau of Prisons, face significant prison gang problems. A National Major Gang

Headline Crime: The Aryan Brotherhood

On July 28, 2006, a jury in Santa Ana, California, convicted four leaders of the Aryan Brotherhood prison gang—Barry Mills, Tyler Bingham, Edgar Hevle, and Christopher Gibson—under the Racketeer Influenced and Corrupt Organization (RICO) law on charges of using murder and intimidation to protect their drug trafficking activities in prison. The four had been charged with 32 murders and attempted murders involving members of the Aryan Brotherhood over nearly three decades. Mills and Bingham were found guilty of ordering the murder of African American inmates from their cells at the super-max prison at Pelican Bay.

Over the years, most of the gang's violence was directed at African American inmates. The bloodiest attack occurred on August 28, 1997, when gang members at the Lewisburg federal prison armed themselves with shivs (homemade knife-like weapons) and stabbed six African American inmates, killing two.

While originally formed to strike at African American inmates belonging to the Black Guerrilla Family, the Aryan Brotherhood soon evolved into a full-fledged criminal enterprise involving extortion, drug trafficking, and the sale of "punks" (inmates forced into prostitution). To be accepted into the gang, a recruit had to "make his bones," which often required killing another inmate. Although only a few hundred inmates belong to the gang, its impact has been far-reaching. For example, the Aryan Brotherhood accounts for most of the drug distribution that occurs in state and federal prisons.

The conviction of the four gang leaders suggests an attempt by prison officials to break up one of the most violent prison gangs and to restore a greater control over prison gangs, even in super-max prisons.

Sources: Greg Risling, "Jury Convicts 4 White-Supremacists," *The Washington Post* (July 28, 2006), available at http://www.washingtonpost.com/wp-dyn/content/article/2006/07/28/AR2006072801079.html, accessed September 2, 2008; Associated Press, "4 Aryan Brotherhood Leaders Convicted," *CBSNews* (July 28, 2006), available at http://www.cbsnews.com/stories/2006/07/28/national/main1847262.shtml, accessed August 1, 2008; David Grann, "The Brand: How the Aryan Brotherhood Became the Most Murderous Prison Gang in America," *New Yorker* 80:156–171 (2004).

Task Force survey of gang activity in U.S. prisons conducted in 2002 reported that six major prison gangs are in operation and pose serious security threats to the institutions, staff, and inmates.[52]

- The *Mexican Mafia* (also known as *La Eme*), a Mexican American/Latino gang formed in the late 1950s in the California Youth Correctional Facility at Duel, is considered to be one of the most dangerous gangs both state- and nation-wide. It uses extremely gruesome killings to establish fear and intimidation.
- *La Nuestra Familia* (NF) established itself in Soledad Prison in California in the mid-1960s to protect younger, rural Mexican Americans from other inmates and the gang's chief rivals—the Mexican Mafia. This gang is involved in drug trafficking, extortion, and pressure rackets.
- *Neta* originated in 1970 in a Puerto Rican prison and is composed of Puerto Rican Americans and Latinos. Members are involved in drug activity, extortion, and the use of violence to deal with disrespect to the gang.
- The *Black Guerrilla Family* (BGF) was founded in San Quentin by former Black Panther leader George Jackson in 1966. Members of this African American supremacist group are highly political and hostile to government and prison officials.
- The *Texas Syndicate* (TS) was formed in the early 1970s in California's Folsom Prison as a direct response to other prison gangs, especially the Mexican Mafia and Aryan Brotherhood.
- The *Aryan Brotherhood* (AB), also known as *The Brand*, was formed in 1967 in the prison at San Quentin in California. This white supremacist group organized to serve the interests of white inmates and has since spread to prisons around the United States. Much of its activities have centered on drug trafficking, prostitution, extortion, and murder, especially of African American inmates.

Sex in Prison

Most inmates serve their sentences in same-sex institutions with no heterosexual outlet, a scheme that leads to a number of problems for inmates and prison staff. The normal need for sexual release by inmates leads to various adaptations. Some inmates engage in homosexual activity; others resort to prostitution, engaging in homosexual sex while maintaining a heterosexual identity.

A national survey of state and federal prisons as well as local jails found that more than 5600 acts of sexual violence were reported in 2006, up from 5386 incidents in 2004. About 36 percent of allegations involved staff sexual misconduct; 34 percent involved inmate-on-inmate nonconsensual sexual acts; 17 percent involved staff sexual harassment; and 13 percent involved inmate-on-inmate abusive sexual contact.[53] While prison rape is frequently motivated by a desire for sexual release, more often it is the result of an inmate's attempt to gain power and control over another inmate.

Female inmates also have to deal with sexual coercion and assaults both by staff and by other inmates. While rates of sexual coercion are much higher in men's prisons, recent research shows that women are sexually victimized more frequently than previously believed.[54] For example, in their study of three Midwestern women's prisons, Cindy and David Struckman-Johnson reported rates of sexual coercion ranging from a low of 8 percent at one of the prisons to 19 percent at a second facility. The prison with higher rates was more racially and ethnically diverse, and nearly half of its inmates had committed violent crimes. Approximately half of the sexual incidents, ranging from sexual grabs to rapes, were carried out by female inmates; the other half were perpetrated by prison staff.[55]

FOCUS ON CRIMINAL JUSTICE

The Prison Rape Elimination Act of 2003

On September 4, 2003, President George W. Bush signed the Prison Rape Elimination Act into law. The unanimous passage of this legislation reflects a national effort to reduce sexual violence in prison and to protect the rights of inmates. The purposes of the Act are to

- Establish a zero-tolerance standard for the incidence of prison rape
- Make the prevention of prison rape a top priority in each prison system
- Develop and implement national standards for the detection, prevention, reduction, and punishment of prison rape
- Increase the available data and information on the incidence of prison rape, thereby facilitating improvements in the management and administration of correctional facilities
- Standardize the definitions used for collecting data on the incidence of prison rape
- Increase the accountability of prison officials who fail to detect, prevent, reduce, and punish prison rape
- Protect the Eighth Amendment rights of federal, state, and local prisoners
- Increase the efficiency and effectiveness of federal expenditures through grant programs dealing with social and public health issues
- Reduce the costs that prison rape imposes on interstate commerce

The Prison Rape Elimination Act also provides $60 million for a two-year study of the actual extent of prison rape and recommendations for its elimination.

Source: Prison Rape Elimination Act of 2003, Public Law 108-79 (2003).

Prison Violence

In 2002, 48 state prison inmates were victims of homicide and another 168 inmates committed suicide.[56] However, both the prison homicide rate and the suicide rate have dropped dramatically since 1980, even as prison populations have soared.

Unfortunately, violence directed by inmates against prison staff, especially correctional officers, has not declined in similar fashion. For example, two inmates at a Maryland state maximum-security prison escaped from their cells on July 26, 2006, and attacked David McGuinn, a 42-year-old correctional officer, repeatedly stabbing him in the upper torso before returning to their cells. McGuinn was the second Maryland correctional officer to be killed during the first half of the year, and the rate of assaults against correctional officers in that state had almost doubled between 2004 and 2005.[57] Individual acts of violence in prison, however, rarely catch the attention of the public or news media. Instead, interest is largely focused on the explosive, collective violence produced in prison riots.

Prison Riots

Prison riots have occurred as long as there have been prisons. The first recorded riot in an American prison occurred in Connecticut in 1774. Most of the riots in the nineteenth century were caused by terrible prison conditions, heat, backbreaking labor, brutality by prison staff, and contaminated or insufficient food. Riots during much of the twentieth century appear to mirror external social movements, including making demands for improvements in educational, medical, and recreational resources, and questioning the legitimacy of imprisonment itself.[58]

The past few decades have experienced some of the nation's most explosive and bloody prison riots. In a 1971 riot at Attica State Prison in New York, 39 people died as a direct result of the riot and another 4 later died whose deaths were attributed to the riot.[59] Only nine years later, the New Mexico State Penitentiary turned into a battlefield as inmates went on a rampage that left 33 dead before police and the National Guard regained control of the prison. Although the New Mexico riot was not the most deadly prison riot, it was one of the most grotesquely violent. All of the inmates killed in the New Mexico riot died at the hands of other inmates. Twelve guards were taken hostage and were seriously beaten and, in some cases, sodomized by inmates.

Prisons have continued to have to deal with riot situations, with riots occurring in prisons in Indiana, Louisiana, Montana, New York, Ohio, and Pennsylvania between 1984 and 2008.

Causes of Prison Violence

When more inmates are confined in a small space, conflicts among inmates or between inmates and staff intensify.[60] Sociologists have also suggested that riots often occur as a result of the breakdown in the traditional inmate subculture and attempts by prison administrators to establish formal control of the prison by strict rule enforcement. When administrators shake things up by imposing new rules and prison routines and attempting to run the prison "by the book," they alter the informal inmate–staff relations that have developed over time. This change may spark disorder and violent outbursts.[61]

Prisoners' Rights

Many people believe persons who have been convicted of serious felonies and sent to prison should lose all of their basic rights and privileges. Most prisoners are citizens of the United States, however, and thus subject to the protections provided by the Bill of Rights. Nonetheless, as discussed in previous chapters, the courts have not always been very clear on just which rights should be extended to certain people under particular circumstances. This is also true when looking at prisoner rights.

In many states, people who are convicted of serious felonies forfeit certain civil rights and privileges. This forfeiture is known as loss of civil liberties and includes the loss of the right to vote, hold public office, enter into contracts, sit on juries, obtain certain jobs or occupational licenses, marry, keep or adopt children, and even procreate. For example, a federal appeals court recently held that while inmates do not have a fundamental right to procreate via a conjugal visit with their spouse, they may exercise that right through artificial insemination.[62] Perhaps the most controversial forfeiture is the loss of the right to vote. All but two states—Maine and Vermont—deny prisoners the right to vote while they are in prison. In addition, 35 states prevent parolees from voting, and two states deny all convicted felons the right to vote.[63]

Historically, the federal courts deferred to prison administrators to make decisions about how prisons should be run, including the treatment of prisoners. The **hands-off doctrine** essentially stated that the courts do not have the power to supervise prison administrators or to interfere with ordinary prison rules and regulations.[64] For the most part, the courts confined themselves to matters involving writs of habeas corpus, which challenge the legality of confinement of certain inmates.

The 1960s brought a new focus on civil rights, not just for minorities in society but also for prison inmates.[65] Over the next three decades, prisoners successfully challenged a variety of policies and practices involving rights of religion, privacy, mail and access to the media, access to the courts and legal services, protection against cruel and unusual punishment, medical care, and general prison conditions.[66]

Freedom of Religion

Inmates may not be prohibited from participating in religious services.

In 1962, the U.S. District Court for the District of Columbia ruled, in ***Fulwood v. Clemmer***, that Black Muslims have the same constitutional right to practice their religion and to hold worship services as inmates of other faiths.[67] This decision opened the door for further expansion and clarification of religious rights of prisoners in several subsequent court cases, including the rights of orthodox Jews to have a kosher diet,[68] of Native American inmates to wear long hair as a requirement of their religious beliefs,[69] and of Wiccan or Satanists to practice their religion unless it undermines prison security.[70] However, the state is not required to provide members of the clergy to conduct services.[71]

Right to Privacy

How much privacy should prisoners have? Given the legitimate concerns of prisons related to the safety of both staff and inmates, it is understandable that the privacy of inmates is constrained. In a series of cases, the federal courts ruled that inmates have little right to privacy. For example, search warrants are not required for prison officials to search an inmate's cell;[72] strip searches of inmates, including body cavity searches after contact visits, may be conducted when the security needs of the institution outweigh the inmate's personal right to privacy;[73] and prison officials may search cells and confiscate any contraband found there. Inmates do not have a reasonable expectation of privacy during their period of incarceration,[74] nor do they have the right to be present during cell searches.[75]

Mail and Access to the Media

If inmates and their cells may be searched, do such policies extend to limiting, opening, reading, and censoring inmate correspondence? Do inmates have the right to have access to the media? The courts have held that limits may be placed on inmates' mail and media access when necessary to maintain prison security. For example, inmates may correspond with newspapers unless their correspondence contains discussion of escape plans, contraband, or objectionable material.[76] Censorship of inmates' mail is constitutional if it is necessary to maintain order or to facilitate an inmate's rehabilitation.[77] Policies prohibiting the delivery of mail written in a language other than English is unconstitutional, however.[78] Inmates do not have a constitutional right to correspond with other inmates if prison administrators believe that such correspondence might undermine prison security.[79]

Access to Courts and Legal Services

Do inmates have a right to legal assistance in petitioning the courts? Must prisons provide inmates with legal access? Legal procedures are complex and formal, and very few inmates have the necessary legal knowledge or resources to take advantage of such access. Until recently, in fact, it was not unusual for prison administrators to discipline inmates who petitioned the courts. Based on rulings in a series of cases, however, prison officials must now provide some legal assistance to inmates and cannot prohibit inmates from assisting one another in preparing legal materials;[80] prisons must maintain adequate law libraries for inmate use;[81] law students and paraprofessionals cannot be prohibited from assisting inmates;[82] and state prisons must provide inmates with law libraries or assistance by people trained in the law.[83]

Protection Against Cruel and Unusual Punishment

According to the Eighth Amendment, inmates are not to be subjected to cruel and unusual punishments. The issue of cruel and unusual punishment was raised in the courts in 1979, in *Bell v. Wolfish*.[84] In this case, the court ruled that the pretrial detention of a group of suspects at the Metropolitan Correctional Center in Manhattan did not constitute cruel and unusual punishment, as they were detained for a valid government purpose. Placing unruly inmates in the "hole" (administrative segregation) for extended periods of time, however, was found to be unnecessary and beyond acceptable standards.

Correctional officers are also restricted in the amount of force they may use to obtain inmate compliance with their demands. Specifically, officers may use no more force than is necessary[85] and "when prison officials maliciously and sadistically use force to cause harm, contemporary standards of decency always are violated."[86]

Right to Medical Care

Prisoners' right to medical care, including mental health treatment, has also been supported by the courts. For example, courts have held that indifference to an inmate's medical needs constitutes cruel and unusual punishment because it is the government's obligation to provide medical care for inmates in its correctional system.[87]

Prison Conditions

One of the most significant developments in defining inmate rights in recent years has been the introduction of the standard of **totality of conditions** for judging possible constitutional violations within a single prison or an entire prison system. This standard means that a pattern of abuses—none of which by itself would justify the court's intervention, but that would meet this criterion when considered together—constitutes a violation of the Eighth Amendment's protection against cruel and unusual punishment.

The federal courts first applied the totality of conditions standard in 1970 in ***Holt v. Sarver***, when it was ruled that the entire Arkansas prison system was in violation of the Eighth Amendment. Prisons in that state had traditionally authorized armed inmate trustees to supervise and punish other inmates, and they frequently resorted to violence to maintain order.[88] Courts in other cases found that the Alabama prison system was unconstitutional;[89] the Texas prison system was found in violation of the Eighth Amendment by a federal district court judge because of its use of inmate trustees in security positions, patterns of inmate discipline, overcrowding, and inadequate medical care;[90] that overcrowding in an Ohio prison violated the Eighth Amendment prohibition against cruel and unusual punishment; and that a prison official may be held liable under the Eighth Amendment for acting with "deliberate indifference" to inmate health or safety if the official knows that inmates face a substantial risk of serious harm and disregards that risk by failing to take responsible measure to abate it.[91]

WRAPPING IT UP

Chapter Highlights

- As they enter prison, inmates are classified according to their security level as well as their housing, work, or educational assignment.
- Changes in the U.S. prison population in recent decades have transformed it into a younger, more violent, but still overwhelmingly male group of inmates.
- Nearly all prisons provide counseling, health and medical services, academic and vocational programs, and prison industries.
- All correctional institutions are managed by a hierarchy of staff, with the warden appearing at the top of the bureaucratic structure.
- Custody staff (known as correctional officers or guards) supervise inmates throughout the institution and often find themselves torn between their roles as keepers and caregivers.
- Inmates charged with rule violations face a disciplinary hearing. Sanctions for rule violations include placement in administrative segregation, loss of the "good time" credit toward early release, or loss of privileges.
- Prisons must manage a variety of special populations, including inmates with HIV or AIDS, inmates classified as mentally disordered or mentally deficient, elderly inmates, inmates with disabilities, juveniles, and female offenders.
- The social order of prisons is largely maintained by an inmate subculture, which prescribes expected relationships among inmates and prison employees.
- Many scholars believe that the traditional inmate subculture has given way to new social arrangements reflecting the emergence of prison gangs. Inmates are now more likely to tie themselves to racial and ethnic groups for protection, solidarity, and power.
- Inmates lose many constitutional rights when they enter prison. Conversely, as a result of a number of Supreme Court decisions over the past three decades, a number of inmate rights have been extended.

Words to Know

administrative segregation The placement of an inmate in a single-person cell in a high-security area for a specified period of time; sometimes referred to as solitary confinement.

classification System for assigning inmates to levels of custody and treatment appropriate to their needs.

correctional officers Also known as guards; the lowest-ranking prison staff members, who have the primary responsibility of supervising inmates.

deprivation model An explanation of the inmate subculture as an adaptation to loss of amenities and freedoms within prison.

disciplinary hearing A hearing before a disciplinary board to determine whether the charge against an inmate has merit and to determine the sanction if the charge is sustained.

Fulwood v. Clemmer U.S. District Court decision that African American Muslim inmates have the same constitutional right to practice their religion and to hold worship services as inmates of other faiths.

good time The practice of reducing an inmate's sentence for good behavior.

hands-off doctrine The position taken by the Supreme Court that it will not interfere with states' administration of prisons.

Holt v. Sarver Supreme Court decision that applied the "totality of conditions" principle to find the Arkansas prison system in violation of the Eighth Amendment.

importation model A view of the inmate subculture is a reflection of the values and norms inmates bring with them when they enter prison.

inmate code A system of informal norms created by prisoners to regulate inmate behavior.

less eligibility The belief that prisoners should always reside in worse conditions than should the poorest law-abiding citizens.

line personnel Prison employees who have direct contact with inmates.

loss of privileges A disciplinary sanction involving the loss of visits, mail, recreation, and access to the prison commissary.

pains of imprisonment Deprivations—such as the loss of freedom, possessions, dignity, autonomy, security, and heterosexual relationships—shared by inmates.

prisonization The process by which inmates adjust to or become assimilated into the prison subculture.

staff personnel Prison employees who provide support services to line personnel and administrators.

surrogate families Fictive families created by female prisoners to provide stability and security.

total institutions Institutions that completely encapsulate the lives of the people who work and live in them.

totality of conditions A principle guiding federal court evaluations of prison conditions: The lack of a specific condition alone does not necessarily constitute cruel and unusual punishment.

warden The superintendent or top administrator of a prison.

Wolff v. McDonnell Supreme Court decision that inmates facing disciplinary action must have a formal hearing, 24-hour notification of the hearing, assistance in presenting a defense, and ability to call witnesses.

Think and Discuss

1. Who really controls prisons: staff or inmates?
2. Should women be allowed to work as correctional officers directly supervising male inmates, and should men be allowed to work as correctional officers directly supervising female inmates?
3. Should pregnant inmates be allowed to keep their babies with them in prison and, if so, for how long?
4. Do you believe inmates should have the same rights as free citizens? What limits would you place on the rights of inmates, if any?
5. What limits, if any, should be placed on prison inmates' right to privacy?

Notes

1. Quoted in Rose Giallombardo, *Society of Women: A Study of a Women's Prison* (New York: John Wiley & Sons, 1966), p. 23.
2. Erving Goffman, *Asylums: Essays on the Social Situation of Mental Patients and Other Inmates* (New York: Doubleday, 1961), p. 6.
3. John Irwin and James Austin, *It's about Time: America's Imprisonment Binge* (Belmont, CA: Wadsworth, 1994), p. 74.
4. William Sabol and Heather Couture, *Prison Inmates at Midyear 2007* (Washington, DC: U.S. Department of Justice, 2008); Bureau of Justice Statistics, *National Prisoners Statistics—1994* (Washington, DC: U.S. Department of Justice, 1994).
5. Sabol and Couture, note 4; William Sabol and Todd Minton, *Jail Inmates at Midyear 2007* (Washington, DC: U.S. Department of Justice, 2008).
6. Philip Williams and Yenna Wu, *The Great Wall of Confinement* (Berkeley, CA: University of California Press, 2004); "The Hidden Gulag: Exposing North Korea's Prison Camps, Prisoners' Testimonies, and Satellite Photographs," available at www.hrnk.org/hiddengulag/executiveSummary.html, accessed September 2, 2008.
7. William Sabol, Heather Couture, and Paige Harrison, *Prisoners in 2006* (Washington, DC: U.S. Department of Justice, 2007).
8. Sabol et al., note 7.
9. James Stephan and Jennifer Karberg, *Census of State and Federal Correctional Facilities, 2000* (Washington, DC: U.S. Department of Justice, 2004).
10. "Pennsylvania Correctional Industries" (March 2005), available at http://www.cor.state.pa.us, accessed May 31, 2008; Section 4122(b) of title 18, United States Code; Joan Mullen, Kent Chabotar, and Deborah Carrow, *The Privatization of Corrections* (Washington, DC: National Institute of Justice, 1985).
11. T. Paul Louis and Jerry Sparger, "Treatment Modalities Within Prison," *Are Prisons Any Better? Twenty Years of Correctional Reform* (Newbury Park, CA: Sage, 1990), p. 151.
12. Sabol et al., note 7.
13. Caroline Harlow, *Education and Correctional Populations* (Washington, DC: U.S. Department of Justice, 2003); Steven Klein, Michelle Tolbert, Rosio Bugarin, Emily Cataldi, and Gina Tauschek, *Correctional Education: Assessing the Status of Prison Programs and Information Needs* (Washington, DC: U.S. Department of Education, 2004).

14. Stephan and Karberg, note 9.

15. Donald Cressey, "Prison Organizations," in James March (Ed.), *Handbook of Organizations* (Chicago: Rand McNally, 1965), pp. 1023–1070.

16. Joseph Rowan, "Who Is Safer in Male Maximum Security Prisons?" *Corrections Today* 58:186–189 (1996).

17. *Grummett v. Rushen*, 779 F.2d 491 (9th Cir., 1985).

18. Melvin Claxton, Ronald Hansen, and Norman Sinclair, "Sexual Abuse Behind Bars: Guards Assault Female Inmates," *Detroit News*, May 22, 2005, available at http://detnews.com/2005/specialreport/0505/24/A01-189215.htm, accessed September 2, 2008.

19. Associated Press, "Pa. to Pay Murderer $35K in Assault Case," available at http://news.yahoo.com/s/ap/20070904/ap_on_re_us/stalking_murder_lawsuit, accessed September 2, 2008.

20. Bureau of Justice Statistics, *Prison Rule Violators* (Washington, DC: U.S. Department of Justice, 1989), pp. 1–8.

21. John Hewitt, Eric Poole, and Robert Regoli, "Self-Reported and Observed Rule-Breaking in Prison: A Look at Disciplinary Response," *Justice Quarterly* 1:437–447 (1984).

22. Hewitt et al., note 21, p. 446.

23. *Wolff v. McDonnell*, 418 U.S. 539 (1974).

24. Irwin and Austin, note 3, p. 91.

25. Laura Maruschak, *HIV in Prisons, 2006* (Washington, DC: U.S. Department of Justice, 2008).

26. William Branigin and Leef Smith, "Mentally Ill Need Care, Find Prison," *The Washington Post*, November 25, 2001, p. A01; Luke Birmingham, Debbie Mason, and Don Grubin, "A Follow-up Study of Mentally Disordered Men Remanded to Prison," *Criminal Behaviour and Mental Health* 8:202–214 (1998).

27. Kenneth Adams, "Former Mental Patients in a Prison and Parole System: A Study of Socially Disruptive Behavior," *Criminal Justice and Behavior* 10:358–394 (1983); Hans Toch, *Living in Prison: The Etiology of Survival* (New York: Free Press, 1977).

28. Brian McCarthy, "Mentally Ill and Mentally Retarded Offenders in Corrections: A Report of a National Survey," *New York State Department of Correctional Services, Sourcebook on the Mentally Disordered Prisoner* (Washington, DC: National Institute of Corrections, 1985), pp. 14–29.

29. *Washington v. Harper*, 494 U.S. 210 (1990).

30. Sabol et al., note 7; Patrick McMahon, "Aging Inmates Present Prison Crisis," *USA Today*, August 10, 2003, available at http://www.usatoday.com/news/nation/2003-08-10-prison-inside-usat_x.htm, accessed September 2, 2008.

31. Pat Shellenbarger, "Aging Inmates Bring Increased Ailments, Expenses," *Grand Rapids Press*, September 25, 2006, p. A3.

32. Ronald Aday, *Aging Prisoners: Crisis in American Corrections* (Westport, CT: Praeger, 2003).

33. Paige Harrison and Allen Beck, *Prisoners in 2005* (Washington, DC: U.S. Department of Justice, 2006).

34. *Pennsylvania Dept. of Corrections v. Yeskey*, 118 F.3d 168 (1998).

35. Sabol and Couture, note 4; Sabol and Minton, note 5.

36. Howard Snyder and Melissa Sickmund, *Juvenile Offenders and Victims: 2006* National Report (Washington, DC: U.S. Department of Justice, 2006).

37. Sabol and Couture, note 4.

38. Paige Harrison and Allen Beck, *Prisoners in 2004* (Washington, DC: U.S. Department of Justice, 2005); U.S. General Accounting Office, *Women in Prison: Issues and Challenges Confronting U.S. Correctional Systems* (Washington, DC: United States General Accounting Office, 1999).

39. Theresa Severance, "'You Know Who You Can Go to': Cooperation and Exchange Between Incarcerated Women," *The Prison Journal* 85:343–367 (2005).

40. Rose Giallombardo, "Social Roles in a Prison for Women," *Social Problems* 13:268–288 (1966); Alice Propper, "Make-Believe Families and Homosexuality among Imprisoned Girls," *Criminology* 20:127–139 (1982); Susan Cranford and Rose Williams, "Critical Issues in Managing Female Offenders," *Corrections Today* 60:130–134 (1998); Severance, note 39.

41. U.S. General Accounting Office, *Women in Prison: Issues and Challenges Confronting U.S. Correctional Systems* (Washington, DC: U.S. General Accounting Office, 1999); Judith Greene and Kevin Pranis, "Growth Trends and Recent Research," in Ann Jacobs and Sarah From (Eds.), *Hard Hit: The Growth in the Imprisonment of Women, 1977–2004* (New York: Women's Prison Association, 2006), pp. 7–28.

42. Harrison and Beck, note 33.

43. Greene and Pranis, note 41.

44. Karen Holt, "Nine Months to Life: The Law and the Pregnant Inmate," *Journal of Family Law* 20:537 (1982).

45. Gresham Sykes, *Society of Captives: A Study of a Maximum Security Prison* (New York: Random House, 1956).

46. John Irwin and Donald Cressey, "Thieves, Convicts, and the Inmate Culture," *Social Problems* 10:142–155 (1962).

47. Stanton Wheeler, "Socialization in Correctional Communities," *American Sociological Review* 26:250 (1961).

48. Donald Clemmer, *The Prison Community* (New York: Holt, Rinehart & Winston, 1940).

49. Charles Tittle, "Prison and Rehabilitation: The Inevitability of Failure," *Social Problems* 21:385–394 (1974).

50. Gresham Sykes and Sheldon Messinger, "The Inmate Social System," in Richard Cloward et al. (Eds.), *Theoretical Studies in the Social Organization of the Prison* (New York: Social Science Research Council, 1960), pp. 5–19.

51. James Jacobs, *Stateville: The Penitentiary in Mass Society* (Chicago: University of Chicago Press, 1977), p. 207.

52. Florida Department of Corrections, "Major Prison Gangs," Gang and Security Threat Group Awareness, available at http://www.dc.state.fl.us/pub/gangs/prison.html, accessed August 1, 2008.

53. Allen Beck, Paige Harrison, and Devon Adams, *Sexual Violence Reported by Correctional Authorities, 2006* (Washington, DC: U.S. Department of Justice, 2007).

54. Cindy Struckman-Johnson and David Struckman-Johnson, "Sexual Coercion Reported by Women in Three Midwestern Prisons," *Journal of Sex Research* 39:217–227 (2002); Leanne Alarid, "Sexual Assault and Coercion among Incarcerated Women Prisoners: Excerpts from Prison Letters," *Prison Journal* 80:391–406 (2000); Agnes Baro, "Spheres of Consent: An Analysis of the Sexual Abuse and Sexual Exploitation of Women Incarcerated in the State of Hawaii," *Women and Criminal Justice* 8:61–84 (1997); Cindy Struckman-Johnson, David Struckman-Johnson, Lisa Rucker, Kurt Bumby, and Stephen Donaldson, "Sexual Coercion Reported by Men and Women in Prison," *Journal of Sex Research* 33:67–76 (1996).

55. Struckman-Johnson and Struckman-Johnson, note 54.

56. Christopher Mumola, *Suicide and Homicide in State Prisons and Local Jails* (Washington, DC: U.S. Department of Justice, 2005).

57. Eric Rich, Hamil Harris, and Nelson Hernandez, "Inmates Kill Guard at Prison in Maryland," *The Washington Post*, July 27, 2006, p. A01.

58. Marilyn McShane, *Prisons in America* (New York: LFB Scholarly Publishing, 2008), pp. 161–162.

59. Tom Wicker, *A Time to Die: The Attica Prison Riot* (Lincoln, NE: University of Nebraska Press, 1994).

60. Paul Paulus, *Prison Crowding: A Psychological Perspective* (New York: Springer-Verlag, 1988).

61. Richard Wilsnack, "Explaining Collective Violence in Prisons: Problems and Possibilities," in Albert Cohen, George Cole, and Robert Bailey (Eds.), *Prison Violence* (Lexington, MA: Lexington Books, 1976), pp. 61–78.

62. *Gerber v. Hickman*, 264 F.3d 882 (9th Cir. 2001).

63. The Sentencing Project, *Felony Disenfranchisement Laws in the United States* (Washington, DC: The Sentencing Project, 2008).

64. *Banning v. Looney*, cert. denied, 348 U.S. 859 (1954).

65. James Jacobs, "The Prisoner's Rights Movement and Its Impacts," in Norval Morris and Michael Tonry (Eds.), *Crime and Justice: An Annual Review of Research*, vol. 2 (Chicago: University of Chicago Press, 1980), pp. 557–586.

66. American Correctional Association, *Legal Responsibility and Authority of Correctional Officers* (College Park, MD: American Correctional Association, 1987), p. 8.

67. *Fulwood v. Clemmer*, 206 F.Supp. 370 (D.C. Cir. 1962).

68. *Kahane v. Carlson*, 527 F.2d 492 (2d Cir. 1975).

69. *Gallahan v. Hollyfield*, 670 F.2d 1345 (4th Cir. 1982).

70. *Cutter v. Wilkinson*, 544 U.S. 709 (2005).

71. *Gittlemacker v. Prasse*, 428 F.2d 1 (3d Cir. 1970).

72. *United States v. Hitchcock*, cert. denied, 410 U.S. 916 (1973).

73. *Bell v. Wolfish*, 441 U.S. 520 (1979).

74. *Hudson v. Palmer*, 468 U.S. 517 (1984).

75. *Block v. Rutherford*, 468 U.S. 576 (1984).

76. *Nolan v. Fitzpatrick*, 451 F.2d. 545 (1st Cir. 1971).

77. *Procunier v. Martinez*, 416 U.S. 396 (1974).

78. *Ramos v. Lamm*, 639 F.2d 559 (10th Cir. 1980).

79. *Shaw v. Murphy*, 523 U.S. 233 (2001).

80. *Johnson v. Avery*, 393 U.S. 483 (1969).

81. *Younger v. Gilmore*, 404 U.S. 15 (1971).

82. *Procunier v. Martinez*, note 77.

83. *Bounds v. Smith*, 430 U.S. 817 (1977).

84. *Bell v. Wolfish*, note 73.

85. *Whitley v. Albers*, 475 U.S. 312 (1986).

86. *Hudson v. McMillian*, 503 U.S. 1 (1992).

87. *Estelle v. Gamble*, 429 U.S. 97 (1976).

88. *Holt v. Sarver*, 309 F. Supp. 362 (E.D. Ark. 1970).

89. *Pugh v. Lock*, 406 F.Supp 318 (N.D. Ala. 1976).

90. *Ruiz v. Estelle*, 503 F.Supp. 1265 (S.D. Tex. 1980).

91. *Farmer v. Brennan, Warden, et al.*, 511 U.S. 825 (1994).

2620
2620
FURNITURE
LIQUIDATION

CHAPTER

Corrections in the Community

OBJECTIVES

1 Understand the history of probation, including why it is used and how it currently operates to provide support for probationers and safety for the community.

2 Become familiar with the research on the effectiveness of probation and parole.

3 Comprehend the variety of intermediate sanctions used in community corrections.

4 Grasp the technology used in electronic monitoring of offenders in the community as well as the major criticisms of the use of this technology.

5 Identify the key principles of restorative justice and understand its strengths and weaknesses.

6 Understand the history of parole, the other types of prison release that are possible, and the process by which decisions are made to release inmates into the community.

PROFILES IN CRIME AND JUSTICE

Betsy Matthews
Associate Professor
Department of Correctional and Juvenile Justice Studies
Eastern Kentucky University

For as long as I can remember, I envisioned myself in a helping role—as a social worker, a counselor, or a teacher. I also have always been intrigued by courtroom dramas, and sat endlessly watching *Law and Order*–type television series. Little did I know that I would end up in a career that allowed me to combine these two seemingly disparate passions.

Like most college students, I had a difficult time selecting a major. After dabbling in journalism and political science, I ended up majoring in sociology. I took a few classes in criminology and knew I had found my niche. As a requirement for my degree, I completed a practicum at the Greene County Adult Probation Department in Xenia, Ohio; this experience solidified my career choice, and I spent the next 10 years as an Adult Probation Officer.

My favorite thing about being a probation officer was that no two days were the same. Through each case, I was introduced to new people and new circumstances. My first major job task with each case was to conduct a background investigation to learn about the offender's past criminal history and the factors that contributed to his or her criminal behavior. My investigation usually began with a detailed interview with the offender. To confirm the information received and gain a better understanding of the offender, I talked with a variety of people involved in his or her life, including teachers, employers, family members, and mental health counselors. Then I requested information and recommendations from the defense counsel, prosecuting attorney, and police officer involved in the case. Lastly, I interviewed crime victims in the case about any physical or emotional harm caused by the crime, any financial losses they incurred, and what they would like to see happen to the offender in court.

Once the investigation was completed, I wrote a presentence investigation report that summarized the criminal and social background of the offender and made recommendations regarding the offender's disposition. Although some cases were fairly cut-and-dried, making recommendations of this sort was not always an easy task. Was it really necessary to send this offender to prison? Could he or she make it in the community? What would happen to the offender's children? What disposition would make the victim feel that justice has been served? There was always so much to consider. Knowing that, in most cases, the sentencing Judge would follow my recommendation, I took this part of my job very seriously.

When an offender was sentenced to probation, my other major job task began—case supervision. Case supervision involved enforcing the conditions of probation and providing the offender with programs and services that would reduce his or her likelihood of engaging in future crime. To ensure the offender was following the rules and regulations of probation, I had to monitor his or her behavior. I did so by making field visits to the offender's home or place of employment, talking with family members, and conducting curfew checks. When I found offenders breaking the rules, I had to hold them accountable by imposing some type of sanction or by arresting them and taking them back to court. Most of my time was spent trying to connect the offender with a variety of agencies and services that addressed his or her physical, emotional, and financial needs. By providing the offender with counseling and other types of services, I hoped that he or she would make better choices and avoid relapsing into problem behaviors.

It was discouraging when, despite all my efforts, an offender committed another crime. I learned quickly that the social and psychological forces at play in offenders' lives were incredibly difficult to counteract, even for the most motivated and remorseful offenders. But there were also those offenders who managed to beat the odds, who did what it took to make a better life for themselves and their families, and who were truly appreciative of the discipline and support that probation provided. It was those offenders who kept me coming back and sustained my belief in offenders' ability to change.

Introduction

Penologist Tom Murton once said that "placing a man in prison to train him for a democratic society is as ridiculous as sending him to the moon to learn how to live on earth."[1] Prison life is significantly different from living in a local community of a democratic society, and inmate adaptation may lead to greater conformity to the criminal norms stressed by the prison subculture than to the conventional norms preferred by the community.

The most common alternatives to long-term incarceration—probation and parole—are community-based sentences that involve supervision of offenders. Many communities also are experimenting with intermediate sanctions such as fines, house arrest, and community service, both for offenders who are diverted from traditional incarceration and for offenders who are released from prison early. Each of these alternatives reflects the belief that offenders can (and often should) be dealt with within the community. Advocates of **community corrections** argue that these alternatives are less expensive and often more effective in rehabilitating offenders. Critics disagree, insisting that the shift away from incarceration places too many criminals into the community too soon.

Nearly two of every three correctional clients in the United States are on probation.

By 2007, of the slightly more than 7 million adult offenders under care or custody of a correctional agency (about 3.2 percent of the adult population of the United States), only 30 percent were incarcerated in jail or prison; the remaining 70 percent were living in the community under probation, intermediate sanctions, or parole.[2]

Probation

Probation is a sentencing option in which an offender is released into the community under the supervision of a probation officer. Many offenders are given incarceration sentences that are suspended by the courts, only to be placed on probation for a period of time specified in the probation agreement. In 2006, 59 percent of all offenders under correctional supervision were on probation. More than 2.3 million adults were admitted to probation supervision in 2006, while 2.2 million were removed from probation during the same year. Approximately 76 percent of these probationers were male, and 55 percent were white (see FIGURE 12–1).

The use of probation varies from state to state. For example, in 2006, New Hampshire had only 450 persons on probation per 100,000 population; by contrast, Idaho had more than 4400 persons on probation per 100,000 population, while the probation rate in Georgia was slightly over 6000 per 100,000 (see TABLE 12–1).[3]

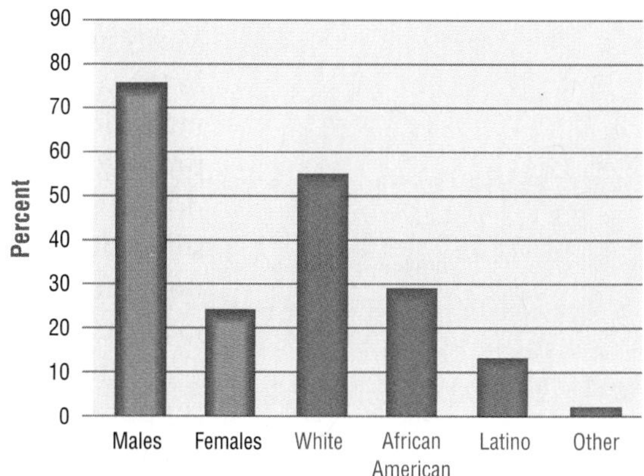

FIGURE 12–1 Probationers by Gender, Race, and Ethnicity

Adapted from Lauren Glaze and Thomas Bonczar, *Probation and Parole in the United States, 2006* (Washington, DC: U.S. Department of Justice, 2007), p. 4.

The Emergence of Probation

The concept of probation was first applied in 1841 by John Augustus, a shoemaker in Boston. Working without pay, he became the nation's first probation officer. For 18 years, Augustus assisted people convicted of crimes: He investigated offenders, evaluated their character, helped them find jobs, and then supervised them in the community. He built friendships with offenders and gained their trust so that they would be more responsive to his counsel about the evils of alcohol and the importance of avoiding further criminal behavior.

In 1878, after recognizing the positive results achieved by Augustus, Boston hired probation officers as extensions of the court. These officers' activities were monitored by the superintendent of police. Probation was implemented statewide in Massachusetts by 1880. Other states soon followed suit. The federal courts authorized the use of probation

TABLE 12-1 State Variations in the Use of Probation

	Number on Probation	Rate per 100,000 Population
States with the Highest Rates of Persons on Probation		
Georgia	422,790	6059
Idaho	48,609	4482
Massachusetts	169,522	3396
Minnesota	127,289	3243
Rhode Island	26,017	3142
Ohio	243,956	2799
Delaware	16,958	2592
Indiana	120,421	2533
Texas	431,967	2515
Michigan	182,650	2398
States with the Lowest Rates of Persons on Probation		
New Hampshire	4590	450
West Virginia	7668	536
Utah	10,426	586
Nevada	13,208	699
Kansas	15,518	748
Maine	7919	760
Virginia	48,144	820
New York	123,418	834
North Dakota	4303	875
Iowa	22,622	993

Source: Lauren Glaze and Thomas Bonczar, *Probation and Parole in the United States, 2006* (Washington, DC: U.S. Department of Justice, 2007), p. 5.

and hired their first probation officers in 1925. By 1956, probation was available for adult offenders in every state.[4]

The Rationale Behind Probation

Much support for probation has been based on the belief that maintaining the offender in the community has a greater rehabilitative effect than incarceration, thereby reducing recidivism (the commission of a new offense). Advocates of probation argue that probation provides more individualized treatment or counseling than is available in prison; it allows offenders greater opportunities to deal with their problems; it avoids subjecting offenders to the negative effects of prison, such as inmate victimization; it is no more likely to lead to recidivism than is incarceration; and it is less expensive than incarceration.

Although the research on most of these contentions is mixed, fairly strong evidence supports the notion that the cost of probation is lower than the cost of incarceration. In Tennessee, for example, the annual cost of keeping an offender in prison is slightly less than $20,000, while the cost of supervising an offender on probation is only $956 per year.[5]

Probation Administration

Several different models of probation administration are currently in use, and approximately 2000 agencies administer probation services at the federal and state levels.

Probation supervision at the federal level is provided by the Division of Probation in the Administrative Office of the United States Courts. Federal probation officers are appointed by judges in the federal district courts.

Probation offices may be located in court houses or in the community near high-crime neighborhoods.

Administration of probation on the state level takes various forms. In more than half of the states, probation is provided by a central, statewide probation office. However, in many states, probation and parole services are organized into a single agency administered by the judicial branch of government. About 25 percent of the states administer probation at the county or local level. This system accounts for nearly two thirds of all offenders supervised on probation in the states.[6] Local probation officers are generally appointed by the local judge and serve at will.

Regardless of probation system, there are extreme variations in caseloads. In counties with small populations, caseloads may be only 15 to 20 clients per officer. In contrast, in large urban counties, such as Cook County (Chicago), probation officers supervise between 120 and 200 clients.

Functions of Probation Officers

Probation officers play an important role in the criminal justice process and have many responsibilities, including the following:

- Investigation and preparation of presentence investigation (PSI) reports
- Intake interviews with offenders to determine the potential for informal disposition of the case
- Diagnostic testing and interviews with offenders to assist in developing a treatment plan
- Risk classification of offenders to determine the type and level of supervision to be required
- Recommendation and assignment of offenders for participation in community treatment programs
- Supervision of offenders in the field
- Meeting with probationers on a regular basis (typically the most time-consuming part of a probation officer's work)

In large agencies with many officers, the investigation function may be carried out by a group of officers who interview offenders, check background sources, assess the offender's potential for completion of community supervision or need for institutional placement, and prepare the PSI for the sentencing judge. Other officers may be assigned to groups responsible for intake tasks, diagnostic testing, supervising offenders in the community, or conducting counseling sessions. In smaller agencies, officers typically perform all of these functions.

Probation officers are usually assigned to conduct PSIs because they will be responsible for supervising the offender if he or she is placed on probation. In addition to conducting interviews with the offender and his or her family, the officer may conduct telephone interviews with school officials, employers, neighbors, and sometimes military personnel in an effort to provide full and accurate information on the offender's background and current situation. The information is then prepared as a final report, with copies being given to the judge, prosecution, and defense before sentencing.

In many jurisdictions, probation officers have taken on the added function of **risk classification**, which assesses the likelihood that an offender poses a continuing risk of reoffending and determines the necessary degree of probation supervision. An offender's risk score is based on a number of factors, including the seriousness of the current offense and the offender's criminal history, education, drug use, age, and employment history. The offender is then assigned to a particular supervisory level, ranging from intensive probation supervision, which may require as many as 20 to 30 contacts between offender and officer per month, to less frequent contact, requiring only a minimum of one contact every three months.[7] Thus offenders who are convicted of more serious crimes and who present greater risks are subject to greater supervision.

Eligibility for Probation

Judges consider a number of factors when evaluating the eligibility of an offender for probation:

- The nature and seriousness of the current offense
- Whether a weapon was used and the degree of physical or emotional injury, if any, to the victim
- Whether the victim was an active or passive participant in the crime
- The length and seriousness of the offender's prior record
- The offender's previous success or failure on probation
- The offender's prior incarcerations and success or failure on parole

Probation is not reserved for people who have been convicted of misdemeanors or minor felonies. Indeed, nearly 20 percent of persons convicted of serious violent offenses in the United States receive probation. Although only 2 percent of those convicted of murder are placed on probation, this sentence is imposed on 17 percent of all offenders convicted of rape and 23 percent of those convicted of assault (see FIGURE 12-2).

About half of all probation cases involve a suspended sentence with incarceration, which is imposed only if the probationer violates the conditions of probation. In about one third of probation cases, probation is the sole sentence; no prison term is attached. Finally, a small portion of probation cases are deferred (also called **informal probation**) before a conviction is entered on the record, and the offender must undergo treatment or follow strict conditions for a specified period; the prosecutor may then decline further prosecution, and the case can be dismissed.

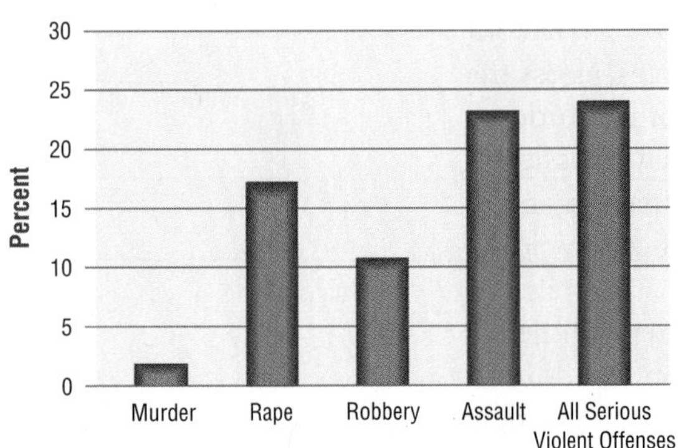

FIGURE 12-2 Percentage of Violent Felons Convicted in Large Urban Counties Receiving Probation, by Offense

Adapted from Brian Reaves, *Violent Felons in Large Urban Counties* (Washington, DC: U.S. Department of Justice, 2006).

Conditions of Probation

Probation is essentially a contract between the offender and the court, and any violations of the conditions could potentially result in revocation of probation. Most state and federal courts have established fairly uniform conditions for probation. In some states, these conditions have been created by the legislature and written into law. The conditions are established to fulfill two broad purposes:

- Treatment or rehabilitation of the offender
- Supervision to ensure law-abiding behavior

The specific conditions of probation often require that the probationer attend school, undergo psychiatric treatment, or participate in drug or alcohol counseling, as well as comply with terms for regular and prompt reporting to the probation officer, restrictions on the offender's geographic mobility, or prohibitions against associating with particular types of people, such as ex-offenders and drug users.[8]

Headline Crime

Talking with Teenage Girl Violates Probation Conditions

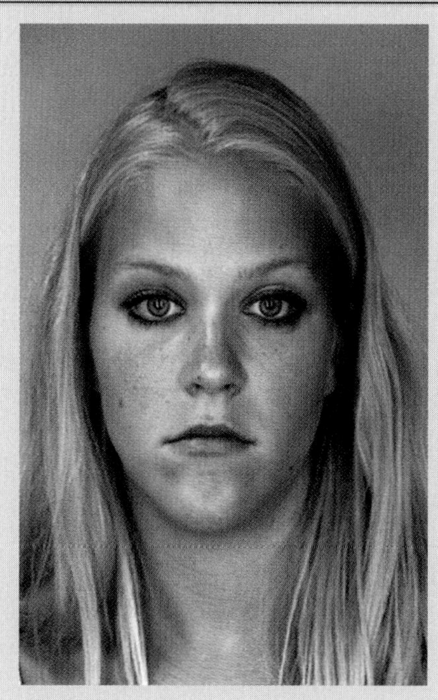

Former middle school teacher Debra Lafave, who had been charged with having sex with a 14-year-old student in her classroom, her home, and in a car, pleaded guilty to a charge of lewd and lascivious battery. She received a sentence of three years of house arrest and seven years of probation. The conditions of her probation included a curfew, treatment in an outpatient program for sex offenders, and staying at least 1000 feet away from schools, parks, and other places where children congregate. In addition, she was prohibited from possessing pornographic material "related to her deviant behavior" and from having unsupervised visits with children younger than age 18.

In December 2007, Lafave was arrested for allegedly violating the condition of her probation regarding contact with children younger than age 18. Lafave was charged with having contact with a 16-year-old female co-worker at the restaurant where they both worked. Police said Lafave frequently spoke in an unsupervised setting with the teenage co-worker about such topics as family problems, high school, friends, boyfriends, and sex. She faces up to 15 years in prison for the probation violation.

Sources: Emanuella Grinberg, "Teacher Pleads Guilty to Sex with Student, Avoids Prison Time," available at http://www.courttv.com/news/2005/1122/lafave_ctv.html, accessed September 2, 2008; "Former Teacher Who Had Sex with Student Back in Trouble," available at http://www.cnn.com/2007/US/law/12/04/teacher.sex/, accessed September 2, 2008.

The courts have also ruled on the permissibility of another condition of probation—reasonable searches. Before 2001, some states and appeals courts interpreted such searches as being limited to those focusing only on probationary issues rather than law enforcement concerns (which would require probable cause). However, the U.S. Supreme Court recently held that reasonable suspicion is sufficient when conducting searches where submission to a search is part of the probationer order.[9]

Supervision of Probation

Since the early 1980s, the supervision and treatment tasks of probation officers have become more complex, often requiring specialized skills beyond the ability of many officers. For example, the increasing number of offenders with drug problems has led many agencies to turn over the treatment of drug addicts to private treatment centers staffed by people with greater expertise in drug rehabilitation.[10] In most probation agencies, however, officers spend the majority of their time in basic supervision, making sure that offenders abstain from drugs and alcohol, seek work or maintain employment, attend counseling sessions, and meet any other conditions of probation.

Probation supervision has historically been organized around caseloads. Thus, as crime rates and prison populations increased from the 1960s to the mid-1990s, so, too, did probation caseloads. Once caseloads in many jurisdictions reached 150 to 200 probationers per officer, experts began to question whether officers were really able to supervise their clients. Many believed that smaller caseloads were necessary to have a positive impact on offenders.

In an attempt to reduce caseloads, many departments hired more officers or developed probation volunteer programs. The increase in crime rates and growing dissatisfaction with the traditional social work orientation of probation that had dominated the field until the mid-1970s eventually brought about a significant change in supervision styles, with officers shifting from a service orientation to an enforcer role.[11] The model of probation officer as enforcer meant that greater attention was given to probationers' compliance with their conditions of probation as well as to the application of more external controls, including drug testing, use of curfews, and increased face-to-face contacts. The demise of the social work model meant that less emphasis was placed on providing services or coordinating services and treatment with community agencies.[12]

Revocation of Probation

An offender's probationary status may be revoked if he or she commits a new crime or violates the conditions of probation (known as a technical violation). If the probationer is arrested for a new crime, the police notify the probation officer so that the probation office may take action. Violations of conditions of probation, by contrast, usually come to the direct attention of the probation officer during the course of supervision.

Probation revocation hearings are conducted with less rigorous due process rights for clients.

In either case, the probation officer has wide discretion in making the decision to initiate probation revocation proceedings. If the new crime is a relatively minor one or if the violation of conditions is deemed insignificant, the officer may choose to warn the probationer. If the offense or violation is serious, however, the officer files a report and places the case on the court calendar for a preliminary hearing before a judge. The probationer is notified of the alleged violation and summoned to appear at the preliminary hearing.

The **preliminary revocation hearing** is similar to the preliminary hearing in a criminal prosecution, with a few important exceptions. First, testimony may include hearsay evidence, and the probationer cannot invoke his or her Fifth Amendment right against self-incrimination. Second, the standard of proof for determining that the probationer is guilty of a violation is a *preponderance of the evidence* (i.e., the greater weight of the evidence suggests guilt), rather than *proof beyond a reasonable doubt.* If no probable cause is established, the probationer is returned to probationary status. If the judge determines there is probable cause that a violation occurred, a revocation hearing is scheduled.

After the preliminary hearing, the **revocation hearing** is held to determine whether probation should be revoked. Minor violations may result in a warning to the probationer and the imposition of additional conditions. If the court determines that the violation is a serious one, the offender's originally deferred or suspended incarceration sentence may be invoked. If no incarceration sentence was imposed at the original criminal trial, the judge may determine an appropriate prison or jail sentence during the revocation hearing.

In 1973, the Supreme Court clarified the probationer's due process rights in ***Gagnon v. Scarpelli.***[13] The Court held that probationers were entitled to the following rights:

- Notice of the alleged violation
- A preliminary hearing to determine probable cause
- The right to present evidence
- The right to confront adverse witnesses
- An independent decision maker (not necessarily a judicial officer)
- A written report of the hearing
- A final revocation hearing

Effectiveness of Probation

The majority of probation cases are successful in terms of probationers getting through their period of probation without committing a new offense or technical violation. In 2006, 57 percent of offenders released from probation supervision in the United States successfully met the conditions of their supervision. Approximately 18 percent were discharged from supervision because of incarceration for a new offense or rule violation, about 4 percent absconded from supervision, and a small number were discharged to the custody of another jurisdiction.[14]

While the majority of probationers meet the conditions of their probation, a number of studies report that probation may not be significantly more effective than incarceration in preventing offenders from committing new crimes. Joan Petersilia and her colleagues tracked 1700 felony probationers for 40 months and found that, within approximately three and a half years, nearly 66 percent had been rearrested, with about one third eventually being sentenced to jail or prison.[15]

Furthermore, probation supervision with smaller caseloads, including intensive probation, proved no more effective in reducing recidivism than did supervision with much larger caseloads. Ed Latessa and his colleagues report that probationers assigned to intensive probation supervision caseloads were just as likely to be rearrested and were no more likely to participate in treatment services offered by the probation department than were probationers assigned as part of regular caseloads.[16]

Intermediate Sanctions

The use of **intermediate sanctions** as alternatives to exclusively probation and prison has become increasingly attractive to policymakers because such sanctions are considered more severe than probation but less expensive than long-term incarceration. Intermediate sanctions include the following options:

- Intensive probation supervision
- House arrest and electronic monitoring
- Day reporting centers
- Fines
- Forfeitures
- Restitution
- Community service

Frequently, multiple sanctions are applied in combination. For example, offenders may be placed under house arrest and also required to pay fines or victim restitution.

Intensive Probation Supervision

Beginning in the 1960s, many states experimented with **intensive probation supervision (IPS)** programs, in which probation officers were assigned very small caseloads (a limit of 25 cases per officer, compared to the normal 100 or more cases assigned). It was believed that IPS would increase the amount of supervision each probationer received and that the increased supervision would, in turn, lead to more positive probation outcomes, including lower recidivism rates. More broadly, IPS was seen as a way to achieve the following goals:

- Reduction in prison crowding
- Increased public protection
- Greater cost-effectiveness (owing to reduced incidents of incarceration)

- Punishment (intensive surveillance and control function as sanctions)
- Rehabilitation of the offender
- Reduction in recidivism[17]

Some IPS programs require 15, 20, or even 30 contacts per month, compared with only three or four contacts in regular probation supervision. In reality, the average number of contacts in IPS programs is slightly less than six per month.[18] An evaluation of 14 IPS programs concluded that IPS contacts of any type amounted, on average, to a total of less than 2 hours per month per offender (assuming that 20 minutes was spent per face-to-face contact). The same is true of drug testing—the average for all sites was just over two tests per month.[19]

Although IPS is used in all 50 states, its effectiveness has been questioned. Most evaluations report somewhat lower rates of new arrests but much higher rates of technical violations for IPS caseloads than for regular probationers.[20] Technical violations by offenders are more likely to be brought to the attention of supervising officers, largely as a result of closer surveillance. In addition to not being significantly more effective than traditional probation supervision, IPS is more costly as a result of the small caseloads, albeit not as costly as incarceration.

Headline Crime: Probation Officer Misconduct

While official misconduct is more widely known in the arena of police behavior, its occurrence among probation officers is not unknown. In 2003, a Havre, Montana, probation officer was found guilty of criminal misconduct for engaging in a consensual sexual relationship with one of his probationers. The woman had stated that she consented to have sex with the officer because "he had significant power over her" and could have recommended revocation of her probation for violating its conditions. Although Montana law forbade corrections officers to engage in consensual sexual activity with inmates, it did not specifically prohibit consensual sex between probation officers and probationers. The officer was found guilty. Following his appeal of the verdict, the Montana Supreme Court threw out the conviction, holding that while the officer's conduct was "reprehensible and opportunistic," it did not amount to official misconduct.

In 2006, a Dakota County, Minnesota, probation officer was charged with having consensual sex on multiple occasions with one of his female probationers. The victim told police she had had sex with the officer several times while under supervision in 2005–2006. Police said that a number of witnesses saw the officer buying the woman drinks at various bars in St. Paul—in direct violation of her conditions of probation. The woman's daughters also told police that the officer visited their mother at her apartment, sometimes late at night. Unlike Montana, Minnesota law specifically prohibits sexual contact between probation officers and probationers.

Hierarchical relationships exist in a wide variety of settings (for example, in businesses, universities, and the military) in which one person has authority over another and always have the potential for abuse. When the relationship is entered into by choice of the two parties, it is less problematic. When the two people are legally required to be in the relationship, however, the abuse of power and authority becomes a significant issue. Even the hint of coercion or the possibility that negative consequences could occur if the client does not agree to the relationship casts is inappropriate in any part of the criminal justice system.

Sources: Frederick Melo, "Probation Officer Accused of Sexual Misconduct," *Pioneer Press* (August 9, 2006), available at http://www.twincities.com/mld/twincities/15228887.htm, accessed September 2, 2008; Jim Adams, "Dakota County Probation Officer Charged with Sexual Misconduct," *Star Tribune* (August 8, 2006), available at http://www.startribune.com/462/story/602433.html, accessed September 2, 2008; Sarah Cooke, "Misconduct Conviction Reversed," *Helena Independent Record* (December 30, 2005), available at http://www.helenair.com/articles/2005/12/30/montana/c01123005_01.prt, accessed September 2, 2008.

House Arrest

House arrest permits punishment while offenders stay integrated into society.

House arrest is a sentence in which the offender is legally ordered to remain in his or her home. While under house arrest, offenders may not leave their homes except to go to work or school or to obtain medical treatment. Offenders are usually required to be in their homes during the evening and on weekends, although some may be allowed to leave their residences to perform community service.

House arrest has a number of advantages over incarceration. First, it is significantly less expensive than incarceration. Second, offenders are able to keep their jobs and avoid adverse effects on families, such as economic hardship and divorce. Third, house arrest is flexible and can be used to cover particular times of the day or control particular types of offenders.[21]

Electronic Monitoring

For individuals who commit more serious offenses, an **electronic monitoring** system may be used in conjunction with house arrest. Such programs require the offender to wear an electronic bracelet attached to the wrist or ankle. The technology involved in electronic monitoring has become increasingly sophisticated in recent years, providing a range of services depending on the degree of monitoring required:[22]

- *Radio frequency (RF) tether*. A transmitter is worn on the ankle of the offender and a receiver is placed in the offender's home. The receiver has a preset range limiting the distance the offender may move during the time he or she is scheduled to be at home.
- *Global Positioning Satellite (GPS)*. The GPS system uses the U.S. Department of Defense's Global Positioning Satellites and provides a real-time map reporting the offender's every move. This system also allows the monitoring agency to establish "hot zones" designating areas that the offender is not allowed to enter.
- *Visual alcohol monitoring*. A visual screen and Breathalyzer are placed in the offender's home. When a randomized computer call is received, the offender is instructed to blow into the Breathalyzer and transmit his or her picture to the monitoring agency. All missed calls and positive readings are logged and reported.
- *Secure continuous remote alcohol monitoring* (S.C.R.A.M.). Offenders wear an ankle bracelet that uses transdermal alcohol testing to measure the amount of alcohol that migrates through the skin, thereby determining the offender's blood alcohol content. The device constantly monitors the blood alcohol level and transmits the information to a receiver in the home, providing 24-hour monitoring by the agency.
- *Voice verification*. The offender receives random telephone calls during the times he or she is scheduled to be home. The offender is then prompted by the computer to repeat a series of numbers. This technology identifies the offender by matching each response to the voice template that was created during the initial enrollment in the program. All missed calls and failed sessions are logged and reported to the agency.

Electronic monitoring and other surveillance devices are an increasing part of correctional supervision.

The use of electronic monitoring, however, raises the fear that the United States may be headed toward the type of society described in George Orwell's book, *1984*, wherein citizens' language and movement are strictly monitored as part of the government's tools of oppression. According to sociologists Ronald Corbett and Gary Marx, "We appear to be moving toward, rather than away from, becoming a 'maximum-security society.'"[23]

Day Reporting Centers

Day reporting centers, which were initially developed to help reduce overcrowding in jails and prisons, often require offenders to spend all or part of each day at a designated reporting center. Offenders may live at home and go to work or attend school, but then must report to the center to meet with a counselor. They may also be required to participate in anger management or drug or alcohol treatment programs.

Fines

U.S. courts have traditionally imposed **fines** on offenders, often in conjunction with other sentences. Although the payment of fines appears to have few rehabilitative advantages, it does expedite the flow of offenders through the criminal justice system. The advantages of traditional fines seem clear:

- Fines can be administered to a variety of offenders
- Fines impose minimal costs on taxpayers
- Fines serve as a form of retribution

Of course, traditional fines also produce inequities between rich and poor offenders. If fines are set at a level great enough to affect the wealthy, they create a proportionately much greater burden on the poor.

Structured fines, sometimes called day fines, are designed to eliminate the proportionately greater financial burden placed on poorer offenders by tying the amount of the fine to the offender's ability to pay.[24]

Forfeiture

Forfeiture is a legal procedure that permits the government to seize property used in the commission of a crime. In 1996, the Supreme Court held that a state could require the forfeiture of a person's vehicle or home even if the owner was not involved in or aware of the use of the vehicle or home in conjunction with criminal activity.[25] In many states, real estate on which marijuana is grown has been seized. Proceeds from the sale of forfeitures generally go to the state or local treasury or are divided among various law enforcement agencies. In some jurisdictions, police agencies retain some or all of the funds to continue their fight against drug traffickers. For example, seized cash may be used to buy illegal drugs in sting operations and to rent or buy buildings used as fronts in such operations.[26]

Restitution

Community service combines the interests of criminal punishment and public service.

The federal government and most states provide for **restitution**, or payment of compensation by the offender to the victim or a victim-assistance program, as an intermediate sanction imposed regardless of whether the offender is incarcerated or placed on probation. Beginning in 1972, the Minnesota Restitution Program gave prisoners convicted of property offenses the opportunity to shorten their jail stays, or avoid prison time altogether, if they went to work and turned over part of their pay as restitution to their victims. Today, many restitution programs also include payment to victims for damages resulting from violent crimes.

Community Service

Through **community service**, an offender provides unpaid service to the larger community. This sentencing option has several benefits:

- It avoids the costs of incarceration.
- It spares the offenders' families undue hardship.
- It provides needed services to the community.[27]

Today, offenders can be sentenced to voluntary work for a specific number of hours, often in charitable organizations, city park maintenance, assisting the elderly, or hospital service work.[28] For example, a convicted accountant might be assigned to help the elderly file their income tax returns; an athlete might speak to school children about the dangers of drug use.

Restorative Justice

Restorative justice focuses on the community and aims to change the way people think about crime.[29] In this model, crime is viewed as more than an individual violation of criminal law—it is seen as a violation of community and relationships. Restorative justice makes the fundamental assumption that crime is a harm committed against an individual victim (more similar to a civil wrong), which is a dramatic shift from thinking about crime as an offense against the larger community or the state. According to this perspective, the government should have a more limited role and victims should be placed at the center of the criminal justice process.

Restorative justice takes many forms:

- *Victim–offender mediation* brings victims and offenders together with a mediator so that both parties can relate what they believe happened and why it occurred and arrive at a mutually agreed-upon reparative agreement.
- *Family group conferencing* requires that an offender admit to having committed the offense and have a representative (usually a family member) attend a conference with a person representing the victim. At this meeting, the two representatives discuss the offense and its consequences and develop a plan of action to repair the harms.
- *Circle sentencing* requires that the victim and the offender meet face-to-face with representatives from local social service agencies, law enforcement, the courts, and the community to talk about how they feel about the offense and the offender. The parties involved also determine the best ways to respond to the offense and attend to the needs of the victim and community.
- *Reparative probation* involves a special hearing board made up of local citizens who question offenders and victims and deliberate (typically in private) to develop appropriate sentencing for nonviolent offenders.[30]

Criticisms of Restorative Justice

Critics such as Sharon Levrant contend that restorative justice does not offer any realistic set of policies for the control of serious crime or methods to reduce the high rates of recidivism by offenders who continue to commit serious crimes. In addition, Levrant believes that:[31]

- Restorative justice approaches do not provide needed due process protections and procedural safeguards for offenders.
- Offenders are often coerced into participating in restorative programs, as they may believe any refusal to do so will result in harsher punishments.
- Policies based on restorative justice may increase punishments for offenders by requiring that they submit to both reparative conditions and traditional probation supervision.
- The current organization of probation departments and their limited resources make it unrealistic to emphasize community reintegration and expand the role of probation officers.

- Unintended race and class bias may occur because more affluent offenders may be better able to mediate or negotiate more favorable sanctions.
- Restorative justice programs target low-risk, nonviolent offenders with little likelihood of recidivism and have not proven to be effective for offenders who commit more serious crimes.
- Restorative justice programs are unlikely to have any long-term impact on the fundamental causes of an offender's inclination to engage in crime.

Other critics, such as Adam Crawford and Todd Clear, suggest that restorative justice advocates assume community consensus without defining the boundaries of community and have not identified clear goals of restoration.[32] Moreover, many communities are too heterogeneous in terms of class, race, and ethnicity to promote consensus, and many—even those with greater homogeneity—have few of the economic and organizational resources needed to successfully bring about the restoration of victims and the reintegration of offenders.[33]

Parole and Other Prereleases

Parole involves the conditional release of an offender from a correctional institution after the individual serves a portion of his or her sentence. Once on parole, the offender remains under community supervision and in the legal custody of the state; if the offender violates the conditions of parole, he or she may be reincarcerated.[34]

In 2006, nearly 800,000 offenders in the United States were on parole and being supervised in the community. Overall, the U.S. parole population grew by 17,586 persons in 2006, which was an increase of 2.3 percent over the 2005 parole population, or slightly more than the average annual increase of 1.5 percent since 1995. Some states, however, saw increases in their parole populations as high as 22 percent or decreases as much as 29 percent.[35] Thirty-seven percent of the offenders on parole in 2006 had been convicted of drug offenses; smaller percentages had committed property crimes and violent crimes. Eighty-eight percent of adults on parole were male. Whites accounted for 41 percent of parolees, African Americans for 39 percent, and Latinos for 18 percent.

Emergence of Parole

The use of parole in the United States actually preceded the concept of probation by several decades. Until the mid-nineteenth century, nearly all prison sentences had to be served in their entirety. With the development of the indeterminate sentence, prisoners began to be released into the community when correctional staff determined they were ready.[36] By 1900, 20 states had established parole systems. By 1932, 44 states and the federal government were using parole as a method of early prison release. Today, all jurisdictions provide for some form of early release and community supervision.

In many states, determinate sentencing laws have resulted in requirements for releasing inmates at the completion of their sentences minus good time. Good time allows prisoners to accumulate days to be subtracted from their terms for good behavior, for attending academic or training programs, or for performing meritorious service. While at least 29 states have "truth-in-sentencing" laws (discussed in Chapter 9) governing when inmates are to be released, four states continue to use good time rules that permit many—if not most—inmates to serve only 50 percent of their sentences. For example, in Indiana in 2005, only 26 of about 15,000 inmates released from prison had reached their sentence release date; the remainder had earned sufficient good time for early release.[37]

Other Types of Release

Not all offenders who are released from prison are placed on parole. Full release from a correctional institution may be unconditional or discretionary. In addition, many inmates are able to take advantage of temporary releases to work or attend educational programs in the community.

Unconditional Release

Unconditional release (also called mandatory release) includes the release, without supervision, of inmates who have served their maximum sentences (minus credits for good time or time served in jail before conviction). It takes two forms: commutation and clemency. **Commutation** is the decision by the governor or president to reduce the severity of an inmate's sentence to allow for immediate release. **Clemency** (also called pardon) is an executive decision by the governor or president to set aside an offender's punishment or exempt the offender from the punishment, and to release the individual instead. A pardon is typically granted after conviction and sentencing in a felony case, usually after the offender has been incarcerated.

Halfway House

The Federal Bureau of Prisons and a number of state correctional systems permit eligible inmates to be transferred to a **halfway house**, sometimes called a community corrections center or reentry center, at a date prior to the inmate's formal release from prison. These facilities provide secure housing of inmates to ensure the public's safety, while also providing inmates with an opportunity to take a controlled step into the community. While at a halfway house, an inmate may attend school, work, participate in a job training program, and receive counseling. If inmates fail to return to the halfway house at the designated time of day or arrive under the influence of drugs or alcohol, they may be returned to prison to serve out the remainder of their sentences.

Temporary Release

Some inmates are released from prison on a temporary basis; that is, they experience a specific period of being back into the community, but remain under the control of prison authorities. Temporary release comes in three forms: furlough, work release, and educational release.

In an effort to help prisoners maintain ties to their families and communities, many states allow qualified inmates who are not considered a danger to the community to go on *furlough*—temporary home visits. Furloughs usually last between 24 hours and one week and are especially common around the Thanksgiving and Christmas holidays. Sometimes inmates are permitted to go on furlough to attend a family funeral, visit seriously ill relatives, or seek employment. Other states allow furloughs only for inmates who are close to their release date.[38]

Work and educational release programs give offenders the opportunity to establish ties to the community before their final release from prison. *Work release* allows an offender to leave the institution during the day to work at a job.[39] As part of the prerelease program, offenders may be assisted in résumé writing and establishing community contacts. Under *educational release*, offenders are allowed to leave the institution to attend classes at nearby colleges, universities, or vocational training schools. Offenders who are involved in work or educational release may be assigned to a prerelease center that houses other inmates in the community.

Parole Board

Inmates who are eligible for conditional release from prison are reviewed periodically by **parole boards** that make discretionary decisions about prisoners' release. Today, only

Most offenders granted early release from prison must meet regularly with their parole officer.

about one fourth of released prisoners are released by parole boards, compared to 65 percent in 1976. In many states, the advent of determinate and structured sentencing systems has meant that numerous offenders now arrive at prison with predetermined release dates.

States differ in how they handle prisoners who have reached their mandatory release dates. Some states require that they serve a year of conditional release (basically one year of parole), during which time released prisoners could be returned to prison if they violate their conditions of supervision. Other states release prisoners with no supervision, no parole officer, and no one legally responsible for their reintegration into the community.[40]

Parole Decision Making

Once an inmate becomes eligible for parole—typically after serving at least one third of the minimum number of years of his or her sentence—a parole hearing is scheduled. Notices are sent to the victim, prosecutor, and defense lawyer involved in the case. Some states also require that the news media be notified of parole hearings.

At the hearing, the parole board reviews the inmate's institutional file, which includes details of the offense, the inmate's criminal background, and his or her behavior in prison. The board questions the inmate about any prison rule violations, participation in treatment programs, and plans for parole. In addition, the prosecutor, the defense attorney, and relatives and friends of both the inmate and the victim may present written or oral statements to the board. The general criteria the parole board considers are based on a number of personal and institutional factors:

- The nature and circumstance of the inmate's offense, including aggravating and mitigating circumstances
- Court statements about the sentence
- The nature and pattern of previous convictions
- The inmate's attitude toward the offense, family members, the victim, and authority in general
- The attitude of the victim or victim's family regarding release of the inmate
- The inmate's insight into the causes of past criminal conduct
- The inmate's adjustment to previous probation, parole, or incarceration
- The inmate's participation in institutional programs
- The adequacy of the inmate's parole plan, including residence and employment[41]

Release of Sex Offenders

Release of sex offenders is a controversial issue, even when convicted sex offenders and child predators have served their full sentences. Although not all convicted sex offenders have committed violent sex crimes, most of those sentenced to prison for sex offenses have done so. When released, they present special concerns for the community.

For example, convicted sex offender Jesse Timmendequas was released from the New Jersey Adult Diagnostic and Treatment Center in 1988 after serving his full term with no mandatory therapy or supervision. In 1994, Timmendequas tricked seven-year-old Megan Kanka into entering his home, then raped and murdered her. Timmendequas lived across the street from the Kanka family, as did two other convicted sex offenders, but their offenses were unknown to the neighbors in the community. Megan Kanka's

Megan Kanka was raped and murdered by a recently released sex offender.

death eventually led to the passage of Megan's Law, which requires both registration and community notification by sex offenders when they move into a community.

Not all paroled sex offenders are known to local police. In spite of laws requiring sex offenders to register with the police when they move into a community, many fail to do so. California authorities, for example, report not being able to account for 44 percent of their state's registered sex offenders. Similarly, police in Seattle cannot account for the whereabouts of more than 20 percent of the registered sex offenders believed to be living in that city.[42] When registered sex offenders fail to notify local police where they live, the police are unable to use Megan's Law to notify residents. Perhaps more importantly, when sex offenders do not notify police of their presence in a community, parole officers are also unaware of their location and cannot provide any supervision. These problems have led many citizens and politicians to call for violent sex offenders' ineligibility for parole via civil commitment.

Unfortunately, even though sex offenders may register with the police, there is no guarantee the offender won't strike again. For example, Corey Saunders, age 26, had been convicted in Massachusetts of attempted child rape and assault and battery on a child—the state's most dangerous designation. However, he spent only four years in prison. The prosecutor had requested Bristol Superior Court Judge Richard Moses to commit Saunders indefinitely based on a state law allowing judges to make such civil commitments if they find an offender to be dangerous and likely to commit a violent sex crime again. Judge Moses denied the prosecutor's motion, citing the defendant's low IQ, his history of being sexually abused when he was a child, and the fact Saunders had committed no sex offenses while in prison. Saunders was released from prison and registered with local police as required. Less than a year later, Saunders was arrested and charged with raping a six-year-old boy at a library while the boy's mother was nearby using a computer. The boy did not scream because Saunders allegedly demanded the boy's address and threatened to rape him again if he yelled out.[43]

Conditions of Parole

The conditions of parole are very similar to the conditions attached to probation. Parolees generally may not leave the community or state without permission, and they may not own a firearm, use alcohol, or associate with people considered to be negative influences. Offenders are required to obtain gainful employment, report regularly to their parole supervisor, submit to unannounced drug and alcohol testing, and enroll in treatment programs if deemed appropriate by the parole officer. Most offenders who are granted parole eventually are discharged from supervision; those found to be in violation of the terms are returned to prison.

Parolees are at a disadvantage as they begin their parole. Upon leaving prison, they typically have few resources; often they set out with only the clothes and small sum of cash provided by the prison. With limited skills and the stigma of a felony conviction, many are unable to find or keep a job. In addition, many jobs are off-limits to parolees, especially if alcohol is present on the premises. Likewise, reasonable housing may be difficult to find. Research suggests that 15 to 27 percent of paroles are likely to go to homeless shelters after being released from prison.[44]

Parole Supervision

Like probationers, when offenders are granted parole, they are placed under the supervision of parole officers and must agree to abide by specific rules. Parolees are expected to

FOCUS ON CRIMINAL JUSTICE

The Civil Commitment of Sex Offenders

In 1994, researchers began a three-year project tracking a group of prisoners released from prison in 15 states to assess their success on parole. Compared to non-sex offenders released from state prisons, these offenders were four times more likely to be rearrested for a sex crime. Forty percent of these new offenses were committed within the first 12 months following their release.

Coupled with the failure of many offenders to register with local law enforcement (which made community notification impossible), the high recidivism rates of sex offenders prompted Minnesota Congressman Mark Kennedy to sponsor federal legislation that would ensure sex offenders and child predators would not be eligible for parole. According to the proposed No Parole for Sex Offenders legislation (H.R. 4621), sex offenders would be committed for treatment for an indeterminate amount of time until they are no longer considered a threat to public safety if they are determined to have a sexual psychopathic personality or to be a sexually dangerous person by the courts.

Minnesota law defines a sexual psychopathic personality as a person who, as a result of a mental or emotional condition:

- Engaged in a habitual course of misconduct in sexual matters
- Has an utter lack of power to control the sexual impulses
- Is dangerous to others as a result of an inability to regulate his or her own behavior

A sexually dangerous person is defined as a person who:

- Has engaged in harmful sexual conduct that creates a substantial likelihood of serious physical or emotional harm to others
- Has a sexual, personality, or mental disorder
- Is likely to engage in harmful sexual conduct in the future

In 1994, Kansas enacted the Sexually Violent Predator Act, which established procedures for the civil commitment of persons who, due to a mental abnormality or personality disorder, are likely to engage in "predatory acts of sexual violence." Unlike a criminal statute, the commitment determination is made based on a mental or personality disorder rather than on a person's criminal intent; thus the commitment is for treatment purposes rather than punishment. In *Kansas v. Hendricks*, and reaffirmed in *Kansas v. Crane*, the U.S. Supreme Court upheld the constitutionality of sex offender civil commitment statutes (involuntary commitments typically made under state mental health laws). The Court held that the Kansas statute violated neither the due process rights of individuals nor their double jeopardy interests.

Thus civil commitment of dangerous sex offenders can allow states to ensure that these offenders no longer present a threat to the community by keeping them incarcerated with no predetermined release date.

Sources: Patrick Langan, Erica Schmitt, and Matthew Durose, *Recidivism of Sex Offenders Released from Prison in 1994* (Washington, DC: U.S. Department of Justice, 2003); H.R. 4621, *No Parole for Sex Offenders* (2005); Section 253B.02.185 *Minnesota Statutes* (2004); *Kansas v. Hendricks*, 521 U.S. 346 (1997); *Kansas v. Crane*, 534 U.S. 407 (2002).

keep appointments with their parole officers and to be available at home, work, or school for regular check-ups with parole officers.

Many parole officers have special caseloads composed of more serious and potentially dangerous parolees who require much closer supervision. Like intensive probation supervision, **intensive parole supervision** involves very small caseloads, which allows officers to meet face-to-face with parolees on a more frequent schedule and make more frequent office, home, or work visits than in typical parole situations.

Revocation of Parole

Parolees, like probationers, may face a revocation hearing as a result of technical violations or commission of a new offense. Often, a new offense also includes a technical violation, as when the parolee robs a store (new offense) using a weapon (whose possession is a technical violation of parole conditions).

Until 1972, parole revocation decisions were often made arbitrarily by individual parole officers. Parolees found in violation of their parole conditions were frequently taken into custody and returned to prison without a hearing. In 1972, the Supreme Court held, in ***Morrissey v. Brewer***, that even though the revocation of parole is not a part of the criminal prosecution, the loss of liberty entailed is a serious deprivation entitling the parolee to his or her due process rights under the Fourteenth Amendment.[45] These due process requirements include the following rights:

- A preliminary hearing and a final revocation hearing
- Written notice of the claimed violations of parole
- Disclosure to the parolee of evidence against him or her
- Opportunity to be heard in person and to present witnesses and documentary evidence
- The right to confront and cross-examine adverse witnesses
- A neutral and detached hearing body
- A written statement as to the evidence relied on and the reasons for revoking parole

Because revocation of parole is not mandatory, many parolees do not return to prison even when they commit new crimes.

Effectiveness of Parole

Overall, parole appears to be ineffective in reducing the likelihood that an offender will reoffend after release. While nearly 800,000 persons were on parole in 2006, approximately 180,000 offenders were returned to prison during that year after failing on parole.[46]

In the most comprehensive study to date, Patrick Langan and David Levin found that nearly one third of parolees were rearrested within the first six months after their release, and 44 percent within the first year after their release.[47] By the end of the second year, nearly 60 percent had been rearrested; by the end of the third year, more than 67 percent had been rearrested. By the end of the three-year period, 47 percent had been convicted of a new crime, and more than 25 percent were resentenced to prison for a new offense. Among this group, property offenders were the most likely to be rearrested and resentenced, but there was relatively little difference for offenders originally convicted of other offenses (see FIGURE 12–3).

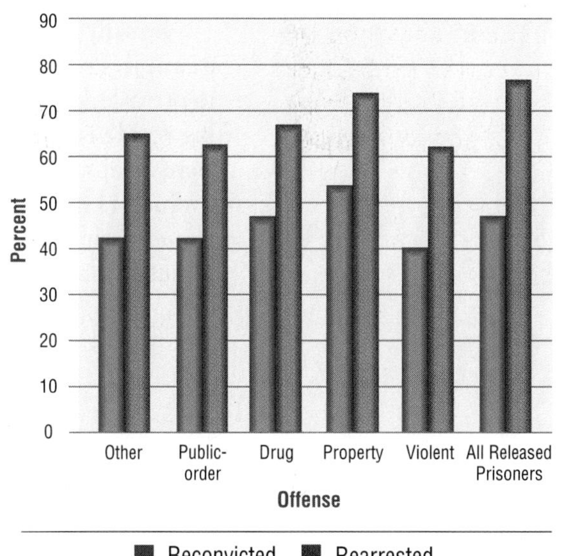

FIGURE 12–3 Percentage of Prisoners Who Are Rearrested and Reconvicted Within Three Years of Release

Adapted from Patric Langan and David Levin, *Recidivism of Prisoners Released in 1994* (Washington, DC: U.S. Department of Justice, 2002).

These reoffenders pose a significant risk to public safety. According to Steven Raphael and Michael Stoll, recently released prisoners are 20 to 50 times more likely to be arrested in comparison to persons in the general public. They also found that the amount of time served in prison had a minimal impact on the likelihood of failure on parole. Sixty percent of prisoners who were released after serving six months or less in prison were rearrested, compared to 63 percent of those who served between three and five years, and 54 percent of those who had served at least five years.[48]

Reentry

When an offender leaves prison, whether supervised on parole or not, the individual's reentry into the community is often difficult. Parole officers can assist parolees with finding jobs, getting into job training or school, or becoming involved in treatment or counseling. Despite this help, the ability of a prisoner to make a positive transition from prison to community often depends on a number of other factors:

- Preprison circumstances—demographic characteristics, job skills, work history, family status, drug or alcohol abuse, and criminal history
- In-prison experiences—length of time served, participation in treatment programs, contact with family members, and prerelease preparation
- Immediate postprison experiences—nature of release, immediate housing needs, family support, and need for transition assistance
- Postrelease integration experiences—family connections, social service support, influence of peers, employment experiences, and community supervision[49]

Unfortunately, few reentry programs have successfully addressed all of these factors. This failure is especially problematic because a large proportion of prisoners released into the community do not have access to the human and social capital required for successful reentry. Many lack a stable family structure, an affordable place to live, and the educational or job skills necessary to establish a routine of stability. Offenders may be viewed in a stigmatizing way by family, friends, neighbors, and potential employers. Moreover, most reentry programs are voluntary and have relatively low participation rates.[50] Regardless of the potential effectiveness of a reentry program, if ex-offenders do not participate, the program cannot succeed.

Equally important for success is the actual implementation of reentry programs. For example, Project Greenlight, a prison-based reentry program in New York, was created to provide specific services to improve the quality of life of new parolees, thereby reducing recidivism. However, evaluations of the program found that participant outcomes were significantly worse than two control groups of inmates who did not participate. Evaluators determined that the program had no real reentry component; the program was entirely prison based, with no community follow-up or provision of services for inmates once they returned to the community.[51]

WRAPPING IT UP

Chapter Highlights

- Since 1992, more than 70 percent of all offenders under some form of correctional care or custody have been supervised in the community.
- While on probation, an individual is expected to obey all conditions set forth in the probation agreement; failure to follow these conditions may result in revocation of probation.
- Intermediate sanctions include intensive probation supervision, house arrest and electronic monitoring, day reporting centers, fines, forfeiture, restitution, and community service.
- Restorative justice seeks to repair relationships broken by crime by balancing the needs of the community, victims, and offenders, although critics question the long-term effectiveness of such programs.
- Parole involves the release of an offender under community supervision from a correctional institution after the offender has served a portion of his or her sentence.
- The unconditional release of inmates into the community comes after they have served their maximum sentence and must be released, often with only a short period of supervision or no supervision at all.
- Some incarcerated offenders may be temporarily placed in the community for furlough, home visits, or work or educational release.

Words to Know

clemency An executive decision by the governor or president to set aside an offender's punishment and release the individual.

community corrections A correctional approach based on the belief offenders can (and often should) be dealt with within the community rather than through prisons.

community service A sentence in which the offender makes reparation to the community.

commutation An executive order in which a prisoner's sentence is reduced to allow for his or her immediate release.

day reporting center A center where counselors meet with offenders who are permitted to remain within the community, live at home, and go to work or attend school.

electronic monitoring A sentence requiring an offender to wear an electronic device to verify his or her location.

fine A sentence in which the offender makes a cash payment to the court.

forfeiture A legal procedure that permits the government to seize property used in the commission of a crime.

Gagnon v. Scarpelli Supreme Court decision identifying the due process rights of an offender during a probation revocation hearing.

halfway house Facilities designed to provide secure housing of inmates and to ensure the public's safety while providing inmates with an opportunity to take a controlled step into the community.

house arrest A sentence requiring that the offender be legally confined to his or her home.

informal probation Placement of an offender on probation before a conviction is entered on the record; upon completion of the probation conditions, the offender is released and the case dismissed.

intensive parole supervision A practice under which caseloads are very small and officers frequently meet face-to-face with parolees to provide greater supervision.

intensive probation supervision (IPS) A practice under which probation officers with very small caseloads are able to provide increased supervision.

intermediate sanctions Sentences that may be imposed as alternatives to traditional probation or incarceration.

Megan's Law A law that requires both registration and community notification by sex offenders when they move into a community.

Morrissey v. Brewer Supreme Court ruling that spelled out the due process rights of offenders on parole.

parole The conditional release of an offender from a correctional institution after serving a portion of his or her sentence.

parole board The group of people who make the discretionary decision about a prisoner's release.

preliminary revocation hearing The first hearing to determine whether there is probable cause that the offender violated the conditions of probation or parole.

probation A sentencing option involving a suspended prison sentence and supervision in the community.

reentry The process in which an inmate leaves prison and returns to society.

restitution A requirement of offenders to pay money or provide services to victims.

restorative justice A punishment philosophy aimed at restoring or repairing relationships disrupted by crime, holding offenders accountable, promoting offender competency and responsibility, and balancing the needs of the community, victim, and offender through involvement in the restorative process.

revocation hearing A hearing to determine whether probation or parole should be revoked.

risk classification An assessment of an offender's likelihood of committing a new offense if granted probation.

structured fines Fines designed to eliminate the proportionately greater financial burden placed on poorer offenders by tying the amount of the fine to the offender's ability to pay.

unconditional release A release from prison that does not require additional supervision in the community.

Think and Discuss

1. Should violent offenders ever be placed on probation? Which characteristics of an offender do you think are most important when determining who should receive probation?
2. Is restorative justice too informal a means for dealing with crime and criminals? Does it threaten the due process rights of offenders afforded by traditional prosecutions and sentencing?
3. Should parolees who are found guilty of minor infractions of their conditions of parole be returned to prison? Why or why not?
4. How much consideration should parole boards give to the views of victims and their families at parole hearings?
5. How much information should residents receive about convicted offenders living in their neighborhoods? Does publicity about released sex offenders violate their right to privacy?

Notes

1. Tom Murton, "Inmate Self-Government," *University of San Francisco Law Review* 6:88 (1971).
2. Lauren Glaze and Thomas Bonczar, *Probation and Parole in the United States, 2006* (Washington, DC: U.S. Department of Justice, 2007).
3. Glaze and Bonczar, note 2.
4. Task Force on Corrections, *Task Force Report: Corrections* (Washington, DC: U.S. Government Printing Office, 1966).
5. Board of Probation and Parole, *Annual Report FY 2004–05* (Nashville: Board of Probation and Parole, 2005).
6. Randall Guynes, "Difficult Clients, Large Caseloads Plague Probation Parole Agencies," *Research in Action* (Washington, DC: National Institute of Justice, 1988).
7. Todd Clear and Vincent O'Leary, *Controlling the Offender in the Community* (Lexington, MA: Lexington Books, 1983).
8. Belinda McCarthy and Bernard McCarthy, Jr., *Community-Based Corrections*, 2nd ed. (Pacific Grove, CA: Brooks/Cole, 1991), p. 376.
9. *U.S. v. Knights*, 534 U.S. 112 (2001).
10. "Drug Treatment Role Increasing for Probation, Parole Agencies," *Criminal Justice Newsletter* 9:6 (1988).
11. Faye Taxman, "Supervision—Exploring the Dimensions of Effectiveness," *Federal Probation* 66:14–27 (2002).
12. Taxman, note 11.
13. *Gagnon v. Scarpelli*, 411 U.S. 778 (1973).
14. Glaze and Bonczar, note 2, p. 2.

15. Joan Petersilia, Susan Turner, James Kahan, and Joyce Peterson, *Granting Felons Probation: Public Risks and Alternatives* (Santa Monica, CA: Rand, 1985).

16. Edward Latessa, Lawrence Travis, Betsy Fulton, and Amy Stichman, *Evaluating the Prototypical ISP: Final Report* (Cincinnati: University of Cincinnati and American Probation and Parole Association, 1998).

17. James Byrne, "The Future of Intensive Probation Supervision and the New Intermediate Sanctions," *Crime & Delinquency* 36:14 (1990); Todd Clear and Patricia Hardyman, "The New Intensive Supervision Movement," *Crime & Delinquency* 36:47 (1990).

18. Joan Petersilia and Susan Turner, *Evaluating Intensive Supervision Probation/Parole: Results of a Nationwide Experiment* (Washington, DC: U.S. Department of Justice, 1993).

19. Joan Petersilia and Susan Turner, "Comparing Intensive and Regular Supervision for High-Risk Probationers: Early Results from an Experiment in California," *Crime & Delinquency* 36:105 (1990).

20. Elizabeth Deschenes, Susan Turner, and Joan Petersilia, *Intensive Community Supervision in Minnesota: A Dual Experiment in Prison Diversion and Enhanced Supervised Release* (Washington, DC: National Institute of Justice, 1995); Benjamin Steiner, "Treatment Retention: A Theory of Post-Release Supervision for the Substance Abusing Offender," *Federal Probation* 68:24–29 (2004); Linda Burrow, Jennifer Joseph, and John Whitehead, "A Comparison of Recidivism in Intensive Supervision and Regular Probation," paper presented at the annual meeting of the Academy of Criminal Justice Sciences, Washington, DC, 2001.

21. National Institute of Justice, *Keeping Track of Electronic Monitoring* (Washington, DC: National Law Enforcement and Corrections Technology Center, 1999); Rene Stutzman, "Ankle Monitors Show a Higher Rate of Success," *Orlando Sentinel*, December 29, 2002, p. A15.

22. House Arrest Services, "Information about Electronic Monitoring Systems," available at http://www.housearrest.com/, accessed September 2, 2008.

23. Ronald Corbett and Gary Marx, "Critique: No Soul in the New Machine: Technofallacies in the Electronic Monitoring Movement," *Justice Quarterly* 8:400 (1991).

24. Barry Mahoney, Joan Green, Judith Greene, and July Eigler, *How to Use Structured Fines (Day Fines) as an Intermediate Sanction* (Washington, DC: Bureau of Justice Assistance, 1996).

25. *Bennis v. Michigan*, 516 U.S. 442 (1996).

26. NIJ Reports, *Controlling Drug Abuse and Crime: A Research Update* (Washington, DC: U.S. Department of Justice, 1987), p. 3.

27. Douglas MacDonald, *Restitution and Community Service* (Washington, DC: U.S. Department of Justice, 1988), p. l.

28. Michael Agopian, "Targeting Juvenile Gang Offenders for Community Service," *Community Services: International Journal of Family Care* 1:99–108 (1989).

29. See, for example, Susan Olson and Albert Dzur, "Revisiting Informal Justice: Restorative Justice and Democratic Professionalism," *Law and Society Review* 38:139–176 (2004); John Braithwaite, *Restorative Justice and Responsive Regulation* (New York: Oxford University Press, 2002); John Perry (Ed.), *Repairing Communities through Restorative Justice* (Lanham, MD: American Correctional Association, 2002); Gerry Johnstone, *Restorative Justice: Ideas, Values, Debates* (Portland, OR: Willan, 2002); Daniel Van Ness and Karen Strong, *Restoring Justice*, 3rd ed. (Cincinnati: Anderson, 2006); Shay Bilchik, Gordon Bazemore, and Mark Umbreit, *Balanced and Restorative Justice for Juveniles: A Framework for Juvenile Justice in the 21st Century* (Washington, DC: Office of Juvenile Justice and Delinquency Prevention, 1997).

30. Braithwaite, note 29; Gordon Bazemore and Curt Griffiths, "Conferences, Circles, Boards, and Mediations: The 'New Wave' of Community Justice Decisionmaking," *Federal Probation* 61:25–37 (1997).

31. Sharon Levrant, Francis Cullen, Betsy Fulton, and John Wozniak, "Reconsidering Restorative Justice: The Corruption of Benevolence Revisited?" *Crime & Delinquency* 45:3–27 (1999).

32. Todd Clear, "Places Not Cases? Re-thinking the Probation Focus," *Howard Journal* 44:172–184 (2005).

33. Adam Crawford and Todd Clear, "Community Justice: Transforming Communities through Restorative Justice?" in Gordon Bazemore and Marie Schift, *Restorative Community Justice* (Cincinnati, OH: Anderson, 2001), pp. 127–149.

34. Wayne Morse, *The Attorney General's Survey of Release Procedures* (Washington, DC: U.S. Government Printing Office, 1939).

35. Glaze and Bonczar, note 2, p. 5.

36. Harry Barnes and Negley Teeters, *New Horizons in Criminology*, 3rd ed. (Englewood Cliffs, NJ: Prentice Hall, 1959).

37. Niki Kelly, "Do the Crime . . . Do Only Half the Time," *Fort Wayne Journal Gazette* (May 28, 2006), available at http://www.fortwayne.com/mld/journalgazette/14685881.htm, accessed June 5, 2008.

38. Howard Abadinsky, *Probation and Parole*, 10th ed. (Upper Saddle River, NJ: Prentice Hall, 2008).

39. Donald MacDonald and Gerald Bala, *Follow Up Study Sample of Edgecombe Work Release Participants* (Albany, NY: Division of Correctional Services, 1985).

40. Christy Visher and Jeremy Travis, "Transitions from Prison to Community: Understanding Individual Pathways," *Annual Review of Sociology* 29:89–114 (2003).

41. Connecticut Board of Parole, *Statement of Organization and Procedures* (Hartford, CT: Connecticut Board of Parole, 1974); Park Dietz, "Hypothetical Criteria for the Prediction of Individual Criminality," in Christopher Webster, Mark Ben-Aron, and Stephen Hucker (Eds.), *Dangerousness: Probability and Prediction, Psychiatry, and Public Policy* (Cambridge, UK: Cambridge University Press, 1985), p. 32.

42. Hector Castro, "Sex Offender Registry Failing," *Seattle Post-Intelligencer*, January 8, 2003, available at http://seattlepi.nwsource.com/local/103212_register08.shtml, accessed June 5, 2008.

43. Associated Press, "Police: Convicted Sex Offender Rapes Boy at Massachusetts Library," available at http://www.foxnews.com/story/0,2933,327590,00.html, accessed February 1, 2008.

44. James Gondles, "Returning to Society," *Corrections Today* 67:6–7 (2005).

45. *Morrissey v. Brewer*, 408 U.S. 471 (1972).

46. Glaze and Bonczar, note 2, p. 8.

47. Patrick Langan and David Levin, *Recidivism of Prisoners Released in 1994* (Washington, DC: U.S. Department of Justice, 2002).

48. Steven Raphael and Michael Stoll, "The Effect of Prison Releases on Regional Crime Rates," in William Gale and Janet Pack (Eds.), *Brookings-Wharton Papers on Urban Affairs 2004* (Washington, DC: Brookings Institution Press, 2004).

49. Visher and Travis, note 40.

50. James Wilson and Robert Davis, "Good Intentions Meet Hard Realities: An Evaluation of the Project Greenlight Reentry Program," *Criminology and Public Policy* 5:303–338 (2006).

51. James Wilson, "Habilitation or Harm: Project Greenlight and the Potential Consequences of Correctional Programming," *NIJ Journal* (June 2007), available at http://www.ojp.usdoj.gov/nij/journals/257/habilitation-or-harm.html, accessed November, 17, 2008.

This final part explores two issues of major concern to criminologists and the public: juvenile offenders and the crimes of terrorism and cybercrime. These issues present the criminal justice system with new and unusual demands.

During most of the twentieth century, actions related to juvenile offenders typically came under the exclusive domain of the juvenile justice system. There, offenders were treated according to a more protective philosophy than they would have had they been cast into the adult system. Today, however, an increasing number of juveniles are being transferred into adult courts and, if convicted, face adult punishments. Chapter 13 examines the history of juvenile justice, explores characteristics of juvenile offenders, and outlines the juvenile justice process, from arrest to disposition. It also investigates those cases in which juveniles are transferred to the adult criminal justice system and the demise of the juvenile death penalty.

Chapter 14 explores terrorism and cybercrime, as well as the unique problems they pose for the criminal justice system. This chapter examines recent legislation, such as the USA Patriot Act, and government efforts to combat terrorism, including the creation of the Department of Homeland Security. It also discusses the widespread problem of identity theft and the criminal justice system's response to the unique problems posed by high-tech crime.

PART

Special Issues

CHAPTER

13

The Juvenile Justice System

OBJECTIVES

1 Know the history of the juvenile justice system.

2 Highlight the distinctions between delinquency and status-offending behaviors.

3 Be familiar with police procedures for arresting juveniles and the effects of legal and extralegal factors when making discretionary arrests.

4 Identify each major stage of the juvenile court process, from intake to adjudication and disposition.

5 Explain the differences between probation, institutional placement, and aftercare of juvenile offenders.

6 Understand the reasoning and methods of waiver for juveniles to the adult criminal justice system.

7 Describe what happens to juveniles once they face prosecution in criminal court.

8 Outline the history of the juvenile death penalty and explain why it was abolished.

PROFILES IN CRIME AND JUSTICE

James Burfeind, PhD
Professor and Chair of Sociology
University of Montana

The boy who sat in front of me in my eighth grade biology class was there one day, gone the next. He returned several months later. We talked often before and after class and I learned of his delinquent escapades and his time in the state training school. His life was so different from mine and that fascinated me. This fascination spurred my interest in juvenile delinquency—an interest I pursued in college by studying sociology, social work, and political science. I also pursued experience in the field through internships in a regional juvenile detention center and a wilderness-based correctional camp for delinquent boys, operated by the state. After college I landed a job with Scott County Court Services in Minnesota as a probation officer.

The position was unique from other jurisdictions in that I managed a caseload of both juvenile and adult offenders, with both probation and parole duties. As a juvenile probation officer, my responsibilities included screening cases referred to the juvenile court, being present at court hearings, conducting predisposition reports (PDR—used to advise the juvenile court judge in case disposition), and supervising youth placed on probation and released on parole. There were always reports to write: PDRs, progress reports, revocation reports, and termination reports. While these duties involved much discretion, they were also carried out according to informally accepted standards and procedures, held commonly by all probation officers.

The job was diverse and I found it to be equally rewarding and frustrating; nonetheless, it was interesting work. Rewarding, because I tried to orchestrate positive change in the lives of delinquent youth. Frustrating, because the caseloads were large and the time and energy that could be given to individual youth were limited. Interesting, because I was given the opportunity to describe, explain, and respond to juvenile delinquency. Using these experiences, I now try to pass on this understanding to students in my juvenile delinquency and juvenile justice classes at the University of Montana.

Introduction

In a 1964 statement, FBI Director J. Edgar Hoover commented on what he saw as the arrogant attitude of youth toward the criminal justice system and noted that many delinquents believed that because they were minors, the full force of the law could not touch them.[1] Most often, they were right. Many arrested offenders who are **juveniles** (typically defined as persons younger than age 18, though this age varies across states) go through a separate juvenile justice system in which they receive lenient treatment and, at most, brief confinement in a detention or juvenile correctional facility. Today, most juvenile offenders have very limited contact with the adult criminal justice system, except for temporary detention in adult jails.

In 2007, juveniles accounted for approximately 15 percent of all arrests (see FIGURE 13–1).[2] While this figure may be a concern to the public, lawmakers, and justice system personnel, the overall juvenile arrest rate has actually declined by 20 percent in the past 10 years (see FIGURE 13–2). In 2007, about 1.6 million juveniles were arrested, with more than 392,652 being charged with serious violent and property crimes.

Numerous studies suggest that most serious juvenile crime is committed by a relatively small number of youths—as few as 6 percent of juvenile offenders have been shown to be responsible for half of all juvenile crime and nearly 70 percent of serious crimes (such as homicide, rape, robbery, and aggravated assault) committed by juveniles.[3] Even

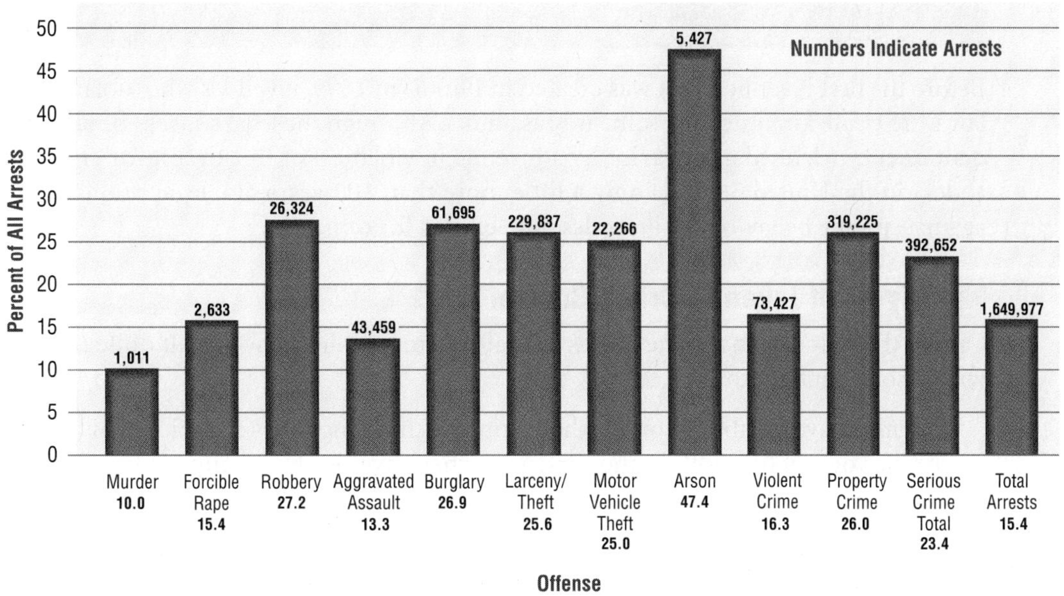

FIGURE 13-1 Arrests of Juveniles in the United States, 2007

Source: Federal Bureau of Investigation, *Crime in the United States, 2007* (Washington, DC: U.S. Department of Justice, 2008), Table 41.

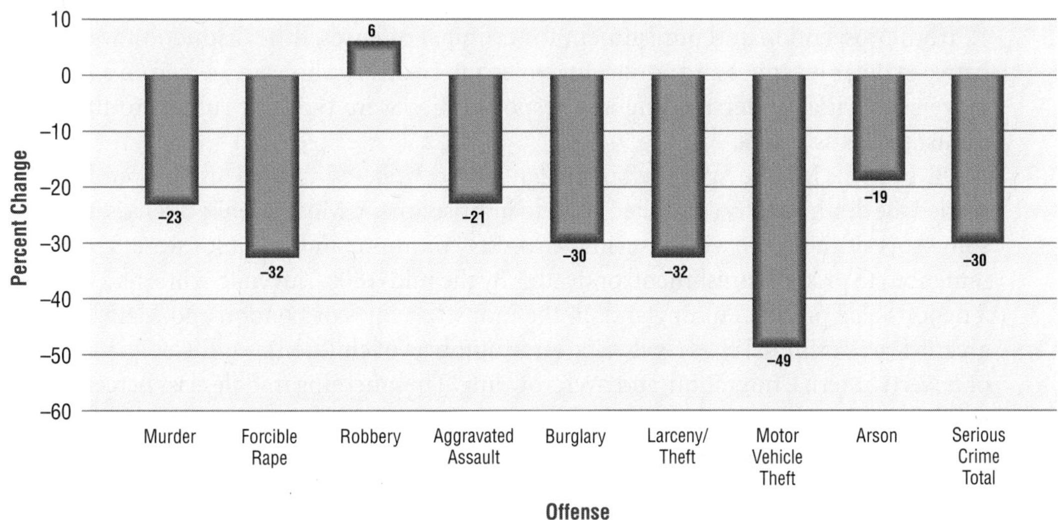

FIGURE 13-2 Percentage Change in Juvenile Arrests in the United States, 1998–2007

Source: Federal Bureau of Investigation, *Crime in the United States, 2007* (Washington, DC: U.S. Department of Justice, 2008), Table 32.

though juvenile crime is a minor part of the larger crime problem, the fact that many juveniles commit very serious crimes—and the fact that some offenders commit such crimes frequently—is a reality that prompts us to explore how society responds to juvenile crime, how the juvenile justice system operates, and how society should deal with the most serious of juvenile offenders. Many of these more serious offenders will grow up to be adult offenders who subsequently find their way into the criminal justice system.

History of Juvenile Justice

Before the first juvenile court was created in Illinois in 1899, juveniles who violated the law were treated in much the same way as adults. Although the legal concept of juvenile delinquency (defined as behavior by a juvenile in violation of the juvenile or criminal codes) in the United States is only a little more than 100 years old, legal prohibitions against specific behaviors by juveniles have existed for centuries.

Origins of Juvenile Crime Control

One of the foundations of the modern legal system—biblical law—dealt quite harshly with disobedient youth:

> If a man have a stubborn or rebellious son, which will not obey the voice of his father, or the voice of his mother, and that, when they have chastened him, will not harken unto them. Then shall his father and mother lay hold on him, and bring him out unto the elders of his city, and unto the gate of his place; And they shall say unto the elders of his city. This our son is stubborn and rebellious, he will not obey our voice; he is a glutton, and a drunkard. And all the men of his city shall stone him with stones, that he die.[4]

Brutal punishment for juvenile offenders in early English law was also common. English King Aethelstan proclaimed in the tenth century that any thief who was more than 12 years old would be punished by death for stealing more than 12 pence, though he later reserved this punishment for those offenders older than age 16 who resisted arrest or ran away.[5] Even though early English law exempted children younger than age 12 from prosecution and punishment for criminal offenses, little distinction was made between older juveniles and adults. Juveniles age 16 or 17, who were perceived as having more substantial understanding and responsibility, were typically subject to the same punishments as adults.

Even in the Middle Ages, theft in England was considered a felony (as was murder) and carried the death penalty as an alternative to imprisonment. Most juvenile offenses involved some sort of theft, but violent crime also was common, and juveniles were frequently sentenced to prison, banishment, or death.[6] By the mid-1800s, juvenile crime had become a major social problem in England. In the industrial cities of London and Manchester, a greatly feared criminal class (including large numbers of children) was linked to problems of poverty, internal migration, and overcrowding. The emerging middle class perceived the children of the urban poor as being thieves or prostitutes, frequently employed by older criminals, often orphaned or deserted, and likely to end up in prison. Given this view, punishing the criminal behavior of juveniles was seen as important for preventing the spread of crime in general. Yet, English law exempted children younger than age 14 from criminal penalties on the assumption that they were not capable of criminal intent (*mens rea*). Even so, children younger than age 10 were occasionally executed for crimes such as theft if they were considered to have sufficient mental maturity.[7]

In the early American colonies, it was not just the criminal activity of children that concerned colonists, but their inactivity as well. Sloth and idleness were considered sinful, corrupting influences to be prohibited by law. In 1646, the Virginia General Assembly passed legislation providing punishments for lazy or indolent children.[8] Massachusetts went one step further in 1672, requiring that "rude, stubborn, and unruly" children be separated from their parents and placed in foster homes, in the hope that stronger disciplinarians might save these children from criminal futures. This law was perhaps an improvement over the previous "stubborn child law" in place in Massachusetts, which, in accordance with biblical law, mandated the execution of stubborn children who disobeyed their parents.[9]

Juvenile Crime Control in Nineteenth-Century America

By the nineteenth century, the view of adolescents had shifted slightly. Children were viewed as corruptible, irritating, and arrogant, but they were also seen as innocent and vulnerable.[10] As such, adolescence was increasingly viewed as a unique period of life in which children needed thoughtful discipline and guidance. To ensure that children developed properly, society recognized that it must closely safeguard children's moral and physical health in preparation for adulthood. Consequently, children needed special treatment and a period of lessened responsibility and demands.[11] To that end, new laws were created allowing the state to take responsibility for improving the lives of children from families who were seen as unable to provide appropriate guidance and supervision.[12] If parents could not or would not produce well-behaved children, then, it was believed, the state should step in to ensure proper training in obedience and conformity.

With the influx of immigrants and growing industrialization of U.S. cities, children of urban workers were often left unsupervised, largely because they were no longer able to participate in their parents' labor in the same manner as their counterparts who had resided on farms. Idleness and lack of supervision allowed many of these children to drift into immoral or criminal behavior. Concerned that these children would eventually become hardened adult criminals, reformers and philanthropists—known as **Child Savers**—sought to save them from their plight through state intervention.

Child Savers, like most other people of that time, believed in the basic goodness of children. Youthful criminality was perceived as being caused by the child's exposure to factors that made for a corrupting environment: poverty, idleness, overcrowded housing, absence of moral training, and lack of proper parental guidance. The Child Savers called for an expansion of the legal authority of the state to regulate the lives of children, including removing problem children from "bad" environments and placing them in rehabilitative milieus with a focus on constructive work programs and healthful surroundings with close supervision.[13]

Perhaps the earliest concrete expression of this desire to save children was the **New York House of Refuge**, which opened in 1825 and was designed to provide for neglected or vagrant children of the poor and immigrant members of the community. Administered almost like a prison, it required children to engage in industrial work and attend classes and subjected them to strict discipline. Children were required to march from one activity to the next, conforming to a rigid time schedule. Uncooperative or indolent children typically faced corporal punishment.[14] Children suffered much at the hands of the adults who ran the New York House of Refuge, as their mixture of hostility and benevolence produced a peculiar atmosphere.[15]

The New York House of Refuge, which opened its doors in 1825, was an institution inspired by the Child Savers' Movement.

Some reformers, such as New York philanthropist Charles Loring Brace, believed that such children posed a threat to the general well-being of society but felt that social agencies should find ways to remove wayward children from the evil and corrupting environment of the cities rather than placing them in cold, sterile, and punitive institutions. To accomplish this goal, Brace established the Children's Aid Society in 1853. The Society sought to place "unwanted" urban children in good homes in the countryside. Over the next 70 years, it ensured that nearly 250,000 children were sent west on trains and placed in foster homes or indentured as servants on farms, where it was hoped they would learn the value of hard work and a love of nature.

The effects of the "orphan trains" were decidedly mixed. There were complaints about how these children were treated, and thousands became drifters and thieves. Some ran away to return to the cities from which they were originally dispatched, whereas others lived lives of indentured servitude. Nevertheless, some found success in life, either as farmers, businesspeople, or even as politicians. The Great Depression brought an end to this practice, as the need for additional laborers in the Midwest decreased.[16]

Creation of the Juvenile Justice System

The first juvenile court in the United States was established in Cook County (Chicago), Illinois, in 1899. It was based on the English common law principle of ***parens patriae*** (literally "parents of the country"), which identified the state as the ultimate sovereign guardian of children and empowered it to act on behalf of the parents to protect the interests of children. This juvenile court was considered a civil—not criminal—court, reflecting the values and interests of the large number of social workers among the reformers. This perspective had several important implications:

- Juvenile offenders were not charged with crimes
- Courts could impose controls without proving guilt beyond a reasonable doubt
- Sentencing goals focused on treatment, not punishment

In an effort to avoid the stigma associated with "criminal" behavior, violators of the juvenile code were considered **delinquent** and were placed in special institutions designed to house juveniles or supervised in the community by probation officers. Delinquency, according to the new code, included all behaviors considered crimes for adults as well as a variety of behaviors prohibited only to juveniles, known as **status offenses**. The latter included the following "undesirable" behaviors:

- Truancy from school
- Running away from home
- Curfew violations
- Incorrigible (habitually disobedient) behavior
- Use of alcoholic beverages
- Knowingly associating with thieves or other malicious or violent persons
- Vile, obscene, vulgar, or indecent language
- Indecent or immoral conduct

Status offenders were handled similarly by the juvenile court and faced the same punishments as ordinary delinquents.

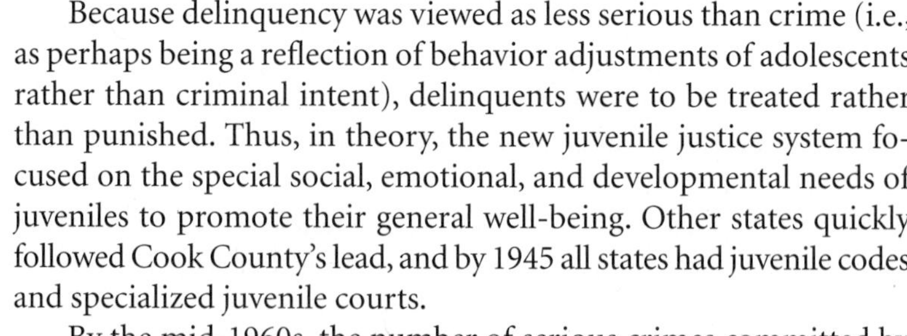

Because delinquency was viewed as less serious than crime (i.e., as perhaps being a reflection of behavior adjustments of adolescents rather than criminal intent), delinquents were to be treated rather than punished. Thus, in theory, the new juvenile justice system focused on the special social, emotional, and developmental needs of juveniles to promote their general well-being. Other states quickly followed Cook County's lead, and by 1945 all states had juvenile codes and specialized juvenile courts.

The juvenile justice system has historically treated youths as both childlike innocents and problems to be controlled.

By the mid-1960s, the number of serious crimes committed by youths had increased dramatically, and high recidivism rates for young offenders led many to believe that the juvenile correctional system was incapable of successfully treating and rehabilitating these youths. Additionally, the courts and correctional facilities were flooded with status offenders, straining the sparse resources of the fledgling juvenile justice system. To help relieve this burden, Congress passed the Juvenile Justice and Delinquency Prevention Act of 1974. Under this Act, only youths guilty of

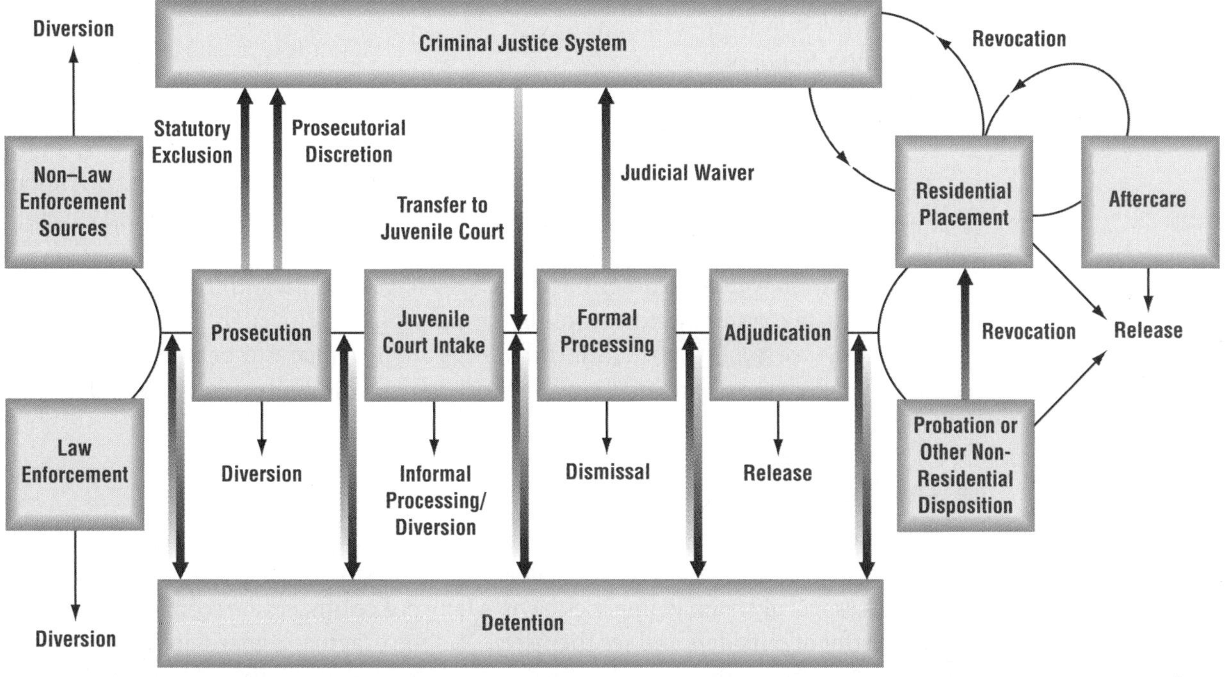

FIGURE 13-3 The U.S. Juvenile Justice System

Adapted from Howard Snyder and Melissa Sickmund, *Juvenile Offenders and Victims: 2006 National Report* (Washington, DC: National Center for Juvenile Justice, 2006), p. 105.

criminal offenses—and not status offenders—could be committed to secure juvenile correctional facilities. In part responding to labeling theorists' concerns, the Act was intended to reduce the stigma and negative consequences of the "delinquent" label being applied to status offenders.

Following passage of the Juvenile Justice and Delinquency Prevention Act, most states revised their juvenile codes to clearly distinguish between delinquent and status offenders. Today, the legal category of delinquency (in all but three states) refers only to those behaviors that violate criminal law, classifying status offenders simply as youths who need special treatment or state supervision. Most jurisdictions call status offenders by one of several terms:

- MINS: minor in need of supervision or services
- PINS: person in need of supervision or services
- CHINS: child in need of supervision or services

In the 1980s, faced with an increasing number of serious and violent juvenile offenders who committed crimes, the courts took a new tack, becoming more adversarial and punitive. A number of states shifted the goals of sentencing away from treatment and toward community protection, thus holding juvenile offenders responsible for their crimes.

The Juvenile Justice Process

The U.S. juvenile justice system is composed of unique judicial and correctional agencies that specialize in dealing with juvenile offenders and operate with specific policies and procedures that are intended to protect youths from the potentially stigmatizing effects of criminal courts (see FIGURE 13-3). Historically (at least until the early 1970s), juvenile justice systems dealt with three types of cases:

- Delinquents
- Status offenders
- Neglected, abused, or dependent (i.e., destitute, homeless, or abandoned) youths

In recent years, many states have established family courts to deal with status offenders and cases of neglect, abuse, or dependency. In these jurisdictions, specialized juvenile courts focus on cases of delinquency.

The terminology used to describe the various stages and procedures associated with the juvenile justice system differs from the terminology employed in the adult criminal justice system (see TABLE 13-1). These differences are not meant to be merely linguistic; rather, they reflect the desire of the juvenile system to avoid unnecessary stigmatization of juvenile offenders.

Law Enforcement

There has always been tension between police and adolescents. Many criminologists believe that this conflict stems from beliefs held by police that separate them from the public, and especially from younger citizens. Many police officers are secretive, defensive, and distrustful of outsiders and see themselves as "the pragmatic guardians of the morals of the community . . . the 'thin blue line' against the forces of evil."[17] Many police view delinquent juveniles as part of that evil force. Conversely, many youths see the police as intrusive, intimidating, and anxious to find fault.

Arrest

Although the police have a great deal of discretion in deciding when to arrest juvenile offenders, most state statutes provide some guidance for arrest procedures. The legal and extralegal factors affecting a police officer's decision to arrest a juvenile are generally similar to those affecting a decision to arrest an adult:

- Seriousness of the offense
- Presence of evidence

TABLE 13-1 Differences in Terminology Used in the Adult and Juvenile Justice Systems

Adult Criminal Justice System	Juvenile Justice System
Crime	Delinquent act
Criminal	Delinquent
Arrest	Take into custody
Arraignment	Intake hearing
Indictment	Petition
Not guilty plea	Deny the petition
Guilty plea	Agree to an adjudication finding
Plea bargain	Adjustment
Jail	Detention facility
Trial	Adjudication hearing
Conviction	Adjudication
Presentence investigation	Social history
Sentencing	Disposition hearing
Sentence	Disposition
Incarceration	Commitment
Prison	Training or reform school, youth center
Parole	Aftercare

- Offender's prior arrest record
- Offender's race, ethnicity, sex, and age
- Offender's attitude and demeanor
- Acceptance or denial of the allegations[18]

In general, the laws that govern juvenile arrests are similar to the laws that apply to adults. There is one significant difference, however: Delinquency cases do not require probable cause (a set of facts and circumstances that would lead a reasonable person to believe that a crime has been committed and that the accused committed it) prior to the juvenile's arrest. Instead, police may take any juvenile into custody if the officer has reasonable suspicion (a suspicion that creates a reasonable belief that the youth committed a delinquent act).

Once an officer arrests a juvenile, some states require the officer to notify a probation officer (or other designated official), who will then inform the youth's parents. In some jurisdictions, a juvenile who is taken into police custody goes to the police station for initial screening. Other jurisdictions give officers discretion to choose another course of action:

- Investigate the offense and the juvenile's background
- Decide to terminate the case
- Refer the offender to a community diversion program
- Send the offender to the juvenile court system

Booking

The procedure used when booking juveniles who have been arrested is essentially the same as in adult cases, with one notable exception: Some states forbid routine fingerprinting and photographing of juvenile suspects unless specifically ordered by the juvenile court.[19] When these identification techniques are used, they are intended only for temporary use and do not become part of a permanent criminal record. Advocates of fingerprinting and photographing all youth argue that these techniques provide complete records of young offenders, which are necessary for dealing with youths who refuse to reveal their identity, such as runaways, gang members, and serious offenders. Critics, however, contend that such permanent records make it more difficult for youths to be accepted by teachers and to find employment.

Courts

Nearly 1.6 million youths are handled by the juvenile courts in the United States each year (see FIGURE 13-4). Several key features distinguish these courts from their adult counterparts:

- Absence of legal guilt
- Nonadversarial, nonconfrontational interactions
- Focus on treatment rather than punishment
- Emphasis on the offender's background (e.g., social history, prior behavior, and clinical diagnosis)
- Absence of public scrutiny (private proceedings)
- Speed in processing cases
- Flexibility with sentencing options
- Short-term incarceration

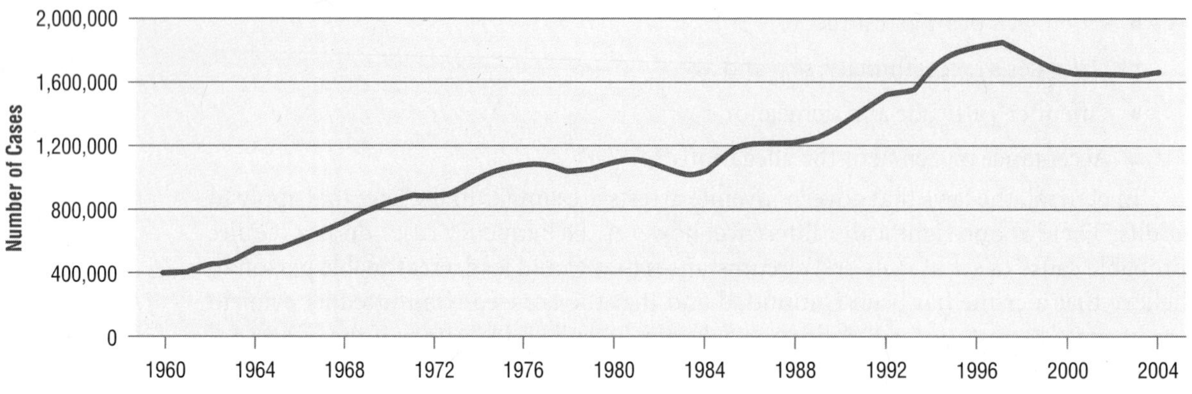

FIGURE 13-4 Delinquency Cases in U.S. Juvenile Courts

Source: Anne Stahl, Charles Puzzanchera, Sarah Livsey, Anthony Sladky, Terrence Finnegan, Nancy Tierney, and Howard Snyder, *Juvenile Court Statistics 2003–2004* (Pittsburgh: National Center for Juvenile Justice, 2007), p. 6.

Intake

Intake screening procedures are designed to screen out those cases that do not warrant a formal court hearing. Typically, cases that are dismissed meet one of the following criteria:

- Lack of sufficient evidence
- Minor law violations that could be handled informally (i.e., through counseling by a probation officer)
- Compensation already made to the victim
- Jurisdiction inappropriate for juvenile courts (i.e., suspects found to be younger or older than the legal age for juvenile court jurisdiction)
- Circumstances that make the case more appropriate for criminal prosecution (i.e., the serious nature of the crime, the extensive criminal history of the juvenile, or a determination that the juvenile is not amenable to treatment in the juvenile system)[20]

To help make this determination, intake officers may order social background investigations or medical or psychological diagnoses. Intake officers are given broad discretion in determining which cases warrant formal handling. In an effort to reduce the court's caseload, they often favor informal hearings, adjudications, or probation supervision rather than referral to a judge. If intake does result in the decision for a formal hearing (which happens in approximately 60 percent of delinquency cases), the intake officer files a **petition**, which states that a delinquent act has been committed by the youth (equivalent to an indictment in criminal prosecutions).[21]

Detention is used for juveniles, like jails for adults, to ensure the youths' appearance at required court hearings.

Detention

Once a juvenile has been arrested, he or she may be temporarily placed in **detention** while the court decides how to proceed. If a juvenile was placed in detention, then a petition must be filed in the case and a hearing held within 48 to 72 hours.[22] The primary goal of detention is to ensure that the youth appears at the necessary court hearings.[23]

Approximately 21 percent of all delinquents are detained at some point in the juvenile justice process—either immediately after arrest, while awaiting a hearing, after sentencing, or before incarceration. In 2004, nearly 342,000 juveniles were held in detention for some period of time. Of these cases, 29 percent involved crimes against a person, 29 percent involved property crimes, 10 percent were related to drugs, and 32 percent involved public order offenses.[24]

Headline Crime

Juvenile Detention Centers

While juvenile detention centers are supposed to provide safe and humane temporary confinement of youths awaiting adjudication hearings or other actions by the juvenile court, lawsuits have been filed by the U.S. Department of Justice in 11 states claiming that their supervision of juveniles is either abusive or harmfully lax. A recent survey of detention centers by the Associated Press inquired about the number of claims of abuse filed since January 1, 2004. More than 13,000 abuse claims were identified, although only 1343 of those claims were confirmed. A total of 1140 claims of sexual abuse were reported, but only 143 were confirmed.

Lawsuits filed against two detention centers in Mississippi include the following claims:

- Thirteen-year-old girls state they were shackled for weeks at a time.
- One girl was cuffed and chained while she ate, used the bathroom, and was being forced to play soccer against other girls.
- Youths were forced to strip and eat their own vomit.
- Multiple youths claim they were held in the "Dark Room," an isolation cell without windows and only a hole in the floor for use as a toilet.
- Some girls were shackled to poles.

Authorities are also investigating claims of physical and sexual abuse in detention centers in Florida, Indiana, Ohio, and Texas. More than 20 girls at a detention center in Indianapolis report guards permitting girls to engage in "networking"—a term used to describe girls who would sneak into each other's cells to engage in sex. One girl also reported that a guard had participated in sex with some of the girls. Since 2000, at least 90 employees of the Texas Youth Commission have been fired or sanctioned for engaging in sexual misconduct with girls in detention centers.

Sources: Ashley Fantz, "Sex Abuse, Violence Alleged at Teen Jails Across U.S.," available at http://www.cnn.com/2008/CRIME/04/04/juvenile.jails/index.html, accessed April 4, 2008; Holbrook Mohr, "Young, Detained and Abused," *The Daily Camera*, March 3, 2008, p. 3A.

Because the juvenile courts view children as being more vulnerable than adults, a number of states have established limits on how long youths may be held in detention before a hearing takes place—generally within 30 days.[25] In ***Schall v. Martin*** (1984), however, the U.S. Supreme Court ruled that juveniles who posed a serious risk of committing additional crimes could be held without determination of probable cause.[26] In this case, the Court reasoned that the protection of society was a sufficiently important goal in itself to justify preventive detention of juveniles.

Diversion

Even after a petition has been filed, efforts may still be taken to avoid formal hearings. Similar to plea bargaining in adult cases, the process of **diversion**—the early suspension or termination of the official processing of a juvenile—favors informal or unofficial alternatives. Officials may implement diversion at any of several points along the juvenile justice process in an effort to avoid the negative stigma associated with formal processing in the justice system. For example, police officers may handle delinquents informally by communicating an expectation of participation in a community recreation program, probation officers may choose to institute restitution rather than recommend a formal hearing, or judges may choose to delay sentencing while the youth is supervised on informal probation.

Good candidates for diversion programs include individuals with the following characteristics:

- First-time offenders charged with less serious offenses
- Repeat status offenders
- Offenders already participating in community-based treatment programs

These youths may be given an opportunity to participate in various diversion efforts, including mediation—meetings that bring the complainant, the juvenile, and a neutral hearing officer together to reach a mutually acceptable solution.

Adjudication

The **adjudication** stage in the juvenile justice system parallels prosecution and trial in adult criminal courts. The purpose of the **adjudication hearing** is to determine whether the juvenile is responsible for the charges outlined in the petition.

Hearings in a juvenile court have traditionally been based more on civil—rather than criminal—proceedings. In addition, juvenile court proceedings have historically been nonadversarial. However, given the public's growing disillusionment with the ability of the courts to reduce serious juvenile crime through informal proceedings, and as a result of a series of Supreme Court decisions holding that juveniles have many of the same due

FOCUS ON CRIMINAL JUSTICE

Due Process in Juvenile Court

From its inception until the mid-1960s, the U.S. juvenile court system tolerated wide differences between the procedural rights accorded to adults and those accorded to juveniles. In practically all jurisdictions, rights granted to adults were withheld from juveniles. It was believed that juvenile court proceedings should not be adversarial or criminal. Rather, the right of the state as *parens patriae* permitted the juvenile court to act informally in the best interests of children. Consequently, juvenile proceedings were described as "civil" and, therefore, were not subject to the requirements that restrict the state when it seeks to deprive a person of his or her liberty. All of this changed in 1967, when the U.S. Supreme Court handed down its decision in what has been considered the leading constitutional case in juvenile law: *In re Gault*.

On June 8, 1964, 15-year-old Gerald Gault was arrested and taken to the Children's Detention Home in Gila County, Arizona, as a result of a verbal complaint by a neighbor, Mrs. Cook, that he had made lewd phone calls to her. No notice was given to Gault's parents that he had been taken into custody, and neither Gault nor his parents were given copies of the petition charging delinquency. At the initial hearing, Mrs. Cook did not appear and no transcript or record of the hearing was made. At a second hearing, Mrs. Cook was still not present. After this hearing, Gault was found to be delinquent and was committed to the state training school for five years.

The State of Arizona did not permit appeals by juveniles in delinquency cases, so the defense filed a writ of habeas corpus with the Arizona Supreme Court, which referred it to the Superior Court for a hearing. The Superior Court dismissed the writ. The defense then sought review in the Arizona Supreme Court, which ruled that the juvenile court had acted appropriately. Gault appealed to the U.S. Supreme Court, arguing that the juvenile court had violated his rights of due process guaranteed by the Fourteenth Amendment.

Justice Abe Fortas delivered the opinion of the U.S. Supreme Court, stating that the basic requirements of due process and fairness must be satisfied in juvenile proceedings and that "neither the Fourteenth Amendment nor the Bill of Rights is for adults only." From this premise, he challenged the very essence of the juvenile court's operation. The court's position that its activities worked for the good of the child was shown to be suspect, and its procedure, in fact, violated juveniles' fundamental rights. According to Justice Fortas, "Under our Constitution, the condition of being a boy does not justify a kangaroo court." He further argued that the proper goal of the juvenile court would not be impaired by constitutional requirements, and expressed his belief that the essentials of due process would reflect a fair and responsive attitude toward juveniles. Justice Fortas then set out the essentials of due process that should apply in juvenile delinquency proceedings, including the right to counsel, the right to confront and cross-examine one's accuser, the right against self-incrimination, and the right to timely notice of the charges.

As a result of the *Gault* decision, the operation of the juvenile court was significantly altered, making it more formal and adversarial in nature.

Source: In re Gault, 387 U.S. 1 (1967).

process rights as adults in criminal proceedings, in recent decades juvenile courts have taken on many of the same characteristics as criminal courts. For example, juveniles may be represented by counsel, cross-examine witnesses, and invoke their Fifth Amendment protection against self-incrimination, largely as a result of the 1967 Supreme Court decision in ***In re Gault***. The Supreme Court also ruled in ***McKeiver v. Pennsylvania*** (1971) that juveniles are not constitutionally entitled to a trial by jury (although currently 12 states allow jury trials in serious cases if juveniles request them).[27]

Additional similarities between the juvenile and adult systems include the presumption of innocence; inadmissibility of hearsay evidence; requirement of adequate, timely, and formal notification of charges; sufficient time to formulate a response; and requirement of proof beyond a reasonable doubt to determine guilt.[28]

Disposition

At the conclusion of the adjudication hearing, the judge may either dismiss the case (equivalent to an acquittal) or sustain the petition (equivalent to a conviction). If the petition is sustained (which happens in approximately 67 percent of cases brought before the court; see FIGURE 13-5), the judge may either immediately determine an appropriate disposition (equivalent to a sentencc) or set a date for a disposition hearing.

A disposition hearing (equivalent to a sentencing hearing) is held to determine the most appropriate sentence for a delinquent. It is often an informal discussion between the following parties (although in some jurisdictions it is a more formal proceeding):

- Judge
- Probation officer
- Prosecutor
- Defense attorney
- Parents of the juvenile

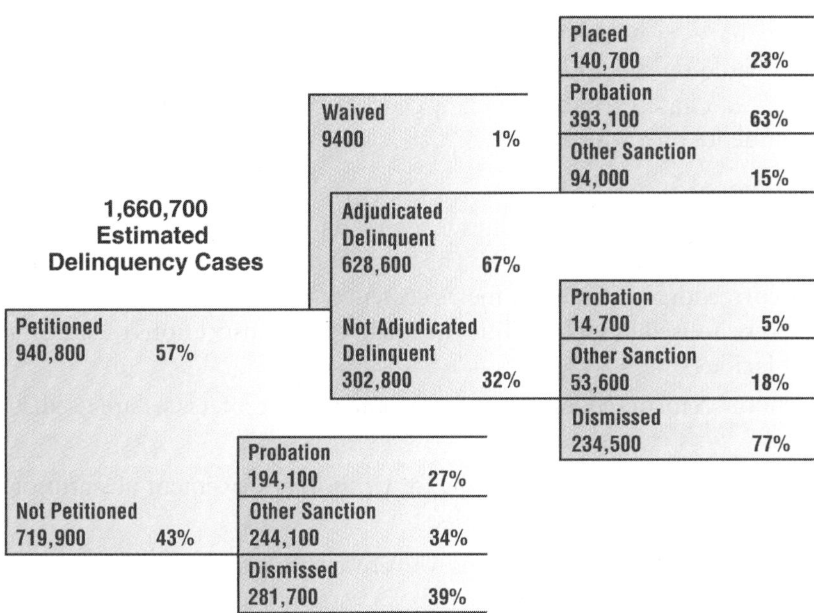

FIGURE 13-5 Processing Delinquency Cases

Source: Anne Stahl, Charles Puzzanchera, Sarah Livsey, Anthony Sladky, Terrence Finnegan, Nancy Tierney, and Howard Snyder, *Juvenile Court Statistics 2003–2004* (Pittsburgh: National Center for Juvenile Justice, 2007), p. 56.

These parties meet to discuss the various sentencing options:

- Probation
- Placement in a correctional facility
- Referral to a drug or alcohol treatment program
- Fines
- Restitution
- Community service

Dispositional orders often include more than one of these options.

Corrections

The juvenile corrections system involves two main components: probation and institutional placement.

Probation

In the juvenile system, probation closely parallels probation within the adult system and involves many of the same key components:

- Conditional freedom within the community
- Close supervision by probation officers
- Rehabilitation through participation in community-based counseling programs

The philosophical foundation of probation is the belief that problem behaviors of youths are more effectively corrected within the community than in institutional settings.

Youths who are placed on probation are required to avoid further law-breaking and to comply with a variety of conditions of probation (i.e., attending school, making restitution, adhering to a curfew, receiving periodic visits from the probation officer, and submitting to random drug or alcohol tests). These conditions aim to further the goals of rehabilitation through treatment and guidance.

Occasionally, controversy arises over exactly which conditions meet this requirement. For example, courts have invalidated conditions requiring juveniles to attend church or religious school based on the notion that to do so would violate the constitutional separation of church and state, even though many people believe such attendance would serve as positive influence on a youth.

Institutional Placement

In general, placement in correctional facilities is reserved for those juveniles who have committed serious violent or property crimes. The United States has approximately 3000 public and private correctional facilities for the placement of juvenile delinquents. Nearly 141,000 juveniles were housed in such facilities in 2004.[29] These institutions include the following types of facilities:

- Training schools, reform schools, boot camps, and youth centers (secure residential facilities)
- Shelter-care facilities (nonsecure housing for temporary placement of status offenders or dependent or neglected youths)
- Jails (secure facilities for holding persons who are awaiting trial or who have been convicted of misdemeanors)
- Ranches, forestry camps, and farms (nonsecure facilities for delinquents who have committed less serious crimes and that provide outdoor environments)

These institutions aim to provide structured programming in a secure environment and further the goal of rehabilitation. In addition, a wide variety of community-based correctional programs have been established for the treatment of youth on probation.

Aftercare

After release from juvenile correctional facilities, delinquent youths typically enter the phase of aftercare (equivalent to parole in the adult system)—that is, the release and subsequent community supervision of an individual from a correctional facility to ensure a more positive and effective transition back into the community. As with probation, delinquents in aftercare are subject to similar conditions and supervision requirements. Youths who violate the law or any condition of their supervision may face revocation (removal from parole) and return to a correctional facility.

Juvenile boot camps frequently use a military-style approach and strenuous physical activities in an attempt to reduce recidivism.

Nearly 100,000 juveniles enter aftercare each year.[30] These youths share several common characteristics:

- Multiple previous commitments (40 percent of juveniles in aftercare have been held five or more times)
- A history of nonviolent offenses
- Residence in a single-parent home or dysfunctional family unit
- Relatives who have been incarcerated
- Educational setbacks when compared to peers
- Extensive time in some form of institutional placement[31]

For serious violent offenders, intensive aftercare programs (IAP) (equivalent to intensive parole supervision) may be used to provide closer monitoring. IAP officers have much smaller caseloads and are expected to conduct a number of face-to-face meetings with their parolees each week. They are also expected to establish and maintain contact with the juvenile's parents or guardians, school authorities, and, if applicable, employer on a regular basis.[32]

These relationships are also the focus of wraparound programs, which are designed to build positive relationships and support networks between youths and their families, teachers, and community agencies. Such programs typically entail a centralized coordination of services through the juvenile court, including clinical therapy, drug and alcohol treatment, special education, medical services, caregiver support, mental health care, and transportation.[33]

Juvenile Offenders in the Adult Criminal Justice System

In response to public and legislative perceptions of judicial leniency and the inability of the juvenile justice system to deal adequately with serious or repeat adolescent offenders, some delinquents—owing to their age, prior delinquent record, or seriousness of their offense—may face prosecution in criminal court and the possibility of sentencing to adult prisons.

Transfer to Criminal Courts

Waiver of jurisdiction is the judicial mechanism by which a juvenile may be transferred from juvenile court to criminal court. Waivers are usually filed in two types of cases:

- *Serious violent offenders.* Criminal courts can impose harsher punishments for serious violent offenders.[34]
- *Chronic offenders.* The criminal justice system is believed to provide more appropriate (i.e., punitive) treatment for offenders with long criminal records who have not responded positively to treatment programs.[35]

Intensive aftercare programs are designed for serious, violent juvenile offenders who are released to the community.

TABLE 13-2 Minimum Age for Judicial Transfer to Criminal Court in the United States

No minimum age specified	Alaska, Arizona, Delaware, District of Columbia, Hawaii, Idaho, Indiana, Maine, Maryland, Oklahoma, Oregon, Rhode Island, South Carolina, South Dakota, Tennessee, Washington, West Virginia
10 years	Kansas, Vermont
12 years	Colorado, Missouri
13 years	Georgia, Illinois, Mississippi, New Hampshire, North Carolina, Wyoming
14 years	Alabama, Arkansas, California, Connecticut, Florida, Iowa, Kentucky, Louisiana, Michigan, Minnesota, Nevada, New Jersey, North Dakota, Ohio, Pennsylvania, Texas, Utah, Virginia, Wisconsin

Minimum ages may not apply to all criminal offense restrictions, but represent the youngest possible age at which a juvenile may be judicially waived to criminal court.

Source: Howard Snyder and Melissa Sickmund, *Juvenile Offenders and Victims: 2006 National Report* (Washington, DC: National Center for Juvenile Justice, 2006), p. 112.

In many jurisdictions, adolescents accused of serious crimes such as murder and forcible rape are waived automatically to the adult criminal justice system for prosecution.

To be eligible for transfer to the adult criminal system, juvenile offenders in many states must be older than some minimum age (see TABLE 13-2). In reality, most offenders waived to criminal courts are older than age 16.[36]

In ***Kent v. United States*** (1966), the U.S. Supreme Court held that the differences between juvenile and adult courts were so great that the transfer decision must be based on clearly established procedures designed to protect the rights of juveniles.[37] Although the Court ruled that the practice of trying juveniles in criminal courts was constitutional, the juvenile may not be deprived of his or her constitutional rights. The decision to transfer offenders must include the following elements:

- A waiver hearing
- Effective counsel
- A statement of the reasons behind the decision to transfer

In its *Kent* decision, the Supreme Court also enumerated several criteria to guide judges in making transfer decisions, including the seriousness of the offense, the presence of violence, and the sophistication and maturity of the youth.[38]

Despite the existence of these guidelines, the transfer of juveniles to criminal courts remains controversial. Many citizens and correctional experts are unsure about the appropriateness of harsher punishments or the possibility of rehabilitation for juveniles in the adult correctional system. At the same time, long-term incarceration is possible only within the adult system and may be necessary to keep chronic or serious offenders off the streets. Approximately 9500 juvenile offenders are transferred to adult criminal courts in the United States each year (see FIGURE 13-6), which equates to less than 1 percent of all petitioned cases.

Several procedures (or remands) are used to transfer youths between juvenile and criminal courts, though they are not all employed in all states.

- **Judicial waiver**: the most common form of transfer to the criminal system. It involves a formal decision by the judge after careful consideration of the relevant issues at a transfer hearing.
- **Statutory exclusion**: the automatic transfer to the criminal system of certain juvenile offenders based on age, seriousness of offense, or prior criminal record.

- Prosecutorial waiver (or direct transfer): a form of transfer that gives the prosecutor the authority to decide whether to file a waiver of jurisdiction.
- Demand waiver: a request by a juvenile offender to be transferred to criminal court. While rare, such waivers are filed by delinquents who are seeking acquittal by jury or shorter sentences.
- Reverse waiver: a request by a juvenile who is being prosecuted in criminal court to be transferred back to the juvenile system.

To avoid situations of double jeopardy, in which the youth is tried for the same crime twice (once as a juvenile and once as an adult), the Supreme Court ruled in ***Breed v. Jones*** (1975) that the waiver process must begin before the evidence is presented at the adjudication hearing.[39]

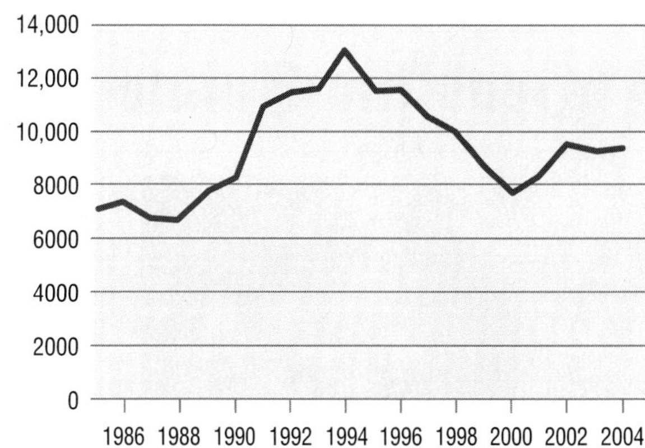

FIGURE 13-6 Juvenile Court Waivers to Criminal Court

Source: Anne Stahl, Charles Puzzanchera, Sarah Livsey, Anthony Sladky, Terrence Finnegan, Nancy Tierney, and Howard Snyder, *Juvenile Court Statistics 2003–2004* (Pittsburgh: National Center for Juvenile Justice, 2007), p. 38.

Prosecution in Criminal Courts

Some juvenile cases that are transferred to criminal court (approximately 16 percent) are dropped before charges are formally filed. Even when charges are filed, some cases (about 11 percent) are terminated by the prosecutor's *nolle prosequi* (decision not to prosecute).[40] If the prosecutor decides to proceed with the case, a trial may still be avoided by the process of plea bargaining.[41]

If the case does go to trial, a juvenile offender is significantly more likely than an adult to be convicted.[42] Researchers have suggested various reasons for this high conviction rate, including impaired competence to stand trial due to immature judgment and decision making. Other studies, however, have shown no significant differences between those youths who are tried in criminal courts and similar peers who are tried in the juvenile system, other than the seriousness of their charges.[43]

Sentencing the Convicted Juvenile

Juveniles subject to criminal convictions have several advantages over adult criminals in obtaining lenient sentencing. First, age is a mitigating factor that is taken into consideration in determining the appropriate sentence. Second, most juveniles do not have adult criminal records, and prior juvenile records are sometimes prohibited from being introduced in criminal hearings (primarily because the courts have traditionally believed that juvenile misbehavior reflects immaturity and should not be held against juveniles once they became adults).[44] Prior criminal records are important because many states' sentencing laws require incarceration of the offender when he or she is convicted of a second felony. Despite these considerations, research has demonstrated inconclusive findings about lenient sentencing of juveniles in general.[45]

Juvenile Offenders in Prison

Although only a small number of juveniles are incarcerated in state prisons (where they account for less than 0.2 percent of the total incarcerated population) (see FIGURE 13-7), this population presents serious challenges for both offenders and correctional administrators.[46]

Life in adult prisons is significantly different from life in juvenile institutions, and juvenile offenders often have difficulty adjusting to

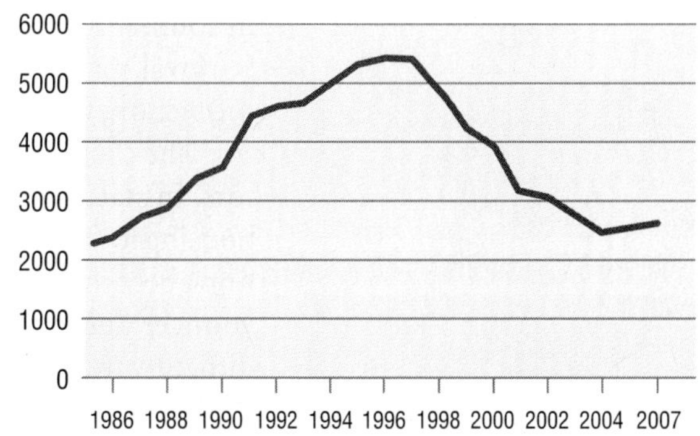

FIGURE 13-7 One-Day Count of Juveniles Held in State Prisons

Adapted from Howard Snyder and Melissa Sickmund, *Juvenile Offenders and Victims: 2006 National Report* (Washington, DC: National Center for Juvenile Justice, 2006), p. 238.

Headline Crime

Sixteen-Year-Old Sentenced to Life in Prison

On October 15, 2005, 16-year-old Scott Dyleski entered the home of 52-year-old Pamela Vitale. Dyleski was planning to steal Vitale's credit cards to use in purchasing marijuana-growing equipment. During the burglary, something went wrong, and Dyleski got into a fight with Vitale. Ultimately, he bludgeoned and stabbed her to death. The brutal attack involved multiple blows to Vitale's head, dislodged teeth, broken fingers, bruises over her entire body, a stab wound to her abdomen deep enough to expose her intestines, and a symbol cut into her back.

Dyleski was a former Boy Scout who refused to eat meat or to wear leather. He lived with his mother in a communal home with two other families not far from Vitale's residence. A friend who was involved in a credit card theft scheme with Dyleski tipped off police after learning about the murder.

Jurors deliberated more than 18 hours before finding Dyleski guilty of first-degree murder with special circumstances (reflecting the unusual brutality of the murder). Dyleski was sentenced to life in prison without parole.

Source: Lisa Sweetingham, "After Guilty Verdict, Vitale Family Reflects on Their Mother's Killing and the Harrowing Trial," *CourtTVnews*, August 30, 2006, available at http://www.courttv.com/news/horowitz/082906_ctv.html, accessed January 20, 2008.

prison subculture. A youth's reputation as being tough, which might have afforded him or her status on the streets or in a juvenile institution, carries little weight among older inmates. Juvenile offenders find themselves at the bottom of the status ladder, subject to both the formal authority of guards and the informal power of other inmates. They may merely resent the authority or, worse, be subject to victimization. Indeed, juveniles in adult prisons are significantly more likely to become victims of violent crime or sexual assault than youths in juvenile institutions.[47]

Daily survival becomes the primary concern for youths in prison. For many, survival means adapting to the inmate subculture. Although this adaptation may improve their daily life in prison, it may also distract or discourage juveniles from pursuing activities that would improve their chances of getting out of prison earlier, such as participating in counseling and educational programs and conforming to institutional expectations.[48] Survival may also include forging an alliance with an older inmate who will provide protection, which all too often comes at the cost of sexual exploitation.

The characteristics of juvenile inmates also create difficulties for prison administrators. In states with very small numbers of juvenile inmates, the cost of building special housing for these juveniles (rather than integrating them into the general inmate population) becomes a serious budgetary concern. Furthermore, because juvenile inmates are younger and proportionately more violent than adult inmates, they may have greater difficulty in adapting to institutional rules and consequently require greater supervision by institutional staff. Unlike juvenile correctional facilities, which try to foster resident and staff interactions that promote the social and personal development of youthful offenders, most adult prisons emphasize custody and control. Adult correctional facilities are not intended to cater to, nor are they typically equipped to provide for, the educational or psychological needs of juveniles. Because most states have only a handful of juvenile inmates, legislatures hesitate to allocate additional expenditures for programs or staff to give these youths specialized treatment.

The recidivism rate among juveniles released from prison also challenges criminal justice professionals. Juveniles who are paroled from prison fare no better than their adult counterparts, with approximately 60 percent returning to prison for a new offense or violation of probation in less than three years. The length of time served appears to make little difference in the recidivism rate.[49]

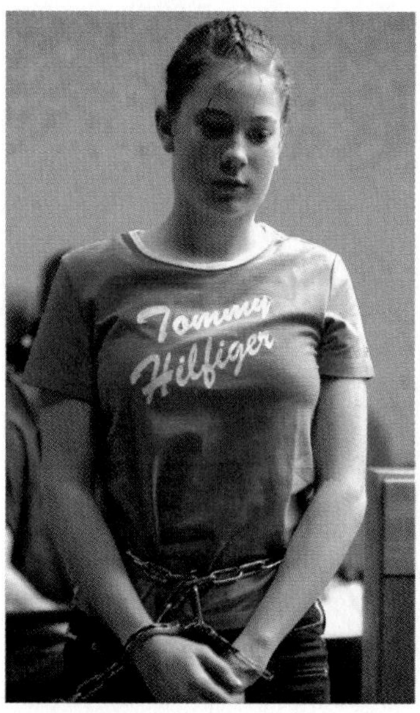

Approximately 60 percent of juvenile inmates return to prison within 3 years after their release.

Abolition of the Death Penalty for Juveniles

Although juveniles have rarely been executed in the United States, at least 366 have been legally put to death since 1642. Since the 1890s, juveniles have accounted for less than 2 percent of all persons executed. From the 1890s to 1930, fewer than 30 juveniles were executed in any given decade. In the 1930s and 1940s, however, an unusual increase in juvenile executions occurred, with 40 and 50 executions taking place in those two decades, respectively. Between 1965 and 1984, no juveniles were executed. However, with the execution of Charles Rumbaugh in Texas on September 11, 1985, juveniles once again faced the prospect of execution. Between 1985 and April 2003, 22 persons who were under age 18 at the time when they committed their crimes were executed.[50]

Beginning in 1982, it became clear that the U.S. Supreme Court was interested in the death penalty as it applied to juveniles when it held that the youthfulness of an offender must be considered as a mitigating circumstance at sentencing, reflecting a growing ambivalence about juvenile executions among policymakers and the public alike.[51] Six years later, in *Thompson v. Oklahoma*, the Court held that the execution of a person who was younger than age 16 at the time of the commission of his or her crime was unconstitutional.[52] The next year, in *Stanford v. Kentucky*, the Supreme Court rejected an appeal that could have prohibited the execution of anyone younger than 18 at the time of his or her crime.[53]

A total of eighteen 17-year-olds and one 16-year-old were executed after the *Stanford* decision. Then, on March 1, 2005, the Supreme Court, in a divided 5-to-4 decision in ***Roper v. Simmons***, ruled that "the death penalty is disproportionate punishment for offenders under the age of 18" and, therefore, is a violation of the Eighth Amendment's prohibition against cruel and unusual punishment.[54] Although the Court and the country remained deeply divided over the juvenile death penalty, it had come to an end.[55]

WRAPPING IT UP

Chapter Highlights

- Public frustration with the inability of the juvenile justice system to respond adequately to serious youth crime has led many states to revise their juvenile codes so as to hold juvenile offenders more accountable for their criminal behavior and to make it easier to transfer juveniles to adult criminal court for prosecution.
- Before the twentieth century, juveniles who violated the law were treated much like adult criminals. However, as a result of the Child Savers' movement, a special juvenile justice system was created that included separate codes, courts, and correctional facilities for youthful offenders.
- A number of features distinguish the contemporary juvenile court from criminal court, including its definition of legal guilt, correctional philosophy, and judicial procedures.
- After a juvenile is arrested or taken into custody, a petition charging delinquency is filed with the court. An adjudication hearing is then held to determine whether the charge should be sustained. If it is sustained, a disposition hearing is held to determine the appropriate treatment or placement for the youth.
- Youths who commit serious crimes may be transferred from juvenile court to criminal court for prosecution as adults via one of three waiver procedures: judicial waiver, legislative or automatic waiver, and prosecutorial waiver. Criminal courts typically gain jurisdiction over persons who are age 18 or older, but most states have set lower minimum ages for waiver eligibility, depending on the offense charged.
- Juveniles who are prosecuted in criminal court face the same prosecutorial process that all adult defendants confront and are afforded all the same constitutional protections. Juveniles are less likely than adult defendants to receive a plea bargain, however, and are more likely to be convicted than their adult counterparts.
- In 2007, approximately 2600 juveniles were incarcerated in state and federal prisons in the United States, accounting for approximately 0.2 percent of the total incarcerated population. Most incarcerated youth are confined in the general adult prison population, which creates special problems for both youths and prison administrators: Youths often have trouble adjusting to prison rules and the inmate subculture and are more likely than older inmates to be victims of assault and exploitation by other prisoners.
- After a series of cases, the U.S. Supreme Court abolished the juvenile death penalty in 2005.

Words to Know

adjudication Stage in the juvenile justice system that parallels prosecution and trial in adult criminal courts.

adjudication hearing A hearing to determine whether a juvenile committed the offense of which he or she is accused.

aftercare The release and subsequent community supervision of an individual from a correctional facility to ensure a more positive and effective transition back into the community.

Breed v. Jones Supreme Court decision that a criminal prosecution of a child following a juvenile court hearing constitutes double jeopardy.

Child Savers A group of nineteenth-century reformers who believed that children were basically good, delinquency was the product of bad environments, and the state should remove children from such environments.

delinquent A juvenile younger than age 18 who is determined to have violated a state's juvenile code.

demand waiver Process by which a juvenile may request to have his or her case transferred to criminal court.

detention The temporary custody and care of juveniles pending adjudication, disposition, or implementation of disposition.

disposition hearing A hearing to determine the most appropriate placement of a juvenile adjudicated to be delinquent.

diversion The early suspension or termination of the official processing of a juvenile in favor of an informal or unofficial alternative.

In re Gault Case in which the Supreme Court held that juveniles could not be denied basic due process rights in juvenile hearings.

intake The initial screening process in the juvenile court to determine whether a case should be processed further.

intensive aftercare programs (IAP) Equivalent to intensive parole supervision; used to provide greater supervision of youths after their release from official institutions.

judicial waiver Most common waiver procedure for transferring youths to criminal court, in which the judge is the primary decision maker.

juvenile A person younger than the age of 18.

juvenile delinquency Behavior by a juvenile that is in violation of a state's juvenile or criminal codes.

Kent v. United States Supreme Court decision requiring a formal waiver hearing before transfer of a juvenile to criminal court.

McKeiver v. Pennsylvania Supreme Court decision that juveniles do not have a constitutional right to a jury trial in juvenile court.

New York House of Refuge The first correctional institution for children in the United States (opened in 1825), which emphasized industry, education, and strict discipline.

parens patriae A principle based on English common law that viewed the state as the ultimate sovereign and guardian of children.

petition Similar to an indictment; a written statement setting forth the specific charge that a delinquent act has been committed or that a child is dependent or neglected or needs supervision.

prosecutorial waiver Process in which the prosecutor determines whether a charge against a juvenile should be filed in criminal or juvenile court.

reverse waiver Process in which a juvenile contests a statutory exclusion or prosecutorial transfer.

Roper v. Simmons Supreme Court decision that the death penalty for anyone who was younger than age 18 at the time of his or her crime is unconstitutional.

Schall v. Martin Supreme Court decision authorizing the preventive detention of juveniles who are identified as "serious risks" to the community if released.

status offenses Acts prohibited to children that are not prohibited to adults (such as running away, truancy, and incorrigibility).

statutory exclusion Process established by statute that excludes certain juveniles, because of either age or offense, from juvenile court jurisdiction; charges are initially filed in criminal court.

waiver of jurisdiction A legal process to transfer a juvenile from juvenile to criminal court.

wraparound programs Programs designed to build positive relationships and support networks between youths and their families, teachers, and community agencies through coordination of services.

Think and Discuss

1. Some critics have argued that the juvenile justice system should be abolished. Do you agree? Why or why not?
2. Should juveniles be granted the right to a jury trial? Which benefits might this change afford? What damages may it cause?
3. Under which circumstances should a juvenile be transferred to adult criminal courts?
4. Should juveniles who are convicted as adults be incarcerated with the general adult inmate population?
5. Are there any circumstances in which the death penalty should be applied to persons who were younger than the age of 18 at the time they committed their crimes?

Notes

1. Statement by FBI Director J. Edgar Hoover, warning against "misguided policies which encourage criminal activity and often result in arrogant and defiant attitudes by youth." Quoted in Thomas Bernard, *The Cycle of Juvenile Justice* (New York: Oxford University Press, 1992), p. 34.
2. Federal Bureau of Investigation, *Crime in the United States, 2007* (Washington, DC: U.S. Department of Justice, 2008).
3. Marvin Wolfgang, Robert Figlio, and Thorsten Sellin, *Delinquency in a Birth Cohort* (Chicago: University of Chicago Press, 1972); Marvin Wolfgang, Terence Thornberry, and Robert Figlio, *From Boy to Man, from Delinquency to Crime* (Chicago: University of Chicago Press, 1987); Simon Dinitz and John Conrad, "The Dangerous Two Percent," in David Shichor and Delos Kelly (Eds.), *Critical Issues in Juvenile Delinquency* (Lexington, MA: Lexington Books, 1980), pp. 129–155; Dora Nevares, Marvin Wolfgang,

and Paul Tracy, *Delinquency in Puerto Rico: The 1970 Birth Cohort Study* (Westport, CT: Greenwood Press, 1990); Lyle Shannon, *Assessing the Relationships of Adult Criminal Careers to Juvenile Offenders: A Summary* (Washington, DC: U.S. Government Printing Office, 1982).

4. *Deuteronomy* 21:18–21, *The Thompson Chain-Reference Bible*, 5th ed. (Indianapolis, IN: B. B. Kirkbride Bible Company, 1988).
5. Fredrick Ludwig, *Youth and the Law* (New York: Foundation Press, 1955), p. 12.
6. Wiley Sanders, *Juvenile Offenders for a Thousand Years* (Chapel Hill, NC: University of North Carolina Press, 1970).
7. John Tobias, *Crime and Industrial Society in the 19th Century* (New York: Shocken Books, 1967).
8. Joseph Hawes, *Children in Urban Society: Juvenile Delinquency in Nineteenth-Century America* (New York: Oxford University Press, 1971), pp. 15–19.
9. Hawes, note 8, p. 14.
10. Phillippe Ariès, *Centuries of Childhood*, trans. by Robert Baldick (New York: Knopf, 1962), pp. 411–412.
11. Ariès, note 10.
12. George Haskins, *Law and Authority in Early Massachusetts* (New York: Archon Books, 1968).
13. Anthony Platt, *The Child Savers: The Invention of Delinquency* (Chicago: University of Chicago Press, 1969).
14. Clifford Dorne, *Crimes against Children* (New York: Harrow and Heston, 1989), p. 30.
15. New York Society for the Reformation of Juvenile Delinquents, *Documents Relative to the House of Refuge* (New York: Mahlon Day, 1832).
16. Charles Brace, *The Dangerous Classes of New York and Twenty Years' Work Among Them* (New York: Wynkoop and Hellenbeck, 1880/1970); Stephen O'Connor, *Orphan Trains* (Boston: Houghton Mifflin, 2001).
17. Robert Carter, "The Police View of the Justice System," in Malcolm Klein (Ed.), *The Juvenile Justice System* (Beverly Hills, CA: Sage, 1976), p. 131.
18. Robert Brown, "Black, White, and Unequal: Examining Situational Determinants of Arrest Decisions from Police–Suspect Encounters," *Criminal Justice Studies* 18:51–68 (2005); Michael Resig, John McCluskey, Stephen Mastrofski, and William Terrill, "Suspect Disrespect toward the Police," *Justice Quarterly* 21:241–268 (2004); Irving Piliavin and Scott Briar, "Police Encounters with Juveniles," *American Journal of Sociology* 70:206–214 (1964); Geoffrey Alpert, John MacDonald, and Roger Dunham, "Police Suspicion and Discretionary Decision Making During Citizen Stops, *Criminology* 43:407–434 (2005).
19. National Advisory Committee for Juvenile Justice and Delinquency Prevention, *Juvenile Justice and Delinquency Prevention* (Washington, DC: U.S. Government Printing Office, 1976).
20. Robert Regoli, John Hewitt, and Matt DeLisi, *Delinquency in Society*, 7th ed. (New York: McGraw-Hill, 2008), p. 426.
21. Anne Stahl, Charles Puzzanchera, Sarah Livsey, Anthony Sladky, Terrence Finnegan, Nancy Tierney, and Howard Snyder, *Juvenile Court Statistics 2003–2004* (Pittsburgh: National Center for Juvenile Justice, 2007), p. 15.
22. Barry Feld, *Cases and Materials on Juvenile Justice Administration* (St. Paul, MN: West, 2000), p. 313.
23. James Austin, Kelly Johnson, and Ronald Weitzer, *Alternatives to Secure Detention and Confinement of Juvenile Offenders* (Washington, DC: U.S. Department of Justice, 2005).
24. Stahl et al., note 21, p. 30.
25. Barry Krisberg, Ira Schwartz, Paul Litsky, and James Austin, "The Watershed of Juvenile Justice Reform," *Crime & Delinquency* 32:5–38 (1986); Barry Krisberg, Robert DeComo, Norma Herrera, Martha Steketee, and Sharon Roberts, *Juveniles Taken into Custody: Fiscal Year 1990 Report* (San Francisco: National Council on Crime and Delinquency, 1991).

26. *Schall v. Martin*, 467 U.S. 253 (1984).

27. *McKeiver v. Pennsylvania*, 403 U.S. 528 (1971).

28. Howard Snyder and Melissa Sickmund, *Juvenile Offenders and Victims: 2006 National Report* (Pittsburgh: National Center for Juvenile Justice, 2006), p. 198.

29. Stahl, note 21, p. 48.

30. Snyder and Sickmund, note 28, p. 232; Howard Snyder, "An Empirical Portrait of the Youth Reentry Population," *Youth Violence and Juvenile Justice* 2:39–55 (2004).

31. Lynn Goodstein and Henry Sontheimer, "The Implementation of an Intensive Aftercare Program for Serious Juvenile Offenders," *Criminal Justice and Behavior* 24:332–359 (1997).

32. James Howell, *Preventing and Reducing Juvenile Delinquency: A Comprehensive Framework* (Thousand Oaks, CA: Sage, 2003).

33. Regoli et al., note 20.

34. Barry Feld, *Bad Kids: Race and the Transformation of the Juvenile Court* (New York: Oxford University Press, 1999).

35. Daniel Mears, "A Critique of Waiver Research: Critical Next Steps in Assessing the Impacts of Laws for Transferring Juveniles to the Criminal Justice System," *Youth Violence and Juvenile Justice* 1:156–172 (2003).

36. Snyder and Sickmund, note 28.

37. *Kent v. United States*, 383 U.S. 541 (1966).

38. *Kent v. United States*, note 37.

39. *Breed v. Jones*, 421 U.S. 519 (1975).

40. Charles Thomas and Shay Bilchik, "Prosecuting Juveniles in Criminal Courts: A Legal and Empirical Analysis," *Journal of Criminal Law and Criminology* 76:439–479 (1985).

41. Cary Rudman, Eliot Hartstone, Jeffrey Fagan, and Melinda Moore, "Violent Youth in Adult Court: Process and Punishment," *Crime & Delinquency* 32:75–96 (1986); David Reed, *Needed: Serious Solutions for Serious Juvenile Crime* (Chicago: Chicago Law Enforcement Study, 1983).

42. Thomas Cohen and Brian Reaves, *Felony Defendants in Large Urban Counties, 2002* (Washington, DC: U.S. Department of Justice, 2006), p. 24; Dean Champion, *The Juvenile Justice System* (New York: Macmillan, 1992), p. 583; Rudman et al., note 41, p. 86; Donna Bishop, Charles Frazier, and John Henretta, "Prosecutorial Waiver: Case Study of a Questionable Reform," *Crime & Delinquency* 35:180 (1989).

43. Thomas Grisso and Richard Schwartz, *Youth on Trial: A Developmental Perspective on Juvenile Justice* (Chicago: University of Chicago Press, 2000); Thomas Grisso, Laurence Steinberg, Jennifer Woolard, Elizabeth Cauffman, Elizabeth Scott, Sandra Graham, et al., "Juveniles' Competence to Stand Trial: A Comparison of Adolescents' and Adults' Capacities as Trial Defendants," *Law and Human Behavior* 27:333–363 (2003); Norman Poythress, Frances Lexcen, Thomas Grisso, and Laurence Steinberg, "The Competence-Related Abilities of Adolescent Defendants in Criminal Court, *Law and Human Behavior* 30:88 (2006).

44. Dean Champion, *The Juvenile Justice System* (New York: Macmillan, 1992), p. 92.

45. Mary Clement, "A Five-Year Study of Juvenile Waiver and Adult Sentences: Implications for Policy," *Criminal Justice Policy Review* 8:201–219 (1997); Megan Kurlychek and Brian Johnson, "The Juvenile Penalty: A Comparison of Juvenile and Young Adult Sentencing Outcomes in Criminal Court," *Criminology* 42:485–517 (2004); Jeffrey Fagan, "The Comparative Advantage of Juvenile Versus Criminal Court Sanctions on Recidivism among Adolescent Felony Offenders," *Law and Policy* 18:77–114 (1996); Carole Barnes and Randal Franze, "Questionably Adult: Determinants and Effects of the Juvenile Waiver Decision," *Justice Quarterly* 6:117–135 (1989).

46. William Sabol and Heather Couture, *Prison Inmates at Midyear 2007* (Washington, DC: U.S. Department of Justice, 2008).

47. Martin Forst, Jeffrey Fagan, and T. Scott Vivona, "Youth in Prisons and Training Schools: Perceptions and Consequences of the Treatment–Custody Dichotomy," *Juvenile and Family Court Journal* 40:1–14 (1989).

48. Zvi Eisikovits and Michael Baizerman, "'Doing Time': Violent Youth in a Juvenile Facility and in an Adult Prison," *Journal of Offender Counseling, Services and Rehabilitation* 6:10 (1982), p. 9.

49. Kathleen Heide, Erin Spencer, Andrea Thompson, and Eldra Solomon, "Who's In, Who's Out, and Who's Back: Follow-up Data on 59 Juveniles Incarcerated in Adult Prison for Murder or Attempted Murder in the Early 1980s," *Behavioral Sciences and the Law* 19:97–108 (2001).

50. Regoli et al., note 20.

51. *Eddings v. Oklahoma*, 455 U.S. 104 (1982).

52. *Thompson v. Oklahoma*, 487 U.S. 815 (1988).

53. *Stanford v. Kentucky*, 492 U.S. 361 (1989).

54. *Roper v. Simmons*, 543 U.S. 551 (2005).

55. Regoli et al., note 20.

CHAPTER

Terrorism and Cybercrime

OBJECTIVES

1 Know the scope of international and domestic terrorist groups and major terrorist events in recent decades.

2 Identify how the United States and its allies respond to Al Qaeda and other terrorist groups via the criminal justice system.

3 Outline the function and rationale for counterterrorism efforts and the USA Patriot Act.

4 Grasp the function of the Department of Homeland Security as a counterterrorism entity.

5 Place the attacks of September 11, 2001, in historical context and understand the role that they played in transforming criminal justice responses to various forms of criminal behavior.

6 Understand the emerging crimes of cybercrime and identity theft and the ways that the criminal justice system responds to them.

PROFILES IN CRIME AND JUSTICE

Scott J. White, PhD
Former Intelligence Officer
Assistant Professor of Criminal Justice
Westfield State College

Upon graduating from the University of Bristol, I looked for a career that would put me at the forefront of homeland security. As an intelligence officer, I worked in an environment that was professional and that respected critical and innovative thinking. I was faced with some of the most challenging issues affecting homeland security on a regular basis. It was a fast-paced environment where my knowledge and creativity were constantly being challenged and assessed. The decisions my colleagues and I made during the course of our work played a major part in the country's efforts to counter terrorism and in protecting critical infrastructure.

Intelligence officers deal with highly classified, important subject matter that is crucial to the security of the nation. Typically, an officer might start his or her career by assessing or investigating threats to homeland security. Over time, he or she might move into one of the specialized areas, such as terrorism, espionage, transnational crime, information security, or the proliferation of weapons of mass destruction, to name but a few options. In addition, intelligence officers have the opportunity to travel abroad and work with agencies from other countries.

An important aspect of any security organization is teamwork. Individuals at all levels and across all specialty areas make important contributions to the overall security mission. While you will have your own areas of specialization, you will also work as part of a team of people from different backgrounds and areas of specialization. For this reason, recruiting people to the various security services is based on the skills, competencies, and personal qualities of each candidate as well as the needs of that particular service. Because threats to our country can come from a wide variety of sources, a strong educational background and a knowledge and understanding of other communities, cultures, and languages are critical. You will meet people from all walks of life in the intelligence field.

Discretion is an integral part of intelligence work. Intelligence officers must meet the highest standards of personal integrity and honesty. Also, because the work is of a classified nature, your successes and those of your team will remain relatively unknown outside of the intelligence community. Nevertheless, working in the field of security intelligence in furtherance of homeland security is a very rewarding and satisfying career.

Introduction

The twenty-first century is a new world for the criminal justice system. Developments in technology have led to new crimes, new criminal methods, and new ways to respond to crime. The leading "new" problem that the criminal justice system must address is terrorism. No longer just a concern of the United States military and intelligence community, criminal justice operatives—from those in policing to prosecution to corrections—now engage in counterterrorism efforts.

Although terrorism is the defining issue of the new century, there are other serious threats to society as well. Emerging crimes, such as cybercrime and identity theft, can produce enormous losses and feelings of panic and uncertainty—just like terrorism. These crimes have grown considerably in the past decade, at a tremendous expense. Besides facing the widespread—and dangerous—computer viruses, email spam, and spyware, each year more than 10 million Americans are the victims of identity theft, with estimated annual costs now approaching $50 billion.[1] These new crimes have inspired innovative responses by the criminal justice system, from the creation of the Department of Homeland Security and restructuring of the Department of Justice to the USA Patriot Acts and increased communication between intelligence agencies.

Terrorism

On September 11, 2001, the United States suffered the worst terrorist attack in its history.

Not long ago, few Americans took the subject of terrorism very seriously. Public opinion polls indicated that terrorism was not considered a national priority compared to other concerns, such as the economy, crime, and civility/public morality.[2] When terrorist events did directly affect the United States, such as the 1993 attack on the World Trade Center and the 1995 bombing of the Alfred P. Murrah Federal Building in Oklahoma City, they seemed to be viewed as horrible, but atypical, and not cause for major concern. Indeed, although domestic and international terrorists have consistently been prosecuted and punished by the U.S. criminal justice system, terrorism was not even the first priority of federal and state authorities.[3]

On September 11, 2001, the world changed, when 19 Al Qaeda terrorists hijacked four U.S. commercial airliners with chilling intent, as described in the 9/11 Commission Report:

> The 19 men were aboard four transcontinental flights. They were planning to hijack these planes and turn them into large guided missiles, loaded with up to 11,400 gallons of jet fuel. By 8:00 A.M. on the morning of Tuesday, September 11, 2001, they had defeated all the security layers that America's civil aviation security system then had in place to prevent a hijacking.[4]

The result of their efforts is well known: The American Airlines and United Airlines passenger flights were turned into deadly weapons, hitting the two towers of the World Trade Center, the heart of the country's financial district in New York City, and the Pentagon, the heart of the U.S. Department of Defense. Passengers on the fourth plane attacked the hijackers, and the plane crashed into a field in southwestern Pennsylvania; its intended target was likely either the U.S. Capitol Building or the White House, the seat of American government. Taken together, these events killed nearly 3000 people, destroyed the World Trade Center, grounded all aircraft in the United States, overwhelmed stock markets around the world, and cost more than $17 billion in immediate costs and 200,000 lost jobs. They also placed terrorism at the heart of policy efforts, federal criminal justice focus, and international debate among the United States and its allies.[5] Ten days after the September 11 attacks, President George W. Bush made clear the purpose of the U.S. government regarding terrorism:

> We will direct every resource at our command to win the war against terrorism: every means of diplomacy, every tool of intelligence, every instrument of law enforcement, every financial influence. We will starve the terrorists of funding, turn them against each other, rout them out of their safe hiding places, and bring them to justice.

By 2002, nearly 75 percent of Americans were very worried that the United States would suffer another major terrorist attack.[6] In 2008, terrorism, counterterrorism, and criminal justice efforts to aid in counterterrorism remained important political items in the presidential election.

Terrorism encompasses not only extreme acts of violence, such as those on September 11, but also widespread attacks that inflict massive victimization, cause financial loss, and spread fear. The Federal Bureau of Investigation (FBI) defines **terrorism** as the "unlawful use of force or violence to intimidate or coerce a government, the civilian population, or any segment thereof, in furtherance of political or social objectives or goals."[7] Federal law defines terrorism as "[a]ctivities that involve . . . violation(s) of the criminal laws of the United States or of any State and . . . appear to be intended (i) to intimidate or coerce a civilian population; (ii) to influence the policy of a government by intimidation or coercion; or (iii) to affect the conduct of a government by mass destruction, assassination, or kidnapping. . . ."[8] Terrorism, in other words, is a politically motivated act of violence.

Osama bin Laden is the most wanted criminal in the world.

Terrorism takes several forms and is differentiated according to two factors:

- The target of the attack (which often holds symbolic and practical value)
- The means by which the terror is inflicted (such as arson, bombing, assassination, or chemical attack)

Some common forms or types of terrorism are summarized here:

- **Eco-terrorism** (or environmental terrorism): the infliction of economic damage to those who profit from development and destruction of environmental resources (such as the logging industry, developers and construction companies, and restaurant chains that are perceived to be harmful to animals).
- **Economic terrorism**: the attack of banks and other financial centers that are seen as symbols of capitalistic oppression (such as the acts committed by the Weather Underground, which robbed and bombed banks, mostly during the 1970s).
- **Racial terrorism**: the use of intimidation and violence against select racial and ethnic groups perpetrated by persons holding extremist views about race (such as the acts of the Ku Klux Klan, which has targeted African Americans, Jewish Americans, and homosexuals as enemies of white, Christian, heterosexual Americans).
- **Cyberterrorism**: threats or attacks on computer or information systems.
- **Bioterrorism**: the introduction of biological toxins (such as ricin, anthrax, or smallpox) into a food or water source or transportation hub in an attempt to inflict massive casualties.

Regardless of the methods used, terrorists share many common characteristics. First, terrorists are extremely motivated by a profound political cause, religious belief, or social grievance that often places them in a state of inequality compared to their stated enemy. Terrorists often deeply resent the enemy, whom they blame for their problems. In this way, terrorism can be viewed as a war of freedom against one's oppressors. From this perspective, one state's terrorist is another state's "freedom fighter." Second, terrorists are extremely aggressive and view the use of violence—even suicidal violence—as appropriate and justified means to strike their enemy. Third, terrorists believe that their violence will produce social change benefiting the terrorist organization or movement; at times the social change is as simple as the destruction of the group's enemy.[9]

International terrorists generally direct their hatred at two nations: the United States and Israel.[10] The reasons why these countries are targeted are longstanding and relate to their religious and cultural differences with traditional Islam. International terrorist groups practice a radical form of Islam that views non-Muslims, or infidels, as eternal enemies.[11] In addition to possessing extreme religious hatred, Islamic terrorist groups view the political, economic, and military power of the United States and Israel as oppressive.[12] Indeed, in the wake of the September 11 attacks, the political motivation behind terrorism has often been conflated with religious fanaticism and Islamic fundamentalism.[13]

Although there are many terrorist organizations, certain groups appear very prominently in discussions of international terrorism:

- **Al Qaeda**, formed in 1988 by Osama bin Laden and Muhammad Atef, was responsible for the September 11 attacks and is the main opposition to the United States in the War on Terror. Al Qaeda has unofficial partnerships with Egyptian Islamic Jihad, Palestinian Islamic Jihad, and Hezbollah in Lebanon.
- **Hamas**, or the Islamic Resistance Movement, was founded in 1987 and has been engaged in a holy war (**jihad**) against Israel with the ultimate goal to "liberate Palestine from Israeli occupation." Hamas specializes in bombings and suicide attacks. It also employs a political organization that has candidates running in local elections.

- The **Palestinian Liberation Organization (PLO)** was founded by Yasser Arafat in 1964 and is considered by many to be the terrorist organization that has achieved the greatest political currency. The PLO developed from Al Fatah, an underground terrorist organization that Arafat founded in Egypt in 1956. Today, the PLO has two offshoot organizations that are even more radical in their mission to destroy Israel: the Popular Front for the Liberation of Palestine (PFLP) and the Popular Front for the Liberation of Palestine–General Command (PFLP-GC). Although their primary target is Israel, these groups have recently established cells across the United States.[14]

Within America's borders, several homegrown, domestic terrorist groups also pose significant threats to the country's security:

- Left-wing (i.e., Marxist or communist) political groups, such as Macheteros, New African Freedom Fighters, and the Provisional Party of Communists, strive to destroy capitalist society and its perceived forms of oppression.
- Eco-terrorists, such as the Animal Liberation Front, Earth Liberation Front, and Earth First, use terrorist methods—especially arson and vandalism—to promote radical environmentalism.
- Islamic fundamentalist groups, like Jamaat Ul Fuqra (Fuqra)—an organization created in Pakistan that consists almost entirely of African American extremists who live in communal environments (called jamaats) in the United States—commit murders, bombings, white-collar crimes, cybercrime, and identity theft to serve Islam through violence.[15]
- Hate groups include the white supremacist group Ku Klux Klan (KKK), which was founded by former Confederate soldiers after the Civil War to terrorize African Americans, Jews, and even whites who sympathized with the Klan's targets.

At one time, the Klu Klux Klan wielded considerable political influence in the United States and had nearly 5 million members.[16] Today, its legitimate power and presence on the domestic terrorism scene are minimal, and the group has fewer than 6000 members nationwide. However, even today, the Klan continues to commit hate crimes nationwide and has become a formidable security threat group in U.S. prisons. For instance, in 2007 in Miami–Dade County, the KKK claimed responsibility for setting a church on fire and painting racial slurs at the scene.[17]

Since 1980, 318 terrorist attacks have occurred within the United States (including the September 11 attacks).[18] Most of these (66 percent) were bomb attacks, followed by arson (14 percent), malicious destruction (6 percent), and shooting (5 percent) (see FIGURE 14-1). During this period, U.S. criminal justice personnel successfully prevented 133 terrorist acts or thwarted plans of known terrorist groups.[19] On an international level, the prevalence of terrorism against the United States is somewhat lower, with 136 terrorist attacks against U.S. targets occurring during the same period. As with domestic terrorist acts against the United States, bombings were the most common form of international terrorism.[20] According to the Federal Bureau of Investigation, since 1980 approximately 17,216 people have been killed or wounded by terrorists.[21]

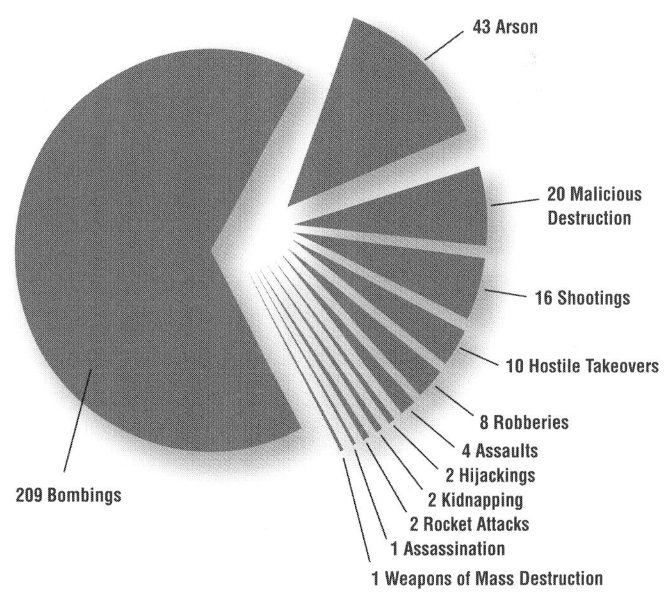

FIGURE 14-1 Domestic Terrorism Events

Federal Bureau of Investigation, *Terrorism 2002–2005* (Washington, DC: U. S. Department of Justice, 2007).

It is important to note that estimates of the deaths caused by terrorists are just that—estimates. Different groups employ different definitions of which types of violence constitute terrorism. For example, United Nations member states have no agreed-upon definition of terrorism, which has proved a stumbling block in enacting meaningful counterterrorism measures. To illustrate, whereas the FBI places the number killed by terrorists at fewer than 20,000, the Tamil Tigers (officially known as the Liberation Tigers of Lamil Eelam, or LTTE) in Sri Lanka are responsible directly or indirectly (as a result of government response) for more than 65,000 deaths and the displacement of 1.6 million people.[22]

Timeline of Major Terrorist Events

The following timeline captures major terrorist events of the last 40 years, including assassinations and attempted assassinations of world leaders, airline hijackings, truck bombings, suicide attacks, kidnappings, and murders.

- June 5, 1968: U.S. Presidential candidate Robert F. Kennedy is assassinated by Sirhan Sirhan, a Palestinian who was motivated by Kennedy's pro-Israel positions.
- June 9, 1970: The PLO attempts to assassinate Jordan's King Hussein.
- September 1970: The PFLP hijacks planes in the Netherlands, Switzerland, and Germany and kills more than 400 passengers. In response, Jordan attacks Palestinian neighborhoods, which results in more than 20,000 deaths.
- September 5, 1972: Black September, an Islamic terrorist group, kills 9 Israeli athletes at the Olympic Games in Munich, Germany.
- November 4, 1979: Fifty-two U.S. diplomats are taken hostage by fundamentalist Islamic students in Tehran, Iran, and held for 444 days.
- May 13, 1981: Pope John Paul II is shot in an assassination attempt by a Turkish assailant who claims PFLP membership.
- October 6, 1981: Egypt President Anwar al-Sadat is assassinated by Muslim extremists within the Egyptian army.
- April 18, 1983: The U.S. Embassy in Beirut is destroyed by a suicide car-bombing by Radical Islamic Jihad; 63 people are killed.
- October 23, 1983: U.S. military barracks are destroyed by a truck-bombing carried out by Muslims associated with bin Laden's mentor, Imad Magniyah, in Beirut, Lebanon, killing 241 U.S. Marines and 58 French troops.
- December 21, 1988: Pan Am Flight 103 explodes over Lockerbie, Scotland, killing 259 passengers, including American students and military personnel. The Libyan government and PFLP-GC claim responsibility.
- February 26, 1993: A truck bomb explodes in the garage underneath the World Trade Center in New York City, killing 7, injuring nearly 1100 people, and resulting in $500 million in damages. Ramzi Yousef and Sheik Omar Abdel Rahman, terrorists with links to Al Qaeda, are sentenced to life imprisonment for their roles in the attack on September 5, 1996.
- April 14, 1993: An assassination attempt on U. S. President George H. W. Bush is foiled in Kuwait.
- October 4, 1993: Al Qaeda militants destroy U.S. helicopters in Somalia, killing 18 soldiers.
- April 19, 1995: A Ryder truck packed with explosives destroys the Alfred P. Murrah Federal Building in Oklahoma City, killing 168 and wounding 600 civilians. The attack is carried out by Timothy McVeigh and Terry Nichols. McVeigh is executed for his crimes on June 11, 2001, and Nichols is sentenced to life imprisonment without parole on August 9, 2004.

- June 25, 1996: The Movement for Islamic Change detonates truck bombs outside the U.S. Air Force complex Khobar Towers in Dahran, Saudi Arabia, killing 19 and wounding 515.
- August 7, 1998: Al Qaeda coordinates truck-bombings of U.S. embassies in Kenya and Tanzania, killing 224 and wounding more than 5000 African civilians.
- October 12, 2000: Al Qaeda operatives ram the *USS Cole* in Aden, Yemen, with a boat laden with explosives, killing 17 and injuring 39 American military personnel.
- September 11, 2001: Al Qaeda operatives crash commercial airliners into the World Trade Center in New York City and the Pentagon in Washington, D.C., killing 2993 and injuring approximately 16,000 civilians.
- September 18, 2001: Letters containing anthrax are sent to five major U.S. media outlets, killing 1 civilian. A second batch of anthrax letters is sent on October 9; they result in 4 deaths and 17 injuries. The FBI claims that the anthrax letters were sent by domestic terrorists, but no terrorist group has taken responsibility. On August 6, 2008, the Department of Justice announces that Dr. Bruce Ivins, a government biodefense researcher who committed suicide on July 29, 2008, was the likely perpetrator.
- October 12, 2002: Al Qaeda members destroy nightclubs in Bali, killing 202 and wounding more than 300 people.
- March 11, 2004: Al Qaeda operatives explode bombs on three commuter trains in Madrid, Spain, killing more than 200 people and injuring 1400.
- September 1, 2004: Chechen terrorists storm a school in Russia and take 1100 people hostage; they ultimately kill 334 hostages, including 186 children.
- July 7, 2005: Four Al Qaeda operatives explode bombs on London Underground trains and a London city bus, killing 52 and injuring more than 700 civilians.
- August 21, 2006: Al Qaeda plot to destroy 10 airplanes en route from England to the United States using liquid explosives is foiled, as 21 terrorists are arrested.
- April 11, 2007: Al Qaeda members detonate two car bombs in Algiers, Algeria, killing 33 and injuring 222 people.
- June 30, 2007: Al Qaeda plots to attack Glasgow (Scotland) International Airport and sites in London are foiled, resulting in 8 arrests.
- December 27, 2007: Al Qaeda terrorists murder Benazir Bhutto, former prime minister of Pakistan, and kill 20 other innocent civilians, escalating the war on terror.
- September 5, 2008: Suicide truck bombs kill 35 and injure 70 in Peshawar, Pakistan.[23]
- November 26, 2008: Terrorists attack hotel, train station, and Jewish community center in Mumbai, India, killing at least 173 people.

The War on Terror

The United States has declared a War on Terror to fight against radical Islamic terrorist groups, such as Al Qaeda, who wish to destroy the United States and its allies.[24] The U.S. Department of Justice (DOJ) has taken broad steps in this war by designating key terrorist organizations, dismantling terrorist threats and cells, freezing terrorist assets around the world, and killing, capturing, or otherwise incapacitating terrorist operatives. The DOJ has also significantly increased its intelligence capacity to produce information on terrorist subjects and track suspected terrorists.

Congress has also worked to prevent future acts of terror against the United States and its allies by passing legislation (such as the USA Patriot Acts, discussed later) to facilitate information sharing and cooperation among government agencies; provide investigators with necessary tools, such as increased wiretapping and surveillance capability; update the law to reflect new technologies and threats; and increase the penalties for those who commit terrorist acts or who assist or harbor terrorists.

The DOJ has been successful at utilizing the federal criminal justice system to apprehend, prosecute, convict, and incarcerate terrorists operating within the United States and abroad. Members or associates of Al Qaeda, the Taliban (the terrorist government that seized power in Afghanistan), Hezbollah, Hamas, and dozens of other terrorist groups from Afghanistan, Colombia, England, Pakistan, and Yemen have been brought to justice. Some of the more high-profile convictions include the following cases:

- Richard Reid was sentenced to life imprisonment in January 2003 for attempting to ignite a shoe bomb aboard a transatlantic flight.

FOCUS ON CRIMINAL JUSTICE

Hamdan v. Rumsfeld

Perhaps the most controversial criminal justice/military policy in the War on Terror has been the detention of enemy combatants (members of Al Qaeda and the Taliban) by U.S. authorities in Camp Delta in Guantanamo Bay, Cuba. According to the doctrine established by President George W. Bush, enemy combatants are not afforded due process rights reserved for members of official state militaries or criminal defendants. However, on June 29, 2006, the U.S. Supreme Court held that terrorist suspects detained in the terrorist prison in Guantanamo Bay must receive due process provisions consistent with the military system and international standards or be released from military custody. The decision was an affront to the Bush administration's plan to try terrorists as enemy combatants in military tribunals, which do not give defendants the same rights as prisoners of war under the Geneva Convention. The Bush administration was sharply critical of the decision.

In *Hamdan v. Rumsfeld* (2006), in a 5-to-3 decision, the Supreme Court held that it had jurisdiction to rule on the matter and that the federal government did not have authority to set up these particular special military commissions, which were ruled illegal under both the Uniform Code of Military Justice and the Geneva Convention. Although the ruling dealt a blow to the Bush administration's efforts in the War on Terror, the Court did not categorically prohibit military commissions. In a concurring opinion with the majority, Justice Stephen Breyer wrote, "Congress has denied the President the legislative authority to create military commissions of the kind at issue here. Nothing prevents the President from returning to Congress to seek the authority he believes necessary."

In his dissent, Justice Antonin Scalia forcefully criticized the Court and its decision. Fundamentally, he argued that no court had jurisdiction to hear court requests of a detainee from Guantanamo Bay. In Justice Scalia's words:

> On December 30, 2005, Congress enacted the Detainee Treatment Act (DTA). It unambiguously provides that, as of that date, "no court, justice, or judge" shall have jurisdiction to consider the habeas application of a Guantanamo Bay detainee. Notwithstanding this plain directive, the Court today concludes that, on what it calls the statute's *most natural* reading, *every* "court, justice, or judge" before whom such a habeas application was pending on December 30 had jurisdiction to hear, consider, and render judgment on it. This conclusion is patently erroneous. And even if it were not, the jurisdiction supposedly retained should, in an exercise of sound equitable discretion, not be exercised.

It is clear that the controversy surrounding counterterrorism measures is hotly debated, even among Supreme Court Justices.

Sources: Hamdan v. Rumsfeld, 548 U.S. 557 (2006); Associated Press, "Gonzales: Gitmo Ruling 'Hampered' War on Terror," available at http://www.cnn.com/2006/LAW/07/01/gonzales.gitmo/index.html, accessed January 12, 2008.

- John Walker Lindh was sentenced to 20 years in prison in July 2002 for supplying services to the Taliban.
- The Lackawanna Six (New York) were sentenced to 7 to 10 years in prison in 2003 for providing material support to Al Qaeda.
- The seven persons in the Portland (Oregon) Cell were sentenced to 18 years in prison in 2003 for money laundering, conspiracy to supply goods to the Taliban, and conspiracy to commit sedition.
- Zacarias Moussaoui was sentenced to life imprisonment in May 2006 for his participation in the September 11 conspiracy.[25]

In general, Americans support the government's efforts in the War on Terror, although some wonder if civil liberties are being jeopardized by the increased surveillance powers of law enforcement and the increased information sharing between intelligence, military, and criminal justice organizations. Furthermore, many people are concerned about violations of the Constitutional rights of persons suspected of terrorist activity.[26]

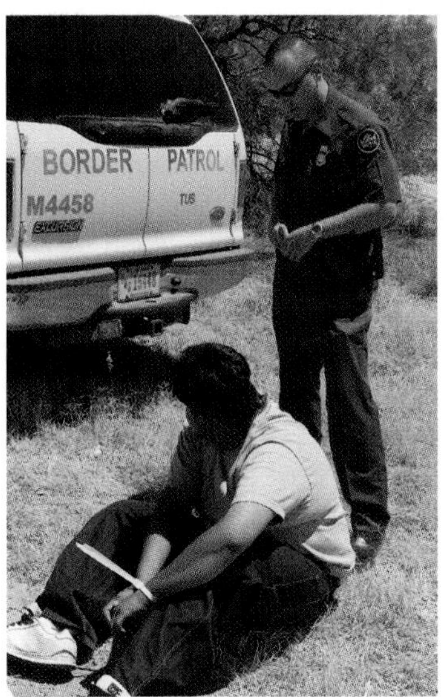

Increased surveillance of the nation's borders is intended to reduce illegal entry into the country and to identify and capture potential terrorists.

Department of Homeland Security

One of the central problems that enabled the terrorist attacks of September 11, 2001, was the lack of information sharing between intelligence and criminal justice agencies. In the wake of the attacks, President George W. Bush proposed the creation of the **Department of Homeland Security** (DHS), a new Cabinet-level federal unit whose primary mission is to protect the United States by coordinating intelligence efforts and communication with law enforcement. The Department of Homeland Security seeks to accomplish the following goals:

- Lead the unified national effort to secure the United States
- Prevent and deter terrorist attacks
- Protect against and respond to threats and hazards to the country
- Ensure safe and secure borders
- Welcome lawful immigrants and visitors
- Promote the free flow of commerce[27]

It aims to achieve these goals by creating better transportation security systems, strengthening border security, reforming immigration processes, increasing overall preparedness, and enhancing information sharing about terrorist activities.[28] Each of these efforts is the focus of specific directorates (or components) of the DHS.

Transportation Security Administration (TSA)

The TSA was created in response to the terrorist attacks of September 11, 2001, as part of the Aviation and Transportation Security Act signed into law by President Bush on November 19, 2001. This agency was originally part of the Department of Transportation but was moved to the DHS in March 2003. TSA's mission is to protect the nation's transportation systems by ensuring the freedom of movement for people and commerce. In February 2002, TSA assumed responsibility for security at U.S. airports and by the end of the year had deployed a federal work force to meet challenging Congressional deadlines for screening all passengers and baggage.[29]

U.S. Customs and Border Protection (CBP)

As the unified border agency, the CBP combines the inspectional work forces and broad border authorities of the U.S. Customs, U.S. Immigration, Animal and Plant Health Inspection Service, and U.S. Border Patrol organizations.[30]

Immigration and Customs Enforcement (ICE)

ICE, which is the largest investigative branch of the DHS, was created by combining the law enforcement arms of the former Immigration and Naturalization Service (INS) and

Headline Crime — Terrorist Attack in India

On November 26, 2008, a group of 10 terrorists hijacked a ship off the coast of Mumbai, India, killed three crew members and ordered the captain to guide them into Mumbai. Once near the shore, they killed the captain. After landing, the terrorists attacked targets popular with tourists, including the Taj Mahal Palace and Tower Hotel, the Oberoi Hotel, the Chhatrapati Shivaji train station, and the Nariman House, an ultra-Orthodox Jewish center. When the attacks were over, at least 171 people had been killed.

The terrorists were members of the Pakistani-based Lashkar e Taiba, a group affiliated with al Qaeda. Mohammad Ajmal Amir Iman, age 21, was the only terrorist captured. Police interrogators report that he and the group participated along with 14 others in a year-long terrorist training course in Pakistan. The group's intention was to blow up the Taj Mahal Palace hotel after executing as many "white targets," primarily America, British, and Jewish tourists, they were able to find. Iman told his interrogators "I have done right. I have no regrets." Interrogators said his account is consistent with evidence recovered from the boat and intercepted satellite phone conversations.

Because a number of the victims of the attack were American citizens, the Federal Bureau of Investigation is sending agents to Mumbai to assist in the ongoing investigation.

Sources: "FBI Sends Agents to Mumbai," available at www.wsj.com/washwire/2008/11/28/fbi-sends-agents-to-mumbai-dead-include-us-citizens/, accessed December 4, 2008; "Mumbai: Where are the 14 Other Pakistani-Trained Terrorists?" available at www.abcnews.go.com/Blotter/story?id=6378603&page=1, accessed December 4, 2008; "'No Regrets:' Captured Terrorist's Account of Mumbai Massacre Reveals Plan Was to Kill 5,000," available at www.dailymail.co.uk/news/article-1090546/No-Regrets-Captured-Terrorists-account-Mumbai-Massacre-Reveals-Plan-Kill-5,000.html, accessed December 4, 2008; "Mumbai's Small Jewish Community in Shock After Attack on Jewish Center in India," available at www.latimes.com/news/nationworld/world/wire/sns-ap-as-india-shooting-jews,1,3632469.story, accessed December 4, 2008.

the former U.S. Customs Service. Before the September 11 attacks, immigration and customs authorities were not widely recognized as an effective counterterrorism tool in the United States. ICE changed this perception by creating a host of new systems to better address national security threats, detect potential terrorist activities in the United States, effectively enforce immigration and customs laws, and protect against terrorist attacks. Key activities of ICE include targeting illegal immigrants; the people, money, and materials that support terrorism; and other criminal activities. ICE is a key component of the DHS "layered defense" approach to protecting the nation.[31]

Additional components of DHS work with local and state law enforcement and other criminal justice officials in the event of emergencies:

- Federal Law Enforcement Training Center—trains law enforcement personnel
- U.S. Citizenship and Immigration Services—establishes immigration services policies and priorities and manages immigration functions and adjudications
- Directorate for Preparedness—identifies threats, vulnerabilities, and targets to protect U.S. borders, seaports, bridges and highways, and information systems
- Office of Intelligence and Analysis—uses information and intelligence from multiple international, national, state, and local sources to identify and access current and future threats to the United States
- Directorate for Science and Technology—acts as the research and development arm of the DHS and assists all other components
- Directorate for Management—represents the budgetary, appropriations and finance, and human resources arm of the DHS and assists all other components[32]

USA Patriot Act

The most important yet controversial counterterrorism measure is the **USA Patriot Act**. The Patriot Act empowers criminal justice and counterterrorism in several important ways. For example, it allows law enforcement personnel to use electronic (wiretap) surveillance to monitor nonterrorism crimes that terrorists commit to build and sustain their resource infrastructure. In other words, when authorities investigate crimes such as immigration fraud, mail fraud, and passport fraud, it often leads to more fruitful information about plans for violence.

After the September 11th attacks, racial profiling became a controversial issue in counterterrorism and law enforcement.

The Patriot Act also allows "roving wiretaps" that permit the surveillance of a particular person rather than a particular telephone or communications device. Because terrorists are trained to move frequently to evade capture, roving wiretaps give law enforcement more latitude to track individual suspects. Similarly, the Act provides that search warrants can be obtained in any district where terrorism occurred, regardless of where the warrant will actually be executed.

Additionally, the Patriot Act permits law enforcement, under narrow circumstances, to delay for a limited time when the subject is told that a judicially approved search warrant has been executed. The delay gives authorities time to identify terrorist associates, eliminate immediate threats, and coordinate the arrests of multiple individuals without tipping them off beforehand.

Federal agents may, under the provisions of the Patriot Act, obtain business records of businesses that are suspected of posing risks to national security through their association with terrorist groups. The Patriot Act also removed the major legal barriers that prevented the law enforcement, intelligence, and national defense communities from sharing information and coordinating their efforts to ensure public safety.

Lastly, the Act increased the legal penalties for an assortment of terrorism-related crimes, enhanced a number of conspiracy penalties, and abolished the statutes of limitations for certain terrorism crimes. It also prohibits the harboring of terrorists, attacks on mass transit systems, and bioterrorism crimes.

The Patriot Act has been criticized for its potential to infringe on civil liberties, but many media accounts fail to inform readers about the actual provisions of the Act. In most cases, the Patriot Act simply gathered together criminal justice policies that were already in place, have been used, and have already passed constitutional muster via judicial review. Nevertheless, some view these provisions as an example of excessive and unconstitutional governmental power. For example, the American Civil Liberties Union has described the Patriot Act in the following manner:

> Just 45 days after the September 11 attacks, with virtually no debate, Congress passed the USA Patriot Act. There are significant flaws in the Patriot Act, flaws that threaten your fundamental freedoms by giving the government the power to access your medical records, tax records, information about the books you buy or borrow without probable cause, and the power to break into your home and conduct secret searches without telling you for weeks, months, or indefinitely.[33]

Despite the controversy, the Patriot Act has been the centerpiece criminal justice initiative used by the United States to wage the War on Terror.

The **USA Patriot Act Improvement and Reauthorization Act of 2005** was passed by Congress in 2005, enhancing the powers of the criminal justice system to combat crime and terrorism. It made several provisions of the original Patriot Act permanent and extended others to facilitate communication between law enforcement and national security, permit victims of computer hackers to request law enforcement assistance in monitoring trespassers on their computers, and make several terrorism-related crimes wiretap predicates. In addition, this legislation reorganized the Department of Justice to create a National Security Division and clarified death penalty procedures for terrorist defendants. In an effort to prevent terrorist weapons from entering the country, the revised Act empowered the U.S. Coast Guard to stop suspicious persons believed to be entering the country with chemical, radioactive, or nuclear materials; sentencing enhancements have also been added for maritime crimes.[34]

Together, the Patriot Acts target the financial backing of terrorist groups in several ways: by holding U.S. banks accountable for their dealings with foreign banks, by strengthening laws on money laundering as they relate to terrorist financing, and by creating asset forfeiture laws in matters involving the funding of terrorist activities.

The Foreign Intelligence Surveillance Act

The Foreign Intelligence Surveillance Act of 1978 (FISA) established a legal procedure for foreign intelligence surveillance that was separate from other types of surveillance carried out by law enforcement.[35] FISA aims to regulate the collection of foreign intelligence information in furtherance of U.S. counterintelligence, including gathering information on the following crimes:

- Espionage and other intelligence activities
- Sabotage
- Assassinations conducted by or on behalf of foreign governments, organizations, or persons
- International terrorist activities

The Foreign Intelligence Surveillance Court reviews the U.S. Attorney General's applications for authorization of electronic surveillance aimed at obtaining foreign intelligence information. The records and files of these cases are sealed and may not be revealed even to persons whose prosecutions are based on evidence obtained under FISA warrants, except to a limited degree.[36]

On August 5, 2007, President Bush signed the Protect America Act into law. The Protect America Act modernized FISA in four ways:

- It permits intelligence professionals to more effectively collect foreign intelligence information on targets in foreign lands without first receiving court approval. The new law accomplishes this by clarifying that FISA's definition of "electronic surveillance" does not apply to activities directed at persons reasonably believed to be outside the United States, thereby restoring the statute to its original focus on appropriate protections for the rights of persons in the United States.
- It provides a role for the FISA Court in reviewing the procedures used by the intelligence community to ensure that collection of intelligence remains directed at persons located overseas.
- It provides a mechanism for the FISA Court to direct third parties to assist the intelligence community in its collection efforts.
- It protects third parties from private lawsuits arising from assistance they provide the U.S. government in authorized foreign intelligence activities targeting individuals located outside the United States.[37]

Police Responses to Terrorism

Federal, state, and local law enforcement agencies also play an important role in the War on Terror by turning their attention toward the white-collar crimes that help terrorist organizations finance their operations and support their infrastructure. Since the September 11 attacks, more than 100 federal criminal cases have been brought against foreign and U. S. nationals who were ultimately convicted of these white-collar crime offenses for the purposes of terrorism.[38]

Additionally, law enforcement agencies are working to respond to the needs of victims of terrorism through the government-sponsored **Terrorism and International Victims**

Unit (TIVU). This organization develops programs to help victims of terrorism, mass violence, and other transnational crimes by providing medical assistance, financial aid, and legal guidance. The government is also funding terrorist research organizations, such as the National Consortium for the Study of Terrorism and Responses to Terror (START); these organizations use state-of-the-art theories, methods, and data from the social and behavioral sciences to improve understanding of the origins, dynamics, and social and psychological impacts of terrorism and enhance the resilience of U.S. society in the face of terrorist threats.[39]

Terrorism is not a traditional problem for U.S. law enforcement, so it might seem that police are poorly prepared to effectively deal with various terrorist threats. However, the community policing effort has helped train police to effectively address the underlying social problems that engender crime. Additionally, local law enforcement officers are now trained and continue to participate in training throughout their careers to address and be prepared for terrorism and terrorism-related criminal activity. Officers must make risk assessments of the potential damage that terrorists pose to their community. These assessments focus on critical infrastructure and likely targets, a sense of how critical the threat is, the vulnerability of the community to a terrorist attack, a calculation of casualties and other risks, and a counterterrorism response.[40]

Within the Department of Justice, the Office of Community Oriented Policing Services (COPS) provides law enforcement and community resources that enable communities to respond to terrorism threats in several important ways:

- Improving data and intelligence collection and processing
- Capitalizing on technological advancements to gather and use intelligence effectively
- Increasing communication between local police and other public safety agencies
- Working with federal agencies and local victim agencies to assist victims of terrorism[41]

Members of "local" law enforcement are no longer doing their job only at the local level. Increasingly, law enforcement agencies have established regional mutual aid agreements under which multiple criminal justice agencies are contracted to respond to specific problems such as terrorism. Mutual aid agreements have also facilitated information sharing between neighboring and regional criminal justice agencies.[42] Overall, the important and growing role of law enforcement in counterterrorism has been referred to as a new paradigm or era in American policing.[43]

Judicial Responses to Terrorism

With increased assistance and cooperation from federal entities, state courts are now assisting in the prosecution, deportation, and sentencing of criminal offenders who are found to be in violation of immigration laws. In some cases, the defendants are involved in or suspected of conspiring to commit terrorism; in the majority of cases, however, the defendants are involved in street crimes of immigration violations. For example, ICE agents recently arrested 154 undocumented immigrants in Columbus, Ohio, with the help of local police. These offenders were then housed in local jails, prosecuted in local courts, and deported from local airports.[44]

Local prosecutors have made concerted efforts to assist the federal government in the War on Terror, especially by focusing on precursor crimes that can be used to establish organized crime or terrorist efforts. Although only 16 percent of local prosecutors have ever prosecuted a terrorism-related case, nearly 75 percent report that they feel actively involved in homeland security.[45] Prosecutors are part of important information-sharing networks, although many complain that federal authorities do not share enough information with local officials, which hampers prosecutors' abilities to make connections in investigating and prosecuting potential terrorists.[46]

Counterterrorism is without question the primary foreign policy concern of the United States and a new facet of traditional criminal justice practice. It is an emerging crime, like cybercrime and identity theft, that has presented unique challenges for lawmakers and criminal justice personnel, and one that will likely shape the future of criminal justice.

Cybercrime

Cybercrime is an umbrella term that describes computer-based criminal behaviors intended to damage or destroy computer networks, fraudulently obtain money and other commodities, and disrupt normal business operations. Although cybercrime is not usually characterized by extremely violent criminal behavior, it is arguably as devastating to society as is terrorism. The global cost of cybercrime is estimated to exceed $500 billion per year. Only some 10 percent of cybercriminals are reported to police, and fewer than 2 percent of cybercrime cases result in conviction.[47] Cybercrime can seriously disrupt or damage travel, commerce, and the normal operating schedule of a society. There are several common types of cybercrime:

- *Computer viruses:* hidden fragments of computer code that spread by inserting themselves into or modifying other programs
- *Cyber-vandalism or -sabotage:* deliberate or malicious destruction or alteration of electronic files, webpages, data, and computer programs
- *Denial of service:* disruption or degradation of an Internet connection or email service that results in an interruption of the normal flow of information
- *Hacking:* unauthorized gaining of access to computers
- *Hijacking:* installation of malicious software that effectively takes over the victim's computer, such as flooding it with obscene pop-up windows
- *Sniffing:* unlawful monitoring of data traveling over a computer network
- *Spamming:* sending of frequent, unwanted email advertisements
- *Spoofing:* gaining unauthorized access to a computer through a message sent from a trusted Internet address
- *Spyware:* illegally installed software that obtains personal information from a personal computer
- *Theft of proprietary information:* illegal electronic copying of copyrighted materials or other data[48]

Estimates suggest that cybercrime is extremely costly. According to former U.S. Attorney-General Alberto Gonzales, cybercrime results in annual losses of $250 billion and have resulted in the loss of more than 750,000 jobs.[49] Nearly 75 percent of businesses claim that they have been the victims of cybercriminals.[50] Nearly 1 in 5 businesses has suffered 20 or more cyberattacks in the past year (FIGURE 14-2). In a single day, Symantec, a computer security provider, aborted 59 million attempts of cybercrime.

On an individual level, about 1 in 3 Americans is the victim of cybercrime each year. More than 60 million Americans have received a "phishing" email, and upward of 90 percent of businesses have suffered a computer breach from cybercriminals. Virtually everyone is

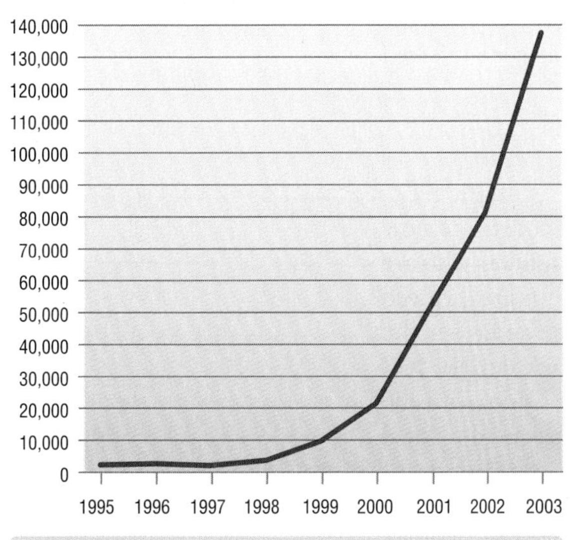

FIGURE 14-2 The Growth of Cybercrime

Source: Prasad Calyam, Network Forensics, available at http://ftp.osc.edu/education/si/projects/forensics/index.shtml, accessed January 14, 2008.

FOCUS ON CRIMINAL JUSTICE

The Melissa Virus

In May 2002, David Smith was sentenced to 20 months in federal prison and fined $5000 for creating the Melissa computer virus, which caused $80 million in damages to computer networks and businesses in 1999. He is liable for state fines in excess of $150,000.

Smith created the Melissa virus and disseminated it from his home computer through email. The Melissa virus appeared on thousands of email systems on March 26, 1999, disguised as an important message from a colleague or friend. The virus sent an infected email to the first 50 email addresses on users' mailing lists, evading antivirus software and infecting computers using Windows operating systems and other Microsoft programs. The Melissa virus was able to spread very quickly by overloading email servers, which resulted in the shutdown of networks and significant costs to repair or cleanse computer systems.

Smith described in state and federal court how, using a stolen America Online account and his own account with a local Internet service provider, he posted an infected document on the Internet newsgroup "Alt.Sex." The posting contained a message that enticed readers to download and open the document with the hope of finding passwords to adult-content websites. Opening and downloading the message caused the Melissa virus to infect victim computers. The virus altered Microsoft word-processing programs such that any document created using the programs would then be infected with the Melissa virus. The virus also lowered macro security settings in the word-processing programs. Smith acknowledged that each new email greeted new users with an enticing message to open it, thereby spreading the virus further. The message read: "Here is that document you asked for . . . don't show anyone else ;-)."

Source: Department of Justice press release, available at http://www.usdoj.gov/criminal/cyber crime/melissaSent.htm, accessed January 29, 2008.

susceptible to cybervictimization because individuals do not control who has access to businesses' information databases. For example, in 2004, a portable computer database containing personal information and credit card information for almost 40,000 customers was stolen from BJ's Wholesale Club.[51] In 2006, a laptop was stolen from the Veterans Administration containing sensitive data for more than 26 million U.S. veterans.[52]

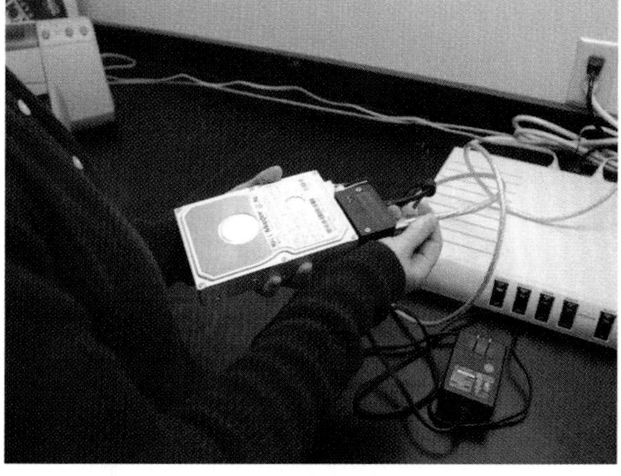

In the twenty-first century, crime has extended into cyberspace with hacking, sniffing, spamming, spyware, and illegal downloading of copyright protected material.

The U.S. government is working hard to combat computer and intellectual property crimes worldwide.[53] The Department of Justice has developed the Computer Crime and Intellectual Property Section (CCIPS) to combat electronic penetrations, data thefts, and cyberattacks on critical information systems. CCIPS aims to prevent, investigate, and prosecute computer crimes by working with other government agencies, the private sector, academic institutions, and foreign counterparts.[54] In addition to CCIPS, the DOJ has taken the following steps:

- Created special Computer Hacker and Intellectual Property units of prosecutors who specialize in the investigation of cybercrime
- Dispatched prosecutors to Asia and Europe to dismantle international organized crime rings that use cybercrime to fund other criminal activities
- Increased prosecution of cybercriminals involved in intellectual property offenses by 98 percent
- Bolstered extradition treaties to include cybercrime
- Sponsored the Intellectual Property Protection Act, which would enhance habitual-offender penalties for certain cybercriminals[55]

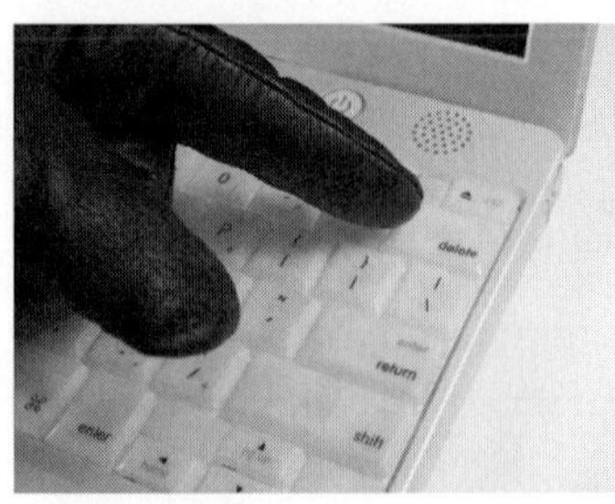
Criminal justice authorities are increasingly cracking down on crimes committed in cyberspace.

Cyberterrorism

Cyberspace is the term used to refer to the hundreds of thousands of interconnected computers, servers, routers, switches, and fiber-optic cables that allow the country's digital infrastructure to work. Cyberspace has been referred to as the nervous system of the United States because computers play a major part in every major area of American life, including agriculture, water, public health, defense, industry, travel, and commerce. Given its key role, controlling and protecting cyberspace is as critical as protecting the homeland from violent terrorist attack. Both terrorists and conventional criminals are keenly aware of the importance of computers to the American way of life and can inflict major damages to American society without bloodshed through cyberterrorism. The bad news is that cyberspace is largely open for exploitation by cybercriminals, making crimes such as phishing and identity theft relatively easy to carry out. For instance, a nationally representative sample of 2000 households reported that nearly 30 percent of households have been victimized by viruses, spyware, phishing, or some other form of cyberattack. Because of these vulnerabilities, an estimated 2.6 million households must replace their computer systems annually. Moreover, about 1 in 5 households does not have antivirus software installed to repel cyberattacks.

The National Strategy to Secure Cyberspace, a Department of Homeland Security program created in 2002, has several goals to increase cyberspace security:

- Establish a public–private structure for responding to national-level cyber-incidents
- Provide for the development of tactical and strategic analysis of cyberattacks and vulnerability assessment
- Encourage the development of a private-sector capability to protect cyberspace
- Support the role of the Department of Homeland Security in coordinating crisis management
- Coordinate processes for voluntary participation in cyberspace protection
- Exercise cybersecurity plans for federal systems
- Improve and enhance public–private information sharing involving cyberattacks, threats, and vulnerability[56]

Fortunately, federal authorities and local criminal justice systems have made headway in their responses to cybercrime. The Computer Security Institute, a national organization devoted to computer security, and the Federal Bureau of Investigation recently conducted the nationally representative Computer Crime and Security Survey and reported promising findings:

- Total financial losses from cyberattacks have declined dramatically, down 61 percent in the past year.
- Attacks on computer systems and misuse of systems have slowly declined.
- More organizations and businesses now guard against cybercrime by using antivirus software, intrusion detection systems, and server-based access control lists.
- Almost 90 percent of respondents conduct security audits to evaluate their readiness against cyberattack.[57]

Thirty states have either passed or are considering legislation targeting cybercriminals who use spyware. Virginia became the first state to pass an anti-phishing bill, which America Online then used to file lawsuits against phishing gangs. Other states, such as California and New York, are also pursuing new statutes to target phishers, and in 2005 the House of Representatives passed an anti-spyware bill.[58]

Identity Theft

One of the fastest-growing types of cybercrime is **identity theft**—the use or attempted use of another person's financial account or identifying information without the owner's permission. In the 1990s, as society became increasingly dependent on computers, cases of identity theft began to increase at a rate of more than 30 percent each year; between 1996 and 2000, identity theft fraud losses incurred by MasterCard and Visa increased more than 43 percent. Since 2000, identity theft cases have plateaued as more consumers have taken steps to protect themselves against identity theft.[59]

The most common types of crimes committed along with identity theft are unauthorized use of existing credit cards, savings accounts, or checking accounts and the misuse of personal information to obtain new accounts, loans, or commit crimes. Often, identity thieves use a method known as **phishing**—the creation and use of emails and websites designed to look like well-known legitimate businesses, financial institutions, or government agencies—to deceive Internet users into disclosing private financial information, such as passwords or personal identification numbers.

Identity theft produces enormous costs and has sometimes severe negative consequences for victims and consumers. The National Crime Victimization Survey (NCVS) estimates that nearly 6.4 million American households (nearly 6 percent of all U.S. households) had at least one family member who had been victimized by identity theft in the past six months. The average identity theft incident resulted in $1620 in losses, and national cumulative losses are in excess of $5 billion.[60]

Identity theft presents a host of problems for the victims of this crime:

- Confrontations with debt collectors or creditors
- Banking problems, such as overdrafts of checking accounts
- Problems with credit card accounts, such as fraudulent charges resulting in damaged credit history
- Higher interest rates
- Denial of phone or utility service
- Higher insurance rates
- Civil lawsuits
- Criminal investigations

It is estimated that in addition to incurring billions of dollars in damages, victims have spent 300 million hours resolving various problems stemming from identity theft. Part of the reason that identity theft thrives is that the criminal justice system was generally unprepared to deal with the threat. There is no single database that captures all investigations and prosecutions of identity theft cases, and it is estimated that 75 percent of identity theft victims do not report the crime to the police.[61] Identity thieves often have technical knowledge about producing fraudulent documents, a working understanding of banking and other financial industries, and savvy social skills that help them evade detection.[62]

In October 1998, Congress passed the Identity Theft and Assumption Deterrence Act of 1998 (Identity Theft Act) to address the problem of identity theft. Specifically, the Identity Theft Act made identity theft a federal crime, including the activities of knowingly transferring or using another person's identification with the intent to commit, aid, or abet any unlawful activity. In addition to the specific charge of identity theft, identity criminals may be in violation of several federal laws, including those related to wire fraud, credit card fraud, bank fraud, and computer fraud, among others.[63] Identity theft is also a crime at the state level. Since 1998, every state except Colorado and Vermont has enacted legislation to deal with identity theft.[64]

In 2004, Congress toughened the penalties for identity theft–related convictions when it passed the Identity Theft Penalty Enhancement Act. This Act added two years

Since Congress passed the Identity Theft and Assumption Deterrence Act of 1998, the criminal justice system has targeted identity thieves and increased penalties for identity theft violations.

of imprisonment onto sentences for crimes involving the use of identity theft and an additional five years when the identity theft facilitated involvement with terrorists or terrorist organizations.

In 2006, President Bush convened the Identity Theft Task Force to advise lawmakers and criminal justice systems how to most effectively respond to the identity theft problem. Among its recommendations were increased penalties for offenders convicted of identity theft, a universal police report to help law enforcement and victims track complaints, and victims' rights laws that would provide compensation for time lost disputing fraudulent charges on credit and debit cards.[65] The Enhancement Act is particularly tough in that it precludes probation as a sentence for identity theft and mandates consecutive—not concurrent—sentences.

Criminal Justice Responses to Identity Theft

Victims and the criminal justice system alike were slow to respond to identity theft offenders because both parties viewed credit card companies as the ultimate victim of the offense. It was not until identity thieves repeatedly used various credit cards or other types of stolen financial information that the criminal justice system got involved.[66] Like all cybercrimes, identity theft cases pose problems for law enforcement because their complexity makes it difficult to get an arrest warrant for most identity crimes and because use of the Internet makes jurisdiction difficult to establish.[67]

In 2006, the Department of Justice launched a National Strategy to Combat Identity Theft, administered by COPS. It includes several key components:

- *Partnerships and collaboration*—for example, with state agencies that provide crime analysis, victim assistance, and statewide investigations, and that promote intelligence sharing among law enforcement agencies
- *Reporting procedures*—uniform data collection on identity theft cases for use in the Uniform Crime Reports
- *Victim assistance*—policies for responding to victims of identity theft, including written standard operating procedures to help victims resolve problems with their financial accounts and credit history
- *Public awareness*—national public awareness campaign focusing on prevention and response techniques as well as reporting of identity theft crime
- *Legislation*—documentation of all state and federal identity theft legislation
- *Information protection*—national public education for consumers and merchants that focuses on information protection
- *Training*—through which all police, prosecutor, victim-assistance, and private-sector organizations dealing with identity theft would conduct an assessment of identity theft training needs[68]

Several federal laws pertain directly to identity theft, including those dealing with identification documents, access devices, loan and credit applications, bank fraud, and Social Security number misuse. The FBI, U.S. Secret Service, and U.S. Postal Inspectors have made more than 10,000 arrests of identity theft offenders, resulting in nearly 3000 convictions secured by United States Attorneys.[69]

Technology makes crimes such as identity theft possible, but technology will also play a vital role in overcoming this threat by improving ways that individuals and organizations conduct financial transactions and by increasing authentication methods. Authentication helps verify the identity of the individual by using personal identification numbers or check verification processes. The next generation of authentication most likely will occur in the area of biometrics, which accurately captures an individual's unique physical attributes through fingerprints, voice, eyes, face, and written signature in electronic format.[70]

WRAPPING IT UP

Chapter Highlights

- Terrorism has emerged as the greatest national security threat to the United States and has resulted in massive restructuring of the way that the criminal justice system responds to a variety of crimes.
- The Department of Homeland Security reflects the new focus of the Department of Justice, which is to prevent and preempt terrorist activity.
- Terrorist groups or organizations may emerge from all over the globe, within the United States, and from extreme ideological positions on the far left and far right.
- The U.S. Patriot Acts have greatly enhanced the surveillance and investigative powers of U.S. law enforcement personnel.
- Cyberspace is among the most important and vulnerable targets to attack from terrorists and nonterrorist criminals.
- Cyberspace is also the location of an assortment of cybercrimes, most notably identity theft.

Words to Know

Al Qaeda Terrorist group led by Osama bin Laden that was responsible for the terrorist attacks of September 11, 2001, and that has the most active international terrorist organization since the 1990s.

bioterrorism The use of biological toxins to inflict mass casualties.

cybercrime Criminal behaviors that are intended to damage or destroy computer networks, fraudulently obtain money and other commodities, and disrupt normal business operations.

cyberspace Interconnected computers, servers, routers, switches, and fiber-optic cables that allow the U.S. infrastructure to work.

cyberterrorism Terrorism that involves threats or attack on computer or information systems.

Department of Homeland Security The federal agency that oversees U.S. counterterrorism efforts.

economic terrorism Terrorism that involves attacks on banks and other financial centers that are seen as symbols of capitalistic oppression.

eco-terrorism The infliction of economic damage on those who profit from the development and destruction of environmental resources.

Hamas A terrorist organization; also known as the Islamic Resistance Movement.

Hamdan v. Rumsfeld Supreme Court decision that ruled the George W. Bush administration's policy of treating terrorists as enemy combatants without due process unconstitutional.

identity theft Any illegal act that involves the use or attempted use of another person's financial account or identifying information without the owner's permission.

jihad Holy war of fundamentalist Islam directed against nations such as the United States and Israel.

Palestinian Liberation Organization (PLO) Terrorist organization that directs violence mostly against Israel.

phishing The creation and use of emails and websites designed to look like well-known legitimate businesses, financial institutions, or government agencies in an attempt to deceive Internet users into disclosing private financial information.

terrorism The unlawful use of force or violence to intimidate or coerce a government, the civilian population, or any segment thereof, in furtherance of political or social objectives or goals.

Terrorism and International Victims Unit (TIVU) The federal agency responsible for developing programs to help victims of terrorism, mass violence, and other transnational crimes.

USA Patriot Act Federal legislation that broadened the surveillance and investigative powers of criminal justice agencies to combat terrorism and removed barriers between military, intelligence, and criminal justice entities so that they could share information on terrorist suspects and threats.

USA Patriot Act Improvement and Reauthorization Act of 2005 Federal legislation that revised the USA Patriot Act of 2001, enhancing the powers of the U.S. criminal justice system to combat crime and terrorism.

War on Terror The global armed conflict between radical Islamic terrorist groups, such as Al Qaeda, and the developed world, principally the G8 nations (Canada, France, Germany, Italy, Japan, the United Kingdom, the United States, and the Russian Federation).

Think and Discuss

1. Should terrorist suspects be treated as prisoners of war with specific rights to due process, or should they be treated as enemy combatants? Does providing terrorists with due process rights hamper the United States' ability to fight terrorism at home and abroad?
2. In what ways is the War on Terror also an exercise in criminal justice?
3. How does the USA Patriot Act empower law enforcement to fight terrorism? Is the controversy surrounding the USA Patriot Act justified?
4. Which crimes are enabled by the advent of cyberspace?
5. How do criminals obtain the information needed to commit identity theft? How common are these methods?

Notes

1. United States House of Representatives Committee on Ways and Means, *Facts and Figures: Identity Theft*, available at http://waysandmeans.house.gov/media/pdf/ss/factsfigures.pdf, accessed January 12, 2008.
2. Dinesh D'Souza, *What's So Great about America* (Washington, DC: Regnery, 2002).
3. Brent Smith and Kelly Damphousse, "Punishing Political Offenders: The Effect of Political Motive on Federal Sentencing Decisions," *Criminology* 34:289–321 (1996); Brent Smith, Kelly Damphousse, Freedom Jackson, and Amy Sellers, "The Prosecution and Punishment of International Terrorists in Federal Courts: 1980–1998," *Criminology and Public Policy* 1:311–338 (2002).
4. National Commission on Terrorist Attacks Upon the United States, *The 9/11 Commission Report* (New York: W. W. Norton, 2003), p. 4.
5. Kevin Strom and Joe Eyerman, "Interagency Coordination in Response to Terrorism: Promising Practices and Barriers Identified in Four Countries," *Criminal Justice Studies* 20:131–137 (2007).
6. Pew Research Center for the People and the Press, *The 2004 Political Landscape: Evenly Divided and Increasingly Polarized* (Washington, DC: Pew Research Center, 2006).
7. Federal Bureau of Investigation, *Terrorism 2002/2005* (Washington, DC: U.S. Department of Justice, 2007).
8. Federal Criminal Code (Title 18 U.S.C. § 2331).
9. Randy Borum, "Understanding the Terrorist Mind-Set," *FBI Law Enforcement Bulletin* 72:7–10 (2003).
10. Jonathan White, *Defending the Homeland: Domestic Intelligence, Law Enforcement, and Security* (Belmont, CA: Wadsworth, 2004).
11. Michael Hronick, "Analyzing Terror: Researchers Study the Perpetrators and the Effects of Suicide Terrorism," *National Institute of Justice Journal* 254:1–5 (2006).
12. Steven Emerson, *American Jihad: The Terrorists Living Among Us* (New York: Free Press, 2002); National Commission on Terrorist Attacks Upon the United States, note 4.
13. Raphael Perl, "Terrorism and National Security: Issues and Trends," *Congressional Research Service* (Washington, DC: Library of Congress, 2004); Bruce Hoffman, "Combating Al Qaeda and the Militant Islamic Threat," testimony presented to the House Armed Services Committee, Subcommittee on Terrorism, Unconventional Threats and Capabilities (February 16, 2006).
14. Emerson, note 12, pp. 177–182.
15. John Kane and April Wall, *Identifying the Links between White-Collar Crime and Terrorism* (Washington, DC: U.S. Department of Justice, Office of Justice Programs, National Institute of Justice, 2005).
16. Rory McVeigh, "Structural Incentives for Conservative Mobilization: Power Devaluation and the Rise of the Ku Klux Klan, 1915–1925," *Social Forces* 77:1461–1496 (1999).
17. Southern Poverty Law Center, "Ku Klux Klan," available at http://www.splcenter.org/intel/map/hate.jsp?T=35&m=5, accessed January 2, 2008; Gregg Etter, David McElreath, and Chester Quarles, "The Ku Klux Klan: Evolution Towards Revolution," *Journal of Gang Research* 12:1–16 (2005).
18. Federal Bureau of Investigation, note 7.
19. Federal Bureau of Investigation, note 7.
20. U.S. Department of State, *Patterns of Global Terrorism, 2003* (Washington, DC: U.S. Department of State, 2004).
21. Federal Bureau of Investigation, note 7.
22. John Parachini, "Putting WMD Terrorism into Perspective," *The Washington Quarterly* 23:37–50 (2003); U.S. Department of State, "Country Reports on Terrorism, 2006," available at http://www.terrorisminfo.mipt.org/pdf/Country-Reports-Terrorism-2006.pdf, accessed April 10, 2008.

23. Bruce Hoffman, *Inside Terrorism*, 2nd ed. (New York: Columbia University Press, 2006); Emerson, note 12; National Commission on Terrorist Attacks Upon the United States, note 4; U.S. Army, available at http://www.army.mi/terrorism, accessed January 13, 2008; Robert O'Block, "Timeline of Terrorism," available at http://www.acfei.com/images/PDF/Final%20Timline%20of%20T.%20color.pdf, accessed January 13, 2008; "Al-Qaeda Claims Murder of Benazir Bhutto," *Jihad Watch*, available at http://www.jihadwatch.org/archives/019342.php, accessed January 4, 2008.

24. U.S. Department of Justice, available at http://www.lifeandliberty.gov/subs/a_terr.htm, accessed January 26, 2008.

25. U.S. Department of Justice, available at http://www.usdoj.gov/opa/pr/2006/June/06_crm_389.html, accessed February 13, 2008.

26. Dinesh D'Souza, *The Enemy at Home: The Cultural Left and Its Responsibility for 9/11* (New York: Broadway, 2007).

27. "Securing Our Homeland: U.S. Department of Homeland Security Strategic Plan," available at http://www.dhs.gov/xabout/, accessed February 14, 2008.

28. Department of Homeland Security, available at http://www.dhs.gov/index.shtm, accessed January 14, 2008.

29. Transportation Security Administration, available at http://www.tsa.gov, accessed January 14, 2008.

30. U.S. Customs and Border Protection, available at http://www.cbp.gov, accessed January 14, 2008.

31. Immigration and Customs Enforcement, available at http://www.ice.gov, accessed January 14, 2008.

32. U.S. Department of Homeland Security, available at http://www.dhs.gov, accessed January 14, 2008.

33. American Civil Liberties Union, available at http://www.aclu.org/safefree/resources/17343res20031114.html, accessed January 13, 2008.

34. U.S. Department of Justice, available at http://www.usdoj.gov/opa/pr/2006/March/06_opa_113.html, accessed January 13, 2008.

35. 50 U.S.C. §§ 1801-1811, 1821-1829, 1841-1846, 1861-62.

36. Federal Intelligence Surveillance Act, available at http://www.fas.org/irp/agency/doj/fisa/, accessed January 14, 2008.

37. Protect America Act, available at http://www.lifeandliberty.gov/index.html, accessed January 26, 2008.

38. Kane and Wall, note 15.

39. National Center for the Study of Terrorism and Responses to Terrorism (START), available at http://www.start.umd.edu/about/, accessed January 14, 2008.

40. Joel Leson, *Assessing and Managing the Terrorism Threat: New Realities* (Washington, DC: U.S. Department of Justice, 2005).

41. Robert Chapman, Shelly Baker, Veh Bezdikian, Pam Cammarata, Debra Cohen, et al., *Local Law Enforcement Responds to Terrorism: Lessons in Prevention and Preparedness* (Washington, DC: U. S. Department of Justice, 2002); David Thatcher, "The Local Role in Homeland Security," *Law and Society Review* 39:635–676 (2005).

42. Phil Lynn, *Mutual Aid: Multijurisdictional Partnerships for Meeting Regional Threats* (Washington, DC: U.S. Department of Justice, 2005).

43. Christopher Ortiz, Nicole Hendricks, and Naomi Sugie, "Policing Terrorism: The Response of Local Police Agencies to Homeland Security Concerns," *Criminal Justice Studies* 20:91–109 (2007).

44. Kevin Mayhood, "Ohio Sweep Nets 154," *Columbus Dispatch*, July 15, 2006, p. B1.

45. M. Elaine Nugent, James Johnson, Brad Bartholomew, and Delene Bromirski, *Local Prosecutors' Response to Terrorism* (Washington, DC: U.S. Department of Justice, 2005).

46. Nugent et al., note 45.

47. Chris Hale, "Cyber Crime: Facts and Figures Concerning the Global Dilemma," *Crime and Justice International* 18:5–26 (2002).

48. Ramona Rantala, *Cyber Crime Against Businesses* (Washington, DC: U.S. Department of Justice, 2004).

49. Alberto Gonzales, "Prepared Remarks to the U.S. Chamber of Commerce," available at http://www.usdoj.gov/ag/speeches/2006/ag_speech_060620.html, accessed July 14, 2008.

50. Rantala, note 48.

51. Dennis Fisher, "Tales of Cyber-crime Running Rampant," available at http://www.eweek.com/article2/0,1759,1597360,00.asp, accessed January 14, 2008.

52. Federal Bureau of Investigation, "Stolen Laptop and External Hard Drive Recovered" (2006), available at http://www.baltimore.fbi.gov/pressrel/2006/laptop_062906.htm, accessed January 14, 2008.

53. Federal Criminal Code (Title 18 U.S.C. § 1030).

54. Computer Crime and Intellectual Property Section, available at http://www.cybercrime.gov, accessed January 14, 2008.

55. Gonzales, note 49.

56. Department of Homeland Security, "The National Strategy to Secure Cyberspace," available at http://www.dhs.gov/interweb/assetlibrary/National_Cyberspace_Strategy.pdf, accessed January 14, 2008.

57. Federal Bureau of Investigation, available at http://www.fbi.gov/page2/july05/cyber072505.htm, accessed January 14, 2008.

58. Consumer Reports National Research Center, "Cyber Insecurity: You're More Vulnerable Than You Think," *Consumer Reports*, September, 2006, pp. 20–26.

59. U.S. House of Representatives Committee on Ways and Means, *Facts and Figures: Identity Theft*, available at http://waysandmeans.house.gov/media/pdf/ss/factsfigures.pdf, accessed January 12, 2008.

60. Katrina Baum, *Identity Theft, 2005* (Washington, DC: U.S. Department of Justice, 2007).

61. U.S. House of Representatives Committee on Ways and Means, note 59.

62. Heith Copes and Lynne Vieraitis, *Identity Theft: Assessing Offenders' Strategies and Perceptions of Risk* (Washington, DC: U.S. Department of Justice, 2007).

63. U.S. Department of Justice, available at http://www.usdoj.gov/criminal/fraud/docs/phishing.pdf, accessed January 4, 2008.

64. Federal Trade Commission, available at http://www.ftc.gov/bcp/edu/microsites/idtheft//index.html, accessed January 4, 2008.

65. Associated Press, "Task Force Recommends Steps to Curb Identity Theft," *USA Today*, September 20, 2006, p. 5A.

66. Graeme Newman, *Identity Theft* (Washington, DC: U.S. Department of Justice, 2004).

67. Stuart Allison, Amie Schuck, and Kim Lersch, "Exploring the Crime of Identity Theft: Prevalence, Clearance Rates, and Victim/Offender Characteristics," *Journal of Criminal Justice* 33:19–29 (2005).

68. Phyllis McDonald, *National Strategy to Combat Identity Theft* (Washington, DC: U.S. Department of Justice, 2006).

69. Baum, note 60.

70. John Pollock and James May, "Authentication Technology: Identity Theft and Account Takeover," *FBI Law Enforcement Bulletin* 71:1–4 (2002).

GLOSSARY

48-hour rule Supreme Court ruling in *Riverside County, California v. McLaughlin*, that a defendant must be brought before a magistrate within 48 hours of his or her arrest.

abandoned property Property that is intentionally left behind or placed in a situation where others may reasonably take it into their possession.

acquit A verdict of not guilty.

actus reus Guilty act; a required material element of a crime.

adjudication Stage in the juvenile justice system that parallels prosecution and trial in adult criminal courts.

adjudication hearing A hearing to determine whether a juvenile committed the offense of which he or she is accused.

administrative segregation The placement of an inmate in a single-person cell in a high-security area for a specified period of time; sometimes referred to as solitary confinement.

affidavit of probable cause A document that lists evidence regarding a crime and asserts there is additional evidence of that crime in a certain location that needs to be searched.

aftercare The release and subsequent community supervision of an individual from a correctional facility to ensure a more positive and effective transition back into the community.

age–crime curve A curve showing that crime rates increase during preadolescence, peak in late adolescence, and steadily decline thereafter.

aging-out phenomenon Older persons commit fewer crimes in part because reductions in strength, energy, and mobility with age make it more difficult to commit crime.

alibi Assertion that the defendant was somewhere else at the time the crime was committed.

Al Qaeda Terrorist group led by Osama bin Laden that was responsible for the terrorist attacks of September 11, 2001, and that has been the most active international terrorist organization since the 1990s.

anomie A social condition where the norms of society have broken down and cannot control the behavior of its members.

arraignment Hearing at which felony defendants are informed of the charges and their rights and given an opportunity to enter a plea.

arrest Action where police physically take a suspect into custody on the grounds that there is probable cause to believe the suspect has committed a criminal offense.

arrest warrant A written court order instructing the police to arrest a specific person for a specific crime.

Ashurst–Sumners Act Legislation passed by Congress in 1935 and amended in 1940 that prohibited interstate transportation of prison goods.

atavistic beings Individuals who are throwbacks to an earlier, more primitive stage of human development, and more closely resemble their ape-like ancestors in traits, abilities, and dispositions.

Atkins v. Virginia Supreme Court ruling that the death sentence is not a suitable punishment for a mentally retarded criminal, and that to execute such a person would be a violation of the Eighth Amendment's prohibition of cruel and unusual punishment.

aversion therapy Therapy in which people are taught to connect unwanted behavior with punishment.

bail Money or a cash bond deposited with the court or bail bondsman allowing the defendant to be released on the assurance that he or she will appear in court at the proper time.

bail bondsman Person who guarantees court payment of the full bail amount if the defendant fails to appear.

bail guidelines Use of a grid to plot a defendant's personal and offense characteristics to determine probability of appearance.

Bail Reform Act of 1966 Act providing for release on recognizance (ROR) in noncapital federal cases when it is likely that the defendant will appear in court at required hearings.

Bail Reform Act of 1984 Act extending the opportunity for release on recognizance (ROR) in many federal cases but also providing for preventive detention without bail of dangerous suspects.

beat The largest geographic area that a patrol unit can patrol effectively; an assigned area for police patrol.

behavioral theory Theory that views behavior as a product of interactions people have with others throughout their lifetime.

bench trial A trial before a judge alone; an alternative to a jury trial.

bifurcated trial Two-stage trial: the first stage determines guilt, and the second stage determines the sentence.

Bill of Rights First 10 amendments to the U.S. Constitution.

bioterrorism The use of biological toxins to inflict mass casualties.

booking The process of officially recording the name of the arrested individual, the place and time of the arrest, the reason for the arrest, and the name of the arresting authority.

boot camp A highly regimented correctional facility where inmates undergo extensive physical conditioning and discipline.

Breed v. Jones Supreme Court decision that a criminal prosecution of a child following a juvenile court hearing constitutes double jeopardy.

broken windows theory A theory that proposes small signs of public disorder set in motion a downward spiral of deterioration, neighborhood decline, and increasing crime.

Brown v. Mississippi Supreme Court case that established involuntary confessions as inadmissible in state criminal prosecutions.

bureaucracy A model of organization in which strict and precise rules are used as a way of effectively achieving organizational goals.

Camp Delta A facility at the Guantanamo Naval Base in Cuba that is used for the confinement of suspected terrorists.

Carroll doctrine Doctrine that permits the warrantless search of a vehicle whenever police have a reasonable basis for believing the vehicle is involved in a crime.

case law Law that emerges when a court modifies how a law in a particular case is applied.

chain of command A hierarchical system of authority that prescribes who communicates with (and gives orders to) whom.

challenge for cause A challenge by the prosecutor or the defense to dismiss a person from a jury panel for a legitimate cause.

charge to the jury Judge's instructions to the jury, which are intended to guide the jury's deliberations.

Child Savers A group of nineteenth-century reformers who believed that children were basically good, delinquency was the product of bad environments, and the state should remove children from such environments.

Chimel v. California Supreme Court case that established the "one arm's length" rule, which allows police without a warrant to search suspects and, to a limited extent, the immediate area they occupy.

choice theories Theories that assume people have free will, are rational and intelligent, and make informed decisions to commit crimes based on whether they believe they will benefit from doing so.

circumstantial evidence Testimony by a witness that requires jurors to draw a reasonable inference.

civil law A body of private law that settles disputes between two or more parties in a dispute.

classical school A school of thought that holds criminals are rational, intelligent people who have free will and the ability to make choices.

classification System for assigning inmates to levels of custody and treatment appropriate to their needs.

clemency An executive decision by the governor or president to set aside an offender's punishment and release the individual.

closing arguments The final presentation of arguments to the jury.

co-correctional prison An institution where men and women are confined together.

common law Case decisions by judges in England that established a body of law common to the entire nation.

community corrections A correctional approach based on the belief offenders can (and often should) be dealt with within the community rather than through prisons.

community policing A policing model that was popular in the 1990s, in which police and citizens unite to fight crime.

community service A sentence in which the offender makes reparation to the community.

commutation An executive order in which a prisoner's sentence is reduced to allow for his or her immediate release.

competency A list of factors that reflect abilities or skills, including qualifications, test scores on promotional exams, and field performance.

concurrent sentences Two or more prison sentences to be served at the same time.

confession A voluntary declaration by someone who has committed a crime in which the suspect admits his or her involvement in the offense.

conflict theory Theory that blames crime on inequalities in power.

congregate system A nineteenth-century model that held prisoners in isolation during the night, allowing them to work together during the day in silence. It was implemented at New York's Auburn Prison.

conjugal visit A private visit that some prison systems allow between inmates and their spouses to help them maintain sexual and interpersonal relationships.

consecutive sentences Two or more prison sentences to be served one after the other.

consent search A legal, warrantless search conducted after a person gives expressed consent to police.

corpus The body of the crime; the material elements of the crime that must be established in a court of law.

correctional officers Also known as guards; the lowest-ranking prison staff members, who have the primary responsibility of supervising inmates.

correctional system Programs, services, and institutions designed to manage people accused or convicted of crimes.

corruption Misuse of authority by officers for the benefit of themselves or others.

courts of general jurisdiction Courts with the authority to hear virtually any criminal or civil case.

courts of last resort In most states and in the federal court system, the final appellate court.

courts of limited jurisdiction Courts usually referred to as the lower or inferior courts, which are limited to hearing only specific kinds of cases.

crime An intentional act or omission to act, neither justified nor excused, that is in violation of criminal law and punished by the state.

crime clearance rate The percentage of crimes for which law enforcement agencies make an arrest, charge at least one person with the commission of a crime, and turn the case over to the court for prosecution.

Crime Index A statistical indicator consisting of eight offenses that was used to gauge the amount of crime reported to the police. It was discontinued in 2004.

crimes of interest The seven offenses in the National Crime Victimization Survey, which asks people whether they have been victims of these crimes during the past year.

criminal career The progression of criminality over time or over the life-course.

criminalists Scientists who work in crime laboratories and examine forensic evidence, which includes fingerprints, DNA analysis, bloodstains, footprints, tire tracks, and the presence of narcotics.

criminal justice process The procedures that occur in the criminal justice system, from a citizen's initial contact with police to his or her potential arrest, charging, booking, prosecution, conviction, sentencing, incarceration or placement on probation, and appeals (if any).

criminal justice system A complex set of interrelated subsystems composed of three major components—police, courts, and corrections—that operate at the federal, state, and local levels.

cross-examination Questioning of a witness by counsel after questions have been asked by the opposing counsel.

cultural deviance theory Theory that proposes crime is the product of social and economic factors located within a neighborhood.

cultural transmission The process through which criminal values are transmitted from one generation to the next.

custody Assumed legal control of a person or object.

cybercrime Criminal behaviors that are intended to damage or destroy computer networks, fraudulently obtain money and other commodities, and disrupt normal business operations.

cyberspace Interconnected computers, servers, routers, switches, and fiber-optic cables that allow the U.S. infrastructure to work.

cyberterrorism Terrorism that involves threats or attack on computer or information systems.

dark figure of crime A term used by criminologists to describe the amount of unreported or undiscovered crime; it calls into question the reliability of Uniform Crime Reports data.

day reporting center A center where counselors meet with offenders who are permitted to remain within the community, live at home, and go to work or attend school.

defense of life standard Policy mandating that officers may use deadly force only in defense of their own lives or another's life.

delegation of authority Decision making made through a chain of command in a bureaucracy.

delinquent A juvenile younger than age 18 who is determined to have violated a state's juvenile code.

demand waiver Process by which a juvenile may request to have his or her case transferred to criminal court.

Department of Homeland Security The federal agency that oversees U.S. counterterrorism efforts.

deprivation model An explanation of the inmate subculture as an adaptation to loss of amenities and freedoms within prison.

detention The temporary custody and care of juveniles pending adjudication, disposition, or implementation of disposition.

determinate sentence A prison sentence with a fixed term of imprisonment.

deterrence A punishment philosophy based on the belief that punishing offenders will deter crime.

developmental theory Theory that focuses on offenders' early childhood and the way these experiences influence the onset of their participation in crime at later stages in life. Same as life-course theory.

differential association theory Theory that proposes that through interaction with others, people learn the attitudes, values, techniques, and motives for criminal behavior.

direct evidence Testimony by an eyewitness to the crime.

disciplinary hearing A hearing before a disciplinary board to determine whether the charge against an inmate has merit and to determine the sanction if the charge is sustained.

discovery Legal motion to reveal to the defense the basis of the prosecutor's case.

disposition hearing A hearing to determine the most appropriate placement of a juvenile adjudicated to be delinquent.

diversion The early suspension or termination of the official processing of a juvenile in favor of an informal or unofficial alternative.

division of labor A system of assigning duties for the routine jobs completed in bureaucracies.

dizygotic twins Twins who do not share the same set of genes (DZ twins).

double jeopardy Trying a person for the same crime more than once; it is prohibited by the Fifth Amendment.

Durham rule An insanity test that determines whether a defendant's act was a product of a mental disease or defect.

economic terrorism Terrorism that involves attacks on banks and other financial centers that are seen as symbols of capitalistic oppression.

eco-terrorism The infliction of economic damage on those who profit from the development and destruction of environmental resources.

ego Component of the personality that represents problem-solving dimensions.

electronic monitoring A sentence requiring an offender to wear an electronic device to verify his or her location.

entrapment The claim that a defendant was encouraged or enticed by agents of the state to engage in a criminal act.

Escobedo v. Illinois Supreme Court case that established suspects accused of felonies may request an attorney during questioning.

exclusionary rule Rule generally prohibiting the introduction of illegally obtained evidence or confessions into a trial.

excuses Claims based on a defendant admitting that what he or she did was wrong but arguing that, under the circumstances, he or she was not responsible for the criminal act.

federal criminal code The legal code that identifies and defines federal crimes.

felony A serious crime, such as robbery or embezzlement, that is punishable by a prison term of more than one year or by death.

fine A sentence in which the offender makes a cash payment to the court.

fleeing felon doctrine Law (prior to 1985) stating that an officer could use deadly force to stop a felony suspect from fleeing.

forfeiture A legal procedure that permits the government to seize property used in the commission of a crime.

full law enforcement Law enforcement approach in which officers respond formally to all suspicious behavior.

Fulwood v. Clemmer U.S. District Court decision that African American Muslim inmates have the same constitutional right to practice their religion and to hold worship services as inmates of other faiths.

Furman v. Georgia Supreme Court ruling that the death penalty, as applied at that time, was unconstitutional.

Gagnon v. Scarpelli The Supreme Court decision identifying the due process rights of an offender during a probation revocation hearing.

general deterrence Punishing offenders to discourage others from committing crimes.

Gideon v. Wainwright Supreme Court ruling that state courts, under the Sixth Amendment of the Constitution, must provide legal counsel in criminal cases for defendants who cannot afford an attorney.

good faith exception Rule that allows for evidence collected in violation of a suspect's rights under the Fourth Amendment to be admitted at trial if the police had good reason to believe their actions were legal.

good time The practice of reducing an inmate's sentence for good behavior.

grand jury A group of citizens who are called upon to investigate the conduct of public officials and agencies and criminal activity in general and to determine whether probable cause exists to issue indictments.

Gregg v. Georgia Supreme Court ruling that the death penalty was constitutional under a state statute requiring the judge and the jury to consider both aggravating and mitigating circumstances.

guilty, but mentally ill (GBMI) A substitute for traditional insanity defenses, which allows the jury to find the defendant guilty and requires that the prisoner receive psychiatric treatment during his or her confinement. Also called guilty but insane (GBI).

guilty plea An admission of guilt to the crime charged.

habeas corpus A judicial order to bring a person immediately before the court to determine the legality of his or her detention.

halfway house Facilities designed to provide secure housing of inmates and to ensure the public's safety while providing inmates with an opportunity to take a controlled step into the community.

Hamas A terrorist organization; also known as the Islamic Resistance Movement.

Hamdan v. Rumsfeld Supreme Court decision that ruled the George W. Bush administration's policy of treating terrorists as enemy combatants without due process unconstitutional.

hands-off doctrine The position taken by the Supreme Court that it will not interfere with states' administration of prisons.

harmless error An error, defect, irregularity, or variance that does not affect substantial rights of the defendant.

hate crime A crime in which an offender chooses a victim based on a specific characteristic, and evidence is provided that hate or personal disapproval of this characteristic prompted the offender to commit the crime.

Hawes–Cooper Act Legislation passed by Congress in 1929 requiring that prison products be subject to the laws of the state to which they were shipped.

hearsay evidence Testimony involving information the witness was told but has no direct knowledge of.

hierarchy rule A rule dictating that only the most serious crime in a multiple-offenses incident will be recorded in the Uniform Crime Reports.

Holt v. Sarver Supreme Court decision that applied the "totality of conditions" principle to find the Arkansas prison system in violation of the Eighth Amendment.

Hopt v. Utah Supreme Court case that established guidelines for involuntary confessions.

hot spots of crime Locations characterized by high rates of crime.

house arrest A sentence requiring that the offender be legally confined to his or her home.

hung jury A jury that is deadlocked and cannot reach a verdict. As a result, the judge may declare a mistrial.

Hurtado v. California U.S. Supreme Court decision that the Fifth Amendment guarantee of a grand jury indictment applied only to federal—not state—trials, and that not all constitutional amendments were applicable to the states.

id Component of the personality that is present at birth, and consists of blind, unreasoning, instinctual desires and motives.

identity theft Any illegal act that involves the use or attempted use of another person's financial account or identifying information without the owner's permission.

importation model A view of the inmate subculture is a reflection of the values and norms inmates bring with them when they enter prison.

incapacitation A punishment aimed at removing offenders from the community through imprisonment or banishment.

incidence The number of crimes committed in a specific time period.

incorporation The legal interpretation by the U.S. Supreme Court in which the Fourteenth Amendment applied the Bill of Rights to the states.

indeterminate sentence A prison sentence that identifies a minimum number and a maximum number of years to be served by the offender; the actual release date is set by a parole board or the institution.

inevitable discovery rule Rule that if illegally obtained evidence would have eventually been discovered by lawful means, it is admissible regardless of how it was originally discovered.

informal probation Placement of an offender on probation before a conviction is entered on the record; upon completion of the probation conditions, the offender is released and the case dismissed.

infraction A violation of a city or county ordinance, such as cruising or noise violations.

initial appearance A defendant's first appearance in court, at which the charge is read, bail is set, and the defendant is informed of his or her rights.

inmate code A system of informal norms created by prisoners to regulate inmate behavior.

in-presence requirement Police may not make a warrantless arrest for a misdemeanor offense unless the offense is committed in their presence.

In re Gault Case in which the Supreme Court held that juveniles could not be denied basic due process rights in juvenile hearings.

intake The initial screening process in the juvenile court to determine whether a case should be processed further.

intelligence-led policing A crime-fighting strategy driven by computer databases, intelligence gathering, and analysis.

intensive aftercare programs (IAP) Equivalent to intensive parole supervision; used to provide greater supervision of youths after their release from official institutions.

intensive parole supervision A practice under which caseloads are very small and officers frequently meet face-to-face with parolees to provide greater supervision.

intensive probation supervision (IPS) A practice under which probation officers with very small caseloads are able to provide increased supervision.

intermediate sanctions Sentences that may be imposed as alternatives to traditional probation or incarceration.

interrogation A method used by police during an interview with a suspect to obtain information the suspect might not otherwise disclose.

intimate partner violence Violent victimization by intimates, including current or former spouses, boyfriends, girlfriends, or romantic partners.

involuntary confession A confession precipitated by promise, threat, fear, torture, or another external factor such as mental illness.

irresistible impulse test An insanity test that determines whether a defendant, as a result of a mental disease, temporarily lost self-control or the ability to reason sufficiently to prevent the crime.

jail An institution to hold pretrial detainees and people convicted of less serious crimes.

jihad Holy war of fundamentalist Islam directed against nations such as the United States and Israel.

judgment of acquittal A defense motion for dismissal of a case based on the claim that the prosecution failed to establish that a crime was committed or that the defendant committed it.

judicial review The power of the U.S. Supreme Court to review and determine the constitutionality of acts of Congress and orders by the executive branch.

judicial waiver Most common waiver procedure for transferring youths to criminal court, in which the judge is the primary decision maker.

Judiciary Act of 1789 An act created by the First Congress establishing the basic structure of the federal court system.

jurisdiction The territory over which a law enforcement agency has authority.

jury pool The master list of community members who are eligible to be called for jury duty.

Justice of the Peace (JP) courts Courts first established in the American colonies to hear minor criminal cases.

justification Defense wherein a defendant admits responsibility but argues that, under the circumstances, what he or she did was right.

juvenile A person younger than the age of 18.

juvenile delinquency Behavior by a juvenile that is in violation of a state's juvenile or criminal codes.

Kent v. United States The Supreme Court decision requiring a formal waiver hearing before transfer of a juvenile to criminal court.

knock-and-announce rule Rule that requires police to announce their presence and wait approximately 20 seconds before entering a home.

labeling theory Theory that examines the role of societal reactions in shaping a person's behavior.

laws Formalized rules that prescribe or limit actions.

less eligibility The belief that prisoners should always reside in worse conditions than should the poorest law-abiding citizens.

lifestyle theory Theory suggesting that people become victims because of the situation in which they put themselves.

line personnel Prison employees who have direct contact with inmates.

line-up A pretrial identification procedure where several people are shown to a victim or to a witness of a crime, who is then asked if any of those individuals committed the crime.

loss of privileges A disciplinary sanction involving the loss of visits, mail, recreation, and access to the prison commissary.

low-security prison An institution that operates between the medium and minimum security levels.

mala in se Behaviors, such as murder or rape, that are considered inherently wrong or evil.

mala prohibita Behaviors, such as prostitution and gambling, that are considered wrong because they have been prohibited by criminal statutes, rather than because they are evil in themselves.

mandatory sentence A requirement that an offender must be sentenced to prison.

Mapp v. Ohio Supreme Court ruling that expanded the exclusionary rule to the states.

Marbury v. Madison The U.S. Supreme Court case that established the principle of judicial review.

mark system System by which prisoners earned "marks" for good behavior to achieve an early release from prison.

master status The status bestowed on an individual and perceived by others as a first impression.

maximum-security prison The most secure prison facility, having high walls, gun towers, and barbed wire or electronic fences.

McKeiver v. Pennsylvania Supreme Court decision that juveniles do not have a constitutional right to a jury trial in juvenile court.

medium-security prison A middle-level prison facility, which has more relaxed security measures and fewer inmates than a maximum-security prison.

Megan's Law A law that requires both registration and community notification by sex offenders when they move into a community.

mens rea Guilty mind, or having criminal intent; a required material element of most crimes.

minimum-security prison A prison facility with the lowest level of security that houses nondangerous, stable offenders.

Miranda v. Arizona Supreme Court case that established criminal suspects must be informed of their right to consult with an attorney and their right against self-incrimination prior to questioning by police.

***Miranda* warning** A warning that police must recite at the time of a suspect's arrest, informing the suspect of his or her constitutional right to remain silent and have an attorney present during questioning.

misdemeanor A crime that is less serious than a felony, such as petty theft or possession of a small amount of marijuana, and that is punishable by less than one year in prison.

mitigating circumstances Factors such as age or mental disease that influence the choices people make and affect a person's ability to form criminal intent.

M'Naghten rule Insanity defense claim that because of a defect of reason from a disease of the mind, the defendant was unable to distinguish right from wrong.

monozygotic twins Twins who share the same set of genes (MZ twins).

Morrissey v. Brewer Supreme Court ruling that spelled out the due process rights of offenders on parole.

National Crime Victimization Survey (NCVS) An annual survey of criminal victimization in the United States conducted by the U.S. Bureau of Justice Statistics.

National Youth Survey (NYS) A comprehensive, nationwide self-report study of 1700 youths who have reported their illegal behaviors each year for more than 30 years.

neoclassical school A school of thought that considers mitigating factors when deciding culpability for criminal behavior, such as the offender's age and whether he or she has a mental disease.

new-generation jails Jails that are designed to increase staff interaction with inmates by placing the staff inside the inmate housing unit.

New York House of Refuge The first correctional institution for children in the United States (opened in 1825), which emphasized industry, education, and strict discipline.

noble cause corruption A type of corruption that some police and civilians believe is justified because it serves the greater public good.

nolo contendere A plea of no contest; essentially the same as a guilty plea except that the defendant neither admits nor denies the charge.

norms The rules and expectations by which a society guides the behavior of its members.

not guilty by reason of insanity plea A plea in which the defendant does not deny committing the crime but claims that he or she was insane at the time of the offense and, therefore, is not criminally responsible.

not guilty plea A plea denying guilt.

official crime statistics Statistics based on the aggregate records of offenders and offenses processed by police, courts, corrections agencies, and the U.S. Department of Justice.

opening statement The initial presentation of the outline of the prosecution's and the defense's cases to the jury.

operational style Within law enforcement agencies, common patterns or styles of policing emerge.

pains of imprisonment Deprivations—such as the loss of freedom, possessions, dignity, autonomy, security, and heterosexual relationships—shared by inmates.

Palestinian Liberation Organization (PLO) Terrorist organization that directs violence mostly against Israel.

parens patriae A principle based on English common law that viewed the state as the ultimate sovereign and guardian of children.

parole The conditional release of an offender from a correctional institution after serving a portion of his or her sentence.

parole board The group of people who make the discretionary decision about a prisoner's release.

penitentiary house An eighteenth-century place of penitence for all convicted felons except those sentenced to death.

Percy Amendment Law that allowed states to sell prison-made goods across state lines as long as they complied with strict rules to ensure unions were consulted and to prevent manufacturers from undercutting existing wage structures.

peremptory challenge A challenge by the defense or the prosecution to excuse a person from a jury panel without having to give a reason.

petition Similar to an indictment; a written statement setting forth the specific charge that a delinquent act has been committed or that a child is dependent or neglected or needs supervision.

phishing The creation and use of emails and websites designed to look like well-known legitimate businesses, financial institutions, or government agencies in an attempt to deceive Internet users into disclosing private financial information.

plain view doctrine Standard that allows police to seize evidence that they discover in places where they have a legal right to be.

plea A defendant's response to a criminal charge.

plea bargaining The negotiation between a prosecutor and a defense attorney in which they seek to arrive at a mutually satisfactory disposition of a case without going to trial.

police brutality The unlawful use of force.

police discretion Authority of police to choose between alternative courses of action.

police subculture Beliefs, values, and patterns of behavior that separate officers from police administrators and the public.

positive school A school of thought that blames criminality on factors that are present before a crime is actually committed.

precinct The entire collection of police beats in a specific geographic area.

preliminary hearing An early hearing to review charges, set bail, present witnesses, and determine probable cause.

preliminary revocation hearing The first hearing to determine whether there is probable cause that the offender violated the conditions of probation or parole.

presentence investigation (PSI) A comprehensive report including information on the offender's background and offense and any other information the judge desires to determine an appropriate sentence.

preservation of life policy Policy mandating that police use every other means possible to maintain order before turning to deadly force.

presumption of innocence The notion that a person is presumed to be innocent unless proved guilty beyond a reasonable doubt.

presumptive sentencing The use of ranges—that is, minimum number and maximum number of years of incarceration—to set punishments for types of particular crimes. The judge determines the number of years to be served from within this range.

pretrial motion A written or oral request to a judge for a ruling or action before the beginning of trial.

pretrial release Release of a defendant from custody while he or she is awaiting trial.

prevalence The number of offenders committing crime during a specific time period.

preventive detention The practice of holding a defendant in custody without bail if he or she is deemed likely to abscond or commit further offenses if released.

prison An institution for the confinement of people who have been convicted of serious crimes.

prison farms Correctional institutions that produce much of the livestock, dairy products, and vegetables used to feed inmates in the state prisons.

prison forestry camps Correctional institutions that provide labor for the maintenance of state parks, tree planting and thinning, wildlife care, maintenance of fish hatcheries, and cleanup of roads and highways.

prisonization The process by which inmates adjust to or become assimilated into the prison subculture.

privatization A process in which state and federal governments contract with the private sector to help finance and manage correctional facilities.

probable cause A set of facts and circumstances that would lead a reasonable person to believe that a crime had been committed and that the accused committed it.

probation A sentencing option involving a suspended prison sentence and supervision in the community.

procedural criminal law A body of law that specifies how crimes are to be investigated and prosecuted.

proportionality A punishment philosophy based on the belief that the severity of the punishment should fit the seriousness of the crime.

prosecutorial waiver Process in which the prosecutor determines whether a charge against a juvenile should be filed in criminal or juvenile court.

psychoanalytic theory Theory that unconscious mental processes developed in early childhood control the personality.

rational choice theory Theory suggesting that offenders are rational people who make calculated choices to commit crime.

real evidence Physical evidence introduced at the trial.

reasonable doubt The requirement that the jury (or the judge in the case of a bench trial) must find the evidence entirely convincing and must be satisfied beyond a moral certainty of the defendant's guilt before returning a conviction.

reasonable suspicion Arises when a reasonable officer could believe that a person has been, is, or is about to be, engaged in criminal activity.

rebuttal The presentation of additional witnesses and evidence by the prosecutor in response to issues raised in the defense's presentation of witnesses.

reentry The process in which an inmate leaves prison and returns to society.

reformatory A penal institution generally used to confine first-time offenders between the ages of 16 and 30.

rehabilitation A sentencing objective aimed at reforming an offender through treatment, education, or counseling.

release on recognizance (ROR) A personal promise by the defendant to appear in court; does not require a monetary bail.

restitution A requirement of offenders to pay money or provide services to victims.

restorative justice A punishment philosophy aimed at restoring or repairing relationships disrupted by crime, holding offenders accountable, promoting offender competency and responsibility, and balancing the needs of the community, victim, and offender through involvement in the restorative process.

retribution A punishment philosophy based on society's moral outrage or disapproval of a crime.

reverse waiver Process in which a juvenile contests a statutory exclusion or prosecutorial transfer.

revocation hearing A hearing to determine whether probation or parole should be revoked.

risk classification An assessment of an offender's likelihood of committing a new offense if granted probation.

Roper v. Simmons Supreme Court ruling that the death penalty for anyone who was younger than age 18 at the time of a crime's commission is unconstitutional.

Schall v. Martin Supreme Court decision authorizing the preventive detention of juveniles who are identified as "serious risks" to the community if released.

search warrant A written order instructing police to examine a specific location for certain property or persons relating to a crime, to seize the property or persons if found, and to account for the results of the search to the judicial officer who issued the warrant.

selective law enforcement Law enforcement approach in which officers under-enforce some laws and over-enforce others.

self-control theory Theory claiming that people who seek pleasure are self-gratifying, and commit crimes owing to their low self-control.

self-defense Claim that a defendant acted in a lawful manner to defend himself or herself, others, or property, or to prevent a crime.

self-report survey A survey that asks offenders to self-report their criminal activity during a specific time period.

sentencing discrimination Differences in sentencing outcomes based on illegitimate, morally objectionable, or extralegal factors.

sentencing disparities Differences in sentencing outcomes in cases with similar case attributes.

sentencing guidelines Sentencing schemes that limit judicial discretion; the offender's criminal background and severity of current offense are weighed to determine the sentence.

sentencing hearing A court hearing to determine an appropriate sentence, which is typically scheduled within three to six weeks after the offender's conviction.

separate confinement A nineteenth-century prison model that separated inmates. It was implemented in Pennsylvania's Western and Eastern penitentiaries.

service function Role of police to assist citizens with noncriminal matters, such as opening locked car doors.

sheriff The principal law enforcement officer in a county.

silver platter doctrine Doctrine that permitted state officers to hand over "on a silver platter" evidence that had been illegally obtained for use at federal trials.

social bond A measure of how strongly people are connected to society.

social control theory Theory that holds people are amoral and will break the law unless obstacles are thrown in their path.

social learning theory Theory that suggests children learn by modeling and imitating others.

sociological theories Theories that attribute crime to a variety of social factors external to the individual, focusing on how the environment in which the person lives affects his or her behavior.

specialization The practice of dividing work among employees so that the work will be completed more effectively and efficiently.

specific deterrence Punishing offenders to prevent them from committing new crimes.

staff personnel Prison employees who provide support services to line personnel and administrators.

stare decisis Literally, "to stand by the decision"; a policy of the courts to interpret and apply law according to precedents set in earlier cases.

status offenses Acts prohibited to children that are not prohibited to adults (such as running away, truancy, and incorrigibility).

statute Legislation contained in written legal codes.

statute of limitations The maximum time period that can pass between a criminal act and its prosecution.

statutory exclusion Process established by statute that excludes certain juveniles, because of either age or offense, from juvenile court jurisdiction; charges are initially filed in criminal court.

stigmata Atavistic beings who possess unique, distinguishing features, such as large and protruding ears.

stop-and-frisk rule Rule that police may stop, question, and frisk individuals who are engaged in suspicious behavior.

strain theory Theory that proposes a lack of integration between cultural goals and institutionalized means causes crime.

stress A condition that occurs in response to adverse external influences and is capable of affecting an individual's physical health.

strict liability laws Laws that provide for criminal liability without requiring either general or specific intent.

structured fines Fines designed to eliminate the proportionately greater financial burden placed on poorer offenders by tying the amount of the fine to the offender's ability to pay.

substantial capacity test An insanity test that determines whether the defendant lacked sufficient capacity to appreciate the wrongfulness of his or her conduct.

substantive criminal law A body of law that identifies behaviors harmful to society and specifies their punishments.

superego Component of the personality that develops from the ego and comprises the moral code, norms, and values the person has acquired.

super-maximum-security prison A prison where the most predatory and dangerous criminals are confined.

surrebuttal Questioning by the defense of witnesses who were presented by the prosecutor during rebuttal.

surrogate families Fictive families created by female prisoners to provide stability and security.

sworn officers Officers who are empowered to arrest suspects, serve warrants, carry weapons, and use force.

Tennessee v. Garner U.S. Supreme Court ruling that eliminated the "shoot a fleeing felon" policy and replaced it with a defense of life standard.

terrorism The unlawful use of force or violence to intimidate or coerce a government, the civilian population, or any segment thereof, in furtherance of political or social objectives or goals.

Terrorism and International Victims Unit (TIVU) The federal agency responsible for developing programs to help victims of terrorism, mass violence, and other transnational crimes.

Terry v. Ohio Supreme Court case in which the Court determined that police investigating suspicious behavior could stop, briefly detain, and frisk a person on a street, without having to meet the Fourth Amendment's probable cause requirement.

testimonial evidence Sworn testimony of witnesses who are qualified to speak about specific real evidence.

theories Integrated sets of ideas that explain when and why people commit crime.

three-strikes laws Laws that provide a mandatory sentence of incarceration for persons who are convicted of a third separate serious criminal offense.

total institutions Institutions that completely encapsulate the lives of the people who work and live in them.

totality of conditions A principle guiding federal court evaluations of prison conditions: The lack of a specific condition alone does not necessarily constitute cruel and unusual punishment.

totality-of-the-circumstances rule Rule that requires a judge to evaluate all available information when deciding whether to issue a search warrant.

traffic enforcement Police duties related to highway and traffic safety and accident investigations.

trait theories Theories that argue offenders commit crimes because of traits, characteristics, deficits, or psychopathologies they possess.

true bill An indictment issued by a grand jury charging a person with a crime; similar to a prosecutor's filing of an information.

truth-in-sentencing Laws that require offenders, especially violent offenders, to serve at least 85 percent of their sentences.

unconditional release A release from prison that does not require additional supervision in the community.

Uniform Crime Reports (UCR) An annual publication from the Federal Bureau of Investigation that presents data on crimes reported to the police, number of arrests, and number of persons arrested.

United States Supreme Court The highest appellate court in the U.S. judicial system; it reviews cases appealed from federal and state court systems that deal with constitutional issues.

United States v. Leon Supreme Court case that established the good faith exception to the exclusionary rule, under which evidence that is produced in good faith and later discovered to be obtained illegally may still be admissible.

United States v. Salerno U.S. Supreme Court ruling that the preventive detention provisions of the Bail Reform Act of 1984 were constitutional.

unofficial crime statistics Crime statistics produced by people and agencies outside the criminal justice system, such as college professors and private organizations.

USA Patriot Act Federal legislation that broadened the surveillance and investigative powers of criminal justice agencies to combat terrorism and removed barriers between military, intelligence, and criminal justice entities so that they could share information on terrorist suspects and threats.

USA Patriot Act Improvement and Reauthorization Act of 2005 Federal legislation that revised the USA Patriot Act of 2001, enhancing the powers of the criminal justice system to combat crime and terrorism.

venire A group of people who are selected from the jury pool and notified to report for jury duty.

victim impact statement (VIS) A statement informing the sentencing judge of the physical, financial, and emotional harm suffered by the crime victim or his or her family.

victimization survey A method of producing crime data in which people are asked about their experiences as crime victims.

victimology The study of the characteristics of crime victims and the reasons why certain people are more likely than others to become victims of crime.

voir dire Preliminary examination by the prosecution and defense of potential jurors.

waiver of jurisdiction A legal process to transfer a juvenile from juvenile to criminal court.

warrantless arrest An arrest without a warrant, which may be performed when an officer has probable cause to believe that a felony has been or is being committed.

warden The superintendent or top administrator of a prison.

War on Terror The global armed conflict between radical Islamic terrorist groups, such as Al Qaeda, and the developed world, principally the G8 nations (Canada, France, Germany, Italy, Japan, the United Kingdom, the United States, and the Russian Federation).

Weeks v. United States Supreme Court case that established the exclusionary rule in federal cases.

Wolff v. McDonnell Supreme Court decision that inmates facing disciplinary action must have a formal hearing, 24-hour notification of the hearing, assistance in presenting a defense, and ability to call witnesses.

working personality A term that distinguishes an officer's off-the-job persona from his or her on-the-job behavior.

work release A program allowing the inmate to leave the institution during the day to work at a job.

wraparound programs Programs designed to build positive relationships and support networks between youths and their families, teachers, and community agencies through coordination of services.

writ of certiorari An order by the U.S. Supreme Court to a lower court to send up a certified record of the lower court decision to be reviewed.

CASE INDEX

T

U

V

W

NAME INDEX

Q

R

S

T

U

V

W

Z

SUBJECT INDEX

R

S

T

U

CREDITS

Section Opener, page 2 © L. Kragt Bakker/ShutterStock, Inc.

Chapter 1

Chapter Opener © Crystalcraig/Dreamstime.com; **page 6** Courtesy of Florida State University; **page 7 (top)** © Virginia State Police/Reuters/Landov; **(bottom)** © Landov; **page 8** © David Pearson/Alamy Images; **page 9 (top)** © British Centre for Durkheim Studies, Oxford; **(bottom)** © Wysiwygfoto/Dreamstime.com; **page 16** © Brett Coomer/POOL/Reuters/Landov; **page 17 (top)** © Santa Monica Police Department/Reuters/Landov; **(bottom)** © Chaiwat Subprasom/Reuters/Landov; **page 18** © Daniel Gluskoter/Reuters/Landov; **page 19** © Steve Helber/POOL/UPI Photo/Landov; **page 21** Courtesy of Heber Brown, III/faithinactiononline.com; **page 22** © CBS/Landov

Chapter 2

Chapter Opener Courtesy of Tim Bommel and the House Communications Office; **page 30** Courtesy of Mark D. Cunningham; **page 31** © James Steidl/ShutterStock, Inc.; **page 36 (top)** © Ian Thraves/Alamy Images; **(bottom)** © David Rae Morris/Reuters/Landov; **page 44** © Rebecca Cook/Reuters/Landov; **page 46** Courtesy of the Special Collections Department, Harvard Law School Library

Chapter 3

Chapter Opener © Ashley Whitworth/ShutterStock, Inc.; **page 54** Courtesy of Cassia Spohn; **page 58** © Bill Fritsch/age fotostock; **page 61** © Jack Dagley Photography/ShutterStock, Inc.; **page 62** © Medical File/Peter Arnold, Inc.; **page 63 (top)** © Mark Green, *Bloomberg News*/Landov; **(bottom)** © Gabe Palmer/Alamy Images; **Page 64** © Eugene Richards/VII/AP Photos; **page 65** © Chris Dean, *Texarkan Gazette*/AP Photos; **page 66** © Chris O'Meara/AP Photos; **page 67** © VStock/age fotostock; **page 69** © Dennis MacDonald/age fotostock; **page 71** © Alex Segre/Alamy Images; **page 73** © AP Photos; **page 74** © Ljupco Smokovski/ShutterStock, Inc.; **page 76** © Crystal Kirk/ShutterStock, Inc.

Section Opener, page 86 © Michael Rubin/ShutterStock, Inc.

Chapter 4

Chapter Opener © Michael Rubin/ShutterStock, Inc.; **page 90** Courtesy of Mark D. Cunningham; **page 92 (top)** © The Print Collector/age fotostock; **(bottom)** Courtesy of The Bancroft Library, University of California, Berkeley. Used with permission; **page 93** © Landov; **page 94** © Jim Parkin/ShutterStock, Inc.; **page 96 (top)** © tatiana sayig/ShutterStock, Inc.; **(bottom)** © Richard D. Green, *The Californian*/AP Photos; **page 98** © Doug Menuez/Photodisc/Getty Images; **page 100** Courtesy of Yellowstone National Park/NPS; **page 101** © Jupiterimages/Thinkstock/Alamy Images; **page 104** © NNS, *The Plain Dealer*/Landov; **page 108** © Donald Swartz/Dreamstime.com; **page 112 (top)** © Michael Dwyer/Alamy Images; **(bottom)** © Larry St. Pierre/ShutterStock, Inc.

Chapter 5

Chapter Opener © Jason Reed/Reuters/Landov; **page 122** Courtesy of Kim Budreau; **page 125** Scott Heckel, *The Repository*/AP Photos; **page 126** © Stockbyte/age fotostock; **page 127** © UpperCut Images/age fotostock; **page 128 (top)** © Paul Chauncey/Alamy Images; **(bottom)** © Jeff Thrower (WebThrower)/ShutterStock, Inc.; **page 130** Courtesy of Gerald L. Nino/U.S. Customs and Border Patrol; **page 131** © Joseph/ShutterStock, Inc.; **page 133** © AP Photos; **page 136** © John Lund/Sam Diephui/age fotostock; **page 138** © U.S. Marshall/AP Photos

Chapter 6

Chapter Opener © Mark C. Ide; **page 146** Courtesy of Lorenzo Boyd; **page 150** © Bill Fritsch/age fotostock; **page 151** © Bob Daemmrich/PhotoEdit, Inc.; **page 152** © Mark Richards/PhotoEdit, Inc.; **page 156** © Pictorial Press Ltd/Alamy Images; **page 158** © Mel Evans/AP Photos; **page 160** © Jack Dagley Photography/ShutterStock, Inc.; **page 161** © Brendan McDermid/Reuters/Landov; **page 164** © Mikael Karlsson/Alamy Images

Section Opener, page 172 © Corbis/age fotostock

Chapter 7

Chapter Opener © Elias H. Debbas, II/ShutterStock, Inc.; **page 176** Courtesy of Diana Reynolds Clayton; **page 181** Photograph by Franz Jantzen, Collection of the Supreme Court of the United States; **page 182** © Tami Chappell/Reuters/Landov; **page 183 (top)** © Corbis/age fotostock; **(bottom)** © Brandi Simons/AP Photos; **page 187** © Lucy Pemoni/Reuters/Landov; **page 188** © Dennis MacDonald/age fotostock; **page 189** © Michael Ging/POOL/AP Photos; **page 193** © Bill Fritsch/age fotostock

Chapter 8

Chapter Opener © Bill Fritsch/age fotostock; **page 202** Courtesy of Jeffrey Cohen; **page 203** © Doug Jennings/AP Photos; **page 205** George Wilhelm, *Los Angeles Times*/POOL/Reuters/Landov; **page 207** © Lucas Jackson/Reuters/Landov; **page 208** © RubberBall/Alamy Images; **page 209 (top)** © maxstockphoto/ShutterStock, Inc.; **(top middle)** Courtesy of the United States District Court; **(lower middle)** © Dennis MacDonald/age fotostock; **(bottom)** © PNC/age fotostock; **page 214 (top and bottom)** Courtesy of Cynthia D. Homer, Maine State Police Crime Laboratory

Chapter 9

Chapter Opener © Steve Griffin/POOL/AP Photos; **page 228** Courtesy of Judge Pablo Cortes; **page 229** Elaine Thompson/UPI/POOL/Landov; **page 230** © AP Photos; **page 231** © Tim Harman/ShutterStock, Inc.; **page 235** © Damian Dovarganes/AP Photos; **page 236** © Pat Sullivan/AP Photos; **page 244** Courtesy of the Florida Department of Corrections

Section Opener, page 256 © Richard Smith/Alamy Images

Chapter 10

Chapter Opener © Corbis; **page 260** Courtesy of Art Beeler; **page 261** Courtesy of Eastern State Penitentiary Historic Site; **page 262** © Eastern Kentucky University Archives, Richmond, KY; **page 264** © AP Photos; **page 269** © Robin Nelson/PhotoEdit, Inc.; **page 270** Mark Wilson/POOL/Reuters/Landov; **page 275** © Jeff Zelevansky/AP Photos

Chapter 11

Chapter Opener © Kimber Rey Solana/ShutterStock, Inc.; **page 284** Courtesy of Judith Garrett; **page 285** © Bill Fritsch/age fotostock; **page 289** © A. Ramey/PhotoEdit, Inc.; **page 291 (top)** © Don Hammond/age fotostock; **(bottom)** Courtesy of the Wisconsin State Journal and photographer Leah L. Jones; **page 293** © A. Ramey/PhotoEdit, Inc.; **page 294** © Renee Sauer/Columbus Dispatch/AP Photos; **page 297 (top)** © Luis Galdamez/Landov; **(bottom)** © A. Ramey/PhotoEdit, Inc.; **page 301** © Mikael Karlsson/Alamy Images

Chapter 12

Chapter Opener © Robert Schroeder/Flickr.com; **page 312** Courtesy of Eastern Kentucky; **page 313** © Bob Daemmrich/PhotoEdit, Inc.; **page 315** © Spencer Grant/PhotoEdit, Inc.; **page 317** © AP Photos; **page 318** © Spencer Grant/PhotoEdit, Inc.; **page 321 (top)** © A. Ramey/PhotoEdit, Inc.; **(bottom)** © Madison/X17online.com; **page 322** © James Shaffer/PhotoEdit, Inc.; **page 326** © Bob Daemmrich/PhotoEdit, Inc.; **page 327** © AP Photos

Section Opener, page 336 Courtesy of Andrea Booher/FEMA

Chapter 13

Chapter Opener © Ablestock; **page 340** Courtesy of James Burfeind; **page 343** © Photos.com; **page 344** © Michael Newman/PhotoEdit, Inc.; **page 348** © Mikael Karlsson/Alamy Images; **page 353 (top)** © Fabrizio Bensch/Reuters/Landov; **(bottom)** © Spencer Grant/PhotoEdit, Inc.; **page 354** © Christopher Berkey/AP Photos; **page 356** © Dan Rosenstrauch/POOL/AP Photos; **page 357** © Don Ryan/AP Photos

Chapter 14

Chapter Opener Courtesy of FEMA; **page 366** Courtesy of Westfield State College, Westfield, Massachusetts; **page 367** © Peter Foley/Landov; **page 368** © CBS/Landov; **page 373** Courtesy of the U.S. Customs and Border Patrol; **page 375** © Sue Ogrocki/Reuters/Landov; **page 379** © Mikael Karlsson/Alamy Images; **page 380** © Lein de León Yong/ShutterStock, Inc.; **page 382** © Peter Baxter/ShutterStock, Inc.